D0301398

MILTON AMONG THE PURITANS

Solidly grounded in Milton's prose works and the long history of Milton scholarship, *Milton among the Puritans: The Case for Historical Revisionism* challenges many received ideas about Milton's brand of Christianity, philosophy, and poetry. It does so chiefly by retracing his history as a great "Puritan poet" and reexamining the surprisingly tenuous Whig paradigm upon which this history has been built.

Catherine Gimelli Martin not only questions the current habit of "lumping" Milton with the religious Puritans but agrees with a long line of literary scholars who find his values and lifestyle markedly inconsistent with godly beliefs and practices. Pursuing this argument, Martin carefully reexamines the whole spectrum of seventeenth-century English Puritanism from the standpoint of the most recent and respected scholarship on the subject. Martin also explores other, more secular sources of Milton's thought, including his Baconianism, his Christian Stoic ethics, and his classical republicanism; she establishes the importance of these influences through numerous direct references, silent but clear citations, and typical tropes.

All in all, *Milton among the Puritans* presents a radical reassessment of Milton's religious identity; it shows that many received ideas about the "Puritan Milton" are neither as long-established as most scholars believe nor as historically defensible as most literary critics still assume, and resituates Milton's great poems in the period when they were written, the Restoration.

IOHN   MILTON

DRAWN AND ETCHED MDCCLX BY I.B. CIPRIANI A TVSCAN AT THE DE SIRE
OF THOMAS HOLLIS F.R. AND A.SS. FROM A PICTVRE IN THE COLLECTION OF THE
RIGHT HON. ARTHVR ONSLOW SPEAKER OF THE COMMONS HOVSE OF PARLIAMENT

HOW SOON HATH TIME THE SVTTLE THEEF OF YOVTH
STOLN ON HIS WING MY *ONE* AND TWENTIETH YEER
MY HASTING DAYES FLIE ON WITH FVLL CAREER
BVT MY LATE SPRING NO BVD OR BLOSSOM SHEW'TH
PERHAPS MY SEMBLANCE MIGHT DECEIVE THE TRVTH
THAT I TO MANHOOD AM ARRIV'D SO NEAR
AND INWARD RIPENESS DOTH MVCH LESS APPEAR
THAT SOM MORE TIMELY-HAPPY SPIRITS INDV'TH
YET BE IT LESS OR MORE OR SOON OR SLOW
IT SHALL BE STILL IN STRICTEST MEASVRE EEV'N
TO THAT SAME LOT HOWEVER MEAN OR HIGH
TOWARD WHICH TIME LEADS ME AND THE WILL OF HEAV'N
ALL IS IF I HAVE GRACE TO VSE IT SO
AS EVER IN MY GREAT TASK MASTERS EYE

Frontispiece: Cipriani etching of John Milton from *Memoirs of Thomas Hollis*
(London, 1760). By permission of Princeton University Library.

Milton among the Puritans
The Case for Historical Revisionism

CATHERINE GIMELLI MARTIN
Dunavant Professor of English, University of Memphis, USA

ASHGATE

Published by
Ashgate Publishing Limited
Wey Court East
Union Road
Farnham
Surrey, GU9 7PT
England

Ashgate Publishing Company
Suite 420
101 Cherry Street
Burlington
VT 05401-4405
USA

www.ashgate.com

British Library Cataloguing in Publication Data
Martin, Catherine Gimelli.
  Milton among the Puritans: the case for historical revisionism.
  1. Milton, John, 1608–1674 – Criticism and interpretation. 2. Milton, John, 1608–1674 – Religion. 3. Milton, John, 1608–1674 – Political and social views. 4. Christianity and literature – Great Britain – History – 17th century. 5. Politics and literature – Great Britain – History – 17th century. 6. Great Britain – History – Puritan Revolution, 1642–1660.
  I. Title
  821.4–dc22

Library of Congress Cataloging-in-Publication Data
Martin, Catherine Gimelli.
  Milton among the Puritans : the case for historical revisionism / Catherine Gimelli Martin.
    p. cm.
  Includes bibliographical references and index.
  ISBN 978-1-4094-0856-7 (alk. paper) – ISBN 978-1-4094-1927-3 (eBook) 1. Milton, John, 1608–1674 – Religion. 2. Milton, John, 1608–1674 – Criticism and interpretation. 3. Christian poetry, English – Early modern, 1500–1700 – History and criticism.
  I. Title.
  PR3592.R4M26 2010
  821'.4–dc22

2010025637

ISBN 9781409408567 (hbk)
ISBN 9781409419273 (ebk)

Mixed Sources
Product group from well-managed forests and other controlled sources
www.fsc.org Cert no. SA-COC-1565
© 1996 Forest Stewardship Council
FSC

Printed and bound in Great Britain by
MPG Books Group, UK

This book is dedicated to Richard, Justin, Matthew, and Jessamyn,
my best Puritan legacy

If a man could succeed … in kindling a light in nature—a light which should in its very rising touch and illuminate all the border-regions that confine upon the circle of our present knowledge; and so spreading further and further should presently disclose and bring into sight all that is hidden and secret in the world— that … man would be the benefactor indeed of the human race—the propagator of man's empire over the universe, the champion of liberty, the conqueror and subduer of necessities.

—Francis Bacon, *Proem, Of the Interpretation of Nature*

So at length … when universal learning has once completed its cycle, the spirit of man, no longer confined within this dark prison-house, will reach out far and wide, till it fills the whole world and the space far beyond with the expansion of its divine greatness. Then at last most of the chances and changes of the world will be so quickly perceived that to him who holds this stronghold of wisdom hardly anything can happen in his life which is unforeseen or fortuitous. He will indeed seem to be one … to whom, lastly, Mother Nature herself has surrendered, as if indeed some god had abdicated the throne of the world and entrusted its rights, laws, and administration to him as governor.

—John Milton, *Seventh Prolusion* (*CPW* 1:296)

Contents

List of Figures   *ix*
Preface and Acknowledgments   *xi*
Abbreviations and Note on Texts   *xvii*

Introduction: Carlyle's Ghost   1

**PART I: THE REVOLUTIONARY ERA: HISTORICAL OVERVIEW
            AND ANALYSIS OF MILTON'S EARLY WORKS**

1   A Brief History of the "Puritan Revolution"   31

2   Milton among the Puritans   65

3   Vocation, Prophecy, and Secular Reform in the Early Poems and
     Prose   105

4   The Humanist Ethics, Metaphysics, and Aesthetics of Milton's
     Spenserian Masque   141

5   Mid-Century Debates on Law, Religion, Rhetoric, Education, and
     Science   175

PART II: RESTORATION CULTURE AND MILTON'S MAJOR WORKS

6   The Secular Cosmology and Anthropology of Milton's Civilized
     Eden   215

7   The Neoclassical Poetics of *Paradise Regained*   249

8   The Classical Republican Tragedy of Defeat in *Samson Agonistes* 279

Afterword: Milton and the Early Development of Toleration in England *305*
Bibliography   *319*
Index   *349*

List of Figures

Frontispiece: Cipriani etching of John Milton from *Memoirs of Thomas Hollis* (London, 1760). By permission of Princeton University Library.　ii

2.1　John Milton at the age of ten, Cornelius Janssen van Ceulen (1618). By permission of the Pierpont Morgan Library.　69

2.2　Portrait of John Milton, Frontispiece to J. Richardson's *Explanatory Notes and Remarks on Milton's "Paradise Lost"* (London, 1734). By permission of Princeton University Library.　91

2.3　Portrait of Richard Baxter, Frontispiece to Baxter's *Paraphrase to the New Testament* (London, 1695). By permission of the Folger Library.　93

Preface and Acknowledgments

The primary function of an academic preface is to thank those who have contributed to the completion of the book, and to explain or to apologize, if only briefly, for any of its shortcomings or omissions. This preface does not differ from the rest in any of those respects, though it must offer more in the way of explanation than most. The reason for that addition is relatively simple: more than one anonymous reader and several friends have made me unusually aware of potential misinterpretations of this book's purpose and conclusions. To state them as clearly and succinctly as possible, I argue that, contrary to long-standing assumptions still widely held in the academic community, Milton was not a Puritan. My project thus requires me to challenge many traditional beliefs about Milton's religious affiliations and milieu, but I must emphasize to my readers as well as to my friends that this challenge is not aimed at any individual critic or historian. My revisionism rather concerns a paradigm which during my career as a Miltonist has come to seem increasingly indefensible, even counter-logical. Deeply rooted in a now defunct historical thesis about the "Puritan Revolution," this paradigm assumes that, as a leading defender of the parliamentary and Protectorate side of the English civil wars, Milton was by definition a religious Puritan himself. Yet none of his fellow polemicists—neither John Hall nor Marchamont Nedham—even remotely belonged to the Puritan camp, and very few of the poet's friends fell into it either. As most Miltonists know, any evidence that their author was ever affiliated with any Puritan congregation is also non-existent, and he was married and buried according to the rites of the Church of England. As early as graduate school, these details, along with the kind of poetry Milton wrote, caused me to ask why his Puritanism remained largely unquestioned. Later, our greatly expanded knowledge concerning the Arminian and perhaps even Catholic persuasions of his immediate family and first wife, Mary Powell, only intensified my awareness of this irony.

At first, however, as a raw beginner in the field I felt completely unqualified to pursue such questions even though both of my dissertation advisers, George Amis and Harry Berger, Jr., were equally skeptical; George actually found the paradigm somewhat amusing. While I was still writing my dissertation, a class taught by Buckingham Sharpe introduced me to the then relatively new school of historical revisionism, but his focus on the economic causes of the civil wars seemed to offer no new insights into Milton's verse. Perhaps even more to the point, I considered it utterly impertinent to question the work of such giants in the field as Stanley Fish, Christopher Hill, Barbara Lewalski, and her brilliant mentor, Ernest Sirluck. Even now, I am sometimes startled by my own temerity, an unease lessened only by the fact that all of the above wrote their major works on Milton when the "Puritan Revolution" thesis appeared impregnable. My unease is also strongly mitigated by my personal respect for all of them, two of whom (Fish and Hill) I have known and liked enormously ever since graduate school. Hill often lectured at my university during my graduate studies and my chief adviser, George Amis, made his old colleague Fish a living presence in his classes. Finally, since my primary interest then lay in Milton's aesthetics, my adherence to the traditional paradigm seemed no more material to my work than my "conversion" to the opposing camp seemed foreseeable. In short, *Milton among the Puritans* is a book I never intended to write about a thesis whose flaws I still only vaguely perceived while completing my dissertation and subsequent book, *The Ruins of Allegory*. Although I was always far from uninterested in the great poet's politics and religion, I then rightly felt that my background in seventeenth-century Protestantism, republicanism, or civil war history was insufficiently strong to permit my entry into these highly contested domains. Yet, after spending nearly half of my career studying these subjects, I now feel qualified to enter the fray.

Nevertheless, my intent is always and everywhere to examine the Puritan paradigm and its factual bases of support, not the intelligence, integrity, or expertise of those who consciously or unconsciously uphold it. I am only too well aware that its principal author was one of the greatest scholars of his age, a man of (so far as I know) unquestionable character, learning, and astuteness. I refer to David Masson, Milton's great Victorian biographer. Yet like his hero, Thomas Carlyle, for all his brilliance, Masson was a man of his age, a period dominated by "grand narratives" whose accuracy late twentieth- and early twenty-first-century historiography has increasing disputed. Although contrary to what some postmodernists have concluded, narrative is by no means dead, the current corrective trend is now toward more modest, concrete, and historical-particular portraits of the past, portraits less obviously driven by the ideologies of the grand narrativists. This is not to say that Masson's magisterial six-volume biography of Milton was ever in any way a pure product of ideology. Masson was a careful empiricist, and although like all "scientists" he got some of his facts wrong, his biography will long be read and appreciated for its richness of detail, its vastness of scope, and its stylistic poise. Yet no work of genius is exempt from the ravages of time, a truism more true in history than in literature, where even in this postmodern age we can still glimpse something of the universal human situation in Milton as in Shakespeare. Grand narrative, on the other hand, has particularly suffered from time's ravages because it attempted to explain too much. Vico, Hegel, Marx, and Weber may still be read for their individual insights, but few any longer read them to discover the *telos* or "end" of history, about which we remain much in doubt. Masson did not of course attempt to tell the history of Milton's time on that kind of scale, but he was strongly influenced by Carlyle, who did. Even more to the point, he was strongly influenced by Carlyle's "heroic" concept of Puritanism, a concept which, more than anything else, this book challenges.

I make this challenge, in part, because in modern Milton studies heroic Puritanism has gone so long unquestioned that few literary specialists have paused to consider its history or impact on their field. This is not to suggest any more than ordinary oversights on their part, so just as in Masson's case, if I disagree with my fellow scholars, it is because they have ideas worth disagreeing with from both a factual and a theoretical perspective. Unfortunately, however, the scholarly stature of Masson's major defenders confronts me with a paradox: I cannot question their paradigm without questioning their work, a necessity which may easily be interpreted as temerity on my part. Yet this situation is actually more ironic than paradoxical, since the revisionism I bring to bear on Milton has long been the mainstream position among historians. Post-revisionists have usefully altered or modified their predecessors' portraits of the civil wars and the role played by Puritanism, but they have not even marginally overturned it. Milton studies are thus exceptional in the extent to which their contributors have ignored this movement; critical works on Shakespeare, Donne, and even more minor metaphysical poets have long incorporated the revisionists' new and (I would add) less binary, more nuanced, and in every respect, more satisfying historiography. Proving it to be so therefore remains my chief, almost exclusive, reason for writing this book.

That said, I must add that the process of acquiring the necessary background for this undertaking has been greatly aided by many sympathetic scholars whom I have met along the way, all of whom will be introduced in due course. Without their strong encouragement, this book certainly would not have been written. Its inception, however, was not sparked by them but by two unforeseen coincidences. The first was beginning my teaching career in the American South, where Protestant theology is still an intense and living presence. That meant that my best-informed students, especially some seniors preparing for the ministry—a type of student I rarely encountered at the University of California, Santa Cruz, where my dissertation was written—insisted rather vociferously that my suspicions were correct: Milton's religious beliefs lie outside the Puritan tradition that ultimately if differently informs the theology of both American Presbyterians and Baptists. Yet originally, the effect of this information was slight: it simply led me to Dennis Danielson's excellent study of Milton's departures from Calvinism, *Milton's Good God*, which seemed to me the last word on the subject. The second coincidence was thus far more important: Michael Fixler, another Sirluck student, vetted one of my articles on Milton's cosmology for *Milton Studies*, which immediately led to a long correspondence and friendship. Initially we meant to collaborate on a book on Milton's science, but in the process Michael introduced me in detail to the Puritan Revolution thesis in which he had been schooled and to which he had made a signal contribution, *Milton and the Kingdoms of God*. After many discussions that failed to overcome my doubts, he insisted that systemically reading through the entire Yale prose edition of Milton's polemical work would do the trick. I agreed, and began the lengthy process with the *Prolusions* and antiprelatical tracts and ended with the *Brief History of Muscovia*. At the same time, I had begun reading through all of Bacon's major prose works to complete my end of our envisioned collaboration, and what I found there soon led me to believe that Milton reformism was far more indebted to Bacon (whom, as many scholars such as Fish and Hill acknowledge, he frequently echoes) than to any Puritan school of thought or the

Smectymnuans with whom he was tangentially associated. How could this be possible?

Two places where I first looked for answers were Hill's *Intellectual Origins of the English Revolution*, which gives prominent credit to Bacon, and Conrad Russell's *Causes of the English Civil Wars*. Professor Sharpe's class had introduced me to the latter but I had never yet read it from cover to cover. Both works made crucial contributions to my increasingly dubious turn of mind: Hill's *Intellectual Origins* presented some startling discrepancies with his later and far more popular work, *Milton and the English Revolution*, while Russell's 1970 essay collection implicitly contradicted the latter. Its most important revelation came in the form of an early essay by Nicholas Tyacke indicating that the initial Puritan contribution to the civil wars was conservative, not radical, although it later evolved in that direction. Even then, however, the Puritans supported radical religiosity and millenarianism, not for the most part republican politics or theories of government. After further reading, I became a confirmed revisionist simply because the new school of history seemed to clarify so many problems presented by the old, especially its untenable assumptions about the religiously unified and proto-democratic nature of the "Puritan revolution." After thoroughly absorbing this and related material, I wrote what is now Chapter 3 of this book, which seeks to explain how and why an antiprelatical Milton is not necessarily a Puritan Milton. My timing proved extremely fortuitous, since soon afterward Marshall Grossman kindly invited me to present any new scholarship I had at the Northeastern Milton Seminar. My presentation proved a true eye-opener, for it made me realize just how much more work I needed to do in order to justify my "radical" thesis. For that realization, I am especially grateful not just to Marshall but also to my fellow presenter and later friend, Jim Nohrnberg, and to Laura Knoppers for her learned advice on my need accurately to define Puritanism in chapters that would precede the current Chapter 3. Soon afterward, I would become equally grateful to Andrew Escobedo and Beth Quitslund for asking me to contribute an article on Milton's very Spenserian but hardly Puritan masque to their special *Milton Quarterly* issue on the theme of Milton and Spenser. With the journal's permission, I include an expanded version of this article, first published in *Milton Quarterly* 37 (December 2003, pp. 215–44), in Chapter 4 of this book.

Finally, I need to mention a far more personal source of encouragement in my early and continuing skepticism about Milton's Puritanism, namely, my husband Richard Martin, who, after taking his senior seminar at Santa Cruz, first told me that "no way" could Milton ever be the kind of Puritan his professor claimed he was. This professor happened to be a specialist in British modernism, so neither of us could then be completely sure that an expert in the field would not have been more convincing. All the same, when many years later I began to find ways of confirming his guess, Richard rendered unremitting aid and comfort whenever I was most discouraged, which was often. Although his own expertise is in Shakespeare studies, he also patiently served as my first non-specialist literary reader. For all those reasons this book is dedicated to him and to our children,

Justin, Matthew, and Jessamyn, my much beloved support group and, in a real sense, my best friends. Yet academic friends have hardly been wanting, and I am most happy to acknowledge them in chronological order, since any other way of ranking them would be as impossible as unwise.

The first of these is John Shawcross, whom I met at my very first academic conference, still not yet out of graduate school. John too taught in the South, and he later kindly accepted an invitation to lecture at my "new" university. At the time, our interests did not strongly overlap, although we continued to meet at conferences and exchange views. Later, especially after the publication of his excellent study of Milton's family, *The Arms of the Family* (2004), and his very positive response to my book chapter in Christophe Tournu and Neil Foryth's volume, *Milton, Rights and Liberties* (2006), on the shortcomings of the front matter and footnotes in the early volumes of the Yale prose edition, we began regularly exchanging ideas and encouragement via e-mail. Next, even before Marshall, Jim, and Laura, I met both Victoria Kahn and David Quint at another academic conference where the overlap between many of our ideas soon became obvious. They have remained strong supporters ever since, and Vicky generously invited me to present my thesis at a faculty seminar at UC Berkeley in 2004. There I met two other distinguished Miltonists, James Turner and Raymond Waddington. In point of fact I had already met Ray more briefly through Jim at another conference, but this meeting marked the beginning of a continuing, most helpful and enjoyable friendship. Ray also uniquely stands out from the rest because he has generously helped me reedit the first draft of this book and has provided much invaluable support and technical advice throughout, especially when the slings and arrows of anonymous readers hit hardest. Far above and beyond all that, he is precisely the kind of person I am most happy and privileged to call my friend.

I am additionally grateful to an Oxford reader of this manuscript who decided not to remain anonymous, Thomas Corns. Although Oxford finally decided not to publish my manuscript, his astute reading and criticism has made it a much better book. So, too, have his many articles and his recent biography, *John Milton: Life, Work, and Thought* (2008), which substantially supports many of the conclusions reached in this book. This biography, co-written with Gordon Campbell, came out much too late really to shape my conclusions, and Tom actually read my manuscript before I read his study. As an empirical rather than an intellectual historical and literary study of the poet, it also differs from mine in not engaging the paradigm I critique. Yet in many ways its complementary research into the primary data surrounding Milton's life makes it a more valuable resource than if it did. I gratefully acknowledge my thankfulness for both that data and for Tom's personal encouragement. My current editor, Erika Gaffney, deserves similar credit for her longtime interest in my work.

Last but hardly least, I must thank a friend who goes back as far as John Shawcross. Achsah Guibbory only recently made me aware of her support for my approach although she has not read any of this manuscript. Her good friend Paul Stevens has also supplied general encouragement, as have much older acquaintances who do not agree with my thesis but have supported me nonetheless. Aside from my late friend Michael Fixler, these are Joan Bennett, Jacki Disalvo, and especially Bill Shullenberger, scholars I deeply admire and have long regretted disappointing due to my departure from their school of thought. All the same, traveling to visit their friend Christopher Hill in Oxford with Joan and Jacki, and receiving Bill's wonderfully expressive poems and reflections in many e-mails only scratches the surface of my warmest memories. Along with Ray's exceptional generosity, the continuing affection of these three is a testimony to the qualities I most admire in the academic community, and which I must now humbly request from my readers: fairness and willingness to judge ideas on their merits alone.

Catherine Gimelli Martin
September 2010

Abbreviations and Note on Texts

Primary Sources

CPW	*The Complete Prose Works of John Milton*, ed. Don M. Wolfe et al. (8 vols., New Haven: Yale University Press, 1953–82).
Hughes	*John Milton, The Complete Poetry and Major Prose*, ed. Merritt Y. Hughes (New York: Odyssey Press, 1957).
PL	*Paradise Lost* in Hughes.
PR	*Paradise Regained* in Hughes.
SA	*Samson Agonistes* in Hughes.
Works	*The Works of Francis Bacon*, ed. James Spedding, Robert Ellis, and Douglas Heath (14 vols., London: Longman & Co., 1860).

Textual Note

References to the prose works are by volume and page number separated by a colon, references to *Paradise Lost* and *Paradise Regained* are by book and line number separated by a period, and references to all other poems are by line number. Many references to the Yale prose works are to editorial opinions or commentary, as clearly indicated. All biblical citations are from the Authorized Version, or King James Bible. Quotations from Milton's *Christian Doctrine* (*De Doctrina Christiana*) are assumed to be by Milton, although, due to Professor William Hunter's questioning of its authorship in *Visitation Unimplor'd*, most are supplemented with citations from the canonical works. Details of the authorship controversy are too extensive to be covered here, but the vast bulk of scholarship presently supports the long-held assumption that Milton composed or was in the process of editing the *Christian Doctrine* at the time of his death.

Introduction
Carlyle's Ghost

These sacred lines with wonder we peruse
And praise the flights of a seraphic Muse,
Till thy seditious prose provokes our rage,
And soils the beauties of thy brightest page

—Thomas Yalden, "On the Reprinting of
Milton's Prose Works in 1698"[1]

For although the scriptures themselves are written by the Spirit of God, yet they are written within and without: and besides the light that shines upon the face of them, unless there be a light shining within our hearts, unfolding the leaves, and interpreting the mysterious sense of the Spirit, convincing our consciences and preaching to our hearts; to look for Christ in the leaves of the gospel, is to look for the living amongst the dead.

—Jeremy Taylor, *Via Intelligentiae, Works* 8:379

Of all great English poets, none but John Milton now holds a reputation so far removed from his contemporary estimation; and of all great religions, few but the religion of the English Puritans has become so distanced from its historical milieu in current literary studies. My primary argument in what follows is that these lapses of historical memory are closely linked: only by simplifying and liberalizing the nature of Puritanism have literary scholars so seriously misconstrued Milton's relationship to the movement. These lapses have also obscured the fact that what Thomas Yalden still found most radical about Milton almost twenty-five years after his death—his secular politics—was usually not found among the Puritans, who for the most part were inspired by apocalyptic or Spirit-based views of reformation.[2] At the turn of the century, the Anglican churchman Yalden still

---

[1] In Samuel Johnson, *The Lives of the Most Eminent English Poets: with Critical Observations on Their Works* (4 vols., London, 1793).

[2] As Sharon Achinstein points out, "We may search in vain for radical political content in the many writings produced by Dissenters," who, like pre-revolutionary Puritans, were above all committed to their Calvinist heritage; see *Literature and Dissent in Milton's England* (Cambridge, 2003), p. 27. Blair Worden even accuses them of "blott[ing] out real politics" in *Roundhead Reputations: The English Civil Wars and the Passions of Posterity* (London, 2001), p. 60.

accurately reflected the common opinions of his age: "sacred wonder" at Milton's biblical poetry, but deep disdain for his "seditious," anti-monarchical prose. By then, however, his political theories had become the property of radical Whigs, many of whom ironically shared Yalden's liberal theology if not his politics.[3] In Milton's own time the situation was reversed: godly politicians like Sir Henry Vane, Henry Ireton, and Edmund Ludlow may have shared his republican convictions but not his theology, his anti-theocratic and anti-clerical biases, or his profoundly humanistic view of sublime art.[4]

These remarks are by no means meant to suggest that Milton had no regard for godliness or little if any reliance on the Spirit he invokes at the beginning of *Paradise Lost*. Like all Protestants, including the Arminian Jeremy Taylor, Milton obviously sought the spiritual guidance promised to all believers in 1 Corinthians 2:12–13: "we have received, not the spirit of the world, but the spirit which is of God; that we might know the things that are freely given to us of God. Which things also we speak, not in the words which man's wisdom teacheth, but which the Holy Ghost teacheth." Nevertheless, this spiritual gift was very differently construed by the godly brethren, who unlike Taylor, Milton, or other heirs of the rationalist Richard Hooker, utterly shunned the natural man and absolutely relied on the Spirit to correct their fallen reason through irresistible grace. Both radical and conservative Puritans affirmed their absolute need for God's "indwelling Spirit" to rectify "carnal reason," the common property of fallen man, while Milton consistently trusts in a synthesis of universal grace and "right reason" to guide him.[5] He also considers spiritual aids not as the property of a narrow "Elect" but of all believers and even right-minded pagans (*CPW* 6:132; *PL* 3.175–202; *PR* 4.351–52). Milton's biblical poetics can thus be directly linked to his rejection of the very sort of certitude Puritans sought through the Holy Spirit. David Sedley points out that sublime verse in general, and Milton's in particular, requires a suspension of judgment, heightened ambiguity, and potential for self-contradiction which, as Stephen Fallon observes, make "Milton's writings ... anything but representative of Puritan practice and perspective." They share nothing of the "anguished soul-searching" or "'experiential immediacy' that marks

---

[3]   See George Sensabaugh, *That Grand Whig Milton* (Stanford, 1952), and also below.

[4]   John T. Shawcross shows that, despite Samuel Johnson's political criticisms, eighteenth-century readers generally viewed Milton in much the same way, and Johnson himself of course considered his verse "sublime." See "The Deleterious and the Exalted: Milton's Poetry in the Eighteenth Century," in Mark R. Kelley, Michael Lieb, and John T. Shawcross (eds.), *Milton and the Grounds of Contention* (Pittsburgh, 2003), pp. 11–36, 284–92.

[5]   See Geoffrey F. Nuttall, *The Holy Spirit in Puritan Faith and Experience*, with a new introduction by Peter Lake (Chicago, 1992), especially p. 48. On the heirs of Hooker, see Robert Hoopes, *Right Reason in the English Renaissance* (Cambridge, MA, 1962). On Milton's debt to Hooker, see Joan S. Bennett, *Reviving Liberty: Radical Christian Humanism in Milton's Great Poems* (Cambridge, MA, 1989).

Puritan individualism."[6] Puritans were famously torn between the poles of despair and conviction, but their soul-searching was meant to provide stronger assurances of their election, not the comparatively cool suspension of judgment that marks what critics frequently call Milton's "poetics of choice." Sedley rightly traces this suspension of certitude to the skeptical methods advocated by Francis Bacon. In science as in religion, Baconianism defers absolute knowledge in favor of experimentation and reevaluation, and "Milton's doctrinal eccentricities" promote this deferral by blocking direct "human access to divine presence and the certainty enabled by it." Predestination gives way to "the contingencies of human free will," and scriptural infallibility succumbs to probability as even the Bible's authors are no longer "amanuenses taking dictation from God." Finally, man's eternal soul itself becomes mortal and fallible. For Sedley, this is the final ingredient in the skeptical pattern: Milton's mortalist heresy makes all humans less intrinsically perfectible or divine.[7]

The revolutionary outlook pioneered by Bacon and embraced by Milton also balances skepticism with a new optimism about nature, matter, and (with qualifications) human progress not found in mainline Puritanism. For Milton, nature and matter may be mutable but not subject to old age or decay, as the title of his *Naturam Non Pati Senium* announces and as his *De Doctrina Christiana* confirms (*CPW* 6:309). Not only do nature's laws remain constant after the Fall, but her works and signs at least partially reveal the divine will, as Michael reminds Adam in *Paradise Lost* (11.349–54). The universe thus becomes more comprehensible and its habitants less susceptible to the belittling forms of doubt that haunt Puritan poetics. Baconian influences on Milton's radically reformist political, educational, and scientific thought have been previously recorded by scholars ranging from the Victorian David Masson to Christopher Hill and Charles Webster. All show that Bacon's attacks on the "idols" of custom, superstition, and tradition in *The Advancement of Learning* and *Novum Organum* are major sources of Milton's thought.[8] His antiprelatical tracts and *Areopagitica* directly cite Bacon as a champion of toleration and anti-ceremonial Protestantism, subjects on which he never cites a single Puritan author to positive effect. Although Puritans certainly shared his anti-ceremonialism, their contemporaneous attacks on the bishops were

---

[6]   Stephen M. Fallon, *Milton's Peculiar Grace: Self-Representation and Authority* (Ithaca, NY, 2007), pp. 21, 27. Fallon refutes N.H. Keeble, "Milton and Puritanism," in Thomas N. Corns (ed.), *A Companion to Milton*, (Oxford, 2001), p. 126, but includes Milton among the Puritans on the basis of doctrines no longer considered exclusively characteristic of the movement: millenarianism, individualism, and "the priesthood of all believers"; see *Peculiar Grace*, chapters 1–3.

[7]   David Sedley, *Sublimity and Skepticism in Milton and Montaigne* (Ann Arbor, 2005), pp. 82–85, 107. Sedley cites *De Doctrina, CPW* 6:382.

[8]   Christopher Hill, *The Intellectual Origins of the English Revolution* (Oxford, 1965), pp. 85–130; Charles Webster, *The Great Instauration: Science, Medicine and Reform 1626–1660* (New York, 1976).

even more deeply motivated by their antipathy to the Arminian or "free will" theology of the Laudians, which Milton either silently shared at the time or soon adopted.[9] His final antiprelatical tract calmly assumes a self-willed capacity to "practice ... all that which is praise-worthy" on one's own initiative. Rather than cultivating humility or praying for grace from above, he relies on self-knowledge combined with a just "self-esteem either of what I was, or what I might be" (*CPW* 1:890).

No comparable position was available within Puritanism until much later, after the rise of Antinomianism, and even then, only through a strongly Spirit-based mysticism. Indeed, at the very time Milton published his remarks on self-esteem in *An Apology against a Pamphlet*, Edward Calamy, one of the Smectymnuans he had been defending, was recommending national humiliation as the only route to reformation. Calamy calls for "seven buckets to 'draw that water of tears withal,' the first two of which are the contemplation of personal sins and the second the consideration of national sins."[10] Antinomians later countered this self-lacerating faith with a belief in saintly "perfectionism" that provided an equal if opposite form of assurance firmly linked to divine grace and spiritual exaltation, not to Miltonic probability, self-knowledge, moral endeavor, or humanistic "self-esteem."[11] These differences become less puzzling once we realize that conservative and radical Puritans had much more in common with each other than either did with Milton. As remote but very real heirs of the mainline Calvinist tradition, Antinomians continued to disparage the capacities of the "mere" natural man and to depend on "free grace" descending from above. This dependence remains relatively unchanged as Puritanism evolves into the broad spectrum of beliefs seminally detailed decades ago by Christopher Hill and Geoffrey Nuttall.[12] All Puritans basically held that any "justification by works was 'an opinion settled in nature'"

---

[9]   Nicholas Tyacke, *Anti-Calvinists: The Rise of English Arminianism c.1590–1640* (New York, 1990). For a differing view, see Achsah Guibbory, *Ceremony and Community from Herbert to Milton: Literature, Religion, and Cultural Change in Seventeenth-Century England* (Cambridge, 1998).

[10]   John Morrill, "A Liberation Theology?," in *Puritanism and Its Discontents*, ed. Laura Lunger Knoppers (Newark, NJ, 2002), pp. 27–48, cited p. 31.

[11]   See Richard Strier, "Milton against Humility," in *Religion and Culture in Renaissance England*, ed. Claire McEachern and Debora Shuger (Cambridge, 1997), pp. 258–86. Ignoring the humanistic sources of this ethic, Fallon in *Peculiar Grace* castigates him for not sharing the deep sense of sinfulness common to Puritans: "by this measure Milton is worse than the [perfectionist] Quakers, for they normally did admit their youthful errors" (p. 22), although he concedes that "Milton never sounds like an enthusiast claiming a personal and ecstatic vision of God" or undergoes a blinding infusion of divine grace (p. 38).

[12]   Christopher Hill, *The World Turned Upside Down* (London,1972), and Nuttall, *Holy Spirit.* Nuttall especially emphasizes the continuities in Puritan belief.

or natural pride; only "self-love and presumption were fostered by the doctrine of free will and merit."[13]

Although much uncertainty remains as to exactly when and how Milton came to espouse an Erasmian or Arminian belief in free will, the mature poet clearly grounds it in the conviction that God's "prevenient" or restorative grace (*PL* 11.3) repairs the faculties of the whole human race soon after Adam and Eve's Fall. This teaching completely counters the Calvinist teaching on man's "total depravity" through Adam, and further explains Milton's less than anxious search for signs of personal salvation, the central quest and hope of the godly. By the 1650s a Puritan form of Arminianism had also emerged, but the differences between the structure and provenance of this new teaching and Milton's beliefs are enormous. Milton's ideas derive from radical Dutch and Italian humanist sources, while radical Puritans with few exceptions were influenced by native Antinomians and mystics like George Fox.[14] Milton's mortalist beliefs are also non-Puritan in origin; mortalism is now understood not as a sectarian position but a view espoused by a diverse group of exegetes influenced by similar scriptures but very different sources.[15]

The foregoing paragraphs outline some of the basic revisions to the portrait of Milton alluded to in the subtitle of this book, although they also refer to the radically new account of the English civil wars produced by "historical revisionists," as they are called, a powerful and now dominant movement still largely neglected in Milton studies. Before detailing the richer portrait provided by their account, precisely what is at stake and why this "heretical" line of thought should be pursued must be clearly spelled out. First, the new historiography accounts for many contradictions and corrects many over-simplifications inherent in the older "Whig" history of the "Puritan Revolution." Second, Milton scholarship has long suffered

---

[13] Peter Lake, "Anti-popery: The Structure of a Prejudice," in Richard Cust and Ann Hughes (eds.), *The English Civil War* (London, 1997), pp. 181–210, cited p. 184.

[14] See Louis Aubrey Wood, *The Form and Origin of Milton's Antitrinitarian Conception* (London, Ont., 1911). As with most rules, there are important exceptions; William Walwyn was influenced by Montaigne, and Ellen More traces other continental influences in John Goodwin's late conversion to Arminianism. See "John Goodwin and the Origin of the New Arminianism," *Journal of British Studies* 21.1 (1982): pp. 50–70. However, as she notes, Goodwin's conversion had little if any influence among the godly, and his most recent biographer shows that he was neither the progressive nor the proto-Enlightenment figure later "Whigs" made him. See John Coffey, *John Goodwin and the Puritan Revolution* (Woodbridge, 2006), pp. 296–97.

[15] See Normal Burns, *Christian Mortalism from Tyndale to Milton* (Cambridge, MA, 1972). Burns locates Milton's position somewhere between that of Richard Overton and Thomas Hobbes, although he is often closer to the latter than to the former (pp. 173–85). Milton obviously opposed Hobbesian absolutism, but his iconoclastic views of religion have definite affinities with those expressed in the second part of *Leviathan*. On mortalism in Milton's poetry, see Raymond B. Waddington, "Murder One: The Death of Abel. Blood, Soil, and Mortalism in *Paradise Lost*," *Milton Studies* 41 (2002): pp. 76–93.

from a sense of stagnation signaled by frequent but largely ineffective rallying cries aimed at freeing Milton from the "hard and definite" outlines imposed on him by Stanley Fish, who ironically voiced precisely the same complaint against scholars of the previous generation.[16] *Milton among the Puritans* approaches both problems in a radically new way. It argues that not just Fish but the Whig historical model he inherited and advanced must be radically reexamined in light of the new historiography of the English civil wars, which alone promises to free Milton from the procrustean bed of religious Puritanism that supports both Fish's anti-scientific exemplar of spiritual certitude and Hill's radical saint. These portraits remain the dominant models for dealing with Milton despite recent explorations of his republicanism and liberalism (in the early modern senses of these terms). Although these developments are welcome, they are still tenuous and often hampered by residual assumptions concerning the "Puritan Revolution" that continue unquestioned.[17]

Yet ironically, even in the heyday of Whig history, Denis Saurat could argue that Milton was not a Puritan, a view that such major scholars as Douglas Bush and C.S. Lewis supported well into the latter half of the twentieth century.[18] Saurat pointed out that Milton's worldly ambition and pride, his lack of religious fanaticism

---

[16]   See especially John Rumrich, *Milton Unbound: Controversy and Reinterpretation* (Cambridge, 1996), and Peter Herman, *Destabilizing Milton: "Paradise Lost" and the Poetics of Incertitude* (New York, 2005), and Stanley E. Fish, *Surprised by Sin: The Reader in "Paradise Lost"* (Berkeley, 1967). Fish responds in "The New Milton Criticism," a paper read at the Ninth International Milton Symposium, July 7, 2008. This paper provides a thorough assessment of these complaints.

[17]   See, for instance, William Walker, in "Reassessing Milton's Republicanism," which contends that the "religious dimension of his [Milton's] thinking conflicts with many of the tenets of the classical and Machiavellian republicanism with which he has been aligned." See Charles W. Durham and Kristin A. Pruitt (eds.), *Uncircumscribed Mind: Reading Milton Deeply* (Selinsgrove, 2008), p. 184; and William Walker, *"Paradise Lost" and Republican Tradition from Aristotle to Machiavelli* (Turnhout, 2009), which questions Milton's classical republicanism. For the opposite point of view, see David Armitage, Armand Himy, and Quentin Skinner (eds.), *Milton and Republicanism* (Cambridge, 1995); Quentin Skinner, *Liberty before Liberalism* (Cambridge, 1998), and *Visions of Politics* (3 vols., Cambridge, 2002), vol. 2, pp. 386–307); Richard Tuck, *Philosophy and Government 1572–1651* (Cambridge, 1993); and David Norbrook, *Writing the English Republic: Poetry, Rhetoric, and Politics 1627–1660* (Cambridge, 1999). Martin Dzelzainis takes a similar perspective in *John Milton: Political Writings* (Cambridge, 1991), and I follow Skinner and Tuck in two articles, "Rewriting Cromwell: Milton, Marvell, and Negative Liberty in the English Revolution," *Clio* 36.3 (2007): pp. 307–32, and "Milton and the Huguenot Revolution," in Catherine G. Martin and Hassan Melehy (eds.), *"The Perilous Wide Ocean": French and English Connections in the Renaissance* (Ashgate, forthcoming). See also Annabel Patterson, *Early Modern Liberalism* (Cambridge, 1997) and *Nobody's Perfect: A New Whig Interpretation of History* (New Haven, 2002).

[18]   C.S. Lewis, *A Preface to "Paradise Lost"* (New York, 1961); Douglas Bush, *John Milton: A Sketch of His Life and Writings* (New York, 1964).

or Bunyanesque dread, his highly cultivated aestheticism, and his intellectual independence all contradicted the case for his Puritanism, and he saw similar traits governing Milton's family as a whole. His father had been disinherited for converting to Protestantism, but this liberally educated and musically skilled composer of secular madrigals showed "no sign of violent religious zeal." Rather than coveting "the fame of a reformer for his richly gifted son," he "brought him up for poetical glory," and peacefully coexisted with the "possibly Catholic family" of Milton's wife, Mary Powell, as well as with his soon-to-be-Catholic brother, Christopher. In such a family, only tolerant respect for personal independence seems to explain their apparent equanimity amidst religious and political diversity.[19] Perez Zagorin's 1992 biography revived many aspects of Saurat's argument, but it was virtually ignored in an atmosphere still dominated by Hill's thesis: Milton's heresies like his politics were indebted to his association with the radical Puritan underground.[20] More recently, however, Gordon Campbell and Thomas Corns have definitively shown that Saurat's intuition was right: Milton's family favored Arminian, not Puritan, theology and practice, and while Richard Stock, the godly minister who moved into their London parish, may have catechized their eldest son, "the process failed to turn the young Milton into a puritan."[21] Yet their findings fill in only one part of the larger puzzle: given his upbringing and early sympathies, why did the mature Milton join the radical "Root and Branch" cause against the bishops in the early 1640s? Campbell and Corns offer one traditional answer: he was strongly influenced by his Puritan tutor, Thomas Young, a view for which there is some but by no means unshakable evidence. Hill offered a similar but ultimately different answer: he was strongly influenced by the "radical Puritan underground." This book offers a third and completely different answer: Milton's place in the Root and Branch movement can be clarified only by examining the revisionist account of the civil wars and the unique nature of his "political Puritanism," both of which are thoroughly explored in Chapters 1 and 2 below.

Despite Hill's undisputed historical credentials, the enormous success of his *Milton and the English Revolution* (1977) was never attributable to the large number of "facts" it produced about Milton's connection to the radical sects. Hill's correction of Fish's dour portrait of Milton in the guise of Richard Baxter was certainly astute, but his radical affiliations remained sketchy, conjectural, and, as many fellow historians complained, improbable. His work's overwhelming success thus stemmed more from the fact that it completed the turn toward a Puritan Milton earlier begun by David Masson and filled in by William Haller, A.S.P. Woodhouse, and Don M. Wolfe (to whom Hill's biography is dedicated). Their studies relied extensively on the work of Whig historians to establish views

[19]   Denis Saurat, *Milton, Man and Thinker* [rpt. 1925] (London, 1944), pp. 2–4.

[20]   Hill, *Milton*; Perez Zagorin, *Milton: Aristocrat and Rebel: The Poet and His Politics* (New York, 1992).

[21]   Gordon Campbell and Thomas N. Corns, *John Milton: Life, Work, and Thought* (Oxford, 2008), pp. 15–16. For a fuller exposition of the evidence, see Chapter 2 below.

since written into the notes and prefaces of Wolfe's widely read Yale edition of
Milton's prose (1953–82), another important reason for the long endurance of this
paradigm.[22] It became especially pervasive once the more belle-lettristic approach
of Lewis, Bush, and "old" new critics like Joseph Summers began to seem naive
in comparison to the technical mastery demonstrated in Fish's *Surprised by Sin*
(1967), the first "close reading" of Milton's epic to embrace the Puritan Milton.
Hill's detailed radicalization of this paradigm simply made it even more appealing
as the cultural revolution of the 1960s and 1970s went mainstream. Its current
vitality is attested in the millennial edition of *Milton Studies* (2000), in which
Kathleen Swaim states the "indisputable" fact that Milton is a prime "exemplar of
the Puritan extreme of Protestantism" whose creative Bible-reading continued his
family tradition of forging a "unique relationship with the divine."[23] This standard
view has been so widely accepted that few seem to question (as Saurat once did)
why Milton never considered a godly ministry or a Puritan bride, never recorded
a conversion experience, and never conformed to any other aspect of the godly
brethren's *modus vivendi*—matters that will be thoroughly considered in Chapters
2 and 3.[24]

In the long run, however, the Puritan Milton is less indebted to any single
defender of the thesis than to the tradition established by Masson's magisterial
Victorian biography, which assumed that, as a prominent spokesman for the "Puritan
Revolution," Milton was self-evidently a Puritan himself. Any successful challenge
to this paradigm must therefore holistically reassess Milton's religious, aesthetic,
ethical, and political beliefs in the context of the demise of the Puritan Revolution
thesis. It must additionally survey the newer understandings of seventeenth-century
English Puritanism that have accompanied this demise, which significantly depart
from the older, more defensive and "apologetic" accounts of the movement often
composed by its direct descendants.[25] Finally, it must emphasize how slender the
evidence for the Puritanism of either Milton or his family actually is. Not only was
the "Puritan poet" a stranger to the earlier Victorian era and to Whigs like Thomas
Macaulay, he was equally unknown to his own contemporaries. As Yalden's lines
suggest, during his lifetime neither Milton's enemies nor his friends considered

---

[22]   This perspective is particularly prominent in the first three and most widely read
volumes; see my essay, "Unediting Milton: Historical Myth and Editorial Misconstruction
in the Yale Prose Edition," in Christophe Tournu (ed.), *Milton, Rights and Liberties* (New
York, 2006), pp. 113–30.

[23]   Kathleen M. Swaim, "Myself a True Poem: Early Milton and the (Re)formation of
the Subject," *Milton Studies* 38 (2000): pp. 66–95, cited p. 66.

[24]   For an important exception, see John T. Shawcross, *The Arms of the Family: The
Significance of Milton's Friends and Associates* (Lexington, KY, 2004). Milton's most
recent biographers, Campbell and Corns, do not consider these details but (as noted above)
supply a thoroughly non-Puritan portrait of the poet's background, family, and early work.

[25]   On this point, see the conclusion to Philip Benedict's important study, *Christ's
Churches Purely Reformed: A Social History of Calvinism* (New Haven, 2002).

him one of the godly, much less their poet laureate. He was briefly linked to John Goodwin at the Restoration when the two famous defenders of the regicide were "miraculously" pardoned, and both were included in Colonel Baker's *The Blazing Star ... or Nolls Nose* in 1660 as Protectorate "propagandists." Milton did not, however, appear in the anonymous *Devils Cabinet Councell Discovered* of the same year, although in 1663 an anonymous Anglican satirist implausibly portrayed the Puritan (and anti-republican) Richard Baxter as secretly "planning" to republish Milton's and Goodwin's political writings. Far more often, however, Milton's fiercest and far from anonymous foes attacked him for espousing a "Jesuit" natural law theory.[26] Roger L'Estrange repeatedly tarred him with this brush, which he apparently found more convincing than trying to link Milton to Puritan resistance theorists such as Samuel Rutherford, one of the poet's detested "New Forcers of Conscience."[27] In general, however, popular and even royalist opinion dismissed his great revolutionary defenses as the work of a talented mercenary, not of a dangerous radical.[28] Thomas Hobbes somewhat more perceptively accused the humanist defenders of the rebellion of naively adopting the classical republicanism they learned with their Latin exercises, but certainly not from their divinity classes at Puritan Cambridge. A contemporary Milton biographer, the Baconian John Aubrey, merely restates Hobbes's view more sympathetically: "being so conversant in Livy and the Roman authors, and the greatness he saw done by the Roman commonwealth, and the virtue of their great commanders induced him to write against monarchy."[29] Major contemporary political historians such as Richard Tuck and Quentin Skinner have learnedly revived Aubrey's understanding of Milton's secular politics, an opinion shared by the radical Whigs who shortly after his death began canonizing him as an important antecedent to Locke. Their strategy was a simple one: by praising what L'Estrange, Baxter, and Hobbes had loathed, they turned Milton into a pillar of enlightened eighteenth-century liberalism.[30]

---

[26] See Coffey, *John Goodwin*, pp. 268–70, 277. As Coffey explains, Anglican polemicists downplayed the internal divisions between Dissenters and other casualties of the Restoration, falsely depicting a unified "conspiracy against church and state" (p. 277). Goodwin cited Milton but not vice versa; Coffey believes that they were personally acquainted (p. 96) but cites no real evidence aside from some unconvincing rhetorical comparisons and the "Whig" tradition.

[27] On L'Estrange and other inveterate enemies of the Whig program in general and Milton in particular, see Sensabaugh, *That Grand Whig*, pp. 21–53.

[28] Campbell and Corns, *John Milton*, pp. 309, 315; see also pp. 312–13.

[29] John Aubrey, *Brief Lives*, ed. Oliver Lawson Dick (London, 1960), p. 203; see also Thomas Hobbes, *Behemoth, or The Long Parliament*, ed. Ferdinand Tonnies (Chicago, 1990), p. 56. Aubrey was well aware of Hobbes's aspersions against Milton in *Behemoth*, which he mentions.

[30] Caroline Robbins, *The Eighteenth-Century Commonwealthmen* (Cambridge, MA, 1961). For Skinner and Tuck, see note 17 above.

Whigs of this era were frequently heirs of the Nonconformist tradition created by the Restoration, but most knew that earlier Puritans were rarely attracted to the secular, neo-Roman republican theories embraced by Milton. When they were, they usually infused them with apocalyptic strains absent from Milton's mature political thought. Rather than promoting a "holy war" or justifying what is today known as terrorism, Milton defended the English people in terms of Hebrew, Roman, and natural law theory, carefully justifying tyrannicide only after clear proof had been produced that the monarch had overstepped his legal rights. [31] Hill himself conceded that Milton made his secular stance evident by debunking the more messianic and theocratic aspirations of his allies, but at the same time, he linked him to "Bible republicans" like Goodwin, Henry Ireton, and Edmund Ludlow.[32] In response, Edward Chaney bitterly complained that Hill's comparison of Milton, Ludlow, and their voyages to Italy suppressed or skewed many important facts and differences, so that Hill "subtly distort[ed] Ludlow's memoirs in order to draw a supposed parallel with Milton's experience." Like H.R. Trevor-Roper and George Whiting, Chaney contrasts the xenophobic, anti-papist attitudes prevailing among English Puritans at the time of Milton's Italian journey with his enthusiasm for the warm reception he received in Rome and throughout the peninsula. Although Ludlow also traveled to Italy, his response to the faults of the Venetian republic significantly differs from the uncritical enthusiasm of Milton, Algernon Sidney, Henry Neville, and James Harrington.[33] In obscuring these differences, Hill was again following the lead of the later Whig historians, who long overlooked relatively obvious evidence that Ludlow's *Memoirs* were forged because it implicitly challenged their conflation of Puritanism and constitutionalism. The hoax at last became evident in 1970, when Ludlow's real work, *A Voyce from the Watchtower*, clearly showed that an anonymous editor (probably John Toland) had stripped away its Puritan sentiments about the imminent return of Christ and the indelible superiority of the Elect. Worden, the modern editor of *A Voyce*, thoroughly details how the Whig "Puritan Revolution" thus lost an enlightened avatar of godly liberty just as other supports of their paradigm began to crumble.[34]

Raphael Samuel traces this paradigm not to Toland or the eighteenth-century Whigs but to the "rediscovery" of Puritanism in the first quarter of the nineteenth century, a time when its seventeenth-century realities had been largely forgotten.

---

[31]   On godly "terrorism," see Achinstein, *Literature and Dissent*, p. 114.

[32]   On Ireton, see David Farr, *Henry Ireton and the English Revolution* (Rochester, NY, 2006), p. 154. On Goodwin's messianic republicanism, see Coffey, *John Goodwin*, p. 193. On Ludlow, see Worden, *Roundhead*, pp. 45–64.

[33]   Edward Chaney, *The Grand Tour and the Great Rebellion: Richard Lassels and the "Voyage of Italy' in the Seventeenth Century* (Geneva, 1985), pp. 250, 43, 37. See also Hugh R. Trevor-Roper, *Catholics, Anglicans and Puritans: Seventeenth Century Essays* (Chicago, 1987), pp. 244–49, and George W. Whiting, *Milton's Literary Milieu* (New York, 1964), pp. 370–73.

[34]   Worden, *Roundhead*, pp. 39–64, 116–18, 339–44.

Toward the middle of the century, the historian Thomas Carlyle popularized the highly romanticized portrait of the "Puritan Revolution" that inspired Masson, Carlyle's great admirer and disciple.[35] In general, this portrait enhanced the Victorian tendency to simplify and sentimentalize seventeenth-century religious zealotry by confusing it with their own much more secular political liberalism. More specifically, it encouraged the habits of thought that allowed Marx, Weber, and the foundational Whig historians, Samuel Gardiner and Charles Firth, to attribute the rise of democracy, modernity, and modern science to Puritanism. Internal strains in these "grand narratives" eventually led later historians to explore the greater role played by skepticism, classical republicanism, natural law theory, and Baconianism in all three developments, factors that had been virtually ignored once the nineteenth-century rage for the "primitive" and the "medieval" replaced the eighteenth-century preference for politeness and polish. Taking umbrage at the ridicule heaped on the godly by Enlightenment historians and aestheticians, Victorians not only brought them back into vogue but turned a term of abuse into a term of endearment. Byron, Keats, Scott, and Tennyson all contributed to the popularity of a Gothic revival that embraced everything from "naive" poets, noble savages, and medieval manors to primitive politics and theology. Coleridge rehabilitated Bunyan and Carlyle restored Cromwell, no longer either the great Puritan "pretender" or hypocrite he had long been for Tories, or the great betrayer of the revolution that he had been for the Whigs, but a misunderstood martyr and noble ancestor of a newly respectable Nonconformity. In the process, he became the model of the primitive warrior-hero Carlyle so passionately admired, the opposite of the over-civilized Englishmen of his own day and the prototype of his own Scots Covenanting ancestors.[36]

Yet Carlyle's real contribution was to English mythology, not to history. Completely ignoring the first-hand accounts of the "great rebellion" by Lord Clarendon and Hobbes, both of which minimized the Puritan role, Carlyle made the godly its driving force.[37] He accomplished this primarily through his immensely influential edition of Cromwell's letters and speeches (1845), which both Samuel and Worden agree is a literally fictional "Cromwelliad," a German Romantic, anti-democratic, and far from accurate portrait of the faith of Carlyle's forefathers—a faith he had himself long since lost. Unlike Carlyle, most Victorian Nonconformists

---

[35] As Raphael Samuel points out in "The Discovery of Puritanism, 1820–1914: A Preliminary Sketch," in Alison Light (ed.), *Island Stories: Unravelling Britain* (London, 1998), the "'Puritan Revolution' was a neologism coined … by Guizot, popularized (though he did not use the phrase) by Carlyle, and assimilated to the constitutional proprieties (as well as domesticated for the university examination syllabuses) by Gardiner and Firth" (p. 280).

[36] Samuel, "Discovery," pp. 279–89.

[37] On Hobbes's and Clarendon's different yet parallel perspectives, see Michael G. Finlayson, *Historians, Puritanism, and the English Revolution: The Religious Factor in English Politics before and after the Interregnum* (Toronto, 1983), pp. 49–53.

were social democrats, but this portrait strongly appealed to them because it glorified their ancestors and upheld their own ideal of the self-sacrificing citizen-warrior hero, the type later featured in Kipling's imperial romances. This type fell out of fashion after the Second World War, but in the meantime, Gardiner and Firth had imported many of Carlyle's assumptions into their seminal reconstruction of the revolutionary era from primary documents. Their pioneering late nineteenth-century scholarship went virtually unquestioned until more recent historians began to realize that it not only promoted erroneously progressive assumptions about the Puritans, but that it also slighted political realities in favor of legal precedents. Finally, by casting the Puritans as heroic constitutionalists, like Carlyle they had actually created an idealized portrait of themselves, their Nonconformist heritage, and their late Victorian values.[38]

Neither Milton's political writings nor his poetry seemed susceptible of being painted into the Puritan paradigm until the belated discovery and translation of his *De Doctrina Christiana* in 1823. Macaulay's famous "Essay on Milton" directly responded to this event by denying that it advocates a primitive Christianity or that its theology resembled that of contemporary Quakers or Baptists. Ironically, *The Evangelical Magazine* (which represented the Nonconformist viewpoint) agreed, saying that Milton "was an Arian, a Polygamist, a Materialist, a Humanitarian, and in fact an abettor of almost every error which has infected the Church of God."[39] The Quakers were less theologically precise, but the list of "errors" cited above suggests the vast difference between the Christian faith of George Fox and someone like Milton, who stands in the liberal theological tradition that gave birth first to Socinianism and then to modern Unitarianism.[40] Samuel Johnson earlier supported this view by noting that Milton's final tracts on religion signaled his reconciliation with the Latitudinarian branch of Anglican tradition, although, as we now know, he was much less orthodox than they.[41] The Latitudinarians nevertheless supported similar causes—secular toleration and pluralism—by skeptically denying the Calvinist belief that truth is an indivisible whole.

---

[38] See, *seriatim*, Samuel, "Discovery," pp. 291–94; Worden, *Roundhead*, pp. 254–56, 264–95, 342, especially p. 270; and Nicholas Tyacke, *Aspects of English Protestantism c.1530–1700* (New York, 2001), pp. 5–7.

[39] Herbert McLachlan, *The Religious Opinions of Milton, Locke and Newton* (Manchester, 1941), p. 23, citing *The Evangelical Magazine* of 1825.

[40] For a Quaker reading of Milton's later work, see David Loewenstein, *Representing Revolution in Milton and His Contemporaries: Religion, Politics, and Polemics in Radical Puritanism* (Cambridge, 2001), pp. 242–91, 294–95. On Socinians, see Michael Lieb, "Milton and the Socinian Heresy," in Kelley et al. (eds.), *Milton and the Grounds of Contention*, pp. 234–83, 318–33.

[41] Samuel, "Discovery," pp. 283–84. For a modern documentation of this rapprochement, see Keith Stavely's editorial notes on *Of True Religion*, *CPW* 8:418–23, 426.

This view has been almost entirely ignored in modern Milton studies for numerous reasons, one of which is that Puritanism has long been the loose, elastic or indefinable concept that Hill rightly labeled "a refuge from clarity of thought."[42] Yet this looseness continues to prevail only in literary studies, not in historical or religious scholarship, which has risen to Hill's challenge by establishing a new and much narrower definition of terms. No longer a vague or virtually meaningless term, Puritanism for the modern historian is a sound way of categorizing men like Baxter, who if they had not called themselves Puritans would have to be considered such by later historians.[43] Another reason is that Miltonists have remained largely unaware that, as Zagorin complains:

> Wolfe's book [on the Puritan revolution], a useful contribution at the time of its appearance, is by now rather outdated. [Arthur] Barker's study, while it continues to stand out in Milton studies for its depth and insight, accorded a greater importance than is warranted to the poet's theological conceptions in shaping his political doctrines and idea of liberty. As for Hill's, the largest and most recent of these works, it is seriously flawed ... despite the author's great knowledge of Milton's time, by its crude decodings of Milton's poetry and its inability to provide any evidence to sustain its novel central thesis that Milton developed his religious and political beliefs in a continuous dialogue with the lower class radical and fringe groups of his society.[44]

Haller does not appear on Zagorin's list, but Nicholas Tyacke considers his "Whig" attempt to link Puritanism and liberty equally outdated; at worst, it even confuses Puritan beliefs with "ideas officially approved" by their episcopal opponents.[45]

Equally defunct is Hill's attempt to dissociate religious radicalism from Calvinism, an important ingredient in most literary assessments of Milton as a Puritan but non-Calvinist. Recent studies by Anthony Milton and many others have shown that, while radicals and conservatives disagreed on narrow points of doctrine, even the most radical saints shared a belief-system descended from Geneva. All Calvinists considered "true doctrine to be essentially constitutive of the church," and regarded "divine truth as an indivisible whole and any deviation

---

[42]   Christopher Hill, *Society and Puritanism in Pre-Revolutionary England* (London, 1964), p. 13. Hill began his career by redefining Gardiner's Puritan revolution as a Marxist or bourgeois revolution, but as Finlayson shows in *Historians*, pp. 27–31, his general outlook remained largely the same even though he later emphasized the religious radicals.

[43]   See Ian Breward, "The Abolition of Puritanism," *Journal of Religious History* 7.1 (1972): pp. 20–34, especially p. 32; Patrick Collinson, "A Comment: Concerning the Name Puritan," *Journal of English History* 31 (1980): pp. 483–88; Tom Webster, *Godly Clergy in Early Stuart England* (Cambridge, 1997), pp. 3–4.

[44]   Zagorin, *Milton*, p. ix.

[45]   Tyacke, *Aspects*, p. 9.

from it as heretical and potentially subversive."[46] Radical Antinomians departed from their more conservative brethren by rejecting Calvin's "double covenant" of works and grace, the "terrors of hell[,] and the need to search for signs and tokens," but these deviations actually strengthened their traditional emphasis on irresistible grace.[47] Imminently anticipating "that union which the divine nature, the Spirit, hath with and in our spirits" worked to "its own glory," Thomas Collier like other Antinomians believed that God would "wholly swallow up the Saints in that spiritual glory, which will be their eternal perfection."[48] The most radical of Hill's "Arminian" Puritans ultimately did support free will, yet as Norman Burns, Dewey Wallace, and David Como all show, they are best understood as anti-legalists who resisted the tendency of the Calvinist covenant of works to create an elect meritocracy at the expense of "free grace."[49] Hence their emphasis on the Inner Light actually made Antinomian Puritans more otherworldly and mystical than their brethren, not more ethically motivated, as Hill often implied. Abandoning the historical Christ and the "legal" Word for a living experience of heavenly rapture, many believed that they had been transformed into Christ.[50] Casting aside their Bibles in favor of this experience, they had no need to pray for the illumination of the Holy Spirit in reading scripture, as Milton and Taylor did; nor did they believe that self-disciplined moral effort, spiritual independence, and secular toleration would "free" them. In fact, religious radicals almost always considered secular or rational restraints as obstacles to the superior workings of the Spirit.[51]

Worden has long resisted the characterization of Puritans as proto-liberals even though he sympathizes with the effort "to soften the Puritan mentality and, as we suppose, to humanize it." Yet too often that effort willfully neglects

> the darknesses of Puritanism, at least in its 17th-century form. The volume of despair engendered by Puritan teaching on predestination is incalculable ... Social and economic explanations of Puritanism have collapsed, and we do not know how to replace them. In what sense can it have been in anyone's *interest* to

---

[46]   Anthony Milton, "The Unchanged Peacemaker? John Dury and the Politics of Irenicism in England, 1628–1643," in Mark Greengrass, Michael Leslie, and Timothy Raylor (eds.), *Samuel Hartlib and Universal Reformation* (Cambridge, 1994), p. 101.

[47]   See Morrill, who also shows that the radicals often went "*through* Puritanism and then *beyond* it" without truly departing from the "spiritual journey" they all sought; "A Liberation Theology?," p. 35.

[48]   Thomas Collier, cited in A.S.P. Woodhouse (ed.), *Puritanism and Liberty* (2nd ed., Chicago, 1951), p. 390.

[49]   Dewey M. Wallace, Jr., *Puritans and Predestination: Grace in English Protestant Theology, 1525–1695* (Chapel Hill, 1982), pp. 112–57, and David Como, *Blown by the Spirit: Puritanism and the Emergence of an Antinomian Underground in Pre-Civil-War England* (Stanford, 2004), pp. 13–72; see especially pp. 29–30.

[50]   Burns, *Christian Mortalism*, p. 46.

[51]   See, for instance, Worden's description of Ludlow's outlook in *Roundhead*, p. 48.

subscribe to … spiritual anxieties, to sit … through 19 long sermons in a week,
to endure endless fasts, to rise in the middle of the night for meditation and
suffer agonies of self-reproach for dozing beyond the appointed hour?[52]

Worden here refers to conservative Puritans, yet their "dream of order" offered
some of the same psychological compensations as Antinomianism. David Leverenz
shows that disciplinary Puritans could allay "conflict at every stage of a believer's
life," but only at the price of turning "what Puritans called self-knowledge" into
"an anxious and incessant effort to make all one's experiences fit the proper
pattern. The self must become God's instrument" in controlling "feelings of guilt,
anger, or inadequacy" through "relentless self-observation of personal sinfulness,
often expressed with meticulous detail in diaries. A private language of agonized
doubt complements a public language of militant submission."[53] Although radical
enthusiasts experienced more exaltation than humiliation, the price was often
equally high, and not essentially different: strenuous fasts, bouts with the devil,
and (particularly for women) torments that Sharon Achinstein links to abject self-
loathing.[54] Thus John Stachniewski hardly exaggerates when he characterizes
exchanges between such women as contests in "one-downsmanship."[55] Some
of Hill's favorite Puritans, men like Lawrence Clarkson, broke the mold by
experimenting in pantheism and amoral libertinism, yet they usually found their
final "rest in a characteristic way," in Clarkson's case, by accepting "the authority
of two fanatic 'Witnesses' whose concept of a transcendent and corporeal God
required" rejecting his previous beliefs and repudiating "human reason as a
deception of the Devil."[56]

These modern reevaluations may appear harsh, but even scholars who stress
the compensations of Puritanism's disciplinary logic no longer deny "the essential
correctness of the recent emphasis on the negative, anxiety-producing, repressed

---

[52] Blair Worden, Review of Paul S. Seaver, *Wallington's World: A Puritan Artisan in
Seventeenth-Century London* (1985), *LRB* (23 January–6 February 1986): pp. 16–17.

[53] David Leverenz, *The Language of Puritan Feeling: An Exploration in Literature,
Psychology, and Social History* (New Brunswick, 1980), pp. 13, 14. On the bruised will
and the repudiation of carnal reason, see also John von Rohr, *The Covenant of Grace in
Puritan Thought* (Atlanta, GA, 1986). Drawing on Keith Thomas, Conrad Russell argues
in his introduction to the *Origins of the English Civil War* (London, 1973) that Puritans
secretly wished to conserve, not to repudiate magic, especially the "magic" of providential
experience (p. 20). These studies strongly qualify Weber's assertion that their "doctrine
of grace made … the idea of the methodical demonstration of vocation in one's economic
behavior" a social ally of capitalism; see Max Weber, *Economy and Society*, ed. Guenther
Roth and Claus Wittich (New York, 1978), p. 575.

[54] Achinstein, *Literature and Dissent*, pp. 63–65, 67, 71–73.

[55] John Stachniewski, *The Persecutory Imagination: English Puritanism and the
Literature of Religious Despair* (Oxford, 1991), p. 41.

[56] Burns, *Christian Mortalism*, pp. 146–47.

aspects of mid-seventeenth century godlyism." John Morrill shows that its political counterpart can be found even in those most clearly liberated by Puritanism, men like Oliver Cromwell, who saw himself "working out his own destiny in relation to God's plan, and God was no democrat." Hence "liberation for most Puritans … meant liberation *for themselves* rather than liberation for others; and all-too-often it meant liberation for themselves but not *from themselves*"—precisely the opposite of what the young Milton sought in struggling to discover not just "what he was" but what "he may be."[57] This difference has far-reaching implications, because, whereas Whigs in the tradition of Samuel Gardiner defined "Puritanism not only as the political harbinger of liberal democracy, but also as 'a great moral force,'" modern historians increasingly depict it as a reactionary force.[58] Modern sociologists like David Zaret find the link between Puritanism and democracy no more sustainable than Hill's belief that religious "experientialism" fueled scientific experiment. Both ideas rest on highly selective, anachronistic, or self-interested readings of the evidence, which, at the most extreme, schematically identify Puritanism with progress and Anglicanism with reaction. Zaret notes that the secular version of this mythos persists in "ritual iterations of Mayflower history in classrooms, Sunday schools, and political rhetoric," but as early as 1973, many historians had already rejected the notion that the American Puritans were proto-democrats who farsightedly sowed the love of liberty.[59]

By 1974, Charles Webster had also successfully challenged the Merton/Hill thesis that Puritans led the scientific revolution, and the idea that they pioneered religious toleration is now equally discredited. Although they certainly fought against the suppression of their own beliefs, Peter Toon concludes that, like John Cotton, Puritans usually permitted "no religious toleration," since God never "'did ordain democracy as a fit government either for church or commonwealth.'"[60] They inherited these views from the theological inspiration behind much seventeenth-century Puritanism, William Perkins, who maintained that in a true Christian commonwealth "there may be no toleration of any other religion. For

---

[57] Morrill, "Liberation Theology?," pp. 29, 45, 33. For a fuller assessment of the non-democratic aspects of Cromwell's regime, see Patrick Little (ed.), *The Cromwellian Protectorate* (Rochester, NY, 2007), especially Blair Worden's essay, "Oliver Cromwell and the Council," pp. 82–104.

[58] John Netland, "Of Philistines and Puritans: Matthew Arnold's Construction of Puritanism," in Knoppers (ed.), *Puritanism and Its Discontents*, p. 68. Netland cites Timothy Lang, *The Victorians and the Stuart Heritage* (Cambridge, 1995), p. 20.

[59] David Zaret, "Religion and the Rise of Liberal-Democratic Ideology," *American Sociological Review* 54.2 (1989), pp. 163–79, cited p. 176. Writing in 1973, Peter Toon observes that "modern scholarship has effectively discounted the notion that Puritans were early democrats"; see *Puritans and Calvinism* (Swengel, PA, 1973), p. 31.

[60] Toon, *Puritans and Calvinism*, citing Cotton, p. 31. See also Charles Webster (ed.), *The Intellectual Revolution of the Seventeenth Century* (London, 1974), which records the debate over the "Merton hypothesis" begun in the pages of *Past and Present*.

that which is the end of God's laws must also be the end of all good laws in all commonwealths and kingdoms, namely, to shut up the people in the unity of one faith."[61] Followers like John Brinsley called upon "the godly magistrate not only to countenance the painful ministry but also to compel all the people to yield obedience thereunto," while others like Thomas Taylor insisted on suppressing offenses not just "against publike peace and humane societie; but blasphemies, heresies, swearing, sabboath-breaking; and such sins as more directly oppose God and his worship."[62] Even the Anabaptists, the driving force behind most radical offshoots of Puritanism, including the Quakers, opposed modern ideas of toleration. Although they maintained that "nobody has a right to take the sword" of justice, they meant "that no worldly person has a right to take the sword. Dominion is founded on grace," without which "you have, strictly speaking, no rights, and therefore no authority either to govern or to make war—least of all on the saints."[63] In fact, as William Lamont observes, even "the impulse to form Independent congregations was, at root, disciplinarian in nature, not libertarian: to create, not asylums from tyranny, but superior vehicles for godliness."[64] Like other Puritans, the Independents only reluctantly accepted toleration as an unforeseen corollary of their "charismatic revolt against those worldly institutions—for example, the universities, the church, law, and the state—that were seen as impediments to the creation of a holy commonwealth."[65]

Philip Benedict's broad study of European and English Calvinism aptly summarizes the new consensus among religious scholars that the movement's "historical importance ... does not lie in its connections to metanarratives of modernization," narratives that unduly obscure its "anthropological otherness."[66] Sociologists like Zaret trace this confusion to the lasting influence of the nineteenth- and early twentieth-century "grand narratives" of Comte, de Tocqueville, Marx, Durkheim, and Weber. Enduring to this day in the prefaces of

---

[61] William Perkins, *Workes of that Famovs and VVorthy minister of Christ* ...(3 vols., Cambridge, 1608–9), vol. 2, p. 289.

[62] John Brinsley, *The Third Part of the True Watch* (1623), p. 471, and Thomas Taylor, *Japhets First Public Perswasion* (Cambridge, 1612), sig. *3.

[63] Ronald Knox, *Enthusiasm: A Chapter in the History of Religion* (New York, 1950), p. 148.

[64] William Lamont, "Pamphleteering, the Protestant Consensus and the English Revolution," in R.C. Richardson and G.M. Ridden (eds.), *Freedom and the English Revolution* (Manchester, 1986), p. 78. On Milton's negative view of the Independents, see especially his public sonnet to Cromwell (Sonnet 16 in Hughes) and *The Likeliest Means to Remove Hirelings.*

[65] Zaret, "Religion," p. 171; on Puritan intolerance before the failure of their revolution, see p. 168. John Coffey is one of the few scholars who disputes this new consensus, but his conclusion concedes its major points; see "Puritanism and Liberty Revisited: The Case for Toleration in the English Revolution," *Historical Journal* 41.4 (1998): pp. 961–85.

[66] Benedict, *Christ's Churches*, p. 543.

widely taught college anthologies which stubbornly place Milton's Restoration poems in the "Puritan era," these narratives are flawed by the same overly abstract, teleological, and unverifiable methods and assumptions that flawed Whig history. Marx, for instance, simply regarded Puritanism as the secret weapon or "mask" of bourgeois capitalism, an empty abstraction that Durkheim corrected by showing that Protestant secularism was the end result of a long process of post-medieval differentiation between church and state. Yet even this improvement was marred by Durkheim's quasi-Marxian "*mimetic* or correspondence theory that makes change in religious and political beliefs a function" of the shift toward an ill-defined "individualism." By adding Puritan asceticism and "rationalism" to his theory of Protestant individualism, Weber constructed the most lasting and influential model of its role in producing modernity, but it, too, has long outlived its historical viability. No one, of course, denies Puritanism's undoubted contributions to the English revolution or its "leveling" effects on culture, but those effects require more careful definition than they usually receive. Puritans were above all true believers "united by shared experiences (social background, cohort, education), by networks of friendship, patronage, and formal organization, and by access to the intellectual precedents of the new ideology," nearly always some form of Calvinist or post-Calvinist orthodoxy. Zaret adds that this ideology was never intrinsically revolutionary, which is why Weber erred in making the saints a kind of "John the Baptist to Thomas Paine." [67] Leading religious scholars like Tyacke and Patrick Collinson support these findings by arguing that, if the monarchy had not upset the earlier and broader Calvinist consensus in the English church and blocked all parliamentary attempts at reform, the godly would have continued to support the King. In fact, many still did support him—or at least they accepted an extremely lenient view of a monarch sadly misled by "evil counselors"—throughout the civil war era.

Nevertheless, Weber was not entirely wrong in linking Puritanism to a dramatic rise in "affective individualism," an intensely religious form of self-fashioning markedly different from medieval modes of piety.[68] Yet as Stephen Greenblatt's work on the subject has shown, this form of self-fashioning was not unique to Puritanism but belonged to the Reformation as a whole. It can thus be found in progressive Catholics like Thomas More and Erasmus, who brought the techniques of radical humanist critique to bear on it.[69] When intensified by the forms of self-scrutiny and discipline inherent in Calvin's and Luther's teachings on man's absolute moral insufficiency to achieve salvation, "affective individualism" naturally increased among both mainline English Protestants and Puritans. Yet,

[67]   Zaret, "Religion," pp. 166, 167.

[68]   Tyacke, *Anti-Calvinists*; Patrick Collinson, *The Religion of Protestants* (Oxford, 1982), and "Sects and the Evolution of Puritanism," in Francis J. Bremer (ed.), *Puritanism: Transatlantic Perspectives on a Seventeenth-Century Anglo-American Faith* (Boston, MA, 1993), pp. 147–166.

[69]   Stephen Greenblatt, *Renaissance Self-Fashioning* (Chicago, 1980), pp. 11–73.

for Collinson, Puritans, including Quakers, chiefly differ from other Protestants in exhibiting a much stronger inclination toward dualism. In every moment of crisis, the Puritan habit of strongly distinguishing between the godly and the "malignant," Christ and Antichrist, the True Church and popery—or in the case of Quakers, the Outer and Inner Word—reasserted itself. This habit could and did "functionally radicalize" devout men like Cromwell, yet Collinson considers that process is not a function of Puritanism per se but an effect produced whenever an extreme ideology confronts revolutionary circumstances. Not all or even most of those who joined the parliamentary side of the revolution were motivated by this ideology. Other incentives ranged from localist resentment of misrule and national resentment of arbitrary government to widespread Protestant fears of international Catholicism. Most historians regard the latter as the *sine qua non* in fracturing the English people's conventional and (as it proved) enduring commitment to the monarchy, but even this issue was far from an exclusively Puritan concern.[70] Politically, the vast majority of Puritans were actually Presbyterians who welcomed back the restored king, as did Richard Baxter, who argued against Milton that even tyrants like Nero should be obeyed.[71] Charles II's invitation to include this faction in the national church was defeated by bitter bishops, biased magistrates, and his Cavalier Parliament, yet the subsequent "Great Persecution" of Puritans proved ironically empowering for the godly; they responded by establishing independent Nonconformist churches and educational institutions that survived into the twentieth century.

Yet even these gains are linked to the Puritans' essentially dualist or separatist vision of society, which is why winnowing the wheat from the chaff had always been a prime purpose of their preaching and teaching. In the 1640s Arthur Hildersam proclaimed that "The elect of God are made the better and the rest the worse by it, and God will be glorified in them both." As in Puritan thought generally, here divine grace and glory are not literally "free" in the sense of freely pardoning all, nor "free" in the sense of "just." They respond "neither [to] the good workes he [God] fore-saw we should doe, nor the faith he fore-saw we should have, ... but his owne good pleasure onely." Once granted, they give the Elect the power of "restraining grace" over the Reprobate, while among the chosen, Perkins says that they "bridle[s] and restrain[s] the corruptions of men's hearts from breaking forth into outward actions, for the common good, that societies may be preserved."[72] As the English revolutionaries became even more "functionally radicalized," this "common good" was often maintained by violent means: "no danger was to be thought difficult when God called for the shedding

---

[70] Patrick Collinson, *The Birthpangs of Protestant England: Religious and Cultural Change in the Sixteenth and Seventeenth Centuries* (New York, 1988), pp. 132–36; on Milton and radical humanist critique, see pp. 96–97.

[71] William Lamont, *Richard Baxter and the Millennium* (London, 1979), pp. 91, 103.

[72] Arthur Hildersam, *CLII Lectures upon Psalm LI* (London, 1642), p. 735; Perkins, *Workes*, vol. 2, p. 131.

of blood" or overthrowing the "temporal governments" he anathematized—or so John Evelyn complained in his diary.[73]

The most repressive aspect of Puritan thought is, of course, the most familiar: its suppression of "almost all forms of music, masques, plays, sport, dancing, painting, modern architecture, most forms of non-theological literature, ... over-high status for women, peace with the Habsburgs, long hair, may-poles, foreigners in general and foreign travel in particular." At times, these Puritan phobias seem to confirm some of Jonson's or Samuel Butler's most exaggerated caricatures of hysterical Puritan legalists and iconoclasts, which certainly contributed to the post-Restoration backlash against the godly. Their draconian laws had included making the sin of adultery—for Milton, a potentially forgivable trespass, even "though repeated" (*CPW* 2:591, 674)—punishable by death for women.[74] Notoriously "judaizing," as Milton complained in *Areopagitica*, the godly feared adultery as "a fire" that even the liberal Roger Williams claimed that this "holy nation, bred up and fed with miraculous dispensations," must root out; for the "gentiles, the nations of the world, will never be proved capable of such laws & punishments."[75] Like iconoclasm itself, these attitudes spring from Puritanism's scriptural or "Hebraic" literalism, its attempt to apply Old Testament sanctions and laws to a new "holy nation."

Ultimately, however, it cannot be said that Milton was never influenced by Puritan thought or that it made absolutely no contribution toward democracy or modernity. While hardly welcomed by the godly, Milton's attempt to harmonize Hebrew and Christian teachings on divorce had, in retrospect, liberalizing implications not unlike Williams's radical belief that all religions should be tolerated by Christians much as they had been by the Jews after their state was established. Levellers like John Lilburne and William Walwyn also contributed to early notions of human rights and republican virtues, as did John Goodwin, although many were less directly inspired by Calvinist tenets than by more humanist theologians such as Grotius and Hooker and skeptics such as Charron

---

[73]   John Evelyn, *Diary and Correspondence* (4 vols., London, 1857), vol. 1, pp. 286–87.

[74]   Chaney, *Grand Tour*, p. 43. On the relevance of the Puritan caricature, see Margaret Aston, "Puritans and Iconoclasm, 1560–1660," in Christopher Durston and Jacqueline Eales (eds.), *The Culture of English Puritanism, 1560–1700* (New York, 1996), pp. 92–121. Chaney notes that Puritans also persecuted witches to an extent impossible under Laud and "without parallel in Europe": see *The Grand Tour*, pp. 318–19, On the adultery law, see Keith Thomas, "The Puritans and Adultery: The Act of 1650 Reconsidered," in Donald Pennington and Keith Thomas (eds.), *Puritans and Revolutionaries: Essays in Seventeenth-Century History presented to Christopher Hill* (Oxford, 1978), pp. 257–82. G.E. Aylmer chronicles the Puritan closure of more than 200 alehouses in *The State's Servants* (London, 1973), pp. 312–14.

[75]   Roger Williams (16 December 1649), *Collections of the Massachusetts Hist. Soc*, 4th ser. 6 (Boston, 1863), p. 276.

and Montaigne.[76] Additionally, while the congregational "contracturalism" of the Independents and other sectarians rarely produced authentically democratic habits of thought, it clearly developed their congregations' ability to participate in the public sphere and (without necessarily making them proto-capitalists) it also expanded their organizational and economic skills.[77] Milton himself was admired by Goodwin, Williams, Walwyn, and other Levellers, including his friend Richard Overton, although Overton seems to have had relatively little influence on the poet's mortalist convictions.[78]

Milton was an eclectic reader and patriotic citizen; his late political sonnets and prose show that he in turn could admire Sir Thomas Fairfax even though he detested most Presbyterians, and could place his hopes in politicians like Cromwell even though he feared the religious Independents supported by him. His political sonnets and prose eulogies nevertheless praise his Puritan heroes mainly in "noble Roman," not in religious terms. Hence, while he lived, lectured, and worked alongside prominent Puritan supporters of the revolution he defended, and while there were many points of agreement between Milton and the godly, his outlook consistently remained closer to the Arminians, Latitudinarians, Baconians, and neo-Roman republicans of his era. In other words, while Milton certainly sustained a career *among* the Puritans, like his fellow polemicists, John Hall and Marchamont Nedham, he was probably never *of* them. Like Thomas Ellwood, many of the broader-minded saints admired his humanistic learning, ethics, and rhetoric, but in the end, he was alienated from a Puritan regime whose "insanities" and other "crimes" he found "worthier of silence than of publication" (*CPW* 7:515), as he frankly informed his friend Henry Oldenburg, a founding secretary of the Royal Society.

In this Milton was hardly alone: John Wilkins, Thomas Sprat, Robert Boyle, John Dryden, and Andrew Marvell (to name but a few) either served or supported Parliament or Cromwell's Protectorate but later openly or quietly recanted. Except for Sprat and Dryden, most were reluctant royalists who lacked Milton's obstinate republican convictions but shared many of his Baconian ideas about progress. Exploring such connections both early and late thus places the poet in a very different milieu from the one he currently occupies—but one in which Saurat might have placed him if he had had the advantage of recent scholarship on seventeenth-century science, politics, and religion. This "place" is at the forefront of a "Protestant ethic" no longer principally the property of Puritans but pioneered by the other progressives surveyed throughout this study. Many began life as

---

[76] Walwyn's humanist reading is well known; on Goodwin, see Coffey, *John Goodwin*, pp. 30–33. Nevertheless, as a Puritan divine, Goodwin's outlook remained firmly scholastic and "overwhelmingly religious" (pp. 34, 35).

[77] David Zaret, *The Heavenly Contract: Ideology and Organization in Pre-Revolutionary Puritanism* (Chicago, 1985). Tyacke shows that Puritanism also had anti-economic implications in *Aspects*, pp. 90–110, especially p. 105.

[78] Burns, *Christian Mortalism*, pp. 169, 174, 179.

Puritans but later migrated toward religious rationalism rather than Antinomian mysticism. Milton's enduring commitment to rationalist ideals even in his less optimistic later years not only explains why the Royal Society virtuosi considered making him their poet laureate, but also why his work found so much success in the anti-Puritan climate of the Restoration.[79] Long afterward, Puritanism would remain an influential and positive ingredient in modernity, but less in pioneering democracy than in spawning conservation and health food movements, and Victorian and modern campaigns for better hygiene, fitness, and more "natural" relationships among the sexes.[80] Milton probably would have approved these reforms much as he probably would have applauded John Wesley's non-Calvinist return to primitive Christianity, but none of these sympathies authentically define him as a Puritan.

It remains to be said that, while the views presented here are obviously "revisionist," they are not faddish. The historiography surveyed in this book now rests on the careful empirical scholarship of the past two generations. Although post-revisionists have made many needed corrections to the model proposed by the "father" of 1970s revisionism, Conrad Russell, the co-authors of his Festschrift—Thomas Cogswell, Richard Cust, and Peter Lake—note that his work was never the complete rupture with the past that it may have at first seemed. Its many pre-revisionist antecedents include work by Gerald Aylmer, J.G.A. Pocock, and William Lamont; Lamont in turn credits C.H. George with first seeing through the "alchemistical tricks" of the Puritanism-and-democracy men, and Murray Tolmie with first clarifying the differences between religious Independents like Goodwin and political independents like Milton. Zaret cites Leo Solt's early work on the New Model Army (1959), and in literary studies, I would also give Lawrence Sasek (1961) an honorable mention. These studies all prepared historians for Tyacke's groundbreaking documentation of the fact that the English Puritans were not radical reformers but reactionaries resisting not just Archbishop Laud's ceremonies but his liberal Arminian theology (1973).[81] In most cases, their

---

[79]   On Milton's proposed career as Royal Society laureate, see Nicholas von Maltzahn, "Laureate, Republican, Calvinist: An Early Response to Milton and *Paradise Lost* (1667)," *Milton Studies* 29 (1992), pp. 181–98; on his Royal Society sympathies, see Joanna Picciotto, "Reforming the Garden: The Experimentalist Eden and *Paradise Lost*," *ELH* 72 (2005): pp. 23–78, and Catherine G. Martin, "Rewriting the Revolution: Milton, Bacon, and the Royal Society Rhetoricians," in Juliet Cummins and David Burchell (eds.), *Science, Literature, and Rhetoric in Early Modern Europe* (Aldershot, 2007), pp. 95–123.

[80]   Samuel, "Discovery," pp. 299–306.

[81]   Thomas Cogswell, Richard Cust, and Peter Lake (eds.), *Politics, Religion and Popularity in Early Stuart Britain: Essays in Honour of Conrad Russell* (Cambridge, 2002). Tyacke's groundbreaking essay is reprinted in *Aspects*, pp. 132–59. Both Lawrence A. Sasek's *The Literary Temper of the English Puritans* (Baton Rouge, 1961) and Leo F. Solt's *Saints in Arms* (Stanford, 1959) established vast differences between Milton and the saints, but neither work has had a noticeable impact on Milton studies. Zaret cites Solt in

objections to this theology made them post-Restoration Dissenters from the very church Milton was working to make even more liberal.

Accepting the less flattering Puritan portraits of modern scholarship does not mean abandoning old political heroes or divorcing history from ideology, modern or early modern. It merely means rejecting the earlier "lumping" of incompatible rebels like Milton, Goodwin, and Baxter along with Whig "inevitability theory," the idea that democracy sprang full-born from a revolution "propelled by capitalist imperatives, led by the bourgeoisie, or animated by revolutionary Puritanism." Cogswell, Cust, and Lake show that even the "'postrevisionists,' who rightly … reject the revisionist claim" that social and constitutional conflict in early Stuart England was either non-existent or had no social basis, agree with this major correction to Whig teleology.[82] They also usefully dispel the myth that post-revisionists have returned to the older paradigm, and that Russell's "high political antiquarianism" has been replaced by "ignored issues of ideology." Sensitive to poststructuralist critiques of "grand narrative," revisionists and post-revisionists commonly adopt a newer definition of "'ideology' … as the operating assumptions, the often implicit, only partially articulated, beliefs and expectations that underpinned the workings of the polity." This more flexible, non-party-based approach to ideology became necessary simply because "previous attempts to establish … long-term continuities and causal links had been botched; that is to say 'Whig' or 'Marxist' historians had too easily assumed or too readily asserted continuities between one period and another in their search for the causes of the Civil War." At present, the issue remains not *if* this period should be related to our own, but *how*, since the older, more anachronistic picture was a "job … done badly, not … [one] that … should not be done at all."[83]

J.H. Hexter is usually singled out for first pinpointing the folly of "compulsive lumping," the kind of over-simplification that first "botched" our understanding of Milton's period, Commenting on this error, Raymond B. Waddington notes that it was especially linked to the Marxist tendency to treat seventeenth-century religion as an epiphenomenon whose real meaning is modern political "radicalism"—a word whose current meaning had not yet been invented. Hill's highly evocative work exhibits this tendency by approving "radical individuals" who claimed to be Christ without specifying how their "religio-hallucinogenic" habits made them more democratic or even more "free."[84] For as Hill surely knew, this mentality often made them more, not less, intolerant, and it rarely if ever contributed to the development of modern constitutional principles or rights. As for the term

---

"Religion," p. 170. Murray Tolmie's *The Triumph of the Saints: The Separate Churches of London, 1616–1649* (Cambridge, 1977) is thoroughly discussed in Chapter 2 below.

[82]   David Zaret, *Origins of Democratic Culture: Printing, Petitions, and the Public Sphere in Early-Modern England* (Princeton, 2000), pp. 37–39.

[83]   Cogswell et al., *Politics*, pp. 9, 10, 12.

[84]   Raymond B. Waddington, "Milton Turned Upside Down," *Journal of Modern History* 51 (1979), pp. 108–12, cited p. 109.

"radical," Burns notes that while Hobbes, Milton, and Overton all certainly deserve the label, that hardly means that "the defender of the absolute power of the state, the defender of the regicides and of minority rule, and the defender of the Leveller ideal of a republic built on … nearly universal manhood suffrage" were of the same camp.[85] All disliked precedent and tradition, yet in the end, their chief contribution to the future lay in attempting to fuse the pagan values of classical antiquity—especially in Milton's and Overton's case, its republican virtue ethic—with various forms of Christian faith. Far more than the Antinomians who rejected standard Christian morality, these three thinkers contributed to modernity by pursuing rational explanations of Christian mystery that Puritans found deeply suspicious. Like Taylor, Milton affirmed that the remains of divine light left to us after the Fall continue as a "kind of gleam or glimmering" of the "unwritten law of nature … given to the first man" in the hearts of all mankind (*CPW* 6:516). Never alien to reason, this "light" resolves apparently conflicting statements about God and man (*CPW* 6:134). The same rationalism—which Milton early encountered at St. Paul's School—lent itself to anti-ceremonialism and "low church" ecclesiology, which was never the exclusive property of Puritans.[86]

In defending a largely untrained, non-preaching parish clergy against Puritan attacks, Richard Hooker seminally applied an exalted "rhetoric of self importance … to the general run of ministers without embarrassment," a rhetoric that soon became available to the humble lay preachers of the "low church" or radical sects.[87] Hence both among more conservative and "hotter" Puritan factions, the godly minister guided the communal ways of thinking of his congregation, which allowed individual experiences to be "collectivised and magnified," so that "the perceived persecution of the individual [became] the persecution of the group and, by the logic of godly rhetoric, … of the visible church." Tom Webster further shows that even among the most radical sects, including the minister-less Quakers, godly communalism tended "to elide the distinction between the visible and invisible church"—a distinction always staunchly maintained by Milton.[88] Stephen

---

[85]   Burns, *Christian Mortalism*, pp. 188, 19. Conal Condren urges that the word "radical" should be used only as an adjective in the seventeenth-century context, not as a noun; see *The Language of Politics in Seventeenth-Century England* (New York, 1994), p. 162. J.C.D. Clark also critiques the term "radical" as an anachronistic label; see *Revolution and Rebellion: State and Society in England in the Seventeenth and Eighteenth Centuries* (Cambridge, 1986), pp. 16, 106.

[86]   On the anachronism of low church/high church distinctions and on the Latitudinarian position, see Tyacke, *Aspects*, pp. 24, 320–39. On Milton's early introduction to liberal theology, see Donald Lemen Clark, *John Milton at St. Paul's School* (New York, 1948), pp. 67, 77–80, and Chapter 2 below.

[87]   Peter Lake, *Anglicans and Puritans? Presbyterians and English Conformist Thought from Whitgift to Hooker* (London, 1988), p. 217.

[88]   Webster, *Godly Clergy*, pp. 142, 139; see also Lake, *Anglicans and Puritans?*, pp. 28–29, 241–42, and "Presbyterianism, the National Church and the Argument from Divine

Honeygosky agrees that his "concept of church … was predominantly mystical, spiritual, invisible, and increasingly internal," but he errs in linking the radical sects to this model, since visible collectivization literally defined the "gathered" churches.[89] Finally, even Milton's "spirit within" is the opposite of the Puritans' Inner Light, since its work is supplementary, not overwhelming or inscrutable. Like the eye-clearing herbs and drops "from the Well of Life" that naturally "purge" the "inmost seat" of Adam's "mental sight" after the Fall (*PL* 11.414–22), Milton maintains that the "illumination of the Holy Spirit" *assists* our reading of "holy scripture," the "*main* foundation of our protestant religion," but it never *replaces* mental insight as it does among the sectaries. The operation of this Spirit is so fundamentally uncertain that it validates biblical interpretations "warrantable only to our selves and to such whose consciences we can so perswade" (*CPW* 7:242). By definition, it thus invalidates all "New Forcers of Conscience," disciplinary or enthusiastic.

Despite this evidence, Miltonists overwhelmingly prefer to associate their poet with some variant of Puritanism rather than with the religious rationalists, in part because they see them as forebears of tepid Christianity or even Enlightenment "neo-paganism." Yet, as Worden notes, Enlightenment Christianity did *not* forsake religion but merely defended the "claims of 'reason' against 'enthusiasm.'" Finding enthusiasts guilty of "'presumption' in 'meddling with the secret councils of God,'" Christian moderates rejected the "'flaming conceit that we have great personal interests with the deity … [who] sets us far above those who have less pride and more sense than ourselves.'" Such conceits, they rightly felt, either intentionally or unconsciously reflected worldly prejudices rather than promoting true love of neighbor, and thus reaped what they sowed: "implacable hatred, animosities, and uncharitableness amongst men of the same nation"—not harmony, brotherly love, practical reform, or real social progress. Hence these "modern" Christians agreed with both Milton and Bacon that "We cannot 'serve God by sequestering for a time all the faculties which he has given us, by sending our wits out of doors to make room for grace'"; God is better served by a faith that "'improves and enlarges the faculties of men, exalts their spirits, [and] … inspires them with generous and beneficent affections to one another.'"[90] Nor did the Enlightenment institute the sudden "fall" into instrumental reason or scientific rationality still widely held responsible for the "one-dimensional man" of Herbert Marcuse and late Marxism generally. Post-Marxists and postmodernists only slightly alter this critique by

---

Right," in Peter Lake and Maria Dowling (eds.), *Protestantism and the National Church* (London, 1987), pp. 193–224.

[89]   Stephen R. Honeygosky, *Milton's House of God: The Invisible and Visible Church* (Columbia, MO, 1993), p. 42; on enthusiasm and the visible church, see Knox, *Enthusiasm*, pp. 173–75, and Geoffrey Nuttall, *Visible Saints: The Congregational Way 1640–1660* (Oxford, 1957).

[90]   Worden, *Roundhead*, p. 197, citing John Trenchard and Thomas Gordon, *Cato's Letters*, ed. Ronald Hamowy (2 vols., Liberty Fund, 1995).

holding science responsible for creating an "n-dimensional," hypertextual man equally devoid of authenticity. Zaret rightly accuses both theories of producing a non-existent "epistemic break" in which "a pristine view of communicative realities" prevails only in the early "pre-commercial" era. Logocentrically supposing "that signification run riot was not an important feature of mediated communication in the age of the printing press," these theories overlook the fact that liberal-democratic values ironically sprang from the same chaotic proliferation of information that they "hold responsible for the dissolution of modernism and liberal faith in reason as a progressive force."[91]

To correct this mistaken view, Zaret argues that Habermas's "public sphere" should be pushed back from the Enlightenment into the seventeenth century, when truly "binary" political parties in the modern sense were not yet formed. This earlier public sphere was inadvertently created by the sudden implosion of the central government and by practical imperatives that far out-paced formal theories about how to reinstate or transform the "ancient constitution." As Achinstein similarly shows, English men and women were spontaneously forced into a newly created public forum simply by exercising their right to petition across lines of religion, rank, or social class.[92] Realizing that these revolutionary opportunities were not created by any single group, movement, or ideology not only encourages focusing on more truly "material" factors such as print culture and popular literacy, but essentially confirms W.K. Jordan's early insight that "The trend of constitutional development in England was determined by compulsive historical events which theorists influenced only very slightly."[93]

Reexploring Milton's creative responses to these events has required dividing this study into two sections, the first of which is much more general and historical in focus. Part I defines Puritanism, the Puritan Revolution, and the historically revised account of the multiple causes and effects of the "Great Rebellion." It also details the very real differences between the godly and what has sometimes been called the "church of Milton"; the non-Puritan dimension of Milton's early poetry and prose; and his Baconian and republican proposals for ecclesiastical, educational, and legal reform. It concludes with a broad historical overview of the different approaches to law, education, science, rhetoric, and the ministry taken by Puritans and by religious rationalists like Milton. Part II traces the effects of these mainly secular-rationalist influences (including classical republicanism) on Milton's major poems. This portion includes one chapter on the proto-modern cosmology and anthropology of *Paradise Lost*, one on Milton's experimentation with post-Restoration neoclassicism in *Paradise Regained*, and one on the "tragic" republicanism of *Samson Agonistes*. It concludes with a brief Afterword

---

[91]   Zaret, *Origins*, pp. 275–79, cited p. 278.

[92]   Ibid., pp. 37–39; Sharon Achinstein, *Milton and the Revolutionary Reader* (Princeton, 1994), especially pp. 9–26, 17.

[93]   W.K. Jordan, *Men of Substance: A Study of the Thought of Two English Revolutionaries, Henry Parker and Henry Robinson* (Chicago, 1942), p. 141.

on Milton's posthumous contribution to the secular theories of toleration advanced by the liberal Latitudinarians, radical Whigs, and Deists who later supported or advanced his cause. Throughout, the novelty of my approach to these questions requires a broad synthesis of traditional source studies and new intellectual history with literary "close-reading," a method best suited to a work midway between literary history and criticism.

PART I
The Revolutionary Era:
Historical Overview and Analysis of
Milton's Early Works

Chapter 1
A Brief History of the "Puritan Revolution"

The Causes and Motives of sedition are, innovation in religion; taxes; alteration of laws and customs; breaking of privileges; general oppression; advancement of unworthy persons; strangers; dearths; disbanded soldiers; factions grown desperate; and whatsover, in offending people, hath joined them in a common cause.

—Francis Bacon, "Of Seditions and Troubles"

Without scholarship there is no history, only fashion.

—Blair Worden, *Roundhead Reputations*

In retrospect, Francis Bacon's essay "Of Seditions and Troubles" seems to prophesy the causes and, as some contemporaries later believed, even the outbreak of the English civil wars. An astute politician and peace-maker, Bacon had long advised the Stuarts against their apparent drift toward "arbitrary government" only to be overruled by the "advancement of unworthy persons." Rather than changing course, however, James I's son vastly increased the widespread discontent produced by "innovation in religion; taxes; alteration of laws and customs; breaking of privileges; [and] general oppression," thus becoming the first European king deposed by his own people. No one denies that all these factors led to his overthrow, or that Charles I's "innovations in religion" were the most crucial cause. Yet contrary to Samuel R. Gardiner's and Sir Charles H. Firth's epochal assumptions about the "Puritan Revolution," not just the godly but a broad spectrum of Protestants rose up to defend their church, and the godly were not an avant-garde factor but much more of a rear-guard force in this movement.[1] Despite much general agreement on this basic reevaluation, no "brief history" of

---

[1] See Samuel R. Gardiner, *History of England from the Accession of James I to the Outbreak of the Civil War, 1603–42* (10 vols., London, 1883–84); *History of the Great Civil War, 1642–1649* (4 vols., London, 1893); and *History of the Commonwealth and Protectorate* (4 vols., London, 1903); Charles H. Firth, *The Last Years of the Protectorate* (2 vols., London, 1909); Godfrey Davies, *The Restoration of Charles II* (London, 1955); and Herbert Butterfield, *The Whig Interpretation of History* (London, 1931); G.M. Trevelyan, *Tudors and the Stuart Era* (Garden City, NJ, 1954). Early critics include J.P. Kenyon, *The Stuart Constitution, 1603–1688* (Cambridge, 1966), and Christopher Hill, *Puritanism and Revolution* (New York, 1964), although Hill's Marxist views ultimately support the Whig

the demise of their Puritan Revolution thesis can possibly cover the many fissures that led to the rise of the new historical consensus or the more minor ones that remain. What follows is thus a broad overview of the main lines of agreement on the root causes of the civil wars and the contributions, positive as well as negative, made by seventeenth-century English Puritanism.

Puritan Religion

Simply defining English Puritanism, let alone its contribution to the civil wars, is almost too large a task for a single chapter, especially since scholars now agree that this movement has no static spiritual or moral "essence." Patrick Collinson cautions against considering Puritanism an "independent, free-standing entity" when it is actually "an oppositional, agitatory movement, frequently in conflict with the secular and ecclesiastical authorities" from the time of Henry VIII through the Elizabethan settlement and the Laudian era. Climaxing in the latter period, Puritan resistance to church policy regularly led its opponents to claim that the godly were fundamentally rebellious and anti-authoritarian.[2] Yet this polemical charge cannot be taken at face value; Collinson among many others believes that English Puritanism might have proved as socially conservative at home as it was on the Continent and in the colonies had it been supported by the crown. Peter Lake has slightly qualified this view, but he agrees that the "hotter sort of Protestants" were never fully radicalized until the Laudians seemed to threaten a return to "popery."[3] This general agreement is the culmination of a long history of challenges concerning the term "Puritan." Christopher Hill, Geoffrey Elton, Basil Hall, and C.H. and Katherine George all complained that the designation had become so vague and misleading that it should be abandoned altogether. That never happened, because scholars soon realized that the term was too useful and, when carefully defined, too accurate to lose.[4] Abandoning it would

---

historians, as does Lawrence Stone, *The Causes of the English Revolution* (New York, 1972). On their overlap, see Finlayson, *Historians*, pp. 27–43.

[2]   Durstun and Eales (eds.), *Culture of English Puritanism*, p. 3; and Collinson, *Birthpangs*, p. 143, and "Comment."

[3]   Collinson, "Sects," pp. 150–51. Collinson aims at discrediting the teleological assumptions of Haller and Hill. Lake slightly qualifies this view in "Defining Puritanism—again?" in the same volume, Bremer (ed.), *Puritanism: Transatlantic Perspectives*, pp. 3–29.

[4]   See, *seriatim*, Basil Hall, "Puritanism: The Problem of Definition," *Studies in Church History* 2 (1965): pp. 283–96, W. J. Sheils, *Puritans in the Diocese of Peterborough 1558–1610* (Northampton: Northampton Record Society, 1979), vol. 30, p. 2; C.H. George, "Puritanism as History and Historiography," *Past and Present* 41 (1968): pp. 77–104; and William Hunt, *The Puritan Moment* (Cambridge, MA, 1983), pp. 145–46. See also Durston and Eales (eds.), *Culture*, pp. 1–31.

also do a grave disservice to the seventeenth-century men and women who knew, used, and in many cases embraced the term as a proud self-description. Even as a term of opprobrium the label remains useful, for as Lake points out, the actual difference between Puritan caricature and sympathetic description is largely one of perspective: contemporaries did not disagree over *what* Puritans believed but over the value, negative or positive, of those beliefs.[5] Serving and being saved by a stern and demanding Maker was a high calling for their brethren even though they acknowledged its "dark side." They knew it often led believers to engage in obsessive bouts of "'self-judging, and to frequent prayer, and reading, and serious thoughts'" of damnation or salvation, much as it did Margaret Charlton, Richard Baxter's future wife. Cromwell, like other lesser-known Puritans, suffered from nagging doubts and fears that formed the typical side-effects of Calvin's emphasis on human unworthiness before divine justice.[6]

This predisposition toward potentially damaging introspection is notably lacking in Milton, John Hales, Henry More, or other English Protestants who early left the rigors of Calvinism aside either on their own (as in More's case) or through outside influences. As a result, tortured conscience is one relatively easy means of distinguishing religious Puritans from other Protestants, especially since other attitudes—millenarianism, providentialism, and anti-Catholicism—are now considered the common property of all Protestants, not of Puritans alone. Protestants were also commonly concerned with eliminating the outdated superstitions, ceremonies, and hierarchies that had crept into the post-apostolic church, pan-European preoccupations diversely taken up by Erasmus, Hus, Wyclif, Foxe, Hooker, More, and Sarpi, to name only some of the more prominent Reformers.[7]

---

[5]   Peter Lake, "'A Charitable Christian Hatred': The Godly and Their Enemies in the 1630s," in Durston and Eales (eds.), *Culture*, pp. 178–9.

[6]   Durston and Eales, *Culture*, p. 11; Margaret Charlton's experience is cited from Richard Baxter, *A Breviate of the Life of Margaret, the daughter of Francis Charlton of Appleby in Shropshire esquire ...* (1681), p. 4. Cromwell's experience is discussed in John Morrill's chapter on "The Making of Oliver Cromwell," in John Morrill (ed.), *Oliver Cromwell and the English Revolution* (London, 1990), pp. 19–48. For another useful portrait of Puritan scruples, see Margo Todd, "Puritan Self-Fashioning," in Bremer (ed.), *Puritanism: Transatlantic Perspectives*, pp. 57–87.

[7]   As Horton Davies pointed out in a classic study, *Worship and Theology in England: From Andrewes to Baxter and Fox, 1603–1690* (Princeton, 1975), both the original Calvinist tradition and the Scottish church actually approved set liturgies, "not only a set order of items of worship, but set prayers as well." These liturgies were based on solid scriptural foundations—the "Psalms and the Aaronic blessing in Numbers" (pp. 189, 190). Later objections to this tradition stemmed from at least five very different criticisms, not all of which are exclusively Puritan. The first three are typical of the godly: interference with the Holy Spirit, with individual ministers or congregations, and with "Christian liberty" narrowly defined (see Coolidge below). Yet, as shown in what follows, the latter two, encouragement of lay hypocrisy and church hierarchy (Davies, pp. 189–94), were shared by a far broader spectrum of English and continental Reformers.

Belief in England as an elect nation with a special relationship to God and even the identification of the pope as Antichrist have also lost their exclusive Puritan status since even extreme rationalists like Hobbes and Locke held these or similar beliefs.[8] For Lake, even the concept of an "elect nation" is much more ambiguous than generally thought: "ultimately Antichrist would lose and Christ would win, [but] it was still an open question whether England would triumph with Christ or be destroyed with Antichrist."[9] Widespread European as well as English attempts to purify the church as the apocalypse approached explain why most historians now prefer to call Puritans "precisians," "professors," the Elect, or "Protestants of the hotter sort"; many conformists and Anglicans (a term now reserved for post-Restoration churchmen and women) simply took a more gradual, peaceable, or (like the group gathered at Little Gidding) less interventionist approach to pure worship. The "hotter sort" rejected gradualism because they were more deeply afraid that the "papist" contamination of church and state was a sign of Antichrist's approaching victory. Puritans—still an accurate synonym for the "precisians" who clung to Calvin's teachings on predestination and irresistible grace—were also more deeply inspired by the Genevan dream of establishing a holy community, as were their Antinomian brethren.

English Puritanism has long roots going back as far as Wyclif, the Lollards, Hussites, and apparently isolated "heretics" like Anne Askew in the reign of Henry VIII.[10] The movement gained much more of a mainstream following in the later sixteenth century, particularly after 1572, when John Field and Thomas Wilcox's "First Admonition" complemented the work of Thomas Cartwright's advocacy of a Presbyterian policy for the church. William Perkins's covenant theology (*c.* 1588) later proved an equally enduring influence on seventeenth-century Puritanism, and continental Anabaptism, its far more radical counterpart, was not far behind. Yet, since Anabaptists focused less on doctrine than practice, most branches of English Puritanism drew more deeply upon Perkins's strenuous interpretation of Calvin's teaching on divine inscrutability in matters of election and "free grace." Ecclesiastically, all tended to believe that even ordinances "not distinctly expressed in the words of the Bible are 'commanded' in some sense by God," including apparently omitted forms of worship. As a result, Puritans almost universally rejected the established church's teaching on the *adiaphora*, the "things indifferent" to salvation such as traditional ceremonies and services. Believing that nothing that fails to purify or "edify" the community could be truly "indifferent"

---

[8]   Durston and Eales, *Culture*, p. 6. On Anglican providentialism, see Blair Worden, "Providence and Politics in Cromwellian England," *Past and Present* 109 (1985): p. 88, n. 157.

[9]   Lake, "Anti-popery," p. 190.

[10]   See David Loewenstein and John Marshall (eds.), *Heresy, Literature, and Politics in Early Modern Culture* (Cambridge, 2006). On Askew, see Loewenstein, "Writing and the Persecution of Heretics in Henry VIII's England: The Examination of Anne Askew," in *Heresy*, pp. 11–39.

or permissible, they came to regard "Christian liberty less as a permission than as a command. To do 'any of those things which God hath not commanded' would be, not an assertion, but a violation of Christian liberty." John S. Coolidge traces this prescriptive approach to scripture to the Judaic or "idiographic" worldview, which uses particular historical incidents as precedents for future action. In contrast, the Greek or "nomothetic" approach to the past abstracts from its events to form general natural and civic laws. St. Paul synthetically balanced these worldviews but Perkins and the English Puritans reverted to a virtually Hebraic notion of the covenant in which Christian "liberty" meant exclusive obedience to God's particular word or concrete precept. According to Coolidge, it was imperative "to hear God's voice of command in all his thoughts," and one could not "feel that he is obeying God if it is 'shut out'. Directions simply found out by reason, reliable or not," were thus considered no more viable "than a good map of the country" when God sent "the pillar of cloud that went before the people ... in Exodus; 'it is necessary', Cartwright says, 'to have the word of God go before us in all our actions ... for that we cannot otherwise be assured that they please God.'" Even in the Antinomian phase of the movement, where tensions between personal and communal "edification" or "upbuilding" finally led to individualistic extremes, Puritanism preserved the same sense of divine ownership and communal exclusiveness.[11] As a result, even its radical wing focused on using Christian liberty to free the "conscience, which God owns," to fight against worldly corruption, not to secure secular rights.[12]

Yet in either case, tensions remained between individual conscience or choice and strict godly obedience, frictions that John von Rohr usefully traces to the difference between the conditional and absolute aspects of the Puritan covenant with God.[13] In the realm of God's absolute and eternal decrees, the covenant is univocal and unilateral: the Elect are called not by but often actually against their wills, which produces the recurrent theme of the broken and bruised will as a sign of God's amazing grace. Peter Bulkeley typically affirmed that "Faith brings nothing to God of our owne, it offers nothing to stand in exchange for his mercy offered; it receives a gift, but giveth no price." John Preston agreed: "faith empties a man, it takes a man quite off his owne bottom," because faith is "infinitely too hard for man," in the words of Robert Bacon.[14] Yet the human *experience* of divine grace is not absolute but temporal and conditional. Responding to the divine "call" to conform ever more closely to God's will thus requires the believer's

---

[11]   John S. Coolidge, *The Pauline Renaissance in England: Puritanism and the Bible* (Oxford, 1970), pp. 111–27, cited pp. 26, 11; see also pp. 47, 56. On idiographic versus nomothetic outlooks, see pp. 16–17.

[12]   Worden, *Roundhead*, p. 294.

[13]   Von Rohr, *Covenant*, pp. 13–17; see also Coolidge, *Pauline*, pp. 39–41.

[14]   Peter Bulkeley, *Gospel-Covenant* (London, 1651), p. 337; John Preston, *Breast-Plate of Faith and Love*, 3 pts. [2nd edn.] (London, 1630), 1:43; Robert Bacon, *Spirit of Prelacie* (London, 1646), p. 18.

full cooperation, without which there could be no assurance of that calling. But even this aspect of conversion remains staunchly communal, because both the initial "awakening" call and subsequent warnings against spiritual complacency are firmly linked to the preached word. Long after receiving signs of "sealing" or justification, Coolidge notes, "If the sight of their infirmities make the 'weak Saints' doubt their election, they are to renew their assurance by performing works of sanctification." These works require both rigorous self-scrutiny and a communal "outreach" of shared experience with other believers, which is why sermons and meetings are centrally important to Puritan faith.[15]

Von Rohr's balanced approach to the covenant leads him to be highly critical of religious historians who have over-simplified and over-secularized Puritan "voluntarism" by focusing only on its individualistic aspects. By ignoring the absolute or divinely decreed aspect of "free grace," historians like Perry Miller made the covenant a form of "'spiritual commercialism,'" while he believes historians like Hill add "an Arminian coloration" even to the saints who most rigorously opposed it. These simplifications sacrifice "all sense of the continuing Calvinism in Puritan thought," that is, all the insecurities generated by the covenant's absolute aspect and the communal props needed to assuage them.[16] Puritans themselves were well aware of these needs, which led them to develop the pastoral practice of "experimental predestinarianism." Here good works and devotions still did not merit election, but they could at least "experimentally" prepare the believer to receive *signs* of grace. This teaching made predestination less "absolute" and yearning souls less helpless before a wrathful and inscrutable God. Rather than seeking a blinding conversion experience such as Paul had on the road to Damascus, they could experience justification (or confirmation of election) as a more gradual and tentative opening of the heart through pious works. Erring souls could then see that God had not forever abandoned them, but that they had merely walked blindly for a while in the sins of the "old man" or original Adam. Here, as throughout the Puritan tradition, the metaphor of "walking with God" through the irregular assistance of the Holy Spirit took on a highly literal meaning.[17]

R.T. Kendall's study of experimental predestination further explains the paradox of how a movement that began by stressing primitive Christian simplicity, faith, and liberty ended up endorsing a quasi-sacramental approach to good works. Perkins played a central role by showing that Calvin's distinction between a "saving" and merely "temporary" faith meant that the true or "saving" version usually required "certaine meanes" or stages, and these gradually took on a ritual character. The first step toward salvation was to recognize that, as heirs of the old Adam, the Elect are born into unbelief and do not so much as "dreame" of their election until becoming acquainted with the Law. The preacher's purpose

---

[15]   Coolidge, *Pauline*, p. 126.

[16]   Von Rohr, *Covenant*, pp. 21, 22; on its insecurities, see p. 122.

[17]   On the importance of journey motifs in Puritan faith, see William Haller, *The Rise of Puritanism* (New York, 1957), pp. 141–65.

is thus to "shew ... a man his sin" under the Law, "and the punishment thereof" (*Works* 1:79), so that Christ may soften his heart and make him "capable of faith." This stage requires humbling the intellect and "bruising" the will so that the sinner can receive an accurate "sight" of and "sorrow" for his incapacity to rectify sin (*Works* 2:5). Mercifully implanting an "accusing conscience" of one's total depravity before God, the preacher "mollifies" the sinner's heart through four principal "hammers": knowledge of the Law, of sin, of divine wrath, and of "holy desparation" before them. Once this desperation is complete, the believer should experience a "miraculous and supernaturall facultie of the heart, apprehending Christ Jesus applyed by the operation of the holy Ghost," which is then "sealed" by his or her reformation of life (*Works* 1:79). Of course, the four hammers will not always achieve the desired effect, but when they do, it will become outwardly manifest: "the sap behind the bark does not assure; but buds and blossoms do." Yet as exclusive gifts of the Spirit, these signs may be as sudden and unpredictable as they are technically "unearned." All the same, failure to increase in holy works shows that the "sap" has congealed in apparently chosen believers unfortunately granted only a temporary faith.[18]

Once their spiritual growth seems complete, the Elect attain a high degree of social "voluntarism" in relation to the "World," but not in relation to their ministers or the holy community. Both during the conversion process and long afterward, the convert must seek reassurance of his or her "perseverance" by humbling the "old man" in the face of otherworldly terrors. The believer's tensions are thus lessened but not removed, since as Perkins tells us, "The foresaid beginnings of grace are counterfeit unlesse they increase" in gifts, good works, subjection to God and his holy people, and resistance to the naturalistic ethics of "the World," the "mere morality" of self-rewarding virtue. Good works were thus unacceptable unless accompanied by spiritual signs of their disinterestedness: deep bitterness at heart for offending God through sin, striving against the flesh, earnestly desiring God's grace, considering grace one's most precious jewel, loving the ministers of God's word, calling upon God earnestly with tears, ardently desiring Christ's second coming, avoiding all occasions of sin, and persevering in these effects until the "last gaspe" of life. By conforming their lives to this pattern, the Elect experienced the beginnings of sanctification, which those of temporary faith "tasted" without digesting. This selfless and otherworldly orientation explains why Puritans typically placed more emphasis on the "first table" of the ten commandments—the decrees dealing with the honor and worship of God—than on the more "humanistic" second table commandments dealing with justice and charity to neighbors.[19]

---

[18]   R.T. Kendall, *Calvin and English Calvinism to 1649* (Oxford, 1979), pp. 59–61, 63; on the natural order, see also pp. 21–22. Kendall cites Perkins's *Workes*.

[19]   Kendall, *Calvin*, pp. 72–75; see also J. Sears McGee, *The Godly Man in Stuart England: Anglicans, Puritans, and the Two Tables, 1620–1670* (New Haven, 1976).

The covenant theology developed by Perkins and his followers produced highly disciplined individuals who were also rigid dogmatists, freely confessing error or temporary relapse into sin only in the service of higher and more certain assurances of election.[20] Yet moderate Puritans such as James Ussher, John Davenant, and John Preston significantly softened high Calvinist teaching on predestination, although, like their pupil John Goodwin, they retained the classical Calvinist emphasis on orthodoxy and rectitude; few besides the liberal Goodwin wavered on the question of certitude.[21] The more classic Puritan emphasis is perhaps most clearly expressed in John Geree's 1646 *Character of an Old English Puritane or Non-Conformist*, which praises the godly brethren for granting not just greater authority but greater "*efficacy*" to the Word preached. Through self-imposed fasting, opposition to sensual delight (including church music), and through daily gravity, sobriety, and asceticism, they eliminated vanity by "rather beating down the body than pampering it." In the process, they turned their households into miniature churches where none was admitted "but such as feared God" and strove to be "born again to God." Geree's whole life was thus "a warfare, wherein Christ was his captain; his arms, prayers and tears; the Cross his banner, and his word *vincit qui patitur* [he conquers who suffers]."[22] After the Restoration, disappointed Nonconformists placed even more emphasis on the virtue of suffering, Christian warfare, and the Word preached.

Both before and afterward, Antinomians, Quakers, and Seekers radically turned against the scriptures themselves, but all shared Geree's basic commitment to the salvific spirit of Christ within. That commitment often included resistance not just to church "forms" but to formal learning and even reason as hindrances to the Spirit. Directly or indirectly inspired by the Anabaptists, radical Puritans either limited the use of the Bible as a mere "form of words" or altogether banned it from their services. Quakers were so anti-formalistic that they freely disrupted the services of other congregations, a practice that made them the most hated sect of the period, although the Baptists were not far behind. As Robert Baillie testifies, many radical Baptists believed "That the reading out of a Book, is no part of Spiritual Worship, but the invention of the Man of Sin; that Books and Writings are in the nature of Pictures or Images; and therefore in the nature of Ceremonies." It is likewise unlawful to have the "Book before the eyes in the singing of Psalms."[23] Like Richard

---

[20]   William Lamont, *Godly Rule: Politics and Religion 1603–1660* (New York, 1969), pp. 122, 130. Lamont's frequent example is William Prynne, whose convictions changed radically throughout the period without once losing their radical sense of rectitude.

[21]   See Coffey, *John Goodwin*, p. 27.

[22]   John Geree's *The Character of an Old English Puritane or Non-Conformist* (1646), quoted in Durston and Eales, Culture, pp. 15–16.

[23]   Horton Davies, *The Worship of the English Puritans* (Glasgow, 1948), pp. 81, 89–90, 95. Robert Baillie is cited from *A Dissvasive from the Errours of the Time* (1645) pp. 18, 19; see also J.F. McGregor, "The Baptists: Fount of all Heresy," in J.F. McGregor and B. Reay (eds.), *Radical Religion in the English Revolution* (London, 1984), p. 50.

Overton, other sectarians were far less anti-intellectual, although their heresies were often tinged with the populism of the sects and the typical Puritan insistence on salvation by grace alone.[24] Most scholars nevertheless regard the extreme Antinomianism of the sects as a logical reaction against the rigorous moralism of covenant theology, which raised charges of legalistic hypocrisy even among the godly. Yet the Antinomian reaction represented a readjustment, not a real departure from the intense otherworldly drive of English Calvinism. Dispensing with the "Protestant ethic" altogether, Antinomians replaced Perkins's covenant of works with a personal covenant of grace. For mystical libertarians like Gerrard Winstanley, private property itself became a form of legalism obstructing man's return to Eden. Fifth Monarchists, Seekers, Ranters, and Muggletonians held similar views, yet, regardless of how socially or politically radical they became, the sects remained deeply antipathetic to the "carnal" man, the fallen world, and the light of nature.

John Webster was not alone in praising grace for "mercifully" bringing man "to the full, and absolute abnegation of all his wit, reason, will, desires, strength, wisdome, righteousness, and all humane glory and excellencies whatsoever." John Saltmarsh similarly held that the Elect's "pure, spirituall, and glorious assurance" could never be attained by any rational "Demonstrations of Salvation," a teaching that even conservative Puritans did not deny.[25] More radical schismatics like William Dell embraced a mystical dualism utterly separating the "two distinct seeds and sorts of people; the one from beneath, the other from above; the one the seed of woman, the other the seed of the serpent; and between these God hath put such an enmity that no man can take away." Hence it is not "the way of peace to mingle the Church and the world, but to separate them, and keep them distinct; that those of one nature may be of one communion among themselves."[26] These sentiments strikingly contrast with the young Milton's plea simply to "take councel of that which counsel'd" the prelates—"reason, ... the gift of God in one man, as well as in a thousand," which is "illustrated by the word of God" (*CPW* 1:684, 685). Here Milton already exchanges the Puritan language of "illumination" for that of logical analogy or "illustration," a language he hoped would "unyoke & set free the minds and spirits of a Nation first from the thraldom of sin and superstition, after which all *honest and legal freedom of civil life cannot be long absent*" (*CPW* 1:853, emphasis added). Herschel Baker long ago observed that such statements express the young Milton's hope that "once the Reformation hindered by the prelates was completed, such consequences as civil liberty and universal civic virtue would come of themselves," yet Baker ironically failed to realize the extent to which this hope falls outside the Puritan lexicon altogether.[27]

---

[24]   Burns, *Christian Mortalism*, pp. 162–63.

[25]   John Webster, *Academiarum Examen* (1654), p. 16; John Saltmarsh, *Sparkles of Glory* (1647), pp. 274–75.

[26]   William Dell, *The Way of True Peace and Unity* (1649), in Woodhouse (ed.), *Puritanism and Liberty*, pp. 303, 311.

[27]   Herschel Baker, *The Wars of Truth* (Cambridge, MA, 1952), p. 298.

Puritan Politics

Godly zeal, not Miltonic reason or "civil honesty," filled first the pulpits and
then Parliament with the anti-Laudian diatribes that soon led to the onset of the
civil wars.[28] Later, however, this zeal proved more of an obstacle than an aid to
constitutional progress or even popular rule, since personal grace proved a schismatic
rather than a unifying force. The godly brethren not only deeply disagreed among
themselves, but often rejected religious moderates who supported their cause for
fundamentally different reasons. Politically, the Puritan revolutionaries ranged
from arch-conservative royalists like William Prynne to utopian visionaries like
Winstanley and the semi-secular Levellers with whom Milton has sometimes been
associated. Religiously, they also ranged from a small handful of "Arminian"
Puritans gathered around Baxter and John Goodwin to moderate Independents and
conservative Presbyterians, who vastly outnumbered all the rest, especially the
colorful "sectaries" of the heresiographers. Much misinformation surrounding the
sects stems from the scare-tactics of the heresy-hunters, who wildly exaggerated
their numbers, beliefs, and even their existence. Such is certainly the case with the
"divorcers," the label that seems to have embarrassed Milton, that "sect" of one.[29]
Yet despite these divergences, the Puritans' success in bringing down Archbishop
Laud and, eventually, the King himself, makes "the circumstantial case for linking"
Puritanism and revolution seem "at first sight overwhelming," even inspirational.
William Lamont nevertheless adds that "When we probe a little further, the case
… becomes more complex. Not all puritans fought for Parliament; not all anti-
puritans fought for the King." If we probe deeper still, we find that both pre-
revolutionary and Restoration "martyrs"—William Prynne, John Bastwick, Henry
Burton, Richard Baxter, and Lodowicke Muggleton—were "legatees, not of a
continuous revolutionary tradition, but of a continuous *counter-revolutionary* one.
They were, for the most part, Protestant imperialists, brought up on a diet of Foxe
and Jewel to recognize the authority of the sovereign." Hence they associated
"'Christian subjection'" with Protestantism and "'Unchristian Rebellion'" with
Papists and with Laud's unchristian "innovations."[30]

At the same time, revolutionaries like Milton were more often motivated by
anti-imperial traditions, which as Hobbes claimed, they found in the classical
republican sources that led the poet to style himself "Junius Brutus" in his
Cambridge "Vacation Exercise." Much later, in *Eikonoklastes*, he would identify

---

[28]   See John F. Wilson, *Pulpit in Parliament: Puritans in the English Civil Wars 1640–
1648* (Princeton, 1969).

[29]   Thomas Edwards's *Gangraena* (the "shallow Edwards" of Milton's "On the New
Forcers of Conscience) famously placed Milton in this invented "sect"; for his response,
see Thomas N. Corns, "Milton's Quest for Respectability," *Modern Language Review* 77.4
(1982): pp. 769–79.

[30]   William Lamont, *Puritanism and Historical Controversy* (Montreal, 1996), pp. 55,
56. On Prynne's "Elizabethan" Royalism, see pp. 20–25, 57–73.

the "beginning of these Combustions" not with the Laudians' "plot" to reintroduce papacy but with a nearly "unanimous ... dislike and Protestation against" the King's "evil Government," his unparliamentary or personal rule. The prelates were also evil, of course, but mainly for helping Charles I reduce his people to a state of "servility" with

> more cunning fetches to undermine our Liberties, and putt Tyranny into an Art, then any British King before him. Which low dejection and debasement of mind in the people, I must confess I cannot willingly ascribe to the natural disposition of an Englishman, but rather to two other causes. First, to the Prelats and thir fellow-teachers ... the Doctrin and perpetual infusion of servility and wretchedness to all thir hearers; ... next to the factious inclination of most men divided from the public by several ends and humors of thir own ... from the time that it became his custom to break Parlaments at home, and either wilfully or weakly to betray Protestants abroad .... . (*CPW* 3:344)

Milton also lists a broad range of other charges—faction, illicit taxation, unworthy promotions, breaking laws and traditional privileges—that basically recapitulate Bacon's classic analysis.

The differences between these grievances and those of the Puritan martyrs illustrate in small why the Whig historians have been accused of inventing a "Puritan Revolution" alien to the understanding of contemporary observers. Contemporary anti-imperialists were as numerous as religious Puritans, not limited to a small party of Milton, who was never actually a major player in the revolution but only its spokesperson. Yet for that very reason, his motives for resisting the King were hardly unique. In retrospect, John Thurloe similarly charged him with exercising an "arbitrary power" at once "incompatible with the Word of God, natural law, and gothic liberty," a view shared by his friend Bulstrode Whitelocke, an exclusively political rebel who had been Laud's protégé. To Whitelocke, Thurloe wrote that "The true foundation and ground of this great war on the Parliament's part" was twofold: "sober Christians were afraid of imposing upon their consciences, and everybody of having arbitrary power set up over their estates to the distraction of their liberties."[31] Yet the primary issue had never been monarchical authority itself but merely its limits. Parliamentarians, including Milton, initially agreed that true authority resided in the king-in-parliament. Nor was there as yet any intrinsic conflict between parliament and the King's court, since national policy could be forged in either arena and many men used both venues. Even during Charles's personal rule, some of his harshest critics agreed to hold court offices because they knew it afforded them the best possibility of dissuading him from his overbearing fiscal schemes, his proliferation of monopolies, and his use of prerogative courts,

---

[31] Steven Pincus, *Protestantism and Patriotism: Ideologies and the Making of English Foreign Policy, 1650–1668* (Cambridge, 1996), pp. 182–83. Pincus cites John Thurloe's letter of 23 December 1653 to Whitelocke.

Star Chambers, and church courts to enforce religious and political uniformity. Hence as the historical revisionists have shown, no unified opposition existed during the pre-revolutionary period, since many of the King's closest advisers also favored reform. Clarendon urged Charles to accept his critics' advice, and many of the King's other allies were ironically more pro-reformist than parliament, whose bywords were Magna Carta, Saxon law, and the reign of good Queen Bess.

Like the King's many other critics, Puritans both in and outside of parliament were not anti-monarchists but patriots concerned to distance him from the "evil counselors" responsible for his "wicked" innovations. Writing from the tower in 1637, Bastwick blamed his imprisonment on the bishops but promised to "maintaine to the vttermost of my power the Kings supremacy," affirming that he would "rather live with bread and water under [Charles's] regiment, then in all plenty under any Prince in the world."[32] Strongly divided factions appeared only after the failure of compromise in 1642, but even then royalists were less an anti-reform party than champions of law and order. Fearful of plebian radicals and of "King" John Pym's willingness to mount a populist offensive, their only choice seemed to be to defend their monarch. Yet as Martin Butler relates, unilateral commitments remained rare: "throughout the 1640s, parliament (and Charles's advisers) continued to include peace and war lobbies and more complex divisions besides ... . Absolute commitment was only for the few, something which large generalizations about Cavalier and puritan disguise." These mixed agendas were further complicated by "neutralist" and "localist" concerns that made true political "parties" in the modern sense impossible. At the same time, national unity had so long been maintained by the fiction of sameness that few Englishmen were ready to favor a truly pluralist society. Parliamentarians thus joined royalists and Puritans in equating dissent with rebellion, neither of which could be tolerated in a stable society. Differences on either side were still customarily aired by referring "to an ideal of harmony between king and people which, however mythical or imaginary, had a theoretical validity" challenged by none but a tiny handful of budding revolutionaries.[33]

Lamont traces the Puritan stake in this brewing conflict not to their "individualism," "voluntarism," or "democracy," but rather to the "centripetal and centrifugal" impulses latent within English millenarianism—the providential view of history reinvented by John Bale, John Foxe, and Thomas Brightman, and passed on to both Puritans and non-Puritans like Bacon and Joseph Mede.[34]

---

[32]   John Bastwick, *The Litany* (1637), pt. 1, p. 2; pt. 4, p. 5.

[33]   Martin Butler, *Theatre in Crisis 1632–42* (Cambridge, 1984), pp. 18, 21; this entire paragraph, like the preceding one, is indebted to Butler's fine synthesis of Gardiner et al. with more recent historiography (pp. 12–21).

[34]   Lamont, *Godly Rule*, pp. 24–25. On the evolution of English millenarianism, see Katharine R. Firth, *The Apocalyptic Tradition in Reformation Britain 1530–1645* (New York, 1979). On Bacon and Mede, see Ernest Lee Tuveson, *Millennium and Utopia* (New York, 1964), pp. 76–84.

Puritans eventually divided over the "imperial" and "popular" interpretation of this tradition, which Hill interpreted as a split between "Arminians of the right and the Arminians of the left"; the right naturally supported the "godly rule" of prince and magistrate, while the left supported the rule of the downtrodden and oppressed.[35] A.S.P. Woodhouse influentially concluded that the leftward shift toward demotic rule was inevitable, since equality in the Puritan order of grace made men equal in the order of nature. Prominent Puritan theologians like Thomas Goodwin seemed to support this belief when they declared that "The saints of God gathered together in a church are the best commonwealths men," the "great ones" and "worthies" who would soon accomplish "the founding of Zion."[36] However, like Baxter and most other Puritans, Goodwin made no provision "for the non-believers, the non-elect, the lost souls arbitrarily assigned to eternal perdition," much less for heretical Christians like Milton. Recognizing this fact, Leo Solt early concluded that "a society of great *inequality* rather than equality would be formed" in the "ideal" Puritan theocracy, a conviction supported by Anne Hutchinson's experience in Puritan New England.[37]

Solt's work on the Antinomians in the New Model Army further shows the error of identifying members of the radical left with Arminianism, a doctrine never adopted by many radicals, including the Leveller leader John Lilburne, who supported a greater degree of popular liberty than any contemporary save Winstanley. Nor were Arminians essentially populist; many who adopted their free will theology were (like Milton) actually committed not to "political equalitarianism but [to] a civil aristocracy of virtue."[38] True populists, on the other hand, were not defeated by royalist reactionaries but by opportunists and extremists within their own ranks. As Jonathan Scott observes:

> The bitter lesson of the revolution for many radicals [was] ... not that "revolution" could not be achieved, but that when it was so little ... was achieved with it. In short, the victors behaved as their oppressors had before them ... . They were defeated by the experience of power-holding itself. George Fox agreed "Oh what a seriousness was in the people at the beginning of the wars, yea both

---

[35] Christopher Hill, "From Lollards to Levellers," in Maurice C. Cornforth (ed.), *Rebels and their Causes* (London, 1978), pp. 58–59, and Hill, *Milton and the English Revolution* (London, 1977), pp. 268–78. Hill's description of Protestant millenarianism as a "heresy" is only the most untenable of his many strained attempts to link Milton to the "radical underground"; see *Milton*, p. 72.

[36] Thomas Goodwin, *The Works of Thomas Goodwin* (12 vols., Edinburgh, 1861–65), 12:73–74, 76.

[37] Solt, *Saints*, p. 66.

[38] Ibid., pp. 33, 67–68.

small and great … oh how is the sincerity choked and smothered and quenched by the fatness of the earth."[39]

Milton typically targeted not "the people" for this failure but the corrupt and greedy clergy who "under Covert of Hypocritical Zeal," confused spiritual with political aspiration—power-seeking with the voice of the Lord (*CPW* 5:444).

Historians nevertheless agree that the Leveller struggle against "Norman slavery" constituted "the most striking attempt of the period to liberate the radical cause from appeals to precedent," although many trace its failure to fulfill its goals to underlying Puritan assumptions. Although the Levellers were never exclusively religious (they relied on both natural law and constitutional theory), their decision to frame their "radical objectives … in a relationship not to time but God" insured that political liberty remained not "an end but rather a means to the appropriate relationship" with the deity. Once that was established, they believed that the "abolition of the church, monarchy, and House of Lords" could be secured "without theoretical assistance and against the wishes of 'the people', Levellers included"; their "God-given" duty to seize the sword and forcefully cleanse the land was all that was required. As a result, Scott shows that "the first phase of the revolution, no less than the second" was doomed to achieve neither "liberty from outward bondage, whether parliamentary or monarchical," nor "the practical government of God."[40] Lilburne's insistence on broadening the franchise, a truly democratic reform, was more successful, although not nearly as "leveling" as his enemies claimed. He merely sought to reorganize the system of proportional representation based on property and radically redistribute parliamentary constituencies. Since the Levellers and the Army officers were agreed on these reforms, the Commonwealth endorsed it and Cromwell implemented it.[41] J.C. Davis nevertheless endorses Solt's complaint that the Leveller program can only be defined as fully democratic (as both Woodhouse and Haller defined it) by reversing the Levellers' real argument. They did not assert that liberty could not exist without toleration, but only that "there could be no toleration without civil liberty." This subtle distinction is far from trivial, since in practice it meant that they grounded liberty in Christian equity and charity, not in civil rights. As a holy people dedicated to God, they believed that practical Christianity would turn society into "the invisible church made visible," which Davis cites as a major reason for their failure to secure dramatic constitutional reform.[42]

Similar confusions of secular and spiritual ideals were widespread among Puritans. Thomas Goodwin claimed that "The very naming" of a fellow saint

---

[39]   Jonathan Scott, *England's Troubles: Seventeenth-century English Political Instability in European Context* (Cambridge, 2000), p. 267.

[40]   Ibid., p. 289.

[41]   Worden, *Roundhead*, pp. 318–19, 338.

[42]   J.C. Davis, "The Levellers and Christianity," in Brian Manning (ed.), *Politics, Religion, and the English Civil War* (London, 1973), pp. 225–50, cited pp. 250, 233.

"dasheth morality and formal profession out of countenance, as light doth a glowworm, as importing a more divine workmanship created, and some singular thing, ... even holiness in truth."[43] As Lake shows, that also meant devaluing "mere" morality as "lukewarmness, coldness in religion and good fellowship." Robert Bolton, another prominent spokesman for the godly, regarded moderation itself as a dangerous "idol" potentially threatening their eternal souls:

> moderation and discretion, truly so called and rightly defined by the rules of God, are blessed and beautifying ornaments of the best and most zealous Christians but being tempered with their coldness and edged with their eagerness against forwardness ... become the very desperate cut throats to the power of godliness.[44]

Not only would such worldly virtues never get anyone into heaven, but as both Lake and Eamon Duffy point out, they gravely threatened the "master division between the godly and the profane," the "'great mystery of godliness'" separating the saints from the worldly "'men of Belial.'"[45] Thus in both religion and politics, the standard Calvinist dichotomy between the Elect and the Reprobate not only disenfranchised ceremonialists but undermined the broader Puritan community. As Solt wryly observers, while "Cromwell's communion with the Spirit of God led him to political views based upon custom and privilege," the Army radicals heard the Spirit endorsing opposing doctrines of natural rights and majority rule. Relying on the Spirit of the Lord could thus justify individualistic *interpretations* of its message without producing secular individualism, toleration, or democracy as we know it. Assuming a rule of grace still rooted in Calvinist ideas of stewardship, Levellers like other Puritans condemned "Carnal Professours" who placed their faith in the "mere forms" taught by learned men. Solt finds these attitudes indicative of "the doctrinal affinity ... between the Antinomian [or radical] concept of Free Grace and Calvinist orthodoxy": for Saltmarsh and the Army chaplains, the free grace of "all men" really referred to the freedom of the Elect. By forgetting this important distinction, Woodhouse (and before him, Firth) erred in identifying Puritanism and democracy.[46] Tending toward an unrepresentative populism at best, Puritan faith also tended to pull converts between the poles of anarchic enthusiasm

---

[43] See McGee, *Godly Man*, p. 177, citing Thomas Goodwin, *Works*, 1:11.

[44] Robert Bolton, *Some General directions for a comfortable walking with God* (1626), pp. 305–6.

[45] Lake, "'Charitable Christian Hatred,'" pp. 170–71; Lake cites Eamon Duffy's important essay, "The Godly and the Multitude in Stuart England," *The Seventeenth Century* 1.1 (1986): pp. 31–55. On the persistent anachronism of earlier twentieth-century scholarship on the Levellers, see Worden, *Roundhead*, pp. 316–38.

[46] Solt, *Saints*, pp. 58, 38, 39, 59–72.

and legalistic authoritarianism, the twin trajectories followed by both Winstanley and Lawrence Clarkson.[47]

This binarism additionally produced theological confusion: many Antinomians acted as if they believed in universal and equal salvation while denying it in principle, while the lowly mystics' claim to perfected union with the divine seemed intolerably elitist to their conservative brethren. Capable of sinning in the flesh but not in their consciences, Antinomians held that no fleshly sin could separate them from God, only from direct communion with God. Thus both imperial and demotic branches of Puritanism felt entitled to take the lead in public life based on spiritual assumptions that seemed far too elitist from the opposing perspective, which fractured the godly themselves over the question of who was fit to rule: Presbyterian elders or magistrates, Independent ministers, Levellers, or "humble" Antinomian saints.[48] J.M. McGregor shows that the final and least successful phases of radical or "demotic" millenarianism merely shifted the Calvinist concept of natural depravity from "the wickedness of the mass of mankind … to the wickedness of the men in power." The Levellers contributed to this phase by insisting that corrupt individuals needed to be restrained not only by new laws but by new magistrates chosen from God's humblest servants, who were most susceptible to the experiential work of the Spirit upon the heart. These views were clearly more "leveling" than their legal reforms, yet in other ways they simply constituted a reverse meritocracy. Another problem was that since most Puritans made "no provision for principled dissent from the will of the congregation except for defection or expulsion," differences could be resolved only by recourse to disputable scriptural or doctrinal authority. Hence even that "fount of all heresy," the Baptists, were torn between rigid "collectivism and … voluntary, egalitarian principles," which continually disturbed their domestic peace despite their official acceptance of a popular free will theology. [49]

Bernard Capp shows that the same fate afflicted the Fifth Monarchists, toward whom many Baptists later gravitated: ultimately, they were torn between humanitarian justice and a draconian legal code based upon "Mosaic laws … imposing death for adultery, blasphemy, and profanation of the sabbath."[50] Still clinging to "the Puritan ideal that reformation of society and its institutions was possible [only] through the action of godly men," not "civilly honest" men, most became mystical Ranters, Seekers, or Quakers after their political agenda imploded. In this final phase of the revolution, the Fifth Monarchists clearly revealed the impractical and undemocratic underpinnings of their program by urging that "'Mere natural and worldly men' … could have no political rights,"

---

[47] See Robert Appelbaum, *Literature and Utopian Politics in Seventeenth-Century England* (Cambridge, 2002), pp. 153–71.

[48] Solt, *Saints*, p. 33.

[49] McGregor, "Baptists," p. 40.

[50] Bernard Capp, "The Fifth Monarchists and Popular Millenarianism," in McGregor and Reay (eds.), *Radical Religion*, p. 173.

since "'the dim light of nature' (frail human reason)" could never "surpass the wisdom of God."[51] These and related findings have fractured the Whig view of history summarized in *Freedom and Authority*, Gerald Cragg's 1975 study of thought in early seventeenth-century England. Cragg claims that, simply by emphasizing the supreme authority of the Word, "Puritanism released the turbulent forces of individualism." It did this by insisting "that conscience could be guided and trained," and also "by teaching that all men stand on the same footing in the sight of God." Although Puritans never claimed that "all men are equal" (which would "ignore the distinction between the just and the unjust, between the Elect and the Reprobate"), "Puritan preachers had struck a mighty blow on behalf of human equality" by teaching that a "good man is equal to any other good man, and both are vastly superior to an unregenerate nobleman or an unjust king." Since Puritans passed easily from religious to civil considerations, their reassessment of an individual's spiritual worth eventually "affected the estimate of each man's place in society." In fact, "the two were in continual interaction. Liberty in the spirit is the gift of Christ; freedom in society is its inevitable sequel." Finally, after laying the foundations of equality, democracy, and liberty, Puritans pioneered modern science, since

> the Puritan emphasis on experience encouraged experiment among those who "believed (in the words attributed to John Robinson) that 'the Lord hath yet more truth to break forth out of his holy word.' ... [T]his willingness to experiment with new forms appeared only when the Civil War had released all the forces working for change, but the way had already been prepared by much earnest Puritan preaching."[52]

The main interest of Cragg's account (which he takes from Woodhouse, Merton, and Haller, who respectively made Puritans the heroes of democracy, science, and equality) lies in the fact that, while still popularly credited, virtually all of its facets have been disproved. Puritans were hardly alone in upholding the supreme authority of scripture, a standard Reformed doctrine. Nor were they centrally concerned with individual rather than with corporate well-being, but often the reverse: reviving the universalist dream of medieval Christianity, they stressed the uniformity of God's chosen people in the true body of Christ. In that spirit, the most radical favored utopian theocracies designed to promote the "primitivist" ideals described by Theodore Bozeman and James Holstun.[53] While the Puritans

---

[51] McGregor, "Baptists," pp. 49–63, cited p. 49, and Capp, "Fifth Monarchists," p. 173.

[52] Gerald R. Cragg, *Freedom and Authority: A Study of English Thought in the Early Seventeenth Century* (Philadelphia, 1975), pp. 156–57.

[53] Thomas Dwight Bozeman, *To Live Ancient Lives: The Primitivist Dimension in Puritanism* (Chapel Hill, 1988); and James Holstun, *Towards a Rational Millennium* (New York, 1987).

of the Hartlib circle were indeed deeply concerned with educational and medical reform, truly proto-modern scientific "experiments" were mainly the preserve of non-Puritan members such as Robert Boyle or secularists such as Robert Hooke. Of course, as Cragg's quotation from Robinson shows, Puritans were staunch millenarians, but most looked forward to a literal Kingdom of God, not to Baconian progress. Ranters like Abiezer Coppe proclaimed this godly kingdom in populist terms, but at the same time refused toleration or inclusion to prosperous or "smug" fellow Christians.[54] Last but hardly least, the Puritan relaxation of clerical/lay distinctions did not truly level all believers in the sight of God. Even moderately Arminian Puritans like Baxter segregated the masses into opposing classes of the "precious" and the "vile," and most gave new and even quasi-"popish" authority to their ministers—a fear initially dismissed by Milton in 1641–42, but seriously revived when he wrote *Areopagitica* two years later. As Carlos Eire perceptively remarks, while Reformed religion turned inward to "an invisible, interior realm," that very invisibility nearly always "depended on the guidance of a clerical elite" marked either by highly specialized training (as in the mainstream churches) or by exceptional gifts of the Spirit (in the populist sects).[55] Radical Quakers and Seekers solved this problem by eliminating ministerial authority, but they also maintained strict barriers between the apostles of the Inner Light and "the World." Finally, while Puritans were deeply preoccupied with social transformation, they imagined the Elect attaining a more disciplinary form of the original Eden, not the highly advanced, immensely prosperous, and only loosely paternal utopia described in Bacon's *New Atlantis*.

Yet the most telling objection to Cragg's identification of Puritanism with individualism or democracy is that it actually became more authoritarian over the course of the revolution. Determined to achieve God's kingdom on earth, most of the godly followed Thomas Collier in changing their minds about the completely spiritual and apolitical nature of the "Kingdome of Christ." Some, like John Saltmarsh, maintained that the spheres of grace and nature had never been exclusive, since one "*perfects* and *glorifies*" the other. The execution of Charles I also supported Collier's conviction "'that those who are saved spiritually, know best what is good for the nations temporall well-being, for they seek not their own, but others good.'" Yet even the most radical were ultimately "no more eager than Cromwell to put [their] views at the mercy of a majority vote." They knew all too well that the majority disbelieved in Free Grace, while their Antinomian convictions prevented them from relying on "theological or ecclesiological covenants" or any "specific forms of political government" because they disbelieved in specific

---

[54] Scott, *England's Troubles*, p. 263.

[55] Carlos M.N. Eire, *War against the Idols* (Cambridge, 1986), p. 317; see also pp. 318–19. Eire does not discuss the sects, but their authoritarianism is well documented by McGregor and other contributors to *Radical Religion*; Ben Jonson's *Bartholomew Fair* is perhaps fairer than we think.

forms of church government.[56] When the Barebones or Nominated Parliament ended the saints' common hope for godly rule by failing to enact much-needed practical reforms, the Fifth Monarchists led the way to further chaos. At this point the educated public, already horrified by radical Puritan proposals to base the government, university curriculum, and ministerial training on the Bible alone, flatly refused to accept reforms justified by "openly claim[ing] to receive visions from heaven."[57]

Of course, this is not to say that more moderate Puritans did not share significant common ground with classical republicans like Milton and Marchamont Nedham, but rather that republicans maintained it by carefully blurring the difference between more secular and "apocalyptic" progressivism.[58] This practice arose from the fact that the more secular neo-Roman polemicists differed from apocalyptic republicans like Edmund Ludlow on the proper role of government. Neo-Roman republicans anticipated its gradual limitation through the moral improvement and liberation of all the people rather than empowering the spiritual elite represented by Ludlow. Scott shows that the more secular republicans similarly desired "not only liberty from tyranny, but (where appropriate) from history," yet they saw this being achieved through individual self-improvement and greater civic participation in the *polis*. Rather than adopting this Aristotelian model, religious republicans sought "liberty *from* public institutions rather than through them," not an anti-monarchic republic of virtue, but a biblical kingdom "of poverty, humility, equality and peace" liberated "from the fleshly snares of selfishness and covetousness." The Quaker James Nayler clearly expresses this ideal in his letter to Fox: "to live upon bread and water is [no] bondage to me, within, or without, for it is my liberty[;] … to be taken out of all created things is perfect freedom."[59] In this spiritual struggle, "arbitrary government" was at best an incidental obstacle. Yet even amid the apocalyptic overtones of Milton's antiprelatical tracts, the secular republican keynote is sounded as voluntary *moral* improvement is posed as the answer to authoritarianism. Its rational basis is equally obvious:

> the perswasive power in man to win others to goodnesse by instruction is greater, and more divine, then the compulsive power to restrain men from being evill by terrour of the Law; and therefore Christ left *Moses* to be the Law-giver, but himselfe came downe amongst us to bee a teacher. (*CPW* 1:722)

---

[56] Solt, *Saints*, pp. 75, 58, 72.

[57] Toon, *Puritans and Calvinism*, p. 44.

[58] Pincus, *Protestantism*, p. 21; on the broad influence of Bacon's "eschatological science" on republican ideology, see p. 47.

[59] Jonathan Scott, "The English Republican Imagination," in John Morrill (ed.), *Revolution and Restoration* (London, 1992), pp. 35–54, cited p. 40; and *England's Troubles*, pp. 265, 248–49, 251; Scott cites Nayler in Geoffrey Nuttall (ed.), *Early Quaker Letters from the Swarthmore mss. to 1600* (London, 1952), p. 88.

Milton's optimistic humanism, like that of the liberal theologians of his day, stems from seeing life not as a vale of tears nor government as an instrument for containing sin, as even the most "Arminian" Puritan, John Goodwin, believed it was.[60]

This pessimistic view was inherent in the Calvinist conviction that the "totally depraved" natural man is incapable of self-government and wholly dependent upon "Soveraignety" in both church and state. Bolton maintained that, without it:

> Men would become cut-throats and canibals one unto another. Murder, adulteries, incests, rapes, roberies, perjaries, witchcrafts, blasphemies, all kinds of villanies, outrages, and savage cruelty, would overflow all Countries. We should have a very hell upon earth, and the face of it covered with blood, as it was once with water.[61]

Similar habits of thought prevented Cromwell's Protectorate from effectively establishing toleration, which would only be achieved after what John Morrill calls the collapse of the "godly ... itch to impose what has been vouchsafed to them as the Will of God for all Men." Hence he locates the true "emancipation of dissent" in the nation's cultural *retreat* from fanatic zeal and fantastic chiliasm, which without defeating Christianity or even Puritanism per se, privatized belief and freed the public arena from sectarian animosity.[62] The nation also became more theologically polarized after the Restoration, but the persecution of Dissenters at the same time became increasingly distasteful to all civilized men and women. Yet the Dissenters themselves generally clung to Bolton's Calvinist conviction that God's unaccountability to man required self-humilation, while religious liberals embraced a more "melioristic view of human life and a more comfortable relationship with God."[63] Morrill and Scott further agree that the cultural turn toward a more life-affirming religion helped create the great masterpieces of revolutionary literature, all of which belong to the period 1660–88.[64] Morrill especially sees the greatness of these works becoming apparent only by turning from the colorful personalities and cults favored by Hill to "a more balanced assessment of other [non-Puritan] groups, a less sentimental attachment to some victims and a less harsh view of

---

[60]   Glenn Burgess, "Was the Civil War a War of Religion?," *HLQ* 2 (1998): pp. 173–201, cited p. 188.

[61]   Cited in Charles H. and Katherine George, *The Protestant Mind of the English Reformation 1570–1640* (Princeton, 1961), p. 217. Bolton was one of the moderate Richard Baxter's favorite divines.

[62]   John Morrill, *The Nature of the English Revolution* (London, 1993), p. 395. On Milton, Morrill favors accounts that stress "his humanism rather than his puritanism, his elitism more than his populism, his basic consistency rather than his inconsistency" (p. 396 n. 15).

[63]   C. John Sommerville, *Popular Religion in Restoration England* (Gainesville, 1977), p. 85.

[64]   Scott, *England's Troubles*, p. 343.

others, and the kind of awareness of nuance in social history that he [Hill] has developed in religious history." It also requires abandoning large canvases where "the civil war remains a struggle between the forces of progress and the forces of reaction," a binarism that (as in Hill) causes political theory, formal theology, and even "the royalists [to] remain in the shadows."[65]

A "happy" casualty of this more nuanced approach is Hill's gloomy account of the extreme Puritan "experience of defeat" after the Restoration, which mysteriously "dooms" the social and scientific energies generated by the "Puritan Revolution" to stagnation. Michael Finlayson traces this extreme "dissociation of sensibility" thesis to assumptions about the godly shared by historians from Hill through Lawrence Stone. From the godly perspective, "the 'Good Old Cause' … was lost and … they themselves were betrayed," yet the overwhelming majority of post-Restoration men and women did not actually "believe that their world had necessarily been permanently or significantly altered."[66] Social and scientific advances not only continued but accelerated after the nation's return to social stability. Finlayson thus ascribes "The assumption that Puritanism was a fundamentally important force in English society before 1640" but relatively insignificant after 1660 to the "almost schizophrenic tendencies" of earlier seventeenth-century English historiography, which stubbornly failed to see the strong continuities in both science and society that would produce the "Glorious Revolution" of 1688–89.[67]

The Multiple Causes and Effects of the English Civil Wars

Historians still legitimately disagree on the exact origins of "true" modernity or democratic thought; some trace them to the second civil war, others to the early years of the Interregnum or to the Glorious Revolution, still others to the eighteenth-century establishment of a fully secular economic agenda for the state. Yet they generally agree that religion was a considerably less important factor in this evolution than previously believed. As Marx seminally theorized, economic forces were as or even more important in the long run, but the difficulties of tracing secular modernity to the decline or rise of the gentry, the growth of the merchant and urban laboring classes, or the growing fiscal predicament of a grossly underfunded monarchy are ultimately matters for social, not intellectual

---

[65] Morrill, *Nature of the English Revolution*, pp. 279, 282; see also Scott, *England's Troubles*, pp. 21–22, 350.

[66] Finlayson, *Historians*, pp. 5, 8, 9, cited p. 10.

[67] Ibid., p. 8. Thomas Sprat was well aware that progress at Oxford during the Interregnum had been substantial, and his *History of the Royal Society* acknowledges its debt to the Puritan era. See also Nicholas Tyacke, "Science and Religion at Oxford before the Civil War," in Pennington and Thomas (eds.), *Puritans and Revolutionaries*, pp. 73–93.

or literary, historians to determine.[68] For the latter, religion remains an undisputed factor in the English wars, although Collinson warns against adopting even the modified revisionist view that religion was their principal if not sole cause. Morrill and Anthony Fletcher adopt this modified view (which also stresses "localist" and "legal constitutionalist" factors) but Collinson still finds it too close to the Whig conflation of constitutional and religious reform. He more cautiously confines the religious factor to sanctioning "otherwise illegal and violent acts" against the King. By bonding elements of society whose "natural inhibitions in codes of conduct and political convention" would otherwise have forbidden them, religion and religious hysteria seemed to justify dethroning a legally and sacrally anointed king. Yet this still does not make the civil wars "entirely or even mostly 'about' religion," much less "religious in content." Men like Baxter may have taken the parliamentary side to save Protestantism from Laud and King Charles, not to alter the English constitution, but many others joined the coalition primarily to enforce legal and constitutional barriers against imperial "tyranny."[69] Military historians like Mark Kishlansky have even shown that religion did not dominate the New Model Army, as Woodhouse supposed. Its Declaration of 14 June 1647 focuses on strictly secular issues: rejecting "any arbitrary power of a state," defending "our own and the peoples' just rights and liberties," and supporting "the Kingdom in Parliament … against all particular parties and interests whatsoever." He thus traces the Army's increasing radicalization to its increasing suspicion first of the King's and then of Parliament's failure to safeguard the public trust against special interests.[70]

Much like Conrad Russell's, Kishlansky's historical revisionism has sometimes been accused of dismantling not just Whig history but the concept of "revolution" itself. Yet the main outlines of their positions have stood the test of time: not just Puritans but most seventeenth-century men and women deeply feared innovation and social disorder, desiring "revolution" only in the sense of a return or "restoration" of the proper status quo.[71] For most, that meant returning to the principles of "good Queen Bess," who unlike the Stuarts, eschewed divine

---

[68]   See R.H. Tawney, "Harrington's Interpretation of His Age," *Proceedings of the British Academy* 27 (1941): pp. 199–223, and "The Rise of the Gentry: A Postscript," *Economic History Review*, 2nd series 7.1 (1954): pp. 91–97; J.H. Hexter, "Storm over the Gentry," in *Reappraisals in History* (Evanston, IL, 1962), pp. 117–62; Lawrence Stone, *The Crisis of the Aristocracy, 1558–1641* (Oxford, 1965); and H.R. Trevor-Roper, "The Gentry, 1540–1640," *Economic History Review*, Supplement I (1953), *Historical Essays* (London, 1957), and *Religion, the Reformation, and Social Change* (London, 1967). On the fiscal problems newly besetting the monarchy, see Kevin Sharpe, *The Personal Rule of Charles I* (New Haven, 1992).

[69]   Collinson, *Birthpangs*, pp. 133, 134, 135.

[70]   Mark Kishlansky, "Ideology and Politics in the Parliamentary Armies, 1645–9," in John Morrill (ed.), *Reactions to the English Civil War 1642–1649* (New York, 1982), pp. 163–83, citing passages from the Declaration of 14 June 1647, p. 183.

[71]   For an overview of the evidence, see Finlayson, *Historians*, pp. 15–41.

right theory and its implications. Hence Milton could claim with some justice that absolutism was radically incompatible with the temper of the English people, although like other vigorous reformers, he, too, lacked a fully modern constitutionalist outlook, chiefly relying on biblical and classical precedent to justify his claims.[72] In that respect, however, he and other radical reformers were following Machiavelli, who similarly used "ancient" precedents to revive classical republicanism, and Francis Bacon, his admirer, who drew on millenarian orthodoxy to justify progress. As the frontispiece to *The Great Instauration* reminded his readers, the prophets themselves declared that in the latter days, "Many shall pass to and fro and knowledge shall be increased" (Daniel 12:4). The resulting overlap between religious and secular factors in the civil wars means that it is often difficult but not impossible to sort out the predominance of one or the other in individual participants. Among Puritans, the prime motivating factors usually included anti-formalism, anti-ceremonialism, and of course, anti-Arminianism. These motives could and did promote personal spirituality, concern for the holy community, resistance to repressive external authority, and social reform. Yet as we have seen, the Puritans' intense preoccupation with relatively narrow doctrinal and anti-formalist issues often proved politically counter-productive or even socially repressive, fostering neither spiritual democracy nor the separation of church and state. In politics, Puritans often sounded like anti-absolutists, but it was "not absolutism per se that most of them objected to" but only its use in advancing "the cause of popery." Once this threat was eliminated, their disagreements over the nature of "godly rule" fractured first the Parliamentarian cause and then the Protectorate.[73]

At the same time, secular anti-absolutists and natural law theorists like John Selden shared the godly repugnance for a "lazy and ignorant clergy," but little else; Selden early espoused the idea of "heresy" as mere "opinion," which supported his anti-Calvinist and anti-Puritan outlook.[74] The fourth earl of Bedford shared the Puritan repugnance for Laud's "sacramental" Arminianism, which for him constituted a thinly disguised reintroduction of Catholicism through ceremonial innovations, but he, too, disliked Puritans.[75] As Russell seminally pointed out,

---

[72] On the obsolescence of divine right theory after James I, see Baker, *Wars*, pp. 246–58.

[73] William Lamont, "The Two 'National Churches' of 1691 and 1829," in Anthony Fletcher and Peter Roberts (eds.), *Religion, Culture, and Society in Early Modern Britain* (Cambridge, 1994), p. 349; see also Derek Hirst, "The Failure of Godly Rule in the English Republic," *Past and Present* 132 (1991): pp. 33–66.

[74] See Richard Tuck, "'The Ancient Law of Freedom': John Selden and the Civil War," in Morrill (ed.), *Reactions to the English Civil War*, pp. 137–61, cited p. 154. Selden's discussion of heresy appears in his *Table Talk*, cited in David Masson, *The Life of John Milton* (6 vols., New York, 1946), vol. 1, pp. 524, 525.

[75] See Nicholas Tyacke, "Puritanism, Arminianism, and Counter-Revolution," in Russell (ed.), *Origins of the English Civil Wars*, p. 136.

one reason for these conflicting allegiances was that until the first Bishops' War broke out in 1641, religion was isolated both from constitutional issues and from broad national debate, and even then, it played a more emotional than intellectual role in the conflict. J.G.A. Pocock's study of *The Ancient Constitution* produced similar conclusions since modified by Morrill, Fletcher, J.P. Sommerville, and Glenn Burgess.[76] All nevertheless agree that even exclusively religious opposition to bishop and king was never limited to Puritans alone. Selden's historical surveys of Hebrew law and institutions were only one of many non-Calvinist sources used in the opposition to prelacy, which included purely political resistance to arbitrary government.[77] Burgess's important studies, *Absolute Monarchy and the Stuart Constitution* and *The Politics of the Ancient Constitution*, provide the most nuanced explanation of the political path toward rebellion, which Charles inadvertently paved by unduly expanding the royal prerogative in style if not actually in substance. Siding with Russell's partially contested claim that no "constitutional" versus "absolutist" factions yet existed in the late Jacobean and early Caroline period, Burgess finds the new monarch's not-so-subtle changes in style fueling the incipient political resistance. Where James I had glossed over the tension between legal monarchy and *jure divino* kingship with fruitful ambiguity and divine mystery, Charles collapsed that ambiguity both through his "personal rule" and through pronouncements that seemed to arrogate truly divine powers to himself and his *jure divino* bishops. This ideological shift unleashed potentially dangerous tensions and widespread distrust on the part of both the nobles and gentry against the King and his "Court-vassals," as Milton and others called his supporters (*CPW* 3:344).[78] As his most recent biographers add, such measures as the "Forced Loan" signally broke the consensus among the government and the governed in 1626, which thereafter allowed the King's short parliaments to link failures in foreign policy and fiscal management to the increasingly authoritarian and ceremonial tendencies of the national church.[79]

Laud's role in this calamity has thus never been disputed, but even among the commons, individual hostility to bishop and king was prompted by many disparate

---

[76]   J.G.A. Pocock, *The Ancient Constitution and the Feudal Law* (Cambridge, 1957); Conrad Russell, *The Causes of the English Civil War* (Oxford, 1990), pp. 73–74, 77, 79–80, 85; Anthony Fletcher, *The Outbreak of the English Civil War* (London, 1981); J.P. Sommerville, *Politics and Ideology in England, 1603–1640* (Harlow, 1986); Glenn Burgess, *Absolute Monarchy and the Stuart Constitution* (New Haven, 1996), and *The Politics of the Ancient Constitution* (Basingstoke, 1992). Sommerville traces earlier and sharper divergences between absolutist and constitutional thought than Russell or Burgess, but Peter Lake and Kevin Sharpe convincingly argue that the choice between these positions is misleading. See Lake and Sharpe (eds.), *Culture and Politics in Early Stuart England* (Basingstoke, 1997), pp. 1–20. Burgess comes to similar conclusion in *Politics*, p. 113.

[77]   Tuck, "'Ancient Law,'" pp. 156–57.

[78]   Burgess, *Politics*, pp. 212–14, 221–31.

[79]   Campbell and Corns, *John Milton*, p. 48.

factors—religion alone, politics above religion, or religion above politics. Many of the King's earliest opponents lacked clearly defined principles or common agendas for change, and even strongly committed Puritans like Colonel John Hutchinson could join the Parliamentary opposition from firm devotion to civil, not religious, liberty.[80] Cromwell followed the same route, as he announced in his famous speech: "Religion was not the thing at the first contested, but God brought it to that issue at last; and gave it unto us by way of redundancy; and at last it proved to be that which was more dear to us."[81] These pronouncements seem to support Brian Manning's somewhat over-generalized claim that gentlemen of their type usually fought first for political liberty while those from the "lower orders" fought more for religion, at times subtly tinged with class warfare.[82] The claim is not groundless, yet as Kishlansky stresses, even the "lower orders" in the Army were not necessarily committed to radical ideology or "leveling." Social determinism simply fails to explain why "social outcasts and social climbers have the same origins" but opposite goals or attitudes.[83] Pym's anti-popery essentially proves his point: it agitated the lower orders, but also Prynne and other men of "middling" origins, while men as socially different as Selden, Milton, and the martyred "hero" of toleration in *Areopagitica*, Lord Brooke, commonly focused on episcopal arrogance, greed, and unscriptural claims.[84] Yet, as Campbell and Corns attest, Milton's critique of episcopacy's support of kingship is far more similar to Brooke's objections than to his putative Puritan allies; unlike theirs, his engagement with the bishops' arguments was neither "close nor vehement."[85]

Puritans of course especially resented the Laudians' admission of any degree of human self-sufficiency in the work of salvation as an insult to the sole majesty and grace of God, but like the general run of Protestants, they were equally offended by their return to ceremonial vehicles of grace such as auricular confession. These innovations not only seemed to reassert Rome's "magical" religion but to realign England with Counter-Reformation practices precisely when the cause of international Protestantism was suffering stunning defeats in France, Spain, and the Low Countries. These threats also roused political patriots who, at the extreme end, could be complete secularists like Henry Marten, an opponent of

---

[80]   Lucy Hutchinson, *Memoirs of the Life of Colonel Hutchinson*, ed. Julius Hutchinson and revised C.H. Firth (2 vols., London, 1885), vol. 1, pp. 137, 141.

[81]   In *The Writings and Speeches of Oliver Cromwell*, ed. W.C. Abbott (4 vols., Cambridge, MA, 1937–47), vol. 3, p. 586.

[82]   Brian Manning, "Religion and Politics: The Godly People," in *Politics, Religion, and the English Civil War* (London, 1973), pp. 83–123.

[83]   Kishlansky, "Ideology and Politics," pp. 163–64.

[84]   On Brooke, see Robert E.L. Strider, *Robert Greville, Lord Brooke* (Cambridge, MA,1958), and George Whiting, "Milton and Lord Brooke on the Church," *MLN* 51 (1936): pp. 161–66. Strider differs from Whiting on whether Brooke borrowed from Milton.

[85]   Campbell and Corns, *John Milton*, pp. 143–44, 148–49, cited 149.

jure divino politics and theology as incentives to French-style absolutism.[86] Other Parliamentarians shared Marten's objections to the King's political and legal abuses—ship money, forced loans, and tyrannous Star Chamber decrees—but relied on "anti-popery" as a propagandistic rallying cry.[87] This strategy netted recruits like Baxter, who naively believed that the Arminian bishops sought the abolition of "good preaching and advance [of] Popery" even though (as he later admitted) he had no understanding of Arminianism. He was not alone: for the Puritan divine Thomas Hooker, Arminianism simply meant that "the gospel is going ... . Christ is departing" from England, since "if Catholicism could reassert itself in the best of reformed churches" abroad, why not here? He thus joined hardline Calvinists like Prynne in waging a rearguard resistance again all innovations as dangerous reversions to Babylon.[88] Other factors in igniting the rebellion include a general suspicion of the Stuart disinterest in supporting the Protestant side of the Thirty Years War, grave disappointment at the death of Prince Henry, fears of the Queen's Catholic allegiances abroad, and the King's encouragement of Counter-Reformation styles of worship, celebration, and entertainment at home.

In sum, then, the appearance of a united "Puritan" front has proved largely illusory. Like Milton, Selden, and Whitelocke, many Parliamentarians were not religious reactionaries but reformers with quite practical objections to the prelates' collusion with Charles's "personal rule." Milton in particular lacked any Puritan conviction that Stuart non-participation in the Thirty Years War constituted a betrayal of their co-religionists, but instead supported James I's self-image as the English *rex pacificus*.[89] Other "Root and Branchers" were neither uniformly anti-episcopalian nor pro-Presbyterian; many wished to root out the Laudians but still supported episcopacy, while anti-episcopalians varied widely in their goals. Their coalition thus collapsed as soon the Presbyterians and the almost equally doctrinaire Independents of the Westminster Assembly tried to impose their conceptions of church government upon a deeply divided nation. Initially unconcerned with the strict Presbyterian doctrines early established by Cartwright, Milton was not alone in abandoning the movement as soon as its disciplinary tenor manifested itself. His *Tenure of Kings and Magistrates* shows that by the end of the 1640s he had read Cartwright (*CPW* 3:248–49), but only for polemical purposes; by then he had already become rabidly anti-clerical. After being successively disenchanted by prelates, Presbyterians ("On the New Forcers of Conscience"), Independents

---

[86] See C.M. Williams, "The Anatomy of a Radical Gentleman: Henry Marten," in Pennington and Thomas (eds.), *Puritans and Revolutionaries*, pp. 118–38.

[87] See Peter Lake, "Anti-popery," p. 96 and *passim*.

[88] Susan Hardman Moore, "Popery, Purity, and Providence: Deciphering the New England Experiment," in Fletcher and Roberts (eds.), *Religion, Culture, and Society*, pp. 257–89, cited p. 263; Thomas Hooker, "The Danger of Desertion" (1631), in *Thomas Hooker: Writings in England and Holland, 1626–1633*, ed. George H. Williams (Cambridge, MA, 1975), pp. 221–52. See also Tyacke, *Anti-Calvinists*.

[89] Campbell and Corns, *John Milton*, p. 38.

(*Areopagitica*) and sectaries (*The Doctrine and Discipline of Divorce*), he was ready to denounce the clergy in general for its merely "verbal" resistance to tyranny and related offenses against political consistency:

> For Divines, if ye observe them, have thir postures, and thir motions no less expertly, and with no less variety then they that practice feats in the Artillery-ground. Sometimes they seem furiously to march on, and presently march counter; by and by they stand, and then retreat; or if need be can face about, or wheele in a whole body, with that cunning and dexterity as is almost unperceavable; to winde themselves by shifting ground into places of more advantage. And Providence onely must be the drumm, Providence the word of command, that calls them from above, but always to som larger Benefice, or acts them into such or such figures, and promotions ... . But if there come a truth to be defended, which to them, and thir interest of this world, seemes not so profitable, strait these nimble motionists can finde no eev'n leggs to stand upon: and are no more of use to reformation throughly [*sic*] performed, and not superficially, or to the advancement of Truth (which among mortal men is alwaies in her progress) then if on a sudden they were strook maime, and crippl'd. (*CPW* 3:255–56)

Not long afterward, Milton's *Likeliest Means to Remove Hirelings* would propose eliminating nearly all vestiges of clerical authority and prestige, including most forms of state support and training. It would also eliminate the need for doctrinal orthodoxy by confining "heresy" to its root sense, "opinion." His anti-Calvinist Hartlib associate, Henry Robinson, shared both this definition of heresy and Milton's resistance to clerical authority. He also similarly blamed the Presbyterian clergy, whose "way of government was never apostolical and good," for incessantly "tyranniz[ing] oer their brethren instead of feeding them, aiming at no reformation soe much as to get themselves into the fattest benefices."[90] Both seem to recall Selden's *Table Talk*, which claimed that "heresies" abounded in primitive times, until "one of these opinions being embrac'd by some Prince, and received into his kingdom, the rest were condemn'd as Heresies; and his Religion, which was but one of the several opinions, first is said to be orthodox."[91]

At the same time the Presbyterians and Independents were engaged in a vigorous battle against the growth of "damnable heresies" which, like the sects,

---

[90]   Henry Robinson, *A Short Answer to A.S. alias Adam Stewart's second part of his overgrown Duply* (London, 1645), p. 8. A.S (Adam Stewart) is also attacked by Milton in his sonnet "On the New Forcers of Conscience." Like Milton and Parker, Robinson supported the Independents against the Presbyterians without being a Congregationalist himself. He similarly believed that monarchy was outdated and objected to the Puritan teachings on predestination, which pitted him against both factions. See Jordan, *Men of Substance*, pp. 86–88, 110–11, 130–31; on heresy, pp. 114–18.

[91]   John Selden, *Table Talk* (1689), "Opinion," p. 4, cited in Joseph Lecler, *Toleration and the Reformation* (2 vols., London, 1960), vol. 2, p. 440.

they loosely associated with Christian rationalism, the pagan classics, advanced humanism, and the new science—all the basic trends that were to shape the coming age. Given these biases, Worden shows that Cromwell and his religious leaders "neither wanted toleration nor provided it, whether we use the term in its pejorative seventeenth-century sense or in its approving modern sense"; they instead embraced a scriptural "literalism" that usually meant adhering to Calvinist interpretation. They sometimes found the very different literalism of the liberal theologians "embarrassingly 'plausible,'" but they were scandalized by their conviction "that not so much a bad opinion, as a bad life, exludes [sic] a Christian out of the Kingdom of Heaven; and that the things necessary to be known for salvation, are very few and easy." For Samuel Gott, such views implied that a "good easy and indulgent God, [is] content with anything," even Socinians like John Biddle.[92] Hence more often "than not in puritan England, toleration was a dirty word, ... an expedient concession to wickedness," "'the whore of Babylon's back door,'" and the "'last and most desperate design of Antichrist.'" Like Coolidge before him, Worden traces these beliefs to a pre-modern view of Christian "liberty" that primarily meant "freedom from the guilt of sin, and ... the release of the will from its bondage to Satan[,] ... 'a power to do what we ought, not what we will.'" Like Lamont, he argues that, since this form of "'liberty' could have nothing to do with the individual dignity and self-assertion with which the modern world invests the word," earlier historians mistakenly imported twentieth-century sociological concerns into pre-modern debates about freedom of conscience. Whether Puritans took the conservative position that "to tolerate heresy is to condemn its converts to eternal torment," or the more liberal, Independent position that "to interpose human authority between God's grace and the soul is to threaten the lifeline of salvation," they commonly feared that toleration made them a damning "'accessory to the blood of that soul.'"[93]

Earlier historians once cited the Independents' famous *Apologeticall Narration* of 1644 as an exception to this rule, but this, too, has proved to be a strong misreading. Their position was actually designed to make common cause with the Presbyterians against the more radical sects, not to establish liberty of thought. The *Narration* indeed allows room for error and later correction, as earlier claimed, but it also confines error to the limits established by Calvinist orthodoxy and ecclesiology and its theocracy of "visible saints." The Independent leader, John Owen, led their determined resistance to liberal theology by condemning the heretical error of liberating "'men's rational faculties'" by teaching "'that religion consists solely in moral honesty, and a fancied internal piety of mind towards

---

    [92]   Blair Worden, "Toleration and the Cromwellian Protectorate," *Studies in Church History* 21 (1984): pp. 199–233, cited pp. 227, 204; and Samuel Gott, *An Essay of the true Happiness of Man* (1650), p. 267.

    [93]   Worden, "Toleration," pp. 200–201.

the deity.'"[94] Of course, many aspects of Puritanism authentically worked toward more modern notions of "liberty of conscience," most notably its emphasis upon individual and evolving spiritual experience. Yet, as we have seen, its final goal was never self-determination but the firm "union of the believer with Christ, and the union of believers with each other. The former was essential to salvation: the latter was essential to the creation of a commonwealth fit for God's eyes." In such a commonwealth, heresy—particularly antitrinitarianism, an intellectualist heresy common among classical republicans of Milton's type—was felt as a wound to the body of Christ.[95]

The non-dogmatic "merciful men" in Cromwell's government held dramatically opposing beliefs even though most had godly sympathies or associations. In return, they were scornfully labeled mere "politiques" or even "cursed Socinians" by strict Puritans.[96] Yet, according to H. John McLachlan, with few exceptions, religious and political rationalists of this type were not secularists: most combined a "scrupulous and vigorous biblicism" with a virtually "Puritan" anti-sacramentalism. They were also classicists who acknowledged "the rights of reason in religion," but maintained an exalted attitude toward the deity as seen in his revealed creation. As a result, their religion, like Milton's, falls somewhere between "'supernatural rationalism'" and "'rational supernaturalism.'"[97] Representing the rebirth of "the true disciples of Hooker," they helped to renew the left wing of the mainstream church which, even "before the coming of toleration ... was often more 'liberal' in doctrine than the sects." However, as in most vital new movements, its leading lights often defy any simple "left/right" alignment. For instance, Jeremy Taylor was in one respect a conservative "high" sacramentalist, but in his free will theology and dedication to intellectual liberty just as radical as Milton.[98] "Mistrustful of externals and extremes, [yet] vigilantly taming the appetites," the "politiques" themselves ranged from liberal Anglicans like Matthew Hale to the "Puritan" Lord

---

[94] Worden, "Toleration," p. 205; Worden cites the *Works of John Owen*, ed. W.H. Gould (6 vols., Edinburgh, 1850–53), 7:5–6, and 15:76. On the Presbyterian/Independent alliance against the sects in the latter years of the Protectorate, see also Tai Liu, *Discord in Zion: The Puritan Divines and the Puritan Revolution 1640–1660* (The Hague, 1973). On the misreading of the *Apologeticall Narration* by modern scholars, see Avihu Zakai, "Religious Toleration and its Enemies: The Independent Divines and the Issue of Toleration during the English Civil War," *Albion* 21.1 (1989): pp. 1–33.

[95] Worden, "Toleration" pp. 209–10, and "Classical Republicanism and the English Revolution" in Hugh Lloyd Jones, Valeries Pearl, and Blair Worden (eds.), *History and Imagination: Essays in Honour of H.R. Trevor-Roper* (London, 1981), p. 195.

[96] Worden, "Toleration," pp. 228–33. On the vast difference between the high churchmanship of Laud and Cosin and "the more liberal and anthropocentric outlook" of the version of the post-Restoration Church supported by Marvell's *The Rehearsal Transpros'd* (cited by Worden, pp. 202–3, n. 16), see Wallace, *Puritans and Predestination*, p. 128.

[97] H. John McLachlan, *Socinianism in Seventeenth-Century England* (London, 1951), pp. 11, 12.

[98] Ibid., p. 54.

Saye and Sele's son-in-law, Sir Charles Wolsely. A close friend of Whitelocke, Dryden, and Cromwell, like the circle around him, Wolsely was known for his vast Hebrew and Greek learning, his willingness to apply it to biblical scholarship, and his association with Selden's circle, one of the most learned of the time.[99] Another group of liberal theologians gathered at Oxford around John Wilkins, Cromwell's brother-in-law, whom Calvinists like Anthony Tuckney criticized for preaching "a kinde of moral Divinitie." Yet both before and after the Restoration Wilkins and his allies practiced the latitude they preached. John Tillotson was not atypical in maintaining friendships across the religious divide with the Socinian Thomas Firmin, the Nonconformist Richard Baxter, and the high churchman Robert Nelson, while Baxter responded in kind by supporting the Latitudinarians' ecclesiology if not their scientific agenda.[100]

Like the classical republicans of the revolutionary era, the "politiques" drew upon a complex of ideals ranging from Cicero's definition of the orator and Aristotle's *Nicomachean Ethics* and *Politics* to the Italian civic humanists of late Trecento and Quattrocento Florence. According to Annabel Patterson, they helped reformulate Christian fortitude by making it less fundamentally "religious in orientation, although its causes include the politics of religion." Their hero was the "public benefactor, whose egoism is justified by the event rather than in spite of it."[101] This outlook gradually made theology seem "a matter for a university, perhaps, not for a kingdom," as Henry Marten had hoped, although Milton would even exclude divinity from the universities. Avid demystifiers, politiques of this type typically went from challenging the "hollow mystery of divine right and hereditary monarchy" to challenging the mysteries of the Trinity and of Calvinist predestination. Like Robinson, the most radical believed "that God 'spares not these erronious beleevers [*sic*] or hereticks that they might seduce ... the faithful,'" but rather to stimulate and animate the vitality of the church.[102] As a result, although they helped shape foreign policy, they had little influence over the ecclesiastical policies of the Interregnum under Cromwell and his Independent ministers. When accused of "real" heresies, like Milton they blamed the "religious intolerance and ... the political and intellectual pretensions of the clergy."[103]

Although it is not difficult to associate Milton with men like the "politiques," Henry Parker's contemporary definition of the varieties of Puritanism at the onset of the civil war era also supplies important insights into his position. Anticipating

---

[99]   Worden, "Toleration," p. 229.

[100]   Isabel Rivers, *Reason, Grace, and Sentiment: A Study of the Language of Religion and Ethics in England, 1660–1780* (2 vols., Cambridge, 1991), vol. 1, pp. 30–31, 37.

[101]   Annabel Patterson, "The Civic Hero in Milton's Prose," *Milton Studies* 8 (1975): pp. 71–101, cited p. 72.

[102]   Henry Marten, *The Independency of England Endeavoured to be Maintained* (1648), p. 12; Worden, "Classical Republicanism," p. 195; and Henry Robinson, *Liberty of Conscience* (1644), p. 12, summarized and quoted in Jordan, *Men of Substance*, p. 115.

[103]   Worden, "Classical Republicanism," pp. 195–96.

the definitions supplied in the first eighteenth-century history of the Puritan and Nonconformist tradition, Parker divided the movement into ecclesiastical Puritans, the descendants of the Elizabethan opponents of ceremony; religious Puritans, or dogmatic Calvinists; moral Puritans, or scrupulous precisians in conduct; and political Puritans.[104] Those who fit all four categories are obviously the most extreme Puritans, whom he finds "in very many things erroneous," although "furious" anti-Puritans are just as bad. In contrast, he defines a "political Puritan" like himself as merely a "civill and honest Protestant which is hearty and true to his religion." Similar distinctions were made by men like Joseph Mede, the most famous tutor of Milton's Cambridge years, although he might not have agreed with Parker that conservative Protestants encourage clerical tyranny by "attribut[ing] too much" to priests, while true "Protestants … have no other ayme but to diminish Ecclesiastical authority."[105] By 1641, Protestants of this type—whom Parker places in an ecumenical tradition associated with Paolo Sarpi—occupied the center of the Root and Branch movement. United by a common resistance to Catholics, dogmatic Calvinists, and conformists, they would eventually turn Protestantism into a layman's religion by making opposition to clericalism a species of piety. Like Parker and Milton, they recognized vague uses of the Puritan label as meaningless catch-all phrases exploited by anti-Reformers (*CPW* 1:784).

Parker's modern biographer places him in the lineage of Richard Hooker, which explains why Protestants of his type could be anti-clerical without being at all secular:

> God suffuses Parker's world and Parker was not ashamed of a robust, practical spirituality. But as Parker's characteristic concerns and modes of argument in his political pamphlets had little to do with theology and heavily prescriptive uses of Scripture (the intellectual provinces of the clergy), his religious pamphlets had much—for his critics too much—to do with politics. Parker's perspective was always the layman's, his spiritual sensibility ever yoked to a political agenda … Amongst well-known contemporaries only Harrington, Hobbes, and Selden (in some of his moods) matched Parker in exuberant, visceral, and unrelenting suspicion of the clergy.[106]

Milton provides another "match" for Parker no doubt overlooked by Michael Mendle because of his current "Puritan" reputation, yet like Parker's, Milton's anti-ceremonialism is far more "mainline reformist" than precisian. His 1645 volume of verse exhibits the same "strong streak of acceptance of traditional

---

[104] Henry Parker, *A Discourse Concerning Puritans* (London, 1641), p. 13. Much the same categories are used in Daniel Neal's four-volume *History of the Puritans or the Protestant Nonconformists* (London, 1730); see Finlayson, *Historians*, pp. 56–57.

[105] Parker, *Discourse*, pp. 4, 10, 11, 30, 23.

[106] Michael Mendle, *Henry Parker and the English Civil War: The Political Thought of the Public's "Privado"* (Cambridge, 1995), p. 52.

worship forms" Mendle finds in Parker, and an even stronger acceptance of "free will and works than most [contemporary] Protestants." In politics, Milton clearly supported Parker's views on Parliamentary supremacy, while in religion, he praised his benefactor, Lord Brooke, as a hero of toleration, not Puritanism (*CPW* 2:560–61). Like Parker, he also seems to have considered Brooke's so-called Puritanism as a "confused imposture" concocted to tar him and his ally, Lord Saye and Sele, with sedition. Although Parker did not live to see the Protectorate, Mendle speculates that he would have similarly defended Cromwell's regime on the grounds of stability and practicality.[107]

It thus goes without saying that political Puritans of Parker's type have little in common with the ecclesiastical Puritans who attacked altar rails, church windows, and organs, or even with the moral Puritans who strictly censured personal conduct in a manner Milton derides in *Areopagitica* (*CPW* 2:523–27). Political Puritans could support their condemnation of Laud for reversing the long retreat from magical religion initiated by the original Israelites, continued by St. Paul, and completed by the Protestant Reformation—which in their view, permanently discredited any "fencing" of the altars, elevation of the priesthood, or excessive ceremony—but still resent his anti-Calvinism less than his authoritarian return to "delusions of magic" that overly enhanced "the dignity of the magician." They thus objected to the very word "priest," which as Russell points out, "until Laud's day ... was almost unused in the Anglican church"; yet they were less puritanically preoccupied with religion than with the increasing "the wealth of the church and the dignity of the priesthood" at the expense of both lay believers and national liberty.[108] Although Milton's antiprelatical tracts are nearly always read in a Puritan context, they merely represent this mainline reformist position in especially strong terms. *Of Reformation* opens with a loose (if suggestive) analogy between the Roman Catholic and the Episcopal aping of the "ancient Hebrew priesthood .... abolished by the coming of Christ" (*CPW* 1:520 n. 3; cf. n. 2) and continues with a bitter condemnation of priests and school divinity, but like the following tracts, it remains "remarkably free from theological disputation" or overt hostility to Arminianism.[109] The same can hardly be said of the Puritan martyrs Burton, Bastwick, and Prynne, whose tracts reflect a far more technical and thorough understanding of Laudian theology. Prynne begins his attack in *A Brief Survay and Censure of Mr. Cozens his Couzening Devotions* (1928), then only a year later broadens it to include the entire establishment in *The Church of Englands Old Antithesis to New Arminianisme* (1629). At this early date, he confines himself to relatively polite protests against this "heathen" theology, yet within a few years—

---

[107] Mendle, *Henry Parker*, p. 53 n. 4. (quoted), and p. 188. Victoria Kahn shows that Parker influenced Milton in *Wayward Contracts: The Crisis of Political Obligation in England 1640–1674* (Princeton, 2004), pp. 95–103.

[108] Russell, *Origins*, p. 21.

[109] See Leo F. Solt, commenting on Milton, in "The Bishops" (Appendix G), *CPW* 1:1010; and only once does he mention the "taint" of Arminianism at *CPW* 1:917.

and fully two years *after* Milton's highly "ceremonial" masque is produced—in his *News from Ipswich* (London, 1636) and *A Looking-Glasse for All Lordly Prelates* (London, 1636), Prynne is already a hysterical anti-Arminian.

Milton's apparent disinterest in these controversies either at Cambridge or afterward, his relative lack of anti-papist xenophobia abroad, and his undated *Commonplace Book* combine to suggest that he was chiefly motivated by resistance to arbitrary government, which was linked to the prelates as early as 1628. Whitelocke at that time publicly denounced the Arminian Richard Sibthorpe's opinion "that the king may make laws; and do whatsoever pleaseth him," noting that Dr. Manwaring "preached the same divinity, and highly against the power of Parliaments." Unlike the quasi-mythical "popish plot" promoted by Pym and his Puritan allies, similar political objections dominate Milton's attack on the bishops. By using their enhanced power to support Charles I's personal and non-parliamentary rule, the Laudians had regained much of the property lost to the laity by the church, which was thus exempted from the King's most burdensome taxations as well as from the oversight of Parliament. Widely ostracized not only as "Baal's priests" but as "Caesar's friends," their usurpation of formerly secular offices incited widespread public fear of continental-style church-state tyranny. As Lord Clarendon later observed, the King's appointment of a clergyman to the post of Lord Treasurer inflamed more men against Laud and his church than nearly anything else. Whitelocke made similar objections to Spottiswood's appointment as Chancellor, a post that had not been filled by a cleric since the Reformation. Thus when the Short Parliament of 1640 ended the King's personal rule, charges of "malignancy against Parliament" redounded upon the bishops not only because of their vastly increased presence there but also because of their ruthless acquisition of high office by treading "upon the neck of the common law," as Richard Martin earlier put it. Whitelocke added that the upper clergy neglected their studies and preaching duties for ceremonies and matters of state, a charge repeated by Milton, and even by moderates like Lord Falkland and Sir George Digby, who would "'make them such as they were in primitive times'" without eliminating episcopacy altogether.[110]

Milton's antiprelatical tracts of 1641–42 further show that the prelates' bold *jure divino* claims for bishoprics and tithes—claims already disproved by Selden's *History of Tithes*, a work important to both Milton and Parker but not to the Puritans, who generally supported tithes—especially infuriated him. The Laudians responded by blaming the public outcry against them on a "handful of puritans," jealous lawyers and laymen, a loose alliance that the Whig historians combined into a unified "Puritan Revolution." The flaws in this account were long obscured by either the severe over-simplification of seventeenth-century

---

[110] Andrew Foster, "The Clerical Estate Revitalised," in Kenneth Fincham (ed.), *The Early Stuart Church, 1603–1642* (Stanford, 1993), pp. 139–60, cited pp. 147, 153–54. Toon cites Digby in *Puritans and Calvinism*, p. 36. Historians remain uncertain whether John Pym truly believed in the Laudians' "popish plot" or merely used it to gain power.

theology exemplified by Cragg or by Marx and Weber's reduction of theology to sociology, errors also promoted by the Whig habit of assuming that all reformers were "somehow" Puritans. Yet no great revolutions, either of the past or of the present, are diminished by demystifying this account. Scott instead proposes that, by abandoning the present-centered teleology that made and marred the last "powerful explanatory analyses of the century as a whole," we are not dooming ourselves to revisionist fragmentation. On the contrary, "undomesticating" and recontextualizing the civil war within its pan-European situation allows us to abandon the powerful but ultimately gloomy portraits drawn by Hill, Stone, and G.M. Trevelyan, thereby gaining a new appreciation of the fact that neither the Restoration, the Glorious Revolution, nor the early English Enlightenment destroyed the centrality of religious belief and enthusiasm.[111] Nor did they derail the revolution's very real gains in religious toleration, Protestant individualism, formal and ethical theology—all of which reaped immeasurable benefits from the cultural retreat of Calvinist teleology.

---

[111]   Scott, *England's Troubles*, pp. 21, 23.

Chapter 2
Milton among the Puritans

It hath pleased thee to call vs to the knowledge of thy holy Gospel, drawing vs out of the miserable bondage of the devil, whose slaves we were, and delivering vs from most cursed idolatrie and wicked superstition, wherein we were plunged, to bring us into the meruailous light of thy truth.

—Middleburg Liturgy of the English Puritans (1586)

What? Must other Churches have Organs, Singing Quires, Altars, Images, Crucifixes, Tapers, copes, and the like, because such is the guise of Cathedralls? Must long chanting Service goe up, & preaching goe downe, because it is so in … Cathedralls?

—Henry Burton, *For God and King* (1636)

But let my due feet never fail
To walk the studious Cloister's pale,
And love the high embowed Roof,
With antic Pillars massy proof,
And storied Windows richly dight,
Casting a dim religious light.
There let the pealing Organ blow
To the full voic'd Choir below,
In Service high and Anthems clear
As may with sweetness, through mine ear,
Dissolve me into ecstasies,
And bring all Heav'n before mine eyes.

—John Milton, *Il Penseroso* (1645)

Aside from the fact that the Whigs' "Puritan Revolution" turned virtually all revolutionaries into saints, Milton has long been identified with the godly due to his anti-formalism, anti-episcopalism, iconoclasm, and "low church" ecclesiology, all of which are seriously called into question by the undated *Il Penseroso* he published in 1645. Milton of course did defend some version of all these positions, but from a perspective significantly different from the broad spectrum of English Puritans. Their strident iconoclasm markedly contrasts with his obvious reverence for stained-glass windows, organs, "full voic'd Choir[s]," "Service high and Anthems clear" expressed in this poem, and also with the Orphic ecstasy, "unreproved pleasures" of revelry, and "antique Pageantry" celebrated in its companion poem, *L'Allegro* (40, 145–50, 128). Both lyrics are generally regarded as early compositions (1631–38?), but the stubborn fact remains that Milton sent them to press without revision after his divorce tracts of 1643–45 ruptured his ties to both the Presbyterians and the Smectymnuans he defended in the antiprelatical tracts of 1641–42. An unanswered question thus remains as to how to relate these and the other "festive" poems collected in his 1645 volume of verse to the Puritan attacks on ceremony, revelry, and tradition in the antiprelatical tracts. One potential answer is already implicit in the previous chapter: political Puritans objected to ceremony and tradition when they served political and spiritual tyranny, not as "papist" evils in and of themselves. Another answer is that, like Bacon, Milton opposed intellectually corrupt or obfuscating customs and "superstitions," but neither pleasure in worship nor the harmless pleasures celebrated in the companion poems. His nephew Edward Phillips tells us that Milton worshiped God with both organ and song all his life, which, like other evidence explored in this chapter, suggests that Macaulay's famous essay was right: Milton never was a moral, ecclesiastical, or religious Puritan.[1]

Seventeenth-century Puritans are often distinguished from Protestants less threatened by "contaminating" rituals or pleasures simply on the basis of differing psychologies or "world-views." Whereas more liberal Protestants saw their world becoming more rational, organic and comprehensible, Puritans conserved a deeper sense of mystery or miraculism based ultimately on their inscrutable God. Additionally, as Conrad Russell (among others) observes, the classes most deeply attracted to Puritanism tended to be the most economically and socially unstable. Whether among the "lower orders" or the upper aristocracy, traditional roles and means of support were undergoing rapid change, and Puritanism's "dream of order" offered solutions to the insecurities it posed. Hence those attracted to a Puritan life-style were generally united by personal experiences of instability, while those attracted to Baconianism or religious rationalism felt more confident about their hopes for intellectual integration and reform. Since Puritanism inspired other intellectuals, members of the rising bourgeoisie, and the aristocrats who lent them support, personality factors were no doubt as important as social or class experience. James Holstun, one of Russell's harshest critics, concedes that Puritanism offered these diverse individuals a stronger and securer "associative solidarity" as opposed to the "individuated serial collective of the Arminian or Catholic parish."[2] Yet Milton's life records show him significantly preferring the looser "individuated collectives" of Protestant culture to the tight-knit associations of Puritan communities, just as they show him favoring attempts at intellectual

---

[1]   Campbell and Corns concur with Macaulay and with my own readings of these poems: they describe the pleasure not "of a radical-in-waiting, but of one who loves cakes and ale"; see *John Milton*, p. 61.

[2]   See James Holstun, *Ehud's Dagger: Class Struggle in the English Revolution* (New York, 2000), p. 36.

integration over more emotive forms of security. Russell and other historians, ranging from John Morrill and Jonathan Scott to Blair Worden, thus regard him as an essentially proto-modern "type," a poet/politician who greatly profited from the astonishing intellectual fertility of his age. They also consider its clash of ideas, not the *sola scriptura* doctrine cited by Weber, as its principal impetus to progress.

The young Milton's London was certainly a hotbed of Puritan activity and the parish in which he was brought up was no exception, but there is very little evidence that he received a strict Calvinist upbringing or ever sought the "associative solidarity" of the Puritan brethren. His parish minister, Richard Stock, was a Puritan, yet David Hawkes has found that his strictness on the issue of usury, a significant source of the Milton family income, very likely distanced the family from their minister.[3] Milton's father hired the Puritan tutor Thomas Young to teach his gifted son, but Milton's surviving letters to Young show that he revered him largely for the humanistic learning proudly displayed in these letters. His former pupil sympathizes with his temporary "exile" in Hamburg, although Young was not literally a Puritan exile but a chaplain to English merchants abroad. The letters never discuss religious matters with Young but merely lament England's "error" in not employing him at home as the Thirty Years War rages nearby. Yet, as Campbell and Corns show, unlike most Puritans Milton signally fails to represent this ideologically charged battle as a crusade of any kind, while his former tutor (who was never actually in danger) soon returned to England.[4] Later in his career Milton's admiration may have waned not only due to Young's Presbyterianism but also to the fact that he accepted a profitable "plurality," or non-residential congregation (*CPW* 1:310–11). Nevertheless, Presbyterians belonged to the most cultured and least anti-intellectual Puritan faction, so Milton's respect for Young was undoubtedly sincere. It must at the same time have been counterbalanced by the influence of the elder and younger Alexander Gil of St. Paul's School, religious rationalists with whom Milton remained in touch for many years, long after the younger Gil fell afoul of Archbishop Laud at Oxford for political reasons. Milton himself ran afoul of the authorities at Cambridge, where he was "sent down" for a term, although the reasons remain unclear. Like most of the university colleges, Christ's was then dominated by Puritans, if less so than Emmanuel, where most of the godly sent their sons to seek out religious role models. Milton not only failed to do this but quarreled bitterly with his tutor, William Chappell, the cause of his temporary dismissal. He also actively disliked his fellow ministerial students, as he remarks in a letter to Gil (*CPW* 1:314). If hardly a complete loner, Milton seems never to have placed "associative solidarity" very high on his list of priorities. In any case, both of the students he was most clearly associated with, Edward King and Robert Gell (who later performed his third marriage), were Arminians.[5]

---

[3] David Hawkes, "Milton and Usury," Paper read at the Ninth International Milton Symposium, July 11, 2008.

[4] See Campbell and Corns, *John Milton*, p. 38.

[5] Ibid., p. 41. King was also a staunch royalist; see pp. 96–97.

His father's failure to enroll his son at Emmanuel College accords well with everything we know about him: he was an easy-going man who loved music, supported the theater, and served as churchwarden of the chapel at Hammersmith, a Laudian foundation dominated by Laudian enthusiasts. He was also a co-trustee of the Blackfriars theater, the winter home of the King's Men, and his gifted son deeply shared his musical and theatrical interests.[6] The only friend from Cambridge that Milton acknowledges and honors was also a Laudian supporter, Edward King, the "Lycidas" he describes as a promising minister and great loss to the church. Significantly, no counterbalancing praise or even mention of the popular Puritan martyrs of the day appears in Milton's early correspondence, his *Commonplace Book*, or his Latin poems, one of which eulogizes an Arminian bishop, Lancelot Andrewes. Milton's 1645 headnote to *Lycidas* does claim that his elegy for King foretold "the ruin of our corrupted Clergy then in their height" (Hughes 120), a clear reference to the Arminians, but it fails to explain whether their corruption was religious or political. Since Milton's friend Alexander Gil, the classical republican lecturer at Cambridge, Isaac Dorislaus, and Milton himself all suffered academic or political censorship at the hands of Laud and his counterparts at Cambridge, the most likely option (as the antiprelatical tracts seem to confirm) is Laudian politics.[7] Both King and Gil (especially the latter) were accomplished poets, while Gil's father, the headmaster at St. Paul's, was a radical language reformer, but none were remotely puritanical. Although his son nearly lost his ears for denouncing the monarchy, the elder and the younger Gil were fully "'conformable to the ceremonies of the Church of England.'" Donald L. Clark shows that the headmaster had so few Puritan sympathies that he was never persecuted by the Bishop's officers while in theology, he belonged to the liberal lineage of Hooker and Andrewes. Clark believes that *Il Penseroso*'s "studious Cloisters" and "dim religious light" actually recall the cathedral where Gil sent his students on hot summer days, while Milton later began his teaching career on the same London street where his former tutor, Alexander the younger, taught after losing his post at St. Paul's to "a very strict Puritan."[8] Later still, Milton would go further than either Gil in carrying "Christian rationalism to the extreme limits of orthodoxy."[9]

---

[6]   See Thomas N. Corns, "Milton before 'Lycidas,'" in Graham Parry and Joad Raymond (eds.), *Milton and the Terms of Liberty* (New York, 2002), p. 27. Corns cites Jeremy Maule, "Milton's Hammersmith" (unpub. paper, British Milton Seminar 15, Birmingham, March 1997).

[7]   See Leo Miller, "Milton's Clash with Chappell: A Suggested Reconstruction," *MQ* 14.3 (1980): pp. 77–87, especially p. 85, which shows that Dorislaus, a progressive lecturer on Roman history and liberty (two of Milton's favorite subjects), was dismissed through Laud's intervention after giving only two or three lectures.

[8]   Clark, *John Milton*, pp. 36, 67 n. 4, 66–68, 96–99.

[9]   Douglas Bush, *English Literature in the Earlier Seventeenth Century* (Oxford, 1945), p. 321.

Clark to the contrary, scholars continue to assume that Young's influence on Milton was greater not only because he was a Smectymnuan but also because he gave his pupil the famous "roundhead" haircut worn in an early portrait of the poet (see Figure 2.1). Yet even this evidence is far more ambiguous than it seems. The contemporary biographer John Aubrey seems to have found it amusing that "his school-master then was a puritan ... who cut his hair short," a style that, as everyone knew, Milton never wore again (Hughes 1021).

Figure 2.1   John Milton at the age of ten, Cornelius Janssen van Ceulen (1618). By permission of the Pierpont Morgan Library.

The clothing his parents chose for the portrait also suggests gentlemanly rather than Puritan inclinations, which Thomas Corns finds completely in keeping with their broad acceptance of ideological diversity and commitment to metropolitan cultural life.[10] Even when the mature Milton later joined Young and the other Smectymnuans in debating the prelates, they formed no united front for the simple reason, noted by Ken Simpson, that "nothing resembling a unified Presbyterian party [yet] existed for those who sought more local autonomy for the church through government by lay elders elected by the congregation." In addition, Milton significantly differed from the Smectymnuans on the key question of church and scriptural authority: they reserved it for ordained ministers, while Milton granted it to all individuals guided by God's Word and Spirit.[11]

Whether or not his father held similar views, Milton's *Ad Patrem* argues that their shared love of the arts should (and did) make him appreciate his son's right to pursue an artistic rather than a ministerial, legal, or courtly "calling." This plea stands on much firmer ground than earlier supposed. The elder Milton probably contributed a poetic tribute to Shakespeare's First Folio (1623), and he seems to have arranged for his son to first publish his own poem "On Shakespeare" in the Second Folio. Timothy Burbery further shows that the earlier assumption that the young Milton never saw a "live" or at least a non-academic play is almost certainly wrong. His family not only lived in close proximity to the Blackfriars theater, but Milton's *Elegia Prima* lists London play-going among the chief joys of his temporary expulsion from Cambridge. Although some of the poem's lines do refer to classical tragedies that Milton either read or saw only in academic productions (37–46), an equal number (27–36) refer not to a composite or fictional play but to Jonson's *Staple of the News*, which was playing at the Blackfriars at the time he was expelled from the university. Burbery also traces the play-going passages in *L'Allegro* and *Il Penseroso* to contemporary productions. Finally, Milton's undated *Commonplace Book* finds nothing wrong with theater, melody, or musical instruments in church worship, all of which it defends against Puritan objections (*CPW* 1: 382–83, 489–91). His second non-academic "performance" was a masque set to music by the royalist Henry Lawes and mounted (at least in part) by Laud's protégé Bulstrode Whitelocke. Burbery finds no contradiction between Puritanism and drama, but he bases this view on a study that too often conflates Puritans with Parliamentarians; he also concedes that Puritans almost uniformly opposed the masque genre.[12]

---

[10] Corns, "Milton before 'Lycidas,'" p. 27.

[11] Ken Simpson, "'That sovran Book': The Discipline of the Word in Milton's Anti-Episcopal Tracts," in P.G. Stanwood (ed.), *Of Poetry and Politics: New Essays on Milton and His World* (Binghamton, NY, 1995), pp. 313–25, cited pp. 313–14.

[12] Timothy J. Burbery, *Milton the Dramatist* (Pittsburgh, 2007), pp. xiii, xvii, 1–24. Burbery refers to Margot Heinemann's work (pp. xiii, 32), *Puritanism and the Theatre: Thomas Middleton and Opposition Drama under the Early Stuarts* (Cambridge, 1986*)*.

Again unlike the Puritans but like his easy-going father, the young Milton at first ignored the burning religious issues of the day, and when he finally turned to them, he closely linked them to politics. He certainly took religion seriously, as did his father, who was disowned for his Bible-reading, and his mother Sara was known for her piety and good works. Yet Milton's decision to pursue a poetic rather than a ministerial vocation clearly jars with standard Puritan practice. Good Calvinists ranging from Donne and Herbert to Baxter and Bunyan intertwined these pursuits, but Milton claimed first that he could not, and then that Laudian dominance meant that he would not, combine them.[13] Yet, whatever animosities he bore them, the Laudians certainly did *not* prevent him from taking holy orders, a contradiction thoroughly explored in Chapter 3. Although this crux has been previously pointed out, no one yet seems to have noticed another one: unlike the Puritans, Milton expresses an unusually low opinion of ordination or ordained ministers.[14] Although the godly considered ordination "inferior" to the gospel sacraments of baptism and holy communion, they observed it with a sacramental laying on of hands signifying that exercising church discipline was an "ordinance of Christ."[15] By contrast, Milton dismisses ordination as a mere "outward signe or symbol of admission ... it creates nothing, it conferres nothing; it is the inward calling of God that makes a Minister" (*CPW* 1:715). This position is certainly anti-formalist, but Milton grounds it in a humanist, and especially Spenserian, belief that (as Annabel Patterson remarks) "'every free and gentle spirit'" has the right to "dub himself knight without 'the laying of a sword upon his shoulder.'" Unconventionally conflating religious with chivalric idealism, Milton's "peculiar insertion of the prudence-fortitude *topos* ('both by his counsel and his arme') in this context suggests strongly that Milton's persona is now true knight as well as true pastor, and that both metaphors are subsumed in the civic heroism of the orator."[16] Milton's contemporaneous defenses of temperance and chastity are similarly subsumed in the cause of civic heroism, which he plainly identifies with both Italian and Platonic sources (*CPW* 1:890–91) and implicitly with the hygienic moral ideals featured in Bacon's *New Atlantis*, the new "virgin of the world."[17]

---

[13] For an overview, see John Spencer Hill, *John Milton: Poet, Priest and Prophet* (London, 1979), pp. 27–29.

[14] On the deference most Puritans paid to their ministers, see Webster, *Godly Clergy*; Kendall, *Calvin*; and Tolmie, *Triumph*,

[15] Davies, *Worship of the English Puritans*, pp. 222–25, 232.

[16] Patterson, "Civic Hero," pp. 83–84, citing *CPW* 1:891.

[17] See Richard Serjeantson, "Natural Knowledge in the *New Atlantis*," in Bronwen Price (ed.), *Francis Bacon's "New Atlantis": New Interdisciplinary Essays* (Manchester, 2002), pp. 82–105, especially pp. 89–95.

Temperamental, Social, and Theoretical Divergences from the Godly

In the long run, however, Milton's humanistic and individualistic ideals are much less at odds with Puritan morality than with godly communitarianism, an orientation that turned Christian fellowship into the "essence of the sacrament." As Bunyan and others clearly show, Puritans equated the loss of fellowship with the loss of religion, and all agreed with William Ames that the saints either needed to join "a particular congregation" or to be severely sanctioned.[18] John Preston taught that neglecting Christian fellowship proved one's incomplete conversion, since the convert's most fervent desire and delight should be the company of the saints, and those who desired any other company could not be true lovers of God.[19] Even among the radicals, the imitation of fellow saints became nearly as important as the imitation of Christ. One reason is that communal evangelism and other forms of proselytizing fulfilled a double function: first, as "'most sure and certain signs of regeneration,'" as Thomas Goodwin declared, and second, by providing a kind of "bank" where the "poor in spirit" could deposit and receive reciprocal charity in moments of weakness. Given Luther's condemnation of popish "assurance policies," J. Sears McGee finds this aspect of Puritan religiosity one of history's richer ironies. Yet, since Calvinism taught that even the Elect could not truly imitate their Savior except in his suffering and death, these assurances fulfilled an important need.[20]

Milton's failure to focus on Christ's suffering and death is well known: the theme is virtually absent from his major works and his early poem on the passion was never completed. Exactly when he rejected Puritan sabbatarianism as a duty commanded only of the Jews (*CPW* 6:704–15) is uncertain, but his nephew Edward Phillips states that he did not attend religious services but reserved Sundays for private Bible-reading, meditation, and music. Ironically, extreme Puritans warned against singing divine psalms for ordinary recreation and even in church services, replacing them with chants to eliminate every element of sensual delight.[21] They were even stricter about the choice of marriage mates, which they communally limited to fellow believers. Bunyan's Mr. Badman exemplifies the fatal folly of ignoring the biblical prohibition against being "'unequally yoked together with unbelievers, for what fellowship hath righteousness with unrighteousness; … what concord hath Christ with Belial; or what part hath he that believeth with an infidel; and what agreement hath the temple of God with idols?'" (2 Cor. 6:13). Although Paul is here warning the Corinthians against marrying pagans, Puritans like Bunyan taught that even among the saints, future mates should be pre-approved by godly ministers. Since "Satan and carnal reason and lust, or at least inconsiderateness, has

---

[18]   See McGee, *Godly Man*, pp. 203, 205; Honeygosky (on Ames), *Milton's House of God*, p. 39; and Nuttall, *Visible Saints*.

[19]   McGee, *Godly Man*, pp. 182–83.

[20]   Ibid., pp. 204–5.

[21]   Lewis Bayly, *The Practice of Piety* (1633), pp. 215–16; cf. p. 184.

the chiefest hand" in courtship, "in the multitude of counselors there is safety."[22] Milton certainly repented his hasty courtship of Mary Powell, but he never blamed this mistake on "carnal reason" or "inconsiderateness" of religious disparity. "Spurred" on by his sad experience, his divorce tracts merely warn "innocent" bachelors not to let maidenly beauty and modesty outweigh more important traits—delightful conversation, liveliness of mind, and personal compatibility. Since Mary lacked these qualities—which he probably expected from a member of her high-spirited, far from Puritan family—he next sought out the "witty Miss Davis" to relieve his solitary scholarly pursuits. When Mary finally returned from her self-imposed absence, Phillips reports that he chivalrously forgave her without any puritanical lectures on her unchristian behavior, since "his generous nature" was always "more inclinable to reconciliation than to perseverance in anger and revenge" (Hughes 1032).

Milton's theory of marriage is obviously the opposite of Bunyan's, who like the authors of most Puritan marriage manuals, emphasized wifely obedience, made no allowance for separation even from a "Mr. Badman," and largely restricted mutuality to the marriage bed—for Milton, an utterly joyless "blessing" without the "spirit" of mental and emotional compatibility.[23] Some sectarians did adopt his radical views on marriage and divorce, but the poet himself was not pleased.[24] Perhaps they came too close to proving his claim that the sexual "ills" that divorce could cure are commonest among the "sort of men who follow *Anabaptism, Famelism, Antinomianism*, and other *fanatick* dreams." Unfortunately "addicted to a zeal of Religion," these radicals suffer from an extreme moral rigidity that "suffocates" the body and drives "natures current" into "the head and inward sense," which results in either the "dotage and idle fancies" of outright madness or libertinism (*CPW* 2:278–79). *The Doctrine and Discipline of Divorce* also blames conforming and covenanting Puritans for attributing an "awfull sanctity" to the man-made pact of marriage, which they worship "like some *Indian* deity, when it can conferre no blessing upon us, but works more and more to our misery" (*CPW* 2:277–78). Like a Baconian idol of the tribe, the irrational fear of divorce cruelly turns Christian liberty into a harsh forbidding as destructive as the Roman Church's anti-Christian "forbidding to marry" (*CPW* 2:280). Yet the "cure" he offered was hardly the libertinism adopted by the radical sects, but a position far closer to Martin Bucer's carefully reasoned provisions for divorce. Finally, although he was happy to rely on such an orthodox Protestant divine, as Campbell and Corns

---

[22] John Bunyan, *The Life and Death of Mr Badman*, in *The Works of John Bunyan*, ed. George Offor [rpt. 1856] (3 vols., New York, 1973), vol. 3, pp. 621, 622.

[23] See Anthony Fletcher, "The Protestant Idea of Marriage in Early Modern England," in Fletcher and Roberts (eds.), *Religion, Culture, and Society*, pp. 161–81, and also my introduction to *Milton and Gender* (Cambridge, 2004), pp. 1–15.

[24] See Corns, "Milton's Quest."

point out, his own divorce tracts became increasingly secular after his discovery of Bucer's support.[25]

Milton is nevertheless placed in the sectarian camp by those who regard him as an ecclesiological Puritan, and his *De Doctrina Christiana* indeed favors a form of sectarian service in which all members have the right to speak and exchange opinions (*CPW* 6:608). Yet the overlap is far from exact: Milton's congregations carefully study the Bible and offer solutions to textual cruxes, unlike the "spirit-filled" Quakers or Baptists who put the Bible aside. Milton's very different approach is explained in *Of Civil Power*, which warns that, since no one can know "the illumination of the Holy Spirit ... to be in himself, much less to be at any time for certain in any other," the biblical word must remain "the main foundation of our protestant religion" (*CPW* 7:242). He does grant that "God hath promis'd by his Spirit to teach all things," but he glosses that to mean only those "things absolutely necessary to salvation" (*CPW* 8:424). Radicals like William Dell believed precisely the opposite: transfused grace "makes a man *invincible*," for "if this power in a *Christian*, should be prevailed against, *God* himself who is that power, should be conquered, which is impossible."[26] Milton's views are thus ironically closer to Hobbes than to the apostles of the Inner Light, since both advocate scripture-based, rational choices about teachers and beliefs. As Hobbes remarks in *Leviathan*, everyone should either become or choose his own teacher in imitation of the "Independency of the Primitive Christians, to follow Paul, or Cephas, or Apollos, every man as he liketh best." For so long as voluntary religion "be without contention" or prejudice generated "by our affection to the Person of his Minister (the fault which the Apostle reprehended in the Corinthians), [it] is perhaps best" (*Leviathan* 4.47).[27] Milton's *Hirelings* and *Of True Religion* closely echo this balanced view: since everyone may be swayed by venal "affections" and "private interest," all "assertion without pertinent scripture" or additions to scripture adopted "for the Teachers sake, whom they think almost infallible[,] ... becomes, through Infirmity, implicit Faith," or false religion (*CPW* 7:293, 8:422). Milton elsewhere cites St. Basil: "*it is a plain falling from the Faith, and a high pride either to make void any thing therin, or to introduce any thing not there to be found*" (*CPW* 1:565; cf. 6:123).[28]

In striking contrast, Quakers like Robert Barclay defended additions to the Bible because they believed the "fundamental Doctrines of the Christian religion are contained in [but] the tenth part of Scripture." In fact, "*any other books*" may "*now* [be] *written by the same Spirit*," since some biblical texts are actually misleading or erroneous. A case in point is the "authentik" Protestant (or Lutheran)

---

[25]   Campbell and Corns, *John Milton*, p. 169.

[26]   William Dell, *Christ's Spirit a Christian's Strength* (London, 1651), p. Av.

[27]   Thomas Hobbes, *Leviathan*, ed. C.B. Macpherson (Harmondsworth: Penguin, 1968), p. 711.

[28]   Campbell and Corns similarly show that the poet's "bibliocentric theology" is ultimately incompatible with Quaker belief; see *John Milton*, p. 320, and also p. 289.

rejection of the teaching of James—"faith without works is dead"— a text Milton favors from his early Sonnet 9 onward.[29] As his religious thought matures, he reiterates the necessity of good works even more strongly: "our whole practical dutie in religion is contained in charitie, or the love of God and our neighbour, no way to be forc'd, yet fulfilling of the whole law; that is to say, our whole practise in religion" (*CPW* 7:256). The entire second book of *De Doctrina Christiana* is devoted to defending this emphasis on good works, since rather than qualifying James, Milton instead qualifies Paul's assertion that man "is justified by faith alone" (Gal. 5:6). He feels certain that Paul must have meant "*faith working through charity*," because the works of faith "may be different from the works of the law," but they are works nonetheless (*CPW* 6:490).

Yet by far the most striking distinction between Milton and the godly is that, in all his vast output of theological writing, much like Jeremy Taylor he says almost nothing about conversion.[30] According to J. Herbert McLachlan, this avoidance of conversion narratives characterizes "once-born" believers, a category embracing Sir Thomas Browne, Robert Boyle, the Cambridge Platonists, and the liberal nineteenth-century Christians who virtually equated right reason with the voice of God.[31] *De Doctrina* expresses their general point of view as follows: "any man who wishes to be saved should work out his beliefs for himself ... by [his] own exertions," "ponder[ing] the Holy Scriptures themselves with all possible diligence," preferably in the original languages and in consultation with "more diffuse volumes of divinity," although theology is often unfortunately "dishonest" or misleading (*CPW* 6:118–20). As for miracles and other special signs of election, they are "not things which go on for ever. They were more necessary in the early days of the church than today. Because then the gospel was a strange, unheard-of and almost incredible thing to the ears of Jew and Gentile alike, but now men are brought up in the apostolic faith from the first, and begin to believe while they are still children. It is enough for us to hear and read about the miracles which Christ performed in the beginning" (*CPW* 6:564). We should thus progress in faith not through miraculous vision but scriptural study, which is apparently why *Of True Religion* fails to list Quakers and Seekers among other Protestant "heretics" deserving official church comprehension. "Lutherans, Calvinists, Anabaptists, Socinians, [and] Arminians" may commit "some errors" but they abstain from the implicit faith of a Dell or a Barclay (*CPW* 8:423; cf. 6:584).

Milton's omission of Quakers from this list does not appear accidental, since fellow republicans like Sir Henry Vane and his apologist Henry Stubbe pointedly *did* urge toleration for Quakers and also for Catholic defenders of "implicit faith."

---

[29]   Robert Barclay, *An Apology for the true Christian divinity, as the same is held forth and preached by the people, called in scorn, Quakers* ([Aberdeen?], 1678), pp. 55, 40 (on James).

[30]   McGee, *Godly Man*, p. 57.

[31]   McLachlan, *Religious Opinions*, pp. 29, 47. On Boyle, see Richard S. Westfall, *Science and Religion in Seventeenth-Century England* (New Haven, 1958), pp. 125–27.

In contrast, Milton defines this kind of faith as the "Will and choice profestly against Scripture" without "sincere endeavours to understand it rightly" (*CPW* 8:423), the same negative definition given in *Of Civil Power* (*CPW* 7:247). *Of True Religion* slightly rewords it, but mainly (as Keith Stavely notes) to indicate his new "alliance with the latitudinarians" and his approval of their distinction between error and heresy.[32] This "new" alliance seems less than surprising given that Milton, Taylor, and the Latitudinarians were all strongly influenced by John Hales, the author of the influential *Golden Remains* and *A Tract concerning Schisme*, which argues that Arius was not a heretic (*CPW* 8:423 n. 27). The liberal Hales has long been presumed to be the Eton friend (Horton was only a few miles from Eton) who introduced Milton to Henry Wotton, who in turn provided him with letters of introduction for his Italian journey. Milton later presented Hales with his first treatise, *Of Reformation*.[33] Like Locke after and Selden before them, they all distinguished between rational error and the heresy of "implicit faith," which would exempt both extreme enthusiasts (always a tiny minority of Puritans) and Roman Catholics from toleration for years to come. Locke's rejection of innate ideas also helped to discredit enthusiasm, as did his insistence that perception, insight, and even "revelation" are naturalistic processes capable of being restored to a fully operable if not "perfectly" unclouded state, as Quakers and other mystics believed.[34]

The modern critic might object that this outline overlooks the apparent Puritan "conversion" behind Milton's attack on the prelates, a thesis that Leo Solt first raised grave doubts about by pointing out that Milton's attacks departed from the usual practice of learned Puritans. Since he made no theological distinctions between Laudian and Calvinist bishops like Joseph Hall (whom Puritans did not criticize), Solt concluded that Milton's rancor was not religious but political. This conclusion was further supported by the fact that his critiques revolved around the prelates' opposition to his own "view that monarchy is made up of two parts: the supremacy of the king *and* the liberty of the subject (*Of Reformation*, ... p. 592)."[35] In failing to register this distinction and in other ways "contriving" to reinstate "popish" absolutism, the prelates seemed to Milton to threaten subjects with an "everlasting slavery" that would sell "your bodies, your wives, your children, your

---

[32]   For a contrary view, see Janel Mueller, "Milton on heresy," in Stephen B. Dobranski and John P. Rumrich (eds.), *Milton and Heresy* (Cambridge, 1998), pp. 21–38.

[33]   Barbara K. Lewalski, *The Life of John Milton* (Malden, MA, 2003) pp. 569 n. 93, 586 n. 49, and 695 n. 49.

[34]   Unlike Locke and ironically more like the Quakers, the Cambridge Platonists remained committed to innate ideas, but mainly as a bulwark against Calvin's doctrine of total depravity. On the Quaker attempt to reintroduce literally "naked" Edenic experience into their lives, see Kristen Poole, *Radical Religion from Shakespeare to Milton* (Cambridge, 2000), pp. 147–81; on the distance between Milton's Eden and Quaker dreams of complete perfectability, see pp. 173–79.

[35]   Solt, Appendix G, "The Bishops," *CPW* 1:1011.

liberties, your Parlaments, all these things … at an out-cry in their Pulpits to the arbitrary and illegall dispose of … a King" (*CPW* 1:851). Other sources of rancor in the antiprelatical tracts include the clerical close-mindedness he encountered at Cambridge, the shallowness of its ministerial candidates, the upper clergy's ignorance and conceit, and their retreat into the "dark ages" of ignorant ceremony. Yet here again, his emphasis is not typically puritanical: ignorant rituals and church hierarchies may be outdated, but they are not literally contaminating; they may inhibit solid Christian *teaching*, but he fails to mention *preaching*, the key Puritan objection. An equally significant divergence lies in his failure to demean the memory of the bishop most typically reviled by Puritan anti-ceremonialists, Lancelot Andrewes, the subject of one of his most "devout" Latin elegies.[36] Finally, whether or not Milton realized it at the time, the underlying tenor of these tracts is already implicitly anti-Puritan. As Zagorin observes, by dismissing "any corporate reason … which could not persuade" on its own merits, their logic is "as fatal to the claims of the Presbyterian ministers as to those of the Laudian clergy."[37] No wonder, then, that the "purple" apocalyptic passages of his antiprelatical tracts rapidly give way, first, to the Baconian but still millenarian expectations of *Areopagitica* (1644), and then to the completely naturalistic account of human ascent, decline, and fall in the early drafts of his *History of Britain* (1648), which is hardly a "prehistory of a chosen people."[38]

Running like a leitmotif through his major poems and prose, Milton's conviction that even revelations above reason must "conform to and not violate the dictates of reason" synthetically underpins his understanding of scripture and politics. The gospel covenant provides a fully "free, elective and rational worship'" (*CPW* 7:260), a theme Lewalski finds recurring in Milton's writings from his divorce tracts to *The Tenure*, *Of Civil Power*, *The Likeliest Means*, and his *Defence of the People of England*.[39] Drawing upon both the Bible and Francis Bacon, Milton first heralds the new era of "universal learning" announced in *The Advancement of Learning* in his final Cambridge Prolusion. As its editors recognize, his argument is a virtual précis of Bacon's claim that

---

[36] See Campbell and Corns, *John Milton*, pp. 148–49; they quite rightly believe that this was because Milton's real concern was not with ceremonialism but with toleration.

[37] Perez Zagorin, *A History of Political Thought in the English Revolution* (London, 1954), p. 109.

[38] Campbell and Corns, *John Milton*, p. 356. On *Areopagitica*'s Baconian agenda, see Blair Hoxby, *Mammon's Music: Literature and Economic in the Age of Milton* (New Haven, 2002), pp. 25–56. On the *History of Britain*, see also Nicholas von Maltzahn, *Milton's "History of Britain": Republican Historiography in the English Revolution* (Oxford, 1991), pp. 88–89.

[39] Barbara K. Lewalski, "Milton and *De Doctrina Christiana*: Evidences of Authorship," *Milton Studies* 36 (1998): pp. 203–28, cited p. 215.

> If a man could succeed ... in kindling a light in nature—a light which should
> in its very rising touch and illuminate all the border–regions that confine upon
> the circle of our present knowledge; and so spreading further and further should
> presently disclose and bring into sight all that is hidden and secret in the world,—
> that ... man would be the benefactor indeed of the human race,—the propagator
> of man's empire over the universe, the champion of liberty, the conqueror and
> subduer of necessities. (*Works* 10:84–85)

Milton similarly foresees that soon "the spirit of man, no longer confined within
this dark prison-house, will reach out far and wide, till it fills the whole world and
the space far beyond with the expansion of its divine greatness" (*CPW* 1:296).
Other key Baconian references surface in debating Hall (*CPW* 1:668, 882, 906–7)
and in maintaining his lifelong conviction that the advancers of learning far excel
military heroes or even law-givers. Bacon had argued that "inventors" alone plant
the "seeds" of an everlasting harvest "without causing harm or sorrow to any"
(*Works* 4:113–14), an idea echoed in Milton's divorce tracts, which claim that the
rediscoverers of domestic liberty will be "reck'n'd among the publick benefactors
of civill and humane life; above the inventors of wine and oyle." They also soar
above the puritanical "austerity of *John the Baptist*" because they have listened to
"the charming pipe of him who sounded and proclaim'd relief to all in distress"—
the good Shepherd who taught that the sabbath of rest was made for man, and not
man for the sabbath (*CPW* 2:240, 241).

Just before this passage, Milton identifies one of "the best learned" progressives
of the time as Hugo Grotius, the Dutch natural law theorist, historian, and staunch
Arminian ally of the anti-Calvinists (*CPW* 2:238). Milton's similarly secular and
non-providential understanding of history—which consistently conflates natural
and divine law—thus marks another crucial departure from the inspirational
mindset of the godly.[40] Wyman Herendeen shows that his progressive outlook
clearly diverges from that of standard Protestant historiographers like Sleidanus,
who sees history as the fulfillment of prophecy and divine predestination. Milton
instead finds human agents providing "an effective force or exemplum in history"
not exclusively governed by "divine revelation," "election," or apocalyptic
intervention. He early rejects the "fading" type of millennialism endorsed by
most of the godly who, "having seen the light of Reformation," see themselves
facing "'the last age of this fading world' when 'Satan shall be Prince,'" the event
immediately preceding Christ's Second Coming.[41] Instead of fading, the "light"
shines brighter day by day in both the divorce tracts and *Areopagitica*, which
foresee an ascending Baconian millennium where human, not divine, agency
alone is at work. Hope and industry, not dogmatic certitude, reconstruct the temple

---

[40]   Campbell and Corns, *John Milton*, pp. 106, 359.

[41]   Wyman Herendeen, "Milton and Machiavelli: The Historical Revolution and
Protestant Poetics," in Mario di Cesare (ed.), *Milton in Italy* (Binghamton, NY, 1991), pp.
427–44, cited p. 441.

of Truth in Milton's *Areopagitica*, and even Puritan military victories are later portrayed in tentative terms: he never regards them as apocalyptically assured, but as active, ambiguous, ongoing, and utterly dependent upon the classical virtue of their agents.

Even liberal Puritans like the Levellers instead tended to see themselves as ideally inert instruments in the hands of a dynamic God who could achieve anything. In September 1641, Jeremiah Burroughs typically claimed that "the greatest human happiness on earth [is] to be instrumentall for God," while a 1643 sermon insisted that the very bullets in battle "were directed by God towards or away from their target." Although Milton's God also has a plan for his Englishmen, it requires their participation, not a "total dependence on God" and his "leadings." J.C. Davis finds the passive Puritan outlook relatively constant throughout the revolutionary period. On the eve of Pride's Purge in 1648, Peter Sterry advised Parliament that avoiding all human forms and constitutions would insure the imminent coming of Christ, while the Fifth Monarchists later opposed Cromwell's Instrument of Government because all human "forms and disputes about them were … 'abominable popery.'" The Quaker James Nayler and the prophetess Mary Cary took the same position since, like Christopher Feake, Henry Jessey, Hugh Peter, and Cary's supporters, they "saw God as a breaker of forms." Ironically, even Cromwell's own chaplain (Sterry) believed in a "God [who] was a destroyer, not a sanctifier, of carnal forms," convictions that made Puritans deeply ambivalent, not just about republican constitutional reforms but also "about the process of re-*form-ation*" itself.[42] Milton's colleague and admirer John Hall (who regarded Milton as a second Bacon) early pinpointed the underlying problem with this outlook, which *The Readie and Easie Way* (1660) later repeats. According to Hall, so long as the "main pretence" of Puritan governmental policy was "Religion, or according to *their* odd and fanatick Notions, the setting up of the Kingdome of *Jesus Christ*," "such *notions* as these, proceeding from ill made brains, and disturbed fancies, strongly tinctured with an hypocondriack melancholy," would unjustly "oblige us to quit our *Discourse*, our natural *reason*, our *experiences* drawn even from common sense, the means God hath ordained to direct us in civil matters, and to follow those *Wills-with-Wisps*, or *ignes fatui* of *revelation* and pretended *Spirit*."[43] Milton's friend Marvell agreed: rather than promoting rational balance or a modern mixed constitution, radical Puritans had erupted into a "frantique army" of Fifth Monarchists, Ranters, seditious "prophets," and other "remnants" of the Munster Anabaptists, a rag-tag assortment of "Wand'rers, adult'rers, liars, … / Sorc'rers, atheists, Jesuits, [and] possessed" who defaced law and scripture "With the same

---

[42] J.C. Davis, "The Millennium as the Anti-Utopia of Seventeenth Century Political Thought," in *Anglophonia: French Journal of English Studies* 3 (1998): pp. 57–66, cited pp. 61, 62, 63, 66.

[43] John Hall, *Confusion Confounded, … Wherein Is Considered the Reason of the Resignation of the late Parliament and the Establishment of a Lord Protector* (London, 1654), p. 3.

liberty as points and lace; / Oh race most hypocritically strict! / Bent to reduce us to the ancient pict" (*The First Anniversarie*, 299, 313–18).[44]

Milton's educational outlook is as basically secular and rationalist as his attitudes toward history and progress. Even in ethics, his tractate *Of Education* provides a moral education almost wholly based on classical or "heathen" authors: Aristotle's *Proairesis*, "all the morall works of *Plato, Zenophon, Cicero, Plutarch, Laertius*, and those *Locrian* remnants." The "study of *David* or *Solomon*, or the Evangels" is naturally recommended, but reserved for more private "nightward studies." This casual, individualistic approach to scripture indicates Milton's clear disinterest in training youths for the Puritan ministry, although, as he sarcastically observes, his methods would vastly improve the quality of what now appears "in Pulpits," which is "oft times to as great a triall of our patience as any other that they preach to us." This remark seems to confirm his disdain for the godly ministers then at their zenith in the London pulpits (*CPW* 2:396–97, 406). Aside from the irenic John Dury, whose "Reformed School" was similarly indebted to the Christian humanist educators of the Renaissance, those influenced by Milton's program were mainly non-Puritans like Hall and Abraham Cowley.[45] Cowley's 1661 *Proposition for the Advancement of the Empirical Philosophy* closely follows Of *Education* in its section on "The School," while the Deist Charles Blount even more carefully reprises *Areopagitica* in his *Just Vindication of Learning*.[46] Like other Protestant rationalists, these men "shared a common dissatisfaction with existing educational institutions and methods," and a firm belief that "educational reform [w]as a necessary condition for the successful reformation of church and state. They also believed in extending education opportunity," an idea not developed in *Of Education* itself but in *The Likeliest Means* (1659) and *The Readie and Easie Way* (1660), where "Milton advocated the use of state revenues to provide a national system of elementary schools and libraries." Hartlib and Milton agreed that "these objectives were best served by association with the Independents," although there is no evidence that they shared their Congregationalist tenets, which Milton rejects in *Areopagitica*.[47]

Self-motivated introspection of the type encouraged in *Of Education* was once considered a Puritan characteristic, but, as Margo Todd insists, if these habits are not situated "in the midst of an over-powering concern with the Christian community," we revert to a confused and "distorted notion of Puritans as individualists."[48] For William Hunt, that overpowering concern means that

---

[44]   Cited from *The Poems of Andrew Marvell*, ed. Nigel Smith (London, 2003).

[45]   Charles Webster, *Samuel Hartlib and the Advancement of Learning* (Cambridge, 1970), p. 42.

[46]   Milton's 1673 reprint emphasizes the priority of his treatise to Cowley's by noting that it was "Written above twenty Years since" (*CPW* 2:362). On Blount, see my Afterword below.

[47]   Webster, *Samuel Hartlib*, pp. 42–43.

[48]   Todd, "Puritan Self-Fashioning," p. 75.

a "man of irreproachable personal piety who nevertheless has no objection to his neighbours' boozing on the Sabbath or fornicating in the haylofts is not a Puritan. A Puritan who minds his own business is a contradiction in terms."[49] Like the Independent divines who fled to America, the vast majority of Puritans thus believed with Thomas Hooker that "'we are our brothers keepers,'" yet *Areopagitica* is all about minding one's own business.[50] In order to end censorship and intolerance, we must not police our brethren but instead recall that "To the pure all things are pure." Therefore "all kinde of knowledge whether of good or evil ... cannot defile, nor consequently ... books, if the will and conscience be not defil'd" (*CPW* 2:512). No one can be outwardly contaminated by previously censorable words or actions, for "a wise man like a good refiner can gather gold out of the drossiest volume," while "a fool will be a fool with the best book, yea or without book" (*CPW* 2:521). These beliefs also implicitly dispute Puritan iconoclasm, which typically insisted (as the Fifth Monarchist John Canne put it) that any "plant which the heavenly Father never planted ... [is] therefore to be pluckt up by the roots"—all forms and "inventions" of men.[51] Milton's position can thus be properly understood as *anti*-iconoclasm, since he permits the free circulation even of forbidden literature: "as for the burning of those Ephesian [magic] books by St. *Pauls* converts," "It was a privat act, a voluntary act, and leaves us to a voluntary imitation: the men in remorse burnt those books which were their own; the Magistrat by this example is not appointed: ... another might perhaps have read them in some sort usefully" (*CPW* 2:514).

Good and evil thus become relative to the reader, not prescribed by authority or tradition. God himself scorns "to captivat [man] under a perpetuall childhood of prescription, but trusts him with the gift of reason to be his own chooser." Temptation, too, is relative, for "to all men such books are not temptations, nor vanities; but usefull drugs and materialls wherewith to temper and compose effective and strong med'cins, which mans life cannot want," despite "all the licencing that Sainted Inquisition could ever yet contrive" (*CPW* 2:514, 521). Both inquisitorial and puritanical censorship are therefore not only impractical but *immoral*, for "If every action which is good, or evil in man at ripe years, were to be under pittance, and prescription, and compulsion, what were vertue but a name, what praise could be then due to well-doing, what grammercy to be sober, just or continent?" Believing that God "esteems the growth and compleating of one vertuous person, more then the restraint of ten vitious" (*CPW* 2:527, 528), Milton forges a conception of conscience more flexible than that of any contemporary except Hobbes, who similarly anticipates Locke.[52] Typically,

---

[49]   Hunt, *Puritan Moment*, p. 146.

[50]   McGee, *Godly Man*, pp. 196–97, 202, 246, and also Haller, *Rise of Puritanism*, pp. 49–127.

[51]   John Canne, *A Second Voyce from the Temple* (London, 1653), p. 4.

[52]   Sharon Achinstein, "Milton Catches the Conscience of the King: *Eikonoklastes* and the Engagement Controversy," *Milton Studies* 29 (1992): pp. 143–63, see especially p. 159.

however, *Areopagitica* is merely seen as marking Milton's departure from the Presbyterians and realignment with the Independents, although a closer reading shows that it actually anticipates his later hostility toward the Independents as hypocritical "Dependents" upon state support (*CPW* 7:318).

Milton's position on other sectarian practices of Christian liberty (*CPW* 2:555–57) is more ambiguous for, while praising all who forego a "fugitive and cloister'd vertue" (*CPW* 2:515), he sternly warns against forming new "cloisters" that support a godly but impractical reformation of manners:

> If we think to regulat Printing, thereby to rectifie manners, we must regulat all recreations and pastimes, all that is delightfull to man. No musick must be heard, no song be set or sung, but what is grave and *Dorick*. There must be licencing dancers, that no gesture, motion, or deportment be taught our youth but what by their allowance shall be thought honest … It will ask more then the work of twenty licencers to examin all the lutes, the violins, and ghittarrs in every house; they must not be suffer'd to prattle as they doe, but must be licenc'd what they may say. And who shall silence all the airs and madrigalls, that whisper softnes in chambers? The Windows also, and the *Balcone's* must be thought on, there are shrewd books with dangerous Frontispices set to sale. (*CPW* 2:523–24)

Modern readers might well take this indignant *reductio ad absurdum* as a mere rhetorical flourish, but the restrictions described here were actually advocated by Puritans still frequently linked to Milton by literary critics.[53] George Wither's *Haleluiah, or, Britans Second Remembrancer* (1641) proposed precisely the measures *Areopagitica* satirizes, while William Prynne wanted to ban all "effeminate music" and all "chromatical harmonies" as an "impudent malapertness" or "whorish music crowned with flowers." Yet, as Campbell and Corns note, Milton on the other hand never really fell out of love with choral music and perhaps not even with ceremony: the funeral he arranged for his beloved second wife Katherine Woodcock, the subject of Sonnet 23, was elaborately ceremonial. Their general summary of Milton's religious position—that he was closest to the Erastians (especially Selden) in intellectual terms, to the Independents in regard to church government, and to the sectarians in terms of heterodoxy—is quite accurate so long as we add that he was never either a religious Independent (ultimately the same as a Congregationalist) or a sectarian.[54] Milton *politically* favored the "Assembly Independent" position on church government without

---

[53]   See, for instance, Guibbory, *Ceremony and Community*, pp. 147–227; John N. King, *Milton and Religious Controversy: Satire and Polemic in "Paradise Lost"* (Cambridge, 2000); Loewenstein, *Representing Revolution*; and Achinstein, *Literature and Dissent*.

[54]   Prynne is quoted in *Histriomastix* (London, 1633), pp. 275. On Milton's love of choral music, see Campbell and Corns, *John Milton*, p. 75; on Katherine Milton's funeral and Milton's sonnet in memory of his "late espoused saint" (which they number 19), see pp. 268–69; for their summary of Milton's "mixed" religious outlook, see p. 161.

remotely admiring Congregationalism. Not only was its theology as staunchly Calvinist as Presbyterianism, but its ideology was equally puritanical. As for Milton's heterodoxies, they were commonly shared by intellectuals like Hobbes as well as by sectarians.

The Independents undoubtedly offered the laity a considerably broadened role in the congregation, but they limited it to sharing personal religious experiences and selecting their own ministers. Radical Independents like Katherine Chidley consistently sought more power for the congregation as a whole, not just for the local minister or the vestry, but even then, these rights were firmly grounded in the spiritual communion of saints. As the term "Independent" implies, the movement was founded on a radical separation from "the world," and as the term "congregational" implies, it rested on publicly attested fellowship and fitness to qualify as a "visible saint."[55] The Independents' separatist tendencies were reinforced by their precisionism concerning the proper administration of the sacrament. Considering both altar-rails and kneeling in communion to be popish practices, they imitated the postures of the apostles at the Last Supper and administered the sacrament either to a seated or a standing congregation informally gathered around the communion table or in individual pews. The strict screening process required for congregational membership also qualifies both the "voluntarism" and the actual "independency" of the Independents, and other Puritans regularly criticized them for hypocritically seeking "saints" of high social or financial status. By accepting members more for their material than for their spiritual gifts, ministers, elders, and individual converts appeared to engage in a self-interested "bargaining" with God.

Milton early satirized these practices in a famous but much misunderstood passage of *Areopagitica*, which slyly paints a portrait of a wealthy man who "finds Religion to be a traffick so entangl'd, and of so many piddling accounts," that he "resolvs to give over toyling, and to find himself out som factor, to whose care and credit he may commit the whole managing of his religious affairs; som Divine of note and estimation … to [whom] he adheres, resigns the whole ware-house of his religion, with all the locks and keyes into his custody." This complacent "heretick in the truth … beleeve[s] things only because his Pastor sayes so," thereby adopting an "implicit faith" worthy of any "lay Papist of Loretto." Most modern readers have conventionally assumed that Milton's "faithful" heretic is a complacent conformist, but the context of the passage clearly indicates otherwise. Milton describes him as a man who "would have the name to be religious" in order to stand out above "his neighbours," not merely as a "conforming" parishioner. Like the Independents, he actively searches for an eminent divine to "invest" in (*CPW* 2:543–44). This investment was mutual, since successful Independent ministers were notorious for maintaining several congregations while residing only in one. They also refused to observe the traditional parish boundaries retained by both unseparating "church"

---

[55] See Nuttall, *Visible Saints*, pp. 70–100; and also Patrick Collinson, "The Godly: Aspects of Popular Protestantism," in *Godly People* (London, 1983), pp. 1–17.

Puritans and Presbyterians, a practice that allowed charismatic preachers to achieve a particularly lucrative "Independence" by retaining both their duly constituted parishes and another congregation drawn from dissatisfied members of surrounding ones. In extreme cases like that of John Goodwin, Murray Tolmie shows that they sometimes maintained two-congregations-in-one, a practice that created great bitterness among "normal" parishioners who were refused the sacrament offered to the gathered or Independent members on the same premises.[56]

Although this kind of conflict was relatively rare, other Independents inspired similar dissensions by reserving the sacrament for visible saints, a ministerial privilege implicit in John Owen's "Humble Proposals," the document so bitterly protested in Milton's Cromwell sonnet but accepted by Goodwin.[57] Presbyterians similarly used suspension from the sacrament or the further step of excommunication as instruments of godly discipline, but, as Tolmie points out, they did not generally "unchurch" the masses in the manner of their more "liberal" Puritan brethren. Of course, the Independents did not completely consign the masses to paganism, but they did destroy the integrity of the parish community. By "insisting that there was a first-class church available to saints in the gathered church," they abandoned the Presbyterian reformers' goal of exercising godly discipline in an inclusive dispensation. The liberal Goodwin forcefully defended this practice and was accordingly ejected, but his beliefs already had much in common with the extreme separatist belief that all parish buildings were eternally polluted by the catholic mass.[58] Many literary critics and even some historians such as John Coffey nevertheless continue the long tradition of aligning Milton with Goodwin even though *Areopagitica* denounces the very ecclesiology he practiced.[59] This confusion is partly justified by the fact that both adopted Arminian positions on free will, and that Milton shared the Independent belief that "a rigid externall formality" is a "grosse conforming stupidity" that contributes "more to the sudden degenerating of a Church then many *subdichotomies* of petty schisms" (*CPW* 2:564). Nevertheless, *Areopagitica* does not plainly endorse separatists and even wryly critiques them for their "implicit faith" in their ministers. It also rejects the very idea of visible saints, since "it is not possible for man to sever the wheat from the tares, the good fish from the other frie; that must be the Angels Ministery at the end of mortall things." It does declare that "all the Lords people

---

[56]   Tolmie, *Triumph*, pp. 99–105.

[57]   See Coffey, *John Goodwin*, pp. 234; Goodwin did, however, reject the other Independents' Triers.

[58]   Tolmie, *Triumph*, pp. 100–101, 111–19; see also Nuttall, *Visible Saints*.

[59]   Coffey, *John Goodwin*, 196. Coffey too often relies on outdated work on Milton and Whiggish assumptions about his Puritanism, but his study still reveals crucial differences between the two (see below). Campbell and Corns largely follow Coffey but warn that any evidence connecting Milton and Goodwin (aside from the fact that the latter used some of Milton's political arguments) is circumstantial and conjectural; see *John Milton*, pp. 319–20.

are become Prophets" in "the slow-moving Reformation which we labour under," but the interminably mixed and uncertain appearances of truth and error in this labor strongly suggest a Baconian, not a Puritan, view of truth (*CPW* 2:564–65, 556). Otherwise, he reveals few if any millenarian sympathies and absolutely no anxiety about the fate of his soul.[60]

Milton's most overt antagonism to the Presbyterians is, like so much of his thought, nevertheless more secular and political than spiritual or theological. His *Tenure of Kings and Magistrates* describes this "frustrated Faction" as "new Apostate Scarcrowes, who under show of giving counsel, send out their barking monitories and *memento's*, empty of ought else but ... madness and vexation of thir ends lost, ... [and] Statutes and Scriptures ... falsly and scandalously ... wrest[ed] against thir [former] Friends and Associates" (*CPW* 3:194–95). Certainly his wrath is mainly political: Presbyterians balked both at rejecting monarchy and at executing the King. By the mid-1640s, however, he was clearly exasperated with both the Puritan right and left. He dashed out angry poetic diatribes against "the New Forcers of Conscience," by which he meant Presbyterian martyrs like Prynne, Presbyterian censors like Thomas Edwards, theologians like Rutherford, A.S. (Adam Stewart), and "Scotch what d'ye call" (8, 12). In Sonnet 11, the rude "names" (10–11) of these "barbarous" Scots not only jar with harmonious Greek titles like "Tetrachordon," but actually herald a new dark age ending the humanistic era of "Sir *John Cheke*" at Cambridge (12). He also lashes out at the sects who hate "Learning worse than Toad or Asp" (13), as his companion Sonnet 12 complains. The raucous prophets who "bawl for freedom in their senseless mood, / And still revolt when truth would set them free" are too ignorant either to understand his divorce tracts or to realize that they want "License ... when they cry liberty" (Sonnet 12, 9–11). There is thus little to choose between their "radical" incomprehension and Presbyterian hypocrisy, for while the conservatives "adjure the Civil Sword / To force our Consciences that Christ set free, / And ride us with a classic [or classis] Hierarchy" ("On the New Forcers," 5–7), the radicals create senseless chaos and combustion—"all this waste of wealth and loss of blood" (Sonnet 12, 14). [61]

Yet, as Nathaniel Henry long ago noted, Milton's targets in Sonnet 12 actually include *all* those who ignore "the known rules of ancient liberty" (2). Rather than "quit their clogs" (1), they form a "barbarous" chorus of "Owls and Cuckoos, Asses, Apes and Dogs" (4), classical symbols of ignorance, and, in this case, of the inability to bear the light of day or even night, the light of Apollo or Diana. Finally, Milton even turned against learned radicals like Stephen Marshall, the widely revered author of the famous Puritan sermon, *Meroz Cursed.* He complains

---

[60]   Campbell and Corns, *John Milton*, p. 52.

[61]   Nathaniel H. Henry, "Who Meant License When They Cried Liberty?" *MLN* 66.8 (1951): pp. 509–13. As Henry observes, Milton's satire is less party-based than it seems, although he believes it was aimed particularly at the "fanatics" of Coleman Street—the Attaways and Jenneys.

that, while this sermon has become "the very *Motto* of thir Pulpits," the godly have fallen "notoriously into the same sinns, wherof so lately and so loud they accus'd the Prelates." Hence their preachers no longer resemble the "true Ministers of the Protestant doctrine, taught by those ... famous and religious men, who first reformed the Church" at home and abroad. Through their "filthy love of gaine" and tyrannical power, they have become "Pulpit-firebrands," not true "Protestant Divines," hypocritical "Ministers of Mammon instead of Christ" (*CPW* 3:242–43). The only solution is for all "Divines," not just prelates (*CPW* 1:598–99), to learn "not to be disturbers of the civil affairs, being in hands better able and more belonging to manage them; but to study harder, and to attend the office of good Pastors" (*CPW* 3:240–41).

This phase of Milton's religious development in the late 1640s also marks the beginning of the disestablishmentarian ideas that he will pursue during the following decade. To attain a ministry that hates "covetousness, which worse then heresie, is idolatry"; which hates "pluralities and all kind of Simony; [and] ... rambling from Benefice to Benefice, like rav'nous Wolves seeking where they may devour the biggest," state religion must be altogether ended (*CPW* 3:241). Like Bacon in "Of Superstition," Milton finds that idolatry—financial or spiritual—is worse than atheism, since it licenses stratagems for ambition and lucre that prohibit progress of any kind. Selfish passions disguised as spiritual zeal also animate Puritan zealots who cannot be content with their own liberty of conscience, but must "violently ... impose what [they] ... will have to be the only religion, upon other men's consciences," a disposition that betrays minds "not only unchristian and irreligious, but inhuman also and barbarous." Uncivilly disrupting parliaments in the name of their "pretend[ed] ... fifth monarchie of the saints," they hypocritically advance "thir own tyrannical designs" (*CPW* 7:380). This outburst in the first edition of *The Readie and Easie Way* (1660) had probably been brewing since Milton excoriated the Independent divine John Owen and his ministers in Sonnet 16 (1652), for if not precisely like the Fifth Monarchists, the so-called Independents had used their committees for the "Propagation of the Gospel" and their Triers "to bind our souls with secular chains." Milton thus vainly asked Cromwell to "Help us to save free Conscience from the paw / Of Hireling wolves whose Gospel is their maw" (Sonnet 16, 12–14). Recalling the false prelate-shepherds of *Lycidas*, this passage also forecasts the vile triad of lucre, ambition, and superstition that in *Paradise Lost* eternally compromises truth, forces "the spirit of Grace," and undermines "His consort Liberty" (*PL* 12.511–26).

Clearly, the names of the guilty have changed but not their methods or motives. Yet Milton also has some very personal reasons to fear Owen and his fellow ministers, Thomas Goodwin, Philip Nye, and Sidrach Simpson, who indicted "heresies" we now know he upheld. The second edition of their proposal for the "Propagation of the Gospel in this Nation" (December 1652) mandates the teaching of trinitarian doctrine and the belief "that all men by Nature are dead in trespasses and sins and no man can be saved unless he be born again, repent, and believe." It also declares "that whosoever shall forsake and despise all the duties of his worship cannot be saved," and censors "persons of corrupt judgements from publishing dangerous Errours and Blasphemies in Assemblies and meetings" or in the public press, as Milton had permitted the Socinians to do in their *Racovian Catechism*.[62] Their teachings also suggested that he could not be saved since he neglected all houses of worship. Zagorin notes that Goodwin and the Independents thereby refused to carry their conviction that "all believers ... are privileged to be heard, since truth might emerge from any quarter" into the secular domain, but took "refuge in ideas at bottom inconsistent" with this belief.[63] Worden adds that Cromwell's failure to heed Milton's warnings about his favorite Independent chaplain (Owen) ultimately distanced him from the Protectorate. Hence, like Sir Henry Vane, he continued to retain the language of popular sovereignty long after the Protectorate had dropped it, referring to the Rump as the "supreme council of the nation" both in 1654 (*Defensio Secunda*) and in 1659 (*A Treatise of Civil Power*). The point was to remind readers of that legitimate exercise of sovereignty of which, in the minds of the Commonwealthmen, Cromwell's coup of April 1653 had deprived it, for Milton was always only too well aware that single rule "'easily slips into the worst sort of tyranny.'" While accepting provisional minority rule, he regarded it only as a temporary and fairly representative solution until the state could be reestablished on more stable grounds. More than anything, however, his dedication to fuller religious toleration distanced him not just from Cromwell, his Independents, and the Army, but also from the Puritan establishment in both church and state which had so disappointed his hopes.[64]

At about the same time, the Leveller William Walwyn acknowledged making the same mistake as the antiprelatical Milton (and many moderns) in forgetting that for most of his contemporaries, religion *was* religion, a means of salvation and not a proto-democratic program. By overlooking this truism, he had unwittingly helped bring about the collapse of his movement, for as Tolmie notes, once the Levellers began to endorse the separation of church and state in virtually secular terms, their "incipient liberalism" proved equally "unacceptable to the politically powerful classes of the nation" and to "the sectarians, who could not free themselves from

---

[62]   Peter Toon reprints these proposals (which were not included in John Owen's *Complete Works*) in *Puritans and Calvinism*, pp. 64–68; on the *Racovian Catechism*, see pp. 63–64. On the Independents' aim of banning the *Racovian Catechism* and Milton's angry response in his Cromwell sonnet, see Campbell and Corns, *John Milton*, p. 245.

[63]   Zagorin, *History*, pp. 81–82, citing John Goodwin, *Right And Might well met* (1649), pp. 81–82.

[64]   Blair Worden, "John Milton and Oliver Cromwell," in Ian Gentles, John Morrill, and Blair Worden (eds.), *Soldiers, Writers, and Statesmen of the English Revolution* (Cambridge, 1998), pp. 243–85, cited pp. 244 n. 2, 257, 259. Richard Tuck defends Milton's belief that the Protectorate council of state at first adequately served the republican ideal of "elective aristocracy"; see *Philosophy and Government*, p. 253. See also Zagorin, *History*, pp. 62–95, and my essay "Rewriting Cromwell." Campbell and Corns point out the when Milton did support the Army, it was for tolerationist reasons; see *John Milton*, p. 196.

lingering aspirations for a Christian magistrate and for 'righteousness' in a Christian society." Unlike Goodwin, however, Walwyn did not blame vestiges of "papism" for his failure, but like Milton, he blamed the Puritans themselves for refusing to "undertake any thing of any nature, Civill or Naturall, but as they are prompted thereunto, (as they imagine) by the Spirit," a "false supposition and assumption" that leads many "to doe such things as the Holy Scriptures abhorre."[65] Thus, as Walwyn now realized, the early separatists had always been ill-equipped to develop secular political principles, in part because in identifying the Church of England as a totally false church, their main concern was to establish the one true church supposedly set forth in the Bible. As well as limiting the extension of toleration to others, this conviction lent all but the most Antinomian saints the severely practical moralistic outlook characteristic of modern fundamentalist sects.

Tolmie also believes that the Puritan practice of engaging their own lecturers not only failed to mitigate clerical authoritarianism but in many cases increased it, while their highly touted "spiritualization of the household" did not encourage true "voluntaryism" but reinforced patriarchal authority. Although joining a sect might seem like an assertion of "spiritual independence ... and female identity," even "radical" Baptists held deeply conservative attitudes toward women.[66] Naturally, there were exceptions, and Walwyn was one. Like Milton,

> he was not a Seeker, he did not believe in a future age of the Spirit, and he did not expect or feel the need of a future revelation to understand the basic doctrine "very plain and easy to be understood," "that is the blood of Christ which cleanseth us from all sin." But he was deeply influenced by the Seeker view that there were no longer "men having authority" to administer the sacraments or to provide an authoritative exposition of the Bible, and hence, by implication, no true churches and no true ministry. Walwyn was especially hostile to the sermons of the clergy, "making merchandise of the blessed word of truth." The Bible alone was sufficient for the Christian, and beyond that he suggests there might be "conferences and mutual debates, one with another, the best way for attaining a right understanding, far excelling that which is called preaching." [67]

These parallels are obviously valid, especially since Walwyn was a fellow member of the Hartlib circle and close friend to Henry Robinson. Yet, in the end, Milton is divided from Walwyn by his deep conviction that Calvin's God was always an intellectually reprehensible construct (*CPW* 6:168–202). Early shared by his friend John Hales, the Cambridge Platonist Henry More, and most of the Latitudinarians,

---

[65]   William Walwyn, *The Vanitie of the Present Churches* (1649), in William Haller and Godfrey Davies (eds.), *The Leveller Tracts, 1647–1653* (New York, 1944), pp. 259, 258.

[66]   Tolmie, *Triumph*, pp. 144, 185–87; on the ambivalent effects of "volantaryism" in the household, see pp. 32–33, and also McGregor, "Baptists," p. 47. Tolmie's correction of Haller and Hill closely parallels Solt's correction of Woodhouse in *Saints*.

[67]   Tolmie, *Triumph*, p. 186.

this belief freed Milton from any tedious obscurantism surrounding God's decrees of reprobation and salvation and supported their common conviction that "zeal and charity could dwell together."[68]

Walwyn finally did abandon the rigors of Calvinist doctrine for the charitable high ground, but, as J.C. Davis's important study shows, Levellers in general replicated Calvinist dualism in new ways. By hypothetically including all of nature in the state of grace, they thought that they could pragmatically reunite all men of good will. Yet this inclusiveness created an important logical contradiction: if all good Christians were "right" in theory, why did they disagree in practice? The Levellers solved this problem by adopting the Puritan devaluation of all human "forms" as potential idols and by appealing to a vague concept of natural law "never divorced from divine influence," although that influence "applied to all men." Yet it was "God's law made known to the elect, [that] became the universal prescript," and since that law was made known by faith alone, Walwyn believed that "Whatsoever is not founded on faith is sin" in the true service of "the Lord." Lilburne agreed that "living upon other mens light, takeing [what] ... Learned men say without tryall" to be true is the mark of "'Carnal Professours' ... satisfied with forms only." These criteria not only ignore the important difference between a truly representative secular government and one that merely represented a vaguely constituted core of "true" Christians, but subtly reintroduce the classic Calvinist distinctions between the Elect who are fit to govern and the Reprobate who are not.[69] The ideal senate of Milton's *Readie and Easie Way* is often accused of relying on a similarly elitist and unworkable selection process, yet there is a central difference: its virtuous senators are not saints but seasoned civic benefactors. Even its so-called "apocalypticism" is ultimately as unsaintly as its pragmatic, anti-utopian premises, as Robert Ayers (*CPW* 7:374 n. 75) and James Holstun variously demonstrate.[70]

Milton's "True" Intellectual and Religious Milieu

Although Masson never placed Milton among the sects, some of the poet's eighteenth-century biographers influenced his account of the "Puritan Milton" by either intentionally or unintentionally blurring his divergences from their tenets. The radical Whig John Toland related the rumor that Milton favored the

---

[68]   Gerald R. Cragg, *From Puritanism to the Age of Reason* (Cambridge, 1950), p. 37. Cragg does not specifically compare Milton to the Cambridge school, but apparently accepts Basil Willey's comparisons in *The Seventeenth Century Background* [rpt. 1934] (New York, 1962), pp. 160–61, 241–43; cf. Cragg, p. 39 n. 1.

[69]   Davis, "Levellers," pp. 230, 231, 245, 246, citing William Walwyn, *A Compassionate Samaritan* (1644), p. 43, and John Lilburne, *An Answer to Nine Arguments* (1645), "To the Reader," and *Come Out of her my People* (1639), p. 4.

[70]   Holstun, *Rational Millennium*, pp. 246–65, 292–93.

"Independents and *Anabaptists"* who allowed "more Liberty than others," yet
even this notoriously unreliable polemicist never claimed he joined either sect,
which he simplistically classified as "free-thinking" Christians. Later, Jonathan
Richardson declared that Milton "Ever was a Dissenter from Our Church as by
Law Established," an opinion derived from the anti-clerical wrath of Milton's
"Long Digression" from *The History of Britain*, which was actually directed not at
the established but at the Puritan clergy who dominated the Long Parliament (*CPW*
5:405–51). Yet even Richardson meant this in a relatively loose sense, as shown by
his relation of the tale that Milton drove a servant from his employ by showing the
"Silly Fellow" how little he gained from the Puritans' "enthusiastic" services. Not
content with "Ridiculing Their Fooleries," *"Milton* thought All National Churches
or Publick Religions had Something in them Political, Something *Corrupted from
the Simplicity that is in Christ*, 2 Cor xi. 3," as shown in his *Areopagitica*.[71] Here
Richardson comes much closer to the opinion of Milton's own contemporaries,
who also rightly believed (as John Shawcross and Nicholas McDowell show) that
his nephews had absorbed many of his anti-Puritan attitudes.[72] The frontispiece to
Richardson's *Explanatory Notes and Remarks on Milton's "Paradise Lost"* further
suggests his overall opinion of the poet by casting him in the guise of a neo-Roman
politician. Dressed in the conventional high-collared costume of his day but
crowned with the eternal laurel wreath of "ethereal Olympus" (100), Richardson's
"excellent original" portrait depicts a clear-eyed, proto-Enlightenment, republican
poet laureate (see Figure 2.2).

Richardson's heroic Augustan fiction is at least partly factual: Milton did
"devoutly" yearn for the laurel, as the attached inscription from his *Mansus* clearly
shows. His 1638–39 poetic tribute to the Italian marquis who had patronized both
Tasso and himself in Naples commemorates his fond memories of a destination
"devoutly" detested by Puritans and even by his episcopal opponent, the Calvinist
Bishop Joseph Hall.[73] Despite some apparent problems with the English Jesuits in
Italy, Milton felt completely at home there and long continued a correspondence

---

[71]   John Toland, "The Life of John Milton," in *Early Lives of Milton*, ed. Helen
Darbishire (New York, 1932) p. 195; and Jonathan Richardson, "The Life of Milton, and
a Discourse on *Paradise Lost*," pp. 232, 237, 238 in the same volume. On the correct
dating of Milton's famous diatribe against the Long Parliament and Westminster Assembly
(which was expunged from his *History of Britain*), see Austin Woolrych, "The Date of
the Digression in Milton's *History of Britain*," in Richard Ollard and Pamela Tudor-Craig
(eds.), *For Veronica Wedgewood These: Studies in Seventeenth-Century History* (London,
1986), pp. 217–46.

[72]   Shawcross shows that more puritanical "Whigs" later drove an artificial wedge
between Milton and his nephews to support their own biases in *Arms*, pp. 95–133; Nicholas
McDowell further details their common anti-Puritanism in "Family Politics: How John
Phillips Read His Uncle's Satirical Sonnets," *Milton Quarterly* 42.1 (2008): pp. 1–21.

[73]   Joseph Hall, *Quo Vadis? A Just Censure of Travell, As It Is Commonly Undertaken
by the Gentlemen of Our Nation* (1617), cited in Whiting, Milton's *Literary Milieu*,
pp. 370–73.

Nectens aut Paphia Myrti, aut Parnaſside Lauri
Fronde comas, at ego secura pace quiescam.
J.R. sen: f.   *MILTON's Mansus.*
From an Excel.ᵗ Orig: (Crayons) in his Collection.

Figure 2.2   Portrait of John Milton, Frontispiece to J. Richardson's *Explanatory Notes and Remarks on Milton's "Paradise Lost"* (London, 1734). By permission of Princeton University Library.

with Catholic friends and priests. Richardson's engraver thus accurately alludes to one of his Latin commemorations of this voyage, *Mansus*. In it he asks someone like his friend to "wreathe my locks with Paphian myrtle and Parnassian laurel, so I should rest in perfect peace" ("Nectens aut Paphia myrti, aut Parnasside lauri / Fronde comas, at ego secura pace quiescam") "after I shall have lived through the span of no silent career" (92–93, 85). At the time, Milton still dreamt of composing an Arthurian epic about the "magnanimous heroes of the [round] table" (81–82) that might equal Tasso's epic about the first crusade. If he succeeded, and "if there be such a thing as faith and assured rewards of the righteous" (94), he would rejoin his heroes on a figurative "Mt. Olympus" (95–100). Given that Puritans almost universally disparaged the pagan classics, the legends of the Round Table, and nearly all "feigned" romances of the kind Milton admired in Spenser, it seems unlikely that any ever dreamt of even a metaphorical reunion with a Roman Catholic on Mount Olympus.[74]

Richard Baxter exemplifies the moderate-to-liberal type of Puritan who sternly disapproved of the "lascivious" and "unedifying" literature frankly beloved of the young Milton. Himself a poet, Baxter was no extreme opponent of secular or semi-secular literature. His list of "edifying" poets ranges from serious "wits" like Abraham Cowley, Sir John Davies, and Lady Katherine Phillips to more predictable Puritan choices: George Wither, Francis Quarles, George Sandys, Fulke Greville, George Herbert, Guillaume Du Bartas, and his English translator, Joshua Sylvester. Yet Milton is not only conspicuously absent from this list, but the words appended to Baxter's posthumous portrait (the frontispiece to his *Paraphrase to the New Testament*) show that, like John Goodwin, he scorned both the "poet's hell" and the poetic paradise that Milton celebrated.[75] No Christian mortalist he, Baxter is shown bidding "Farewell" to this "vaine world" of "dust and a shadow," as he gratefully enters heavenly bliss. There, like his own writings, all this world's "LEAVES & FRUIT" will have "dropt, for soyle & seed" to sow future heirs of heaven—not to immortalize their author, but to encourage the saints to follow his example in resisting this vain world. Though it will continue to "flatter and molest" them, by ignoring its temptations, his heirs will join him in finding an "everlasting Rest" for his soul's "unseen VITALL SUBSTANCE" (see Figure 2.3). Reinforcing this warning, his "true effigy" (*vera effigies*) gloomily frowns at the reader with one eye and squints sadly with the other, his right hand firmly clasping his Bible as his "sword" against the authors of worldly temptation. According to Baxter's *Christian Directory* (1677), these authors include Shakespeare and other

---

[74] See Sasek, *Literary Temper*, pp. 59–64; and Achinstein, *Literature and Dissent*, pp. 182–83, 194–200.

[75] See Sasek, summarizing the preface to Baxter's *Poetical Fragments* (1781), in *Literary Temper*, p. 75; even liberal Puritans like John Goodwin had "little respect for the poet's hell" (p. 64).

Figure 2.3   Portrait of Richard Baxter, Frontispiece to Baxter's *Paraphrase to the New Testament* (London, 1695). By permission of the Folger Library.

dramatists Milton admired, since Baxter never knew or heard "of a lawful stage-play, comedy, or tragedy, in the age I have lived in."[76]

Lawrence Sasek's early study of Puritan literature demonstrates that this rigorously didactic aesthetics was shared by all the godly, including liberals like Goodwin. Yet Sasek finds Milton's literary outlook so profoundly different that even the most "sympathetic studies of puritans" (which meant "practically all" at the time) could not establish any connection between them.[77] *Mansus* suggests why: like many other classical republicans who flocked to Italy before the outbreak of the civil wars, Milton not only ardently admired his host culture but was directly encouraged by its patriots to defend the English cause of liberty (*CPW* 2:537–39, 4.1:555). In other words, it was the Italians, not the English Puritans, who chiefly made him aware that when the "cause of God and his Church was to be pleaded," his duty was to give up the "ease and leasure" of his "retired thoughts" and labor for liberty (*CPW* 1:804–5). Like Spenser and Jonson, Milton also believed that the work of the true Protestant poet was to "civilize, adorn, and make discreet our minds by the learned and affable meetings of frequent Academies" and other assemblies, "not only in Pulpits, but after another persuasive method, at set and solemn Paneguries, in Theaters, porches, or what other place, or way may win most upon the people to receiv at once both recreation, & instruction" (*CPW* 1:819–20). These "academies" are modeled on those he found in Italy, which similarly aimed to inaugurate "true learning …, where true grace, and our obedience" to God not only "abounds," but through "right establisht discipline" insures that "hee will replenish us with all abilities in tongues and arts, that may conduce to his glory, and our good" (*CPW* 1:721). Milton's final political treatise, *The Readie and Easie Way*, recommends the same educational goals in strictly secular terms. Last but hardly least, his humanistic view of poetry as the combined fruit of craftsmanship, training, and natural talent jars with the Puritan theory, *nascitur, non fit poeta*, which traces the poetic gift to heaven alone.[78]

All these factors explain why anti-Puritan contemporaries like Samuel Butler criticized him not as a Puritan but as a notorious "politique," regicide, and republican long suspected of religious heresy.[79] This opinion persisted long after his death, although the blame soon turned to praise. Early Whig historians began to regard their greatest epic poet as the great apostle of English liberty (a reputation clearly sought by the poet himself) while distancing him from everything Puritan: "their

---

[76] Richard Baxter, *Christian Directory* (1673), pp. 877–78.

[77] Sasek, *Literary Temper*, pp. 95–98, 102, 122, 13.

[78] On this tradition, see Sasek, *Literary Temper*, pp. 65–66, 71, and Nigel Smith, *Perfection Proclaimed: Language and Literature in English Radical Religion 1640–1660* (Oxford, 1988), p. 32. On Philip Sidney's very different view of poetry (and Milton's agreement with him), see Sasek, pp. 64, 95.

[79] Nicholas von Maltzahn, "From pillar to post: Milton and the attack on republican humanism at the Restoration," in Gentles et al. (eds.), *Soldiers, Writers, and Statesmen*, pp. 265–85, and "Samuel Butler's Milton," *SP* 92 (1995): pp. 482–95.

savage manners, their ludicrous jargon, their scorn of science, and their aversion to pleasure. Hating tyranny with a perfect hatred, [Milton] had nevertheless all the estimable and ornamental qualities" of the cavaliers except their royalist politics. Refuting Masson's post-Carlylean biography in advance, Macaulay thus declared:

> He was not a Puritan. He was not a free thinker. He was not a Royalist. In his character the noblest qualities of every party were combined in harmonious union. From the Parliament and from the Court, from the conventicle and from the Gothic cloister, from the gloomy and sepulchral circles of the Roundheads, and from the Christmas revel of the hospitable Cavalier, his nature selected and drew to itself whatever was great and good, while it rejected all the base and pernicious ingredients by which those finer elements were defiled ... Any person who will contrast the sentiments expressed in his treatises on Prelacy with the exquisite lines on ecclesiastical architecture and music in the Penseroso, which was published about the same time, will understand our meaning. This is an inconsistency which, more than anything else, raises his character in our estimation, because it shows how many private tastes and feelings he sacrificed, in order to do what he considered his duty to mankind.[80]

Macaulay's famous "Essay on Milton" of course ignores the parallels with Parker, Robinson, Walwyn, and other members of the Hartlib circle observed here and in the previous chapter, yet in many ways both Milton's religious pragmatism and his highly individualistic application of the "priesthood of all believers" doctrine place much of his mature religious thought as close to the progressive Anglican theologians gathered at Great Tew as to these liberal/intellectual Puritans or "true" independents. Like the rational theologians, he believed that the primary purpose of worship was private communion with God, and only secondarily with like-minded Christians. He dispensed with the formal covenants, confessions, and testimonies of the gathered churches, for, as Austin Woolrych remarks, "public confessions of faith were obnoxious to Milton in principle" (*CPW* 7:45). This attitude also distances him from most post-Restoration Dissenters, whose Savoy *Declaration of Faith and Order* of 1658 reiterated Calvinist teachings on total depravity and its sole "solution," the covenant of works and grace.[81] Long after the Restoration, these teachings played a central role in Nonconformist thought, which also continued to teach that "God was pleased, according to His wise and holy counsel, to permit" sin, "having purposed to order it to His own glory." Criticizing these and other passages in the Savoy *Declaration*, Peter Toon complains that its enthusiasm for "the sovereignty of the grace of God" failed

---

[80]   Thomas Macaulay, "Milton" (August 1825), in *Literary Essays Contributed to the Edinburgh Review* (London, 1913) pp. 45, 46.

[81]   John Owen and Philip Nye, *A Declaration of Faith and Order* (rpt. 1688; London, 1658).

"to emphasise adequately the equally important responsibility of men to God."
He finds this problem endemic in the "hyper-Calvinism" into which most post-
Restoration Puritans, including the Baptists, retreated as the Arminianism they
detested advanced among other Protestants. [82]

Since Milton and his great Protestant epic, *Paradise Lost*, participated in this
advance, later biographers questioned his religious aloofness. Richardson wonders
why had he so "little Regard to the Exterior of Religion ... even in his Last hours;
... frequented no Publick Worship in his Latter years, nor used any Religious
Rite in his Own Little Family." No adequate answer has ever been forthcoming,
especially not from the Nonconformist tradition in which some recent literary
critics have placed him: Dissenters certainly did observe religious rites not only in
their own families and conventicles but also in the educational institutions that the
Savoy *Declaration* helped establish.[83] Richardson's final answer to the question is
thus more reasonable than most: Christianity for Milton mainly meant the rule of
"Holy Scripture ... Interpreted by his Own Judgement Ultimately," and no better
rule "can Any of Us Have, Desire or Pretend to"; the best Protestants, who are
no heretics, adhere to "what we in our conscience apprehend the scripture to say,
though the visible church with all of her doctors gainsay."[84] Since here as always
the emphasis falls on rejecting implicit faith, a broad interpretation of this criterion
could explain why Milton sincerely respected thoughtful, literate Roman Catholics
abroad and converts at home, like his brother Christopher and his admirer and
versifier, Dryden.[85]

Evidence that *Paradise Lost* could not have been written by either a conventional
Calvinist or radical "Free Gratian" accumulated throughout the twentieth century,
culminating in Dennis Danielson's important demonstration that Milton's epic
theodicy violates all five Calvinist "heads" of doctrine.[86] Although contemporary
evidence is lacking, it is hard to suppose that, if Baxter or Bunyan ever read the

---

[82]   Toon, *Puritans and Calvinism*, pp. 80, 83; on Arminians and moderate Presbyterians,
see pp. 85–86. On the continuities between the Savoy *Declaration* and the *Westminster
Confession* and *Larger Catechism*—and their enduring influence on Nonconformist
education—see Rivers, *Reason, Grace, and Sentiment*, pp. 13–15.

[83]   Richardson, "The Life of Milton," in Darbishire (ed.), *Early Lives*, p. 237. N.H.
Keeble places Milton in the Nonconformist tradition in *The Literary Culture of Nonconformity*
(Athens, GA, 1987), and Sharon Achinstein regards him as a post-Restoration Dissenter in
Literature and Dissent.

[84]   Richardson, "The Life of Milton," p. 233; Richardson paraphrases *Of Civil Power*,
CPW 7:249.

[85]   See Rueben Márquez Sánchez, Jr., "'The Worst of Superstitions': Milton's *Of
True Religion* and the Issue of Religious Tolerance," *Prose Studies* 9.3 (1986)*:* pp. 21–
38. Sanchez argues that Milton's treatise ambiguously extends recognition to Catholics
who rejected "implicit faith" and the Church's imperialistic political agenda. On Milton's
Catholic family members, see Shawcross, *Arms.*

[86]   On the five heads of Calvinist doctrine, see Dennis Danielson, *Milton's Good God*
(Cambridge, 1982).

epic, they would not have been keenly aware that it attacks the central Calvinist mysteries, unmerited election and reprobation (*PL* 3.111–34), along with the Savoy *Declaration*'s assertion that God need not be justified for "pleasing" to permit sin. Mainline Protestants no longer adhered to this theology, but as conventional trinitarians, most preferred to overlook Milton's relatively plain poetic admission of Arianism (*PL* 8.404–7), a "problem" not generally conceded until *De Doctrina Christiana* came to light in 1823. Ironically, had it come to light earlier, it would have exerted a far greater influence on the liberal eighteenth-century clergymen who leaned in this direction.[87] Later, twentieth-century Christians balked at admitting Milton's unorthodoxy, but their views have not stood the test of time.[88] Hence, at present, the real question is when and how he adopted these anti-Calvinist positions.

Milton's rejection of trinitarian doctrine, once thought to be his most radical position, is now understood as relatively common among religious rationalists of the era. Both the *Racovian Catechism*, licensed by Milton, and the Cambridge Platonists steered many (including Locke and Newton) in this direction. On the other hand, like John Biddle, who was imprisoned and nearly executed by the Cromwell regime for his Arian convictions, Milton may have arrived at this position from reading of scripture alone, or, like Taylor, he may have been influenced by pre-Augustinian Fathers like Julian. Julian cut the mysterious, imponderable Gordian knot of the Incarnation and Atonement by simply turning Christ's sacrifice into a supreme act of literally "kindly" charity. Reasoning that if God's Son is actually of the same "kind" as his other creatures but unique in freely choosing to die for his brethren, his sacrificial Atonement could be understood as an even more glorious and humanly *exemplary* achievement. No longer a miracle performed by an Almighty God, Christ's voluntary act makes him mankind's elder brother and natural role model rather than our infallible father. The first modern exponents of this belief were the Polish and Italian Anabaptist sect whose most prominent member, Faustus Socinus, "stamped the sect with his theology and name." Milton was certainly familiar with their teachings, for like other "politiques," he was always attracted to theological doctrines that naturalized or demystified divine

---

[87] McLachlan, *Religious Opinions*, p. 25, citing Richard Garnett, *The Life of Milton* (London, 1890), p. 191.

[88] Following William B. Hunter's rebellion against Maurice Kelley's Arian reading of Milton's poetry in the light of *De Doctrina*, many Miltonists considered the Son's relationship to the Father as "subordinationist" rather than antitrinitarian. See William B. Hunter, Jack H. Adamson, and C.A. Patrides, *Bright Essence: Studies in Milton's Theology* (Salt Lake City, 1971). Yet as Leonora L. Brodwin early observed, "the Son's creation from the substance of God does not accord the Son divine status" different from the rest of his *ex deo* creation. Milton's Christology thus "parallels that of Servetus, which was considered to be Arian by the Calvinists"; Brodwin, "The Dissolution of Satan in *Paradise Lost*," *Milton Studies* 8 (1975): pp. 165–207, cited p. 207, n. 70.

mysteries.[89] Yet he seems sincere in claiming to adhere only to scripture and to "follow no other heresy or sect," although he admits that "unthinking distortions of ... scripture" (*CPW* 6:123–24) by the orthodox played a part. This cautious phrasing shows that, like the Latitudinarians, Milton accepted only the aspects of Socinian rationalism endorsed by his reading of scripture and rejected refusals of Christian "mysteries" based on reason alone. This allowed him to retain an undeniably "lofty doctrine of the atonement," so that, like the eighteenth-century Arian Dr. Clarke, he could long retain his reputation for Protestant orthodoxy despite the antitrinitarian implications of key passages in his epic.[90]

The date of Milton's conversion to "free will" theology is much more conjectural. Arthur Barker dated it to the divorce tracts of the mid-1640s, but Lewalski argues that it is already implicit in the antiprelatical tracts of the early 1640s, which present human agency in ways implicitly at odds with predestinarian orthodoxy. Although the tracts reject the "Laudian belief in grace gained through sacraments," they apparently accept some version of the Arminian teaching on free will.[91] Corns dates Milton's departure from predestination even earlier, to Milton's 1634 masque.[92] A more radical but not unlikely alternative is suggested here: that Milton (and very likely his father) departed from this orthodoxy very early on, perhaps while he was still at St. Paul's School. In his antiprelatical tracts the only favorable references to Calvin are either placed in the mouth of the "Remonstrant," Joseph Hall, or used to disprove him, while the divorce tracts simply use Calvin as prop for Bucer's "preferable" views (*CPW* 2:709). Both references to Calvin in *Areopagitica* are entirely negative: had Englishmen listened to their own reformers, they would already have surpassed him, and should do so now (*CPW* 2:550, 553). The two favorable references to him in the *Tenure* are either purely historical or oddly trivial: Milton cites one of Calvin's digressions rather than a passage in the *Institutes* that would have been much more to the point (*CPW* 3:246 n. 202). As a whole, these references seem to be minor concessions to his Calvinist contemporaries or subtle suggestions of his own less than favorable attitude. They once again demonstrate his distance from Puritan Arminians like Goodwin, a moderate Calvinist until 1651, when his *Redemption Redeemed* greatly upset the godly brethren by reversing his former position. His latest biographer shows that Goodwin's break was partly influenced by reading Acontius and Grotius and partly by troubling logical contradictions inherited from his moderate Calvinist mentors, mainly John Preston. Yet, unlike Milton, Goodwin continued to regard Calvin as a great theologian and to cite him more than any other. In concession to his followers he also refused to accept the "label 'Arminian' for his own position" because "the

---

89   Brodwin, "Dissolution," p. 193. See also Sedley, *Sublimity*, p. 107.

90   McLachlan, *Religious Opinions*, pp. 40–51, cited p. 44. For a more detailed consideration of Milton's relationship to Socinianism, see Michael Lieb, "Milton and the Socinian Heresy."

91   Lewalski, *Life*, pp. 421, 139.

92   Corns, "Milton before 'Lycidas,'" p. 34.

term … sent shivers down Puritan spines.'" In the end, he even denied that the controversy over *Redemption Redeemed* was a "debate between 'Calvinists' and 'Arminians,'" not only because he found the terms misleading but also because he was an entirely orthodox trinitarian and anti-Socinian. Both Milton's intention to publish *De Doctrina* and his willingness to place Arminian views in the mouth of God himself suggest he had no such qualms (*PL* 3.173–202); as Lewalski shows, he even considerably liberalizes Arminius.[93]

Yet if Milton always favored a more Arminian than Puritan position on free will, why did he portray Arminius as "perverted" by heretical works in 1644? Lewalski notes that the passage in *Areopagitica* (*CPW* 2:519–20) implies Milton's admiration for the Dutch theologian's scholarly independence, yet some self-censorship may also be involved.[94] His nearly contemporaneous *Doctrine and Discipline of Divorce* acknowledges his countrymen's common resentment of the Arminian claim that Calvinists make God responsible for sin, but he himself credits this charge in the first and (probably) contemporaneous drafts of *De Doctrina Christiana*. In any case, since *Areopagitica* argues *against* banning books, Milton surely means that even apparently "corrupting" doctrines must be openly debated, not censored. What, then, are we to make of *An Apology against a Pamphlet*, which erroneously describes Arminians as full-fledged Pelagians who "deny originall sinne" (*CPW* 1:917) by making recuperative grace available to all? Three explanations are possible: (1) Milton was still an anti-Arminian at this point; (2) the remark refers only to Laud's "Pelagianism"; or (3) he was not yet fully versed in the intricacies of Arminian and Calvinist disputes over supra- and infra-lapsarian predestination. These debates were not only highly technical but banned from public discussion during Milton's Cambridge years, when even staunch Calvinists disagreed on the correct interpretation, in part because the exceptionally harsh doctrine of double or supralapsarian predestination does not appear in Calvin's *Institutes*. Modern theologians trace it to his successors, Beza and Zwingli, and in England to William Perkins, who developed a stricter version of Calvinist theology than any continental variant.[95]

These facts, along with Milton's declared dislike for technical theology and his claim to derive his beliefs solely from the Bible, suggest that his *Apology* may register real confusion over Arminianism, not just an anti-Laudian jibe. Since his family used the King James Bible, which lacked the "Puritan" Geneva Bible's closely printed Calvinist glosses in the margins, he may have adopted the Gils' free will assumptions without realizing their technical heterodoxy. The Cambridge scholar George Hakewill ably defended Bacon in his *Apologie for the Power and*

---

[93] Coffey, *John Goodwin*, pp. 12, 22, 27, 37, 212, cited pp. 246, 247,48. Milton's position is more nearly Pelagian, but he avoids that extreme; see Lewalski, *Life*, p. 423.

[94] See Lewalski, *Life*, p. 422; and Corns, "Milton before 'Lycidas,'" and "Milton's antiprelatical tracts and the marginality of doctrine," in Dobranski and Rumrich (eds.), *Milton and Heresy*, pp. 39–48.

[95] Davies, *Worship of the English Puritans*, pp. 35–45.

Providence of God's Government of the World (1627), but stumbled badly in defining predestination. When asked to defend Calvinist orthodoxy on the point, he unwittingly upheld the Arminian position he incorrectly ascribed to Augustine: the Elect were "chosen before the foundation of the world because God foresaw wee would be good [and] not that himselfe would make us good.'"[96] One reason for his mistake is that most English Protestants did not deeply question Calvinist doctrine until the increasingly powerful Arminian factor in the church began to identify "Calvinists as Puritans," predestination as the root of Puritanism, and "Puritanisme [as] the roote of all rebellions and disobedient intractableness in parliaments etc. and all schisme and sauciness in the countrey, nay in the Church itself.'" So wrote Samuel Brooke in 1630, but, as Nicholas Tyacke adds, "it was more truly the case that the victory of Arminianism meant the recrudescence of militant Puritanism," which mainline Protestants at first merely saw as an agent of liturgical and organizational reform.[97]

Earlier, proto-Arminian theologians like Richard Hooker and Lancelot Andrewes could still present themselves as faithful upholders of mainstream Protestant doctrine despite the indelible Calvinist imprint on the Thirty-Nine Articles of the Church. Ambiguities about when and how grace intervened made the Articles broadly acceptable to a wide variety of English believers before Puritans began to resist "innovators" who allowed greater scope for human agency than grace alone.[98] As Jeremy Taylor later reaffirmed, questions of salvation could then be solved simply by "regularly, day by day overcom[ing] our sin," and problems of backsliding addressed by understanding that one's state of grace might be "disordered but not destroyed."[99] *De Doctrina* adopts a similar position against "irresistible grace" and the "preservation of the saints" by reevaluating what John meant when he says "that *he cannot sin*." Milton concludes that he must "mean that he does not sin easily or willingly or intentionally. It must mean that he does not devote his mind and energies to sin, but sins with reluctance and remorse, and that he does not persist in sin, as a habit": "*the just man falls seven times, but gets up again, but the wicked fall headlong into evil*, Matt. xxv. 3" (*CPW* 6:512–13). "Repulsive and hateful" both to the Creator and to the creature, sinful works are naturally shunned by all who do not (like Satan) actively desire their own impairment (*CPW* 6:173). As Hooker insisted, sin not only runs counter to a providential design never intended for the death of the sinner, but betrays a basic misrecognition of the purpose of freedom, which is necessarily good. This reasoning neatly does away with the other three principal heads of Calvinist doctrine—total depravity, unlimited [or predestined] election, and limited

---

[96] See Tyacke, *Anti-Calvinists*, pp. 6, 29.

[97] Ibid., p. 57.

[98] For a short summary, see A.D. Nuttall, *Overheard by God* (London, 1980), pp. 21–26.

[99] Jeremy Taylor, *Unum Necessarium*, Ch. IV, Sect. II, p. 39, quoted in H.R. McAdoo, *The Structure of Caroline Moral Theology* (London, 1949), p. 50.

atonement—by simplifying salvation to the point where (as Lewalski suggests) one need not even say "yes" to the Spirit, but only *not* say "no" to God.[100]

This theology has some affinities with the "New Methodism" taught at Protestant Saumur, the home of the French Enlightenment, "which ... plac[ed] the decree of (universal) redemption before the decree of election, and which denied that there was a decree [either] of reprobation" or of "particular redemption." In England, both Baxter and Milton's friend Marvell borrowed these ideas, but Milton's theology is more radical in collapsing the separate covenants of works and grace retained by the New Methodists into a single, eternal dispensation of charity.[101] Believing that the Mosaic law had completely lapsed and that grace fulfills without abrogating the law, Milton's combination of charity and good works is strenuous in a very different sense (*CPW* 6:532–34). According to this synthesis, the *letter* of the law may be dispensed with for some higher need or "important cause" but its charitable essence cannot; nor (as his Samson recognizes) can one voluntarily "comply" with anything "scandalous or forbidden" simply for convenience sake (*SA* 1379, 1408–9). This position is often confused with Antinomianism, but Milton's divorce tracts (which the tragedy frequently echoes) flatly reject the idea that "dispensation" is a special favor from God. Indirectly citing Paolo Sarpi, he terms this idea a *"fond perswasion"*; *"dispencing is"* rather *"good distributive justice, ... for it is nothing else but a right interpretation of law"* (*CPW* 2:300; cf. n. 3). Hence, even in acting as a proto-Christian, Samson may violate the Hebrew ceremonial law that forbids him to perform feats in the Philistine temple, but only to fulfill a higher purpose. David obeyed this concept of "higher charity" when he allowed his famished troops to eat the show-bread in the Hebrew temple; such acts remain technically lawful so long as they "never run contrary to the love of God and of our neighbour, which is the sum of the law" (*CPW* 6:640).

In obeying an "inward Law" that is both "ethical and rational in character," the only real conflict for believers is between love of God and charity to neighbors.[102] Face with this conflict, Milton's Samson rightly honors the Creator over the creature, a decision not derived from the superior "motions" of his Spirit, but from his logical debate with himself and his countrymen. Unlike Milton's erring Eve, Samson spends the bulk of his lengthy drama carefully weighing his differing obligations to God, neighbor, father, wife, and nation, in each case placing the highest and most universal categories—God and nation—first. Eve's failure to do this causes her to sin in ways technically closer to atheism—she distrusts God's power and justice, if not his existence—than to "voluntarist antinomianism," as Joan Bennett would have it. Eve thus does not need Adam's "humanist antinomianism" to correct her error, because violating the Creator's generous covenant solely to

---

[100] Lewalski, "Milton and *De Doctrina*," p. 220.

[101] Toon, *Puritans and Calvinism*, p. 86. Both New Methodists and Presbyterians upheld federal or "double covenant" theology, while the Congregationalists remained "high" Calvinists.

[102] Woodhouse, *Puritanism and Liberty*, p. 65 n. 2.

satisfy selfish pleasures or desire for power was never an option at all.[103] Her sin is doubly blameworthy because she has access to what Andrewes calls "the Common Law of the World" originally "written in the hearts of all men," a law that clearly dictates (as she knows) that covenants must be either upheld or forfeited.[104]

The persistence of this common law in the fallen world ultimately allows Milton to restrict the function of the Holy Spirit in ways no Puritan would. *De Doctrina* speculates that since the Bible nowhere defines its nature or unique function, neither "what the Holy spirit is like, how it exists, or where it comes from," whether it is "generated or created," or "how else it exists," the Spirit must be substantially inferior to both the Father and Son (*CPW* 6:281–98). Since even "the sacred writers are noncommittal about it" (*CPW* 6:282), they, too, must be read by the light of reason (*CPW* 6:582–85). This drastically decreased role of the Spirit (which at times is no more than "right reason") parallels an increase in the role of free will in successive drafts of *De Doctrina*. Here, as Arthur Sewell summarizes, it seemed necessary to Milton "that the renovation of man should not only involve an enlightenment of the mind, but also a quickening of his will. For the end of faith is good works, freely willed out of an understanding of spiritual things."[105] Hence, as in Taylor's *Unum Necessarium*, God's prevenient grace progressively renews reason through benign "'powers and inclinations' and 'new aptnesses'. It assists us and 'inclines us sweetly' and is as a grafting upon another stock, converting the energies of the latter into its own nature," and enlarging the powers of the regenerate.[106] Politically, these beliefs also explain Milton's "invariably optimistic" attitude toward the "perfect correlation among the law of nature, the law of nations, and the law of Scripture" noted both by his Yale editor, William Grace (*CPW* 4.1:289 n. 18, 294), and by Lewalski. Milton's *Defence of the People of England* categorically states: "I am of the opinion, ... and *always have been*, that the law of God does exactly agree with the law of nature," which is at once "gentle" and "kind" (*CPW* 4.1:342; emphasis added).[107] As Grace points out, this position is closer to Aquinas than to Calvin (*CPW* 4.1:289–90) or to any subsequent Calvinist, including even the early Arminians he misunderstands or

---

[103] Bennett, *Reviving Liberty*, pp. 94–118, cited pp. 98–99, 109, 116–17. Bennett's misunderstanding of Antinomianism (which has no truly "humanist" version) stems from Gertrude Huehns's inaccurate study, *Antinomianism in English History, with special Reference to the Period 1640–1660* (London, 1951). For a critique of Huehns and some of Bennett's other sources—Haller, Hill, and A.L. Morton, *The World of the Ranters* (London, 1970)—see Wallace, *Puritans*, p. 226, n. 2.

[104] Lancelot Andrewes, *XCVI Sermons* (1629), p. 163.

[105] Arthur Sewell, *A Study in Milton's Christian Doctrine* (New York, 1939), p. 20. See also Lewalski, *Life*, p. 423.

[106] McAdoo, *Structure*, pp. 54–55, citing Taylor, *Unum Necessarium*, Chapter 5, Sect. 5, 51, 52.

[107] The first quotation is translated by Lewalski, "Milton and *De Doctrina*," p. 215, from the Columbia edition of Milton's prose, vol. 7, pp. 266–67.

misrepresents in *An Apology Against a Pamphlet* (*CPW* 1:917). As in Aquinas, "sin does not destroy entirely the good of nature," since "there remains in man the inclination to act in accordance with the eternal law."[108] Milton's *De Doctrina* refers to this as the "unwritten law … given to the first man" and preserved in the hearts of all mankind (*CPW* 6:516). Grace directly links this anti-Calvinist denial of human corruption to Milton's willingness to rest his arguments "upon the 'Law of Nature' rather than on Scripture" or the Spirit (*CPW* 4.1:290), views that easily explain why he shocked so many conservative contemporaries, not just Puritans but solid churchmen like Thomas Yalden.

Yet Milton was not alone: the Latitudinarians' theological rationalism also caused them to be labeled radically sectarian and "rebellious," a charge that led to Simon Patrick's retort that they were indeed a new and improved "sect" of "primitive" Christians as he and Edward Stillingfleet waged war on a double front against the "implicit faith" of Rome and hide-bound Calvinists.[109] They also joined Goodwin in critiquing William Perkins, whom Matthew Scrivener boldly decried as "a servile and credulous spirit, so far addicted to such Modern Divines, that scarce any thing so new, harsh, or inconsistent with Antiquity fell from them, that Perkins presently took it up for scripture and Catholic doctrine, and transcribed the same into his works." His high Calvinism required no "care or pains to look into the Scripture, or the Doctrine of the Ancient Church, but through such men's spectacles."[110] Thus, by the time *Paradise Lost* was published, a new breed of religious thinker had begun to use anti-Calvinism to forge what Gerald Cragg calls the "charter of the liberty of the Christian" in an authoritarian age.[111]

Both Cragg and Isabel Rivers attribute this "charter" not to Dissenters but to Latitudinarians like Edward Fowler who, like Milton and his cohort, unified the spheres of nature and grace. While Dissenters upheld declarations of faith in which God's will remains darkly secret and inaccessible, Fowler maintained that:

> *moral good and evil are not only such because God commands the one, forbids the other; but because the things themselves are so essentially and inalterably. That there is an eternal Reason, why that which is good should be so and required; and why that which is evil should be so and forbidden; which depends not so much on the divine will as the divine nature.*[112]

---

[108] McAdoo, *Structure*, p. 17.

[109] W.M. Spellman, *The Latitudinarians and the Church of England, 1660–1700* (Athens, GA, 1993), pp. 11–13; Rivers, *Reason, Grace, and Sentiment*, pp. 46–47.

[110] McAdoo, *Structure*, p. 7, quoting Scrivener's *Entrance to the Course in Divinity* (1674). John Goodwin shared this view; see Coffey, *John Goodwin*, p. 213.

[111] Cragg, *From Puritanism*, p. 47; see also pp. 41–49, 59.

[112] Edward Fowler, *The Principles and Practices, of Certain Moderate Divines of the Church of England* (1670), pp. 12–13. Fowler is always identified as a Latitudinarian, and he seems to have had some connection with St. Giles Cripplegate, Milton's final resting place.

Although believers of Goodwin's type were hardly unenlightened, a new rhetoric of rational light divinely inscribed on each human soul was fast becoming the common property of Latitudinarians, Cambridge Platonists, Socinians, Deists, and, of course, the poet of *Paradise Lost*, who similarly believed that the light from above is mirrored by natural light from within.[113] Revelation further illuminates God's bright darkness (*PL* 3.380), but the "light of Nature" still teaches "moral virtue" even to pagans (*PR* 4.351–52). In thus reconciling reason, pagan virtue, and Christian charity, Milton's major poems unquestionably herald a new age.

---

[113] Rivers, *Reason, Grace, and Sentiment*, pp. 63–64, 69–70, 74.

Chapter 3
Vocation, Prophecy, and Secular Reform in the Early Poems and Prose

Do not persist, I beg of you, in your contempt for the sacred Muses, and do not think them futile and worthless whose gift has taught you to harmonize a thousand sounds to fit numbers ... Now, since it is my lot to have been born a poet, why does it seem strange to you that we, who are so closely united by blood, should pursue sister arts and kindred interests? Phoebus himself, wishing to part himself between us two, gave some gifts to me and others to my father; and father and son, we share the possession of the divided god.

—Milton, *Ad Patrem*, 56–66

As this epigraph suggests, the young Milton's "divided god" of secular music and poetry was already remote from the Calvinist deity who required the exclusive devotion of human gifts to his service. Theodore Bozeman explains that the godly were always inclined "to *limit*," not "to *extend* the reach of human wit toward the things of God," "to *expand* ... biblical authority" over the entire range of human life, including all the sister arts. Since human beings were naturally "'prone ... to evil,'" they felt that Holy Writ should provide precepts for virtually all human activities. This central aspect of Puritan belief has led recent scholars to qualify the once "widely promulgated idea" that Puritanism inherited or advanced Renaissance humanism's "emphasis upon human reason" and optimistic view of human capacity.[1] Milton himself seems to have arrived at a similar realization after enrolling at Cambridge, where his parents hoped that he would successfully prepare for the ministry, but where he would instead be attracted to older humanist ideals modernized (in his case) by Baconian notions of reform. The exact date or cause of his decision against taking holy orders is unknown, but *Ad Patrem* addresses his father's surprise and disappointment soon after the fact. Milton thus reminds him that it was he who first shared and encouraged his love of the muses, and he who still pursued the musical version of his own Apollonian "calling."

---

[1]   Bozeman, *To Live Ancient Lives*, pp. 64, 65, paraphrasing and citing Thomas Jackson, *Works* (12 vols., Oxford, 1844), 9:238, and William Perkins, *The Works of William Perkins*, ed. Ian Breward (Abingdon, 1970) on "total depravity" (p. 192) in n. 26, pp. 65–66. On the differences between Puritanism and Renaissance humanism, he cites John Morgan, *Godly Learning: Puritan Attitudes toward Reason, Learning, and Education, 1560–1640* (Cambridge, 1986), pp. 41–61.

His regretful tone strongly suggests that the poem is meant as a consolation, and not (as some believe) as a celebration of an early success. His intent apparently prevailed, since his father continued to support his son's ambitions and eventually agreed to his departure on an extensive European tour.[2] Yet the elder Milton's initial reluctance to approve his son's decision is also strongly implied throughout *Ad Patrem*, most likely because John senior could not have foreseen any conflict between a poetic and a clerical career. Both at the university and in the ministry the two were commonly combined, and Milton's close contemporary, Peter Heylyn, shows that humanistically inclined students could be and were doctrinally earnest Calvinists. As such, Heylyn actually fit into university life better than the young Milton, and while he later converted to Laudianism, that hardly explains the difference between them. True, Milton's early letters, prose, and poetry all reveal a deep distaste for the clerical ambition that may have led Heylyn in this opportunistic direction, yet they also suggest an equal aversion to the increasingly reactionary direction embraced by the Puritans.[3]

In opposing Laud's "beauty of holiness," the godly increasingly adopted the severe anti-aestheticism of Calvin's Geneva, a city Milton mentions without any note of approval when he later recalls his European tour. By the time he returned to England in 1639, not just the "papist" ceremonies objectionable to most Protestants, but an entire range of traditional rural festivities, rites of spring, holy days, and courtly entertainments had been severely censured by the "hotter sort." Since many of Milton's early poems either celebrate or participate in these activities, it is not surprising that he expressed considerable anxiety about his vocation both before he left and after his return. William Haller's famous chapter on Milton in *The Rise of Puritanism* (1938), "Church-outed by the Prelates," claimed that these were classic Puritan anxieties, but scholarly support for this view has slowly eroded. Although neither questioned the poet's Puritanism, by the mid-1960s Michael Fixler and William B. Hunter both concluded that his "church-outing" was at best ambiguous, at worst an exercise in "passionate self-deception."[4]

Church-outed by the Prelates?

Milton's claim that he was "Church-outed by the Prelates" occurs only once in his writings, in the midst of a passionate protest against all "speaking bought,

---

[2]   For the alternate reading that it marks the success of Milton's masque, see Lewalski, *Life*, p. 71.

[3]   On Heylyn and his fellow Laudians, see Anthony Milton, "Licensing, Censorship, and Religious Orthodoxy in Stuart England," *The Historical Journal* 41.3 (1998): pp. 625–51. On the alienating effects of Cambridge's dogmatic Puritanism, see Tyacke, *Anti-Calvinists*, pp. 29–47.

[4]   Michael Fixler, *Milton and the Kingdoms of God* (Evanston, IL, 1964), p. 48; Haller, *Rise of Puritanism*, pp. 288–323. For Hunter, see n. 5 below.

and begun with servitude and forswearing" in *The Reason of Church Government* (1642). Here he berates the Laudian prelates for effectively enslaving ministers with their tyrannical regulations, and complains that he himself was barred from the ministry by such tyrants. His own refusal to "subscribe slave" thus establishes his "right ... to meddle" in church matters (*CPW* 1:823). Yet in reality, we know that Milton cannot have been a literal victim of Laudian tyranny. His decision against taking holy orders came long *before* swearing the oath that he denounces here was required and even before Laud became archbishop. Since he had already taken all the requisite oaths for ordination upon earning his M.A. degree, no barrier existed against his taking holy orders in 1631–32, the normal time-frame in which he would have taken them.[5] Throughout this period zealous Puritans were still eagerly entering the church to "save" it from the Arminians. When Milton left Cambridge, the radical Puritan minister William Dell had recently received his B.A. from Emmanuel College, and in 1632 the High Calvinist John Owen graduated from Laud's own Oxford, the future archbishop's first truly influential sinecure.[6] Moreover, none of Milton's contemporary letters or poems list any legal or official factors behind his decision, but like the famous disquisition on poetry that follows the remark on church-outing in *The Reason of Church Government*, his poems and letters strongly suggest that he left Cambridge to single-mindedly pursue the "holiness of beauty," not to protest the "beauty of holiness." Long noted for producing Puritan clerics in the direct lineage of their theological father, William Perkins, Cambridge was a most unlikely place either for "outing" Puritans or for ignoring their demands for further ecclesiological reform. Milton's contemporary letters fail to record any interest in these issues, which he virtually ignored until the early 1640s—fully eight years after his departure. He similarly failed to use the university to forge the Puritan friendships, spiritual ties, professional contacts and patronage opportunities that both godly clergy and laymen usually formed there.[7]

For these and related reasons, Dayton Haskin has dismissed Haller's reconstruction of Milton's "conversion experience" as an unconvincing invention. Collecting Milton's scattered rebuttals to Bishop Joseph Hall's charges of libertinism, envy, and self-interest in attacking the prelates, Haller created a non-existent experience. He himself admitted that "Milton never revealed a 'precise moment when he first felt the conviction of grace,'" yet, as Haskin details, he "nonetheless managed to create the impression that Milton had had the requisite conversion." He did this partly by obscuring the polemical and defensive context

---

[5]   See William B. Hunter, *The Descent of Urania: Studies in Milton 1949–1988* (Lewisburg, PA, 1989), p. 181. Donald A. Roberts, the Yale editor of the autobiographical account in Milton's *Second Defence*, suggests 1628 as the probable date for the decision against taking holy orders, which would even more definitely preclude any Laudian influence; see *CPW* 4.1:614 n. 270.

[6]   Wilson, *Pulpit in Parliament*, pp. 131, 133.

[7]   Ann Hughes, *"Gangraena" and the Struggle for the English Revolution* (Oxford, 2004), p. 24.

of the poet's remarks, and partly by interpreting *Lycidas* as a Puritan testimony.[8] Since the poem actually eulogizes a Laudian friend, this interpretation now seems as suspect as Milton's "church-outing." An early "Letter to a Friend" further shows that soon after receiving his M.A. and contemplating ordination, Milton already suspected his temperamental unfitness for the ministry (*CPW* 1:319–21). *The Reason of Church Government* returns to that period when it states that "by the intentions of my parents and friends I was destin'd [for the ministry] of a child, and in mine own resolutions, till comming to some maturity of yeers." It goes on to say that he changed his mind upon "perceiving what tyranny had invaded the Church" (*CPW* 1:822–23), but it does not indicate exactly why or when (long before *Lycidas*) that perception occurred. Its Yale editor, Ralph Haug, thus suggests that the "church-outing" remark in this passage (823) is meant merely as a rallying cry for fellow-sufferers of prelatical tyranny. Yet, however heartfelt Milton's outrage may have been, he voluntarily left Cambridge without taking holy orders a full year before Laud replaced the Calvinist George Abbott as archbishop and eight years before ministerial candidates were forced to "subscribe slave" (823) by swearing the new "Et Cetera" oath. This new oath of 1640 was indeed "a burning issue in 1641" when *The Reason of Church Government* was published, but not earlier, certainly not during Milton's Cambridge years (n. 161).

During that time the Puritan faction at Cambridge remained securely in power—wooed by the influential Buckingham until his death in 1628 and supported by Abbott until his death in 1633—and it remained a dominant force at least until 1634. In that year Thomas Goodwin resigned his post at Trinity rather than conform to the new dispensation, but throughout Milton's residence at Christ's College, Puritans retained as strong a presence as they had since the royalist injunctions of 1547 licensed all Englishmen to read and interpret scripture for themselves.[9] Most treason and heresy statutes concerning religion had been repealed in the reign of Edward VI, so the later Laudian oath of 1640 seemed like an unwarranted innovation not just to Puritans but to most Protestants.[10] Milton's remark is thus an extremely tenuous reason for linking him to the Puritan prophets and early "martyrs" of the anti-Laudian movement—Alexander Leighton, John Bastwick, Henry Burton, and William Prynne. Don M. Wolfe justified this connection because they all regarded themselves as prophets (*CPW* 1:37), yet by his own admission, the martyrs were so militantly "blind to the implications of … persecution" that they urged the destruction of the homes, means, and even

---

[8]   Dayton Haskin, *Milton's Burden of Interpretation* (Philadelphia, PA, 1994), pp. 29–30.

[9]   Haller, *Rise of Puritanism*, pp. 75–78; Tyacke, *Anti-Calvinists*, p. 29. As Haller also points out, Laud's power was checked both by the Calvinist Archbishop George Abbott and "by Puritan leanings in other members of the higher clergy" until Abbott's death in 1633 (p. 230).

[10]   On the changes instituted by Edward I, see John N. King, *English Reformation Literature: The Tudor Origins of the Protestant Tradition* (Princeton, 1982), p. 85.

the lives of "heretics" like the Dutch Arminians (*CPW* 1:39). It is thus virtually impossible to believe that they considered themselves "prophets" in anything like Milton's sense. His conception of prophecy was fundamentally poetic, humanistic, Italianate, and neo-Roman (especially in denouncing "slavery"), yet as William Lamont observes, "The idea of freedom had never stirred Prynne, Bastwick, and Burton; not even in the 1630s, when opposition to Laudian coercive policies could make all three appear to be defenders of liberty. On the contrary, they offered at that time a Calvinist *critique* of what was seen as years of laxity."[11] Finally, if Milton had ever admired Wolfe's prophets, he was strangely silent on that point; he mentions only one, "marginal Prynne," and not in any remotely favorable way. The simple reason seems to be that Milton always detested self-righteous, narrow scripturalism and the Calvinist certitude behind it. Thus, despite his "agreement with the Smectymnuans and other Presbyterians on the sufficiency of the Word in church discipline," they adopted radically different conceptions of its role. Ken Simpson finds Milton approving the equality of all believers and forms other than the sermon (*CPW* 1:819–20), "while the Smectymnuans speak only of the equality of ministers and their right to preach." Milton also refers to more than one discipline found in scripture, while the Smectymnuans outline only their own; he writes of the liberty of each Christian in the Word and Spirit, while they endorse the authority of the Word established by the church, including the narrow authority of words like "presbyter."[12]

These divergences soon led Milton to side with men like Henry Robinson, who between 1645 and 1648 led an amorphous group of political independents and rationalists devoted to a skeptical and irenic religious toleration.[13] Robinson's circle consistently favored an empowered laity over an empowered clergy, hardly the goal of the Puritan martyrs, who typically conflated pastors and preachers with prophets. Thus Robinson, his friend Henry Parker, and Lord Brooke, Parker's patron, all joined the Root and Branch movement for fundamentally different reasons from the prophets, reasons ranging from political and educational reform to ending the crown's control of the church. Parker was particularly skillful in pressing the latter issue, which he regarded as the first step toward "a limited rather than an absolute monarchy," as Wolfe duly notes. He also concedes that Parker's approach to religion was remote from either a Prynne or a Cromwell (*CPW* 1:73), but ignores the extent to which Milton's antiprelatical tracts support the same goals. Much like Parker's, Milton's synthesis of constitutional and scriptural arguments stresses Christian liberty and charity, not Puritan rigor. Wolfe's influential preface to the Yale volume containing the antiprelatical tracts is further flawed by an outdated view of Puritanism, which he describes as a combination of providentialist, millenarian, anti-ceremonial, and anti-Catholic beliefs rooted in the *sola scriptura* principle and a strong work ethic (*CPW* 1:2). Yet these attitudes

---

[11] Lamont, "Pamphleteering," p. 79.

[12] Ken Simpson, "'That Sov'ran Book,'" p. 322.

[13] Jordan, *Men of Substance*, p. 53.

are now considered characteristic of English Protestants in general, while the more truly definitive traits on Wolfe's list—sabbatarianism, distrust of sensual beauty, preference for justice over charity, and rejection of Arminian free will, the pagan classics, and beauty in worship (1:2)—were never shared by Milton.

Thus in many respects Haller was more insightful, for he clearly realized that a significant number of the antiprelatical reformers "sympathized with the Puritan preachers ... for no other reason than that they resented the steady intrusion into politics of churchmen like Laud." Although somewhat inclined toward the Puritan way of life and its "saga" of self-development, their objectives were far less theocratic: "a strong nation, led not by preachers but by energetic, God-fearing gentlemen." He hesitated over whether to label men of this general type "liberal aristocratic Puritans" or "secular humanists" since their rationalism, Neoplatonic idealism, and secular utopianism conflicted with the Calvinist theocratic tendencies of the godly. They also differed in favoring toleration for all, not just "the more moderate Puritan reformers within the church but also ... the independents and the sects."[14] Haller did not of course place Milton in this camp, but nothing, not even *The Reason of Church Government*'s vaguely puritanical defense of Milton's calling, supports Haller's construction of his conversion experience:

> He that hath obtain'd to know ... that God even to a strictnesse requires the improvement of these his entrusted gifts, cannot but sustain a sorer burden of mind, and more pressing then any supportable toil, or waight, which the body can labour under; how and in what manner he shall dispose and employ those summes of knowledge and illumination, which God hath sent him into this world to trade with. (*CPW* 1:801)

Like Sonnet 7 and the closely related *Ad Patrem*, this description of the Christian "calling" alludes to Milton's favorite parable of the talents (Matthew 25:14–31), and thus to standard Christian teachings no Protestant or Catholic would deny. More remarkably still, the broader context of all three of these works shows him plainly anxious to defend his *poetic*, not his religious, vocation.

Milton's lofty goal of glorifying God and country naturally fit into this calling even when, as in Sonnet 7, his late "budding" spring makes him doubt his ability to fulfill it. Yet even these dutiful doubts are often colored by secular rivalry, not religious anxiety. Alan Rudrum suggests that Milton's self-deprecating remarks on his late "bloom" in Sonnet 7 wryly pun on the fifteen-year-old Abraham Cowley's recent publication, *Poetical Blossoms*.[15] Thus as Milton approached the ripe age of twenty-three still relatively "barren," he turned to Pindar's *Nemean Odes* IV, 43, to relieve his anxiety about his "talents": "Whatever merit King Fate has given

---

[14] Haller, *Rise of Puritanism*, pp. 331; see also pp. 194, 350. On Milton's lifelong opposition to theocracy, see Fixler, *Milton*, especially pp. 165–210.

[15] See Alan Rudrum et al., *The Broadview Anthology of Seventeenth-Century Verse & Prose* (Petersborough, ON, 2000), p. 521 n. 1, and p. 770.

me, I shall know that time in its course will accomplish what is destined" (Hughes 77). Milton's allusion to these lines does not cancel out the idea of his "talents" as spiritual "investments," but it does mean that the secular language of untapped aesthetic "capital" remains dominant:

> Yet be it less or more, or soon or slow,
>   It shall be still in strictest measure ev'n
>   To that same lot, however mean or high,
> Toward which Time leads me, and the will of Heav'n;
>   All is, if I have grace to use it so,
>   As ever in my great task-Master's eye.

(Sonnet 7, 9–14)

Here, Milton's "task-Master," like Pindar's Fate, foresees the "height" of a destiny or lot that will gradually unfold in human time, yet like the Father of *Paradise Lost*, he makes his "son" sufficient to stand on his own, to increase his "talents" and render his account without any interference from his foreknowledge.[16] Like the vocational account included in *The Reason of Church Government*, this divine inscrutability is reassuring, not anxiety-producing; it means that Milton may choose to serve God, country, and religion outside the church by cultivating the arts with which he can best "adorn" them, poetry and rhetoric. Since God alone knows the final outcome, the poet is free to choose how and where to dedicate his gifts, whether to a sacred or secular cause or to some synthesis of both, the choice Milton typically prefers.

The most obvious result of that synthesis is his rapid extension of religious free speech in *The Reason of Church Government* into the domain of secular free speech in *Areopagitica*. From that perspective, his penultimate antiprelatical tract is only a partial down-payment on his vocational talents, the first-fruits of his desire "to lay up as the best treasure, and solace of a good old age, if God voutsafe it me, the honest liberty of free speech from my youth, where I shall think it available in so dear a concernment as the Churches good." Yet he can only make that down-payment from a secular position, since he is "either by disposition, or what other cause too inquisitive, or suspitious of my self and mine own doings" to pursue a ministerial career (*CPW* 1:804). As in the "Letter to a Friend," which originally contained Sonnet 7, Milton somewhat regrets that his overly introspective or "suspicious" nature prevents his dedication to the ministry,

---

[16]   Milton's citation from the *Nemean Odes* is noted by Hughes (77). Warren Chernaik rightly identifies "the theology of the closing lines [as] ... Arminian," but wrongly places Milton in the Puritan tradition by confusing "Free Grace and Universal Grace, a distinction which" (according to Lamont) eluded A.L. Morton in *The World of the Ranters* and still confuses those who conflate "predestinarian élitism" with egalitarianism. See Lamont, "Pamphleteering," pp. 84, 86; and Chernaik, "Christian Liberty in Marvell and Milton," in Richardson and Ridden (eds.), *Freedom and the English Revolution*, p. 50.

but his dominant emotion seems to be a sense of relief and liberation, not regret. That no doubt explains why, after initially declining holy orders, he never sought ordination in an independent or "gathered" church. Another reason is that he hardly admired the "wretched[ly] ... bescraull[ed] ... Pamflets" of the enthusiastic utopians whose new "formes of government for our Church" (*CPW* 1:753) already seem impractical to him. No wonder, then, that Bishop Hall never associated his anonymous attacker with the godly faction, but identified him as a university "wit" who deeply resented the pride and perfidy encouraged by clerical privilege.

Despite the residual truth of Hall's accusation, Milton's motives in some ways seem as selfless as he claimed. After a decade of rigorous study and solitary research with little concrete result, he earnestly desired to put his learning to work. If, as some critics suspect, both *Ad Patrem* and Sonnet 7 were composed in 1632 (Hughes 82), Milton must have been acutely aware almost ten years later that he still had little or nothing to offer his father or country "except what golden Clio has given and what has been the fruit of dreams in a remote cavern and of the laurel groves of the sacred wood and ... shadows of Parnassus" (*Ad Patrem*, 14–16).[17] Having won only a few shadowy rewards from his study of history ("golden Clio") and his worship of poetry ("sacred Apollo"), he was still not only deeply "suspicious" of himself but also deeply resentful of a socio-political climate where "some spark of Promethean fire and ... the unrivalled glory of the heaven-born human mind" are not properly honored (20–25). No longer "the usual ornaments of royal tables in the times before luxury and the bottomless appetite of gluttony were known" (41–43), true poets and poetry are now ignored. Fortunately, however, his father has respected his plea not to

> go where the broad ways lies wide open, where the field of lucre is easier and the golden hope of amassing money is glittering and sure; neither do you force me into the law and the evil administration of the national statutes. You do not condemn my ears to noisy impertinence. But rather, because you wish to enrich the mind which you have carefully cultivated, you lead me far away from the uproar of cities into these high retreats of delightful leisure beside the Aonian stream, and you permit me to walk there by Phoebus' side, his blessed companion. (*Ad Patrem*, 68–76)

These details strongly suggest that Milton wrote these lines at Hammersmith (1632–35) before the successful production of *Comus* but after rejecting the "broad way" of a legal career, a lucrative benefice, or an academic appointment (the latter two of which required holy orders).

Yet, even after the production of his Ludlow masque (1634), Milton experienced a long dry period that brought him no closer to composing the English epic promised first in *Ad Patrem*, again in *Mansus*, and yet again in his antiprelatical tracts. During this period his father was residing with Milton's married younger

---

[17]   The lines cited are from the Latin poem, not Hughes's unnumbered translation.

brother, and, while they were never estranged, *Ad Patrem* suggests that his father's keen disappointment in his more gifted son's career choices did not soon subside. Many critics have spotted autobiographical-sounding echoes in the disagreement between Manoa and Samson in *Samson Agonistes*, and certainly, Milton's actual return on his father's "investment" still fell absurdly short of "the ancient treasures of Austria and the lucre of Peru" or the "ivy and laurel of a victor" that *Ad Patrem* promises him (93–94, 102). The tone of exultation in the antiprelatical tracts may thus be traced to a Samson-like sense of vindication as the church establishment he once seemed "destined" to join began to tumble down. Not only was a once-prestigious career path now widely reviled, but the young Milton's refusal to capitulate to time-servers like his former tutor, William Chappell, now seemed justified. After their quarrel, Chappell traded his Puritan convictions for a place in the Laudian hierarchy, but by report, he still vigorously detested the student he had "sent down" from Cambridge.[18] The sentiment was mutual, and Milton's glee at the national ire against the establishment emerges in his tracts' strangely boastful sense of self-righteousness. Filled with autobiographical digressions, they frequently blend personal anxiety and frustration with renewed hope, perhaps at recovering the "self-esteem" that he so unpuritanically cherished (*CPW* 1:890). Spurred on by the encouragement of his Italian admirers, the newly purposeful poet entered the Root and Branch movement full of "big-mouthed prayers" that offended Bishop Hall and probably most Puritans, who had little use for "self-esteem."[19] Not only did they link it to spiritual pride, but they considered even "self-confidence" the equivalent of *self-conceitedness* and *self-fullness*, the diametric opposite of the *self-emptiness* that directed their "utter dependence on God in all … actions."[20] Regarding Root and Branch as the beginning of their bleak battle with Antichrist, they hardly saw the campaign as a means of salvaging wayward literary careers. Although it succeeded with little or no help from Milton, who was scantly noted by anyone but Hall and his son, Milton felt secure enough to marry. When that marriage began to fail, he characteristically set about trying to alter the laws of

---

[18]   On Chappell's Puritanism, see Joseph Levine, who shows that the contemporary Cambridge student body was split between Chappell's Puritans, William Powers's liberal "Powritans," and Joseph Mede's moderate "Medians." Levine, "Latitudinarians, Neoplatonists, and Ancient Wisdom," in Richard Kroll, Richard Ashcraft, and Perez Zagorin (eds.), *Philosophy, Science, and Religion in England 1640–1700* (Cambridge, 1992), pp. 85–108, cited p. 93. Chappell later converted to the Arminianism cause, probably for the sake of the promotion that he later received. H.R. McAdoo dates the change to around the time Chappell tutored Henry More eight years after Milton left Cambridge; see McAdoo, *The Spirit of Anglicanism* (New York, 1965), pp. 99–100.

[19]   For a fuller discussion, see Joshua Scodel, *Excess and the Mean in Early Modern English Literature* (Princeton, 2002), pp. 270–74; and Chapter 6 below.

[20]   Marinus van Beek, *An Enquiry into Puritan Vocabulary* (Groningen, 1969), p. 69.

England to allow divorce on largely humanistic grounds at the very time the saints were expecting the imminent overthrow of all human "forms."[21]

Milton's frankly unpuritanical discussions of his own motives also explain why his tracts abruptly dismiss the "word Puritan" as a meaningless term that now "seemes to be quasht" by newer labels. Without identifying his allies, he merely lumps his opponents together as anti-reformers and "faithlesse spies, whose carcasses shall perish in the wildernesse of their owne confused ignorance, and never taste the good of reformation" (*CPW* 1:784). Then, just where one would most expect either a spiritual defense of himself, the godly ministers, or their common program for reforming the church, we find only broad condemnations of "precisian" pamphlets, strong denials of divine right or biblical authority for prelatry, and heated rebuttals of the charges of libertinism brought against him by Hall and his son. Through it all, Milton is far more seriously concerned to discredit antiquarian arguments than to defend Presbyterian forms of church government. He learnedly denies that any episcopal system can be derived from either Leviticus or the gospels, and asserts that the epistles favor a loose system of presbyters and deacons, but rarely extols Presbyterianism except when pressing a more comprehensive political program. As a then-anonymous layman claiming his "natural" right to advance the cause of reform, Milton's arguments for Presbyterianism are in fact far more conspicuously populist than truly "godly."

As in his early Latin poem on the Gunpowder Plot, Milton's general outlook fits easily into the mainstream Protestant rubric inherited from John Foxe, Matthew Hutton (future archbishop of York), and Thomas Scott, the author of *Vox Populi*. According to Peter Lake, these three Elizabethans established as unassailable truth the idea that "the mindless acceptance of beliefs and practices merely because they had been held for centuries" is "a defining mark of popish darkness," qualities later associated with the Laudian hierarchy. Hutton in particular anticipates Bacon in proclaiming that "custom without truth is but old error," an aphorism Milton recites in his antiprelatical tracts (*CPW* 1:561).[22] Yet Lake finds all three advancing a broadly Protestant, "essentially word-based vision of rationality, enlightenment, and knowledge" as the antithesis to secular and spiritual tyranny. In this vision "true reformation could only be brought about as each individual came to a proper understanding and possession of his spiritual liberties and duties as a Christian, [so] Protestant enlightenment was, almost by definition, popular enlightenment." Presbyterianism at first seemed the logical culmination of the popular opposition to priestly hierarchies and persecutions, since it defined "the rule of one minister over another as the direct emanation of the pope's tyrannical rule over the Church." This tyranny wrongly deprived ordinary believers of both freedom of thought and civil liberty to elect church governors, yet as Lake concludes, it "would be absurd"

---

[21]   On the humanist and non-Puritan sources of the divorce tracts, see John Halkett, *Milton and the Idea of Matrimony: A Study of the Divorce Tracts and Paradise Lost* (New Haven, 1970).

[22]   Lake, "Anti-popery," p. 185.

to see this tradition as "unequivocally populist."[23] Milton was soon to discover this fact, but *Of Reformation* clearly reflects his belief in the tradition's main outlines: church reform is a natural corollary of civil reform and protection from tyranny. Given the "kind of Apostolicall, and ancient *Church* Election" practiced "in our State," Milton asks what kind of "perversnesse" must make "us of all others to retain forcibly a kind of imperious, and stately Election in our *Church?*" Since the English Parliament's lower house (technically, its "popular" element) is chosen by vote, Englishmen should demand a comparably "full and free Election ... to that holy and equall *Aristocracy*" of presbyters. The obvious advantage of this system is that their appointment will "nothing concerne a *Monarch*," which is Milton's way of saying that it will replace Stuart absolutism with mixed government (*CPW* 1:600).

Milton here has obviously not yet rejected monarchy itself as a fundamentally "idolatrous" institution, but *Of Reformation* already argues that church reform will restore the balanced government, "natural" both in the providential scheme of things and in the "Common-wealth of *England*." Its "divinely and harmoniously tun'd" scheme, "equally ballanc'd as it were by the hand and scale of Justice," wants only the election of "the *godliest*, the *wisest*, the *learnedest* Ministers" to oversee the "instructing and disciplining of *Gods people*" (*CPW* 1:599, 600). As for the state, "besides the diffusive blessings of *God* upon all our actions, the King shall sit without an old disturber, a dayly incroacher, and intruder; shall ridde his Kingdome of a strong sequester'd, and collateral power: a confronting miter, whose potent wealth, and wakefull ambition he had just cause to hold in jealousie; not to repeat the other present evills which only their removal will remove" (*CPW* 1:599). Additionally, of course, the new hierarchy will enact the religious reforms previously blocked by the prelates, who have historically "polluted [the church] with idolatrous and Gentilish rites and ceremonies" already eliminated by "our neighbour Churches" (*CPW* 1:761). Yet this final point is based less on strictly anti-ceremonial grounds than on the necessity of safeguarding free speech. By falsely pretending to prevent schism, the bishops have actually adopted "inquisitorial" practices that increase it. Like Lord Brooke, Milton thus aims to end the persecution of "all knowing and zealous Christians by the violence of ... [the bishops'] courts (*CPW* 1:784; 785 n. 42). Haug reminds us that these courts had proved "particularly useful to Stuart absolutism": Laud's "main weapon in the enforcement of his policy of 'thorough'" was to regulate all "matrimonial offences, church irregularities, ... nonconformity, heresy, and schism" (*CPW* 1:784 n. 41).

Thus *Of Reformation* already anticipates *Areopagitica* as well as the divorce tracts, which together would end the church's control of both censorship and marriage at a time when Puritan views of "civil and religious liberty did not march, if they marched at all, to the beat of the same drum."[24] True, Milton's strong synthesis of these liberties sometimes borrows the prophetic Puritan rhetoric of

---

[23]   Ibid., pp. 185–86.

[24]   J.C. Davis, "Religion and the Struggle for Freedom in the English Revolution," *Historical Journal* 35.3 (1992): pp. 507–30, cited p. 514.

biblical denunciation against oppressors, yet this biblical language is common to all English Protestants of the era. Milton also modifies it in crucial instances. Issuing a "dolorous blast" against the prelates, he cites the example of *both* Jeremiah and Tiresias, not just Jeremiah's "stomach, virulence and ill nature," as some scholars still maintain (*CPW* 1:803–4).[25] The reason is that Milton's primary goal was very different from the Puritan attempt to "create, not asylums from tyranny, but superior vehicles for godliness," which, as Lamont notes, did not favor liberty so much as whatever "discipline is the most effective."[26] He traces Milton's departure from this disciplinary quest to the mid-1640s, yet it already seems implicit in *Of Reformation*'s division of "the hinderers of *Reformation* into 3. sorts, *Antiquitarians* (for so I had rather call them then *Antiquaries*, whose labours are usefull and laudable) 2. *Libertines*, 3. Polititians," who uniformly lack not the "sword of the spirit" but enlightened minds. All three thus bring what *The Reason of Church Government* calls "a num and chil stupidity of soul, an unactive blindnesse of minde upon the people by their leaden doctrine" either through their venal motives, their conformist mentality, or their bureaucratic sterility (*CPW* 1.541, 784). Yet, while Milton never tires of berating hide-bound traditionalists, corrupt church officials, and greedy politicians, he never returns to the "libertines" again. This omission may have prompted Hall to accuse him of being one himself, thus provoking the furious testaments to his chastity and probity that led Haller to label him a Puritan.

In fact, at this very time Milton was writing Latin poems ripe with lush erotic and seasonal symbolism, many of which skillfully combined these tropes with the radical reformist zeal that he himself claims to have learned from the great humanist poets—Dante, Ariosto, and Tasso among the Italians, Chaucer and Spenser among the English (*CPW* 1:558–60, 579–80, 595, 722). This strategy is hardly libertine, but it does (as Victoria Kahn remarks) turn both Puritan and royal "policy on its head … to … justify the *virtù* of the individual Christian and poet." This stance leads Richard Helgerson to consider Milton a Caroline synthesizer, not a conventional Puritan iconoclast, an opinion clearly borne out by Milton's astonishingly ecumenical 1645 volume of verse.[27] As Zagorin summarizes, the volume presents its author as a patriot, "a gentleman, scholar,

---

[25]   John R. Knott, *The Sword of the Spirit* (Chicago, 1980), p. 106. Knott omits Tiresias yet admits that Jeremiah is invoked only "by way of analogy, chiefly to justify the vehemence of his writing"; nevertheless, Milton was indeed "assuming a prophetic role" (p. 106).

[26]   Lamont, "Pamphletering," pp. 78, 77. Davis's findings in "Religion" lend strong support to Lamont.

[27]   Victoria Kahn, *Machiavellian Rhetoric: From the Counter-Reformation to Milton* (Princeton, 1994), p. 194, and Richard Helgerson, *Self-Crowned Laureates: Spenser, Jonson, Milton and the Literary System* (Berkeley, 1983), pp. 185–282. On the standard mode, see Barbara Lewalski, *Protestant Poetics and the Seventeenth-Century Religious Lyric* (Princeton, 1979).

and poet whose dedication to the external values of art soared far above local conflicts." Published by Humphrey Mosely, a man of royalist sympathies like "Mr. Henry Lawes Gentleman of the Kings Chappel," its contents (according to Mosley) were comparable to "choice peeces" by the royalist Edmund Waller. They include early elegies on several bishops, an epitaph on a Catholic noblewoman (the Marchioness of Winchester), Latin poems to several of Milton's Italian Catholic friends, tributes to the poet from other Italians, and also from Sir Henry Wotton, a courtier, ambassador, and man of letters. Zagorin adds that this list would seem strange indeed unless, in line with "the more explicit political observations in the antiprelatical tracts," Milton's goal or "art of policie" remained unchanged: to "'train up a Nation in [the] true wisdom[,] ...vertue[,] ... and *godliness*,'" which alone insure the "true florishing of a Land" by overcoming selfish "rapine" and "subjection," luxury and ignorance (*CPW* 1:571).[28] To this Campbell and Corns add that these puzzling royalist sympathies are largely explained by cultural affinities and personal loyalties, although several of the volume's poems (especially those on the nativity, passion, and circumcision) additionally indicate ritualist and even Laudian sympathies.[29]

Later, Milton will come to believe that the land's "true flourishing" primarily demands safeguarding the "authority of the Spirit, which is internal, and the individual possession of each man" (*CPW* 6:587), yet as even Hill admitted, Milton's joint insistence upon the Bible's *rational* authority safeguards against enthusiastic anarchy.[30] It even more clearly safeguards civil liberty and toleration, his life-long concerns. In the early years of parliamentary rule conservative saints posed a far greater threat to liberty than enthusiasts or sectarians, yet even then, Arthur Barker finds that "Milton's sympathy with the left wing of Puritanism was real" but primarily oppositional; just "as his support for the Smectymnuans resulted from common opposition to episcopacy, so his defense of the sects arose from common opposition to Presbyterianism, not from any identity of fundamental principles."[31] His antiprelatical tracts already forecast this opposition by warning his countrymen against being satisfied "with *Calvins* name, unless we be convinc't with *Calvins* reason" (*Animadversions*, *CPW* 1:707). Milton hints at his own hesitation about "Calvin's reason" by paying far greater attention to Luther and Bacon. As Haller points out, the same hesitation is apparent in his defense

---

[28] Zagorin, *Milton*, pp. 62, 34; I closely follow Zagorin's factual summary of the volume's contents and production. See also Annabel Patterson, "'Forc'd Fingers': Milton's Early Poems and Ideological Constraints," in Claude J. Summers and Ted-Larry Pebworth (eds.), *"The Muse's Common-Weale": Poetry and Politics in the Seventeenth Century* (Columbia, MO, 1988), pp. 9–22.

[29] Campbell and Corns, *John Milton*, p. 51.

[30] Hill, *Milton*, pp. 248–49; as he adds, those who "rejected the Bible tended to be those who also rejected the Protestant ethic" (p. 248).

[31] See Knott, *Sword*, p. 114, and Arthur E. Barker, *Milton and the Puritan Dilemma 1641–1660* (Toronto, 1942), p. 80.

of Presbyterianism "in a spirit and on grounds which the Smectymnuans and the godly divines who presently devised the Westminster Directory of Worship could not have conceived and were certain to repudiate. Their advocate of 1641 was already prepared to be their Abdiel of 1644."[32] In that year *Areopagitica* even more boldly flaunts common Puritan attitudes and pays tribute to only one "martyr," Lord Brooke, who (according to Parker) was ironically no Puritan. Besides Bacon, it also praises John Selden, a man who openly held the godly in contempt. Milton may not have yet gone that far, but he was already deeply resistant to their attempts to end "the old separation between religious and secular, between the Church and the State," that is, to copy "Calvin's attempt to identify the holy community with the Genevan community at large." Geoffrey Nuttall finds this goal inherent in the Puritan belief that the "obverse of 'the liberty of the Spirit'" is "the 'government of the Spirit,'" a belief apparent in Peter Sterry's 1645 sermon to Parliament. Exalting the Spirit over both reason and "sense," which is the mere "brute part of the world," Sterry denies "that all truths which come by revelation of the Spirit, may also be demonstrated by Reason, ... [for] if they be, they are then no more Divine, but humane truths; They lose their certainty, beauty, efficacy; ... Spirituall truths discovered by demonstrations of Reason, are like the Mistresse in her Cook-maid's clothes."[33]

Observing that Thomas Goodwin and other major Puritan theologians say much the same thing, Nuttall concludes that "All parties, really, are agreed about this: it is the essential Puritan emphasis." The radical left differed mainly in even more strongly rejecting dead rational "notions" and conventional morality, which they replaced with "a spiritual perception analogous to ... physical perception" in its experiential immediacy.[34] Milton first indicated his opposition to this spiritualist outlook by abandoning Cambridge for purely intellectual or "notional" reasons. Deriding its divinity students as shallow and its scholastic curriculum as an "asinine feast of sowthistles and brambles" (*CPW* 1:314, 2:377), like Bacon, he early resisted the dogmatic dominance "of Aristotle in an age when he no longer claimed the assent of European philosophers." Since the Puritan regime proved sadly indifferent to his obsolescence, the educational reforms advocated by Bacon, Milton, and the Hartlib circle were never adopted and the university entered a period of steep academic decline.[35]

---

[32]   Haller, *Rise of Puritanism*, p. 340.

[33]   Nuttall, *Holy Spirit*, pp. 119, 37; Nuttall cites Peter Sterry, *The Spirits conviction of Sinne* (1645), pp. 11, 16, 26.

[34]   Nuttall, *Holy Spirit*, pp. 39, 38.

[35]   Richard S. Westfall, "Isaac Newton in Cambridge: The Restoration University and Scientific Creativity," in Perez Zagorin (ed.), *Culture and Politics: From Puritanism to the Enlightenment* (Berkeley, 1980), pp. 135–64, cited p. 137.

Drama, Romance, Rhetoric, and Reform

Milton may have objected to the bad taste and "finicall goosery of your neat Sermon-actor" (*CPW* 1:935) or clergyman at Cambridge, but there is absolutely no evidence that he considered play-acting itself a "degraded and unworthy recreation," as many scholars still believe.[36] He not only wrote a drama for child actors but he also played a central role in informal college theatricals ("A Vacation Exercise"). In his antiprelatical tracts he happily admits frequenting the London theater (*CPW* 1:887–88), and *L'Allegro* imagines a perfect country day ending with a play in the city. His remark about weak clerical "acting" thus seems to reflect his poor opinion of the clergy in general, particularly their sermonizing. Even *Eikonoklastes*, a work whose very title suggests an anti-theatrical orientation, fails to justify the King's execution on the basis of his "idolatrous" devotion to drama, popular romance, or ceremony. It does condemn his "heathen" use of a prayer taken from Sir Philip Sidney's *Arcadia*, and it also repeats *Of Reformation*'s condemnation of "gaming, jigging, wassailing, and mixt dancing" on Sundays (*CPW* 1:589). These remarks led Merritt Hughes to suppose that Milton always shared "the Puritan opposition to Sunday theatre" (*CPW* 3:358 n. 26), although the earlier passage in *Of Reformation* fails to mention the theater. A closer look at *Eikonoklastes* also shows that Milton never condemns courtly masques or expresses any regret at writing one. He simply rebukes the court's "licentious remissness" (358), and *The Reason of Church Government* actually defends "artfull recitations" and theatricals as morally instructive forms of recreation worthy of being performed in churches (*CPW* 1:819, 820 n. 136).

On sports, *The Reason of Church Government* and *Eikonoklastes* consistently soften *Of Reformation*'s position. The former approves of "publick sports, and festival pastimes, that ... may inure and harden our bodies by martial exercises to all warlike skil and performance" (*CPW* 1:819). These remarks concede two points first made by King James: (1) forbidding "honest mirth or recreation... cannot but breed a great discontentment" which could be fatal to a "true" Protestant conversion; and (2) barring "the common and meaner sort of people from using such exercises as may make their bodies more able for war" can only be detrimental to the state.[37] Milton thus tries to have it both ways: he concedes the Puritan objection to licentious forms of Sunday entertainment, but also sanctions the court's support for healthful forms of holiday recreation. Yet even *Of Reformation*'s harsher attitude toward Sunday recreation stops short of accusing the King's *Book of Sports* of diverting the people from Puritan preaching; it merely distracts them from their private meditations, personal "communion" of faith, and study. Ever the rational individualist, Milton considers these personal activities vital to the sober "knowledge of God ... and exercise of Charity" (*CPW* 1:589). As

---

[36]   Lewalski, *Life*, p. 43.

[37]   Samuel R. Gardiner (ed.), *Constitutional Documents of the Puritan Revolution 1625–1660* [rpt. 1889] (Oxford, 1958), pp. 100–101.

well as confirming Milton's life-long habit of failing to commend Puritan sermons or preachers, this attitude further identifies him with the Hartlib circle's irenic goal of reuniting a newly polarized Protestant culture through educational, not disciplinary, means. Although he seconded the Puritan protest against the prelates' outdated and "sencelesse *Ceremonies*," he added that until the "*buried Truth*" of sound understanding is restored (true "*Doctrine*" as well as true "Discipline"), reviving "*Pulpit Preaching* is but shooting at Rovers" (*CPW* 1:526).

Yet Milton also differed from the Hartlib circle in combining educational with aesthetic reform, an issue on which he is often closer to Sidney. Closely echoing the latter's *Defence of Poesy, The Reason of Church Government* argues that the best art teaches "sanctity and vertu through all the instances of example with such delight to those especially of soft and delicious temper who will not so much as look upon Truth herselfe, unless they see her elegantly drest" (*CPW* 1:817–18). As in Sidney, this positive view of rhetorical art reflects continental rather than Puritan opinion. Godly rhetoricians in the lineage of Perkins believed that the style which "'best beseemeth the majesty of God' is 'plaine, easie, and familiar,'" while continental rhetoricians such as Richard Bernard felt that any style that "'can paint out vice in the deformitie to make it hatefull, and set out vertue in her beauty, to make her be desired, ... speaketh ... a godly eloquence approued by Scripture and vsed in it, which is to be laboured for.'"[38] Although all recognized with Milton that the talent behind this craft is "the inspired guift of God rarely bestow'd, but yet to some ... in every Nation" (*CPW* 1:816), he clearly sides with both Bernard's figurative description of beauty-as-truth and his emphasis on "eloquence and decorum." Debora Shuger notes that a comparably strong "sense of the drama, grandeur, and rhetorical exuberance of Holy Scripture ... [is] seldom found in the English tradition" apart from Catholic or continental Protestant influences. Puritans opposed these influences because they wanted to strip "the figurative language off the plain, naked meaning of Scripture," to make the spiritual power of God's Word operate almost independently of language or art. While not literally plain, the "passionate plain style" of the Puritans looks back to the early medieval period, which retained "the affective orientation of the grand style" but dropped the classical assumption that heightened eloquence is necessary for divine matters or for producing emotion. For Puritans like Sterry, eloquence is beside the point, since "the power of preaching moves invisibly like a spiritual laser from the Spirit to the preacher's heart to his words," thus obviating the need for art and even reason, which "sensually" hinders the transfer of divine energy.[39] Since Milton is no more anti-rhetorical than he is anti-theatrical, he places considerable value on

---

[38]   Debora K. Shuger, *Sacred Rhetoric: The Christian Grand Style in the English Renaissance* (Princeton, 1988), p. 96, citing Richard Bernard's *The Faithful Shepherd* (London, 1621), p. 96.

[39]   Shuger, *Sacred Rhetoric*, pp. 97, 108–9. See also Perry Miller, *The New England Mind: The Seventeenth Century* (Cambridge, MA, 1956), pp. 342–43, and Knott, *Sword*, pp. 4–5.

craft, which is consciously gained by "labour and intent study … joyn'd with the strong propensity of nature" (*CPW* 1:810).

This aesthetics justifies not only "delicious" didactic poetry but even "libidinous" prose romances such as Sidney's *Arcadia*. Thus, even where Milton's polemical purpose most demands debunking Sidney's romance, *Eikonoklastes* declares it "full of worth and witt" so long as one reads the tale with "good caution" and does not confuse it (as the King has done) with a prayer book (*CPW* 3:362). This broadly inclusive theory of art ironically allows him to condemn Charles for the same aesthetic reasons he mounted against Hall, his fellow prelates, and their bad "Sermon-actors." Exactly like those "libidinous and ignorant Poetasters" (*CPW* 1:818; cf. 1:697, 719, 915), Charles not only promotes bad art but is himself a bad artist who pompously presumes that his "bad lines" will gain him such

> honour and reputation that like the Sun shall rise and recover it self to such a Splendour, as Owles, Batts, and such fatal Birds shall be unable to beare. Poets indeed use to vapor much after this manner. But to bad Kings, who without cause expect future glory from thir actions, it happ'ns as to bad Poets; who sit and starve them-selves with a delusive hope to win immortality by thir bad lines. (*CPW* 3:502)

Here, as throughout *Eikonoklastes*, Milton clearly enjoys sneering at Charles's shallow "poetic" rhetoric and his "Sonnetting" manner of addressing his queen (*CPW* 3:406, 420–21), complaints later leveled at courtly romance in *Paradise Lost* (4.765–70), but no more generally applicable to poetry or music than to theater or painting. The language of Milton's Sonnet 12 clearly shows that he imagines himself as precisely the opposite kind of poet: one at whom "Owls and Cuckoos, Asses, Apes and Dogs" screech in vain (4).

Eikonoklastes also pointedly praises Shakespeare's portrait of *Richard III* (*CPW* 3:361) for capturing the true essence of the ham actor turned tyrant, a role that Charles carries off even less well than his infamous predecessor. Much like the tasteless bishop–artists who populate the antiprelatical tracts, the King actually has the bad sense to believe in his own false performance (*CPW* 3:530–31). Yet rather than intrinsically corrupting him, the royal "performance" demeans him by trading true ceremony, honor, civility, and sincerity for the "dissembling" applause of captive court flatterers (*CPW* 3:539). Rather than the living art that *The Reason of Church Government* promises to produce, the court and King can only create dead or "wooden" allegories lamely supported by crude cue cards or "pointers": "He who writes himself *Martyr* by his own inscription, is like an ill Painter, who, by writing on the shapeless Picture which he hath drawn, is fain to tell passengers what shape it is; which els no man could imagin" (*CPW* 3:575). Milton had oddly enough made much the same joke about the inept work of the artist who produced his portrait in his 1645 volume of verse, which lends his attack a sense of irony lacking in the Puritan propagandists. Thus, while royalists usually portrayed the King's detractors as conniving Puritan divines, Joseph Jane simply attacked Milton as an "oratour" employed by Parliament to defend its "sinful," king-killing power.[40]

The only authentically Puritan position contained in either *Eikonoklastes* or Milton's antiprelatical tracts is the rejection of set liturgies, a position also maintained in *Paradise Lost* (5.144–52). Yet, unlike a godly iconoclast, Milton does not argue his case on grounds of "papist" contamination. He simply states that mechanically "set" devotions are empty and valueless. His objections to the remnants of the mass in the Book of Common Prayer are purely factual and historical; he exhibits no superstitious fear of holy relics or any "holy dread" of offending the Old Testament God who forbids religious imagery. Citing the well-established opinion of Edward VI that the prayer book conserves the Roman Catholic liturgy (*CPW* 3:504), he considers it antiquated and often meaningless, but he never broaches the standard Puritan objection that it impedes the operation of the Holy Spirit. Eliminating it will simply further a deeper understanding of scripture and of charitable duties, which is not "proportionable to a certain doss of prepar'd words" learned by rote without real comprehension. Like other Protestants, he believes that spontaneous words in prayer and meditation take wing from "that Divine Spirit of utterance that moves them" (*CPW* 3:505). This same Spirit sustained Christians before "*Constantine* with his mischievous donations poyson'd *Silvester* and the whole Church" (*CPW* 3:514; cf. 1:551), a statement that anticipates Milton's later objections to a "bought" or hireling clergy. Yet, both early and late, Constantine was highly regarded by Puritans who supported public "donations" as essential aids to the ministry. From Foxe onward, they saw the Roman emperor as a pillar of uncorrupted Christianity and a useful precedent for tithes.[41]

Of course, Milton's task in *Eikonoklastes* naturally required some concessions to the Puritan left, such as Milton's disapproval of the King's fondness for antiphonal responses (*CPW* 3:552–53), yet this point is so ambiguously stated as to cast doubt on Milton's actual convictions. The doubt deepens when we consider his *Commonplace Book*, which cites patristic defenses of antiphonal song and instrumental accompaniment in worship. His sonnet to Henry Lawes highly praises that composer of complex, polyphonic music, and in *Paradise Lost* angelic choirs

---

[40]   Joseph Jane, *Eikon Aklastos, The Image Unbroken* (1651), pp. A1, 12. The King's other detractor was the anonymous author of the *Eikon Alethine*, who was then anonymously attacked in *Eikon E Piste* (1649). While *Eikon Alethine* and *Eikon E Piste* respectively display antiprelatical or anti-Puritan frontispieces, *Eikonoklastes* is merely prefaced with Milton's portrait.

[41]   On the singularity of Milton's departure from Foxe, see Janel Mueller, "Embodying Glory: The Apocalyptic Strain in *Of Reformation*," in David Loewenstein and James Grantham Turner (eds.), *Politics, Poetics, and Hermeneutics in Milton's Prose* (Cambridge, 1990), pp. 9–40.

praise the Almighty with this type of song.[42] As for other forms of iconoclasm, *Eikonoklastes* flatly dismisses them as the "enormities the Vulgar may committ in the rudeness of thir zeal" (*CPW* 3:535; cf. n. 5). Although it accepts legal, publicly decreed acts of Parliamentary iconoclasm, zealots who act on private inspiration are no more defensible than Charles, who believed that private acts of conscience placed him among the Christian martyrs. To this Milton violently objects that only those willing to die in the *public* defense of truth and justice can claim this title, and anticipates his own Samson by proclaiming that "privat reason, ... to us is no Law" (*CPW* 3:360; cf. *SA*, 1211–16). John Knott, Janel Mueller, and Margaret Dean all confirm Milton's intellectual consistency on this point: from *Of Reformation* to his final poems, he broke with Foxe by failing to identify martyrdom with the true church (*CPW* 1:533).[43] Finally, *Eikonoklastes* connects the King's false identification of himself as a martyr to his habit of superstitiously "spelling" events that signify God's will (*CPW* 3:567). Yet this habit was also ironically prominent among Puritans, who regularly sought divine "leadings" in natural or fortuitous occurrences, and were "noted for their vocabulary of 'in-coming, out-lettings, and in-dwellings.'" Yet *Paradise Regained* (4.385) actually associates this practice with Satan, thus definitively rejecting one form of mysticism at the very heart of Puritan experience: the experience of "'being irradiated with the holy and divine nature.'"[44]

Of course, both *Samson Agonistes* and *De Doctrina Christiana* allow that "leadings" may provide signs of divine purpose but, like the Holy Spirit, they are neither omnipresent, infallible, nor even capable of being invoked (*CPW* 6:288, 292, 295). *De Doctrina* therefore warns that Christians must "beware above all of exposing ourselves to the charge which Christ brought against the Samaritans in John iv.22: *you worship something you do not know*" or something "contrary to human reason" (*CPW* 6:288, 289). This refreshingly anti-dogmatic skepticism is already apparent in *Eikonoklastes*, which also condemns any attempt "to set up a distinct Faith or Goverment" as "a Scism and Faction, not a Church. It were an injurie to condemn the Papist of absurdity and contradiction, for adhering to his Catholic Romish Religion, if we, for the pleasure of a King and his politic considerations, shall adhere to a Catholic English" (*CPW* 3:572). This anti-sectarian principle explains Milton's resistance to the Westminster Assembly of

---

[42] For a supporting view, see Raymond B. Waddington, "A Musical Source for *L'Allegro?*", *MQ* 27.2 (1993): pp. 72–74. For a very different view, see Stephen M. Buhler, "Counterpoint and Controversy: Milton and the Critiques of Polyphonic Music," *Milton Studies* 36 (1998): pp. 18–40.

[43] See Mueller, "Embodying Glory," pp. 23–25; John R. Knott, Jr., "'Suffering for Truths sake': Milton and Martyrdom," in Loewenstein and Turner (eds.), *Politics, Poetics, and Hermeneutics*, pp. 153–70; and Margaret Justice Dean, "Choosing Death: Adam's Temptation to Martyrdom in *Paradise Lost*," *Milton Studies* 46 (2007): pp. 30–56.

[44] On Puritan "leadings," see Smith, *Perfection Proclaimed*, pp. 15, 17, ff.

Divines, for in *Eikonoklastes*, as in *Areopagitica*, he consistently demands public, not private or "selective," demonstrations of truth:

> For if we be sure we are in the right, and doe not hold the truth guiltily, ...
> [or] condemn not our own weak and frivolous teaching, and the people for an
> untaught and irreligious gadding rout, what can be more fair, then when a man
> judicious, learned, and of a conscience, for ought we know, as good as theirs that
> taught us what know, ... openly by writing publish to the world what his opinion
> is, what his reasons, and wherefore that which is now thought cannot be sound.
> (*CPW* 2:547–48)

To further distinguish this freedom from sectarian versions of Christian liberty, Milton adds that urging teachers or preachers to go "privily from house to house, ... is more dangerous" then pre-publication censorship, for even "Christ urg'd it ... to justifie himself, that he preacht in publick." While private preaching may not be illegitimate, strong Protestants should prefer the written word, since print "is more publick then preaching; and more easie to refutation, if need be, there being so many whose businesse and profession meerly it is, to be the champions of Truth" (*CPW* 2:548). A clearer defense of the public sphere or of public rationality was never offered by any Puritan but Walwyn, whose thought was becoming increasingly secular during this time.

In contrast, Puritan Root-and-Branchers like Thomas Wilson firmly maintained that "a pious mans greatest care is that ... vile persons that speake villany, may have their mouthes stopped[,] ... that *the purity of discipline, ... very necessary to the condition of the Church*, may be introduced."[45] William Dell believed that neither open debate nor human reason, but only the "gift of the spirit, without human learning," could save the church, and even Roger Williams placed an enormous gulf between the principles of Christianity and public civility: the "world lies in wickedness, is alike a wilderness, or a sea of wild beasts innumerable, fornicators, covetous, idolaters, &c; with whom God's people may lawfully converse and cohabit ..., else they must not live in the world." Yet even this "worldly conversation" is more or less nominal, since "outward peace and plenty of all things, of increase ... of honour, of health, of success, of victory, suits not temporally" with the "spiritual and soul-blessedness" of the godly.[46]

By contrast, greater civility and progress in public discussion was precisely what men like Milton, Robinson, and Parker strove to achieve, in part because they felt that publicly debated religion would also "make the people more zealous for liberty, and Liberty would impower the people the better to defend Religion."[47] With the

---

[45]   Thomas Wilson, *Davids Zeale for Zion* (London, 1641), pp. 14–15.

[46]   William Dell, *Way of True Peace*, in Woodhouse (ed.), *Puritanism and Liberty*, p. 313; and Roger Williams, *The Bloody Tenant of Persecution* (1644), in *Puritanism and Liberty*, pp. 268–69, 290.

[47]   Henry Parker, *Scotlands holy war* (London, 1651), p. 16.

Baconians of the Hartlib circle and with John Wilkins, they also believed that "those in 'search of Truth' must 'preserve a Philosophical Liberty' ... to make impartial inquiries."[48] Kahn places Milton in this category since he was one of the "happy few" who recognized that skepticism usefully enlarged rather than contracted the sphere of "things indifferent" in public life. Rejecting the "usual puritan position" on the *adiaphora* where "'nothing is indifferent,'" he embraces a semi-secular sphere where almost everything is indifferent (*CPW* 2:563).[49] Ernest Sirluck puts this conclusion somewhat differently, but generally agrees that Milton boldly "jeopardized the persuasiveness of the doctrine of Christian liberty (received by all, however variously interpreted) by attempting to extend the scope of indifferency to areas which few would think indifferent." Distinguishing between the divines of the Westminster Assembly and the general populace, he portrays "a liberty-loving nation" whose free-born language and love of learning rejects timorous restraints on intellectual and personal freedom (Sirluck, *CPW* 2:170, 175).

Milton's *Commonplace Book* entry "Of Religion. To what extent it concerns the state" reveals that at least some of these ideas are drawn directly from Machiavelli and Dante and not from the skeptical Baconians alone. The entry begins by noting that "among the most excellent of mortals are those who instruct the minds of men in true religion, more excellent even than those who have founded, however well, kingdoms and republics by man-made laws. Machiavel, discors Book 1.c[hapter] 10." Yet those who combine "ecclesiastical and political government (when, that is to say, the magistrate acts as minister of the Church and the minister of the Church acts as magistrate)" destroy "both religion and the State," as Machiavelli's countryman Dante "shows in his Purgatorio. Canto. 16." Thus "the opinions of men concerning religion should be free in a republic, or indeed under good princes. While Machiavelli praises such princes, he says, among other good things, that under them you will see golden times, 'where each man can hold and defend the opinion he wishes.' discors Book 1. c[hapter] 10" (*CPW* 1:475–77). Although the *Commonplace Book* is undated, these ideas or similar ideas are already adumbrated in the antiprelatical tracts, which similarly make ecclesiastical and religious reform the precondition of both civil virtue and liberty.

---

[48]   Barbara Shapiro, *John Wilkins 1614–1672: An Intellectual Biography* (Berkeley, 1969), p. 55.

[49]   Kahn, *Machiavellian Rhetoric*, pp. 169, 171; on Saltmarsh and Dell's similar sounding but ultimately very different uses of this rhetoric, see pp. 152–53. Lord Brooke comes closer to Milton's objection to bishops who cynically bound "up the Peoples *Liberty* ... with the chaines [of] *Indifferency*." See Robert Greville, Lord Brooke, *A Discourse opening the nature of episcopacy* (1642), in Haller (ed.), *Tracts on Liberty*, vol. 2, p. 59.

Baconian Prophecy in the Early Poems

Although Milton's "prophetic," if postdated, 1645 headnote to *Lycidas* is usually linked to his "church-outing" remarks, neither need be regarded as deliberately deceptive even though neither can be literally true. The new headnote (absent from the poem's 1638 version) famously glosses St. Peter's apocalyptic diatribe against false shepherds as foretelling "the ruin of our corrupted clergy then in their height." It thereby presents the poet foreseeing the triumph of a newly popular cause at a time when the 1644 trial and 1645 execution of Laud had already confirmed its victory. Yet in Milton's era, the word "prophecy" was often used in the broad sense of "testimony" or participation in a debate to be judged from its results. Shakespeare's history plays show that "prophecy" could also refer to completely naturalistic insights into where human motives and methods will ultimately lead.[50] The young Milton's refusal to "subscribe slave" to Chappell no doubt gave him sufficient insight into clerical tyranny to intuit its ultimately ruinous results, and he very probably debated the state of the church and the nation with friends like Alexander Gil the younger and Edward King, who held mixed Laudian and reformist sympathies. *Lycidas* pays tribute to the mixed sentiments he partially shared by ceremoniously imagining his deceased friend participating in a heavenly "communion" as all "the sweet Societies / That sing, and singing in their glory move, / And wipe the tears for ever from his eyes" (179–81). Milton's scorn for those who failed to share his budding interest in educational and ecclesiological reform surfaces in a letter to Gil before reappearing in the famous digression in *Lycidas* and again in the "spleen" of his antiprelatical tracts.[51] Significantly, this spleen most frequently erupts during discussions of scholastic logic and divinity, university subjects which he despised and which provided further stumbling blocks to his projected clerical career. His alienation from fellow ministerial students no doubt increased after King's premature death, an obvious reminder to seek a more suitable vocation before it was too late.

This abrupt, and for his father disappointing, change of course seems to have significantly coincided with his early "conversion" to the Baconian faction at the university. Either promoted or produced by his inveterate hostility to scholasticism, "custom, and antiquity," it continues through his antiprelatical tracts and beyond. This hostility probably deepened his dislike of Puritan theology, since godly divines from Perkins onward relied heavily on scholastic methods and logic to argue their theological points; the "liberal" John Goodwin was certainly no exception to this rule.[52] Puritan traditionalism in these subjects thus seems to be

---

[50] See, for instance, *Henry IV part 2*, which repeatedly refers to prophecy in this sense.

[51] On Milton and Hall's contrast with the Smectymnuans in this respect, see Knott, *Sword*, pp. 106–10, which provides a useful bibliography of earlier explanations.

[52] Coffey, *John Goodwin*, pp. 33–34. On Puritan scholasticism generally, see Miller, *New England Mind*, pp. 100–108 and Westfall, "Isaac Newton."

one factor in the stultifying university atmosphere he protested both early and late. Milton's Baconian cast of mind is later evident in his mature defenses of the regicide, for although these required careful attention to historical precedent, Zagorin finds him consistently avoiding "arguments founded on the idealization and normativity of the past." As "his frequently expressed contempt of custom showed, ... [he] was apt to view the history of earlier centuries as filled with errors and superstition."[53] These attitudes explain both his angry treatment of precedent in his divorce tracts and his failure to appeal to the "Ancient Constitution" in his anti-monarchical prose, which commonly rely upon rationally accessible laws of God and nature which (as his Abdiel later puts it) always "bid the same." Of course, Milton does cite Hebraic and Roman precedent, but usually to confirm an underlying law of nature superior to both. Throughout his career, as Mueller remarks, he is keenly aware that even the best times, men, and writings of the church have been "dangerously adulterated" (*CPW* 1:549), and pristine purity may be an illusion even in Eden.[54]

In a particularly frank letter of 1628 to Gil (whose own clerical career was soon to be cut short by academic treachery), Milton lamented that his fellow students are "almost completely unskilled and unlearned in Philology and Philosophy alike," from which they "flutter off to Theology unfledged, quite content to touch that also most lightly, learning barely enough for sticking together a short harangue by any method whatever and patching it with worn-out pieces from various sources— a practice carried far enough to make one fear that the priestly Ignorance of a former age may gradually attack our Clergy" (*CPW* 1:314). Years later, in his final confrontation with Hall and son, his low opinion of his alma mater led him to retort that the humble "suburb wherein I dwell, shall be in my account a more honourable place then his University. Which as in the time of her better health, and mine owne younger judgement, I never greatly admir'd, so now much lesse" (*CPW* 1:885). Yet, unlike the Puritans who abandoned the establishment's merely "notional" or "discoursive knowledge" to find a more direct spiritual experience or "taste" of the divine Word, Milton obviously resented the fact that he could find "almost no intellectual companions among them."[55] The letter to Gil also shows him deciding against returning to London—already a hotbed of Puritan activity—in favor of "a deeply Literary leisure ... hiding as it were in the Cloisters of the Muses" (*CPW* 1:314). In all these letters—including his 1628 letter to his Puritan tutor Thomas Young—the ambitious student's natural aversion to the sloth and ignorance as well as the more mundane aspirations of the clergy turns him toward all the muses *except* scholastic divinity, to which he seems to have been as naturally allergic as Bacon himself. These attitudes are already well developed

---

[53]   Zagorin, *Milton*, p. 83. Essentially the same political outlook was shared by Parker; see Jordan, *Men of Substance*, p. 161. Campbell and Corns support Zagorin's assessment in *John Milton*, p. 356.

[54]   See Mueller, "Embodying Glory," p. 24.

[55]   On the contrasting Puritan response, see Nuttall, *Holy Spirit*, pp. 34–61.

in his academic *Prolusions* (1625?–1628) and in *Of Reformation*, which eagerly
anticipate the removal of those "Scholastick, and pusillanimous upstarts," the
prelates. Their exile will liberate both "the Common, and Civill *Lawes* ..., the
former from the controule, the other from the meere vassalage and *Copy-hold* of
the *Clergie*" (*CPW* 1:601). This anti-scholastic zeal burns ever brighter in later
antiprelatical tracts, which directly trace the schoolmen's "unprofitable questions,
and barbarous sophistry" to both clerical and educational corruption. All England's
"noble atchievments" have been diminished by these "unskillful... monks and
mechanicks"(*CPW* 1:677, 812; cf. 923).

Instead of pursuing these "unprofitable" methods, Milton tells Diodati only
two months before completing *Lycidas* that (to borrow Bacon's famous phrase)
he intends to make "all knowledge his province" and achieve "an immortality of
fame."[56] He finds his "Pegasus" already "growing wings and practising flight"
toward what God "has instilled into me, if into anyone, a vehement love of the
beautiful" (*CPW* 1:327, 326). He was then reading deeply in the "real" opposed to
the "monkish" history of European civilization, and by the time he was officially
employed by Parliament, Milton had already begun his *History of Britain*. As he
promised, this work replaces monkish miraculism and providentialism with an
increasingly naturalistic account of the role of "ordinary" rather than "extraordinary
providence" in human affairs.[57] His letter to Diodati also stresses his overriding
concern with the loss or attainment of civic liberty, beginning with "the affairs of
the Greeks to the time when they ceased to be Greeks," and proceeding from "the
obscure history of the Italians under the Longobards, Franks, and Germans, to the
time when liberty was granted them." He particularly studies "what each State
did by its own Effort," and wherever he finds "anyone who, despising the warped
judgment of the public, dares to feel and speak and be that which the greatest
wisdom throughout all ages has taught to be best, I shall cling to him immediately
from a kind of necessity." Even if "by nature or by my fate" he fails to emulate that
noble example, Milton knows that "neither men nor Gods forbid me to reverence
and honor those who have attained that glory or who are successfully aspiring to
it" (*CPW* 1:327). These lines suggest the birth of a historian/poet deeply imbued
with the ideology of classical republican *virtù*, not Puritan piety.

Milton's growing aspirations also seem to have been a major factor in his
quarrel with Chappell. Leo Miller speculates that it was precipitated by the entry
of Isaac Dorislaus into a "musty and stagnant atmosphere" dominated by Chappell,
Thomas Bainbridge (Vice-chancellor of Christ's), and Joseph Mede (its chief
Fellow). The last of these wrote a famous apocalyptic commentary that may have
impressed the young Milton, but Mede fit a fairly standard academic mold and
refused Hartlib and Dury's request to assist their Baconian reforms. In contrast,
Dorislaus filled a chair proposed by Bacon and financed by Fulke Greville, the

---

[56] On the equal applicability of the phrase to Milton, see *CPW* 1:354.

[57] See von Maltzahn, *Milton's "History,"* p. 89; his study also details classical
republican influences on Milton's anti-clericalism.

predecessor of the Lord Brooke eulogized in *Areopagitica* along with Bacon and Selden. In this position, Dorislaus gave radically new lectures on the historical roots of classical and modern liberty that probably stimulated Milton's studies. In his sixth and most public Prolusion, he already adopts the name of the Roman republican so often extolled in Dorislaus's lectures, "Junius Brutus."[58] Later, both men defended the regicides, and *Eikonoklastes* uses Dorislaus's assassination as a prime example of the King's perfidy (*CPW* 3:577–78 n. 26). Milton himself relates no specific cause of his quarrel with Chappell but defiantly tells Diodati:

> At present I feel no concern about returning to the sedgy Cam and I am troubled by no nostalgia for my former quarters there ... How wretchedly suited that place is to the worshippers of Phoebus! It is disgusting to be constantly subjected to the threats of a rough tutor and to other indignities which my spirit cannot endure ... I have no objection to the name or to the lot of a fugitive and I am glad to take advantage of my banishment ... free to be dedicated to the quiet Muses. (*Elegia Prima*, 11–12, 14–16, 19–20, 25).

Given these reflections on his "rough tutor," Miller plausibly identifies Milton's third Cambridge Prolusion, *An Attack on the Scholastic Philosophy*, as the spark igniting the quarrel with his staunchly Aristotelian mentor. Cleverly invoking Aristotle only to support Bacon, the Prolusion would have provoked Chappell by describing scholastic methods as "inane and petty squabbling." Afterward, and quite probably as a punishment, Milton was required to perform perfunctory scholastic exercises explaining two Aristotelian "laws" that his great epic would definitively reject: (1) that nothing can be dissolved back into "First Matter," and (2) that there are no "partial forms."[59] After his sequestration, he returned to Cambridge, was assigned a new tutor of decidedly Arminian leanings, and in the final and "finest of [all] the *Prolusions*," produced a Baconian "Praise of Knowledge" closely based on *The Advancement of Learning* (*CPW* 1:287).[60] This final "revenge" suggests that Milton may have considered himself "church-outed" more by the prevailing status quo at Cambridge than by the Laudian prelates themselves. It also prefigures the enormous sense of relief suggested in Milton's "Letter to a Friend" after leaving the university. Although *Ad Patrem* expresses regret at disappointing his father, his letter to the unnamed friend frankly admits that his "Love of Learning" would soon "spoyle all the patience of a Parish." It also adds that he is anxious that his gifts "be quickly diverted from the emptie & fantastick chase of shadows & notions to the solid good flowing from due & tymely obedience" to his calling (*CPW* 1:320–21), but it admits no anxiety about disappointing God. *Ad Patrem*

---

[58] Miller, "Milton's Clash," pp. 85, 84. For a different reading of Milton's relation to Mede, see John Rumrich, "Mead and Milton," *MQ* 20.4 (1986): pp. 136–41.

[59] Miller, "Milton's Clash," p. 81.

[60] The new tutor was Nathaniel Tovey, whose Laudianism, as Campbell and Corns show in *John Milton*, caused him to be deprived of his position in the 1640s (p. 40).

reechoes his secular motives by assuring his earthly father that "however humble my present place in the company of learned men, I shall sit with the ivy and laurel of a victor. I shall no longer mingle unknown with the dull rabble and my walk shall be far from the sight of profane eyes" (*Ad Patrem*, Hughes 101–4). The same theme reappears in *Lycidas*, where he subtly tells "his Cambridge contemporaries why the role of poet-prophet transcends even the honorable role of poet-pastor" to which the dead Edward King had aspired.[61] Later, mindful of the Baconian bias against an inactive life of contemplation yet without a secure epic subject in hand, Milton gleefully exposed the "inquisitorius and tyrannical duncery" of prelates who permitted "no free and splendid wit ... [to] flourish" (*CPW* 1:820).

The personal note is in *Animadversions* unmistakable; Milton bitterly resented a university regime whose

> divinity is moulded and bred up in the beggarly, and brutish hopes of a fat
> Prebendary, Deanery, or Bishoprick, which poore and low pitch't desires, if they
> doe but mix with those other heavenly intentions that draw a man to this study,
> it is justly expected they should bring forth a baseborn issue of Divinity like that
> of those imperfect, and putrid creatures that receive a crawling life from two
> most unlike procreants the Sun, and mudde. And in matters of Religion, there
> is not anything more intollerable, then a learned foole, or a learned Hypocrite,
> ... sowing the World with nice, and idle questions and with much toyle, and
> difficulty wading to his auditors up to the eyebrows in deep shallows that wet
> not the instep. (*CPW* 1:720)

Like St. Peter's diatribe in *Lycidas*, this outburst essentially continues Milton's controversy with his tutor by other means. As late as 1654 Chappell still believed that Milton "well deserved to have been [turned] both out of the University and out of the society of men."[62] No doubt with Chappell in mind, Milton insisted that it is bad enough that "the Universities, that men looke should be fountaines of learning and knowledge, have been poyson'd and choak'd" by "wooden, illiterate, or contemptible" divines, but even worse that their "lazinesse, ... Tavern-hunting, ... neglect of all sound literature, and ... liking of doltish and monasticall Schoolemen daily increase" (*CPW* 1:718) and defeat all hope of progress. As the Yale editor Rudolf Kirk notes, here again Milton's antipathy to custom and antiquity indicates an "attitude toward the ancients ... at one with the thought of Bacon and the [future] Royal Society"; he has already entered the "Battle of the Ancients and Moderns" on the modern side (*CPW* 1:700 n. 9).[63] For in Milton's

---

[61]   Stella Revard, *Milton and the Tangles of Naera's Hair* (Columbia, MO, 1997), p. 204.

[62]   See Gordon Campbell, *A Milton Chronology* (Basingstoke, 1997), p. 153, quoting John Bramhall, who apparently cites Chappell himself.

[63]   On the Ancients' battle with the Moderns and the Moderns' characteristic debunking of the "Giants," see Richard Foster Jones, *Ancients and Moderns* (St. Louis, MO, 1936).

view, devotion to the Ancients (chiefly, the Aristotelians) explains why truth is no longer the daughter of time: "Custome without Truth is but agednesse of Error" (*CPW* 1:561). Paraphrasing Bacon (*Works* 4:15), he declares that time has become a river that sinks solid matter while useless flotsam rises to the top (*CPW* 1:626). Thus the task at hand is to use "all the helps of Learning" to revive the "transparent streams of divine Truth" (*CPW* 1:568, 569). A similar Baconian figure appears in *Areopagitica*, where Milton significantly confuses it with scripture: "Truth is compar'd in Scripture to a streaming fountain; if her waters flow not in a perpetuall progression, they sick'n into a muddy pool of conformity and tradition" (*CPW* 2:543). Milton's editors can find no precise biblical reference here (*CPW* 2:543 n. 194), so the more likely source is again Bacon's *Great Instauration:* by failing "to seek their knowledge at the fountain" men do "great detriment" to truth, for, "knowledge being as water," it "will not rise above the level from which it fell" (*Works* 4:16).[64]

This vision further explains Milton's savage attack on Hall's anti-utopian satire, *Mundus Alter et Idem*, which predicts that the new age of discovery will merely repeat the same foibles and vulgar passions as the old (*CPW* 1:881). *Areopagitica* is often misconstrued as taking a similarly anti-utopian perspective because it objects to "sequester[ing] out of the world into *Atlantick* and *Eutopian* polities" (*CPW* 2:526). Yet that was actually the point of Bacon's *New Atlantis*: his utopian community may have profited from its isolation for a time, but his narrative ends with them actively "opening" their knowledge to all of Europe. A more astute reading of both works shows that Milton resented not only Hall's satire of Bacon but also one of his favorite subjects, the "geographical knowledge exemplified in a work like Heylyn's *Microcosmus* (1621)." Often considered an early influence on the poet, this work was (according to Paul Salzman) a "typical example of the comprehensive geographical description available in the seventeenth century." It was also an embodiment of Milton's Baconian theory of history, since it insists that "History without Geographie like a dead carkassse hath neither life nor motion at all."[65] Setting Hall right on these points, Milton also bitterly accuses him of distorting Bacon's views on the church.

The same views later underpin many of *Areopagitica*'s major arguments, a fact still unjustly overlooked by most critics. A few, like Stanley Fish, early recognized Milton's ample use of Baconian imagery but drew an anachronistically firm line between theology and science.[66] Yet Bacon's language is itself scriptural and

---

[64]   The parallel is loose but far closer than the verse from Psalms 85:11 cited by the Yale editors: "Truth shall spring out of the earth."

[65]   Paul Salzman, "Narrative Contexts for Bacon's *New Atlantis*," in Price (ed.), *Francis Bacon's New Atlantis*, pp. 28–47 cited pp. 34–35; Peter Heylyn, *Microcosmus* (Oxford, 1621), p. 11. On Milton's use of the new "synthetic" geography in *Paradise Lost*, see Chapter 6 below.

[66]   Stanley E. Fish, *Self-Consuming Artifacts: The Experience of Seventeenth-Century Literature* (Berkeley, 1972), pp. 88 n. 11, 152–53. For a correction, see my book chapter,

(especially) pastoral: "I bear myself soberly and profitably, sowing in the meantime for future ages the seeds of a purer truth" (*Works* 4:104). Organically "wound" into threads or "life-lines" like Ariadne's thread, Bacon's "seeds" turn into ideas, and then into books that are not commodities to be traded but organic "skeins or bottoms of thread which may be unwinded at large when they are wanted" (*Works* 4:472). *The Doctrine and Discipline of Divorce* uses the same Ariadnean image when it promises to wind the human race "out this labyrinth of servitude" into the "light" of rational liberty (*CPW* 2:240). *Areopagitica* even more strikingly repeats Bacon's insistence that silencing or "killing" words "of a ventrous edge" does a disservice to "every knowing person alive." Not a commodity "to be monopoliz'd" (*CPW* 2:534, 535), Bacon saw truth as ever alive and "growing":

> the images of men's wits and knowledges remain in books, exempted from the wrong of time and capable of perpetual renovation. Neither are they fitly to be called images, because they generate still, can cast their seeds in the minds of others, provoking and causing infinite actions and opinions in succeeding ages … that whatsoever motions the spirit of man could act and perform without the organs of the body … might remain after death. (*Works* 3:318)

Areopagitica paraphrases this passage almost verbatim, adding only some poetic flourishes:

> For Books are not absolutely dead things, but doe contain a potencie of life in them to be as active as that soule was whose progeny they are; nay they do preserve as in a violl the purest efficacie and extraction of that living intellect that bred them. I know they are as lively, and as vigorously productive, as those fabulous Dragons teeth; and being sown up and down, may chance to spring up armed men … [;]as good almost kill a Man as kill a good Book … the pretious life-blood of a master spirit, imbalm'd and treasur'd up on purpose to a life beyond life. (*CPW* 2:492, 493)

Bacon's gentler seeds may not turn into Milton's "dragon's teeth," the "pretious life-blood" both of their author and the body politic, but Milton here also recalls Parker's use of the Cadmus myth for the same polemical purpose: to show that multiple branches of "knowledge in the making" are essential to "the reforming of Reformation itself" (*CPW* 2:554, 553).[67]

"The Feminine Birth of the Mind: Regendering the Empirical Subject in Bacon and His Followers," in Julie R. Solomon and Catherine G. Martin (eds.), *Francis Bacon and the Refiguring of Early Modern Thought* (Aldershot, 2005), pp. 69–88.

[67] On Milton's reference to Henry Parker, see Nigel Smith, "*Areopagitica*, Voicing Contexts 1643–5," in Loewenstein and Turners (eds.), *Politics, Poetics, and Hermeneutics*, pp. 103–22; on Parker himself, pp. 109–10.

Bacon had long held that the new frontier belongs to those who refuse to let "a few received authors stand up like Hercules' Columns, beyond which there should be no sailing or discovering." By venturing beyond them, the heroes of the future will reap an "amplitude of reward, ... soundness of direction, and ... [fruitful] conjunction of labours" (*Works* 3:321–22). Referring to this famous image, Milton condemns those who would "stop up all our hav'ns and ports" from "the importation of our richest Marchandize, Truth" (*CPW* 2:548), the only proper "seed" for England's "pregnant soile." As a nation always "prone to seek after knowledge," studying, "musing, searching, revolving new notions and idea's," and "as fast reading, trying all things" as "the force of reason and convincement" allows (*CPW* 2:554), England must follow the example of Bacon and his fellow workers in the field, chiefly Selden and the second Lord Brooke, Robert Greville (*CPW* 2:513, 534, 542, 560–61). Championing a speculative, provisional attitude toward truth, Greville had praised "that learned wit, Sir Francis Bacon" for abandoning scholastic logic and its search for final "causes to those, who are content, with Icarus, to burn their wings at a fire too hot for them."[68] Milton in turn proclaims Brooke a "martyr" in the cause of toleration, and like Selden, he also abandoned sterile scholastic disputation. "By exquisite reasons and theorems almost mathematically demonstrative," Selden proved that "all opinions, yea errors, known, read, and collated, are of main service & assistance toward the speedy attainment of what is truest" (*CPW* 2:513).[69] Milton agrees with them and with Bacon that experiment or "triall ... by what is contrary" (*CPW* 2:515) is the key to progress, and he also supports *The Advancement of Learning*'s claim that a catalogue of popular errors would prove conducive to truth. Selden had already demonstrated that, by accumulating facts on both sides of a question, "the balance turned of itself to advance a distinct opinion"; he is also the most probable source of Milton's understanding of "heresy" in its root sense of "opinion."[70]

Selden of course epitomized the "politique" or secular type of reformer who joined the Root and Branch movement, but Robinson is another important influence on *Areopagitica*. He had recently argued that God "spares not these erronious beleevers or hereticks that they might seduce and pervert the faithfull, for that is impossible, but that the faithfull might in due time reduce the misbeleevers unto the truth."[71] John Goodwin held some similar opinions (*CPW* 2: 561–62 n. 266), although he hardly concurred that heresy had "the positive merit of stimulating the vitality and animating the evangelic strength of the church," whose errors could not be vanquished unless they were "'with all possible freedome examined and debated" alongside "'the most acknowledged truths themselves.'" Since "what

---

68   Robert Greville, Lord Brooke, *The Nature of Truth* (1640), pp. 125–26.

69   Milton refers to the preface of Selden's *De Jure Naturali et Gentium juxta Disciplinam Ebraeorum* (1640), which is cited at length in *CPW* 2:513 n. 95.

70   Masson, *Life*, vol. 1, pp. 524, 525.

71   Henry Robinson, *Liberty of Conscience* (1644), p. 12, in Haller (ed.), *Tracts on Liberty*, vol. 3, p. 128.

one man, church or nation takes to be truth, another perhaps accounts no lesse then heresie," for Robinson anyone might become a Miltonic "heretic in the truth" without carefully examining conflicting opinion. Puritans, however, understood heresy very differently, largely as any major variation from their core Calvinist beliefs. Even Goodwin falls into this category, for as Ernest Sirluck observes, his type of "Independency is perfect in its hatred of heresy, diligent in its pursuit, and relentless in its excommunication when persuasion fails," although it liberally rejects using the civil sword against it (*CPW* 2:113). Robinson instead realized that even this "liberal" position too often masked an "ill-defined and frequently malicious" means of quelling the opposition; heresy has been the "convenient excuse of sect after sect that has sought nothing else than its own aggrandizement under the spurious claim" of righteousness.[72] No sectarian himself, Robinson nevertheless believed that the growth of the sects could be beneficial if rightly understood as a sign of religious vitality subject to future correction and refinement. In the meantime, "all such as shall propound their thoughts touching any part of the discipline and doctrine of Gods worship and mans salvation" should not only be tolerated but encouraged, "though they seem never so strange and novel."[73]

Like most members of Hartlib's circle, Robinson also agreed with Bacon that, as Herschel Baker summarizes, "man's sensory knowledge is prone to error, but such as it is it suffices, if properly disciplined, to attain at least limited truth." Investing in limited as opposed to certain truth, they all sought probable knowledge and rejected ideas derived "deductively from innate moral or metaphysical principles in the human mind." Since all intellectual systems are fallible and "deductive systems can never command universal assent," tentative truths are "entertained as 'hypotheses' rather than paths to a 'comprehensive, scientifical, and satisfactory knowledge of the works of nature,'" as Locke later put it.[74] *Areopagitica* advocates an early version of Lockean method when it states that "To be still searching what we know not, by what we know, still closing up truth to truth as we find it (for all her body is *homogeneal*, and proportionall) this is the golden rule in *Theology* as well as in Arithmetick" (*CPW* 2:551). Milton's "homogeneal" knowledge is thus no more unitary or comprehensive than his Temple of Truth; both require

> many dissections made in the quarry and in the timber ... And when every stone is laid artfully together, it cannot be united into a continuity, it can but be contiguous in this world; neither can every peece of the building be of one form; nay rather the perfection consists in this, that out of many moderat varieties ... not vastly disproportionall arises the goodly and the gracefull symmetry that commends the whole pile and structure. (*CPW* 2:555)

---

[72]   Robinson, *Some few considerations* (London, 1646), p. 7, summarized and quoted in Jordan, *Men of Substance*, pp. 115, 116.

[73]   Robinson, pref. to *John the Baptist* (London, 1644).

[74]   Baker, *Wars*, p. 184.

The same logic applies to religious truth:

> if the men be erroneous who appear to be the leading schismaticks, what witholds
> us but our sloth, our self-will, and distrust in the right cause, ... that we debate
> not and examin the matter throughly with liberall and frequent audience; if not
> for their sakes, yet for our own? (*CPW* 2:567)

This language may be far from "scientific," but Bacon's prophetic trumpeting of
the new science was equally visionary:

> I conceive that I perform the office of a true priest of the sense (from which all
> knowledge in nature must be sought, unless men mean to go mad) and a not
> unskillful interpreter of its oracles; and that while others only profess to uphold
> and cultivate the sense I do so in fact. (*Works* 4:26)

Bacon's "oracles" are of course classically ambiguous: they can only be read
by encouraging doubt and examining error, literally "sifting" fact from fiction.
Thus, rather than "raising a capitol or pyramid to the pride of man," they lay "a
foundation in the human understanding for a holy temple after the model of the
world" that we may never complete (*Works* 4:106–7).

W.K. Jordan shows that Robinson skillfully used this Baconian concept of
"positive" doubt to advance the cause of toleration, to reject both "an exclusive
church based upon a complete and infallible body of truth," and all who would
"fasten a yoake of their owne doctrine and opinions on others." "Godly" oppressors
such as these are actually "the most ignorant, absurd, presumptuous, and the
greatest enemies both to God and man of any people under heaven." Jordan further
observes that "this wholly individualistic philosophy was of course in flat denial
of the organic conception of truth to which most Englishmen still lent lip service
and which underlay the strong conviction that some ordered national church must
replace the episcopal establishment."[75] Selden's pioneering work in the science
of comparative religion is equally distant from this outlook and, like Milton and
Brooke, he preferred the language of citizens to that of saints. His Greek motto
was "in all things, above all things, Liberty," and liberty required the collaborative
recovery of learning "from the time before ... [it] had become encrusted" with
error.[76] Brooke similarly proposed that we will "improve in what we know" by
acknowledging that truth is "one, onely bearing different shapes." All thus rejected
the operation of irresistible revelation, for, as *Areopagitica* similarly affirms,
Truth "may have more shapes then one" (*CPW* 2:563).[77] Though Brooke's death

---

[75]   Jordan, *Men of Substance*, pp. 94, and Henry Robinson, *An answer to Mr. William
Prynn's Twelve Questions concerning Church Government, etc.* (London, 1644), pp. 4–5.

[76]   Jason Rosenblatt, *Torah and Law in "Paradise Lost"* (Princeton, 1994), p. 80.

[77]   Greville, *Nature of Truth*, p. 126. Cf. "truth which is but one, doth variegate it selfe,
and take divers shapes" (p. 104).

was accidental, not truly self-sacrificial, Milton imagines that his anti-dogmatic "meeknes and ... charity" made him as a symbolic "saint" of toleration. For by teaching Protestants "to hear with patience and humility those ... that desire to live purely" according to "the best guidance of their conscience," he showed how "to tolerat" all, "though in some disconformity to our selves" (*CPW* 2:561).[78]

However, of all these role models, only Bacon could have influenced St. Peter's "prophetic" outburst against the authoritarian example set by the prelates in *Lycidas*.[79] The first draft of Milton's elegy can be securely dated to late 1637, but Brooke's work, *The Nature of Truth*, and Selden's seminal study of natural law, *De Jure Naturali et Gentium*, both appeared after the poem's 1638 publication. In 1637, however, Bacon's 1589 *Advertisement Touching the Controversies of the Church of England* was not only available to Milton, but there can be no doubt that it deeply influenced him. He explicitly cites it five times: once in his *Commonplace Book*, once in *Animadversions*, once in *An Apology against a Pamphlet*, and twice in *Areopagitica* (*CPW* 1:450, 668, 882; and *CPW* 2:534, 542).[80] Printed in 1640 as *A Wise and Moderate Discourse* (*Works* 8:74–95), it supplies unusually satisfactory

---

[78] Greville's *Discourse Opening the Nature of ... Episcopacie* was printed later in 1641 or 1642, and George Whiting ("Milton and Lord Brooke on the Church") believes that Brooke borrowed from Milton, and, to some extent, vice versa.

[79] Campbell and Corns conclude that "there is nothing recognizably puritan in the poem's attack on ecclesiastical failures," noting that its hero, Edward King, "was not remotely an oppositional figure," though Milton's unease with the establishment is real. See *John Milton*, p. 99.

[80] As Spedding notes (*Works* 8:74–95), the *Advertisement* originally circulated only in manuscript; he was not able to determine the number of manuscripts or the names of those possessing them (p. 73). However, it seems quite likely that Bacon would have shown this manuscript to his own chaplain, Edward Franklin, who had been a tutor at Cambridge until at least late 1623 and quite possibly later; Milton entered in 1625. On Franklin, see Harris Francis Fletcher, *The Intellectual Development of John Milton* (2 vols., Urbana, IL, 1961), vol. 2, p. 29. Bacon had planned to return to Cambridge after being deprived of office and made many arrangements for his move, although it was never completed. Another possible possessor of a manuscript version is that great Baconian proselytizer, Samuel Hartlib, who was certainly given at least one of Bacon's unpublished documents by Sir Christopher Hatton in the late 1630s; see Tyacke, "Science and Religion," p. 92. Milton's earliest reference to Bacon's *Advertisement* occurs in his *Commonplace Book*, whose entries are undated, but scholars agree that the earliest of these entries predates the composition of *Lycidas*. See James Holly Hanford, "The Chronology of Milton's Private Studies," *PMLA* 36.2 (1921): pp. 251–314, a useful essay that unfortunately contradicts itself by placing Milton's note on Bacon's text both before 1640 *and* after it, when the *Advertisement* appeared as *A Wise and Moderate Discourse* (p. 276 n. 111). Hanford also confuses the *Advertisement* with *Certaine Considerations*, but shows that it clearly influenced Milton's ideas on the freedom of the press (pp. 300–301). Whiting notes, in *Milton's Literary Milieu*, that his knowledge of both Bacon's *Advertisement* and his treatise, *Certaine Considerations*, clearly precedes his pamphlet war with Hall (pp. 268–69) since he mentions Bacon "independently of any reference... by Hall" (p. 269).

answers to heretofore unanswered questions about St. Peter's notorious "two-handed engine": why Milton links it to St. Peter, why it stands at a door, and what the engine and the door together symbolize. Earlier solutions to this famous literary puzzle have only deepened the crux. If, as one group of interpreters insists, the engine is the two-handed sword of Revelation or Psalms, why is it not named as such, and why does it stand at a door? If, as another group insists, it refers to St. Peter's keys, why should keys that unlock doors become weapons that "smite once, and smite no more" (*Lycidas*, 131)? Swords or axes cut, and keys open or shut, but Milton's peculiar "engine" does both.

The best way to unmix these metaphors is by returning to the passage of the *Advertisement* that it radically condenses. Here Bacon denounces tyrannous teachers who

> carry not an equal hand in teaching the people their lawful liberty, as well as their restraints and their prohibitions; but they think a man cannot go too far in that that hath a show of commandment. They forget that there are *sins on the right hand, as well as on the left;* and that *the word is double-edged*, and cutteth on both sides, as well the superstitious observances as the profane transgressions. Who doubteth but it is as unlawful to shut where God hath opened, as to open where God hath shut? to bind where God hath loosed, as to loose where God hath bound? (*Works* 8:92)

All the elements contained in Milton's famous passage coexist here along with an explicit warning to those who forget that the two-edged power of the Word will smite *all* extremists with both the right and the left hand. As in Protestantism generally, this two-handed Word is synonymous with the "sword of the spirit" in the Pauline armor of God, biblical truth. Yet since Bacon refers to the *combined* power of the word/sword, he leads Milton to think of it as an "engine" which, through its Latin root, *ingenium*, conveys the multiple senses of mental power or genius and insemination or inspiration. The multiple senses of the word *engine* also appear in the Tacitean aphorism that Milton so often cites from Bacon: "*punitis ingeniis gliscit auctoritas.*" *Areopagitica* translates this as "*The punishing of wits enhaunces their autority*" (*CPW* 2:542). Both senses of *ingenium*—"wit" or "inspiration"—accurately describe St. Peter's "two-handed engine," which may also open or shut, loose or bind, smite the wicked or restore the saints. Laud's *jure divino* clergy believed that they held this power on earth as in heaven, but both Bacon's *Advertisement* and *Lycidas* reject this teaching by considering that power an exclusively heavenly "engine" abused by the corrupt clergy who would unlawfully "shut where God hath opened, ... [or] open where God hath shut." As a result, much like the "*forbidd'n writing*" they seek to repress, the engine retroactively ignites a "*spark of truth that flies up in the faces of them who seeke to tread it out*" (*CPW* 2:542, quoting Bacon's *Advertisement*, *Works* 8:78). Foreseeing this recoil, Milton's St. Peter sternly shakes his "Mitred locks" (*Lycidas*, 112) at the shepherds who would use the "door" or gate of salvation for mere earthly gain, not for truly heavenly or inspirational power. In contrast, true or "witty" ministers like Lycidas at once hear "the unexpressive nuptial song" in heaven (176) and remain on earth as a Virgilian "Genius of the shore," a guide to all who "wander in that perilous flood" (183, 185)—a double, even quasi-sacramental apotheosis strikingly different from Puritan "election."

Milton's reliance on Bacon's *Advertisement* also explains the most mysterious if also most unasked question about the passage: if in 1638 Milton did not believe that St. Peter sanctioned the episcopal tradition, why is his saint wearing a bishop's "mitred" hat? The answer seems to be that, like Bacon, who condemns both the idolatrous "tyranny" of the bishops (*Works* 8:87–90) *and* the precisionism of the Puritans, the young poet takes aim at everyone who would inhibit liberty of conscience on the right or the left. Thus, while the engine is properly two-handed in the grip of the true *episcopos* or overseer (as bishop literally means), only the heavenly St. Peter has the right to condemn extremists on either side of the controversy. From an earthly perspective, then, the only legitimate use of the engine is to wield the two-handed sword of free thought "indifferently," so free speech can generate (as *ingenium* also implies) probable truths until the balance falls where it should. Of course, like Bacon's, Milton's approach to these problems is hardly nonpartisan. Emphasizing that "*Injuries come from them that have the upper hand*," that is, from the established Church (*Works* 8:88), Bacon faulted the bishops for "standing so precisely upon altering nothing," when "the good husbandman is ever ... stirring in his vineyard or field." Moreover, since all legalistic solutions to problems of conscience are bound to fail (*Works* 8:87–88), Bacon rejects both their stance and that of Puritans who would judge the *adiaphora* or "things indifferent" too strictly. He thus foresees the very issue that will prompt the first Bishops' War and incite Milton's pamphlet attacks upon Hall: not "things indifferent," which pose no real threat to salvation, but episcopal abuse of and tyranny over the flock.[81]

Bacon's second, equally unheeded advice to James on the subject of church reform proved equally central to the young poet's thought. First published in 1604 and reprinted twice in 1640, this second treatise, *Certaine Considerations Touching the Better Pacification and Edification of the Church of England*, took an even more liberal position than the earlier one. At once reasserting the reformed emphasis on teaching as opposed to sacrifice, and recommending the role of ministers as opposed to priests, Bacon here condemns the two corruptions most odious to educational reformers like Milton, non-residency and plurality: "That men should live of the flocke that they doe not feede, or at the Altar at which they doe not serve, is a thing that can hardly receive just defence."[82] After his death,

---

[81] Lord Brooke argued that, since no man and no church could fairly decide what another man's conscience might or might not approve, the episcopal "adiaphora" were a contradiction in terms. Milton did not reject Presbyterianism as early as Brooke.

[82] Wolfe, *CPW* 1:26, and Bacon, *Certaine Considerations Touching the Better Pacification and Edification of the Church of England*, in Charles R. Gillet (ed.), *Catalogue*

these words would seem even more prophetic, and Milton's St. Peter would put the case even more strongly:[83]

> Blind mouths! That scarce themselves know how to hold
> A Sheep-hook, or have learn'd aught else the least
> That to the faithful Herdman's art belongs!
> What recks it them? What need they? They are sped;
> And when they list, their lean and flashy songs
> Grate on their scrannel Pipes of wretched straw.
> The hungry Sheep look up, and are not fed,
> But swoln with wind, and the rank mist they draw,
> Rot inwardly, and foul contagion spread.
>
> (*Lycidas*, 119–27)

Since the bishops are false "seers" with large bellies (114), like the allegorical Death of *Paradise Lost*, they are doomed to become all mouth or "maw" without eyes: "blind mouths" who creep into the fold to pillage, waste, and devour, not to shepherd and "see." And since, unlike true shepherds, these wolves in sheep's clothing know no arts of Pan, they play no panpipes but blow upon wretchedly hollow straw. Finally, since their flock can draw no nourishment from mere straw, like Dante's ignorant sheep, they are swollen with "wind" caused by the false sustenance of false shepherds who share their digestive "rot" (*Paradisio* 29, 106–7; Hughes 123 nn. 126–27).

Joining humanist critics like Dante, Bacon always insists that the authentic leader, *buccinator* or "trumpeter" of the new order should adopt the opposite role. He "must not only continually draw his strength from encounters with the utterly novel, but he must never allow his identity to slip … into the encumbrances of the past." Thus, as Charles Whitney adds, Bacon characteristically displaces the court of "authority … from ideas founded, built, molded and reformed in a continuous and cumulative tradition, to ideas arising, changing, and developing or passing away in consciousness undetermined by tradition."[84] His radically reformist notions not only synthesize spiritual and secular horizons of change, but in regarding the unceasing "trials" or changes of the church in a wholly positive, non-sinful light, anticipate Milton and Robinson:

---

of the McAlpin Collection of British History and Theology (5 vols., New York, 1927–30), vol. 1, pp. 21–22.

[83]   Bacon also seems to have foreseen the very situation Milton protests in "On the New Forcers of Conscience"; many of the bishops' opponents were motivated by mercenary aims, and they impugned them only "to have the spoil of their endowments and livings" (*Works* 8:90).

[84]   Charles Whitney, *Francis Bacon and Modernity* (New Haven, 1986), pp. 85, 89, 90.

as it is the condition of the church militant to be ever under trials, so it cometh to
pass that when the fiery trial of persecution ceaseth there succeedeth another trial,
which as it were by contrary blasts of doctrine doth sift and winnow men's faith,
and proveth them whether they know God aright, even as that other of afflictions
discovereth whether they love him better than the world. (*Works* 8:74)

Here, as in *Areopagitica*, the reformed soul or true Psyche must ceaselessly "cull
out," winnow, and sift the "confused seeds" of truth. For, even if "all the windes
of doctrin were let loose to play upon the earth," Truth will only more effectively
"grapple" with and overcome Falshood in a "free and open encounter" (*CPW*
2:514, 561).[85] In the process, reformed "truth" retains its providential horizon but
sheds its closed theocratic design, so like the swain of *Lycidas*, it finds closure
only in continually opening toward "pastures new." No wonder, then, that not only
Milton's antiprelatical tracts but his rousing defense of toleration were ignored
by the godly brethren, most of whom (as he himself suspected) never bothered
to read the divorce tracts that they branded as heretical.[86] In their aftermath, he
no longer bothered to cast his arguments for the elimination of press censorship
and religious intolerance in the sermonizing rhetoric of the godly. Beginning with
The Reason of Church Government, but even more obviously in *Areopagitica*,
he replaces their vocabulary of spirit, conscience, and the gathered church with
images of free trade and the unlimited commerce of ideas.[87] Shedding his centrist
hopes, he clings ever closer to Bacon's vision of the true leader as an entirely new
kind of prophet who must reason, guide, and, at times, prod his sheep into ever
steeper pastures of truth.

---

[85]   On Robinson's similar ideas, see Jordan, *Men of Substance*, pp. 128, 136. In
Mammon's Music, Blair Hoxby notes that these similarities are based on the analogy of
expanding free exchange and equilibrium over time (pp. 26–27, 34–35) drawn from a
common Baconian context (pp. 31–56) partially shared by Joseph Mede (p. 31), who was a
millenarian but definitely not a Puritan.

[86]   Haller concedes his failure to confirm Masson's belief that Milton's pamphlets
played an important place in the Puritan discussions of 1644 in Appendix B, "Milton's
Reputation and Influence, 1643–1647," in *Tracts on Liberty*, vol. 1, pp. 28–39. Von
Maltzahn adds that "It has been suggested that because Milton 'wrote prose like a poet'
that he was especially effective as a 'rabble rouser,'" but the evidence points to the fact that
apart from his much later anti-monarchical tracts, he had little popular influence (although
he definitely influenced the Hartlib circle). See "Samuel Butler's Milton," p. 489.

[87]   See Smith, "*Areopagitica*," pp. 105, 108, 115. On Milton's economic advocacy of
free trade from *The Reason of Church Government* through *The Readie and Easie Way*, see
Hoxby, *Mammon's Music*, pp. 25–56, 77–90, 234, 237.

Chapter 4

The Humanist Ethics, Metaphysics, and Aesthetics of Milton's Spenserian Masque

Not so diligently is Ceres, according to the Fables, said to have sought her daughter Proserpina, as I seek for this idea of the beautiful, as if for some glorious image, through all the shapes and forms of things ("for many are the shapes of things divine"): day and night I search and follow its lead eagerly.

—Milton to Diodati, 1637

Despite Milton's purported hostility to the "politics of mirth," his first major work, a masque or festive "aristocratic entertainment," was frequently and successfully produced well into the eighteenth century. The current consensus that *Comus* is a "Puritan masque" thus overlooks the many paradoxes involved in this characterization: why should a "festive" Puritan production survive long after Puritanism had become widely unpopular, and why do its metaphysics, ethics, and aesthetics all seem so pointedly unpuritan?[1] Neither its richly sensuous poetics, its monist metaphysics, nor its humanist ethics seems to support the current view, which has turned a Spenserian morality play into a thinly disguised anti-Laudianism protest. Of course, as the previous chapters show, anti-Laudianism was never an exclusively Puritan position, but masques in particular fall outside of Puritanism altogether. Godly objections go far beyond the genre's links to the court and include most of the facets included in *Comus*: women dancers and singers, exotic settings and risqué costumes (including, in this case, bestial heads on human bodies). Although William Prynne's *Histriomastix* (1633) vitriolically attacked all these aspects of masquing on the very eve of *Comus*'s first production

---

[1]   See Leah S. Marcus, who situates "Milton's Anti-Laudian Masque" in the context of the Puritan critique of holiday mirth in *The Politics of Mirth: Jonson, Herrick, Milton, Marvell, and the Defense of Old Holiday Pastime* (Chicago, 1986), 169–212. Other prominent defenders of this view include Maryann Cale McGuire, *Milton's Puritan Masque* (Athens, GA, 1983); Guibbory, *Ceremony and Community*; and Barbara K. Lewalski, "Milton's *Comus* and the Politics of Masquing," in David Bevington and Peter Holbrook (eds.), *The Politics of the Stuart Court Masque* (Cambridge, 1998), pp. 296–320. On the masque's broader social context, see Cedric C. Brown, *Milton's Aristocratic Entertainments* (Cambridge, 1985), and on its eighteenth-century popularity, see Don-John Dugas, "'Such Heav'n-Taught Numbers should be more than read': *Comus* and Milton's Reputation in Mid-Eighteenth-Century England" *Milton Studies* 34 (1996): pp. 137–57.

(1634), it concedes no ground to his complaints and, according to a minority view, may have been partly written to protest Prynne's ultra-conservative but by no mean anomalous Puritan attack. Milton never changed his pro-theatrical stance; he approved three more productions of the masque in his lifetime (1637, 1645, and 1673) and used his penultimate antiprelatical tract (1642) to protest the Puritan closing of the public theaters in September of that year.[2] His earlier tract, *Animadversions*, also placed Spenser's *Shepheardes Calender* in a reformist context at a time when his poetics was more often associated with courtly or elaborately "visual" style than with word-centered critiques.

Contrasting "the divine gift of learning" and its "spacious art" with the bishops' "lean and flashy songs," as *Lycidas* calls them (123), *Animadversions* also alludes to Spenser when it asserts that any "cleare spirit nurst up" to temperance would never trade these divine gifts for the whole "den of *Plutus*, or the cave of *Mammon*" (*CPW* 1:719). The exclusively material "gifts" offered by the Laudians are thus implicitly juxtaposed to the devout "love of the beautiful" Milton shared with his friend Charles Diodati. His letter of 1637 emphasizes that this beauty takes many forms—ethical, spiritual, and philosophical—a fact already apparent from his 1634 masque. Spenser's celebration of temperance and chastity is obviously central to its ethical theme, but Bacon's practice of accepting even the wildest fable as a potential "shape" of truth or beauty is another important ingredient in its aesthetic and philosophical myth-making. Three fables in Bacon's *Wisdom of the Ancients* are particularly relevant: "Prosperina, or Spirit," "The Sirens, or Pleasure," and "Orpheus, or Philosophy." According to Bacon, the myth of the sirens teaches that the "search for the beautiful" may be easily distinguished from the illicit passions that inhibit the soul or spirit. Since "meditations on things divine excel the pleasures of the sense, not in power only but in sweetness," spiritual beauty easily overcomes sensual charm (*Works* 6:764). The myth of Orpheus supports this truism not only through his musical conquest of bestial natures but also because Orpheus surpassed Ulysses himself in resisting the sirens. Although Ulysses remained "unshaken ... in the steep-down paths of pleasures," he needed to stop his ears to prevent the weaker sailors' "pernicious counsels and flatteries" from infecting him. As the union of divine and human philosophy, Orpheus needed no such device: he simply overcame the sirens by "singing and sounding forth the praises of the gods" (*Works* 6:764). Here, as in Milton's masque, divine harmony at once exposes and quells the "dissonance" of hedonist delight because higher pleasures naturally triumph over lower ones. Rather than drugging or lulling "the sense" in the "pleasing slumber" of spiritual forgetfulness, divine beauty purges it of the "sweet madness" of illicit desire, and, as Comus himself testifies, instills "such a sacred and home-felt delight, / Such sober certainty of waking bliss, / I never heard till now" (*A Mask*, 260–64).

---

[2]   Burbery, *Milton the Dramatist*, pp. 32–34. Besides Burbery (33), Ethyn Kirby proposes that *Comus* mounts a protest against Prynne, an argument also entertained by William R. Parker, who cites Kirby in *Milton: The Life* (Oxford, 1968), p. 337.

This ethic is later fully developed in *Areopagitica*, which argues that true virtue is won only by experiencing and resisting, not by avoiding or "censoring" dangerous temptations or tempters. It further shows that the allegorical meaning behind the Lady's trial derives from Book II of *The Faerie Queene*: "cloister'd vertue" cannot make anyone chaste any more than locking up Mammon's gold can make him less covetous. In fact, subjecting "all objects of lust" to "the severest discipline that can be exercis'd in any hermitage" cannot make anyone good (*CPW* 2:515, 527). Yet at this very time, Puritan converts like George Wither found it necessary to renounce even the milder temptations presented by Spenser's "pastoral and satiric guises." Richard Helgerson points out that, while Milton may already have been dissatisfied with the Laudians' antiquated liturgy, his response was quite different; he joined the Caroline "sons of Orpheus" in diligently seeking a higher "harmony" that would support the cause of reform.[3] David Sedley similarly finds Milton adopting and refining Neoplatonic and other courtly motifs as ingredients in what will later become his grand style, while John Hollander adds that the young poet seems to be looking both backward and forward: he looks back to a time when "the harmony of word and sound" had not been soured by the approaching culture wars, and forward to a future whose horizons remain ever open and renewable.[4] As the letter to Diodati further shows, long before he became an ecclesiastical reformer Milton was already intent on reforming poetry. *Comus* does this by at once adopting and implicitly critiquing the excessively visual, Neoplatonic rhetoric of earlier courtly masques, which tended to support both Laudian ritual and Stuart divine right theory.[5] It thus employs a morally instructive version of the visual effects, stage machinery, and exotic fairyland scenes common to other masques. John Creaser finds these devices apparent both in the masque's explicit stage directions and the "vice-regal" setting it creates for its occasion, the Earl of Bridgewater's inauguration as Lord President of Wales and the Marches.[6]

Leah Marcus, the most influential defender to date of the idea that Milton wrote a "Puritan masque," also agrees that the poem at times seems to stage a visual and "liturgical pageant." Pointedly employing scriptural references typically cited against the godly (Mark 2:23–28), it plainly alludes to traditional holidays like the harvest festival of St. Michael, the occasion of its first performance. In

---

[3] See Helgerson, *Self-Crowned Laureates*, pp. 276, 262–63, 268–69.

[4] David Sedley, *Sublimity*, pp. 82–107, and John Hollander, *The Untuning of the Sky: Idea of Music in English Poetry 1500–1700* (Princeton, 1961), pp. 330–31. See also Helgerson above, and Graham Parry, who takes the minority position that Milton's 1645 volume of verse reflects a positive engagement with Caroline aesthetic values: "There is much pastoral writing of a kind fashionable at court," and Milton frequently "appears sympathetic to a ceremonious Anglicanism." Parry, *The Seventeenth Century* (London, 1989), p. 83.

[5] See Kahn, *Machiavellian Rhetoric*, pp. 196–97.

[6] John Creaser, "'The present aid of this occasion': The Setting of *Comus*," in. David Lindley (ed.), *The Court Masque* (Manchester, 1984), pp. 111–34, cited p. 113.

fact, the masque's lack of any anti-ceremonial or anti-symbolic orientation is so obvious that Marcus believes that drawing "a simple equation between the court of Comus and the court of Charles I would be recklessly facile." In the end, however, she does see its villain as an upholder of "organized religious authority" and its heroine as the representative of Laud's Puritan opponents.[7] The vast majority of Milton scholars now side with some version of this thesis, although, unlike other major reevaluations in the scholarship, the turn toward a "Puritan masque" has occurred without a struggle.[8] Despite Milton's own word on the subject and Dryden's confirmation that the humanist Spenser was his "Great Original," this debt is no longer generally accepted.[9] Even Milton's public tribute to Spenser as a supreme ethical teacher is commonly disregarded, in part because *Areopagitica* misrepresents some details of the Cave of Mammon episode. These and other objections have allowed critics not only to overlook the Lady's Spenserian/ Arminian defense of free will but also to turn her somewhat conventional devotion to chastity into a thoroughly Puritan ethics of abstinence.[10] Her would-be seducer, Comus, thereby becomes the representative of everything that Puritans most detested in the Caroline court: its self-indulgent aestheticism, its Laudian bishops, and its reissue of James I's *Book of Sports*.

Of course, since Milton later joined the national outcry against most of these abuses seven years later, it seems only logical to suppose that he was already a thorough-going anti-Laudian in 1634—or so the reasoning goes. Marcus justifies these assumptions by stressing later jurisdictional conflicts between the masque's sponsor, the Earl of Bridgewater, and Archbishop Laud. Yet at the time of its production, Bridgewater's close friend Attorney General William Noy was working closely with Laud on republishing King James's *Book of Sports*. Bridgewater himself would later reject Laud's Arminian theology, but as an ecclesiastically moderate Royalist, he never rejected established ritual or holiday mirth.[11] As for his poet, he received much honor from its aristocratic audience, its royalist musician Henry Lawes, and later from the royal ambassador, Henry Wotton, who praised it highly and happily supplied Milton letters of introduction for his European tour. Milton's willingness to take the oaths of allegiance to the Thirty-nine Articles of

---

[7]   Marcus, *Politics of Mirth*, pp. 177, 201–2, 193, 195.

[8]   Major exceptions to this rule are Maureen Quilligan, *Milton's Spenser: The Politics of Reading* (Ithaca, NY, 1983), and John M. Steadman, *Moral Fiction in Milton and Spenser* (Columbia, MO, 1995).

[9]   For an especially spirited argument against Milton's debt to Spenser, see Annabel Patterson, "Couples, Canons, and the Uncouth: Spenser-and-Milton," in *Reading between the Lines* (Madison, WI, 1993), pp. 36–56.

[10]   William and Malleville Haller first made this identification in "'Hail Wedded Love,'" *ELH* 13 (1946): pp. 79–97. On their errors, see Halkett, *Milton*, pp. 5–7.

[11]   Marcus, *Politics of Mirth*, pp. 174, 172. Marcus admits her contention that "Bridgewater was unaware of" Charles's support for Laud's "innovations" at the time is not supported by civil war historians (p. 297 n. 14).

the Church required upon receiving his B.A. and M.A. degrees in 1629 and 1632 also suggests that in 1634 he may have been at least relatively comfortable with the liturgical context of the Anglican church, as Marcus concedes.[12] Perhaps still hoping to restore the broader toleration he identified with the earlier church, he showed little or no interest in "precisian" issues like sabbatarianism even *after* he joined the Root and Branch movement.[13] His antiprelatical tracts regard the *Book of Sports* not as an example of Laudian sacrilege but rather of episcopal tyranny, which erred chiefly in enforcing recreations that might otherwise provide "eloquent and gracefull inticements to the love and practice of justice, temperance and fortitude" (*CPW* 1:819; cf. 1:588). As the previous chapter shows, Milton also never registered any hostility to human eloquence or theatricality.

Puritans, on the other hand, notoriously feared not just traditional "papist" symbols and ceremonies but an enormous range of symbolic representations: court festivities, country games, masques, maypoles, and morrises, all of which they considered "palpable occasions of sin" and (where applicable) "profanations of the Sabbath." They particularly resisted the sophisticated pastoralism of Queen Henrietta's court entertainments, which Neoplatonically idealized her as a type of the Virgin Mary or of "pure" Platonic beauty and love.[14] The stricter sort, men like Prynne, bluntly accused both queen and court of profanely seeking the spirit in sensual "matter." Yet Milton's portrait of Alice Egerton, Bridgewater's "Lady" daughter, ironically draws on nearly every element of the courtly style, even boldly featuring her exquisite singing ability at a time when aristocratic young ladies rarely joined in such potentially "scandalous" public exhibitions. Milton's villain, Comus, is indeed far more courtly, ceremonious, and elitist than the Lady, but her strictures against empty ceremonies and rituals are again more Baconian than Puritan. Bacon's popular *Wisdom of the Ages* interpreted the myth of Prometheus as teaching that religious or cultic "pollution" stems from the treacherous human tendency to substitute the "solid meat" of sound teaching with "dry and bare bones" disguised to resemble "a fair and noble" sacrifice. Referring to Prometheus's attempt to deprive Jove of his proper rites or "portion," Bacon likens his feigned or "boney" sacrifice to the "external and empty rites and ceremonies with which men overload and inflate the service of religion: things rather got up for ostentation than conducing to piety." Thus where "the truly religious man" offers up the "wholesome and useful meat" of charity, strong "affection," and

---

[12] Marcus, *Politics of Mirth*, p. 177.

[13] Lewalski, *Life*, p. 4.

[14] Lewalski, "Milton's *Comus*," p. 297. Lewalski resolves the apparent paradox of Milton's involvement with the form by supporting Marcus's contention that his familial legacy of Puritanism (which is dubious at best) naturally supported the Earl's nascent anti-Laudianism, but this solution fails to explain the masque's Arminian ethics and ceremonial aesthetics. On this point, see Creaser, "'The present aid,'" p. 117, which also explains the historical basis of the mistaken idea that the Bridgewater family had Puritan leanings (pp. 116–18).

burning zeal "for the glory of God," the religious hypocrite is like a Promethean trickster. He not only performs ceremonial "mockeries to God" but pretends that this is what he has commanded even though his true prophets repeatedly warn against it ("Prometheus," *Works* 6:750–51).

Milton's *Of Reformation* later takes up this critique in nearly identical language: the Laudians' "over-bodying" of the spirit of worship substitutes hypocritical, irrational, and empty ceremonies for the wholesome "meat" of Christian teaching. Forsaking both God's will and his "quickning power," their idolatry "under the name of *humility*" confines worship to the "upper skin, and there harden[s] into a crust of Formallitie" (*CPW* 1:522). Yet Milton never entirely rejects "the office of the senses as an aid to faith and worship" (*CPW* 1:522 n. 12), as the tract's Yale editor (Wolfe) assumes; in fact, his protests are filled with the sensuous imagery of Baconian and Spenserian allegory. One passage even portrays Milton and his countrymen as new Redcrosse Knights taking up the sword of "*Divine* and *Humane Learning*" to finish the work of reformation. Striking off the "huge overshadowing traine of *Error*," their fatal "blow" for truth makes her disgorge all that the "settled Night of *Ignorance* and *Antichristian Tyranny*" has swallowed and frees the "Christian Common-wealth" to pursue "true wisdom and vertue" (*CPW* 1:524–25, 571; cf. *FQ* I.i.18–24).[15] A less violent and more "Orphic" plot governs the Egerton children's symbolic victory over Comus: divine and human learning join forces in the Lady's song, which protects her from Comus's ethical and spiritual corruption. Yet knight-like, she succeeds by combining Sir Guyon's temperance with Britomart's chastity in order to overthrow Comus's anti-Christian tyranny. That tyranny consists mainly in the "idolatrous" or Promethean acquisitiveness that Milton later associated with the prelates and the amoral mirth he condemned in their "Poetasters." The Lady's main weapon against them is the twinned power that "At a Solemn Music" associates with Voice and Verse, a quasi-physical union of sensual with sensible song. The power of these "blest" twins (1–4) can transcend life and death much as the Lady can create "a soul / Under the ribs of Death" (*A Mask*, 561–62). Hence, like *L'Allegro* and *Il Penseroso*, they are not actually the logical contraries they seem but polar powers meant to be synthetically joined. Annabel Patterson traces this type of mythic configuration to the second book of Spenser's *Faerie Queene*, and Patricia Vicari agrees that *Comus* is one of its prime descendants, since it uses a similar "Neoplatonic–Lucretian–Orphic" mythos "to show the controlling place of love and fertility

---

[15] Wolfe's interpretation is also invalidated by *Paradise Lost*, where the angels, Adam, and Eve all worship God in highly sensuous hymns of praise. Their worship even follows the traditional cycle of matins and vespers, and includes ceremonious bowing in prayer (*PL* 5.144–45). Significantly, the Puritan refusal to bow at the name of Jesus is shared only by Milton's Satan. Annabel Patterson similarly notes the Spenserian language of the antiprelatical tracts in "Civic Hero." Spenser's epic (abbreviated *FQ*) is cited here and below by book, canto, and stanza number from *Edmund Spenser, "The Faerie Queene,"* ed. A.C. Hamilton [rev. edn.] (Harlow, 2007).

in the cosmos."[16] Its Attendant Spirit and Sabrina, respectively a heavenly and a fertility spirit, are the masque's main synthetic contraries, for while the former can exorcize Comus, the two together are needed to release the Lady from his enchanted chair. The villain's powers are equally dialectical since they combine the deceptive powers of Bacon's sirens and his Prometheus, although, as we will see, he also unites the temptations offered by Spenser's Mammon, the "god of this world" and Phaedria, his spirit of amoral mirth.

From a more strictly Miltonic perspective, the plot of *Comus* can be compared to that of *Paradise Regained*, yet even this similarity confirms its Spenserian basis. A conventional gloss on Guyon's "trial" in the Cave of Mammon identifies it with the three temptations that Christ experienced in the wilderness: "bread" or material comfort, including "world[ly] blis," or "riches" (*FQ* II.vii.32–33); all the kingdoms of the earth; and the temple or "pinnacle" of godlike power.[17] Milton's "steel-clad" Lady faces the same three temptations as Comus first offers her food and drink more powerful than the famous potion of *Nepenthes* (*A Mask*, 421–675); his kingdom's vast dominion and glory if she consents to be his queen; and the opportunity to "boast" the secret of her godlike power, the holy "flame" or "high mystery" contained in her "sage / And serious doctrine of Virginity" (785–87). She wisely seals her lips in his presence much as Milton's Son refuses to prove his godlike power at the temple, yet her abstinence also recalls Guyon's refusal to "taste" any of Mammon's "gifts." Both protagonists employ a form of self-restraint that the mythical Proserpina lacked, although Guyon's escape from his "Hades" is more specifically linked to his awareness that he will become Mammon's permanent "pray"

> If euer couetous hand, or lustfull eye,
> Or lips he layd on thing, that likte him best,
> Or euer sleepe his eie strings did vntye.

> (*FQ* II.vii.27)

Guyon's self-reliant, essentially Arminian ethic anticipates Jeremy Taylor's later reflections on human self-sufficiency and survival not just despite, but actually *through*, evil. Perhaps recalling *Areopagitica*, Taylor's *Ductor Dubitantium* or "rule of conscience" (1660) affirms that "the avoiding of evil is neither good nor bad unless by a positive act of will. It is what we do against evil, not our avoiding of it, that makes us virtuous." Calvinists typically regarded Taylor's

---

[16]   Annabel Patterson, "*L'Allegro, Il Penseroso* and *Comus*: The Logic of Recombination," *MQ* 9.3 (1975): pp. 75–79; Patricia Vicari, "The Triumph of Art, the Triumph of Death: Orpheus in Spenser and Milton," in John Warden (ed.), *Orpheus: The Metamorphoses of a Myth* (Toronto, 1982), pp. 207–30, cited p. 218.

[17]   James Nohrnberg, "Paradise Regained by One Greater Man: Milton's Wisdom Epic as a Fable of Identity," in Eleanor Cook (ed.), *Centre and Labyrinth: Essays in Honour of Northrop Frye* (Toronto, 1983), pp. 83–114.

position as "intolerably optimistic and latitudinarian" because he claimed that Adam's Fall did not introduce a natural necessity of sinning.[18] "Liberty of choice" is here simply "part of the Divine plan for tempering human souls. Without it, ... actions [would be] pre-determined, [and] there would be no meaning or aim in the spiritual life." Thus for Taylor as for Milton, "difficulty" not only begets "virtue," but "liberty is the hand and fingers of the soul by which she picks and chooses; ... if she gathers flowers, she makes herself a garland of immortality."[19] The Lady's actions depict another version of this view of Christian liberty, since only through independent and unconstrained choice can she attain the "Golden Key" that opens the "Palace of Eternity" (*A Mask*, 13–14). *Comus* also anticipates Taylor's "rule of conscience" by demonstrating that true virtue must be active, not passive. As in *Areopagitica*, "blank" or "white-washed" idols of purity are not truly "clean," because real purity stems from the power to "see and know, and yet abstain" from Mammon's false "goods"; as Milton says, "our sage and serious Poet *Spencer* ... better teache[s] then *Scotus* or *Aquinas*" (*CPW* 2:515–16). This famous passage does misquote his "Great Original" when it claims that Guyon is assisted by his Palmer when he is actually alone. Yet Raymond Schoen plausibly interprets this misquotation as intentional, as a subtle but sure announcement of Milton's resistance to Puritan orthodoxy. By keeping his Palmer firmly by Guyon's side when they have actually been parted for several cantos, Milton shows his determination to prove the inseparability of Reason (symbolized by the Palmer) from free moral choice. This decision suggests that by 1644 Milton's virtue ethic was already more rationalistic than Spenser's "enlightened" synthesis of Christian Neoplatonism and Aristotelianism, although in Spenser, too, both virtue and vice lie in our own power.[20] According to Lewalski, Milton's version of this ethic first appears *Arcades*, which like *Comus* develops "a stance toward art and recreation that repudiates both courtly aesthetics and Puritan wholesale prohibitions. Associating this better aesthetics with the values of the virtuous Protestant aristocracy, Milton's entertainments seek both to confirm and to educate these noble families" in the values taught by Spenser and upheld by their common patron, the Dowager Countess of Derby.[21]

---

[18] Jeremy Taylor, *Ductor Dubitantium* (1660) in *The Whole Works of the Right Rev. Jeremy Taylor*, ed. Reginald Heber (12 vols., London, 1828), vol. 12, IV.I.I, pp. 17–18. The commentary is Baker's in *Wars*, p. 64.

[19] McAdoo, *Structure*, p. 44, and Taylor, *Ductor Dubitantium*, Book IV, Chap. I, rule I, 4.

[20] Raymond Schoen, "Milton and Spenser's Cave of Mammon Episode," *PQ* 54 (1975): pp. 684–89; and Sean Kane, *Spenser's Moral Allegory* (Toronto, 1989), pp. 17–19. Ernest Sirluck similarly shows that Milton is here less Aristotelian than Spenser because he is "less disposed to rely on the security of habit" and more on "active reasoning" (*CPW* 2:516 n. 108)

[21] Lewalski, "Milton's *Comus*," p. 297. On Milton's publisher and performers, see Helgerson, *Self-Crowned Laureates*, pp. 257–58.

Spenserian and Arminian versus Puritan Ethics

In Milton's masque, Providence or heavenly grace clearly supports the Lady's moral choices, but, as Thomas Corns reminds us, it actively aids only those striving for salvation "through a synergetic relationship." Hence the Lady and her brothers are not

> predestined to be saved but [must] achieve salvation through an active process: "some there be that by due steps aspire / To lay their just hands on that golden key / That opes the palace of eternity" (lines 12–14) ... [This] theory of salvation differs from that later *radical* Arminian doctrine in that it admits a role for external agencies, the role that Laudian Arminianism assigned to the church and clergy, and which is represented in *Comus* in part by the Attendant Spirit, in part by the Brothers, and perhaps most significantly by Sabrina[, whose] ... intervention is characterised by a powerful element of ceremonialism ... redolent of church sacraments.[22]

Corns's summary is entirely accurate, yet it somewhat understates the Lady's moral self-reliance in fending off the villain's "Savage heat." Before divine providence intervenes, the Elder Brother has assured the younger that her "Virtue could see to do what virtue would / By her own radiant light, though Sun and Moon / Were in the flat Sea sunk" (358, 373–75). This assurance not only turns out to be true, but his point is reemphasized as he answers his brother's doubts about the complete self-sufficiency of feminine virtue: their sister has a "hidden strength," which is not merely "the strength of Heav'n." Of course, she has "that too," but even "if Heav'n gave it," this strength "may be term'd her own," since it stems from her willing embrace of true chastity or virginity (415–20). Such virginity is neither simply a natural endowment, or condition of "intactness," nor a divine gift; it may be compared to classical temperance, which the masque's final song synthesizes with the cardinal Christian virtues of "*faith, ... patience, and ... truth*" confirmed through "*hard assays*" or trials (971, 972). These virtues are the diametrical opposites of "*sensual Folly and Intemperance*" (975), but not of holiday mirth.

This general line of thought emboldens Milton to replace the cardinal virtue of Christian charity with a semi-classical notion of "chastity" as charity to oneself and one's personal integrity (213–15). His antiprelatical tracts later describe his own vow of chastity in similar terms: it expressed a form of "self-esteem" or "honest haughtinesse ... of what I was, or what I might be, (which let envie call pride)" (*CPW* 1:890). As Joshua Scodel points out, this remark invents a "modern" concept of "self-esteem" almost two decades before any other contemporary even

---

22   Corns, "Milton before 'Lycidas,'" p. 34. For an exploration of why the monistic theology of *Paradise Lost* still requires ritual "vehicles" to mediate between the orders of grace and nature, see Catherine G. Martin, *The Ruins of Allegory: "Paradise Lost" and the Metamorphosis of Epic Convention* (Durham, NC, 1998).

mentions it. Completely at odds with the Puritan stress on both godly humiliation
and radical, unmerited grace, this ethical "invention" indicates Milton's "anti-
Calvinist commitment to human merit long before his unequivocal rejection of
the Calvinist doctrine of grace in his *De Doctrina Christiana*." [23] Traditionally,
of course, Milton's vow of chastity has been seen as evidence of his Puritanism,
but Scodel notes that this view jars with the broader context of the passage in
An Apology Against a Pamphlet. Closely echoing the earlier words of the Lady,
Milton asks that "rude eares be absent" from his explanation of his vow, since a
"grosse and shallow judgement, and withal and [*sic*] ungentle, and swainish brest"
can only misunderstand what "the noblest dispositions above other things in this
life have sometimes preferr'd." This "noble" preference is to combine the "good
and faire in one person," or the chaste with the comely "virtues" (*CPW* 1:889–90).
The masque's younger brother questions his sister's ability to do this, but the real
answer comes not from the Elder Brother but from the Lady herself.

Milton's beautiful but good Lady warns Comus that his rude and "swinish"
ear will prevent his "profane" Soul from understanding her answer, but even so,
her confident silence fills him with quaking and "shudd'ring" astonishment at the
force of her conviction (776, 781, 784, 802). As her Elder Brother had predicted:

> She that has that, is clad in complete steel,
> And like a quiver'd Nymph with Arrows keen
> May trace huge Forests and unharbor'd Heaths,
> Infamous Hills and sandy perilous wilds,
> Where through the sacred rays of Chastity,
> No savage fierce, Bandit or mountaineer
> Will dare to soil her Virgin purity:
> Yea there, where very desolation dwells,
> By grots and caverns shagg'd with horrid shades,
> She may pass on with unblench't majesty,
> Be it not done in pride or presumption.

(421–31)

"Pride or presumption" are indeed at once disarmed and redeemed by the Lady's
Diana-like "Virgin purity" and "modest" self-esteem, which protect her as she
wanders through the savage forest. Stoic ethics certainly inform this aspect of the
plot (as do the chaste loves of Dante and Petrarch cited in *An Apology*), but the
subtext is again Spenserian. Milton had been reading *The Faerie Queene* since

---

[23] See Scodel, *Excess and the Mean*, p. 271. Scodel believes that Milton "invented the
term 'self-esteem' as a positive alternative to such negative terms as 'self-love' and 'self-
regard,'" and shows that "his use of the term ... predates the first *OED* citation of 'self-
esteem' in a Catholic (!) meditational work of 1657" by fifteen years (p. 271). Milton's non-
or even anti-Calvinist ethical sources are Xenophon, Seneca, other Stoics, and probably
Ficino (pp. 255–74).

boyhood and rereading Spenser when he later wrote *An Apology* (*CPW* 1:857 n. 52), yet even less avid readers would easily recall Una's safety among the rude foresters and "wild men" in Book I of *The Faerie Queene* and Florimell's escape from the den of the witch's "sonne" in Book III (vii.7–17). In either case, the heroine's beauty, innate goodness, and acquired virtue surround her with steel-clad integrity and "unblench't majesty."

As in his later works, Milton's emphasis on acquired virtue overturns the central Calvinist doctrine of *sole fides* and upholds the Arminian position that man is *not* "justified by faith alone, but *by faith working through charity* Gal.v.6" (*De Doctrina, CPW* 6:490). Long before *De Doctrina, Of Education* (1644) similarly explains that charitable works are not the exclusive gift of grace but of virtue acquired through "good generall precepts ... furnisht ... distinctly with that act of reason which in [Aristotle's] *Ethics* is call'd *Proairesis*." As in *Areopagitica*, sound instruction and good character guide the free choice between "morall good and evill" (*Of Education, CPW* 2:396). This rational choice has little to do with the "passive emptiness" which in Puritan thought requires the irresistible "help" of the Spirit of Grace and spiritual milk "sucked" from the Puritan ministers of the Word.[24] It also flies in the face of William Twisse's Calvinist insistence that a complete separation between natural morality and all-redeeming grace must be maintained to avoid the "foul tayle [or untruth] of *Arminianisme*, in the doctrine of Election." For Calvinists, God's will, not the believer's, is so central to the redemptive process that grace never rewards foreseen merit, not "even obedience of faith, repentance, and good works."[25] Milton instead depicts divine providence rewarding both merit and works because he adheres not to Calvin's but to Hooker's God. And as Joan Bennett observes, this God designs "human as well as 'natural agents' ... to operate ecologically as well as individually" in a world not overruled by total depravity.[26] Like Robert Hoopes, a long line of scholars have found that Spenser's God similarly offers sufficient "prevenient or antecedent grace" to incline "the will to choose the good" rather than evil.[27] This teaching is especially evident in the final book of *The Faerie Queene*, where the "sweet tongued" Meliboe explains that, since "each hath his fortune in his breast," "the heauens" are not responsible for either "fortunes fault" *or* favor; only

---

[24]   See von Rohr, *Covenant*, pp. 67, 82, and Leverenz, *Language*, pp. 1–10.

[25]   William Twisse, *A Treatise of Mr. Cottons, Clearing Certaine Doubts Concerning Predestination. Together with an Examination thereof ...* (London, 1646), p. 46.

[26]   Bennett, *Reviving Liberty*, p. 14.

[27]   Hoopes, *Right Reason*, p. 156. On this point Hoopes cites Virgil K. Whitaker, *The Religious Basis of Spenser's Thought* (Palo Alto, 1950) and A.S.P. Woodhouse, "Nature and Grace in 'The Faerie Queene,'" *ELH* 16 (1949): pp. 194–228, and "The Argument of Milton's *Comus*," *UTQ* 11 (1941): pp. 46–71. More recently, John N. King argues that Spenser was not a Puritan (as his *Shepheardes Calendar* causes some modern critics to believe) but merely (like Milton in my view), a "progressive Protestant"; see *Spenser's Poetry and the Reformation Tradition* (Princeton, 1990), pp. 8–10, 28–29, 34–43,147, 187, 233–38.

the free choice of the unconstrained will and "the mynd ... maketh good or ill" (*FQ* VI.ix.29, 30). That choice in turn invites providential *assistance*, as shown when Milton's "*Meliboeus* old," the "soothest Shepherd that ere pip't on plains" (822–23), supplies the haemony that "supplementally" if not sacramentally allows the Lady's brothers to overcome Comus. Often understood as a figure for Spenser himself, Meliboeus and his "herb" reconcile the realms of nature and grace much as the central action in Book II does: by promoting the cooperation of individual effort, natural magic, and heavenly "help."[28]

In this "Legend of Temperaunce," Guyon relies on a highly similar synergy of moral effort, right reason (signified by his Palmer's return), and divine intervention, in his case figured through the combined intercession of his guardian angel and Prince Arthur. Arthur wields magical powers not unlike Sabrina's, yet like his other external helpers, he intervenes after—and only after—Guyon has successfully tested the natural limits of human virtue by reaching the mouth of Mammon's Cave on his own. The Lady's comparable success in single-handedly fending off Comus and the details of her subsequent release follow the same pattern: three separate kinds of helpers—human, heavenly, and natural/magical—reward her integrity under trial. In the process, she confirms Milton's Areopagitican claim that "the knowledge and survay of vice is in this world ... necessary to the constituting of human vertue, and ... the confirmation of truth" (*CPW* 2:516). He specifically links this moral to Spenser's temperate knight, who, like the Lady, teaches that "mortals" who willingly "love virtue" (which "alone is free") are not only rewarded but assisted, for if their "Virtue feeble were, / Heav'n itself would stoop to her" (*A Mask*, 1019, 1022–23). In contrast, Puritans like William Ames—for whom "Originall Sinne ... is the corruption of the whole man," including "the understanding, the conscience, the will, the affections of every kind"—believed that *only* grace can make the corrupt human "wil ... stoop to God's Will," as John Preston puts it. The human conscience on its own is at best a diseased "Remembrancer" and "false register" of divine law, so that without the Holy Spirit's all-encompassing protection, the "merely moral" man or woman is not only "rudderless" but effectively the same as the wicked.[29] Even moderates like Richard Baxter averred that "not onely the open profane, the swearer, the drunkard, and the enemies of godliness, ... will prove hurtful companions to us, though these indeed are to be chiefly avoided; but too frequent society with ... persons meerly civil and moral, whose conversation is empty and unedifying, may much divert our thoughts from heaven."[30]

---

[28] Woodhouse, "Nature and Grace," p. 211.

[29] See, *seriatim*, William Ames, *The Marrow of Sacred Divinity* (London, 1642), p. 50; John Preston, *A Liveles Life: Or, Mans Spirituall death in Sinne* 2 pts. (London [3rd ed.], 1635), p. 4; von Rohr's commentary on Ames in *Covenant*, p. 41; and Peter Lake, "'Charitable Christian Hatred,'" in Durstun and Eales (eds.), *Culture*, pp. 170–71.

[30] Richard Baxter, *The Saints Everlasting Rest* (London, 1650), p. 652.

Arminians like Lancelot Andrewes contradicted these views by affirming that, while Adam's Fall may have hurt, bruised, or soiled us, it has not killed us in the sense of destroying our will and our rational faculties. While man "is very far gone from original righteousness, … he is not an outlaw." This line of thought represents a turn away from Calvin and Augustine toward Aquinas, where, rather than a "natural" will toward evil, mankind instead retains a *positive* "inclination to act in accordance with the eternal law. For … sin does not destroy entirely the good of nature."[31] Milton's *De Doctrina Christiana* agrees: "A kind of gleam or glimmering" of "the unwritten law[,] … the law of nature given to the first man" remains in the hearts of all mankind (*CPW* 6:516). As a result, the human conscience *can* dutifully act as God's "Secretary" (*CPW* 1:822) or "Umpire" (*PL* 3.195). It may either willingly "stoop" to his just dictates or ask "Heaven" to "stoop to her." This belief is equally far from echoing the Antinomian desire for the "Holy Ghost … [to] come and take [the] place" of one's natural faculties and works.[32] Milton instead insists that all human actions must be completely "elective and unconstrain'd" (*CPW* 2:342), for his God desires no such "artificiall *Adam[s]*" or human "puppets" that could be so constrained (*CPW* 2:527). Refusing to make a "drudge of virtue" (*CPW* 2:342), the Almighty renews man's "lapsed powers" (*PL* 3.176) at the very moment he foresees his Fall. Susanne Woods further shows that, whenever Milton uses Calvinist terms like "elect," "elected," and "elective," they always refer to the proper exercise of free will guided by reason and conscience, not to irresistible grace. This vocabulary distinguishes him even from the Puritans to whom he was most sympathetic; unlike Sir Henry Vane, he never identified the godly as the sole safeguard or source of national virtue.[33]

By far the most notable difference between Milton's virtue ethics and Puritan morality, however, is that the godly never portray personal trial by "what is contrary" as an "ingredient of virtue." Puritans considered trial beneficial, but only in offering believers the humbling opportunity to experience a version of Christ's suffering for their sins. Rather than affirming a Spenserian or Miltonic ethic of "'comprehension and ascent,'" they valued trial principally as a means of humiliation, not as a means of moral self-improvement or instruction.[34] In Bunyan's *Pilgrim's Progress*, the trials Christian experiences on the "ascent" to the Celestial City thus fail to increase either his strength or his self-reliance as he goes along. He gains insights that may be valuable to others, but no preparation for his forthcoming trials, which are either unrelated or even *more* perilous as he

---

[31] St. Thomas is cited and paraphrased in McAdoo, *Caroline*, p. 17.

[32] Thomas Welde's *Rise, reign, and ruine* (London, 1644), p. 1, cited in Von Rohr, *Covenant*, p. 136.

[33] Susanne Woods, "Elective Poetics and Milton's Prose: *A Treatise of Civil Power* and *Considerations Touching the Likeliest Means to Remove Hirelings Out of the Church*," in Loewenstein and Turner (eds.), *Politics Poetics, and Hermeneutics*, pp. 193–211, cited pp. 196–97, p. 211 n. 17.

[34] Hoopes, *Right Reason*, p. 158, and Woodhouse, "Argument," p. 61.

proceeds toward his final justification by faith alone. The moral plots of Milton's *Comus* and *Paradise Regained* conversely show their protagonists' growing ease in refusing temptation after they have met the central "test" at the classical climax of the dramatic action. This contrast also illuminates the central difference between Miltonic and Puritan "voluntarism." In the Puritan view, all offences against God are equally soul-threatening, so "To do 'any of those things which God hath not commanded' would be, not an assertion, but a violation of Christian liberty."[35] This belief often empowered the saints to challenge social authority, yet with the possible exception of the Quakers, the godly remained ethically or religiously prescriptive throughout the period.[36] Milton's anti-authoritarianism is far more sweeping and secular because it replaces this prescriptive morality with just "self-esteem" balanced by Aristotelian temperance. Thus, like Spenser's but unlike Bunyan's, his moral fictions are open-ended: they refuse to impose "virtue on an ever-changing world" and reject all external regulation of desire as a false "myth of power."[37]

Milton's Spenserian Plot

Much like Milton's Lady, Spenser's temperate Guyon exhibits considerable natural immunity to the deceptive "lightness" of license, which he first shows in his encounter with Phaedria, the spirit of torpor and idleness who accosts him on his way to Mammon's Cave. His final encounter will be with Acrasia, who like Phaedria, Mammon, and the rest of her "family," promotes ease, indulgence, and the effortless, irresponsible exploitation of all material goods and honors. Besides these tempters, this family includes two male antagonists, Pyrochles and Cymochles, the "twin" sons of Acrates. As their lineage shows, they all represent not just misrule but anti-rule (a-kratos), the antithesis not just of temperance but also of heroic action. Like Acrasia's other literary prototypes—Ariosto's Alcyna, Tasso's Armida, and Homer's Circe—the antecedents of Milton's Comus and his mother Circe are all island or "inner-worldly" gods or goddesses of self-indulgence. Spenser most clearly spells out their ethical threat in the sixth and central canto of Book II, which defines the hardest and highest type of abstinence:

> A Harder lesson, to learne Continence
>   In ioyous pleasure, than in grieuous paine:
>   For sweetnesse doth allure the weaker sence
>   So strongly, that vneathes it can refraine

---

[35] Coolidge, *Pauline*, p. 26. Modern-day exponents of the Puritan tradition such as Iain H. Murray also support this conclusion; see *The Puritan Hope: A Study in Revival and the Interpretation of Prophecy* (London, 1971), especially pp. 85–103.

[36] Sommerville, *Popular Religion*, p. 71.

[37] Kane, *Spenser's Moral Allegory*, p. 22.

> From that, which feeble nature couets faine;
> But griefe and wrath, that be her enemies,
> And foes of life, she better can abstaine;
> Yet vertue vauntes in both her victories,
> And *Guyon* in them all shewes goodly maysteries.
>
> (*FQ* II.vi.1)

Before meeting Phaedria, Guyon has already mastered "grieuous paine" during his battle with Pyrochles and Cymochles, the latter of whom leads him to her island bower. The harder victory is thus reserved for the range of dangers posed by her "*immodest Merth*" or sensuality, which prepare him for his final encounter with Acrasia in the Bower of Bliss.

Like Acrasia, Phaedria is a female Comus: a deceptively bright, joyful, or shining one (*phaidros*) whose fair outside hides the physical and spiritual death (*phaedo*) lurking within.[38] As the antithetical Greek words embedded in her name show, the common cause *and* effect of her seductive misrule is deadly and ultimately joyless license. Like the god who lives in the "navel" of the wood, his mother Circe, and her "sister" goddess, Calypso (whose name means navel in Greek), Phaedria infantilizes her victims by keeping them tied to the umbilical cord of the mythically smothering mother. Like Acrasia, she derails the Homeric or Miltonic hero's homeward voyage by encouraging a fatal imbalance or deviation from the Aristotelian "mean." One form of this imbalance is symbolized by Pyrochles, the "fiery" man liable to extremes of anger. The opposite form is symbolized by his brother Cymochles, the "watery or wavering" man too liable to the extremes of sensuality and sloth. Lacking the benign balance of Milton's "blest Sisters," Voice and Verse, these "brotherly" contraries either overemphasize the masculine judicial "virtues" (rigor, wrath, and violent retribution) or the sensual feminine qualities associated with "sound" as opposed to "sense"—unrestrained mirth, softness, and singing. Yet true to his moral, Spenser soon removes Pyrochles from the action in order to illustrate Cymochles's more fatal and lasting attraction to Phaedria. The same lesson is also taught by *Comus*: the heroine's greatest peril lies not in the violence feared by the Lady's younger brother (350–58, 393–407), but in the twin lures of Phaedrian license and Mammonish luxury.

Like Guyon, the Lady confronts the twin attractions of Phaedria and Mammon in quick succession. Bearing the "*Charming Rod*" or Bacchic thyrsis of his father in one hand and the enchanted glass of his mother in the other, Comus first appears to her as a "buxom, blithe, and debonair" but fallen L'Allegro (*L'Allegro*, 24) or Phaedria. When repulsed, he turns to the "daemonic" secrets "found / In fire, air, flood, or underground" (*Il Pensoroso*, 93–94), replacing L'Allegro's benign *Euphrosyne* with the nocturnal Venus (definitely *not* the mother of the three Graces featured in *L'Allegro*, 12–16; cf. *A Mask*, 124–35). The dark "Dragon womb" of

---

[38] "Phaedo" does not mean "death" in Greek but has taken on that connotation through Phaedo's famous description of the death of Socrates and through the mythic Phaedra.

his mother Circe (*A Mask*, 131) similarly contrasts with the nurturing powers of Il Penseroso's light-giving, dragon-yoked Cynthia (*Il Pensoroso*, 59). Comus's first ploy, however, is not to seal up the Lady in a Mammon-like "cave," but to attract her to "*glistering*," Phaedria-like companions unmindful of their bestial "crowns." Their light-hearted attractions clearly recall those of Phaedria's floating island and Lake of Idleness, which are similarly filled with "foolish humour, and vaine iolliment" (*FQ* II.vi.3) that hide the high price of heroic forgetfulness. Participating in these "sports" thus means far more than simply forsaking "sour Severity" (*A Mask*, 128, 109) or trivial care, as it does for L'Allegro. It means creating the secret cares wrought by turning day into night, by not merely "allying" daily duties, but "drowning" them with the sun in oceanic streams (96, 97). Hence the Phaedria-like Comus replaces the regulating "clock" set by the "starry ... Court" of Jove (1) with a time told by the fluctuating moon and his own "Starry Choir" of fallen spirits (112). Like the pliable Cymochles in Phaedria's engulfing arms, he and his crew dance a "wavering Morris" seconded by the soft, swift, and effortless motions of the "Seas with all their finny drove," and by "tripping" elves and fairies beside "dimpled Brook and Fountain brim" (115–16, 118–20). Their unfettered "merry wakes and pastimes" abolish both sleep and "daylight ... [which] makes Sin," but only by sinisterly "hailing" the "Goddess[es] of Nocturnal sport"—the dark Venus, Cotytto and Hecate—to infernally "bless" their watery rites by smothering them in the "dun shades" of spiritual slumber (121, 126–8). Comus himself is associated with a floating, Phaedria-like sterility, an inconstancy that ruins his art by exchanging the true "vine" or delightful wine of poetry with jingling rhymes that merely "seeke to please" rather than to instruct (*FQ* VI.xii.41).

These rituals clearly mark Comus's domain as a fluctuating and false imitation not just of Jove's but also of Neptune's and Sabrina's court. The Attendant Spirit identifies the latter with England's fertile land and nurturing waters, and (to honor Bridgewater) particularly with Wales (18–36). As a result, even strong defenders of the "Puritan masque" concede that Comus mainly represents the "dark side" of honorable pastoral exercise, endeavor, and revelry: the illicit, enslaving inversion of the innocent sports defended in Milton's sixth Prolusion. Since both good and bad "shepherds" can compete in "smooth-dittied song," Marcus finds that "the audience is stymied" in trying to place holiday pastimes on either side of "the rigidly polarized positions that fueled the *Book of Sports* controversy."[39] Like L'Allegro, the Lady may thus enjoy the healthful effects of native, "nut-brown ale" while shunning the foreign "poison of [Bacchus's] misused Wine" (*A Mask*, 47). Comus leads his gulls to this "wine" by teaching that effort, abstinence, and trial are evils to be avoided, not goods to be embraced. This ethical "poison" embarks them on the moral equivalent of Phaedria's "shallow ship," which "away did slide, / More swift, then swallow sheres the liquid skye, / Withouten oare or Pilot it to guide" (*FQ* II.vi.5). Caught in her "toils," Cymochles mindlessly sinks into the "*Idle lake*" where neither "swelling *Neptune*" nor "lowd thundring *Iove*" can interrupt Phaedria's hollow "cheare,"

---

[39]   Marcus, *Politics*, p. 190.

which drowns the beneficial effects of "euer mourne[ful]" melancholy in "false delights, and … pleasures vayn" (*FQ* II.vi.10, 14).

Milton's and Spenser's seducers also commonly disguise their shallow wares with a "dear Wit and gay Rhetoric" (*A Mask*, 790) that perverts the true meaning of Christ's parable on the lilies of the field. Since Mother Nature seems carelessly to scatter her "fruitfull" blooms without requiring "carefull paines" on man's part, Phaedria considers this an apt "ensample" (*FQ* II.vi.15) to live as carelessly as one pleases. She thus asks why should Cymochles, the

> … Lord, and eke of nature Soueraine,
> Wilfully make thy selfe a wretched thrall,
> And wast thy ioyous howres in needlesse paine,
> Seeking for daunger and aduentures vaine?
> What bootes it al to haue, and nothing vse?
> Who shall him rew, that swimming in the maine,
> Will die for thrist, and water doth refuse?
> Refuse such fruitlesse toile, and present pleasures chuse.
>
> (*FQ* II.vi.17)

These fatal words complete the spell woven by her music, as "she with liquors strong his eies did steepe" (*FQ* II.vi.18). Comus uses the same "fair pretense of friendly ends / And well-plac't words of glozing courtesy, / Baited with reasons not unplausible" to wind himself into "the easy-hearted man" and "hug him into snares" (160–64). Yet like Phaedria's, his siren songs only entrap his lightest, most wavering victims, so he sometimes disguises himself in the same humble rustic or "rusty" cloak worn by both Spenser's Archimago and Mammon. Suddenly appearing in "a gloomy glade, / Couer'd with boughs and shrubs from heauens light," (*FQ* II.vii.3; *A Mask*, 167), Mammon similarly tests his victim's ability to "Pilot well" (*FQ* II.vii.1) without a guide, and with only "such a scant allowance of Star-light, / [As] Would overtask the best Land-Pilot's art" (*A Mask*, 308–9).

The Lady soon penetrates this Mammonish disguise, so, as in Spenser, the deeper and "blind[er] mazes of this tangl'd Wood" (181) are the toils of Comus's Phaedrian logic. Since Mother Nature seems an endless storehouse—a Lady Bountiful whose "green shops" plenteously fill every "corner" (716–17)—he encourages his victim to follow her licentious "ensample":

> Wherefore did Nature pour her bounties forth
> With such a full and unwithdrawing hand,
> Covering the earth with odors, fruits, and flocks,
> Thronging the Seas with Spawn innumerable,
> But all to please and sate the curious taste?
> …
> Th'all-giver would be unthank't, would be unprais'd,
> Not half his riches known, and yet despis'd,

And we should serve him as a grudging master,

...

[If] Beauty ... nature's coin, ... be hoarded

(A Mask, 710–14, 723–26, 739)

Yet the wise Lady evades these Phaedrian snares as easily as Guyon, so Comus then plays the Mammon card he holds in reserve: he offers her all the wealth and glory of all the kingdoms of the world if she will become his queen. In a legitimate court like Gloriana's or Bridgewater's, these "goods" might be legitimately sought and enjoyed; yet the true Christian knight understands that even there they should not be regarded as goods in and of themselves. Only Comus and Mammon, the pagan "God[s] of the world and worldlings" since time immemorial, teach the reverse: that external "Honour, estate, and all this worldes good," "crownes and kingdoms ... heape[d] with glory and renowne," should be selfishly enjoyed without undergoing the "swinck and sweat" of human labor (*FQ* II.vii.8, 11).

Guyon shuns Mammon's hedonistic and by no means exclusively Laudian shortcuts to renown as the "roote of all disquietnesse." Unearned pleasures leave their victims "Spent with pride and lauishnesse," "griefe and heauinesse," and they also subject whole communities to innumerable "michiefes": "Strife, and debate, bloudshed, and bitternesse, / Outrageous wrong, and hellish couetize." Since in destroying the "noble heart" they destroy just rule (*FQ* II.vii.12), rather than a true king-maker, Mammon is merely a corrupter of kingdoms, one who turns "loyall truth" to treason and wealth to "wrongfull gouernment" (*FQ* II.vii.13). Under such misrule the "priuate state" is not only "vnsweet" but even more perilous than the knight's trackless journey through foreign seas and woods (*FQ* II.vii.14). Milton's Lady shows herself equally well-versed in true "Princely lore" (34) as she reminds her escort that "honest offer'd courtesy" is "sooner found in lowly sheds / With smoky rafters, than in tap'stry Halls / And Courts of Princes, where it first was nam'd, / And yet is most pretended" (*A Mask*, 323–26). Yet as befits a proper scion of the country elite, she values the virtues of "lowly sheds" even more than Guyon, whose encounter with Mammon primarily teaches that England's increasingly centralized plutocracy threatens to corrupt the ancient values of selfless valor, industry, and unwavering service to the highest national interest.[40] Of course, the weakening of these values similarly threatens the ancient landed nobility, so the Lady and Guyon uphold essentially the same communal values of hospitality, respectful conviviality, and distributive justice.[41] This ethos works equally well for the Bridgewater family and their proto-republican poet, who had already begun assimilating it to Machiavelli's classical republican *virtù* (*CPW* 1:421, 475–77). Rooted in the same Aristotelian and Stoic doctrine as Spenser's

---

[40] See Stone, *Crisis*; although the aristocratic "crisis" may have been more imaginary than real, Spenser was alarmed by fears of decline, imaginary or not.

[41] See for instance Felicity Heal, "The Idea of Hospitality in Early Modern England," *Past and Present* 102 (1984): pp. 66–93.

temperance, Machiavelli's *Discorsi* similarly promote a movement back toward the "purer" traditions of political life.[42]

Since these "purer" traditions are not necessarily Puritan, the Lady must be absolved of the "shrill and rigid" rhetoric that many critics find in her response to Comus, which simply paraphrases Guyon's rejection of Mammon's ill-gotten goods.[43] As Guyon rightly objects, these so-called "goods" neither end want nor benefit nature but only lure "frayle men" into the "fowle intemperaunce" of "couetise." This lifestyle is repellent to anyone who merely stops to "thinke, with how small allowaunce / Vntroubled Nature doth her selfe suffise." If they did pause to consider, "Such superfluities they would despise, / Which with sad cares empeach our natiue ioyes." Unfortunately, luxury's ill-effects are cumulative: "At the well head the purest streames arise: / But mucky filth his braunching armes annoyes, / And with vncomely weedes the gentle waue accloyes" (*FQ* II.vii.15). The Lady has precisely the same concerns about the "trickle-down" effects of corruption, which, like Guyon, she would reverse:

> If every just man that now pines with want
> Had but a moderate and beseeming share
> Of that which lewdly-pamper'd Luxury
> Now heaps upon some few with vast excess,
> Nature's full blessings would be well dispens't
> In superfluous even proportion,
> And she no wit encumber'd with her store.
>
> (*A Mask*, 768–74)

In fact, Guyon objects more vigorously to the "mucky filth" of greed concealed within Mammon's "command economy" than the Lady objects to Comus, but both expose the stagnation lurking within the fetid "waves" of intemperance, which "neither wind ... / Nor timely tides ... [can] driue out of their sluggish sourse" (*FQ* II.vi.20). By "congealing" and commandeering all the bounty granted by Neptune's "imperial rule of all the Sea-girt Isles" of Britain, both Mammon and Comus prevent them from shining "like to rich and various gems" upon "the unadorned bosom of the Deep" (*A Mask*, 21–23).

---

[42] On Milton's references to Machiavelli in his *Commonplace Book*, see Chapter 3 above, which duly notes that the entry is undated. David Norbrook places Spenser in a politically reformist tradition in *Poetry and Politics in the English Renaissance* (London, 1984), pp. 59–90, and Richard F. Hardin shows both Milton and Spenser drawing on Erasmian and native English anti-absolutist traditions in *Civil Idolatry: Desacralizing and Monarchy in Spenser, Shakespeare, and Milton* (Newark, DE, 1992); see especially pp. 15–40, 164–207. Puritans were attracted mainly to the utilitarian aspects of civic humanism; see Margo Todd, *Christian Humanism and the Puritan Social Order* (Cambridge, 1987).

[43] See especially Marcus, *Politics*, p. 198; and Guibbory, *Ceremony and Community*, pp. 169–70.

Selfishly overlooking the vast difference between "guifts of soueraine bounty" accepted with "glad thankes, and vnreproued truth" and the greed of "licentious lust," "fat swolne" beyond all proper measure (*FQ* II.vii.16), Comus and his friends foolishly claim that the All-giver is truly "thank't" by their avarice. Yet, as the Lady objects, good shepherds or leaders know that true thanks means feeding the poorer flocks, while "swinish gluttony / Ne'er looks to Heav'n amidst his gorgeous feast, / But with besotted base ingratitude / Crams, and blasphemes his feeder" (776–79). In reply, Comus combines Phaedria's "lilies of the field" argument with Mammon's offer of all that "can thy wantes at will supply" (*FQ* II.vii.11):

> Why should you be so cruel to yourself,
> And to those dainty limbs which nature lent
> For gentle usage and soft delicacy?
> But you invert the cov'nants of her trust,
> And harshly deal like an ill borrower
> With that which you receiv'd on other terms,
> Scorning the unexempt condition
> By which all mortal frailty must subsist,
> Refreshment after toil, ease after pain [?]
>
> (*A Mask*, 679–87)

When this *carpe diem* falls on deaf ears, Comus urges the Lady to drink from an enchanted cup that will "restore all" (689), but she again preserves the freedom of her mind, not by dashing the cup to the ground as Guyon does (*FQ* II.xii.49), but by dashing his arguments one by one.

First, this offer cannot accomplish what Comus claims because it cannot restore "truth and honesty," which, as her captivity and his lies show, he has perverted by turning "loyall truth to treason" (*FQ* II.vii.13; cf. *A Mask*, 690–92). Second, the "ugly-headed Monsters" and "brew'd enchantments" (695, 696) of his Mammonish court plainly show that his "lickerish baits [are only] fit to ensnare a brute" (699). Third, his "false rules prankt in reason's garb" (759) cannot prove that "most innocent nature" intends that "her children should be riotous / With her abundance; she, good cateress, / Means her provision only to the good / That live according to her sober laws / And holy dictate of spare Temperance" (762–67). Possessed of this understanding, the Lady knows that her captor can "startle well, but not astound / The virtuous mind, that ever walks attended / By a strong siding champion Conscience" on one side, and the cardinal Christian virtues of Hope, Faith, and Charity/Chastity on the other (210–15). In spirit, she has already seen these protectors "visibly," which assures her that the "Supreme good ... Would send a glist'ring Guardian, if need were, / To keep my life and honor unassail'd" (216, 217, 219–20). Long before her "corporal rind" is freed (664), this semi-inchoate prayer is answered as she glimpses the silver lining within a "sable cloud" temporarily hiding Jove's moon and stars (221); the Attendant Spirit is already on his way. Thus, just as Guyon's steadfast faith and conscience silently "summon" first his guardian angel, then his Palmer, and finally Prince Arthur to his aid, the Lady's ethical and spiritual "works" summon first the Spirit, then her brothers, and finally the nymph Sabrina to free her.

Significantly, this rescue immediately precedes the Lady's defense of a golden mean between an extreme Puritan regime where men are nature's outcasts— "Nature's bastards, not her sons"—and an extreme Antinomian or Comus-like regime where temperance and even sin have become meaningless.[44] Antinomianism was not yet an issue at the time, but the libertinism later connected to it had long posed a threat to aristocratic values. To balance between the two extremes, Milton's Lady refuses either to be a wanton consumer, a "grudging master," or "penurious niggard" of natural bounty (725–26). Firmly rejecting Comus's jewels, silks, feasts, and finally his cup, much as Guyon sternly rejects Mammon's "fountaines of gold and siluer" (*FQ* II.vii.17), she avoids the corporeal captivity that Spenser associates with Proserpina, the "queen" of Mammon's "hell." By refusing to hoard nature's bounty, she also symbolically redistributes it to those whose "homely features" and "coarse complexions" bar them from Comus's court (748–49). Guyon obeys a similar logic in spurning "Mammon's" deceptively polite offer to "Take what thou please of all this surplusage." Since it is not "well be gott," his refusal proves his concern for what might be "bereaue[d] / From rightfull owner by vnrighteous lott" (*FQ* II.vii.18, 19). Both heroes of temperance thus reject the indiscriminate consumption of all the "pleasures / That fancy can beget on youthful thoughts" (*A Mask*, 668–69) when these are not based on true mutuality but only on mutual lust for "eye-glutting gaine" (*FQ* II.vii.9). Even more importantly, they realize that since "none / But such as are good men, can give good things," ill-gotten goods are not "delicious / To a well-govern'd and wise appetite" (*A Mask*, 702–5). Far from the "prim" Puritan or stoic denial that Comus would make it, the Lady's refusal of his "stolen" goods is socially and personally liberating.

Yet her Aristotelian/Spenserian virtue ethic can only go so far in overcoming evil. Given her mortal state, her sensual self can only temporarily endure the monstrous world of "internall Payne," envy, and strife that afflict Guyon in Mammon's cave. Having corporally or outwardly inured the exhausted Lady to his bestial court, Comus can bring his enchanted cup ever closer to her lips, for like Guyon's, her "mortal coil" remains humanly susceptible to "*Plutoes* griesly raigne" (*FQ* II.vii.21). Although guiltless, she is no "blank" or "whitewashed" image of virtue but a frail wayfaring maiden (*CPW* 2:515–16) whose ethical choices can go only so far in overcoming Comus's magical worldly powers. Her spiritual "ears," like her echoing words and song, can defend her only so long as her body endures; beyond that point, corporeal sleep will inevitably overtake

---

[44] On the Antinomian aspects of Comus's "orgiastic cult," especially its mixture of sexual and religious impulses that at once equate corporeality with evil and relish it, see B.J. Sokol, "'Tilted Lees.' Dragons, *Haemony*, Menarche, Spirit, and Matter in *Comus*," *RES* n.s. 41.163 (1990): pp. 309–24, especially p. 316; on Milton's distaste for these religious excesses, see p. 314 n. 22.

her "wary watch and ward." Although far from the fatal slumber of Mammon's or Comus's careless, soon-to-be-careworn guests, which is "next to death ... to be compared" (*FQ* II.vii.25), she requires more potent help than haemony or the shielding wings of Guyon's Cupid-like guardian angel (*FQ* II.viii.5–8). Yet even more than in Spenser's "Legend of Temperaunce," in Milton's masque providential grace works through nature.

To free her, the river spirit Sabrina sprinkles pure water "thrice" on the Lady's breast, then on her finger-tips, and finally upon her lips. Her "chaste palms moist and cold" provide material signs of temperance (*A Mask*, 918) traditionally linked both to pure "palmers" or pilgrims and to Christ's triumphant entry into his symbolic kingdom on Palm Sunday.[45] By applying her palms to the place where the Lady has unwillingly touched Comus's orgiastic throne, Sabrina also purifies the "seat" of her feminine sexuality and earthly pilgrimage to chaste womanhood. Since the Lady's breast, finger-tips, or lips have touched nothing in this palace, the need to cleanse these other physical "channels" of human creativity or nurture seems more mysterious. None of these creative sources have been truly corrupted by her presence in Comus's palace, but they seem to have been soiled, hurt, or "bruised" by its smokey air, as Andrewes might put it. Sabrina therefore applies her waters first to the Lady's breast (her emotional or proto-maternal "heart"), then to her sense of touch or material "making," and finally to her lips, the source of her verbal and intellectual expression. This cleansing allows Milton's new Prosperina to "remarry" her body in anticipation of her earthly marriage, the purity of which is guaranteed by Sabrina's ritual cleansing.[46] By freeing her from the "gums of glutinous heat" on Comus's enchanted chair (917), Sabrina also prefigures the release of her father's lands from his sensual yet infertile reign, which "perverts" procreation by converting it to exclusively pleasurable uses.

Nevertheless, it is only Comus, not pleasure, that has been banished, as he is in Jonson's *Pleasure Reconciled to Virtue*, the masque generally credited as the source of his name. There "the voluptuous Comus, god of cheer, / [is] Beat from his grove, and that defaced," a harsher ending than Milton's mere routing of the villain, and much more like Guyon's merciless destruction of Acrasia's bower.[47] Tacitly acknowledging his debt to both predecessors, Milton nevertheless prefers Jonson's less ascetic moral: "Pleasure, for his delight, / Is reconciled to Virtue," which brings forth virtuous offspring bred upon "the hill of knowledge," "the

---

[45]   Shakespeare famously features this punning association in both *Romeo and Juliet* and *Othello*.

[46]   Earlier versions of the masque overtly compare Ceres's daughter to the Lady, who "fares as did forsaken *Proserpine* / when the bigg rowling flakes of pitchie clouds / and darkness wound her in." See *A Maske: The Earlier Versions*, ed. Samuel E. Sprott (Toronto, 1973), pp. 92–93.

[47]   Ben Jonson, *Pleasure Reconciled to Virtue*, ll. 159–60, in David Lindley (ed.), *Court Masques: Jacobean and Caroline Entertainments 1605–1640* (New York, 1995), hereafter cited by line number.

chief of whom / Of the bright race of Hesperus is come" to guide them "to the Hesperides, Fair Beauty's garden" (175–76, 178–79, 183–4). These lines seem to allude to Spenser's Garden of Adonis, which similarly unites masculine and feminine principles in eternal bliss, and Milton closely echoes both predecessors as his Attendant Spirit returns to "the Gardens fair / Of *Hesperus*, and his daughters three / That sing about the golden tree." In the eternal spring of those gardens, "young *Adonis*" again rejoins his Venus, while Cupid "holds his dear *Psyche* sweet entranc't / After her wand'ring labors long" (981–83, 999, 1005–6). Jonson's poetic gifts may not have been of the same order, but as a humanist and moralist, he was as good a teacher as Spenser or Bacon, both of whom he deeply admired. Although Milton borrows less from Jonson than either of the latter, his debt to Jonson's concluding moral is obvious in the masque's finale. After learning "To walk with Pleasure, not to dwell," Jonson's heroine reaches the final "height and crown" of her journey: "There, there, is Virtue's seat. / Strive to keep her your own / 'Tis only she can make you great," if not "here on earth," then in "heaven [where] she hath her right of birth" (284, 293, 300–304). The Heavenly Attendant's previously cited lines clearly echo this teaching: "Mortals that would follow me, / Love virtue, she alone is free, / She can teach ye how to climb / Higher than the Sphery chime" (1018–21). As Lawrence Sasek long ago suggested, this highly sophisticated synergy "can prove nothing about" Milton's Puritan allies or about "normative" Puritan art. Puritanism and humanism were never mutually exclusive, but the dualism at the root of the Calvinist belief system inevitably raised a "Malvolio-like spectre" utterly absent from Milton's monist ethical and metaphysical vision.[48]

The Materialist and Monist Metaphysics of Haemony

Critical curiosity surrounding the provenance of Milton's mysterious herb has turned it into critical crux almost as notorious as *Lycidas*'s "two-handed engine." Its lengthy reception history prevents a thorough consideration of every possible source, especially since the real source seems wholly unexplored. Bacon's *Wisdom of the Ancients* again provides an important clue, this time in his myth of Prosperina or "Spirit." Even more than Spenser's "Legend of Temperaunce," the fable considers the problematic captivity of spirit to matter and arrives at a fully monist solution: unlike Ovid's Proserpina, Bacon's "root-bound" goddess escapes from the "cave" of Hades not by leaving behind her earthiness but by successfully "marrying" spirit and matter. According to Bacon, this marriage exemplifies the proper "nourishing of the 'soul' by the 'body'" once the soul's material "seed" is "quickened" by immortal flame. Escaping Hades not by

---

    [48]   Sasek, *Literary Temper*, p. 13. Todd's study, *Christian Humanism*, shows that Puritans drew deeply on humanism but confined it to disciplinary purposes that ultimately disrupted the great "Chain of Being" (p. 234).

renouncing crude matter but by reconciling Proserpina's heavenly "flame" with her material roots, Bacon's goddess is no longer either a captive "bride" or a discardable "mortal coil," but a material body reawakened to Spirit, which in this allegory she is. Her soul thus becomes "a natural body, rarified to a proportion" within matter "as in an integument." Bacon imagines Spirit "feeding" this material integument by converting dense to rare, which according to Charles Lemmi makes Bacon's retelling of the tale a quasi-alchemical or "hylozoic" fable. By linking Proserpina's "refining" process to natural digestion or "concoction," her body's rarer "spirits" retain all of the natural motions of corporeal substance without its grosser limitations (*Works* 6:758–61).[49] This "concoctive" monism is also a likely source for the symbiosis underlying Milton's epic cosmos, where lower degrees of matter are similarly refined by natural or quasi-alchemical processes that Raphael compares to digestion (*PL* 5.435–42). Like Bacon's immanent Spirit (Proserpina), matter in *Paradise Lost* vitalistically ascends from its dark seed or root to its highest "flower," "one first matter all" *(PL* 5.469–90).

Bacon himself declared that he metaphysically "figured" this vitalist continuum "in our *Sapientia veterum* [*The Wisdom of the Ancients*] in the fable of Proserpina," and physically in his *Sylva sylvarum* (*Works* 2:381). In the former work, Proserpina is able "to rise" partly through the power of a golden "misseltoe" (*Works* 6:759) strikingly similar both to Milton's haemony and the "one first matter" of *Paradise Lost*. Like haemony, the mistletoe is a "small unsightly root, / But of divine effect"; it bears "darkish" prickly leaves that "in another Country" will bear "a bright golden flow'r, but not in this soil" (*A Mask*, 629–33). Like the "plant" of immortal glory in *Lycidas*, it will at last flower, "live … and spread … aloft" in that rarer soil under the "perfect witness of all-judging *Jove*" (*Lycidas*, 78, 81–82). Joan Larson Klein observes that Andrew Marvell's "Upon Appleton House" refers to a very similar plant as

> *Conscience*, that heaven-nursèd plant,
> Which most our earthly gardens want.
> A prickling leaf it bears, and such
> As that which shrinks at every touch;
> But Flowers eternal and divine,
> That in the crowns of saints do shine.
>
> ("Upon Appleton House," 355–60)[50]

Either Marvell or Milton could have found the idea of eternal glory as a flower "sprung" from the "mixed seeds" of human virtue and "crude" matter in Spenser,

---

[49]   See Charles W. Lemmi, *The Classic Deities in Bacon: A Study in Mythological Symbolism* (Baltimore, 1933), pp. 75, 80. Lemmi traces the wide variety of sources involved in Bacon's reinvention of this myth—Paracelsus, Lucretius, Empedocles, Heraclitus, and the standard Renaissance mythographer, Natale Conti (pp. 74–91).

[50]   Cited in *Poems of Andrew Marvell*.

yet as Klein shows, Milton's poem first mentions the idiosyncratic detail of the "prickling leaf" that Marvell later picks up.[51]

Milton's apparent source is again Bacon's fable of Proserpina, where the divine "spark" of human glory is *materially*, not just spiritually, immanent within conscience. Bacon uniquely links its power to the uneaten seeds of Prosperina's pomegranate, which Milton in turn interprets as the immortal "seeds" of innocence in the Lady and her brothers. In both cases, these innate seeds are quickened by a golden or a green mistletoe-like plant capable of translating spirit into matter and matter into spirit. Like Wordsworth long after him, Bacon probably derived this "plant" from the Platonic idea that human souls retain an essence which, when from "heaven new-sundered," "some seeds retain, / Some sparks and motions of its kindred sky" (*Works* 6:759). As Lemmi points out, Bacon's myth also stems from the popular belief that mistletoe had "the power of revealing the presence of gold."[52] While unorthodox, this idea can be reconciled with St. Paul's account of the rebirth of the natural body "sown" in the earth like a seed and raised up as a spiritual body (1 Cor. 15:37–44).[53] Unlike Paul or Plato but like Milton, however, Bacon regards this spiritual body as naturally immanent in all of matter. Proserpina's "ethereal spirit which, having been separated by violence from the upper globe," can thus be only temporarily "enclosed and imprisoned beneath the earth." Released by a beautiful and "chaste wedlock" of art and nature, she finds her final "home" in a new material/spiritual synergy (*Works* 6:759). Yet her ascent is also common to all matter not deliberately "deprav'd from good" (*PL* 5.471). Bacon ascribes this impaired condition to the heavier "smoke-souls" who impurely "coagulate into the things of earth."[54] Following Paracelsus, he also traces the fate of a third or intermediate type of soul who is not innately "smoky" but suffers from a temporary "torpor" or "coagulation" of creative energy. Such souls share the "torpid" fate of Narcissus, which "explains" why Proserpina was gathering flowers in the fields of Narcissus when she was ravished away to the underworld. Yet in Bacon's retelling, even Narcissus can be redeemed by "marrying" his true lover, Echo, whom he alternately identifies as the handmaiden or "bride" of Pan, here both a figure of nature and Christ (*Works* 6:713–14). Like Prosperina's, their marriage redemptively transmutes the soul's "ethereal emanations … into more material things," so that "'instead of the body being carried upward with the soul, the soul remains with the body, the work is crowned with success, and the spirit will abide with the two in indissoluble union forever.'"[55]

---

[51]   Joan Larson Klein, "Some Spenserian Influences on Milton's *Comus*," *Annuale mediaevale* 5 (1964): pp. 27–47, cited p. 45.

[52]   Lemmi, *Classic Deities*, p. 88. Lemmi also points to Virgil's golden bough as a likely source of the plant, although he does not identify Bacon's poetic quotation.

[53]   On the influence of Pauline monism in *Comus*, see David Gay, "'Rapt Spirits': 2 Corinthians 12.2–5 and the Language of Milton's *Comus*," *MQ* 29.3 (1995): pp. 76–86.

[54]   Lemmi, *Classic Deities*, p. 77.

[55]   Ibid., p. 86. Lemmi cites Bonus of Ferrara on the latter point.

Milton not only associates this reunion of spirit and matter with the Lady and her brothers, but seems to credit Bacon's speculation that Theseus and Pirithous could have helped Proserpina escape from Hades if they had only been virtuous enough to find the golden, mistletoe-like branch that would release her. This discovery requires a synthesis of art and nature that would transcend "any medicine or method which is simple or natural" (*Works* 6:761), yet Theseus and Pirithous could have discovered it simply by relying on Ceres's torch. Physically, the torch stands for the natural "art" of the "Sun, which does the office of a lamp over the earth, and would do more than anything else for the recovery of Proserpina, were the thing at all possible" (*Works* 6:760). Metaphysically, it represents the divine "light" of conscience or conscious self-restraint, powers latent in the "seed" of the branch that these failed heroes cannot find. Milton seems to allude to this interpretation as the Attendant Spirit's enlivening "torch" or immortal flame reveals the natural, herbal gift of haemony, for passing it on to the Lady's brother allows them partially to succeed where Theseus and Pirithous failed: they dispel Comus's subterranean enchantments, although they forget to seize the wand that created them. This oversight symbolizes their lack of mature knowledge or wisdom, the shepherd's art of rightly applying "every virtuous plant and healing herb / That spreads her verdant leaf to th' morning ray" (622–22). Hence only Sabrina—the natural/supernatural agent whose Proserpina-like rebirth from the depths makes her both a water and a vernal spirit—can complete the Lady's final reunion of grace and nature. At that point, the "smoke-soul" temporarily detained in Comus's court becomes a clear spirit who easily reascends to her natural, earthly home.

Although arcane, this Baconian allegory explains three no less arcane questions surrounding Milton's masque: (1) how and why the Lady's mysterious "Echo" song "saves" her from Comus; (2) why the Heavenly Attendant needs haemony to reinvigorate her "Narcissus-like" brothers (236–37); and (3) why all of the above are unable to free her until Sabrina intervenes. Once she does, Milton introduces a closely related mythic vision of the marriage of Cupid and his "eternal Bride," Psyche (1008). This union represents the "wedding" of all true lovers of virtue, which can alternately be understood as the soul's final release from the smoky prison of Comus/Pluto/Mammon and as a proleptic vision of Christ's marriage with his bride the Church. In either case, the marriage of body and soul is appropriately "crowned" with the redeemed "fruits" of holy wedlock, "two blissful twins ... / Youth and Joy" (1010–11). In the process, Milton's multi-leveled demonstration of the cooperation of human and divine agency fulfills what Bacon considers the highest function of human art: "moving" or inciting "*great love and affection*" toward the otherwise invisible shape of virtue. Although inaccessible to the corporal sense, art makes virtue visible to "the Imagination ... [through] lively representation" in bodily form (*Works* 3:410). This task obviously corresponds with the Attendant Spirit's mission: he leaves behind heaven's serene but invisible air for "the smoke and stir of this dim spot" so that all those striving "to keep up a frail and Feverish being, / Unmindful of the crown that Virtue gives," may "see" her glorious shape and become "her true Servants" (*A Mask*, 5, 8–10).

The Elder and Second Brothers rank high on the list of servants who deserve his help, for while they preserve the seeds of innocence and virtue, they remain uncreatively attached to the unsatisfactory moral extremes more playfully represented by Milton's *L'Allegro* and *Il Penseroso*. The "sober, steadfast, and demure" Elder Brother is on the right path (*Il Pen*, 32), but too complacent in his "sage and holy" (*Il Pen*, 11) belief that his nunlike sister can fend off any captor, as in "clear dream and solemn vision" she apprehends angelic words that "no gross ear can hear" (*A Mask*, 457–58). He believes that her constant "converse with heav'nly habitants" has already allowed her "outward shape" perfectly to reflect the "unpolluted temple of the mind" until *almost* "all be made immortal." Unlike those whose "unchaste looks, loose gestures, and foul talk" produce the confirmed habit and "act of sin," she is completely immune to all carnally "imbodie[d] and imbrute[d]" evil (459–61, 463–65, 468). Yet his attempt to reassure his younger brother backfires since, as the latter realizes, his "charming" but impractical "divine Philosophy" (476) exaggerates Neoplatonic ethics to the point of parody. None of Spenser's purest knights ever experienced full immunity from evil, nor does the Lady, as both brothers almost immediately learn from the Attendant Spirit. Unfortunately, the doubting Second Brother's skepticism is as inadequate as his sibling's idealism. Troubled by the unseen evil lurking in the "Chaos" of the starless night (334–35), the daylight-loving brother brushes aside the Elder's modest longing for some "rush Candle" to guide their way (338), and hopes for nothing less than the complete return of pastoral mirth: the "cheering" sound of "the folded flocks penn'd in their watttled cotes / Or ... pastoral reed with oaten stops, / Or whistle from the Lodge, or village cock / Counting the night watches to his feathery Dames" (344–48). Like L'Allegro in a bad corner, the Second Brother's affinity for the "lively" world of the Lark makes him forget the beauty of night, which his imagination populates with "wild amazement and affright." Particularly fearing "the direful grasp / Of Savage hunger or of Savage heat" (356–58), he rightly suspects that a greedy "Miser" is plotting to seize their "fair Hesperian Tree / Laden with blooming gold" (393–94, 99), but wrongly supposes that his sister cannot find "her best nurse Contemplation" in the "retired Solitude" of her "own clear breast" (376–77, 381).

As a result, the Elder Brother is closer to the truth: not just a passive treasure but an active female Guyon, the Lady's combined temperance and chastity is no "mere negation, or a capacity for remaining unmoved." For, like Spenser, Milton conceives chastity "as a vital, energizing force," both a "saving virtue ... identified with ... poetic inspiration" and a "preparatory stage for a later fruition in mature married love" and its "illustrious progeny." According to Vicari, this explains why the masque ends not with "a vision of the 144,000 virgins" entering a Celestial City or dancing upon Mount Acidale, but "in a country dance in a domestic setting" that foreshadows both the Lady's eventual marriage and the heavenly feast of the soul. Uniting the best instincts of both brothers, its finale combines Neoplatonic ascent with an earthy, "bacchic" wedding not just of Cupid and Psyche but of the wounded "young *Adonis*" and his "*Assyrian* Queen."[56] These weddings complete Milton's implicit contrast of Comus's dark Venus with L'Allegro's and Il Penseroso's higher pleasures: Comus's far too "light fantastic round' (144) is danced to the beat of Hecate's sinister spells (135), while the dances of true shepherds are blissfully unencumbered by "*sensual Folly and Intemperance*" (975).[57]

This finale also reframes the Lady's opening censure of intemperate shepherds. It now appears not as a Puritan complaint against sensuous dances, musical instruments, or "singing choirs," all of which celebrate her victory, but as a classically Spenserian protest against the bad songs which, as in *Lycidas*, drive out the music of the "true ear" (170). This higher music comes from shepherds who worship the true "*Pan*," the counterpart of the Good Shepherd, not the false shepherds who indulge in "Riot and ill-manag'd Merriment, /Such as the jocund Flute or gamesome Pipe / Stirs up among the loose unletter'd Hinds." By thanking "the gods amiss" for "their teeming Flocks and granges full" (172–77), they only produce a spiritual "drought" unknown when true pastors

> had none inheritance
> Ne of land, nor fee in sufferance,
> But what might arise of the bare sheep,
> (Were it more or lesse) which they did keep.
> ...
> For *Pan* himselfe was their inheritance
> And little them served for their maintenance,
> The Shepheards God so well them guided,
> That of naught they were unprovided
>
> ("May Eclogue," 105–8, 111–14; cited *CPW* 1:723)

Milton's *Animadversions* cites Spenser's May Eclogue to make the familiar Protestant point that false pastors are "*wolves full of fraud and guile*," predators who rather than accepting their just "mead" greedily devour the flock ("May," 127) much as Comus seeks to "devour" the Lady. "Our admired *Spencer* inveighs against" them because their "whole life is a recantation of their pastorall vow ... to forsake the World" while their clerical position merely "boggs them deeper into" it (*CPW* 1:722).

Thus the masque does anticipate *Lycidas* and the antiprelatical tracts, but only from a broadly reformist, not a Puritan, perspective. While circumstantially wrong, the Lady is not *essentially* wrong in associating the unruly "trippings" of Comus's crew with "unfetter'd Hinds" who greedily care only for their "granges full," not

---

[56]   Vicari, " Triumph," p. 218. See also Sokol, "'Tilted Lees,'" p. 321, and William Shullenberger, who like Vicari sees the Lady as "a kind of Orpheus" (Vicari, p. 221), although Shullenberger mainly compares her to female figures of "virgin power" in *Lady in the Labyrinth: Milton's "Comus" as Initiation* (Cranberry, NJ, 2008).

[57]   See Patterson, "'L'Allegro,'" p. 76.

for their true "maintenance" or Master. Yet like Orpheus and Edward King, this "hapless Nightingale" (*A Mask*, 566) remains secure from peril by singing more exalted songs, not by eliminating them altogether. Despite his over-confidence, the Elder Brother's basic conviction is therefore vindicated: "Virtue may be assail'd but never hurt, / Surpris'd by unjust force but not enthrall'd" (589–90). Supported by Spenser's "sage / And serious doctrine" (786–87) of temperance, the Lady fends off captors that have neither "Ear nor Soul to apprehend" (784), seize, or "arrest" her mental powers, as Milton's ambiguous verb suggests. Comus cannot "touch the freedom of [her] mind" even though her outer "rind" remains "immanacl'd," for her technically unutterable but vividly imagined "doctrine" cooperates with "Heav'n" in defending the monistic harmony of her mind, soul, and body (663–65). Materially "embodied" in an Orphic "flame of sacred vehemence" (795), this harmony proves far more "arresting" than the swords of her immature brothers, which merely drive Comus away.

Puritan versus Miltonic Aesthetics

As proposed in earlier chapters, the central difference between Puritans and other English Protestants was that they reacted more traumatically to the loss of visible assurances of salvation supplied by the "old religion." They famously responded to this loss by developing an exaggerated dread of the visible signs of salvation and holiness associated with "papism"—the surplice worn by ministers, the sign of the cross in baptism, the ring in marriage, altar rails facing the East, kneeling during communion, and, eventually, altars and crucifixes themselves. Mainline Protestants tended to find more moderate means of compensation than the godly, who developed iconophobic attitudes toward nearly all symbols and rituals: wedding or funeral prayers and ceremonies, seasonal or other rites of passage, baptism with the sign of the cross, and finally, infant baptism of any kind.[58] The Puritan opposition to Laud pushed the saints even further from both Geneva and the mainline English church on ceremonial issues, ultimately leading them to abandon Calvin's practice of tolerating a wider range of practices.[59] Puritans particularly seized upon Old Testament proscriptions against religious images and began shattering not just new cathedral decorations and altar rails but old churchyard crosses, "idolatrous" stained glass windows, church organs, and religious art on an unprecedented scale. Margaret Aston shows that even highly refined Puritans like Brilliana Harley rejoiced when her father Sir Robert shattered "'a most horrible picture of the great God of heaven [and] earth,'" and Lady Brereton of Cheshire was thrilled when her man obeyed her orders and "'most zealously broke all the windows'" in the local church. In this, however, they were merely adhering to a principle enshrined in Calvin's *Institutes* and reaffirmed by William Perkins: that

---

[58]   Davies, *Worship of the English*, pp. 41, 45, 135–36.

[59]   Ibid., pp. 35–42, 50.

it is wrong "that God should be represented by a visible appearance, because he himself has forbidden it and it cannot be done without some defacing of his glory." Utterly unlike the author of *Paradise Lost*, Perkins rejected any representation of the divine "'even in those shapes in which God himself hath heretofore testified his presence,'" presumably including light, smoke, and cloud.[60] In his first volume of verse Milton celebrates most of the holy days proscribed by Puritans—the feasts of the nativity, circumcision, passion, resurrection, ascension, and in *Comus*, the harvest feast of St. Michael—while his great epic violates their strict proscription again fallen humans kneeling in prayer. The epic's exalted angelic hymns not only draw on the Anglican liturgy but have little in common with Puritan "chants."

Puritans did not, however, object to poetry per se, although they anathematized nearly every kind of theatrical entertainment. Their anti-theatricalism was originally rooted in their critique of the Catholic mass as a deceptive play or "show" that claimed to bring the living Christ on stage. Yet it was also encouraged by their quasi-Manichean conception of the path to salvation, which required the repression of most traits or emotions represented by successful playwrights or actors: ambition, vanity, sexuality, lies, anger, idleness, conflict. Stigmatizing every aspect of "the unchecked self in worldly panoply," as David Leverenz puts it, their didactic literature did portray vice but neatly divided the action between exemplary heroes and cautionary villains, with little if any middle ground for "things indifferent." Literary ambiguity and aesthetic pleasure were thus circumscribed since both presuppose the reader's or viewer's ability to appreciate or empathize with charmingly evil as well as only moderately good characters.[61] Puritan art therefore emulated the didactic closure of the printed, not the performed, morality play, and shunned the mimetic standards of Jonsonian and Shakespearean theater. Leverenz believes that mimesis was probably "too honest for the Puritans": not only did "it show ... fathers who are weak[;] it exposed fantasies that are illusions. It enacted the changes that every human rigidity must undergo. It presented angers and desires that can be transformed but never wholly dismissed. For those visions of mixture, flexibility, and limitation—for such a merely *human* world—Puritans could tolerate no forgiveness." These observations cause him to dismiss William Haller's "dramatistic" understanding of Puritans as "faithful ... actors in a universal drama, 'the grand outlines of which they all knew.'" For while they may have "responded more to the 'dramatic violence' of tracts like [Prynne's] *Histrio-mastix* than to the [preacher's] reasoned explications of the Bible," in fact, "what drama joined ... —high and low plots, high and low speech, high and low audience—the sermon tore asunder. Where clarity prevailed, and Elect and Reprobate were clearly demarcated in opposition to each other, combat could be righteously pursued. Drama embodied the spirit of the age. But Puritans could allow themselves dramatic experience only in forms that encouraged strict self-control."[62] This "Manichean"

---

[60]   Aston, "Puritans and Iconoclasm," pp. 112, 116, 96.

[61]   Leverenz, *Language*, pp. 27, 31.

[62]   Ibid., pp. 40, 39.

impulse is closely associated with the Puritan inclination not only to segregate the realms of nature and grace but to improve upon an overly ambiguous "nature."

Puritans also objected to subtler ambiguities: like a host of other Puritans, Robert Cleaver and John Dod exhorted the godly to "Love not mirth and pastime" since these pleasures invited literally "mixed" or ambiguous company.[63] The theater was especially demonized because male actors who dressed as women clearly "adulterated" or ambiguated the male sex, while women who portrayed themselves—even an idealized image of themselves—were equally culpable for potentially arousing lustful desire rather than disinterested admiration. Prynne complained that the "luscious" rhetoric of such women could raise a whole "tempest of unchaste affections, yea kindle a very a hell of lust within your soules," thus causing you *"to commit, if not actuall, yet contemplative adultery with them in your hearts."*[64] His views were admittedly extreme, but so was the widespread Puritan suspicion of most non-didactic fiction, "poetical raptures," and "feigned romances," which they considered not "plays" of imagination but falsehoods. Their own literature demanded more as well as less: the careful strictures of "the guidebook, the sermon, the moral exemplum" to resolve all conflicts or potential ambiguities.[65] In contrast, Milton hoped to raise fiction, romance, and even "luscious" rhetoric to dazzling new heights. As his letter to Diodati particularly shows, he consciously sought the "glorious image" of the beautiful "through all the shapes and forms of things." His "feigned romance," *Comus*, participates in this quest by including nearly every dramatic element denounced by Puritans: an unwed female freely displaying her physical and musical attractions; a highly ambivalent, sexually attractive male villain; two well-meaning but feckless guardian brothers; shape-shifting personas on both sides of the fence; and, of course, a very high degree of verbal ambiguity and intellectual complexity. In generic terms alone, John Creaser finds *Comus* ambiguously wavering "between the opposed modes of masque and drama," but tending toward the latter.[66]

Calvin set the opposing standard of art by contrasting "eloquence" with "fruitfull doctrine" and equating "glorious shewes of woordes" with "vaine boasting."[67] Puritans like Lewis Bayly continued this tradition when they cautioned against singing even "divine psalms for an ordinary recreation," unless one was "sure that the matter makes more melody in your hearts, than the music in your ear."

---

[63] Robert Cleaver and John Dod, *A Godlye Form of Household Government* (London, 1621 [1st ed. 1614]), section E 4.

[64] Prynne, *Histriomastix*, pp. 374–75. Leverenz believes that Prynne's "fears of mixture and disrupted male identity" were driven by a need for a pure (and purely authoritarian) father (*Language*, pp. 32–37).

[65] Leverenz, *Language*, p. 36.

[66] Creaser, "'The present aid'," pp. 127–28. Burbery emphatically agrees; see *Milton the Dramatist*, pp. 57–65.

[67] John Calvin, *A Commentarie upon S. Paules Epistles to the Corinthians*, trans. T. Timme (London, 1577), "Argument of the First Epistle."

Generally considering art to be only "an embellishment of content, an addition of extrinsic ornaments to the logical core of meaning," Puritans typically justified rhetorical inflation only in stern didactic lessons or examples—as in their famous fire and brimstone sermons.[68] Nigel Smith links the Puritan ambivalence about rhetoric to a failure to distinguish between the syllogistic logic and "elaborately contrived language" they practiced and the traditional "dispute" and "eloquence" they attacked. This oversight caused them to insist that human reason had nothing to do with *the things that are freely given to us of God*," which would apparently imply that God had somehow dictated the rhetorical organization of their works.[69] At the most extreme, other sympathetic critics such as Sharon Achinstein concede that they not only attacked high-flown metaphors and all the follies of human "Wit," but often admired "inelegant performance," "rough verse" and "poor aesthetics."[70] The Puritan William Geddes holistically condemned all "the whorish dress of human eloquence, or high flowing notions," and, perhaps with *The Shepheardes Calendar* in mind, he even rejected "the sluttish Garb of rustick expressions"; his "chast Lady of Divinity" wore only "the grave Matronal habite of Godly, pertinent, and Spiritual simplicity." Although Baxter approved a wide range of religious poetry, he would banish all "Play-books, and History-Fables and Romances" and "other Pestilent Vanities" from the Commonwealth. In diametric opposition to the aesthetic stance outlined in *The Reason of Church Government* and practiced in *Paradise Lost*, the Baptist Joseph Stennett vilified "those very bold Flights and those Heathenish Phrases which some have indulg'd even in divine Poesy."[71] Sasek shows that less extreme Puritans sanctioned a far broader use of pagan authors, although more often in writing than in preaching, and much more often the "moralists, historians, and philosophers—in roughly that order—met the fewest objections and appeared more frequently." Typically, however, their virtues were used either to condemn lukewarm "professors" or to illustrate the "ineffectuality of all heathen good works" due to man's natural depravity and divine predestination. Only a tiny, unpopular minority suggested that pagans might be saved through the "light of nature," and almost none freely borrowed from their "superstitious" mythology.[72] As a result, much Puritan art is marked by the "'intense bibliolatry, ... intolerance, and ... Philistinism'" earlier ascribed to

---

[68] Sasek, *Literary Temper*, pp. 52–53, 117–19; Lewis Bayly is cited in *The Practice of Piety* (1611), pp. 312–13. On the Puritan "seasons of humiliation" and the closure of the theaters, see Leverenz, *Language*, p. 25; on Puritan hymns, see Achinstein, *Literature and Dissent*, pp. 210–42.

[69] Smith, *Perfection Proclaimed*, pp. 315–16.

[70] Achinstein, *Literature and Dissent*, pp. 232, 227; on the anti-poetic bias of Quakers, see pp. 233, 235–36; on the role of Puritan iconoclasm in these biases, see p. 232.

[71] William Geddes, *The Saints Recreation, Third Part* (Edinburgh, 1683), Preface, n.p.; Richard Baxter, *A Treatise of Self-Denial* (1659), in *The Practical Works of Richard Baxter* (4 vols., 1707), pp. 111, 377; and Joseph Stennett, *Hymns* (London, 1705), fol. A4.

[72] Sasek, *Literary Temper*, pp. 83–86, cited pp. 84, 86.

Bunyan, for, as Smith shows, Puritans lacked Milton's complex *literary* notion of the "*vates* or inspired poet who can prophesy the future [or past] in a mythic vision" incorporating pre-Christian elements.[73] Thus, even after appropriate qualifications are made, we are forced to conclude that Sasek was right: there is little if any common ground between Miltonic and Puritan aesthetics.

---

[73] On Bunyan, see Achinstein, *Literature and Dissent*, citing V. De Sola Pinto, "Isaac Watts and the Adventurous Muse," *Essays and Studies* 20 (1934): pp. 86–107, at p. 239; on poetic prophecy, see Smith, *Perfection Proclaimed*, p. 32.

Chapter 5
Mid-Century Debates on Law, Religion, Rhetoric, Education, and Science

But now our understandings being eclipsed, as well as our tempers informed, we must betake our selves to wayes of reparation, and depend upon the illumination of our endeavours. For, thus we may repair our primary ruines, and build our selves Men again.

—Sir Thomas Browne, *Pseudodoxia Epidemica* (1646), I.5

The end then of learning is to repair the ruins of our first parents by regaining to know God aright, and out of that knowledge to love him, to imitate him, to be like him, as we may the neerest by possessing our souls of true virtue ... [and] by orderly conning over the visible and inferior creature.

—Milton, *Of Education* (1644)

By learning man ascendeth to the heavens and their motions, where in the body he cannot come.

—Francis Bacon, *The Advancement of Learning*

Like the scholastic philosophy in which Calvin was steeped, his theological system was eminently logical, essentially syllogistic, and enormously useful in confuting Catholic systems constructed along similar lines. Most modern theologians recognize that these advantages are also responsible for its underlying flaw: Calvin's abstract, essentially medieval methods privileged doctrinaire metaphysics at the expense of a more naturalistic concern for the visible world and the human condition.[1] At the heart of his metaphysical structure lay the famous "double decrees" of election and reprobation which, according to Henry R. McAdoo, marked a deterministic "point of no return" dictated by "the inner logic of the system's own presuppositions." In one sense, these decrees merely spring from the Pauline assertion that "election is not of merit" but of faith; yet, by supposing that absolute election to salvation entailed a corresponding condemnation to destruction, Calvin and his followers narrowed Paul's meaning and erased the paradoxes at its heart. Ignoring the abundant contextual evidence against their narrower interpretation,

---

[1]   See Stachniewski, *Persecutory Imagination*, pp. 17–61.

they committed themselves to almost insuperable dichotomies between the dispensation of grace and the realm of nature.[2] In England, the "judicious" Richard Hooker considerably modified this divide by placing God's decrees within the broader context of natural law and human notions of rational justice. The striking contrasts between these two theologians largely shaped the opposing sides of the great seventeenth-century debates over natural reason, free will, and the role of both in human life that are surveyed in this chapter. While the Calvinist side generally adhered to the metaphysical dualism of its founders—not just Calvin, but also Beza and Zwingli—the rational theologians descended from Hooker increasingly reconciled the orders of nature and grace. By mid-century, a large middle ground also emerged, creating a potential for compromise between moderate Puritans and pious Anglicans weary of Calvinist rigor and zeal.[3]

John Stachniewski explains that devout Calvinists resisted this humanistic compromise because it seemed to threaten God's supreme power over the world, which included his absolute foreknowledge of the saved and the damned. Believing either that Christ had not died for all men (Beza), or that while his death atoned for them they had been denied sufficient faith for salvation (Calvin), this branch of Protestantism focused on seeking evidence of divine election.[4] While strenuous, achieving assurances of one's Elect status could transform mere lifeless, worthless "clay" into worthy vehicles of the Almighty. This transformation demanded a denial of free will and a depreciation of reason, but it also "voluntaristically" freed believers from any technical responsibility for salvation. Since men were sinners by nature, and since weak human reason and will could never ascertain God's eternal decrees, emotional relief was available by relying solely on the Holy Spirit. Although the Spirit "knows that all the thoughts of the wisest of men are vain, ... and plainly pronounces every imagination of the human heart to be only evil," humble acceptance of this wretched state is the first step toward regeneration.[5] Once men like Bunyan or Cromwell accepted their natural helplessness, they had the advantage of placing their hopes for redemption on a divine agency completely divorced from their past actions or failures. As well as appealing to ordinary men and women, this theology attracted serious intellectuals who agreed with Calvin that it is God's will that "our nature is destitute of all those things ... confer[red] ... through the Spirit of regeneration" and utterly dependent on his mercy. To further manifest his glory, the Almighty grants sinners only "an imputation of righteousness" through "justification," the means by which "God is pleased to receive us into his favor" by faith alone. And since "no works of ours can render us

---

[2]   McAdoo, *Spirit*, p. 26.

[3]   For a useful study of Hooker's reception, see Michael Brydon, *The Evolving Reputation of Richard Hooker: An Examination of the Responses 1600–1714* (Oxford, 2006).

[4]   Stachniewski, *Persecutory Imagination*, pp. 25–26.

[5]   John Calvin, *The Institutes of the Christian Religion*, trans. John Allen (2 vols., Philadelphia, 1936), II.ii.25.

acceptable to God" except as we are regenerated, and that regeneration is, without exception, entirely of God, our new righteousness has everything to do with Him and virtually nothing to do with man.[6]

For anyone searching for a radical intervention or "turn-around" in his or her life, anyone diffident of his or her moral or intellectual merit, or simply searching for "hard" logical answers, Calvinism thus offered some obvious advantages. These included the emotional benefits of no longer depending upon a "sterile" or "fallen" self. After heroically "wrestling" one's stubborn will and intellect into submission, believers experienced saving grace as a miraculous new ability to resist sin. Yet thanks to the "experimental predestination" pioneered by William Perkins and his fellow covenant theologians, this miracle need not be the fruit of a sudden, drastic conversion. Perkins's pastoral work effectively expanded conversion from a "one-step" to a "twelve-step" process, every stage of which emphasized complete faith and commitment to God, not to rational comprehension or self-justification. Calvinism therefore produced the tormented consciences documented by Stachniewski, but it also produced believers who rose above their doubts and rested secure in their highly voluntaristic, "Spirit-driven" faith. While it did not "free" the saints in the modern sense of the word, believing that God or the Holy Spirit led them to salvation gave them a comforting sense of spiritual rectitude and reassurance. As late as the mid-nineteenth century, the Puritan sensibility continued to appeal to "enlightened" thinkers like Thomas Carlyle even though they personally regarded Christianity as a myth. Unlike earlier Whig historians who praised godly self-determination but condemned its irrational and authoritarian excesses, Carlyle rejoiced that his ancestors had decreed

> "that England should all become a church", and that "God's own law", "the hard-stone tables, the God-given precepts and eternal penalties", should be brought "into actual practice in men's affairs on the earth". Under Cromwell Puritanism had stood "erect, with its foot on the hydra Babylon, with its open bible and drawn sword", chaining and punishing those evils which the laissez-faire philosophy ... was wantonly indulging. Now as then England needed rulers who would enforce the distinction between right and wrong ... [and] give the people, as Cromwell himself had put it, not what they want but what's good for them, ... a "divine right" to exact obedience.[7]

Although Puritans were far from uniformly hostile to reason, science, art, or education, Carlyle's emphasis on their resistance to more open-ended or "laissez-faire" philosophies was hardly counterfactual. As Barbara Shapiro observes, "While Puritans avoided the formal claim of infallibility because of its Roman Catholic associations, they were absolutely certain of their monopoly on religious truth." Early Puritan scientists like John Wilkins adopted a far more open-minded

---

[6]   Ibid., II.ii.20, III.xi.3,4, and III.xiv.13.

[7]   Worden, *Roundhead*, p. 271.

outlook because he "appears to have carried over from scientific investigation to religious thought" certain skeptical habits of thinking: "tentativeness of judgement and unwillingness to find solutions based on authority, together with insistence that quiet discussion rather than violent argument or the clash of authorities was most likely to yield truth." Temperamentally as well as ideologically wary of the Baconian "idols" of the mind, he liked to remind others "that men were naturally prone to error, and that impartiality" was all too rare a quality among them. Shapiro traces this irenic attitude to the example of Wilkins's Puritan grandfather, John Dod, yet as he certainly knew, it was not a typical attitude. At Oxford Wilkins had to overcome godly "fervor and zeal" as he led the "Moral, Sober Party" against the "fiery," zealous faction. Similar irenic principles later allowed Wilkins's "Latitude-men" to ally with moderate Puritans like John Wallis, Anglicans, and even some Quakers in the early Royal Society. Yet like Wilkins's friends Dury and Hartlib, who introduced him to the anti-Calvinist Remonstrants, many of these individuals either traveled in Arminian circles or, like Dod, avoided narrow disputes over doctrine and ritual for the sake of church unity and Christian morality. In many important respects this outlook made them practically "indistinguishable from ... moderate Anglican reformers" like the mature Wilkins.[8]

Moderates principally differed from Puritans in worshipping a God-in-nature very different from the deity of William of Ockham, who, next to Augustine, was the primary influence on Calvin. In opposing Thomistic rationalism, Ockham effectively denied God's hand in secondary causes and exalted God's direct agency to a degree that came perilously close to making him a divine tyrant so transcendent both in himself and in his design that nothing could be known of him even from the empirically knowable laws of nature.[9] Yet Ockham's separation of God from secondary or natural causes also had a number of positive consequences, the chief of which was to undermine the mystical "World Soul" that supposedly mediated between God and his creation. With this dubious force called in question, early scientists began to search for efficient natural causes of phenomena without considering their "Final Cause." Ockham's nominalist position is therefore credited with inspiring both Bacon's empiricist program and Boyle's "proto-deist" universe. Richard Jones seminally associated Boyle's mechanist or "godless" universe with the Royal Society as a whole, and later scholars like Robert Hoopes and Margaret Jacob still support versions of this thesis, which continues to fuel postmodern objections to early modern science. Yet in fact, the vast majority of Royal Society rationalists were anti-Cartesian vitalists who simply replaced the old World Soul with a semi-divine "plastic nature."[10] Jones's faulty conclusions

---

[8]   Shapiro, *John Wilkins*, pp. 67, 66, 23, 123, 9. Sprat's irenic *History of the Royal Society* was written under Wilkins's direction (p. 28).

[9]   Hoopes, *Right Reason*, pp. 91–93.

[10]   Richard Jones, *The Seventeenth Century* (Palo Alto, 1951), and *Ancients and Moderns*, raised intriguing problems but his solutions were simplistic. His many critics, including Shapiro (*John Wilkins*, pp. 79, 99), now accept Han Aarsleff's description of

stemmed partly from his overly vague definition of "voluntarism" and partly from confusing Ockham's nominalist *linguistics* with his nominalist *deity*. Following Duns Scotus, Ockham indeed anticipated Calvin by elevating the divine will above the moral or rational laws of his universe, which are correct only because God decrees them so, not due to their innate rightness or objective "goodness." As a good grammarian, Ockham had recognized that the relationship between words, things, and syntax was arbitrary, and as a good anti-Thomist, he believed that the relationship between God and nature was equally arbitrary. Francis Oakley shows that he thus exchanged the ancient Greek and Thomistic assumption that nature expressed God's "indwelling and immanent reason" for one that subordinated his reason to his will. The thirteenth-century Ockhamists continued his tradition by claiming that, since God freely willed the laws of both nature and salvation, both had to be understood in radically antinecessitarian terms. This position was conducive to mysticism since it undermined "the very possibility of a truly reliable empirical knowledge of the natural world," yet it also enabled anti-mystical empiricists like Bacon to undermine long-held Platonic assumptions about the ontologically "Real" nature of the relation between words and things.[11]

Ockham's essential contribution to this skeptical–empirical line of thought was to expose Plato's ideal forms as mere figments of his imagination. As a result, matter no longer needed to be regarded as merely a copy or "species" of an immaterial order preestablished in the mind of God. Hoopes points out that this skeptical move particularly invalidated futile scholastic inquiries into the processes whereby immaterial species produce matter, although as Milton's anti-scholastic third Prolusion shows, such inquiries persisted well into the seventeenth century. Hence like Bacon, Wilkins, and other founders of the "new science," Milton still needed to defend the Ockhamist position that real knowledge must be based on material sense perceptions of particular, concrete objects, not abstract "forms." Although universals did exist, they represented conceptual likenesses among concrete particulars, not "Real" or immaterial ideas preexisting in the divine or human mind.[12] In making this case, the new empiricists also needed to confront the Christian dilemma created by Ockham's abandonment of universals, which, according to Hoopes, either meant renouncing "certain key dogmas of the faith or ... admit[ting] the independence of reason and religion and abandon[ing] all

---

Jones as "always a poor guide and ... now thoroughly outmoded." See *From Locke to Saussure* (Minneapolis, 1982), p. 275 n. 81; see also p. 273 n. 60. Margaret Jacob's studies in this vein include *The Newtonians and the English Revolution, 1689–1720* (Ithaca, 1976), and *The Radical Enlightenment: Pantheists, Freemasons, and Republicans* (Boston, 1981). Jacob's conclusions have been largely invalidated in numerous studies by Michael Hunter; see especially *Establishing the New Science: The Experience of the Early Royal Society* (Woodbridge, 1989).

[11]   Francis Oakley, *Omnipotence, Covenant, and Order* (Ithaca, 1984), pp. 80, 63, 65.

[12]   Hoopes, *Right Reason*, pp. 89–90; on Milton's relation to this tradition, see pp. 186–200.

efforts to demonstrate a rational basis for Christianity. As a believer, Ockham did not hesitate to take the second alternative"—he accepted the fact that the entire structure of the universe was established by arbitrary decree.[13] This essentially medieval choice nevertheless left the first option open: renouncing or revising key Christian dogmas according to the light of skeptical reason, which (as Hoopes failed to see) is precisely the position taken by the early Baconians and later virtuosi. A supremely reasonable God could still construct his universe according to hidden laws not immediately accessible to the lesser faculties of the human mind without being ultimately arbitrary or unknowable. Nevertheless, his laws could not be determined by human logic alone, but only by careful inductive reason and experiment. Thus, in their view, Plato's abstract ratiocination combined the worst Idols of the cave, tribe, marketplace, and theater. Much the same principles applied to scripture, since Bacon's good God wisely hid his laws both in his revealed Word and in nature's "book" in order to stimulate man's godlike creativity and industry. This view was particularly compatible with Hooker's rationally accessible God-in-nature, who, still partly transcendent and mysterious, had little in common with Ockhamist arbitrariness or Calvinist mystery. Like the Thomistic creator, this deity operates upon rationally comprehensible principles shared by his human creatures, who, while lacking both divine omniscience and angelic intuition, can still cooperatively reconstruct them through the skeptical methods suggested by practical reason. In time, reason itself will rise to new heights as it begins to comprehend the hidden order and beauty of creation, which at once demonstrates and exalts divine goodness.[14]

This brief overview of the contrasting foundations of rationalist and Calvinist theology suggests that, in either system, the creature mirrors his Creator, and vice versa: a rational God gives birth to reasonable, law-abiding creatures, while a voluntarist God gives birth to worshippers arbitrarily elected by his inscrutable Spirit. From that perspective, Christian rationalists like Milton's friend John Hales, who famously bade "John Calvin good-night" after the Council of Dort, could justifiably consider their opponents dogmatic and unreasonable. Hales complained that the Calvinist theologians openly "profess they oppose themselves, first against those opinions concerning predestination, which the authors themselves called horrida decreta," and second, by forcing others to separate from the church because of principles that they could not rationally understand or defend.[15] Like his friends at Great Tew and like the Cambridge Platonists, the liberal Hales embraced rational discussion and dissent as the sole means of ascertaining truth, although, as H.R. McAdoo points out, this did not completely free any of them from paradox.

---

[13]   Ibid., p. 91.

[14]   On the rapid rise of this God among seventeenth-century empiricists, see Oakley, *Omnipotence*, pp. 74–75, 81–92; on Wilkins's role in promoting it, see Shapiro, *John Wilkins*.

[15]   John Hales, *Golden Remains of the Ever Memorable M. John Hales* (London, 1659), pp. 422–24.

They preached tolerance but accepted the Church's authority to set bounds to both legitimate controversy and sectarian dissent. Regarding the visible church as an important part of society's rational life, they felt the need to safeguard it from schism. Yet in many ways they truly were less dogmatic than the Calvinists. Believing with Hales that toleration of "sundry opinions even amongst the Fathers themselves" had not led to the "sceptic theology" their enemies accused them of promoting, they probabilistically defended their beliefs from the scriptures and solid reason, not from Calvin, the Schoolmen, Augustine, or any other of the Church Fathers alone.[16]

Their rejection of the Schoolmen's logical abstractions also ironically made the rationalists more consistent linguistic nominalists than the Calvinists despite their Ockhamist lineage. Guarding against the tendency of words to create signifieds without concrete referents, they valued linguistic simplicity and monosemy over universals, etymologies, or other "signatures" of transcendent truth derived from the scholastic synthesis of Plato and Aristotle. Milton's linguistic practice clearly places him in this empirical tradition, since, as Daniel Fried points out, he includes no transcendent signifiers in Eden and no fallen signifiers even in satanic language. Satan's rhetoric can be regarded as an extreme example of the free play of "slippery signifiers," yet since for Milton "slipperiness" is the condition of all language, it can be overcome only by carefully framing terms and clarifying their referents, as the Son does in debating the tempter of *Paradise Regained*. Like the virtuosi, however, Milton also rejects a Hobbesian or "strong nominalism" in favor of the discursive or "weak" nominalism of the kind advocated by Wilkins, Boyle, and Wilkins's protégé, Thomas Sprat, who commonly insist that well-defined terms may suggestively illuminate but never dictate meaning. This qualification successfully prevents words from becoming arbitrary signifiers of sovereign power as they do in Hobbes.[17] Yet "weak nominalism" is not merely a linguistic term since it actually grew out of the arguments for free inquiry mounted by the commonwealth of the 1640s, as shown both by Milton's *Areopagitica* and Nathaniel Carpenter's comparable writings. Wilkins and his followers followed suit in linking their "Philosophical Liberty" to a positive suspension of belief: "any doubt or obscurity" could only be settled after first refusing to give "our Assents" to any settled "Opinion on either side." If final "Victory cannot be had, Men must be content with Peace" in their "Philosophical Contentions," religious or scientific. In the meantime, "Tis an Excellent rule to be observed in all Disputes, That men should give *Soft* Words and *Hard Arguments*," and "not so much strive to *vex*, as to convince an Enemy. If this were but diligently practiced in all Cases, ... we might ... in a good measure be freed from ... Vexations in the search of

---

[16] McAdoo, *Spirit*, pp. 22–23, 14–21, cited p. 20.

[17] Daniel Fried, "Milton and Empiricist Semiotics," *MQ* 37.3 (October 2003): pp. 117–38; cited pp. 133–34, 126, 128–29.

Truth."[18] This probabilistic seventeenth-century tradition only gradually came
under assault as Romantic thinkers turned from empirical reason to "voluntarist"
authenticity, which, in Carlyle's case, led him to see Cromwell's grammatical
flaws as "witnesses to ... soul[ful] ... depths far below the level of words."[19]

Yet, as Richard Tuck's survey of the natural law tradition shows, the downside
of voluntarism is that it hindered the development of natural rights theories.
Because Calvinists privileged God's divine right to make covenants of all kinds—
religious, legal, and political—thinkers like Samuel Rutherford failed to create a
legal legacy comparable to that left by Arminian or proto-Arminian thinkers like
Hooker and Grotius. Although they were all concerned with the social problems
that arose when rulers failed to comply with their divine obligations, early Calvinist
resistance theorists thought more about their duty to God than about individual
rights. Even humanistic Calvinists such as George Buchanan were ultimately
forced to deny "that men construct political institutions for their own benefit: their
political life is a direct gift from God, without being fully natural to them (i.e.
coeval with them)."[20] Milton's neglect of or disdain for such thinkers—he barely
mentions Buchanan and considers Rutherford a "New Forcer of Conscience" in
a poem so entitled (ll. 7–8)—and his praise of natural law advocates like Grotius
and Galileo again seems most directly influenced by Grotius's English descendant,
John Selden. Although more conservative members of the Great Tew circle also
contributed to the development of natural rights theories by refuting Hobbes's
determinist "laws of nature," Selden's signal contribution was to harmonize local
and universal law in ways that set the example for Milton's defenses of the English
republic. For Selden, both the Decalogue and the Hebrew laws of marriage were
merely local and adjustable derivatives of higher and more universal laws.[21] On
the left, Levellers like Richard Overton and William Walwyn contributed to the
legal development of natural rights theory, while on the right, the Cambridge
Platonists anticipate eighteenth-century notions of the common rights of mankind.
Yet in every case, these developments were more indebted to Hooker than to the
Calvinist resistance theorists who rejected the Thomistic and Ciceronian belief
that "that the law of nature is in *all* humanity, pagans, prechristians and Christians
alike."[22] Bacon also played an important role in these developments by thoroughly
reinterpreting Christian charity to include not just "the absolute primacy of the

---

[18]   See Shapiro, *John Wilkins*, pp. 55–56, who cites Wilkins, *A Discourse Concerning
a New Planet* (1640), pp. 145, 153,146, 140.

[19]   Worden, *Roundhead*, p. 274.

[20]   Richard Tuck, *Natural Rights Theories: Their Origin and Development* (Cambridge,
1979), p. 43; see also p. 44, and on Rutherford, pp. 144–45.

[21]   Tuck, *Natural Rights*, pp. 95–96. For a fuller comparison of Milton and Selden, see
Rosenblatt, *Torah*; on natural law in the defenses, see Chapter 2 above.

[22]   R.S. White, *Natural Law in English Renaissance Literature* (Cambridge, 1996),
p. 228; Tuck, *Natural Rights*, pp. 107–55, especially pp. 149–50. See also Robert Eccleshall,
"Richard Hooker and the Peculiarities of the English: The Reception of the *Ecclesiastical*

love of God, and ... care for the heavenly destiny of one's neighbor," but the invention of corporate and institutional means for aiding one's fellow man through advances in education, law, science, and the liberal arts.[23] The common if far from identical interests of these rationalists explain why most belonged to circles with overlapping memberships not strictly divided by religion or politics.

A cautionary word is nevertheless needed here, since in its pre-modern sense, the term "rationalism" embraced an enormously flexible and expandable set of categories. All of these intellectual circles (Hobbesians excepted) were still strongly influenced by elements of mystical Neoplatonism or Pansophism, and Bacon himself was something of a "mystical" visionary, as were early Baconians like Comenius and Joseph Mede.[24] Mede conducted experiments but also seized upon Bacon's millenarian emphasis, which partly inspired him to compose his famous *Key to the Apocalypse*. Even the strong critical spirit that dominated Great Tew was fused with a millenarianism that transcended any particular style, founder, or even standard of belief.[25] All of these groups included poets, mathematicians, and political theorists along with religious and educational reformers, and all contained members of opposing political persuasions. Nevertheless, most members of the Hartlib circle supported Parliament, while, with the important exception of Selden, those congregated at Great Tew were royalists like their leader, Lord Falkland. Social and temperamental factors also played a part in these allegiances: the more aristocratic Great Tew circle mainly emphasized the obligatory or "dutiful" aspect of natural law, while their more progressive social counterparts in the Hartlib circle focused more on natural and humanitarian rights.[26]

W.K. Jordan believed that the most radical of them all was the religious moderate, Henry Robinson, whose ambitious projects during the Protectorate included legal, land, and economic reform; republican government; and free universal education and health care. Perhaps the only man of his age to understand that the liberal society of the future must combine religious liberty and self-government with a free economy, Robinson was a Baconian pragmatist with few ideological biases.[27]

Polity in the Seventeenth and Eighteenth Centuries," *History of Political Thought* 2.1 (1981): pp. 63–117.

[23]   Richard Kennington, *On Modern Origins*, ed. Pamela Kraus and Frank Hunt (Lanham, MD: 2004), p. 5.

[24]   See Strider, *Robert Greville*, pp. 16–17, 131. As Strider shows, Brooke was early linked to the Hartlib–Comenius–Dury group that John Wallis refers to meeting around 1645, which contained the core of the Invisible College that later sponsored the Royal Society; see also John Wallis, *A Defence of the Royal Society* (London, 1678). Strider believes that the strong Baconian elements in Brooke's thought (pp. 16–17) would have made him a fellow founder (p. 131).

[25]   See Sarah Hutton, "Mede, Milton, and More: Christ's College Millenarians," in Juliet Cummins (ed.), *Milton and the Ends of Time* (Cambridge, 2003), pp. 29–41.

[26]   Tuck, *Natural Rights*, pp. 101–10.

[27]   Jordan, *Men of Substance*, pp. 178–258, especially pp. 215–17.

Yet both Boyle's Invisible College and Wilkins's Oxford group shared this socially progressive orientation, and both either supported the Protectorate or maintained a tolerant neutrality. Along with Seth Ward at Oxford and Milton's friend Henry Oldenburg, these kindred spirits later formed the experimental Royal Society, while those gathered at Great Tew mainly contributed to Latitudinarian theology. Even this loose division will not strictly hold, however, since both Wilkins and Sprat were important Latitudinarians as well as Royal Society founders, as were many members of the generally more Puritan and Parliamentarian Hartlib circle. Like Milton's, their intellectual affinities thus overrode simple Puritan versus Anglican dichotomies. Charles Webster traces Milton's association with both Boyle's Invisible College and Hartlib to the period surrounding his post-graduate studies. He also corrects the long-held misconception that Boyle's Invisible College consisted of "learned and curious gentlemen, who, after the breaking out of the civil wars," diverted "themselves from those melancholy scenes ... [with] experimental inquiries, and the study of nature, which was then called the new philosophy, and at length gave birth to the Royal Society."[28] Boyle's eighteenth-century editor, Thomas Birch, is the source of this misinformation, repeated in most standard histories, both specialist and generalist. Yet, in fact, his Invisible College supported both parliamentary politics and pan-European social reforms. Broadly stimulated by the "new philosophy," his "college" was at once more utilitarian, philanthropic, and utopian than Wilkins's Oxford circle, but it was not uninterested (as long supposed) in solving classic scientific problems.[29]

Boyle's group was at first chiefly involved in schemes for improving their estates, but it rapidly progressed to more abstruse experiments in practical chemistry and agriculture. After the Irish Rebellion, Boyle, his sister Katherine Ranelagh, and their close friend Benjamin Worsley continued these efforts throughout the mid-1640s both in Worsley's laboratory in London and in Lady Ranelagh's home in Pall Mall. From there, their circle rapidly widened to include Parliamentarian intellectuals like Milton, Hartlib, Dury, and John Sadler. Milton's educational innovations especially attracted Lady Ranelagh's attention, who soon placed both her son Richard Jones and Richard Barry, second earl of Barrimore, under his tutelage.[30] After Milton became Latin secretary under Cromwell, Oldenburg took over Jones's education along the same lines set forth in *Of Education*, and his correspondence with the poet frequently touches not only on this subject but on the continental reception of Milton's anti-monarchist tracts. Webster's work also dismisses two long-standing conclusions: that Hartlib was disappointed with Milton's *Of Education*, and that it exerted little if "any influence on contemporary writers or practices within his own lifetime" (*CPW* 2:359) since it rejected

---

[28]   *The Works of the Honourable Robert Boyle*, ed. Thomas Birch (6 vols., London, 1772), vol. 1, p. xlii.

[29]   Charles Webster, "New Light on the Invisible College," *Transactions of the Royal Historical Society*, 5th series, col. 24 (London, 1974), pp. 19–42, cited pp. 21–23.

[30]   Webster, "New Light," 26–29.

Comenius's "*Janua's* and *Didactics*" (*CPW* 2:364). Hartlib in fact immediately sent copies to John Dury and John Hall, and the latter's 1649 *Advancement of Learning* later placed Milton beside Bacon as a harbinger of enlightenment. Since Hartlib collected many different educational programs aimed at different classes, Milton's tractate filled an important gap not addressed by Comenius: a simplified, anti-scholastic, and neo-humanist program for the upper echelon.[31]

Webster thus concludes there was "no basic antagonism between the Hartlib circle and Milton" but rather that Sir Cheney Culpeper's judgment was representative: "Milton was enlightened and should be supported, but was not intimately concerned with detailed pedagogical issues of the kind familiar to the disciples of Comenius." Hartlib nevertheless included Milton on his "'Councel for Schooles,'" and the reformer John Aubrey's unpublished but widely circulated educational manuscript also promotes his ideas and texts. Later, Abraham Cowley's *Proposition for the Advancement of the Experimental Philosophy* (1661) included much of Milton's educational program in his proposal for building a real "Salomon's House" based on Bacon's *New Atlantis*.[32] In response, Milton republished his tractate *Of Education* in 1673, noting that it was "written above twenty Years since" (*CPW* 2:362 n. 1). Finally, despite the Hartlib circle's religious and political diversity, it was united by the most radical corollary of the Baconian program: the "defence of freedom of religious and secular communication …[,] liberty of conscience and civil liberty." In general, that meant ending the "restrictions of the *ancien régime*" on religious association, the press, trade, and professional practice. These utopian dreams were finally destroyed by the "Barebones" or "Saints Parliament," a mismatched assembly of utopian reformers and anti-intellectual iconoclasts who undermined its reforming committees.[33]

Many Puritans were also attracted to the experiential and idealistic aspects of Bacon's empirical program, although they typically rejected his skeptical critique of the irrational elements in religion and his skeptical approach to language as well.[34] Since converts usually relied on mediate or immediate certitude (signs, voices from heaven, or other "leadings"), their emphasis on the Spirit at times—and especially among the radicals—tended to override their Baconian pragmatism.[35] This tendency is also evident among the Puritan members of the Hartlib circle who trusted in a sudden apocalyptic "cleansing" of the darkened glass of the mind to usher in the Joachimists' third "Age of the Spirit." In the Comenian version

---

[31]   Webster, *Samuel Hartlib*, pp. 41–42.

[32]   Ibid., p. 43. See also Michael Hunter, *John Aubrey and the Realm of Learning* (New York, 1975), and Abraham Cowley, *A Proposition for the Advancement of the Experimental Philosophy*, in *The Complete Works in Verse and Prose of Abraham Cowley*, ed. Alexander B. Grosart (2 vols., New York, 1967), vol. 2, pp. 280–91.

[33]   Webster, *Samuel Hartlib*, pp. 41, 61.

[34]   Hoopes, *Right Reason*, pp. 58–63, 54.

[35]   Richard L. Greaves, *The Puritan Revolution and Educational Thought: Background for Reform* (New Brunswick, NJ, 1969), pp. 80–92.

of this vision, spiritual transformation and education proceed hand in hand as microcosmic man (the *imago dei*) regains the original simplicity and harmony enjoyed by Adam in Eden. The sharp contrast between this suddenly "clarified" vision and the Baconian tentativeness advocated by Wilkins, Boyle, Carpenter, Robinson, Milton, and, later, Sprat, ultimately explains their very different views on education. In anticipation of the coming age, Comenians believed that a comprehensive or "Pansophic" key to the three books of God, man, and nature would supplant the gradual, skeptical, and virtually endless Baconian task of reassembling the building blocks of Truth. Comenius also believed that this "key" would unlock the magical microcosmic/macrocosmic homologies inherent in the older conception of the World Soul rejected by both Ockham and Bacon. Even the most mystical Comenian would not, however, have agreed with a strict Calvinist like the Independent Thomas Goodwin, who maintained that, since "divine omnipotence would be threatened if reason could work unaided by the Spirit," "'all wisdom and reason in man is against the way of faith.'" Others like Thomas Hall warned that "Wee must not bring down the mysteries of Religion to be scored by Philosophy, but we must make Philosophy wait and submit to Divinity." Less extreme spiritualists like the author of *The Marrow of Modern Divinity* simply urged that speculative reason must be subordinated to "communion with God," who is chiefly known "by powerful experience." The radical sectarians more often regarded spiritual "experience" as altogether inconsistent with philosophy, but in general, all Puritans accepted some version of the axiom *credo ut intelligam*, which Christian rationalists in the tradition of Hooker reversed.[36] Basing belief on right reason and sound hermeneutics, most accepted Benjamin Whichcote's anti-Calvinist credo that "true *Reason* is so far from being an Enemy to any matter of faith; that a man is disposed and qualified by Reason, for the entertaining those matters of Faith that are proposed by God."[37]

As the most socially disruptive opponents of this credo, Quakers were frequently condemned by everyone from the Platonist Whichcote to Milton's nephew Edward Phillips, who decried them as "Enthusiasts" and "Confounder[s], of both Reason and Religion." As we have seen, Milton excluded them from the list of "non-heretics" who could be regarded as good Protestants, since they accepted new revelations that Paul warned neither the apostles nor even "*an Angel from Heaven*" had the right to promulgate (*CPW* 8:419, Gal. 1:8). More conservative Protestants

---

[36] Ibid., pp. 116–17, see also pp. 118–21; and Keeble, *Literary Culture*, p. 179. Keeble includes Milton in the Nonconformist tradition because he believes that the "intellectual positions" of his *Christian Doctrine* and *Of True Religion* "count for very little" (p. 178). Greaves cites Thomas Goodwin in *Works* (12 vols., Edinburgh, 1861–66), vol. 2, p. 344, vol. 4, p. 239; "E.F." in *The Marrow of Modern Divinity*, ed. C.G. McCrie (Glasgow, 1902), pp. 225–26, and Thomas Hall in *Vindiciae Literarum* (London,1554), p. 51.

[37] Benjamin Whichcote, *Moral and religious Aphorisms, to which are added Eight Letters ... between Dr. Whichcote ... and Dr. Tuckney*, ed. Samuel Salter (London, 1753), p. 98.

were far harsher, accusing the Quakers of cultivating a peculiar "cant" that (as among Baptists like Bunyan) constituted their badge of belonging. Men like Boyle agreed, although he was far from reactionary. A Puritan in sensibility but a Latitudinarian in theology, he worked both with men like Robert Hooke, who had no deep personal commitment to religion, and die-hard Presbyterians like John Wallis. Another prominent Latitudinarian, Joseph Glanvill, also condemned the Quakers' "babbling" enthusiasm as mere "'*Gibberish*,'" but many rationalists were more tolerant. The Royal Society's founding secretary, Henry Oldenburg, regarded then sympathetically at a time when Boyle was ready to condemn even the Cambridge Platonists as "enthusiasts." Yet, as Jackson Cope shows, Boyle and Glanvill were not entirely wrong about the Quakers: rejecting virtually all humanistic learning in favor of personal revelations and "auditory hallucinations" produced by chanting scripture to bring the Spirit into their hearts, they were among the most extreme "Seekers" of the era.[38]

Puritan versus Rationalist Paths toward Truth, Goodness, and Utility

Less extreme Puritans generally sought the same kind of authenticity through some version of the Neoplatonic "mystery" that Ockham rejected while retaining a mysterious God. Although they still admired both Bacon's pragmatism and his disdain for scholastic method, the Comenians' "Pansophy"—a hermetic form of universal knowledge that would simplify and reform human learning—led them to abandon his empiricist emphasis on secondary causes.[39] At once more mystical and more genuinely plain and "anti-poetic" than Bacon, they also abandoned *The Advancement of Learning*'s high regard for poetry as a vehicle of ethical instruction. Even in science itself, Bacon mainly sought to make language more serviceable and knowledge less gullible, while his own rhetorical style was always enriched with "choice conceits of the present state of learning, and with worthy contemplations of the means to procure it," as even anti-innovators like Sir Thomas Bodley conceded.[40] Since Bacon drew liberally on both the Bible and the classics, contrary to modern "legend," the strongest assaults on metaphorical "conceits" and the pagan classics came not from the new scientists but from the Puritans.

---

[38]　Jackson I. Cope, "Seventeenth-Century Quaker Style," *PMLA* 71.4 (1956): pp. 725–54, especially pp. 745, 733, 737; see also Ann Hughes, "The Frustrations of the Godly," in Morrill (ed.), *Revolution and Restoration*, p. 83. Nuttall admired the Quaker theology of grace and was perplexed by the hostility it provoked; see *Holy Spirit*, pp. 150–66.

[39]　Dagmar Capkova, "Comenius and his ideals: escape from the labyrinth," in Mark Greengrass, Michael Leslie, and Timothy Raylor (eds.), *Samuel Hartlib and Universal Reformation* (Cambridge, 1994), pp. 75–91, especially pp. 78, 81, 84. Ockham's deity could, however, dispense with secondary causes; see Oakley, *Omnipotence*, p. 64.

[40]　Sir Thomas Bodley is quoted in Thomas Macaulay, "Lord Bacon" (July 1837) in *Literary Essays*, p. 328.

The Comenians joined this assault by opposing the use of "the ancient classics in teaching Latin. Pagan authors, except possibly a few moralists whose writings were unobjectionable, were to be banned from the curriculum."[41] Believing that the Ancients could teach nothing about physical or human nature, not even the ethical knowledge of good and evil, Comenius taught Latin through abbreviated *Januas* and *Linguas*—the dictionary-like shortcuts despised by Milton—supplemented by a Universal Christian Encyclopedia. Summarizing every kind of practical and spiritually uplifting knowledge, Comenius's program was at once anti-Ancient, anti-humanist, and, to a considerable extent, anti-modern. These attitudes are all apparent in his complaint that

> *Plato's* philosophy seemed most elegant, and divine; but the Peripateticks accused it of too much vaine speculation. And *Aristotle* thought his *Philosophy* compleat, and trimme enough: but Christian Philosophers have found it neither agreeing with the holy Scriptures, nor answerable enough to the Truth of things. Astronomers for many ages carried away the bell with their Spheres Eccentricks, and Epicycles, but *Copernicus* explodes them all. *Copernicus* himself framed a new and plausible Astronomy out of his Optick grounds, but such as will no way be admitted by the unmovable principle of naturall Truth. *Gilbertus* being carried away with the speculation of the Loadstone, would out of it have deduced all Philosophy: but to the manifest injury of naturall principles. *Campanella* triumphs almost in the principles of the ancient Philosopher *Parmenides*, which he had reassumed to himselfe in his naturall Philosophy, but is quite confounded by one Optick glasse of *Galileus Galilei*. And why should we reckon any more?[42]

Virtually quoting Bacon on the excesses of Gilbert's magnetic theory and the "doubtful" effects of Galileo's discoveries, Comenius's final question—"why should we reckon any more?"—nevertheless rejects the Baconian solution of carefully sifting provable fact from "vulgar errors."

Yet the Comenian program was enlightened in comparison with the schemes of radical Puritans more fully invested in the classic Calvinist suspicion of human reason. Believing that no return to Eden was possible without utter reliance on the Spirit, Antinominians like William Dell and John Saltmarsh, Quakers like Isaac Penington, and the followers of the mystic Sebastian Franck demanded a denial "of the sufficiency of man's creatureliness" equivalent to a complete rejection of self.[43] More moderate Puritans like Baxter wittily complained that Dell went so

---

[41]   Greaves, *Puritan Revolution*, p. 94. Arthur Barker notes Milton's quite different principles in *Milton*, p. 183, but they should be obvious from his tractate *Of Education* alone.

[42]   John Amos Comenius, *Reformation of Schooles* …, trans. Samuel Hartlib (London, 1642), p. 16.

[43]   Solt, *Saints*, p. 31; cf. William Poole, *Milton and the Idea of the Fall* (Cambridge, 2005), pp. 67–68.

far in this direction that he "took Reason, Sound Doctrine, Order and Concord to be the intollerable Maladies of Church and State, because they were the greatest Strangers to his Mind."[44] Yet unfortunately, Dell was not unique: the London cobbler and separatist Samuel How opposed all "learning" but that of his native tongue, including "the knowledge of arts and sciences, diverse tongues, much reading, and persisting in these things, so as thereby to be made able to understand the mind of God in his word." Citing 1 Corinthians 2:13, How defended these beliefs on orthodox Calvinist grounds: "Carnal man, though learned, 'cannot perceive the things of God', and those who 'have had this kind of learning, when they came to know Christ, they forsook it all.'" The Baptist William Kiffin commended the new 1655 edition of How's *The Sufficiencie of the Spirits Teaching without Humane Learning* (1640) for making the Spirit all-sufficient, which as N.H. Keeble remarks, is a "distinctive feature of the enthusiasts and lower-class Interregnum sects" who opposed a state-supported, university educated clergy. The Seeker William Erbery firmly agreed with Penington "that education is no alternative to, or substitute for, spiritual vocation, but that it is antipathetic to it."[45]

These views remained relatively constant or were actually intensified later in the period, when post-Restoration Dissenters emphasized an ultra-Augustinian rejection of corporality, sexuality, and even concrete historical referents, which all but disappear from their literature. As Sharon Achinstein adds, their ideal was "an alternate literary economy in which ownership of literature was open to all and to none, since all human creativity properly came from, and belonged to, God." This emphasis nevertheless allowed them to approve of the "high art" of George Herbert, whose struggles to discover and follow the path of redemption and grace resonated strongly with men like Baxter. Despite his emphasis on church "furniture" and ritual, Herbert's penitentialism lent authority to the godly ministers' "cult of commemoration," which Achinstein finds creating a kind of "Real Presence" for Dissenters despite their official theological stance against it.[46] This "cult" contrasts with the virtuosi's renewed interest in primitive or non-ceremonial Christianity, which drew Wilkins and even staunch Anglicans like Glanvill and John Evelyn toward either "natural religion" or greatly simplified forms of faith and worship.[47]

Puritans, particularly the radicals, often shared the scientific interests of this group but their strong focus on the Spirit more frequently drew them toward natural magic. Even highly sympathetic scholars such as Margo Todd, Allison Coudert, Nigel Smith, Derek Hirst, and James Holston agree with Richard Greaves that they were far too addicted "to credulity, especially with respect to

---

[44]   Richard Baxter, *Reliquiae Baxterianae*, ed. Matthew Sylvester (London, 1696), Book I. Pt. 1, sect. 99, p. 64.

[45]   Keeble, *Literary Culture*, pp. 162–63.

[46]   Achinstein, *Literature and Dissent*, pp. 202, 200, 36–37.

[47]   On Evelyn, see W.G. Hiscock, *John Evelyn and Mrs. Godolphin* (London, 1951), pp. 74–99.

homemade medicine." It was thus no "accident that the works of Paracelsus were published in English, and by radicals, in the 1640s," or that most Hartlibians who adopted a strong millenarian outlook were at best quasi-scientific.[48] Christopher Hill suggestively links this interest in magic to their drive to identify spiritual with physical perception, to conflate mystical, infused knowledge with systematic higher learning, although it no longer seems credible that "the saint 'speaking experienced truths' ... and the scientist describing experiments which can be tested by other scientists" performed the same tasks.[49] Coudert confirms that the radicals' interests were inspired by a yearning for divine *gnosis* (the experience of "one who knows"), an offshoot of the dream of human perfectability shared by the alchemists, cabbalists, Quakers, and Seekers. Like Agrippa, Dee, Fludd, and other natural magicians, the radicals believed that one "divine spark" of the purified soul could redeem all of creation by reuniting fallen microcosmic matter with its macrocosmic source. These magical beliefs freed them from the conservative Puritan emphasis on original sin, but they usually failed to further the pragmatic Baconian project of careful empirical progress toward a more perfect world.[50]

Lucy Hutchinson is often considered an exception to this rule, since she produced an accomplished translation of Lucretius' *De Rerum Natura*, a principal source of Baconian atomism. Composed partly under the influence of the Cavendish circle before the civil wars and partly in the spirit of Comenius's belief that "*Democritus* erred not altogether, in making Atomes the matter of the world," Hutchinson's translation is nevertheless "selective and defensive," and "on one occasion even slants the Roman poet's words towards a belief in immortality and providence." Comenius, too, edited out the atomists' "godless" vacua included in *Paradise Lost*; yet by 1675, no amount of editing was sufficient for Hutchinson. Reid Barbour shows that after translating John Owen's theology, she flatly condemned her "wanton dalliance" with the "atheist dog" and rejected "the errors and evils of paganism" wholesale. Heaping scorn on Lucretius, she recast her translation effort as a conversion narrative: after "'walking in the darke, [she] had miraculously scapd a horrible precipice'" and had become a "'seamarke, to warne incautious travellers' about the sweet poison of human learning." Although Barbour compares this stance to that taken by the Son in Milton's *Paradise Regained*, its learned hero merely condemns the *replacement*

---

[48]   Greaves, *Puritan Revolution*, p. 86, and Derek Hirst, *Authority and Conflict in England 1603–1658* (London, 1986), p. 92. On the views of Smith, Todd, Coudert, and Holstun, see below.

[49]   Christopher Hill, *Change and Continuity in Seventeenth-Century England* (London, 1974), pp. 127–48, cited p. 135. For a summary of how and why Hill erred in claiming that "Dell, Winstanley and other radical critics were looking forward ... to the modern secular and scientific university as well as to the modern secular state" (p. 148), see Hirst, *Authority and Conflict*, pp. 89–95, and Shapiro, *John Wilkins*, pp. 7–9, 131.

[50]   See Allison Coudert, "Henry More, the Kabbalah, and the Quakers," in Kroll et al. (eds.), *Philosophy, Science, and Religion*, pp. 31–67, especially pp. 40–41.

of biblical teachings on the soul with pagan "theologians" like Plato and or with Stoics who would make themselves little gods.[51]

Hill similarly used theology to place Milton among the Puritans, in this case because he agreed with the radicals that the universities could not make a minister, whose vocation was determined by his spiritual calling alone. Yet in endorsing this commonly accepted principle, Milton did not reject "Logic, natural Philosophie, Ethics or Mathematics" as appropriate university subjects either for ministers or other students; he merely condemns "Sophistic Subtilties" and "Scholastic Notions, not to be found in Scripture" (*CPW* 7:302, 8:425). He also believed that ministers should not pursue purely secular subjects at the public expense, a proviso added not "in contempt of learning or the ministry," but only in the interest of combating ministerial pride and dereliction of duty. "Hating the common cheats of both" learning and the ministry, he was furious that "they who have preachd out bishops, prelats and canonists, should, in what serves thir own ends, retain thir fals opinions, thir Pharisaical leaven, thir avarice and ... ambition, thir pluralities, thir nonresidences, thir odious fees, and ... thir legal and Popish arguments for tithes" (*CPW* 7:318). Milton's entry into the "learned ministry controversy" was thus obviously motivated by practical rather than "spirit-filled" considerations: over-educated ministers frequently became too pompous and overbearing to "feed their flock."[52] Greaves shows that Puritan thought veered in the opposite direction because its epistemology was neither "truly rational ... [nor] truly intuitive," but an attempt "to juxtapose Spirit and reason, at times going so far as to identify the Spirit in man with man's rational faculties." They did this in different ways: radicals asserted that "reason [w]as markedly inferior to Spirit," while moderates like Richard Baxter insisted that the two worked in tandem, although only after the Spirit "awakens" reason to aid it in curbing the will. Even this distinction remains alien to Milton and other "once-born" heirs of Hooker, whose God universally restores man's lapsed powers immediately after the Fall.[53]

Christian rationalists of this type believed that things done by the light of nature obey the same law that gives all men a "title and interest" in faith, which for Hales is simply maintained by "faithfully ... keep[ing] the commandments of God ... as we are men," not as narrow dogmatists. For William Chillingworth as well, faith means obeying the divine edicts in harmony with "right reason, grounded on divine revelation and common notions written by God in the hearts of all men" without debating imponderable scriptural obscurities, since the fundamentals of

---

[51]   Comenius, *Naturall philosophie reformed by divine light, or A synopsis of physicks* (1651), p. 38; Reid Barbour, "Lucy Hutchinson, Atomism and the Atheist Dog," in Lynette Hunter and Sarah Hutton (eds.), *Women, Science and Medicine 1500–1700* (Phoenix Mill, 1997), pp. 122–37, cited pp. 135, 122–23.

[52]   Barbara Lewalski, "Milton on Learning and the Learned Ministry Controversy," *HLQ* 24.4 (1961): pp. 267–81, describes this as a moderate position.

[53]   Greaves, *Puritan Revolution*, p. 115. On Milton, see White, *Natural Law*, p. 228.

saving faith are clear and accessible to all.[54] If any have unwittingly erred after "sincerely searching all things according to the rule of Scripture," the rationalists agree with Milton that God "hath pardon'd their errors, and accepts their Pious endeavours" because "the assistance of his Spirit … [has] made no man Infallible" (*CPW* 8:426). Virtually paraphrasing Hales at this point, in *Of True Religion* Milton declares Socinians and Arminians "no Hereticks" (*CPW* 8:423, cf. n. 27), a Latitudinarian position which no Puritan endorsed. Explicitly referring to official Anglican documents, Milton here silently quotes "the best-known works of moderate or latitudinarian Anglicans, including one [Hales] that says that an antitrinitarian is not necessarily a heretic." Keith Stavely regards this alliance not as a retreat but rather an advance in his religious thought, which had long been moving in this direction, as Arthur Barker previously noted.[55] According to Greaves, this course was largely closed to Puritans, who were all too well "aware of the dangers of a rationalist epistemology to their ideology, for the unhindered use of reason led to freedom of inquiry and moral choice, and hence to a life of self-determination. Puritanism never became that liberal, though throughout its history it spawned rationalists who did and were consequently condemned."[56] Todd shows that faithful, well-educated Calvinists like the Cambridge scholar and minister Samuel Ward (who deeply shared Milton's love of classical learning) typically subjected themselves to an anti-individualist regime aimed at erasing his anti-Christian pride in "academic excellence, in spiritual accomplishments, in being seen with admired men." Struggling to turn his frivolous, fun-loving, proud self into a penitent Christian ever mindful that "no sin can fail to separate the sinner from God," and none is ever "too small to bewail," Ward was obsessed with imitating his ministerial role models at Emmanuel College and embracing the persecution of those who branded them "Puritans and precisians."[57]

Hill's beloved radicals were of course far less austere and more eager to attain spiritual knowledge; many in fact aspired to a version of Baconian monism. Yet, rather than bringing spirit down to earth or making it a particularly "vital" aspect of matter—as Milton was already doing in his early masque— they tended to transcendentalize matter. Quakers like George Fox actually believed that pronouncing certain letters of the Hebrew alphabet could reproduce the divine creation by recreating God's cosmic building blocks, the cornerstone of which

---

[54] McAdoo, *Spirit*, pp. 17, 14, citing Hales, *Golden Remains*, pp. 48, 42, and Chillingworth, *Religion of Protestants* (1637), ch. III, pt. I, p. 81.

[55] Stavely, preface to *Of True Religion*, *CPW* 8:413; he also notes contemporary allusions. Barker notes the similarity between Milton's and Chillingworth's Latitudinarian positions in *Milton*, pp. 230, 244; see also White, *Natural Law*, p. 233.

[56] Greaves, *Puritan Revolution*, pp. 115–16.

[57] Todd, "Puritan Self-Fashioning," pp. 83, 68, 70. Puritans officially renounced dogmatism but, like Bunyan's Christian, they often remained highly dependent on teachers, preachers, and other approved authorities.

was the "Christ within," who would return them to Adamic purity.[58] Their spiritual possession or "quaking" was another important route to transcendent experience, yet, according to Coudert, it also reintroduced "the rationale for the continual, intense, and in some instances pathological, self and social scrutiny characteristic of much protestant thought. The idea of a sacred community enshrined in covenant theology made it essential for everyone to be his brother's keeper lest one erring individual spoil everyone's chance at heaven."[59] James Holstun confirms the role that similar ideas played in Puritan utopianism. Unlike natural law theorists who emphasized the pre-Christian sources of virtue outlined in Romans 2:14–15, godly utopists believed that "the City of God and the City of Man" would combine in creating a theocracy directly guided by "God's shaping hand." Although they acknowledged that God works through secondary causes in the natural world, his approaching apocalypse would remake the world from a new *tabula rasa*.[60] Walter Cradock expresses the flip side of this belief when he proclaims that "*Gospel Religion*" dictates that "our *main reformation* is in *pulling down*, and not in *setting up*: for we have a world of *institutions* set up that will never hold."[61] For Holstun, this claim marks the divide between the "hermeneutic millennialism" of the Baconians and the "catalytic millennialism" of the Puritans. The latter would create "a machine" disciplining "civil or 'bad' conscience" out of existence, so that, in their new order, no "democratic notions of natural rights, ancient liberties, or the fundamental equality of men as moral agents" would be needed. All would be "fundamentally equal," but "only so far as they" were "equally susceptible to being written on by ... [theocratic] authorities."[62] Calvinist assumptions like these eventually divided the nation more deeply over questions of human agency in law, religion, rhetoric, science, and education than Hobbes ever divided the natural law tradition.

The Background and Aftermath of the Ward–Webster Debates

This growing divide has long been traced to the debates between Seth Ward (Hobbes's one-time friend but later his enemy) and John Webster, whose Calvinist-inflected Antinomianism led to radically different conclusions about reforming the universities. Yet even before the famous debates of 1654 began, conflicts over the role of human agency in educational and scientific progress had surfaced in

---

[58]   See Smith, *Perfection Proclaimed*, pp. 71, 76, 229–30, and Coudert, "Henry More," pp. 39–41, 44–47.

[59]   Coudert, "Henry More," p. 46.

[60]   Holstun, *Rational Millennium*, p. 43.

[61]   Walter Cradock, *Divine Drops Distilled* (1650), p. 212.

[62]   Holstun, *Rational Millennium*, pp. 45, 290. Nuttall supports Holstun's assessment, observing that Puritan equality is "essentially an equality before God, not before man"; see *Holy Spirit*, p. 120, also pp. 121, 166.

the 1651 epistolary free will debate waged between Benjamin Whichcote and his former tutor, Anthony Tuckney. Tuckney had been made master of Emmanuel six years earlier in 1645, but even in this Calvinist stronghold, many Cambridge theologians were already turning to "the more liberal and anthropocentric outlook" popularized by irenic anti-Calvinists like Hales, Chillingworth, and the Cambridge Platonists. Although heirs of the godly tradition, men of this type joined Henry More in objecting to the *horrida decreta*, which like Calvin's teaching on total depravity, More found horrid indeed. Both he and Whichcote also critiqued the Antinomian reaction because it seemed to make free grace an occasion for "wantonness." Yet Whichcote's objections predictably led men like Tuckney to accuse him of "moralism" and Socinianism, since his old-fashioned Calvinist tutor failed to understand his student's growing commitment to religious toleration and free will ethics. Whichcote's frank self-defense is usually regarded as marking a hardening of opinion on both sides of the controversy, although some Puritans like Baxter also softened or moderated their positions in its wake. Baxter's centrist position on free will allowed that it was sufficient in matters of rational, secular self-determination but not in matters of salvation, which remained wholly dependent on divine grace. Even this position differs from the "true" or self-determining Arminianism of men like Milton, who believed in universal grace if not in universal salvation.

Laud's biographer, Peter Heylyn, supported the free will side of these controversies by claiming that "good old" English Protestants like Wyclif, Tyndale, and Foxe had never accepted Calvin's teachings on predestination, a claim that allowed him to sidestep the charge of "papism" that brought down the Laudian Arminians.[63] Taylor contributed to the controversy by arguing for the sufficiency of rational free will in every aspect of life; like Milton, who earlier declared that "reason is but choosing" (*CPW* 2:527, cf. *PL* 3.108), he believed that "even our acts of understanding are acts of choice" demanding careful rational evaluation. The common sources of this belief are Aristotle's *Nicomachean Ethics* 3.2.6 (Hughes 260) and the pre-Augustinian Fathers, especially Lactantius and Julian of Eclanum. Taylor, however, relied more on Julian, and Milton more on Lactantius; Milton's *Commonplace Book* cites Lactantius's belief that God permits evil so "that reason and intelligence may have the opportunity to exercise themselves by choosing the things that are good, by fleeing from the things that are evil" (*CPW* 1:363). Taylor's reliance on Julian to overturn "total depravity" was much bolder, since, as McAdoo observes, he knew that restricting the effects of "original sin could not escape criticism from the dominant Augustinianism of the day" even though he qualified Julian's "Pelagianism." Yet, like Milton, Taylor did this simply by giving prevenient grace a central role in assisting fallen reason: "'right reason proceeding upon the best grounds it can, viz. of divine revelation and human authority, and probability is our guide (stando in humanis) and supposing the assistance of God's

---

    [63]   Wallace, *Puritans*, pp. 140–42. On the growing resistance to predestination doctrine among Calvinists themselves, see Stachniewski, *Persecutory Imagination*, pp. 53–61.

Spirit.'"[64] Following the liberal Mede and More, his pupil, Taylor also rejected Calvin's inscrutable God as a tyrant who damns all but a select few for Adam's sin. This view promoted religious toleration by limiting "revealed," prophetic, and doctrinal certitude and grounding most scriptural interpretation in probability.

Whichcote further illuminates the anti-authoritarian aspect of the free will or "anti-inscrutability" argument in flatly rejecting the idea that anyone should "be limited and confined by will and pleasure, where there is no reason that the mind of man can discern, why he should be restrained."[65] Without making reason entirely self-authenticating, this position replaces the Calvinists' *credo ut intelligam* with the Cambridge Platonists' more naturalistic understanding of mental powers perfected but not overcome or supplanted by grace.[66] These attitudes continued to gain ground as the century progressed and the nation increasingly became impatient with both Calvinist dogma and Antinomian excess. After the Restoration, Calvinists were increasingly "convicted" not only of making God responsible for sin but also of depriving humans of independent authority for their actions, a turn of events that intensified the Dissenters' bitter sense of isolation and betrayal. William Clagett could then openly attack prominent Protectorate ministers like John Owen not only for forcing their beliefs on free consciences but also for "demoting human moral capacity and reducing conversion to an 'irresistible Operation' ... [in which] the human has become an automaton, a piece of mechanical action, and God's calling a form of '*Violence and Compulsion*.'" Baxter by now fully agreed that "this extreme position would diminish people's plans to do good works here on earth," although he still looked to the Holy Spirit as the most efficacious guide in daily life, an indispensable aid to human understanding.[67]

In general, then, except for hard-core Dissenters, a generation nourished on exaltations and agonies began to turn away from narrow doctrinal squabbles toward a more systematic exploration of the new world opened up by the new natural philosophy and religion. Emphasizing experience and a careful consideration of facts as a guide to reason, they worked toward a more unified world of knowledge, more human responsibility, and more confidence in a benign and comprehensible Creator. Yet this new world was still remote from the mechanistic universe depicted by Jones, Foucault, and their followers. Inhabiting a cosmos as "immanentist and creationist" as the world of *Paradise Lost*, the new philosophers neither sanctioned not produced a purely "instrumental" or utilitarian worldview. Both McAdoo and C.E. Raven place the arrival of the instrumental or mechanist era in the early

---

[64]   McAdoo, *Spirit*, pp. 76, 74, citing Taylor, *The Liberty of Prophesying* (1647), Sect. X, in Taylor, *Whole Works*, vol. 5, p. 170. McAdoo traces this general line of thought to Lancelot Andrewes, who is commemorated in Milton's *Elegia Tertia*.

[65]   Benjamin Whichcote, *Select Sermons* (1698), p. 345.

[66]   McAdoo, *Spirit*, p. 123.

[67]   Achinstein, *Literature and Dissent*, p. 165, summarizing Baxter and quoting William Clagett in *A Discourse Concerning the Operations of the Holy Spirit* (1678), p. 282.

nineteenth century. Earlier, at least until Locke—and in religious thought, long afterwards—S.L. Bethel shows that reason remains an extremely rich concept encompassing not just experience and intuition but also feeling, love, beauty, goodness, and faith. Throughout Milton's era, this synthetic view was prominently championed by Christian rationalists, vitalists, and Cambridge Platonists ignored by Foucault, many of whom were also staunch anti-Calvinists.[68]

Later in the era reactionary scholars like Meric Casaubon may have claimed that the new science destroyed all "verbal" learning, yet this charge is no more verifiable than any steep decline of religion at the time. Anthony Grafton shows that Casaubon vastly exaggerated the sudden death of humanism in an age when men like Richard Simon and Richard Bentley worked in harmony with the new scientists. Abrupt Foucauldian "dissociation" theories, particularly the idea that "humanistic scholarship did not regain intellectual profundity or popular appeal until it was transformed, after the French revolution, by the rise of a new German hermeneutics and historiography," ignore the fact that these seventeenth-century humanists forged "many of the technical methods still applied by the supposedly revolutionary German philology of the late eighteenth century." They continued to apply them to modern warfare and administration as well as to oratory and epic poetry, while formal Latin eloquence continued to provide a supple and expressive tool for both technical and literary purposes. Hence classical humanists rarely confined themselves to literary areas of study, since "the two cultures" were never "locked in the battle that the pamphleteers of the New Philosophy called for; they coexisted and often collaborated, and sometimes the scientists proved to be better readers of texts than their scholarly friends."[69] Shapiro's work supports the same basic conclusion: in Milton's era the activities of "*poet, philologist, antiquarian, historian, scientist, virtuoso*" were profoundly interrelated and overlapping.[70]

While rapidly gaining ground in the aftermath of the Ward–Webster debate of 1654, the main elements of this new outlook were set in motion by Hartlib's invitation to Comenius to visit England in the fateful year of 1641. Although Comenius left after the outbreak of the civil war in 1642 destroyed any hope for establishing his Baconian Universal College, his departure catalyzed other reformers. In the decade from 1642 to 1652, a host of educational tracts began attacking scholastic science and divinity, and proposing non-dogmatic alternatives. The Comenian project of unlocking the secrets of nature, culture, and scripture through a universal language or symbol system itself belongs to an earlier, more mystical phase of Baconianism,

---

[68] McAdoo, *Spirit*, pp. 130–31, 144; Charles E. Raven, *Organic Design: A Study of Scientific Thought from Ray to Paley* (London, 1954), pp. 5–7, 12, and *Science, Religion, and the Future* (New York, 1943), p. 27; and S.L. Bethell, *The Cultural Revolution of the Seventeenth Century* (London, 1951), p. 57.

[69] Anthony Grafton, *Defenders of the Text* (Cambridge, MA, 1991), pp. 3, 4, 5.

[70] Barbara Shapiro, "History and Natural History in Sixteenth- and Seventeenth-Century England: An Essay on the Relationship between Humanism and Science," in *English Scientific Virtuosi in the 16th and 17th Centuries* (Los Angeles, 1979), p. 38.

yet it helped discredit Puritan iconophobia. Influenced by classical humanism as well as by Puritanism, the Comenians did not share the extreme iconoclastic view of most images, emblems, or "'sensible' pictures as 'popish,'" and in this as in many other ways they helped to further a belief in a unified, empirically knowable, and "visible" cosmos.[71] Comenius himself clearly stated:

> If any be uncertain if all things can be placed before the senses in this way, even things spiritual and things absent (things in heaven, or in hell, or beyond the sea), let him remember that all things have been harmoniously arranged by God in such a manner that the higher in the scale of existence can be represented by the lower, the absent by the present, and the invisible by the visible. This can be seen in the *Macromicrcosmus* of Robert Flutt, in which the origin of winds, of rain, and of thunder is described in such a way that the reader can visualise it. Nor is there any doubt that even greater concreteness and ease of demonstration than is here displayed might be attained.[72]

Of course, the hermetic and Paracelsan view of nature expressed here is hardly modern; Comenius believed that the semi-magical "sciences" promoted by Fludd would confirm the Mosaic account of creation and abolish all the "heretical" works of Aristotle. Yet his fundamental faith in reason was furthered by the more skeptical Oxford Baconians, who anticipated the anti-mystical turn reformers would take after the Ward–Webster debate.

Along with Wilkins and Wallis (1616–1703), the latter group included Robert Boyle (1627–91), Thomas Willis (1621–65), and Jonathan Goddard (1617–75), who, as Allen Debus shows, formed the nucleus of both the "Philosophical Society of Oxford" and of the future Royal Society.[73] Except for Boyle, they were all men of Milton's generation, and Boyle was exactly the same age as Milton's admiring Parliamentarian ally, John Hall (1627–56). Like Milton, they all pursued postgraduate studies in mathematics and astronomy (*CPW* 4.1:614), and some (but not all) defended the Copernican system, as Wilkins did in his *Discovery of a New World in the Moone* (1638) and *Discourse Concerning a New Planet* (1640).[74] Unlike Comenius, all heeded Bacon's warning against pseudo-philosophical works like Fludd's *Macrocosmus* and the "credulous and superstitions conceits"

---

[71]   On the extreme view, see Patrick Collinson, *From Iconoclasm to Iconophobia* (Reading, UK, 1986), p. 23. On the events surrounding Comenius's visit to England, see Allen G. Debus, *Science and Education in the Seventeenth Century: The Webster–Ward Debate* (London, 1970), pp. 36–37. See also Comenius, *A Reformation of Schooles ...*, trans. Samuel Hartlib (London, 1642), p. 35.

[72]   Comenius, *The Great Didactic*, trans. M.W. Keatinge (London, 1896), p. 339.

[73]   Debus, *Science and Education*, p. 43.

[74]   John Wilkins, *A Discourse Concerning A New Planet* (London, 1640) and *A Discovery of a New World in the Moone* (London, 1638).

of the natural magicians (*Works* 3:361). According to Bacon's *Advancement of Learning*:

> The ancient opinion that man was Microcosmus, an abstract or model of the world, hath been fantastically strained by Paracelsus and the alchemists, as if there were to be found in man's body certain correspondences and parallels, which should have respect to all varieties of things, as stars, planets, minerals, which are extant in the great world. (*Works* 3:370)

Thomas Browne was among the first proto-moderns to follow him by placing this "ancient opinion" in his catalogue of popular errors, *Pseudodoxia Epidemica*, which as (Karen Edwards has shown) Milton clearly knew and followed.[75] Refusing to describe Adam, Eve, or even Eden as microcosmic "little worlds," *Paradise Lost* also participated in the new anti-mystical turn by savagely satirizing the "vain philosophy" of the alchemists (*PL* 3.598–605).

Webster's 1654 *Academiarum Examen*, which dates to about the time when Milton began composing his epic, took the opposite stance by siding with the Comenians, Fludd, the Paracelsans, and other chemical philosophers, whom he believed would provide a sound Christian alternative to the "stale" Aristotelian learning already fast disappearing from the universities.[76] In doing so, Webster acted as the spokesman for a wide variety of Puritan radicals commonly associated with gnostic philosophy. Like John Everard, all were unaware that Isaac Casaubon had disproved the supposed antiquity of the *Corpus hermeticum*, which Everard translated and published in 1649 with the claim that it long pre-dated Moses.[77] Thus Ward easily proved that Webster's uninformed attack on the universities actually had less to do with their curriculum than with his deep Puritan sympathies and suspicions of "worldly wisdom." These sympathies had attracted Webster to the mysteries of chemical medicine sometime before he served as both a surgeon and a chaplain in Cromwell's army. He dedicated his *Academiarum Examen* to Major-General Lambert and, like most radicals and Nonconformists (which he later became), he did not follow Bacon in condemning Aristotle as an overly deductive or outdated natural philosopher, but rather as a "heathen" philosopher whose works had no place in Christian education.

Webster took the same position in his contribution to the learned ministry controversy, *The Saints Guide*. Like his other writings, it shows that, although he shared Bacon's general animus against the "Ancients," his approach was far less critical or analytical.[78] Not only did he indiscriminately devalue the Ancients in favor of "Moderns" who—as in the case of Galileo and Tycho Brahe—did not even remotely agree, but he inconsistently declared "Ancients" like Plato and

---

[75] Karen Edwards, *Milton and the Natural World* (Cambridge, 2001).

[76] See, for instance, Hirst, *Authority and Conflict*, pp. 89–95.

[77] Poole, *Milton and the Idea*, p. 18.

[78] Debus, *Science and Education*, pp. 37–43.

his modern follower Ficino more reliable than Aristotle. His treatment of Bacon is equally contradictory, even though Webster's four rules for rejecting ancient authority closely resemble Bacon's four "idols." Yet, like Comenius, Webster converts Bacon into an exponent of natural magic who "*leadeth cognition of occult forms unto wonderful works, and by conjoining actives to passives, doth manifest the grand secrets of nature.*" These "wonderful works" are supposedly the fruits of inductive method, but to achieve them, Webster relies on a drastic and un-Baconian simplification of language much closer to the Comenian ideal. Thus, rather than "poring continually upon a few paper Idols," students should learn a universal language that Webster assumes is already within reach.[79] These remarks show his ignorance of the actual problems encountered during Wilkins's and Ward's attempt to construct such a language, which he overlooks, in part because he still believes in a magical means for uncovering hidden signs and signatures able to unlock the wisdom of the ages. This enthusiasm for the medieval doctrine of signatures revived by Fludd tends to devalue the study of both conventional and universal language by promoting the illusion that the secret emblems and hieroglyphics of the alchemists and occult philosophers would soon replace both. Considering the occult philosophers equal or superior to Bacon, Puritan mystics of this type attempted to recover the natural language "stamped by the Creator on his Creation" in the hidden virtues and the micro/macrocosmic correspondences exalted by the Rosicrucians and their favorite sage, Jacob Boehme.[80] Hence Webster typically exalts the "Macrocosm" as

> the great unsealed book of God, and every creature as a Capital letter or character, and all put together make up that one word or sentence of his immense wisdom, glory and power; but alas! who spells them aright, or conjoyns them so together that they may perfectly read all that is therein contained? Alas! we all study, and read too much upon the dead paper idols of creaturely-invented letters, but do not, nor cannot read the legible characters that are onely written and impressed by the finger of the Almighty.[81]

Since throughout the Interregnum the universities had been under assault not only from Puritans like Dell but also from royalists like Hobbes, Ward's response to Webster is two-pronged. Hobbes's knowledge of the university curriculum was ironically as outdated as Webster's, but since he represented the mechanical–mathematical method currently advocated by continental science, Wilkins and Ward decided to focus on Webster as the most alarming and vulnerable of their

---

[79]   Webster, *Academiarum Examen*, pp. 69, 68 (quoting Bacon's discussion of magic in *De Augmentis Scientiarum* Book 3, chapter 5), rpt. in Debus, *Science and Education*, pp. 151, 150; see also Debus's summary of Webster's views in *Science and Education*, pp. 40–41.

[80]   Debus, *Science and Education*, p. 40.

[81]   Webster, *Academiarum Examen*, p. 28, and Debus, *Science and Education*, p. 110.

detractors. Although just as mystical, Dell was closer to the "disciplinary" strand of Puritan utopianism than Webster: he promoted the idea that university students should support themselves by learning a trade, an issue ignored in this debate. Ward therefore focuses on showing that Webster's *Secret Messenger* advocates the use of cryptographs and hieroglyphs mainly "invented for the *concealement of things*," and not—like grammar, language, and logic—for their explanation. This in turn allows him to ridicule Webster for promoting natural magicians better known for deceit rather than discovery.[82] This critique is partly inspired by Ward's awareness that Wilkins's work on the "real character" had revealed vast differences between linguistic and mathematical signs, which meant that any universal language would require an almost infinite number of characters. Hence he could agree with Webster's opinion "that my L. Bacons way may be embraced. That Axioms be evidently proved by observations, and no other be admitted," but also reject his corollaries as cabbalistic, Rosicrucian, and Behemist fantasies. In approaching "the Symphonies of nature," for Ward "the rules of applying agent and materiall causes to produce effects, is the true naturall Magick, and the generall humane ends of all Phylosophycall enquiries." Since these objectives were already being pursued at Oxford in medicine, chemistry, magnetism, and atomism, Ward concludes that Webster's disapproval of Oxford's "reformation of learning" stems from a combination of misinformation and gullibility: "Mr *Webster* expects we should tell him, that we have found the Elixar, (surely we are wiser than to say so)."[83]

Ward next discredits Webster's claim that the teaching of "strict *Logicall Method*" had turned university theology into a "confused Chaos," first, by showing that he plagiarized it from von Helmont and Bacon; and, second, by showing that Bacon's objections to logic applied only to scientific demonstration and experiment, not to the proper definition of terms.[84] In the latter capacity, logic remained indispensable in both the sciences and liberal arts. Cleverly anticipating Swift's satire of new philosophers who thought that they could communicate purely through "things," Ward asks why Webster harps on "things" as the proper substitute for "notions": "Was there ever, or can there be a Disputation about anything else but Notions? Would he have them bring forth Bread & Cheese and Dispute *de gustibus*? Or would he have the Consecrated Host brought in, and paper-Idols converted into Wafer-Idols of more favour?"[85] By thus accusing Webster of yearning for a pseudo-scientific "Real Presence," Ward finds this supposedly "great ... favourer of Sciences" guilty of a discursive "Catachresis ... [that] equally runnes against the Schooles, and the arts themselves." His "Pilfering, & ... Plagiarisme" of misunderstood books may qualify him to "rant amongst the Levellers" or with "*such an Author* [as] *is* Dr. Fludd," but his proposed reforms are

---

[82] Seth Ward, *Vindiciae Academiarum* (Oxford, 1654), pp. 18–19; rpt. in Debus, *Science and Education*, pp. 212–13. See also Debus's commentary, p. 44.

[83] Ward, *Vindiciae Academiarum*, pp. 46, 34–35; Debus rpt., pp. 240, 228–29.

[84] Ward, *Vindiciae Academiarum*, pp. 5, 11; Debus rpt., pp. 199, 205.

[85] Ward, *Vindiciae Academiarum*, p. 41; Debus rpt., p. 235.

no more truly grounded "upon sensible, Rationall, Experimentall, and Scripture Principles" than they are truly "new" or consistent.[86]

Webster's inconsistency is especially damning:

> he that even now was for the way of strict and accurate induction, is fallen into the mysticall way of the *Cabala*, and numbers formall: [while] there are not two waies in the whole World more opposite, then those of the L. *Verulam* and D. *Fludd*, the one founded upon experiment, the other upon mysticall Ideal reasons.

Vacillating between both, "and all this in the twinkling of an eye, O the celerity of the change and motion of the Wind," Webster "windily" proposes replacing the astronomy of Ptolemy with that of Copernicus, which, from a cautiously inductive Baconian perspective, is far too premature.[87] Rather than dogmatically maintaining either astronomical system, Ward defends the Oxonian "Method ... observed in our Schooles," which "is first to exhibit the *Phenomena*, and shew the way of their observation, then to give an account of the various Hypotheses, how those Phenomena have been salved." Since until Newton (1687) the Ptolemaic system remained a plausible way of saving the phenomena, it could arguably coexist with the Copernican system "as it was left by him, or as improved by *Kepler, Bullialdus*, our own Professor and others of the *Ellipticall* way."[88]

Another important part of Ward's refutation lies in countering Webster's Puritan objection that "the Universities doe undertake to teach spirituall knowledge, and to furnish men with such gifts, as do only proceed from the Spirit of God." Replying that "no man, (that ever I heard of) ... hath believed or affected any such thing," Ward (or his colleague N.S.) defends "the common opinion ... that there are three kind of gifts materially requisite to compleat a man unto the Minsteriall function":

1. Something to be infused by the Spirit of God, which must illuminate him to understand the misteries of the Gospell, and affect his heart with an experimentall flavour, and acquaintance with those sacred truths wherein he is to instruct others.

2. Some naturall abilityes in respect of solidity of judgment, strength of memory, warmenes [sic] of affection, readinesse and volubility of speech, by which he may be rendered much more serviceable in that worke, then those that want these abilities.

---

[86]   Ward, *Vindiciae Academiarum*, pp. 23, 46; Debus rpt., pp. 217, 240.

[87]   Ward, *Vindiciae Academiarum* p. 46; Debus rpt., p. 240.

[88]   Ward, *Vindiciae Academiarum*, pp. 30, 29; Debus rpt., pp. 224, 223.

3. Something to be acquired by our own industry and the teaching of others;
   Namely, a distinct and methodicall comprehention of the severall subjects to
   be treated of, together with meanes or advantages that helpe to facilitate the
   worke of instructing others.[89]

Ward further argues that the "meanes or advantages" included in the third category
are only accidentally the cause of ministerial pride, while Webster believes that the
clergy's elite training and privileges are fundamentally at fault. Although Milton
agrees with Webster on this point, he agrees with Ward on all the rest, including
the fact that "it can be no hindrance to a man" or the spirit of grace to have "all
the most materiall notions upon any subject, put together, cleared up and stated by
the concurrent labours of many wise and good men, after much consideration and
experience."[90] This collation was in fact a principal aim of Milton's *De Doctrina*:
to collect the most material notions and evidence on scriptural truths, which it
defends in similar terms (*CPW* 6:117–24).

Milton's *Hirelings* also sides with Ward's rejection of the radical Puritan
belief that "Tongues" or languages are "unnecessary to *Theology* ... because they
teach but the Grammatical sense, and a literal understanding." Both Milton and
Ward require ministers to know all the original biblical languages, while Milton's
De Doctrina actually prefers the literal, grammatical sense of scripture to the
"logical ingenuity" and "constant linguistic quibbles" of scholastics *or* mystics
whose "prejudices" override the natural sense "of Conscience, or right reason"
(*CPW* 6:120, 132). Milton's preference for plain speech and "humane reason"
over metaphysics is also the immediate source of his "heretical" antitrinitarianism
(*CPW* 6: 133–42). Ward never went so far in this direction, yet, like Milton,
his stoutly rejects Webster's objection to ancient languages even though (as he
wryly adds) their [Hebrew] "Letters ... have taught a way of Mysticall Theology,
as mysticall as need to be, and not unworthy to be compared to his [Webster's
metaphysics] ... 'tis pitty he had not heard of the mysteries of the *Gnosticks.*"[91]
Challenging Webster rationally to defend his "cabbalistic" approach to the gifts of
the Spirit, Ward also counters him by observing that "unless this Author will say,
that he who has grace, and is without these [rational] gifts, is better able to Teach,
then he that hath both grace and these gifts too, he hath no reason to complaine of
the uselesnesse and danger of Academicall education, in reference to the worke of
the Ministry."[92] Except for the word "academicall" in this sentence, Milton might
have written it himself. For like other Christian rationalists, his positions on both

---

[89] Ward, *Vindiciae Academiarum*, p. 3; Debus rpt. p. 197. Debus does not distinguish
the separately numbered prefatory letter by "N.S." from Ward's treatise itself, a practice
I usually follow, since "N.S." may be a fictional "new scientist." Debus includes no
speculation as to "his" identity.

[90] Ward or N.S., *Vindiciae Academiarum*, p. 4; Debus rpt., p. 198.

[91] Ward, *Vindiciae Academiarum*, p. 5; Debus rpt., p. 207.

[92] Ward, *Vindiciae Academiarum*, p. 4; Debus rpt., p. 198.

the learned ministry and on "godly rule" reject the Calvinist dependence on direct inspiration and gnostic "wisdom" in favor of a skeptical, tolerant view of both empirical and scriptural truth.

Milton, Hartlib, and the Latitudinarians on True Religion, Education, and Science

Besides emphasizing the spiritual calling of ministers in ways not very different from Ward, Milton's much misunderstood *Likeliest Means to Remove Hirelings* constitutes a not-too-subtle warning against giving political power exclusively to the Elect, as the Nominated or Barebones Parliament had in fact attempted to do. Since no uniquely "inspired" individual or group can positively prove their "gifts," the tract implicitly discredits enthusiasts who use their inward illumination to do "'nothing else but ... run to and fro to declare to souls ... the light in their consciences,'" as George Fox said he did.[93] It also discredits "disciplinary" Puritans for authorizing no ministers "but such whom by thir committies of examination they finde conformable to their interest and opinions" (*CPW* 7:318). This objection stems not just from Milton's commitment to freedom of opinion but also from his belief that rather than merely instilling a "saving" fear in the Elect, ministers should serve as rational teachers, physicians, and exemplars to their flock, thereby curing "both soul and bodie" (*CPW* 7:306). The same idea can be found in the most pragmatic utopian among the Hartlib circle, Gabriel Plattes, whose *Macaria* proposes that "the Parson of every Parish" should also be "a good Physician, and ... execute both functions, to wit, *cura animarum, & cura corporum*; ... for a Divine to be without the skill of Physick ... is to put new wine into old bottles; and the Physicians being true Naturalists, may as well become good Divines, as the Divines doe become good Physicians."[94] Milton wholly agrees that ministers should devote themselves to the study "of physic and surgery as well as ... the studie of scripture (which is the only true theologie) that they might be no burden to the church; and by the example of Christ, might cure both soul and bodie; through industry joining that to their ministerie, which he joind to his by gift of the spirit" (*CPW* 7:306). This "industry" is necessary because the "gift of the spirit" is no more always available to ministers than to the rest of mankind, who can never be certain of its presence (*CPW* 7:242).

Both Plattes and Milton obviously favor a more primitive version of Christianity than Ward or Wilkins, who do not envision such drastic reform. Besides the Bible,

---

[93] Huehns, *Antinomianism*, p. 139. Huehns cites William Dewsbury, *A True Prophecy of the Mighty Day of the Lord* (Feb. 6, 1654), p. 5.

[94] Samuel Hartlib, *A Description of the Famous Kingdome of Macaria; shewing its Excellent Government* (London, 1641), p. 6. Webster shows Gabriel Plattes to be the actual author in "The Authorship and Significance of Macaria," in *Intellectual Revolution*, pp. 369–85.

a probable common source of this "primitivism" is Bacon's *New Atlantis*, where the Holy Fathers of Salomon's House practice both spiritual and physical healing through their "industrious" inquiries into nature and its God. Milton may also have read *Macaria*, since its publication coincides with his most active and utopian period of collaboration with the Hartlib circle. Nevertheless, like Plattes himself, who focuses almost entirely on practical agricultural, economic, and empirical reforms, Milton was never a Comenian mystic but a pragmatic Baconian particularly loath to support a "peculiar tribe of levites ... bred up for divines in babling schooles and fed at the publick cost, good for nothing els but what was good for nothing" (*CPW* 7:319). This "tribe" specializes in "schoole terms and metaphysical notions, which have obscur'd rather than explan'd our religion, and made it seem difficult without cause." Hence he would replace them with teachers grounded in "solid reason," supplied with the "entire scripture translated into English with plenty of notes," and educated in decentralized "schooles and competent libraries to those schooles, where languages and arts may be taught free together." By this means "all the land would be soone better civiliz'd, and they who are taught freely at the publick cost" would repay their communities by teaching those among whom they have been born and bred (*CPW* 7:304, 305). This position is obviously light years away from Webster's "enthusiastic" suspicion of solid learning. Both R.S. White and Austin Woolrych agree that Milton's ecclesiastical thought is instead rooted in the same natural law tradition he uses in his defenses of tyrannicide and divorce, a tradition principally derived from Selden.[95] In fact, the "natural laws" of Hebraic divorce ultimately allow him to argue for a "divorce" between church and state, for once God "hath ... severd them," he maintains that further cohabitation would be "presumptuous fornication" (*CPW* 7:260; cf. n. 59).

Milton's views on education even more obviously respond to the standard Baconian critique of the "pride and perpetual contention" (*CPW* 7:319) engendered by formalism and traditionalism, particularly their scholastic counterparts. Yet this critique is semi-secular in comparison with either Webster or the Comenians; in *The Readie and Easie Way*, his final pre-Restoration tract on the subject, he simply points out that a good liberal education supports sound religion and good morals, manners, and first principles, a far cry from the Comenians' insistence on reforming education in strict conformity with Christian belief.[96] Like his much earlier *Of Education*, *The Readie and Easie Way* actually places religion last on Milton's agenda. By establishing more national academies,

> children may be bred up ... to all learning and noble education, not in grammar
> only, but in all liberal arts and exercises. This would soon spread much more
> knowledge and civilitie, yea religion, through all parts of the land: this would

---

[95]   White, *Natural Law*, pp. 217–33, and Woolrych's note, *CPW* 7:260 n. 59.

[96]   On Milton's largely secular approach to education, see Guari Viswanathan, "Milton and Education," in Balachandra Rajan and Elizabeth Sauer (eds.), *Milton and the Imperial Vision*, (Pittsburgh, 1999), pp. 273–93, and also Chapter 2 above.

soon make the whole nation more industrious, more ingenuous at home, more potent, more honourable abroad. To this a free Commonwealth will easily assent; ... for of all governments a Commonwealth aims most to make the people flourishing, vertuous, noble and high-spirited. (*CPW* 7:384)

Yet he and his friend Moses Wall also remain in essential harmony with the Hartlib circle's general refusal to make "the Christian magistrate ... the custodian of both tables of God's law," a position which Milton maintains against Baxter and "countless other exponents of the central Protestant and Puritan tradition."[97] Another member of the Hartlib circle, the reformer William Petty, promoted more utilitarian views on education, although Richard Greaves believes that they influenced the technological and agricultural components of Milton's *Of Education*. Like Petty's educational proposals, his other reforms failed because they were considered too close to the "recently rejected leveling tendencies" associated with his favorite causes: relief for the helpless, the poor, and the unemployed; more equitable taxation; liberty of conscience and religion; a liberalized franchise; and drastic educational, legal, medical, governmental, and ecclesiastical reform.[98] Yet Petty's unpublished religious papers establish a personal, rational, tolerant, and highly ethical basis for faith often intriguingly similar to positions taken in Milton's *Of Civil Power*, *Hirelings*, and *De Doctrina*.[99]

Like Robinson and Milton, Petty believed that rediscovering the fundamentals of Christian belief would end sectarian strife by eliminating its irrational elements: the theological conundrums, empty metaphors, and technical squabbles encouraged by the clergy. Turning against everything "vulgarly meant by worshiping, honoring and glorifying God" to a more primitive form of Christianity, he similarly objected to:

Enriching, obeying, and fighting for those who pretend to be [God's] priests ...; praying to God for such benefits as man cannot give us; and setting forth God's power, wisdom, and mercy in a general way by metaphorical expressions and allusions when we either ignore or deny them in particulars. From these mistaken notions many disadvantages have flowed—the unnecessary expense of a luxurious church establishment, useless study of inexplicable matters, wars and destruction, superstition, hypocrisy, and inattention to useful arts. God would be more honored by the study of natural phenomena[,] ... [since]

---

[97]   See Austin Woolrych's "Historical Introduction" to these tracts of 1659–60 (*Hirelings*, *Of Civil Power*, and both editions of *The Readie and Easie Way*), *CPW* 7:53. On Wall, see Woolrych, *CPW* 7:83–84, 510–13.

[98]   See Greaves, *Puritan Revolution*, p. 51, and Richard Olson, *Science Deified and Science Defied: The Historical Significance of Science in Western Culture* (2 vols., Berkeley, 1990), vol. 2, pp. 82–83.

[99]   Barker compares Petty's religious outlook to Milton's in *Milton*, p. 233, and "Petty was no Puritan" (p. 119).

natural and universal religion consists of studying God's works, worshiping Him
in proper assemblies, praising Him in suitable ceremonies, and promoting the
welfare of other men. If anyone believes in any further doctrines, let him go
beyond the public worship in his private family. [Otherwise,] ... no one should
interfere with the religion of others if it fosters moral uprightness, gives comfort
and courage, and promotes good citizenship.[100]

Except for allowing more room for "suitable ceremonies," Petty's anti-priestly
program closely parallels Milton's position in *Of Civil Power*, *Hirelings*, and the
final books of *Paradise Lost*. By using reason both to support religion and as a tool
of criticism, Petty also provides a logical bridge between the positions of Milton
and Locke, whose *Letter Concerning Toleration* privatizes without overruling
conscience.

Locke employs a calmer rhetoric suited to calmer times, but precisely like
Milton and Petty, he insists that the only "true" church is "a voluntary society of
men, joining themselves together of their own accord in order to publicly worship
God in such a manner as they judge acceptable to him, and effectual to the salvation
of their souls."[101] The point was not to remove religion from public life (as too
many commentators still assume) but to safeguard it from state interference.
Locke went further than Milton in pruning Christianity "of every doctrine not
susceptible to rational demonstration or corroboration," although both in many
ways anticipate younger Royal Society virtuosi like Edmond Halley, the discoverer
of the comet named for him. Richard Westfall notes that Halley later forfeited the
Savilian chair of astronomy by taking "the tendency of other virtuosi to exalt the
Father above the Son" to its logical conclusion—that is, by turning them into two
separate persons.[102] The same skeptical anti-authoritarianism ultimately led both
the Latitudinarians and the circle gathered at Great Tew to conclude with Milton
(*CPW* 7:293) that neither the Protestant martyrs nor the Church Fathers have any
authority apart from the combined force of scripture and right reason.

Milton was apparently always of this opinion, which in later years he slightly
modified to support the view of Simon Patrick's "Latitude-Men" that the ancient
Fathers at least helped to distinguish between "modern corruptions, and [the]
ancient simplicity of the Church."[103] Yet in neither case does the discovery of

---

[100] Westfall, *Science and Religion*, pp. 132–33. Westfall summarizes and cites *The Petty Papers: Some Unpublished Writings of Sir William Petty*, ed. Marquis of Lansdowne (2 vols., London, 1927), vol. 1, pp. 117, 130–31.

[101] John Locke, *The Second Treatise of Government and A Letter Concerning Toleration*, ed. J.W. Gough (Oxford, 1946), p. 129.

[102] Westfall, *Science and Religion*, pp. 135, 134; On Milton's antitrinitarianism, see John P. Rumrich, "Milton's Arianism: Why It Matters," in Dobranski and Rumrich (eds.), *Milton and Heresy*, pp. 75–92. .

[103] Stavely (*CPW* 8:419, n. 7) cites Simon Patrick's *A Brief Account of the New Sect Called Latitude-Men* (London, 1662), p. 9.

those corruptions have any compulsory force. Since even those matters expressly "enjoind or forbidden by divine precept" are "liable to be variously understood by humane reason," and "likewise must needs appeer to everie man as the precept is understood," Milton maintained that the state should not be in the business of licensing opinion of any kind (*CPW* 7:242). Church discipline thus becomes a strictly pastoral matter, aided perhaps by the Spirit but mainly by the force of rational, scriptural demonstration (*CPW* 7:242–49). Such ideas ultimately derive from Hooker's contention that scripture itself could not be intelligible apart from the light of reason, which lies behind Milton's contention that any minister *or* saint who makes his conscience or illumination "infallible" is guilty of "presumption too high for any mortal" (*CPW* 7:243–44).[104] At once overturning the incontrovertible authority of the Spirit, the licensed state clergy, and the national church, these positions had as little appeal for Puritans as for high church prelates. As one admiring contemporary noted, Milton's tract *Of True Religion* said more "in two elegant sheets of true religion, heresy, and schism than all the pr[elates] can refute in 7 years." The same contemporary rightly compares his irenic stance to both Taylor and William Penn, although Milton's burial beside his father in an Anglican church suggests that he ended his life closer to Taylor than to Quakers like Penn.[105] More like John Wesley, who also never left the church, he simply sought the truer spirit of Christianity.

Wesley had little regard for the Latitudinarians, but in Milton's day they and their Royal Society allies held comparably "enlightened" views on both religion and science. They flatly rejected the "tyranny" of the Ancients in either area, but unlike Webster or the Comenians they continued to find large grains of "probable" truth in some of their writings, particularly in Aristotle's *Politics* and *Nichomachean Ethics* (cf. *CPW* 3:199, 202, 361). Milton's heavy use of both texts throughout his writings explains why Aristotle fails to appear on his list of "fabling" Greeks in *Paradise Regained*. His *Readie and Easie Way* also hails Aristotle's *Politics* as "our chief instructer [*sic*] in the Universities," a tribute that significantly occurs in a passage dismissing both "*Sectarian*" schemes of government and the royalist idolization of "a single person." However "good" that person may be, he is too liable to corruption through "the excess of his singular power and exaltation," the natural opposites of both Christian and civil liberty (*CPW* 7:448, 449).

---

[104] On Richard Hooker's identical stance, see Olson, *Science Deified*, vol. 2, pp. 91–92.

[105] This anonymous letter is quoted in William Riley Parker, *Milton's Contemporary Reputation* (Columbus, OH: Ohio State University Press, 1940), p. 50 n. 5. On Milton's burial, see William B. Hunter, *Visitation Unimplor'd: Milton and the Authorship of De Doctrina Christiana* (Pittsburgh, 1998), p. 14. Milton's home was adjacent to a Dissenter graveyard, which his third wife (a Baptist) would probably have preferred, so Hunter concludes that Milton chose this site. *Of True Religion* considers Baptists good Christians, and *De Doctrina* joins them in rejecting infant baptism; but, in making the sacrament optional, he remains remote from Puritan belief.

This passage essentially rehearses the anti-absolutist position earlier adopted in *Areopagitica*: the most "unconstraining laws of virtuous education, religion, and civill nurture" are the essential "bonds and ligaments of the Commonwealth, the pillars and sustainers of every writt'n Statute" (*CPW* 2:526). Removing rather than instituting new "idols" (in this case, new laws rather than persons) will thus promote the "grave and noble invention[s]" anticipated in both *An Apology* and here in *Areopagitica* (*CPW* 1:881, 2:551–54). In the interim, *Of Civil Power* only slightly varies *Areopagitica*'s famous argument that these inventions will flourish only by freely allowing Truth to "grapple" with "Falshood" (*CPW* 2:561): by considering all "powerfull demonstration to the contrarie," "truth the strong" will triumph over "error the weak though slie and shifting." In this match "Force is no honest confutation; but ineffectual, and for the most part unsuccessfull" (*CPW* 7:261). Thus, on the eve of the Restoration, Milton continued his Baconian program of promoting the discovery of "better and exacter things, then were yet known" (*Apology*, *CPW* 1:881) on the model of the *New Atlantis*, where a combination of toleration and experiment has perfected both religion and science.

After the Restoration, Milton's correspondence with Oldenburg continued as the new Royal Society secretary became the intermediary between the poet, Evelyn, and Evelyn's friend John Beale, men impressed by Milton's intellectual range but not his politics.[106] Beale especially admired his post-Restoration *History of Britain* (1671), which traces the non-deterministic causes of social decay. It characteristically warns that "when the esteem of Science, and liberal study waxes low in the Common-wealth, wee may presume that also there all civil Vertue, and worthy action is grown as low to a decline: and then Eloquence, as it were consorted in the same destiny, with the decrease and fall of vertue corrupts also and fades; at least resignes her office" as "illiterat and frivolous" men unable to "survay" or critique over-credulous beliefs come to power (*CPW* 5:40). Beale's Royal Society included many observers, some dilettantes, and only one fully "professional" scientist, Robert Hooke, along with humanist rhetoricians and historians like Sprat, who as Michael Hunter has long insisted, did not exaggerate its religious "latitude."[107] Charles Webster further shows that it was their depth of disagreement on religion and politics rather than their adherence to a uniform Latitudinarianism that caused the Royal Society's leaders to ban discussion of such volatile matters, an effort that hardly served any controlling "High Anglican party" interest.[108] The Society was open to men of all political and religious persuasions who did not disrupt its objective and pacific forms of inquiry, although it did maintain the "anti-enthusiastic" policies for which it has long been noted. Nevertheless, these policies were mainstream, not conservative: the nation as a

---

[106] See William Poole, "Two Early Readers of Milton: John Beale and Abraham Hill," *MQ* 38.2 (2004): pp. 76–99.

[107] Michael Hunter, *Science and Society in Restoration England* (Cambridge, 1981), and *Establishing the New Science*.

[108] Webster, *Great Instauration*, p. 94.

whole was weary of Seekers, Ranters, Quakers, and others who would impose their personal revelations upon others without objective authority.[109] All the same, both Oldenburg and Wilkins were tolerant and even sympathetic to undogmatic Dissenters, Quakers, or Catholics despite their differing convictions.

Milton himself welcomed a similar "latitude" of acquaintances. Still concerned with educating the nation he had earlier declared "so pliant and so prone to seek after knowledge," so exulting in every kind of experiment—"musing, searching, revolving new notions and idea's [*sic*]"—he also continued to despise those who "know" only "by statute" or untested conviction (*CPW* 2:554, 562). His frequent foreign visitors assured him that what he earlier called England's "deepest Sciences" continued to be sought around the globe (*CPW* 2:551), and he was encouraged to learn from Oldenburg that Oxford had been transformed from a Laudian bastion to the kind of liberal and enlightened educational institution recommended in *The Readie and Easie Way.* The "contentious and garrulous learning" that merely "disturbs the mind" was no longer practiced there, for under Wilkins, students learned to "apply themselves actively" to the contemplation of "nature and its Author," while not "neglect[ing] the refinements of the liberal arts." Oldenburg lamented that some scholastic disputers who "contend over the superiority of their talent rather than over the truth" continued in their old paths, but he also assured the poet that "God will eventually cause this evil to be torn out root and branch, and the minds of men to unite in the pursuit of truth and virtue" (*CPW* 7:490, 491). These comments suggest his awareness that the poet currently engaged in writing *Paradise Lost* still supported the agenda set forth in his Baconian Cambridge *Prolusions*, *Of Education*, and all his reformist "Root and Branch" writings.

During this time, other remnants of the Oxford and Hartlib groups continued to collaborate with the Society on a wide range of practical and philosophical concerns. Both founding secretaries of the Royal Society, Wilkins and Oldenburg, had been seen as suitable heads for Hartlib's projected Agency for the Advancement of Universal Learning, and although Oldenburg's far greater knowledge of the work of the Continental mechanical philosophers better qualified him to supervise the Royal Society correspondence, "at no stage did he react against the work of Hartlib, or lose sight of the ultimate humanitarian goal of experimental science."[110] Like Milton, all these circles were deeply opposed to Hobbesian mechanism, which is why the Oxford group focused on discrediting Hobbes, Webster, and Dell but "tactfully avoided answering the equally severe criticisms of Dury, Hartlib, and Hall," the most outspoken and liberal reformers in Hartlib's group.

---

[109]   See Michael Hunter, *Science and the Shape of Orthodoxy: Intellectual Change in Late Seventeenth-Century Britain* (Woodbridge, 1995), pp. 151–79, 225–44. George Williamson early documented these changes in "The Restoration Revolt against Enthusiasm," *SP* 30 (1933): pp. 571–603. On the authoritarian tendencies of early Quakers and other religious radicals, see Knox, *Enthusiasm*, pp. 145–49; and on this tendency among Calvinist Reformers in general, see Eire, *War against the Idols*, pp. 313–18.

[110]   Webster, *Great Instauration*, p. 501.

Their mutual cooperation was further promoted by the fact that all had turned from Bucer's narrower conceptions of educational reform toward a non-sectarian, humanistically inclusive form of instruction that was religious in spirit rather than in doctrine. Here natural history coexisted with "the history of civilisation and Christianity, elementary rules of reasoning, the principles of natural justice and the constitutional history of England," topics long taught and studied by Milton.[111] Finally, Henry Stubbe's contemporary letters reveal that the Presbyterian Wallis was relatively isolated from the rest of the Royal Society on the question of church government, for the new consensus was that "'no forme of Church-gouernment is *jure diuino.'*"[112] Like Milton, all hoped for a new Christian synthesis of "science, religion, and art" to open what Robert Hinman calls a freer "sphere for [modern] man."[113]

Yet, as Blair Worden shows, this hope was balanced by a deep sense of culpability that crossed both political and religious lines: the civil wars had been an "affront to God," "society bore the guilt of it," and its sins "had diverted Christian history from its proper course."[114] This ambiguously religious *and* political sense of national failure fuels the broad concern with divine providence evident in all of Milton's post-Restoration poems. Far from Puritan anticipations of divine vengeance, they attempt to recuperate a nation and culture that Milton felt had already been punished by what to Oldenburg he called the "insanities" and "crimes" of the revolutionary era. Refusing his request to write their history, Milton's letter adds that these "crimes" were best left in ignominious silence (*CPW* 7:515). This repudiation suggests neither a general scorn for history or science, much less what William Poole calls a "devastating, literally catastrophic vision" of an irrecuperable Fall that "not only cracked the frame of the cosmos" but severely "damaged our ability to describe" it.[115] Poole contends that this anti-scientific vision explains Milton's disinterest in performing experiments, which overlooks the fact there is no record of Aubrey, Cowley, Hartlib, or even Wilkins—despite his tremendous contributions to linguistics, mathematics, and mechanical "magic"—performing an "experiment" in the modern sense of the word. Wilkins shared Milton's interests in astronomy, mathematics, religious and language reform, but in practical terms, he preferred "to stimulate imaginations rather than provide blueprints" for future experiments or scientists.[116] William Lynch further shows that the wide diversity of

---

[111] Ibid., pp. 500, 211.

[112] See Noel Malcolm, "Hobbes and the Royal Society," in G.A.J. Rogers and Alan Ryan (eds.), *Perspectives on Thomas Hobbes* (Oxford,1988), pp. 55–56; this new consensus was shared by both Wilkins and Hobbes.

[113] Robert B. Hinman, *Abraham Cowley's World of Order* (Cambridge, MA, 1960), p. 185.

[114] Blair Worden, "The question of secularization," in Alan Houston and Steven Pincus (eds.), *A Nation Transformed: England after the Restoration* (Cambridge, 2001), p. 27.

[115] Poole, *Milton and the Idea*, p. 180.

[116] Shapiro, *John Wilkins*, pp. 39–42, 44.

interests in the new Royal Society closely reflects Bacon's three-pronged approach to the advancement of learning. Its members pursued manual, or "constructivist" experiment, "specular" or non-experimental fact-gathering, and "generative" or theoretical inquires into new arts, such as Wilkins's universal language and Sprat's rhetorical reforms.[117] Rather than ending the revolutionary progress toward modernity, as Hill and other "dissociationists" believe, the post-Restoration period thus witnessed its beginning, as Milton's major poems eloquently attest.

---

[117]   William T. Lynch, *Solomon's Child* (Palo Alto, 2001).

PART II
Restoration Culture and Milton's Major Works

Chapter 6

The Secular Cosmology and Anthropology of Milton's Civilized Eden

The first acts which man performed in Paradise consisted of the two summary parts of knowledge; the view of creatures, and the imposition of names. As for the knowledge which induced the fall, it was ... not the natural knowledge of creatures, but the moral knowledge of good and evil; wherein the supposition was, that God's commandments or prohibitions were not the originals of good and evil, but ... man aspired ... to make a total defection from God, and to depend wholly on himself.

—Francis Bacon, *The Advancement of Learning*

We look with a superstitious reverence upon the accounts of praeterlapsed ages: and with a supercilious severity, on the more deserving products of our own. A vanity, which hath possess'd all times as well as ours; and the Golden Age was never present.

—Joseph Glanvill, *Essays*[1]

The sacred, even puritanical basis of Milton's great epic has gone so long unquestioned that readers and critics remain relatively ignorant of the many secular resources surveyed in this chapter. This survey is not intended to suggest that the author of *Paradise Lost* was not a devout biblical scholar or that his poem lacks strong scriptural, spiritual, and devotional support, but rather that its stated goal of justifying God's ways to man additionally requires a secular philosophical, cosmological, and anthropological framework. His complementary goal of at once justifying and compensating for man's exile from Eden further means that, like Joseph Glanvill, he needed to avoid over-idealizing its "golden age" society as a static, closed state of perfection completely cut off from our present state of mutability and change. Yet that static state was precisely how most conservative Christians and Puritans imagined Eden, as did radicals who associated it with the effortless existence led in the fabled Land of Cockayne. As a Church of England theologian, Glanvill naturally accepted the Genesis account, but (much like the author of *Paradise Lost*), he amplifies it in the *Vanity of Dogmatizing* by famously

---

[1] Joseph Glanvill, *Essays on Several Important Subjects*, in *Collected Works of Jospeh Glanvill*, ed. Bernhard Fabian (9 vols., Hildesheim, 1979), vol. 6.

speculating that the unfallen Adam had super-human powers of perception. Milton partly accepts this idea in giving his first humans perfected logical and observational faculties that allow them to comprehend astronomical debates not foreseen or understood by their children many thousands of years later. These debates at once "modernize" his biblical epic and support his stated aim of soaring "Above th' *Aonian* Mount" by presenting "Things unattempted yet in Prose or Rhyme" (*PL* 1.14–15). Further gifted "by the genial power of nature," honed by exercise in "the tongues, and some sciences," and perfected by studying all that "the greatest and choycest wits of *Athens, Rome*, or modern *Italy*, and those Hebrews of old" could teach about the "inriching of art" (*CPW* 1:808, 809, 812, 813), he wisely glossed and supplemented without providing any "inspired" additions to the Genesis account, a presumption that he, like most of his countrymen, regarded as heretical.

As a result, Thomas Thomkins, a high churchman and strict proponent of Uniformity, consented to license Milton's epic even though he published it at a time of national crisis and repentance. According to Nicholas von Maltzahn, Thomkins no doubt saw that "the complexity and coherence" of Milton's version of sacred history "bore it far beyond the disruptive self-assertion associated with the Dissenters' inner light." He thus credits the story that the Cavalier poet John Denham immediately proclaimed it "the Noblest Poem that ever was Wrote in Any Language or Any Age" before the assembled House of Commons.[2] Yet, as John Stachniewski points out, even the opening pages of *Paradise Lost* would have upset strict Calvinists who denied any human being the capacity to "justify the ways of God to men" (1.26). From their point of view, Milton's initial invocation openly challenges the common Calvinist orthodoxy that God's justice cannot and should not be measured by human understanding. In announcing his determination to oppose this tradition, he joined ranks with the Cambridge Platonists, one of whom— Henry More's pupil, George Rust—anticipated many aspects of Milton's theodicy.[3] Other early admirers of Milton's "free will defense" of God range from the liberal, proto-Whig Presbyterian, Sir John Hobart, to strident anti-Calvinists like Abraham Hill and anti-enthusiasts like John Dryden, an early and influential admirer of his epic accomplishment.[4]

Milton concedes that he had been "long choosing" and late beginning his epic (*PL* 9.26), but long before he portrayed an angel wisely discussing the merits of geocentrism and heliocentrism with Adam, its foundations were already being laid at Cambridge. His second Prolusion expresses awe at the divine justice and scientific order of a universe that is already implicitly sun-centered. For in praising the "universal concord and sweet union of all things which Pythagoras

---

[2]   Nicholas von Maltzahn, "The First Reception of *Paradise Lost*," *RES* 47.188 (1996): pp. 479–99, cited p. 487.

[3]   Stachniewski, *Persecutory Imagination*, pp. 333–34.

[4]   Von Maltzahn, "First Reception," p. 490; on Hill, see Poole, "Two Early Readers"; on Dryden, see Chapter 7 below.

poetically figures as harmony," the second Prolusion champions an early defender of heliocentrism (*CPW* 1:236, 235 n. 2) more than a decade before *Areopagitica* made Galileo a symbol of Reformed truth (*CPW* 2:538). As the previous chapter shows, the debate over Copernicanism had already entered the universities by mid-century, as had the Baconian attack on the science of "Aristotle, the rival and constant detractor of Pythagoras and Plato," as the Prolusion terms him. Closely echoing Bacon's *Advancement of Learning*, which similarly condemns Aristotle's "impetuous and overbearing wit," Milton reprimands the philosopher for building "a road to fame on the ruin of [his] ... great masters' theories" and defends his despised predecessors, Pythagoras and Homer (*CPW* 1:236).[5] In both Bacon's *The Advancement of Learning* and his *Descripti Globi Intellectualis*, Aristotle's "road" leads to an unscientific segregation of earthly from heavenly matter. Yet neither Pythagoras nor the other Presocratics had erred in this regard, as Milton was already well aware in composing his defense: his Pythagoras is not the mystic who "held any [literal] doctrine of the harmony of the spheres, or taught that the heavens revolve in unison with some sweet melody[;] it was only as a means of suggesting allegorically the close interrelation of the orbs and their uniform revolution in according with the laws of destiny for ever" (*CPW* 1:235).

Like Milton's denial of the literal doctrine of the unheard symphony (a notion commonly used to discredit Pythagoras), his early support for the uniform, non-decaying cosmos defended in *Naturam Non Pati Senium* looks forward to *Paradise Lost*. There he will use precisely the same "remarkable and apt metaphor of the golden chain suspended by Jove from heaven" that the Prolusion finds signaling Homer's agreement with Pythagoras and other "poetic" philosophers on the question of cosmic unity (*CPW* 1:236; *PL* 2.1051). *The Advancement of Learning* also promoted this unity by undermining the artificial barriers and homologies that had previously segregated the Aristotelian–Ptolemaic universe. Literally "putting out" its outer ring of fire, as Donne famously complained, Bacon also cast grave doubt on "those supposed divorces between ethereal and sublunary things," those "figments, superstitions mixed with rashness: seeing it is most certain that very many effects, as of expansion, contraction, impression, cession, collection into masses, attraction, repulsion, assimilation, union and the like, have place not only here with us, but also in the heights of the heaven and the depths of the earth" (*Works* 5:512).

After Milton first published his *Prolusions* in 1674, his support for this "modern" cosmos would have been more obvious than ever. The best and last of them declares:

> when universal learning has once completed its cycle, the spirit of man, no
> longer confined within this dark prison-house, will reach out far and wide, till it

---

5   See Benjamin Farrington (ed.), *The Philosophy of Francis Bacon* (Liverpool, 1964), p. 42, which cites Bacon's attitude toward Aristotle's "impetuous and overbearing wit" both in the *Advancement* and in earlier writings.

fills the whole world and the space far beyond with the expansion of its divine greatness. Then at last most of the chances and changes of the world will be so quickly perceived that to him who holds this stronghold of wisdom hardly anything can happen in his life which is unforeseen or fortuitous. He will indeed seem to be one ... to whom, lastly, Mother Nature herself has surrendered, as if indeed some god had abdicated the throne of the world and entrusted its rights, laws, and administration to him as governor. (*CPW* 1:296)

As noted in Chapter 2 above, this passage not only paraphrases but even amplifies Bacon's belief that "if a man could succeed ... in kindling a light in nature—a light which should in its very rising touch and illuminate all the border-regions that confine upon the circle of our present knowledge; and so spreading further and further ... into ... all that is hidden and secret in the world,—that man ... would be the benefactor indeed of the human race,—the propagator of man's empire over the universe, the champion of liberty, the conqueror and subduer of necessities (*Works* 10:84–85).

What has not been previously noted is that the same enthusiasm for the advancement or increase of learning persists in *Paradise Lost*, where the Archangel Uriel authoritatively announces that the

> desire which tends to know
> The works of God, thereby to glorify
> The great Work-Master, leads to no excess
> That reaches blame, but rather merits praise
> The more it seems excess, that led thee hither
> From thy Empyreal Mansion thus alone,
> To witness with thine eyes what some perhaps
> Contented with report hear only in Heav'n.

(PL 3.694–701)

Here Uriel praises his visitor's "virtual witnessing" of God's divine "experiment," a form of observation that Steven Shapin and Simon Schaffer identify as an important contribution to laboratory science at a time when few members of the Royal Society could perform experiments, but all could "witness' or give objective testimony to experimental demonstrations.[6] No longer "contented with report ... only," Milton's good angels actively explore and glorify the "wonderful ... works" of God (702). True, Uriel's visitor is Satan, who is engaging in "intelligence work" of a much more malevolent kind. Yet, as Milton certainly realized, the potential for evil is always inherent in free will, discovery, and experiment. As a result, his epic follows *Areopagitica* in rejecting the "forbidden knowledge" tradition

---

[6]   See Steven Shapin and Simon Schaffer, *Leviathan and the Air Pump: Hobbes, Boyle, and the Experimental Life* (Princeton, 1989), and also Westfall's standard account of the pietistic aims of the virtuosi in *Science and Religion*.

continued in such works as Cornelius Agrippa's celebrated critique of learning, *Of the Vanitie and Uncertaintie of Artes and Sciences* (English translation 1569). Here Agrippa supports gnostic secrecy and cautions against intellectual curiosity in ways that influenced mystical English Puritans, Anabaptists, and Quakers like Isaac Penington long after the Restoration.[7]

Baconians did, however, agree that it was wrong to seek eternal secrets accessible only to an infinite God, although they denied that those secrets included the structure of the visible universe. Uriel reflects this outlook in reminding the supposed "cherub" that he may discover only "what created mind can comprehend," not the uncreated "wisdom infinite / That brought them forth but hid their causes deep" (*PL* 3.705–7). His fellow Archangel Raphael's practical advice to Adam to focus on the visible matters most useful to "this Paradise And thy fair *Eve*" (*PL* 8.171–72) only further bears out this Baconian reservation:

> To ask or search I blame thee not, for Heav'n
> Is as the Book of God before thee set,
> Wherein to read his wond'rous Works, and learn
> His Seasons, Hours, or Days, or Months, or Years:
> This to attain, whether Heav'n move or Earth,
> Imports not, if thou reck'n right; the rest
> From Man or Angel the great Architect
> Did wisely to conceal, and not divulge
> His secrets to be scann'd by them who ought
> Rather admire.
>
> (*PL* 8.66–75)

Yet, while Raphael insists that practical astronomy is preferable to theoretical speculation, the allure of the latter is apparent throughout his lengthy discussion of the respective advantages of the two major "world systems." Milton clearly shared this fascination (Hughes 189) despite his ironic admission that God long hid the correct answer "perhaps to move / His laughter at thir quaint Opinions wide" (*PL* 8.77–78). In one sense, this admission is a concession to orthodoxy as well as to the contemporary conflict between the differing systems proposed by Ptolemy, Copernicus/Galileo, Tycho Brahe, and Descartes.[8] Yet, in another sense, it serves to distract attention from one of the most forbidden "quaint opinions" entertained by Milton—not heliocentrism per se, but one its chief corollaries, the concept of plural worlds.

———

[7]   For an overview of Agrippa et al., see Poole, *Milton and the Idea*, pp. 59–72.

[8]   For a fuller exposition of this situation, see my essay, "What If the Sun Be Centre to the World?': Milton's Epistemology, Cosmology, and Paradise of Fools Reconsidered" *MP* 99.2 (2001): pp. 231–65.

The Science Fiction Epic versus the Saints' Eternal Rest

This concept appeared particularly dangerous to contemporaries not because it contradicted the Bible but because it entirely superseded it. Many scientists, Galileo included, had ably argued that Genesis did not literally teach geocentrism but merely used it as a metaphor for the "natural" human perspective, yet strongly discouraged speculation about the possibility of extraterrestrial, non-angelic life. Kepler thus earned Galileo's disapproval for his conjectures about moon men in his *Somnium* or "dream" of a lunar voyage, but other new philosophers speculated that, since God creates nothing in vain, the stars *should* sustain many habitable planets with humanoid or possibly superior life forms. Milton apparently sided with Kepler, for he shows both Raphael and Satan passing other, quite possibly inhabited, worlds on their voyages to earth (*PL* 3.565–71, 5.268), which Adam could presumably have explored himself had he continued to grow in obedience and love. Most astonishingly of all, *Paradise Lost* regards this type of curiosity as perfectly natural and proper to Adam, who is "to lead thy offspring" in probing the stars (*PL* 8.85–86). John S. Tanner believes that Milton qualifies his cosmological boldness by having Raphael warn Adam to "be lowly wise"— to confine his speculations to earth and to the observable heavens rather than joining Kepler in trying to imagine what "other Creatures" may "serve and fear" God on other planets (*PL* 8.173, 168–70, 175). This warning also conveniently moots the question of whether the miracles of Christ's incarnation and redemption were offered for Adam's offspring alone or for his unknown "brothers" as well.[9] Despite Milton's obvious interest in the question (which he might easily have omitted), Raphael's refusal to discuss "other Worlds, what Creatures there / Live, in what state, condition or degree" preserves the poem's aura of orthodoxy, as does Adam's contentment with what "thus far hath been reveal'd / Not only of Earth only but of highest Heav'n" (*PL* 8.175–78).

Nevertheless, Adam is *not* warned against increasing his knowledge of what Raphael has already said about the structure and course of the heavens or the competing merits of the chief world systems. Presumably, he will continue his habit of not letting "th' occasion pass / Given him by this great Conference [with an angel] to know / Of things above his World, and of thir being / ... whose high Power so far / Exceeded human" (*PL* 5.453–55, 458–59). This freedom to explore is potentially limitless, since, as Raphael informs him, he may later "wing'd ascend" to heaven. That would apparently include flying to the other "Heavenly Paradises" (*PL* 5.498, 500) or other "happy" extraterrestrial isles the reader glimpses with Satan in "the World's first Region" (*PL* 3.562):

> Amongst innumerable Stars, that shone
> Stars distant, but nigh hand seem'd other Worlds,

---

    [9]   John S. Tanner, "'And Every Star Perhaps a World of Destined Habitation': Milton and Moonmen," *Extrapolation* 30.3 (1989): pp. 267–79.

> Or other World's they seem'd, or happy Isles,
> Like those *Hesperian* Gardens fam'd of old,
> Fortunate fields, and Groves and flow'ry Vales,
> Thrice happy isles, but who dwelt happy there
> He stay'd not to enquire.
>
> (*PL* 3.565–71)

Satan would no doubt have stopped to visit these starry worlds were he not filled with rage and resentment that God has given his "vacant room" to Adam's "unworthy" race—emotions that obviously prevent objective exploration. Along the way, however, we find that the moon is a natural "star" reflecting the sun's light to earth (3.722–31), just as Wilkins's *Discovery of a New World* (1638) and his *Discourse concerning a New Planet* (1640) proposed.

Like the earth, Milton's moon is clearly inhabited, although not by the lost "wits" that Ariosto found there, which Milton consigns to his own Paradise of Fools (*PL* 3.457–59). The moon's inhabitants are instead either "Translated Saints" or "middle Spirits ... / Betwixt th' Angelical and Human kind" (*PL* 3.461–62), a mixed species that Milton may have derived (according to Merritt Hughes) from the speculations of Giordano Bruno, Jerome Cardan, or Henry More (Hughes 269). In fact, they seem to be a version of Francis Godwin's lunarians, the superior race described in the first English work of science fiction, *The Man in the Moone* (1638). Godwin's early romance is only semi-Copernican, but Milton's epic contains such fully modern details as Archangels with telescopic vision and a sun powered by "a "Magnetic beam, that gently warms / The Universe" (*PL* 3.583–84). The English discoverer of magnetism, William Gilbert, first proposed this theory, which would make magnetism the early modern equivalent of nuclear power. Galileo's sunspots also prove to be real, not illusory; the poet believes they are formed from solar matter with some "Terrestrial Humor mixt" (*PL* 3.610). All these details suggest that no absolute gulf exists between earthly and heavenly matter, although many of them still derive from the natural magic tradition that Wilkins himself never left behind. Wilkins proposed that the precious stones set beside the biblical Urim and Thummim on Aaron's breastplate must have been fueled by chemical powers, hardly a subject of "scientific" thought, but Milton also credits this opinion (*PL* 3.591–605). There is also a loose resemblance between the "Potable Gold" manufactured by his "Arch-chemic Sun" (*PL* 3.608–9) and the "inflammable oyl" that Wilkins expected to find flowing in the "rivers" of the sun.[10]

Yet this type of speculation was generally as alien to strict Calvinists as Milton's attempt to justify the ways of God to man. Most Puritans also shared the anti-heliocentric bias of Calvin and Luther, which modern historians of science trace to both their scriptural traditionalism and their residual scholasticism. The first systematic expositor of Luther's theology, the converted humanist Philipp

---

[10]   John Wilkins, *Mathematical Magick: Or, the Wonders That May be performed by Mechanichal [sic] Geometry* [rpt. 1638] (London, 1680), pp. 252–53.

Melanchthon, declared that Christians should reject the bare possibility of other worlds "both on the basis of Aristotelian physical principles and Scriptural doctrine." Although Protestantism generally encouraged innovative scriptural hermeneutics, Steven Dick shows that on this point most Reformers ironically took a narrower view than medieval theologians, who after 1277 upheld God's power to order the universe however he saw fit. That teaching offered the possibility of other worlds, but Melanchthon rejected it partly on anti-Catholic principles. Like the English Puritans, he also maintained that the Genesis account of God's completion of his cosmic work on the sixth day meant that no further creation could afterward occur on earth or in other worlds during his current Sabbath rest.[11] As Theodore Bozeman explains, this completed work established a closed, all-sufficient, and timeless pattern that mainline Puritans believed to be incapable of improvement or change. Although divine illumination would increasingly enlarge the minds of believers, their growth or "progress" only spurred fuller conformity to this divine paradigm. The radical saints placed far more emphasis on the progressive revelations of the Spirit, which they often associated with the pantheistic World Soul of the hermeticists and natural magicians. Yet they, too, hoped to be translated back into the prelapsarian purity of a mythic primordium untouched by time, corruption, or evolution.[12]

The new philosophers and natural theologians ironically evaded this logic by returning to medieval thought. Resurrecting Ockham's more "advanced" belief that God's creative will must be completely uncircumscribed, they believed that he could order or progressively change the natural laws of the universe as he saw fit. Moreover, since Ockham's world was no longer conceived as the deified expression of a static divine essence or *Spiritus Mundi*, its matter could hypothetically evolve. Underlying these changes, the new scientists sought contingent natural laws to explain an atomically malleable universe where (as Milton puts it) the divine will can "ordain / ... more Worlds" (*PL* 2.915–16). For, although Moses accurately taught how *our* cosmos was created in Genesis, he revealed nothing about God's universal activity for all time or even for all possible species. Finally, since God's logic is superior to our own, we cannot know his plan abstractly but only by observing the continuities evident in natural history. This proto-modern perspective is everywhere apparent in *Paradise Lost*, as when Raphael warns Adam that cosmic laws do not obey mere human conceptions of "greater" and "lesser," "logical" idols of the tribe he must root out. Yet at the time when Milton wrote, even Wilkins's French translator, Pierre Borel, balked at this Baconian belief. In his view, "natural reason doth sufficiently disswade us to believe, that the greater things serve the lesser; and that those that are the

[11]   Steven J. Dick, *Plurality of Worlds: The Origins of the Extraterrestrial Life Debate from Democritus to Kant* (Cambridge, 1982), p. 88.

[12]   Bozeman, *To Live Ancient Lives*, pp. 17, 16.

noblest, serve the vilest."[13] This was, of course, one way of proving that the sun does not "serve" or circle the earth, but it could also prove the reverse if the earth is considered God's last and best creation, as Raphael clearly recognizes. Hence he teaches that natural reason cannot dictate anything about the exact order of the universe except through empirical proof: "Great / Or Bright infers not Excellence" (*PL* 8.90–91) because other worlds may be inhabited by living "souls," the true test of "greatness" in his account.

Exact empirical proof of the universe's heliocentric structure was not available until the mid-nineteenth century, so Raphael wisely leaves the matter open, although Milton would no doubt have been pleased to learn of Newton's startling new theoretical proof in 1687.[14] In the interim, he adopts Bacon's "Ockhamist" approach to Genesis: the world can and does undergo moral and physical change, both negative—as when God's creatures "invent" evil—and positive, as they cooperate with his plan for a better world. Yet even in Newton's day, Aristotelians and biblical traditionalists remained uninterested in new and "improved" ideas about the expanded universe or about plural worlds. David Knight shows that these ideas belonged to those seeking to establish "'laws of nature' during the seventeenth century" and the early Enlightenment. These pioneers felt that their search exalted rather than detracted from God, a lawgiver "who like the founder of a city could choose" a contingent but still orderly set of laws. As a result, only inductive, not deductive, logic could reveal the structure of these laws.[15] This quest was actually stimulated by ongoing conflicts over scriptural interpretation among the Reformed churches; the new philosophers hoped that knowledge of God's book of nature might stabilize biblical uncertainties about divine Providence and purpose. In this new environment, the appeal of a universe filled with inhabited worlds dramatically increased since, as Dick observes, it promised to provide even "better arguments for God's glory than did Scripture."[16] The works of both Wilkins and Milton grew rapidly in popularity during this period, for while adhering to the plain reason and "sense" of scripture, they freely used the book of nature to support or supplement ideas on which scripture was ambiguous or silent. As the eighteenth century progressed, the triumph of the empirical program not just in England but on the continent began to make both Bacon and Milton appear as prophets of a distinctly non-biblical kind: conductors of "glorious" thought experiments about cosmic mechanics. The early Newtonians were especially inspired by Milton's

---

[13]   Pierre Borel, *Discours nouveau prouvant la pluralité des mondes* (Genève, 1657); English edn., *A New Treatise Proving a Multiplicity of Worlds* (London, 1658), chapters 6 and 7, cited in Dick, *Plurality of Worlds*, p. 119.

[14]   F.R. Johnson, *Astronomical Thought in Renaissance England* (Baltimore, 1937), p. 221.

[15]   David Knight, "Science Fiction of the Seventeenth Century," *The Seventeenth Century* 1.1 (1986): pp. 69–79, cited p. 71.

[16]   Dick, *Plurality of Worlds*, p. 156.

epic since their main access to the "heavens" remained mathematical rather than observational.[17]

At this time no one believed that Milton needed to predict the success of the heliocentric hypothesis to be considered "scientific," although his Copernican sympathies have been suspected by many readers (Hughes 189). Tanner agrees that, by showing Raphael and his curious students respectfully qualifying their hypotheses with an ever-present "perhaps," the "extraordinary, though tentative, possibilities couched in Milton's conditional syntax" signal his affinity with the inductive explorers of the expanded universe.[18] Many earlier, well-informed readers also recognized that his speculations were really only possible against a Copernican background, for (as Knight observes) in the Ptolemaic system there could be no real analogy between the moon, planets, stars, and the earth, and "no reason why they should be inhabited except by spiritual beings quite different from us." Yet

> When Galileo saw the mountains of the Moon with his telescope, and was even able to calculate their height: when he described the craters there; and when he interpreted the faint light on the dark part of the Moon ... as thrown there from the Earth: then the analogy between the Earth and Moon became much closer. When he found that Jupiter had moons as we do, this indicated an analogy between the earth and the planets: they might be the abode of rational beings. Instead of the Sun being a planet, its analogies were with the stars, which on the Copernican theory were much further away than had been supposed; and which might even be expected to have planets themselves.[19]

Based on these analogies, Milton's moon, earth, and other planets are all solid, compact, opaque bodies utterly unlike the diaphanous crystal or glass spheres posited by the older cosmology, although his universe naturally supports both the traditional Christian belief in God as final cause and the traditional argument from design.[20] Despite his skepticism, Bacon agreed that the common "light of nature" illuminating human reason, sense, induction, and judgment can reveal the divine "laws of heaven and earth," laws imprinted "upon the spirit of man by an inward instinct, ... which is a sparkle of the purity of his first estate" (*Works* 3:479). Yet this concession to final causes is not strictly an early modern habit of mind; even now it continues in semi-disguised form in many branches of scientific inquiry. Dick finds the age-old yearning for cosmological meaning in the current search for extraterrestrial life, even though this search is largely used to support the theory of evolution, not a neo-Christian theory of Intelligent Design. In the seventeenth

---

[17]   Ibid., p. 159–6.

[18]   Tanner, "'And Every Star,'" p. 277.

[19]   Knight, "Science Fiction," p. 72.

[20]   On the stark contrast between the "celestial bodies" of the old and new cosmologies, see Dick, *Plurality of Worlds*, p. 100.

century the opposite situation prevailed: Milton, Lucy Hutchinson, and the virtuosi all used Lucretian atomism to show that while Satan might pervert atoms, only God can create them.[21] Hence the search for God's "track Divine" (*PL* 11.354) is common to both early science and science fiction, from which it never entirely disappears, but merely spreads beyond our star to unknown worlds and galaxies.

Milton's Epic Theory and Sources

Guided by this search, as well as by the neoclassical "rules" of decorum he recommended to his pupils (*CPW* 2:404–5), Milton's great epic thus fulfilled his early ambition of exploring kernels of truth hidden in the "golden Poetick ages of such pleasing licence, as the fabl'd reign of old *Saturn*" (*CPW* 2:298). As in his early masque, he freely employed the creative allegoreisis of fable furthered by Bacon's *Wisdom of the Ancients*. In order to rival his admired Italian predecessor, Torquato Tasso, then the reigning "Christian Lucretius," he situated these speculations in an expanded universe. Frank Prince shows that he fulfilled this goal in two other important ways: by avoiding the excessively "prosy or quaint piety" that mars both Tasso's *La Sette Giornate del Mondo Creato* and Guillaume Du Bartas's *Devine Weekes and Works*, and by constructing the newly unified, dramatically charged type of creation narrative advocated by the Italian theorists and experimenters. Where they "pointed the way[,] Milton brought to this literary heritage the full heroic temper it required."[22] His two letters to Henry de Brass (*CPW* 7:500–501, 506–7) reveal that he was also influenced by modern theories of historiography, which aimed to produce realistic, probable, yet also morally engaged comparative accounts.[23] As his *History of Britain* indicates, these theories permit the historian to introduce quasi-legendary alternatives to the standard chronicles if they seem to offer more probable "kernels" of truth than the conventional narrative. Samuel Johnson's biography of Milton shows that he clearly understood and appreciated his epic fusion of these "rules":

> History must supply the writer with the rudiments of narration, which he must
> improve and exalt by a nobler art, must animate by dramatic energy, and diversify

---

[21] See Dick, *Plurality of Worlds*, pp. 1–5, and Philip Hardie, "The Presence of Lucretius in *Paradise Lost*," *MQ* 29.1 (1995): pp. 13–24.

[22] Frank T. Prince, *The Italian Element in Milton's Verse* (Oxford, 1954), pp. 57, 13. As Prince also shows, Milton's experiments in importing Latin grandeur into his native tongue were influenced by Italian experiments with word order and line endings (pp. 20–21, 42, 54). On Milton and Tasso, see also Mindele Anne Treip, *Allegorical Poetics and the Epic: The Renaissance Tradition to "Paradise Lost"* (Lexington, KY, 1994).

[23] See Barbara Shapiro, "History and Natural History," pp. 3–55; on the rise of probabilism, see Shapiro, *Probability and Certainty in Seventeenth-Century England* (Princeton, 1983).

by retrospection and anticipation; morality much teach him the exact bounds and different shades of vice and virtue, from policy and the practice of life ... To put these materials to poetical use is required an imagination capable of *painting nature and realising fiction* (emphasis added).[24]

A final requirement for the advanced Renaissance epic is set forth in Puttenham's *Art of English Poesy*: the poet traditionally sings in the guise of a priest or prophet whose autobiography provides ethical and "'rhetorical aids to proof,'" one of the three principal proofs listed in conventional rhetorical handbooks.[25]

Modern critics overlook these conventions when they interpret the bard as a literal prophet preaching a new biblical revelation, not even pausing to consider why earlier commentators rarely supposed that Milton literally believed his poem had been "dictated" by the Holy Spirit.[26] Not only does *De Doctrina Christiana* deny that the Spirit can be literally invoked, but Milton closely follows the style of his Renaissance predecessors in presenting a highly literary personification of God's "voice" and poetic guidance.[27] A.D. Nuttall finds that these epic conventions are "so prominent, the style so patently governed by human precedent, that there can be no mistaking these lines for the real or even the probable thoughts of God himself."[28] These precedents include both Tasso's and Abraham Cowley's opening invocations to their biblical epics. Tasso prays that "Divine Love" will "from the Father and the Son descend in me, and lodge in my heart and ... bring me grace"; he also asks God to "inspire my senses and my songs, that I may sing that first, exalted work, that was done by you," "the first eternal occasion of created things."[29] Richard Helgerson believes that Milton is even closer to Cowley. Milton's invocation to that "Spirit, that dost prefer / Before all Temples th' upright heart and pure" (*PL* 1.17–18) recalls Cowley's opening lines, where in "'strong verse I raise / A temple, where if thou vouchsafe to dwell, / It Solomon's and

---

[24]   Samuel Johnson, *Life of Milton*, in *Lives of the English Poets* (2 vols., London, 1925), vol. 1, p. 100.

[25]   Puttenham is cited in *English Literary Criticism: The Renaissance*, ed. O.B. Hardison, Jr. (New York, 1963), pp. 161–63. On rhetorical proof, see Steadman, citing John Diekoff, in *Moral Fiction*, p. 44.

[26]   For a summary of these views, Steadman, *Moral Fiction*, pp. 3–8, who points out that critics from Mary Ann Radzinowicz to John Shawcross and James Holly Hanford have supported Maurice Kelley's view, which is consistent with *De Doctrina Christiana* (p. 4). But the strongest support comes from Milton's nephew, Edward Phillips, whose biography notes that Milton's muse was often uninspired or faulty, entailing extensive revision, delay, and wasted pages before his epic was complete. Johnson repeats this information in his *Life of Milton*.

[27]   Smith, in *Perfection Proclaimed*, notes the Puritan lack of a sophisticated tradition of poetic prophesy (p. 32).

[28]   Nuttall, *Overheard by God*, p. 85.

[29]   Tasso's *Mondo Creato* is cited in Prince, *Italian Element*, p. 55 n. 1.

Herod's shall excel.'" Cowley's *Davideis* also traces a similar progress from hell, to heaven, and thence to earth, and Milton even seems to borrow specific details such as its initial description of Satan and his staff, its repeated use of sonorous proper names, the division of labor in his Pandemonium, and a digression on gold's "fatal attractions." Helgerson also believes that Milton's final decision to discard Arthurian or Homeric epic for a Virgilian mode essentially "answers" Cowley's introductory invitation to better his unfinished epic: his failure should open "'a way to the courage of other persons ... better able' to give England a Virgilian epic on a Biblical theme." Given the fact that Cowley was reputedly one of Milton's three favorite English poets, and that Milton borrowed more from his epic than from any other English work, these conjectures appear sound.[30]

Yet Milton was hardly a slavish follower of anyone, and certainly not of Cowley. Both poets were commonly inspired by Spenser's use of "prophetic" fictions to "entertain and, still more, to instruct a nation," and both inherited the new "set of artistic and self-presentational problems" occasioned by England's bloody civil wars. Helgerson explains that "Where Spenser and Jonson had found the divine order mirrored in the monarch," the recent obsolescence of monarchical, courtly, and military grandeur led Milton and Cowley to seek a new kind of divine truth "in the order of nature, as that order was being revealed by scientific investigation."[31] Literary Puritans like Du Bartas were prevented from taking this step since they were even more aware (and more fearful) of the taboo against adding to the word of God than Milton was. They also tended to be much more cautious both in their mythic expansions of scripture and in their invocations. Du Bartas summons a "heedfull *Muse*, trayned in true Religion" to keep him cautiously to "the middle Region" lest "Heau'ns glowing flame should melt her waxen plume." His modern editor finds his epic voice equally conservative and old-fashioned: he figuratively stands "before the flock, exhorting, praying, leading the chorus, instructing, and warning of things to come" protected by an ultra-virginal muse, a "Urania" who detests Venus and her love poets.[32]

In contrast, both the "energetic operation" of Milton's fancy and his free incorporation of Greek mythology allowed him to appeal to eighteenth-century readers like Johnson. Far from detesting Venus, Milton shows her son's "purple wings" and "golden shafts" lighting the "constant Lamp" over that marriage bed where Adam and Eve consummate their love. Here the poet passionately condemns

---

[30]   Helgerson, *Self-Crowned Laureates*, pp. 234–5, citing Cowley's *Poems*, ed. A.R. Waller (Cambridge, 1905) p. 243.

[31]   Ibid., pp. 214, 226; see also pp. 236–42.

[32]   See Guillaumne de Salluste du Bartas, *Bartas: His Devine Weekes and Works* (rpt. 1605) trans. Joshua Sylvester, ed. Francis C. Harber (Gainesville, FL, 1965), p. ix, and "Urania," stanzas 59–70 (*Devine Weekes and Works*, pp. 538–39). George Coffin Taylor, in *Milton's Use of Du Bartas* (Cambridge, MA, 1934), claimed that Milton owed a prominent debt to Du Bartas but Whiting later corrected him, noting far more differences than similarities; see *Milton's Literary Milieu*, p. 9.

the entire Augustinian tradition carefully followed by Du Bartas, who safely followed Grotius and Vondel in accepting the "pre-sexual" view of Edenic life canonized by Augustine. Rather than banning sexuality, that "Perpetual Fountain of Domestic sweets" (*PL* 4.763–64, 760), Milton makes it prominent in Eden. Not only failing to introduce Eve until the moment of her Fall after the manner of Du Bartas, he actually dwells on Adam's courtship, romance, and conjugal embraces after censuring the "Hypocrites austere" who deny or forbid them (*PL* 4.744). This is strikingly modern position on Edenic sexuality may not have been entirely unique, but *pace* Merritt Hughes (295 n. 744), John Salkeld's *A Treatise of Paradise* (1617) did not in fact establish a new Protestant "orthodoxy" on prelapsarian sexual relations. Even Vondel—whose *Lucifer* is often considered an important predecessor—never took this position, and "no other writer of the 'celestial cycle' [but Milton] inquired into the nature and history of marriage, religion, and society nearly so searchingly" or with such "enlightened attention" to detail. Drawing widely on classical, Hebraic, and Christian sources, as Joseph Duncan shows, Milton's synthesis was often boldly unorthodox.[33]

Milton was not even simply content to portray a perfect garden; Duncan finds him producing an encyclopedic account of the origin, development, and enduring values of human culture before, during, and after its decline. Not just innocent gardeners, his Adam and Eve are the first "authors" of human civilization because, just "as Aeneas was to found Rome," they "were intended to establish on earth the City of God."[34] At this point the Virgilian mode becomes problematic, since Roman militarism and imperialism obviously conflicted both with Edenic peace and the values of Milton's militarily disillusioned generation. He thus consigns his epic games, battles, debates, and empire-building to hell and its hellish successors on earth, reserving even the final victory in the War in Heaven for the Son of God alone. Nevertheless, Milton's Eden is not simply a pastoral "Rome" minus martial values, but a vision of a complex culture that is actually higher than any subsequent civilization. Exploring natural history, astronomy, philosophy, and ethics, Adam and Eve even touch on Milton's lifelong concern with domestic, religious, and civil liberty (*CPW* 4.1:624). The vast scope of this epic description can be traced to Bacon's call for new "kind of Mixed History," which Milton also answers in his *Brief History of Moscovia* (*CPW* 8:470). Bacon believed that a competent overview of historical sites should include "Natural History, in respect of the regions themselves, their sites and products; ... History Civil, in respect of the habitations, government, and manners of people;" and a mathematical/astronomical history "of the climates and configurations of the heavens, beneath which the regions of the world lie. In which

---

[33] Vondel's *Lucifer* avoids the subject of sexuality by having his Adam leave his newly wedded Eve for a private chat with God; Grotius's *Adamus Exul* avoids it in the same way as Du Bartas—by not introducing Eve until the temptation scene. See Joseph E. Duncan, *Milton's Earthly Paradise: A Historical Study of Eden* (Minneapolis, MN, 1972), pp. 185–86.

[34] Ibid., p. 159.

kind of history or science we may congratulate our own age" and "plant also great expectation of the further proficience and augmentation of the sciences" (*Works* 4:311). This plan for the "proficience and augmentation of the sciences" obviously alludes to the titles of Bacon's two most famous works, his Latin *De Dignatate et Augmentis Scientiarum*, and its shorter English version, *The Proficience and Advancement of Learning*. Milton's thorough documentation of Eden's "habitations, government, and manners" not only follows Bacon's geographical model but includes a condensed astronomical history of the entire cosmos.

Eden's Baconian Anthropology

While *Paradise Lost* never shows exactly what a perfect earthly government would have looked like, it supplies strong hints that Edenic rule would have been as "mixed" as its geography and civilized pursuits. Adam would remain Eden's original patriarch and authority, but his powers would be far from kingly. Even before he has any sons to rule, Adam bitterly denounces the hubris of the first king without any prompting from the Archangel Michael. When Nimrod usurps human "Authority … from God not giv'n" ("He gave us only over Beast, Fish, Fowl / Dominion absolute"), he not only misappropriates the rights of his "Brethren" but contradicts the divine plan: "Man over men / He made not Lord; such title to himself / Reserving, human left from human free" (*PL* 12.65–71). A clearer denunciation of Filmer's *Patriarcha* could hardly be imagined. Not only refuting Filmer's royalist argument that all kings descend from Adam, Milton replaces the princely epic hero with the "one just Man" who reappears throughout history to free his people (*PL* 11.818). Since he "who hath best aided the people, and best merited against tyrannie" by employing "all reason and good policie" alone deserves any eminence above his brethren, no one can be a king simply by inheritance (*CPW* 7:482). Without establishing either a modern democracy or a Harringtonian republic, these principles reflect the anti-slavery rhetoric of neo-Roman thought that dominates Milton's depiction of postlapsarian life.[35] Most likely for that reason, his Eden seems to include natural property rights, which are lightly touched on as we learn that its animals maintain a "spontaneous" respect for Adam and Eve's privacy. Their own relationship is freely founded upon a classical ethic of mutually balanced "just self-esteem" largely "consonant with the anti-Calvinist stress upon the self-respecting, self-restrained individual in late-seventeenth- and eighteenth-century theology and ethics."[36] If Adam and Eve had not failed to preserve this balance, all decisions and disputes would presumably have been settled at something very much like the "Feast of the Family" described in Bacon's *New Atlantis*, where the family head amicably resolves all disagreements among his children. For as Michael tells Adam, "All generations … had [perhaps]

---

[35]   See Skinner, *Liberty before Liberalism*, pp. 38–52.
[36]   Scodel, *Excess and the Mean*, p. 283.

hither come / From all the ends of th'Earth, to celebrate / And reverence thee thir great Progenitor," and presumably to seek his advice (*PL* 11.344–46). Yet, instead of this Edenic "summit," his descendants tragically inherit a wilderness of savage warriors, envious politicians, and ignorant religious leaders who recognize neither the Spirit of Grace nor her consort Liberty (*PL* 12.525–26).

This tragic inheritance is not immediate but is set in motion soon after Cain's materialistic daughters corrupt the contemplative Sons of God. By focusing exclusively on sensuous arts and crafts, Cain's daughters not only divert attention from nature's proper study and cultivation (*PL* 11.556–627), but ensure that fallen human art will not "perfect and exalt Nature" but instead "wrong, abuse, and traduce" it, as Bacon complains of the Greeks (*Works* 3:387).[37] Bacon's remarks on Cain's murder of Abel are the most likely source of this Miltonic passage, since Bacon interprets Cain's murder as initiating man's "second fall" through the wrongful triumph of action over contemplation. This iniquity is the most fatal result of Adam's moral "defection from God" and decision "to depend wholly upon himself," which reaps only alienation, not real freedom (*Works* 3:297). The ongoing curse on Adam and his sons is thus the widening gap between "Cain's" action and "Abel's" contemplation, which can only be cured by Bacon's "Georgics of the mind," a harmonious balance of active "husbandry and tillage," and passive "shepherding" or contemplation. The new inventions and restored Eden that would result from this "georgics" might ordinarily lead to luxury and materialism, as they do among Cain's daughters in *Paradise Lost*, but Bacon insists that, if his method is correctly employed, the growth of true reason and religion will supplant all "base impulses."[38] Milton's lesson is strikingly similar: Cain's daughters may be "inventors rare" in metallurgy, musical instruments, and dancing (*PL* 11.610), but his unfallen humans and angels put their musical gifts and implements to much better and more harmonious use.

Both Bacon and Milton also provide more gender-balanced analyses of the perversion of reason than the mini-allegory of Book 11 superficially suggests. The Scylla of Bacon's *Advancement of Learning* is a "specious" and dangerous siren whose flattery bears a hidden sting, yet the real sources of her "poison" are the false lovers and false philosophers who pervert her much as Satan perverts his "daughter," Sin. Similarly, when the Sons of Seth abandon "all thir study ... / To worship God aright, and know his works" for fleeting pleasures (*PL* 11.577–78), the real cause is their own susceptibility to the lust of the eye and ear—to flashy females "so blithe, so smooth, so gay / ... To dress, and troll the Tongue, and roll

---

[37] No other sources for Milton's episode have been found aside from three terse verses in Genesis 4:20–22, and a possible reference to Lucretius' *De rerum natura*, 5.1241–68. On Bacon's "husbandry," see Annabel Patterson, "Pastoral versus Georgic: The Politics of Virgilian Quotation," in Barbara K. Lewalski (ed.), *Renaissance Genres: Essays on Theory, History, and Interpretation* (Cambridge, MA, 1986), pp. 241–67, at pp. 242–45.

[38] Stephen A. McKnight, *The Religious Foundations of Francis Bacon's Thought* (Columbia, MO, 2006), p. 101.

the Eye." This weakness causes both their enslavement to sirens "empty of all good wherein consists / Woman's domestic honor and chief praise" (*PL* 11.615–17, 620) and the loss of real science. Adam of course sets the original bad example by abandoning the mutual self-esteem he originally shared with Eve for lustful uxoriousness, whose hidden "sting" is misogyny (*PL* 10.867–908). By pursuing what Bacon calls the mere "shews which first offer themselves to our senses" and succumbing to what Milton calls "Man's effeminate slackness" (*PL* 11.634), Adam's sons will incline to atheism and idolatry as the true "use for which God hath granted" knowledge is forgotten (*Works* 3:221). After physically and mentally seducing the Sons of Seth, Milton's "fair Atheists" (*PL* 11.625) also induct them into a false and hollow religion which, according to Bacon, "consisteth in rites and forms of adoration, and not in confessions and beliefs." Its joint consequences are scientific, spiritual, and political corruption, since formalist worship is as "averse to knowledge" as a dogmatic religion is "jealous of the variety of learning, discourse, opinions, and sects" (*Works* 3:251).

The City of God and the City of Man thus continue their eternal warfare at the end of *Paradise Lost*, but Milton's Edenic anthropology is actually much more optimistic than his postlapsarian history, and this optimism survives in Adam and Eve's "paradise within" (*PL* 12.587). One reason is that work retains its Baconian value both before and after the Fall, which for Calvinist theologians instituted a wholly new and perverted order. Milton strikingly modifies this belief by failing to make Eden a static golden age society even before the Fall. As the original home of an active civil society, his Eden departs from both classical legend and the "land of Cockayne" legend popular among Antinomians. Covenant theologians rejected Antinomian idleness but also supposed that God instituted a disciplinary society even in paradise. Since he universally "condemned all indolent repose" and required all to "employ themselves in some work," and not to "lie down in inactivity and idleness," Puritans like Elnathan Parr declared that absolutely no "Idleness and lawlesse liberty was … permitted to Adam in Paradise."[39] This assumption conflicts both with Milton's portrayal of Adam's paradisal existence and with Bacon's belief that Adam's work, like his pursuit of knowledge, had been "joy" of leisure that we may even now recapture if "delight in the experiment, and not labour" (or strict utilitarian considerations) inspire us (*Works* 3:297, 296).

Milton had experienced a version of this ideal in the Italian academies, voluntary associations for pursuing knowledge mainly flawed by the fact that

---

[39] See Elnathan Parr, *Grounds of Divinitie* (London, 1651), p. 29, and John Calvin, *Commentaries on the First Book of Moses*, p. 125, both cited in Duncan, *Milton's Earthly Paradise*, p. 153. For the opposing view that Milton followed Calvinist traditions about paradise, see Georgia Christopher, *Milton and the Science of the Saints* (Princeton, 1982), and Keith F.M. Stavely, *Puritan Legacies: "Paradise Lost" and the New England Tradition, 1630–1890* (Ithaca, NY, 1987).

Counter-Reformation politics precluded their active intervention in society.[40] They thus failed to attain Bacon's utopian dream of an Edenic reunion of action and contemplation, which Milton projects back into Eden itself. While conceding that Eve's proposed division of labor is well "motion'd ... to study household good" (*PL* 9.229, 233), Adam wisely justifies the joys of "godly" leisure:

> Yet not so strictly hath our Lord impos'd
> Labor, as to debar us when we need
> Refreshment, whether food, or talk between,
> Food of the mind, or this sweet intercourse
> Of looks and smiles, ...
>
> ...
>
> For not to irksome toil, but to delight
> He made us, and delight to Reason join'd.
>
> (*PL* 9.235–39, 242–43)

Given their relaxed afternoon with Raphael and the ultimately fatal result of Eve's reasoning, Adam proves correct: in Eden, labor and delightful contemplation are inseparable components of "household good," while strict utilitarianism may be conducive to the pride that goeth before a fall. Although not sinful in itself, Eve's over-zealous work ethic undermines the balance that is Eden. After the Fall, the balance tips even further as the ideal unity of faculties—active and contemplative, male and female—devolves into conflicting camps or orientations. Satan's hordes experience the same fall as they divide into camps either "idly" contemplating those insoluble Calvinist conundrums of "Fixt Fate, Free will, Foreknowledge absolute" (*PL* 2.560), or over-actively pursuing Moloch's military ethos or Mammon's work ethic.[41]

Antinomians rejected both conservative Calvinists' overly abstract theology and their rigorist work ethic, but in rethinking Eden they fused the biblical book of Revelation with the age-old fantasies of oppressed peoples. They thus envisioned their new Eden or Jerusalem as an effortless, lawless state "ruled" by perfect contentment, peace, and plenty. John Fenwick predicted that after the Second Coming a "land of corn and wine ... shall make young men merry" with bread, and maids with new wine. Bunyan similarly believed that the Lord should "make unto his people a feast of fat things, a feast of wine on the lees of fat things," while Mary Cary "simply promised 'joy without any mixture of sorrow at all.'" All "the grinding toil of the labourer would cease," and as the "resurrected" Nottinghamshire maid attested, "'our charge ... and our travail shall have an end.'" Bernard Capp shows that the paradise of these Puritan prophets seamlessly

---

[40] Anna K. Nardo, "Academic Interludes in *Paradise Lost*," *Milton Studies* 27 (1991): pp. 209–41, cited p. 220.

[41] See my essay, "Self-Raised Sinners and the Spirit of Capitalism: *Paradise Lost* and the Critique of Protestant Meliorism," *Milton Studies* 30 (1994): pp. 109–33.

merged the peasant myth of Cockayne where men and women would be free from both conventional morality and the conventional "other-worldliness of the biblical New Jerusalem." Yet, like conservative Puritans, they still envisioned their sabbath rest as a return to a static and timeless harmony with God and nature.[42] Puritan mystics and Antinomians influenced by the *Theologica Germanica* or by Sebastian Franck's similarly inflected thought believed that this rest meant the very opposite of civilization and all of its arts, for, as Isaac Penington put it, "ignorance is better than knowledge."[43] William Poole shows that Penington closely followed Franck in believing that "our best state is when we quite literally vegetate," for according to the latter, "man, like a Logge," enjoys a paradisal state only "while he doth nothing, knows & desires nothing, but, keeping a holy Sabbath or rest; dyes wholly unto himself, and being void of will or wit, resignes himself over unto God." Penington was Thomas Ellwood's spiritual mentor, and like other Quakers he idealized a "Franckean pre-ethical, almost pre-human bliss, recaptured through self-abasement" and the "unlearning" of any distinction between good and evil, which would be completely blotted out as man literally returns to "'one lump of Clay.'"[44] Mainline Puritans obviously placed far more emphasis on human responsibility, but, as noted above, they similarly imagined paradise as a passive "reversion to a fixed order of precept and form that must shape human society and development, not the other way around."[45]

The contrast with the poet who never tired of citing Christ's dictum that the sabbath was made for man and not man for the sabbath (Mark 2:27) could hardly be greater. Combining innocence and experience in a progressively unfolding paradise, Milton's Eden is neither tightly regulated, blissfully effortless, nor ignorant. Its inhabitants are neither pre- nor super-human; they possess no gnostic, "instant wisdom" and are constrained by no static covenant of nature and grace. Still less is Adam the perfect theologian, natural magician, or little god posited by the Antinomians.[46] "Born" into the world without any innate ideas and only the natural linguistic and logical capacities he passes on to his heirs in slightly disordered form, Milton's Adam lacks any spontaneous understanding of his Creator. He must gradually learn who he is and what his God expects, ultimately through a debate that actually reveals as much about Adam as about the Almighty.

---

[42]   Capp, "Fifth Monarchists," pp. 186–89. Capp cites John Fenwick, *Zions Joy* (1643), p. 57, John Bunyan, *Works* (1856) vol. 3, p. 444, and Mary Cary, *The Little Horns Doom* (1651), p. 279.

[43]   Isaac Penington, *Divine Essays; or, Considerations about Several Things in Religion* (London, 1654), p. 3.

[44]   Poole, *Milton and the Idea*, pp. 63, 65, 67, citing Sebastian Franck, *The Forbidden Fruit* (London, 1642), pp. 60, 24, 92, and Isaac Penington, *Light or Darknesse* (London, 1649), pp. 3, 10, 12..

[45]   Bozeman, *To Live Ancient Lives*, p. 73.

[46]   On Milton's departure from this tradition, see Duncan, *Milton's Earthly Paradise*, pp. 148–55.

Its chief revelation is that sinless curiosity is mankind's fundamental trait, not its fundamental flaw, as the mystics supposed; Adam's bold questioning of his God is praised and rewarded. Before that discussion, his independent awakening to life simply parallels Henry More's recollection of his unfallen childish delight in the beauties of "this outward world, whose several powers and properties touching variously upon my tender senses, made me such enravishing music, and snatched away my soul into so great admiration, love, and desire of a nearer acquaintance with that Principle from which all these things did flow."[47] Like the young More, Milton's Adam eagerly seeks the smiling but invisible face of his unknown Creator through "Hill, Dale, and shady Woods, and sunny Plains," seeing it reflected in all "Creatures that liv'd, and mov'd, and walk'd, or flew"; on him "all things smil'd, / With fragrance and with joy my heart o'erflow'd" (*PL* 8.262, 264–66). After his Fall, Adam's faculties are impaired but not "depraved" so, like Seth's sons, his children retain his instinct to seek God by "know[ing] his works, / Not hid" and studying "those things ... which might preserve / Freedom and Peace to men," although they also inherit his tendency to go astray (*PL* 11.578–80).

Since Milton's humans are more "discursive" than the "intuitive" angels, even in Eden Adam's "sudden apprehension" of creation is limited to simply naming the beasts—in what language, we are not told. Thus, unlike Du Bartas and his translator, Joshua Sylvester, who in common with most Puritans believed that "the very words of Hebrew were divinely significant," Milton gives Adam no privileged dialect and no distinct communicative advantages over his heirs but innocence.[48] God communicates with him in dreams, but, as Eve's final revelation shows, divine dreams do not cease after their Fall. The same continuities apply to ethical knowledge. Before the Fall, Raphael advises Adam that "Oft-times nothing profits more / Than self-esteem, grounded on just and right / Well managed; of that skill the more thou know'st," the more his wife will acknowledge his leadership. In the process, both will climb higher in the natural "scale" of love and reason (*PL* 8.571–73, 586–92). The same ethic permits the human recovery of republican self-reliance first by the Jews, next by the apostles, and then by "all who in the worship persevere / Of Spirit and Truth" until the final "respiration to the just" restores the whole earth (*PL* 12.532–33, 540). The gradual ascent of both pre- and post-lapsarian humans in *Paradise Lost* sharply contrasts with the religious radicals' belief that "intuitive knowledge led directly to [a] power" capable of instantly returning them to Eden. Nigel Smith links this belief to their preoccupation with self-referential dream visions that at times bordered on solipsistic fantasies of redemption. Adopting an essentially Platonic dream theory that required no external confirmation if the impression is "strong" enough, visionaries like

---

47   Henry More, *Immortality*, Preface, 2, in *Philosophicall Poems* (Cambridge, 1647), cited in McAdoo, *Spirit*, p. 116.

48   See David S. Katz, "The Language of Adam in Seventeenth-Century England," in Hugh Lloyd Jones et al. (eds.), *History and Imagination*, p. 143. On similar Antinomian beliefs, see Capp, "Fifth Monarchists," pp. 176–86.

Winstanley relied on purely internal testimonies to justify their beliefs.[49] One result was Winstanley's conviction that the law-giving Christian God was merely an illusion to be cast off so that the mystical fullness of Christ could take his place: "Your Saviour must be a power within you, to deliver you from that bondage within; the outward Christ or the outward God are but men [or false] Saviours."[50]

Since Winstanley also believed that heaven and hell are mere allegories of our earthly human condition, he doubly contrasts with Milton, for whom the law-giving Father is no illusion and heaven and hell no mere allegories. While they are not strictly local—the joys of heaven are comparable to those on earth, and the pains of hell are at once internal and externally portable—both clearly exist within a very real material cosmos.[51] These differences partly stem from the fact that Milton's dream theory is not Platonic but Aristotelian: dream visions can only be considered prophetic if confirmed by external means, as when Eve's dream in Book 12 is verified by the Archangel Michael's waking lessons. Adam adopts the same theory in predicting that Eve's "evil dream" tells nothing of the future unless she *chooses* to sin in "real time," not merely in an unconscious and unwelcome dream. When she does choose to sin, the circumstances of her Fall are utterly different from those in the dream. Vanishing with her confused "animal spirits," it leaves no "spot or blame" behind. As Bacon suggests in *The Advancement of Learning*, her Fall instead results from a *conscious* decision to rely on herself and a flattering serpent rather than on God, who has already sent an angel warning her and Adam not to "suborn" the plain light of reason and the real meaning of God's moral interdiction on the fruit—maintaining their covenant with God (*PL* 9.360–62). When she fails to heed the warning, the circumstances of her "reasoned" decision are almost the opposite of her transgressive dream, in which she unwillingly flew heavenward with a beautiful, apple-bearing angel. Ironically, Adam had hoped that this frightening vision would strengthen her resolve not to sin by teaching that even an imaginary experience of evil is not the painless "nothing" that the serpent/Satan later claims it is. Her failure to reflect on this experience after the serpent offers her an implausible new "revelation" about the divine edict thus parallels a mistake frequently made by the radicals, whose "expectation high" of mystical knowledge (*PL* 9.789–90) and bliss tended to founder upon the problem of the imagination itself.

J.C. Davis and Robert Appelbaum commonly point out that the radicals' utopian schemes tended to disintegrate because their search for mystical, apolitical unity forced the utopian imagination constantly to reinvent itself. It finally came to rest, in Winstanley's case, on a severe form of social coercion grounded in Mosaic law.[52] Yet James Holstun finds that all Puritan utopists eventually encountered

---

[49] Smith, *Perfection Proclaimed*, pp. 73–76, 80, 229–30.

[50] Quoted in Hill, *World Turned*, p. 113.

[51] See Whiting, *Milton's Literary Milieu*, pp. 36–93.

[52] Appelbaum, *Literature and Utopian Politics*, pp. 166–68. Davis surveys the full range of these fictions in *Utopia and the Ideal Society* (Cambridge, 1981); his introductory

Winstanley's dilemma: in seeking a release from bondage into a formless, timeless "self-consuming artifact," they too often achieved only a "personal mortification of the flesh and spirit in anticipation of a universal presence of the spirit." Holstun perceptively adds that the Miltonic imagination actually works in reverse: since he was "unable to find any scripturally sanctioned mechanisms for producing virtuous citizens," his most characteristic use of scripture is anti-utopian.[53] Milton's Eden also works in reverse since its "artifacts" are anything but self-consuming. As outlined above, Milton's highly civilized paradise contains an astonishing range of institutions completely absent from Genesis but present in our world: courtship and marriage rituals, rudimentary property laws, formal rites of worship, culinary arts, horticulture (including the use of tools), liberal education (including legal, ethical, and scientific debates), empirical observation (including astronomy), and arts of married love strikingly absent from any Puritan vision of paradise. This highly civilized *modus vivendi* can be derived neither from God's biblical command to "dress and keep the garden" nor from Adam's "sudden apprehension" of the animals' names and natures. Milton actually pays scant attention to these conventional details, although he gives more gender parity to Eve by giving her a complementary ability to name and "know" her flowers.

In this, as in other important details, the older assumption that the paradise of the great Protestant poet features the self-disciplinary Puritan asceticism that Weber associated with him proves illusory. Milton's Eden completely lacks the double covenant of work and worship that mainline Calvinists located in paradise through God's original prohibition on the forbidden fruit. Milton instead stresses that his interdiction represents a simple test of his children's obedience, love, and faith, which makes both their work and their worship strictly natural and voluntary. Yet, as in his sonnet on his blindness, man needs "day-labor" and trust in God more than the Father needs or requires them from him. *De Doctrina Christiana* also rejects covenant theology by denying that the ten commandments were given to Adam in paradise (as the Calvinists maintained) and making them strictly Mosaic laws. Hence Christians, or proto-Christians like Adam and Eve, must simply love God and neighbor (in that order) above themselves.[54] This simplified "New Law" does not mean they have no need for moral guidance, although it does mean that God establishes no covenant of works for them to obey. Adam and Eve's prelapsarian labor is un-laborious and it serves as its own reward, yet, even after the loss of Eden, work is still not a covenant, a curse, nor even a duty, but rather a blessing in disguise—a Baconian cure for Adam's lost "idyll" of contemplative bliss.

Bacon's *Novum Organum* explains that the Fall did not fundamentally alter Adam's condition because God's apparent curse—"in the sweat of your brow ye

---

remarks (pp. 12–40) on the socially controlling aspects of most seventeenth-century utopias are especially illuminating.

[53] Holstun, *Rational Millennium*, pp. 100, 255.

[54] On this point, see Chapter 2 above, and Lewalski, "Milton and *De Doctrina*," p. 223.

shall eat bread"—was actually intended to ease his fallen state both materially and psychologically (*Works* 4:248). Not only distracting him from his loss of paradise, work also materially repairs it. Milton's Adam "apprehends" this fact long before Michael explains his new condition, virtually paraphrasing Bacon as he remarks, "On mee the Curse aslope / Glanc'd on the ground, with labor I must earn / My bread; what harm? Idleness had been worse; / My labor will sustain me; ... / And teach us further by what means to shun" the disadvantages of their new climate (*PL* 10.1053–56, 1062; cf. *PL* 11.349–65). He immediately applies this insight by "discovering" fire, which additionally means that no Prometheus has cursed technical knowledge. Adam and Eve will simply warm themselves by kindling flame either from dry matter exposed to the "gather'd beams" of the sun or from the friction of "two bodies" rubbed together (*PL* 10.1072–79). These empirical observations redeem all the inventions associated with fire in advance—metallurgy, agriculture, and sailing—from the "Titan's curse" that golden age mythology attached to them. Without a Jupiter to revenge Prometheus's double-pronged "gift" by sending a fatal Pandora to mankind, the curse of fire is redeemed along with the curse on Eve. Like Adam's labor, her labor pains thus become a relatively mild punishment, toil "soon recompens't with joy" (*PL* 10.1052). This Baconian revisionism even removes the taint on vain, "feminine" curiosity, since Adam and Eve's curiosity is as important in recovering from the Fall as in causing it.[55] Before that, Eve's Fall is not actually the result of "feminine" vanity, but (as Victoria Kahn observes) of failing to "think hard" about use value.[56] Allured by the "instant wisdom" sought by Puritan mystics and Antinomians, she ignores the central distinction between useful and fanciful knowledge that Kahn finds in Milton's *Areopagitica*.

Kahn's distinction is based on *Areopagitica*'s differentiation between "productive division" and mere "faction." This distinction closely parallels the difference between useful labor and unproductive friction, which yields only harmful fixations, illusory goods, and fixed commodities "that can be transferred from one person to another without regard for intention or right use." A similar distinction underlies *Areopagitica*'s separation of flexible from fixed "goods" in the moral sense of the word. Whereas flexible goods are products of the dialectical sphere of "things indifferent" and free exchange, fixed commodities are products of a factional and monological monopoly of goods and ideas. Thus where the flexible sphere produces open-ended or "probable" truths fruitfully combining experimental contemplation with action, fixed economies block new knowledge by limiting both action and experiment. These contrasts culminate in the tract's most famous distinction, the difference between actively acquired virtue and passive or "blank" purity. Kahn believes that the same contrast ultimately separates

---

[55]   See Howard Schultz, *Milton and Forbidden Knowledge* (New York, 1955); on the typical Puritan cautions against "forbidden" curiosity and human aspiration (derived from Agrippa and others), see Poole, *Milton and the Idea*, pp. 61–82.

[56]   Kahn, *Machiavellian Rhetoric*, p. 227.

Milton's open-ended Eden from the traditionally enclosed garden of the golden age. Reversing a long tradition, Milton actually identifies closure with hell and openness with Eden, thereby converting the boundless sphere that "Christianity has traditionally marked with the fall" into the essence of paradise.[57] On the positive side, this radical revision of paradise ultimately equalizes human and angelic, male and female opportunity; on the negative side, it leaves Eden as open to Satan's false merchandise as to Raphael's true wares.

Overall, however, Milton's "open" garden allows both Adam and Eve to experience emotions and make choices denied them by virtually all of his poetic predecessors. As noted at the outset, his most obvious and drastic departure from Christian convention is including sexual passion in Eden. Doubly departing from Augustine and his Puritan heirs, for Milton paradisal marriage is no longer solely for procreation but also for physical pleasure as well as for a form of intellectual companionship formerly reserved for males. Returning to the Platonic myth of the union of Eros and Anteros, or Penury and Plenty, first explored in his divorce tracts, Milton all but erases Augustine's central distinction between *caritas* and *concupiscentia*, since passion's "transported touch" and its "commotion strange" have both become natural components of love (*PL* 8.530–31). Passion is thus no longer a "dark" horse to be reined in by the Phaedrian charioteer, or Reason, but a primary source of Edenic bliss.[58] Even after the Fall, Eve's passionate refusal of the "penury" that her vindictive spouse would force upon her is redemptive, not transgressive. Cooperating with God's removal of "the stony from thir hearts" (*PL* 11.4), her resistance to either an emotional or erotic "divorce" from her mate makes Eve the first truly heroic female in epic tradition. Much as the loss of Patroclus spurred Achilles to defeat Hector, and the loss of the young Pallas spurred Aeneas to slay Turnus, the loss of Adam impels Eve to overcome the wrath of Satan—paradoxically, by making love, not war. Adopting the peaceful role usually reserved for very young or very mature warriors, she becomes Adam's confidante and "second" in their long struggle with their newly discovered enemy, Satan, and all his "forces." Since Eve does this by synthesizing aspects of *eros* long regarded as opposites not just by Christian but also by classical tradition, she ultimately lacks the meekness that most Reformed marriage theorists advocated in a wife. Puritans in particular (who did not pioneer completely new forms of companionate marriage, as earlier believed) made only minor alterations in the common Calvinist belief that the prime purpose of marriage was to propagate the church and the family. Milton's "primitivist" preference for spontaneous, unchurched worship and "conversational" marriage is far more civilized, in part because he draws on quite different sources. These include courtesy book writers like the humanist Ludovicus Vives, whose conversational ideal of marriage particularly influenced him. Milton's own divorce tracts had already introduced another major innovation

---

[57]   Ibid., pp. 176, 225.

[58]   For this reading, see Gregory Chaplin, "'One Flesh, One Heart, One Soul': Renaissance Friendship and Miltonic Marriage," *MP* 99.2 (2001): pp. 266–92.

by making "soul relationships" superior to most considerations of bodily or religious "fitness."[59]

John Halkett finds this position at least loosely comparable with that of liberal Puritan marriage manuals, which acknowledged that "meet conversation" between husband and wife would ideally be social as well as sexual, although "only Milton makes so insistent a plea for the fundamental primacy of the spiritual bond in matrimony."[60] Ironically, Antinomian Puritans were even less egalitarian, for in attempting to recover an Adamite relationship that might "involve either naturalistic sexual freedom or ascetic hatred of the flesh and sometimes both at once," they typically engaged in sex or sin in order to cast it out. According to James Turner, they also "abused Genesis" by indulging in "excesses of neo-Gnostic myth making" that produced conceptions of marriage as foreign to Milton's civilized Eden as their mystical dream theories.[61] Milton's other innovations in the conventions of Edenic marriage are presented more subtly than his frankly anti-Augustinian position on prelapsarian sexuality, but for their original audience they would have seemed equally dramatic. Vastly expanding the biblical "scene" where God simply hands the newly made woman to her spouse, Milton makes Adam and Eve's wedding contingent on her acceptance of his (admittedly brief) courtship. He further improvises on Genesis by giving both spouses much lengthier and more independent periods of maturation than any previous poet. At least for Eve, this maturation includes a phase of same-sex attraction before she finds "true" wisdom and beauty in her heterosexual mate, yet even afterward, she does not lose her capacity for independent growth and experimentation. Other important aspects of Eden's anthropology gradually emerge during Raphael's discourse, which ironically proposes "to Adam what is essentially a Baconian project in restorative utilitarian science well before there is anything to restore."[62]

At another level, however, Adam and Eve simply represent "archetypal" or innate human characteristics that Milton derives from epic (and particularly Homeric) tradition. The most prominent of these traits is the native "majesty" (*PL* 4.290) of our "Primitive great Sire" (*PL* 5.350) and his spouse, which includes their innate nobility, courtesy, and hospitality. Adam greets his angel guest with princely but not lordly grace, full of solemn but not "tedious pomp," proud but not puffed up like worldly princes. "Bowing low" but not "agape" with servile awe (*PL* 5.354, 357–60), Adam spontaneously honors Raphael as he is honored by his

---

[59]   See Halkett, *Milton*, pp. 24–30; Scodel, *Excess and the Mean*, pp. 263–83; and Chaplin, "'One Flesh,'" pp. 280–81.

[60]   Halkett, *Milton*, p. 62.

[61]   See James Grantham Turner, *One Flesh: Paradisal Marriage and Sexual Relations in the Age of Milton* (Oxford, 1987), pp. 84, 87–88. For a contemporary example of the Antinomian attempt to indulge in sex and sin in order to "cast it out," see Lawrence Clarkson (Claxton), *The Lost Sheep Found* (1660).

[62]   Holstun, *Rational Millennium*, p. 297.

presence. Both he and his fair spouse admirably succeed in their gracious, even
elegant reception of the angel:

> So to the Silvan Lodge
> They came, that like *Pomona*'s Arbor smil'd
> With flow'rets deck't and fragrant smells; but *Eve*
> Undeckt, save with herself more lovely fair
> Than Wood-Nymph, or the fairest Goddess feign'd
> Of three that in Mount *Ida* strove,
> Stood to entertain her guest from Heav'n; no veil
> Shee needed, Virtue-proof, no thought infirm
> Alter'd her cheek.
>
> (PL 5.377–85)

Ensconced on "mossy seats" around an "ample" table of level turf, they begin their
urbane dinner "discourse" (*PL* 5.391–93, 395) by discussing the pressing "new"
question of material monism, which springs naturally from the occasion itself.
Because the dinner guests include two different species, Adam raises the question
of universal digestion or "transubstantiation" (*PL* 437–43), terms that staunch anti-
papists like Patrick Hume condemned as "barbarous Latin words that have much
disturbed the world."[63] Yet, in Milton's Eden, these discussions are as natural as a
naked but innocent Eve serving luscious "meats and drinks" and "crowning" their
"flowing cups" with "pleasant liquors" (*PL* 5.451, 444–45). Enjoying a classical
epic banquet stripped of all postlapsarian "sting," the hosts and their guest drink
"inoffensive must" (*PL* 345), not the wine that first made Noah drunk. Presiding
over it all, Milton's natural but not artless hostess requires no veil to hide guilt or
defend against it: "O innocence / Deserving Paradise!" (*PL* 5.445–46).

Homer once dreamt of this perfect union of nature and culture but removed it
from history and geography into a fantasy world that Neptune has since hidden
from human sight. Not so Eve's festal meal, whose "vessels pure" are clearly part
of the real world. Purifying her dinner setting with fragrant essences of "Rose
and Odors from the shrub unfum'd" (*PL* 5.348–49), she does not augment the
banquet with incense, but there is no reason why she should—the banquet is
celebratory, not sacrificial or sacramental in either a satiric or a normative sense.[64]
In fact, Milton's point in stressing that these fragrances are "unfum'd" seems to be
that he is not quite so untraditional as to admit fire into Eden—although he does
speculate that some sort of heavenly fire may have sharpened its gardening tools

---

[63]   Patrick Hume, cited in King, *Milton and Religious Controversy*, p. 141.

[64]   King, in *Milton and Religious Controversy*, p. 136, believes that Eve's vessels "are
reminiscent of the simple wide-mouthed beakers (or wooden cups) used in the administration
of Communion in Puritan parishes" as opposed to more traditional "decorative chalices,"
but Eve's "vessels" are most likely the brilliantly colored rinds from which she has extracted
the liquid of "juiciest Gourds."

(*PL* 9.391–92). Yet apart from these hospitable exercises, his Eden includes largely undifferentiated work and informal coeducation conducted within the household as an alternative to the vocational training that Comenius believed Adam and Eve established in paradise. Both of Milton's ideal pupils instead participate in the truly liberal education advocated in his early treatise on the subject, further supplementing their courses on history and natural philosophy with first-hand observation and interaction with their world. Eve is absent during Raphael's discussion of the alternate world systems, but this detail conveniently allows the poet to announce that women are no less capable of astronomical studies than men. She does, however, conform to Pauline teaching by remaining silent in the angel's presence, but she freely discusses the heavens, horticulture, household economy, domestic and divine liberty with Adam.

Both spouses are keenly interested in their own and in cosmic creation history, so even prior to Raphael's disquisition on astro-biological chemistry, Eve has already invented a new "chemistry" for the home. Her culinary arts—in Milton's day, a new and specifically male craft—are much more advanced than commonly observed.[65] Eve serves her angel guest not just an uncooked vegetarian meal but also offers a careful selection of "tasteful" niceties: "fruit of all kinds, in coat, / Rough, or smooth rin'd, or bearded husk, or shell," which she then "tempers" or blends to suit her palate (*PL* 5.341–42, 347). Her "hospitable thoughts" (332) also consider

> What choice to choose for delicacy best,
> What order, so contriv'd as not to mix
> Tastes, not well join'd, inelegant, but bring
> Taste after taste upheld with kindliest change;
> … and from each tender stalk
> Whatever Earth all-bearing Mother yields
> In *India* East or West, or middle shore
> In *Pontus* or the *Punic* Coast, or where
> *Alcinöus* reign'd.
>
>   (*PL* 5.333–341)

Since, like the Phaiakian garden of Alkinöos, Eden includes all the climes of the known world, Eve can produce the most elegant combination of "each Plant and juiciest Gourd" (327) from innumerable new extracts and fusions. Her dinner beverage blends grape juice with "meaths / From many a berry," and her dessert course is even more refined than anything the super-civilized Phaiakians could offer: a dish of "dulcet creams" pressed from "many a berry" and from "sweet kernels" of an unspecified and perhaps still unknown species (5.346–47). Milton's

---

[65] See Elaine Hobby, "A Woman's Best Setting-out Is Silence: The Writings of Hannah Wooley," in Gerald Maclean (ed.), *Culture and Society in the Stuart Restoration: Literature, Drama, History* (Cambridge, 1995), pp. 179–200, especially p. 193.

anthropology thus most dramatically alters the overall portrait of Eve, to whom previous creation poets gave no unfallen passion and no work but to fall. Instead, her sufficiency to stand (*PL* 3.99) is now closely linked to Adam's through a classical virtue ethic in which active honor, not birth or gender, determines inner worth. Joshua Scodel explains that in this ethic, natural "inner *pudor*" must be alike maintained by virtuous men and women who, like Raphael, blush not as a sign of shame or of conventional gender distinctions but as a sign of true self-respect. This essentially gender-neutral ethic teaches both genders to moderate their desires in order to honor their partners as themselves.[66]

Aside from guiltless blushes and paradisal sexuality for both humans and angels, Milton's most startling innovation is to include sweat and tears in paradise (*PL* 5.130–35, 302; 8.255–56). This addition seems inspired not just by Bacon's redemption of work but by the Cambridge Platonist John Smith's intriguing speculation that God planted the tree of knowledge near the tree of life because "the labour and sweat of the Brain" is an essential part of the "warmth" of life.[67] Milton first depicts this "warmth" in Adam's initial awakening (or "birth pains"), which causes him to perspire (*PL* 8.255–56). Later, the "heat" of Eve's unchecked imagination produces painful tears. In between these extremes we find disturbing but not agonizing emotions such as Adam's prelapsarian anxieties about his spouse and his own headship, moderate pain when "tempered" by right reason and self-restraint. Before vice makes these feelings much less tolerable, Adam and Eve experience the emotional equivalent of Milton's thornless roses: mutable and mutual sensations stripped of sharp grief or lasting pain. Even after the Fall, the pains of their newly mortal state are lessened by Michael's reminder that God still presides over "All th'Earth he gave thee to possess and rule, / No despicable gift." Here "every kind that lives" is still "fomented by his virtual power and warm'd" by God (*PL* 11.337–40), and nature is so far from being "depraved" that it does not need to be totally redeemed. Physically "Not Subject to Old Age," as Milton's early Latin poem announced, nature's frame remains although earth's climate is altered. The human pair will certainly suffer from its worsened physical, moral, and emotional "weather," but their Father relieves them with "many a sign" of his "goodness and paternal Love" (*PL* 11.351–53). The signs of his approval also redeem just human aspiration and curiosity moderated by humble respect for natural and human life, the enduring legacy of the just "sons of Seth."

Milton's Pre-Augustinian and Arminian Sources

Jeremy Taylor's *Unum Necessarium* (1655) may have prepared the way for Milton's radical reevaluation of human choice and potential by mounting the most

---

[66]   Scodel, *Excess and the Mean*, pp. 263–75, cited p. 273. Scodel does not argue that the gender hierarchy is thereby eliminated.

[67]   John Smith, *Select Discourses* (1660, 1673), pp. 3–4.

serious intellectual assault on Calvinist doctrine since Laudianism had collapsed. Taking up the standard Anglican critique that Calvinists not only fostered devout ignorance and discouraged secular learning but suppressed free conscience—which Arminians like Taylor experienced under Cromwell—Taylor mounted a strong case against predestination. Frank Huntley shows that, unlike the "populist Pelagians" among the sects, Taylor like other Arminian theologians drew heavily upon the pre-Augustinian Fathers in affirming with Milton that "Calvinist doctrines of original sin ... impute to God motives which it were a sin to impute to our fellow man."[68] They particularly favored Chrysostom, whom Milton cites to prove that clerical corruption and avarice leads to tyranny in both church and state (*CPW* 3:518). More generally, Elaine Pagels finds Chrysostom defending a classical form of Christian liberty where "The tyranny of external government sharply contrasts with the liberty enjoyed by those capable of autonomous self-rule—above all, those who, through Christian baptism, have recovered the [Adamic] capacity for self-government." Chrysostom thus stressed the responsibility of Christian leaders to refrain not only from "the use of force but even from the subtler measures of fear and coercion," since the essence of Christianity is voluntary participation and consent.[69] These views especially contrast with Augustine's belief in man's irremediable bondage to sin and need for corrective discipline, convictions that found favor after worldliness had deeply invaded the church. As a former worldling struggling to overcome his own corruption, Augustine anxiously questioned "What man is there, who, being aware of his own weakness, dares so much as to attribute his chastity and innocence to his own virtue?" (*Confessions* 2, 7).

Augustine's controversies with the Pelagians forced him ever further into the extreme position that "original" human nature ceased to exist after the Fall, which unleashed the complete physical disobedience of man's bodily members and especially his libido. Given man's subsequent helplessness, even tyrannical government could provide a just remedy for original sin. These views again attracted believers during the violent years of the early Reformation and Counter-Reformation, when Calvin championed Augustine's dim view of humanity as a mortally wounded "patient" whom the Good Physician or holy community must mend and comfort.[70] By locating the source of sin and death in his corrupted will, the guilty sufferer could review his past choices, amend his behavior, redress his

---

[68]   See Frank L. Huntley, *Jeremy Taylor and the Great Rebellion* (Ann Arbor, 1970), p. 86. On Taylor's persecution over the issue of original sin, see pp. 56–94, and on Milton's comparable positions see pp. 73, 79, 82, 100–102.

[69]   Elaine Pagels, *Adam, Eve, and the Serpent* (New York, 1988), p. 103. Milton was no doubt impressed by Chrysostom's connection of church corruption to the growing wealth, power, and prestige of the upper clergy: "clerics, infected by the disease of 'lust for authority,' are fighting for candidates on the basis of family prominence, wealth, or partisanship" rather than "excellence of character" (p. 104).

[70]   Augustine's "hard" position on original sin competed with many others throughout church history; see Huntley, *Jeremy Taylor*, pp. 67–76. On the Reformation anxieties

negligence, and thus partly restore his helpless condition. Pagels concedes that the "guilt culture" generated by these beliefs is a high but not necessarily unreasonable price to pay for explaining and at least partially controlling human fallibility—at least for some. For others, scripture was better interpreted by Chrysostom, who believed that Paul's words on humanity's abject need to be subjected to "higher powers" (Romans 7:13, 15–25) applied only to unbaptized Christians.[71] Taylor's decision to endorse this pre-Augustinian position caused him to be attacked as a "second Julian"—a moderate and somewhat less heretical follower of Pelagius— and theologically informed readers of *Paradise Lost* have always been aware that it too reflects Julian of Eclanum's position in a number of important ways.[72] For instance, Julian makes the primary result of sin not physical but moral death (although they are naturally related), but moral sin remains entirely within the scope of the human will, since the will has not been so thoroughly "infected" by Adam's sin that "the flesh lusteth always contrary to the Spirit."[73] Although the final books of *Paradise Lost* clearly show the increased unruliness of man's postlapsarian appetite, like Julian and Taylor, Milton emphasizes their mitigation through the rule of temperance and the power of right reason (*PL* 11.530–37). Since these consistently guide God's people, as with Adam and Eve's labor, pain is no longer an inevitable punishment of original sin but a partially controllable aspect of the natural order.

Pace conservative Puritans, Julian also believed that sexual desire is not a guilty but a "vital fire," and, like Bacon long after him, Julian justified his non-literal understanding of the Genesis curse by pointing out that not all men literally "sweat" to earn a living in a landscape that is not literally choked with weeds and thorns. Milton himself adds that pain is often overcome with joy (as in Eve's child-bearing) or with artificial aids (as with Adam's invention of fire). The heightened difficulties of the fallen condition thus become highly subjective: increased responsibility and asceticism are required, although (Pelagius and the Stoics to the contrary) these virtues do not guarantee a good death for all the good. Yet Abel's death shows that it is not necessarily a bad thing to die—dust to dust is merciful (*PL* 11.60–66)—and Enoch's "translation" additionally shows that the righteous are often the first to go. Death, for both Milton and Julian, is therefore our "last enemy" but also our friend, although, for those who follow Cain in choosing to sin, Satan's "daughter" is a very real foe—no hallucination but an unremitting misery inflicted by one's captive and vitiated nature. This spiritual death nevertheless remains a matter of choice, and while physical death is not, it either offers release or spiritual victory to people of faith who pass from corruptible life on earth to

---

that generated the return to these teachings, see Stachniewski, *Persecutory Imagination*, pp. 61–84.

[71] Pagels, *Adam, Eve*, pp. 105–6 (citing *Confessions*, p. 106), pp. 113, 145, 147.

[72] Huntley, *Jeremy Taylor*, p. 92.

[73] Article IX of the Anglican Church, Taylor's main bone of contention; see Huntley (who cites this portion of the Article), *Jeremy Taylor*, pp. 88–89.

eternal life with God. No one, saint or sinner, ever escapes suffering, but all are free to choose temperate habits that guide them in life, and in their last hours, they feel no anxious Puritan need to make a "good death."[74]

This relatively naturalistic view of sin, desire, and death suggests that Milton includes sweat and pain even in the heavenly paradise (*PL* 6.327–34) to support a fully monistic moral continuum. Like Taylor's Adam, his first man is inexperienced, immature, and potentially imperfect. He is subject to natural concupiscence before the Fall, and, after it, he is not utterly depraved because he remains an incomplete and partially self-creating agent. Neither his intellect nor his body has become irreparably "crooked," although both are more unstable and more in need of temperate balance than they were in paradise. Yet since only his will, not his whole nature, has sinned, as in Taylor's *Unum Necessarium*, sin has "disrobed" us of Eden's veil of innocence, but not made us the fundamentally new species postulated by Augustine and Calvin. Taylor even believed that original sin is not inherited from Adam; we merely retain a certain willful proclivity towards fallen desire. Milton did not go that far in overturning Pauline doctrine but, like the Arminians, he places great emphasis on the Son's Atonement as a compensation for Adam and Eve's lapse even before they fall. Hence his portrait of sin's human consequences veers nearly as far from the Augustinian tradition as Julian's did. One reason is clearly political: like Chrysostom, but unlike Samuel Rutherford, who describes mankind as almost completely "fallen and broken, even under all the fractions of the powers and faculties of the soul," Milton would free conscience, not enslave it to "the promises of reward, feare of punishment, and the coactive power of the sword."[75]

Citing Rutherford, Merritt Hughes's introduction to *The Tenure of Kings and Magistrates* claims that Milton followed him in accepting "Augustine's doctrine of original sin as infecting organized society" (*CPW* 3:121). Yet the passage in *The Tenure* that he refers to fails to confirm this assumption:

> No man who knows ought, can be so stupid to deny that all men naturally were borne free, being the image and resemblance of God himself, and were by privilege above all the creatures, born to command and not to obey: and that they liv'd so. Till from the root of *Adams* transgression, falling among themselves to doe wrong and violence, and foreseeing that such courses must needs tend to the destruction of them all, they agreed by common league to bind each other from mutual injury, and joyntly to defend themselves against any that gave disturbance or opposition to such agreement. Hence came Cities, Townes and Common-wealths. And because no faith in all was found sufficiently binding,

---

[74]   Pagels, *Adam, Eve*, pp. 132, 137–39, 142. Julian is also strikingly modern in displacing humans from the unique moral center of the universe and making them "one species among others" (p. 144). Milton does not endorse this position but his unfallen Adam seems to understand animal language and enjoy their companionship.

[75]   Samuel Rutherford's *Lex, Rex* (1644), Question LXIV, p. 455.

they saw it needfull to ordaine som authoritie, that might restrain by force and
punishment what was violated against peace and common right … Not to be thir
Lords and Maisters (though afterward those names in som places were giv'n
voluntarily to such as had been Authors of inestimable good to the people) but,
to be thir Deputies and Commissioners, to execute, by vertue of thir intrusted
power, that justice which else every man by the bond of nature and of Cov'nant
must have executed for himself, and for one another. (*CPW* 3:198–99)

This is not an Augustinian but an essentially *Aristotelian* account of the gradual
growth of government, which closely matches the postlapsarian history of
Paradise Lost. There for some unspecified time men manage their own affairs
in small families or tribes, for like their forefather Adam, they are all born free,
and "liv'd so" under the mild paternal rule symbolized by the sons of Seth. Yet,
as their tribes came into conflict and patriarchs became corrupt or ineffective,
their inherited proclivity toward Adamic concupiscence created a "war of all on
all" that required them to forge Hobbesian social contracts, although not with
Hobbesian consequences. Milton foresees no universal law of sovereignty taking
effect but simply a choice between two alternate societies: the imperial tyranny of
Nimrod, or the republics of the Jews, who rule through judges and "senates" in the
wilderness (*PL* 12.224–26).

Thus, while not free from the violence introduced by sin, humanity never forfeits
its right to a government based on "intrusted," not alienated. power. Governments
remain completely human and variable institutions, not curses, although, like true
worship, they undergo cyclical corruption and rehabilitation (*PL* 12.79–101, 482–
540). Milton seems to take these progressive ideas from a wide variety of sources.
One is George Hakewill's defense of the Baconian idea that since "men have
uniform capacities at all times," their productivity and competence are predicated
only upon their "studiousnesse, watchfulnesse and love of truth." Another is
probably Lord Brooke's Platonic idea that only willful ignorance prevents
progress, for "The Light, still, will, must, cannot but encrease; why then doe wee
shut our eyes?" Henry Robinson's conviction is also relevant—"though a Christian
live never so long, yet he both may, and ought still to grow from grace to grace,
from knowledge to knowledge"—as is Taylor's even more radical insistence that
while the propensity or even the necessity of sinning may be inherited, "choice and
election still remains [*sic*] to a man." For someone "is not naturally sinful, as he is
naturally heavy, or … apt to laugh, or weep," or anything else that "he is always,
and unavoidably"—a concept that marks the final terminus of "total depravity."[76]
In the end, however, Milton seems closest to Henry Parker, who promoted the

---

[76]   Baker, citing "The Preface," sig. C3v, of Hakewill's *Apologie or Declaration …*
(1627) in *Wars*. Baker (p. 230) also comments on Taylor's *Unum Necessarium*, VI.v.71 in
Works, vol. 7, p. 279. Lord Brooke is cited in *Discourse Opening the Nature*, in Haller (ed.),
Tracts on Liberty, vol. 2, p. 160, Henry Robinson in *Liberty of Conscience*, in *Tracts on
Liberty*, vol. 3, p. 166.

proto-Rousseauian idea that man is naturally born free and capable of casting off the unjust chains of absolutism. Parker's famous *Observations* opens by declaring that any reasonable person should know that government was "originally inherent in the people" and remains so "by common consent and agreement." His *Jus populi* admits that government and order are divinely endowed, but not misgovernment or tyranny, which God disapproves. Like Milton, he therefore compares government to marriage, which, while divinely instituted, does not preclude freedom of choice or require complete subjection.[77] Parker also assumes that humans were intended to enjoy this happier and more equitable organization in small, informal units, although postlapsarian corruption requires adaptation to political necessity over time. Yet those needs are still no justification for absolute monarchy, an "Asiatic vice" unknown to scriptural precedent except through the negative example of Pharaoh; otherwise, "We must go beyond God and natures workmanship and impressions, before we can discover anything but parentall majestie, or gentle aristocracie, or compounded or mixed monarchie."[78] *Paradise Lost* certainly agrees that despotic government is an "Asiatic vice", as both Pharaoh and Nimrod show, for in this as in other respects Milton's postlapsarian political anthropology is founded squarely on his own *Tenure* and other liberal contract theories of the era.[79]

In either case, God's "fatal curse annext" to human misgovernment is mostly self-imposed, since whenever decadent nations lose all their "virtue, which is reason," their punishment fits their crime—they lose "thir outward liberty, / Thir inward lost" (*PL* 12.97–101). This assessment rounds out the epic's virtually "curseless" extra-biblical anthropology, one that fully complements the poet's Reformed account of human history, endeavor, and potential by offering enlightened Christians a liberal interpretation of scripture supplemented with the "natural laws" of observable human culture, history, geography, and politics. Yet, in the end, the frustration of the political ideals to which Milton dedicated his life meant that his need to struggle against the forces of "worldly strong, and worldly wise" (*PL* 12.568) became an even more fundamental duty than knowing "All secrets of the deep, all Nature's works, / Or works of God in Heav'n, Air, Earth, or Sea, / And all the riches of this World" (*PL* 12.578–80). Yet such knowledge is worthy—and Adam's "invention" of fire shows its utility—if internal struggle is more so. Jonathan Scott observes that this knowledge was always central to Milton's republican values and that it naturally became "more important than ever" after the Restoration, the only period in which *Paradise Lost* could have been written.[80]

---

[77] Henry Parker, *Observations upon some of his majesties late answers and expresses* (London, 1642), p. 1; *Jus populi* (London, 1644), p. 4, summarized by Jordan, *Men of Substance*, p. 149.

[78] Henry Parker, *Jus populi*, p. 47.

[79] Baker, *Wars*, p. 274.

[80] Scott, *England's Troubles*, p. 347; as Scott notes, this view is shared by Blair Worden, Armand Himy, David Norbrook, and Mary Ann Radzinowicz.

Chapter 7

The Neoclassical Poetics of *Paradise Regained*

Three poets, in three distant ages born,
Greece, Italy, and England did adorn.
The first in loftiness of thought surpass'd,
The next in majesty, in both the last:
The force of *Nature* could no further go;
To make the third, she joined the former two.

—John Dryden, "Epigram on Milton"

Our Saviour himself did first shew his power to subdue ignorance, by his conference with the priests and doctors of the law, before he shewed his power to subdue nature by his miracles.

—Francis Bacon, *The Advancement of Learning*

Milton's late poetics traditionally have been isolated from neoclassical aesthetics, in part because he eschewed two of its most characteristic forms: the heroic couplet and the drama of empire.[1] Thunderously rejecting the "bondage of Riming," the second edition of *Paradise Lost* contains a famous headnote proclaiming rhyme "no necessary Adjunct or true Ornament of Poem or good Verse, ... but the Invention of a barbarous Age, to set off wretched matter and lame Meter" (Hughes 210). This antipathy to "jangling" rhyme is commonly thought to reflect Milton's low opinion of the "barbarous dissonance" of Restoration poetry and politics, and thus to wage a thinly veiled assault on Dryden's (un)heroic couplets. Yet Milton's denunciation is also clearly defensive; his note on "The Verse" was added at the request of his printer, who complained that many readers were puzzled or put off by his epic's absence of rhyme. Like Andrew Marvell, most of Milton's poetic friends and sympathizers—including his amanuensis, Thomas Ellwood—employed rhyme, so it seems doubtful that they were included in his sweeping attack on the "barbarous Age" that needed "the jingling sound of like endings" to disguise poor matter. Milton may have had some Restoration poetasters in mind,

---

[1]   As an example of this common assumption, see Barbara K. Lewalski, "'To try, and teach the erring Soul': Milton's Last Seven Years," in Parry and Raymond (eds.), *Milton and the Terms of Liberty*, pp. 175–90.

but his primary objection is to the precedent of the past. At present, he admits that rhyme has been "grac't indeed ... by the use of some famous modern Poets, carried away by Custom," although as usual in Milton, Custom only makes things "for the most part worse than else they would have" been. Without naming names, his protest against the "vexation, hindrance, and constraint" (Hughes 210) of their limping verse may target Spenserian stanzas, Cowley's over-elaborate Pindarics, or Lydgate's even more "barbarous" stanzas, but since Dryden was justly famous for the smoothness of his heroic couplets, he remains an unlikely object of Milton's diatribe. Another probable source of his ire is suggested by his silent quotation of Sir Philip Sidney, whose wise words seem to have been forgotten during the current "rage" for heroic couplets: "verse [is] ... but an ornament and no cause to poetry, since there have been many most excellent poets that never versified, and now swarm many versifiers that need never answer to the name of poets."[2]

At the time of Milton's writing, Dryden had just begun his first spectacularly successful experiments with the heroic couplet in two dramas, *The Indian Queen* and *The Indian Emperor* (1665), although Milton's blindness probably kept him from attending either play. His famous comment that his fellow-worker in the Protectorate was a "no poet, but a good rimist" was probably gleaned from having heard printed poems like *Annus Mirabilis* or earlier works read to him, perhaps by Dryden himself. In any case, he graciously accepted the younger poet's request to rewrite *Paradise Lost* in operatic couplets, perhaps as a gesture of thanks for the high tribute paid him in his "Epigram" and in similar accolades at a time when Milton was still "much more admired abroad than at home" (Aubrey, Hughes 1023). He naturally could not admire Dryden's royalist politics, but Cowley's royalism did not prevent Milton's admiration for his unfinished epic, and all three poets promoted a Senecan ethic of mutual benevolence and heroic sacrifice.[3] Before his later conversion to Catholicism, Dryden's views on religion were equally compatible with Milton's. Dryden's *Religio Laici* adopts an independent, lay perspective that emphasizes the Reformed dictum that scripture alone "is a rule; that in all things needful to salvation, it is clear, sufficient, and ordained by God Almighty for that purpose." On this basis he challenges both the sectarian "fanatics" who "have assumed what amounts to an infallibility in the private spirit" and the orthodox creed of the "Holy Bishop Athanasius." Arguing that not all early church Fathers are authoritative, and that "whatsoever is obscure is concluded not

---

[2] Sir Philip Sidney, *An Apology for Poetry*, in Hazard Adams (ed.), *Critical Theory Since Plato* (San Diego, 1971), p. 159. Susanne Woods points out in "The Context of Jonson's Formalism," in Claude J. Summers and Ted-Larry Pebworth (eds.), *Classic and Cavalier* (Pittsburgh, 1982), pp. 77–89, that Jonson's "Fit of Rime against Rime," like his view of poetry generally, agrees with Sidney; he thus "thought not Bartas a Poet but a Verser"; see pp. 81, 85, 89 n. 15. Milton apparently recalls this remark in his famous comment that Dryden was a rhymer, not a poet.

[3] John M. Wallace, "John Dryden's Plays and the Conception of an Heroic Society," in Zagorin (ed.), *Culture and Politics*, pp. 113–34.

necessary to be known," Dryden opposed his own private reading of scripture to both papist and sectarian "orthodoxy." In politics, too, even overtly royalist poems like *Absalom and Achitophel* (1681) trace a middle way between a social contract founded upon individual rights and a somewhat ironic patriarchalism.[4] Finally, Dryden's long preface to *Religio Laici* (1682) suggestively defends the "rough" yet majestic verse some critics had found objectionable in *Paradise Lost*:

> If anyone be so lamentable a critic as to require the smoothness, the numbers and the turn of heroic poetry in this poem; I must tell him that, if he has not read Horace, I have studied him, and hope the style of his *Epistles* is not ill imitated here. The expressions of a poem, design'd purely for instruction ought to be plain and natural, and yet majestic: for here the poet is presum'd to be a kind of lawgiver, and those three qualities which I have named are proper to the legislative style. The florid, elevated and figurative way is for the passions; for love and hatred, fear and anger, are begotten in the soul by shewing their objects out of their true proportion; either greater than the life, or less; but instruction is to be given by shewing them what they naturally are. A man is to be cheated into passion, but to be reason'd into truth.[5]

Although Dryden is here defending his own poem, these remarks are equally applicable to both *Paradise Lost* and *Paradise Regained*. The latter in particular is designed for "reasoning into truth" rather than exalting the passions, as its "plain and natural, and yet majestic" language "legislatively" reveals things as "they naturally are." This language contrasts with "the florid, elevated and figurative way" of Milton's grand style, which was better suited to lamenting how mankind was "cheated" out of paradise. Realizing this, Dryden justifies Milton's decision to dispense with the neoclassical rules of heroic poetry in *Paradise Lost*:

> As for Mr Milton, whom we all admire with so much justice, his subject is not that of a heroic poem, properly so called. His design is the losing of our happiness; his event is not prosperous, like that of all other epic works; his heavenly machines are many; and his human persons are but two. But his thoughts are elevated, his words sounding, and no man has so happily copied the manner of Homer; or so copiously translated his Grecisms, and the Latin elegancies of Virgil.[6]

---

[4]   Su Fang Ng, *Literature and the Politics of the Family in Seventeenth-Century England* (Cambridge, 2007), p. 137.

[5]   Dryden, *Religio Laici*, "The Preface," in *The Poetical Works of Dryden*, ed. George R. Noyes (Boston, 1950), p. 162.

[6]   John Dryden's "Discourse Concerning ... Satire" prefaces his translation of Persius and Juvenal's Satires; see *Of Dramatic Poesy and Other Critical Essays*, ed. George Watson (2 vols., London, 1962), vol. 2, pp. 71–155, cited vol. 2, p. 84. As Earl Miner points out, Dryden was the first and least ambivalent contemporary to pronounce Milton's epics

Dryden's Milton is thus far too astute an artist to fall into the neoclassical straitjacket that had helped to ruin the epic aspirations of lesser poets like Cowley. Although he will not absolutely "justify Milton for his blank verse," he "excuse[s] him by the example of Hannibal Caro, and other Italians who have used it." Yet many critics have suspected that the new poet laureate's attitude toward his role model is somewhat too facile, an opinion confirmed by Dryden's more ironic "excuse," that Milton "had neither the ease ... nor the graces" required for rhyming, "which is manifest in his juvenilia, or verses written in his youth, where his rhyme is always constrained and forced"—even "at an age when ... almost every man [is] a rhymer, tho' not a poet."[7] While credited by subsequent scholars, this enduring critical opinion hardly squares with the virtuoso exhibition of rhyme in early poems ranging from Milton's Nativity Ode to *L'Allegro* and *Il Penseroso*.

Dryden's aspersion (1693) postdates Milton's death, but there is also good reason to believe that the elder poet may have resented the "rimer's" sudden and overwhelming success after the Restoration.[8] When he agreed to the request of this foremost apologist, theorist, and practitioner of the neoclassical mode to "translate" *Paradise Lost* into verse, Milton reportedly told him to feel free "to *Tagg* my Points," since "some of 'em are so Awkward and Old Fashion'd that I think you had as good leave 'em as you found 'em."[9] Stephen Zwicker thus sees Milton directly confronting, questioning, and controverting the new poetics, but also positively engaging with a form, style, and ethos he had in many ways anticipated by thoroughly modernizing Spenserian poetics. Not merely an "aging republican beached on the shores of an alien culture" but still the indefatigable reformer, Milton seems to have written *Paradise Regained* in "response to something other and more formidable than Thomas Ellwood's question about what he had to "'say of Paradise Found?'"[10] Zwicker's conjectures are fully supported by Milton's theoretical prefaces to the 1668 edition of *Paradise Lost* and to the heroic drama, *Samson Agonistes* (1671), both of which partially respond to Dryden's *Essay of Dramatic Poesy*(1668). These prefaces not only help explain the greatly altered style of *Paradise Regained* (Hughes 540), but suggest why it was Milton's personal favorite. Rising to the challenge of the new mode, he had at last achieved the lofty goal that Dryden proposed but never attained: to compose a dramatic "'imitation,

---

"classics." See "Dryden's Admired Acquaintance, Mr. Milton," *Milton Studies* 11 (1978): pp. 3–27.

[7]   Dryden, "A Discourse Concerning ... Satire," vol. 1, pp. 84, 85.

[8]   Campbell and Corns find a possible challenge to Dryden's apparent monopoly of the Virgilian mode in Milton's recasting *Paradise Lost* into its current twelve-book form; see *John Milton*, p. 373.

[9]   *The Monitor*, vol. 1, no. 17, April 6–10, 1713.

[10]   See Steven N. Zwicker, "Milton, Dryden, and the politics of literary controversy," in Maclean (ed.), *Culture and Society*, pp. 137–58, cited pp. 138, 139. Campbell and Corns agree that Ellwood's report of Milton's reason for writing the poem admits various interpretations; see *John Milton*, p. 329.

in little, of a heroic poem'" that redefined both valor and desire in thoroughly modern terms.[11] This achievement builds upon Milton's earlier experiments in modernizing heroic poetry, which, contrary to common opinion, was still being written in blank verse by poets other than him. Nor were neoclassical couplets ever essentially "royalist": Lucy Hutchinson translated Lucretius into couplets and Marvell used them in his anti-royalist satires. Finally, there is increasingly little reason to believe that, apart from the relative isolation induced by his blindness, Milton was utterly alienated from the Restoration, its stage, or its "modern" poetic experiments. Robert Hume for instance points out that "the 'libertism' almost universally ascribed to 'Restoration comedy'"—which often blurs into its heroic mode—is actually "found only in a minority of the comedies of the time, and more often than not the libertine is punished (or reformed and married off) at the end of the play."[12]

Defining and Historicizing the Neoclassical Mode

Hutchinson's example reminds us that, while the neo-Epicureanism of the Restoration era was deeply suspicious to the godly, this later development of the new philosophy was more anti-authoritarian than conservative. The same applies to its neoclassical offspring, although, like other literary modes, neoclassicism was a profoundly malleable form. Richard Kroll points out that neither this mode nor its predecessors could ever monolithically protect themselves from critique or cooptation. For all literary

> communities establish their claims to discursive authority by exploiting possibilities of choice provided by the accepted discourse, though in the process they risk compromising their peculiar and alienated vision … If neoclassical discourse fragmented the claims of dissent by appealing to sceptical modes, its own magisterial claims to authority were instantly threatened by an identical sceptical move, a strategy Catholic apologists were quick to exploit.[13]

As Kroll explains, this "model places rhetoric and ideology into a mutually constitutive relationship" because, "contrary to a largely unstated assumption in many current Anglo-American discussions of language, discourse, and ideology— there exists no necessary logic that binds a certain … form of representation to a certain set of ethical and political points of view." From that perspective, there can be (*pace* N.H. Keeble) no necessary link between the culture of dissent and

---

[11]   Zwicker, "Milton, Dryden," pp. 145–46.

[12]   Robert Hume, "The Aims and Limits of Historical Scholarship," *RES* 53 (2002): pp. 399–422, cited p. 416.

[13]   Richard W.F. Kroll, *The Material Word: Literate Culture in the Restoration and Early Eighteenth Century* (Baltimore, 1991), p. 78.

the media of early modern print culture any more than between neoclassicism and authoritarianism. Kroll also finds the mode far more sensuous, concrete, and open-ended than the Whig stereotype has allowed, for while it was "anti-enthusiastic" in limiting the mind to narrow confines that cannot and should not be exceeded except in rapt meditation, its skeptical habits of mind eventually led to the eighteenth-century cult of sacred wonder or "sublimity" shared by both conservatives like Edmund Burke and radicals like William Blake.[14] Led by John Dennis, the great neoclassical theorist and radical Whig, this later movement was already well under way in the 1690s, little more than a decade after Milton's death.[15] Isabel Rivers's study of Restoration religion further supports Kroll's claims that neither Restoration culture, the contemporary Royal Society, nor its neoclassical views of rhetoric were predominantly conservative. While rejecting what Dryden refers to as the Dissenters' "infallibility in the private spirit," it produced real gains in religious toleration and social reform.[16]

True, the new age widely disapproved of both supernaturalism and Antinomianism, but this disapproval drew much of its energy from a perceived connection between enthusiasm, atheism, and libertinism. Thomas Sprat's *History of the Royal Society* links this seemingly unlikely trio by noting that enthusiasts and libertines commonly combine anti-rational with "carnal" excess. In demanding earthly verification of his faith, the *"Enthusiast"* over-multiplies "miracles" and inadvertently diminishes their power and authority, which in turn leads to atheism and libertinism.[17] Milton's *History of Britain* implicitly agrees when it repeatedly criticizes the early Britons for relying on superstitious omens, prodigies, and signs long after Christ had caused oracles to cease. Miracles have not wholly ceased for either Sprat or Milton, but, as Bacon suggests in the epigraph above, they both largely confine "true religion" to more naturalistic prodigies. The fact that the Son of *Paradise Regained* performs no miracles at all further suggests that Milton agrees that the genuine novelties discoverable by religion and science should be explained rationally, not miraculously, lest the proliferation of "miracles" make

---

[14] Kroll, *Material Word*, pp. 53–54; on Keeble, see p. 21; on Hutchinson, see pp. 95–96; on the "peculiar open-endedness" of neoclassicism's apparent limitations, see pp. 276–77. Kroll does not directly discuss the later culture of sublimity but sets up the assumption discussed above by noting the "vital dynamic" between its "empirical criteria," inferences, and analogies, and the linguistic "enactment and embodiment" they demand. Ultimately, neoclassicism's probable and positional linguistics means that even its "rational theology is hardly rationalist in tenor" because it supplementarily requires "some sufficient model of spiritual apprehension" (p. 241).

[15] See Nicholas von Maltzahn, "Acts of Kind Service: Milton and the Patriot Literature of Empire," in Rajan and Sauer (eds.), *Milton and the Imperial Vision*, pp. 233–54, especially pp. 236–43.

[16] Rivers, *Reason, Grace, and Sentiment*, pp. 33, 165–73.

[17] Thomas Sprat, *History of the Royal Society*, ed. Jackson I. Cope and Harold Whitmore Jones (St. Louis, MO, 1966), pp. 364–65, 370, 372, 376, 417–19.

them appear implausible. As Sprat adds, this mistake leads the errors of dogmatic philosophy to be repeated in reverse, since it causes wits and railleurs to attack the new science with "dogmatic" or close-minded doubts. The proper use of Socrates' skeptical method is rather to defend the truly good, virtuous, useful, and beautiful, which dogmatic skeptics undermine by indolently shrugging off truly worthwhile, achievable prodigies of science and discovery as mere utopianism.[18]

Similar defenses of the new empiricism were mounted by pan-European progressives ranging from Dutch Arminians such as Grotius and Jean Le Clerc to French philosophers such as Descartes and Gassendi, all of whom fought on a double front against the twinned enemies of libertine skepticism and pietism. Their preferred weapons included paying careful attention to "words and stile" and painstakingly contextualizing overly abstract, potentially "superstitious" language. They particularly criticized the "heavy types" of late orality and allegory, not as literary practices, but as overly naive approaches to reality. Connecting them to both enthusiastic vision and Catholic sacramentalism, they particularly vilified enthusiasts because their stereotypical exempla and compulsive memorialization of their "saints" ran counter to the progressive trends of literate, late Reformation culture. Despite their supplemental dependence on printed sermons and their resistance to "high" or multi-leveled symbol systems, Puritans of Bunyan's type continued to rely on ancient oral and symbolic devices.[19] Sharon Achinstein shows that Dissenting culture especially exalted the living, oral memory of the dead saint, whose life and works were "read" as a faithful copy of the saving word. Thus, more than simply commemorating the godly, "to make a 'living [funeral] sermon' was to participate in a kind of transubstantiation, to revive in one's own actions and person those of the departed minister."[20]

In contrast, Milton represents the very epitome of the literate mode; he is a poet who consistently corrects naive "oral" faith and treats scripture as ordinary language rather than as extraordinary illumination. In *Paradise Regained* in particular, his literary handling of the narrative places him at the furthest possible remove from late orality. His final epic in fact goes much farther than either the Puritans or his own "grand" epic in sacrificing typology and allegory to the primary sense of scripture. In that respect alone, his brief epic must be regarded as his most advanced expression of the late literate mode, which (according to Walter Ong) he exemplifies.[21] *Paradise Regained* also exemplifies the common neoclassicist belief that Hebrew narrative was more truly observant of the natural unities of space and time, the natural attributes of human beings, and the simple

---

[18]   Ibid., *History*, pp. 362, 417–19.

[19]   On Bunyan, see Roger Sharrock, introduction to *Pilgrim's Progress* (London, 1966), pp. 15–22; on the "heavy types" of oral culture, see Walter J. Ong, *Orality and Literacy* (London, 1982).

[20]   Achinstein, *Literature and Dissent*, p. 38; see also pp. 35–37.

[21]   Walter Ong, *Interfaces of the Word: Studies in the Evolution of Consciousness and Culture* (Ithaca, NY, 1977), pp. 210–12.

revealed Word of God than either Greek epic or philosophy, which in Plato's hands came too close to "ecstatic" vision.[22] Following the example of Christ and his apostles, neoclassicists wished to return to "real" scripture and nature, to first-hand observation and "humble" reason as opposed to extraordinary "signs." Believing that "true wit" or understanding thrives only when nature, human customs, history, and religion are concretely understood, they turned the gospels themselves into "modern" anthropological accounts much like Milton's anthropocentric rendering of Christ's wilderness temptation.[23]

The more balanced portrait of the neoclassical mode offered by recent criticism further explains why late seventeenth-century prose was anything but starkly "plain." Favoring a dramatic, skeptical, but also "particularist" mimesis, neoclassicists aimed at and achieved a concrete, elegant, semi-ironic, and, at times, even elaborate precision. Simultaneously hostile to mystical essentialism, scholastic schematism, and metaphysical abstraction, they rejected the "violently yoked" metaphors and mysteries of the metaphysical poets as too elitist. Treating words not as mystical devices but as cultural symbols or conventionally agreed-upon signs, they pioneered a proto-Peircean pragmatism. That meant replacing radical metaphor with more "tangible" synecdoches, metonymies, and similes. In general, Kroll shows that they believed that the closer we go toward truth, the more our words should "assert their palpability, like the famous flea under Hooke's microscope." This belief was accompanied by a staunch anti-determinism that undermined the mechanistic aspects of their outlook by redefining "knowing" not as a "matter of static, absolute, and transparent apprehension," but as a human activity made real by the natural instruments of discrimination and choice. Kroll also points out that the neoclassical emphasis on the fundamentally interpretive aspects of textuality produced a careful if limited scriptural literalism. Its adherents preserved the harmonies of the synoptic gospels, but mainly through a sophisticated resolutive–compositive method borrowed from the new science, which allowed them to reweave the "broken Narrative" of the Evangelists according to the principles of true "wit."[24]

Milton early pioneered similar linguistic methods in attempting to "reweave" the "four chords" of the Bible's conflicting views on marriage and divorce, a project that ultimately led to a commonsensical representation of Christ derived from his "desire to naturalize, or [even] ... 'demythologize' the gospel narrative."[25] His admirer John Hall advocated using a similar kind of "wit" to reconstruct the missing knowledge of Christ's life, which he thought would reveal secret deeds as good or

---

[22] Kroll, *Material Word*, pp. 256–59, 269–70; on Plato, see pp. 98–99.

[23] Sprat, *History*, pp. 364–72, 413–14.

[24] Kroll, *Material Word*, pp. 13, 21–22, 257–58, 274 .

[25] Harold Fisch, *Jerusalem and Albion* (New York, 1964), p. 153. "*Tetrachordon*" of course means "four chords" or strands.

better than any contained in scripture.[26] Yet, following Bacon, he found "broken knowledge" (*Works* 3:405) far superior to gnostic certitude. The latter epitomizes "artful" Greek philosophy; the former, the realistically "broken" narrative of Hebrew scripture. Recovering its hidden lessons drew on the tradition of "Egyptian gold" employed in Bacon's *Wisdom of the Ancients*, which regards all texts as potentially containing lost "nuggets" of truth obscured by "superstitious" additions. Milton's fictional "reweaving" of Christ's "deeds / Above Heroic, though in secret done" (*PR* 1.14–15) in his greatly expanded account of his wilderness temptation may thus doubly respond to Hall's suggestions and to Ellwood's request to relate a tale of "Paradise Found," though neither prompting was personally noted by Milton. More holistically, the poet undoubtedly responded to the neoclassical challenge of reinterpreting the Ancients, Moderns, and scriptures in stricter conformity to rational probability. Like Homer's allegorical interpreters, only more so, poets from Cowley to Dryden "corrected" the Greek poets' "ignorant" tributes to wicked deities and erring heroes. Anglican theologians ranging from Edward Stillingfleet and John Wallis to Samuel Bochart went even further in blaming the Greeks for muddying the "'plain and native dress'" of Hebrew learning with their "'fabulous and ambiguous manner'"—but unlike the Puritan enemies of "heathen" literature, they felt free pick out the gold from the dross.[27]

The Royal Society's motto, *nullius in verba* ("on no man's word") has long been considered *prima facie* evidence of its bias toward plain or even "no style," but this evidence has crumbled as scholars have realized its founders' own awareness that all attempts to produce linguistic transparency had ended in failure. After the collapse of Wilkins's universal language project, the Royal Society limited its rhetorical reforms to restraining excessive verbiage, extravagant digressions, abstruse language, and radical metaphors. Such reforms did not replace but rather strengthened rhetoric by replacing the remnants of Ciceronian *copia* with concrete, naturalistic, and historically grounded similes and metaphors. Although the new rhetoric instituted the strong fact/fiction distinctions still associated with modern prose, ambiguity remained an aspect, not the opposite, of neoclassical truth. Foucault was by no means wrong in supposing that these developments produced an explosion of new taxonomies, dictionaries, and tables of classification, but the new rhetoricians never spoke or sought a language of scientific abstraction or condensation.[28] Particularly in England, they idealized the vivid, direct, and

---

[26]   John Hall, *The Advancement of Learning* (1649), ed. A.K. Croston (Liverpool, 1953), pp. 10–11, 18. Despite his equal admiration for Bacon, Hobbes, and Henry More, Hall's political principles were so closely akin to Milton's that one of his essays was long credited to him; see Croston's preface, p. viii.

[27]   Sarah Hutton, "Edward Stillingfleet, Henry More, and the Decline of *Moses Atticus*: A Note on Seventeenth-Century Anglican apologetics," in Kroll et al. (eds.), *Philosophy, Science, and Religion*, pp. 68–84, cited p. 72 (quoting Stillingfleet), and p. 81 n. 23.

[28]   Kroll criticizes Michel Foucault's *The Order of Things* in *Material Word*, pp. 17–18.

naturally "flowing" language Sprat famously associated with merchants and artisans.[29] Neo-Epicurean philosophy also supported this ideal by decreeing that the divide between public and private meaning could only be negotiated by concrete images balanced by a marginal "scripting" of oneself into the act of writing. Neoclassicists thus came to reject the holistic "presence" built into older works like Burton's *Anatomy of Melancholy* for a more fragmentary or contingent "author effect" that provokes as many questions as answers.[30] Hence, as Robert Adolph details, after the Restoration "plain style" began to mean "an impersonal style in which the emotional attitudes of the observer did not appear," a stark contrast to the intensely personal plain style featured in Milton's early prose. Yet the new style was never starkly unemotional or abstract. It no longer retraced the personal process of acquiring truth or fully displayed the ethos of the inquirer, but it continued graphically to expound ideas buttressed by the scattered observations of an authorial persona who was less overwhelming but also more clear.[31]

In general, then, there were both gains and losses: the new style discouraged "lyric force" along with the "organic" assumptions of dogmatic religion, sectarian revelation, and "Platonic" enthusiasm. Successfully recasting the utilitarian as the ideal, neoclassicists appealed to the standard originally established in Bacon's *Aphorisms on the Composition of Primary History*:

> Never cite an author except in a matter of doubtful credit; never introduce a controversy unless in a matter of great moment. And for all that concerns ornaments of speech, similitudes, treasury of eloquence, and such like emptinesses, let it be utterly dismissed. Also let all those things which are admitted be themselves set down briefly and concisely, so that they may be nothing less than words. (*Works* 4:254)

Although this standard was never designed for poetry, the ever-tightening bonds between natural history, human history, and heroic poetry tended to close the gap, especially in biblical poetry. Yet neither the "Moses" of the new Royal Society, as Cowley pronounced Bacon, nor his followers ever eliminated metaphor or allegory. They simply limited the organic, outward expansion of tropes typical of the holistic grand style while progressively tightening, clarifying, and illustrating their essential meaning. Even when reverting to the older plain style, they thus relied on Bacon's debate format and his "businesslike marshaling of evidence pro and con ... without emotive language" to firmly separate "'Reason' and the 'The Passions.'" Adolph contrasts this careful analytical style with the "ambiguous

---

[29]   See Sprat, *History*, p. 113.

[30]   Kroll, *Material Word*, pp. 108–9.

[31]   Robert Adolph, *The Rise of Modern Prose Style* (Cambridge, MA, 1968), p. 130; on Robert Burton's style, see p. 150.

words, violent asyndeton, or terse anaphora" that Tacitus and his English admirers used to describe the mysterious motives and events behind "secret deeds."[32]

Yet, like other earlier chroniclers of the shift toward modern prose, Adolph forgets that a "businesslike" antipathy to emotive or fanciful language characterized only the Lockean pole of the Baconian spectrum. Unlikely as it seems, the Hobbesian pole of this spectrum instead endorsed the imagination's capacity to move, educate, and inspire the mind in ways inaccessible to reason alone. These values are inherent in Hobbes's theory of motion, which makes sensation and desire, not reason, the primary "movers" of human action. Reason remains vital both to the social contract and to the civilized arts and sciences it fosters, but mainly through a creative or vital union of fancy or imagination with solid judgment. While Hobbes agreed with Locke that all thought arises from experience, not from innate ideas, he believed that, without imaginative "wit," reason would fail to address the appetites, passions, or interests of men. In order to stimulate a real appetite or desire for knowledge, and thus real advances in the arts and sciences, the acquisitive instincts had to be diverted by simple curiosity or free play. The ungoverned fancy might still mislead the judgment by fostering irrational expectations and assumptions, but when properly informed by "sensible" words, it usefully sorts similarities and differences among its mental "phantasms," revealing differences to those of strong judgement and similarities to those of "good fancy." When united, these differing sensibilities produce prudential action, improved scientific theories, and more refined arts. Like Sidney, Bacon, and Milton, Hobbes thus set a high value on the ability of great artists to educate the "weaker sort" by superseding the duller operation of reason: by "exciting" the mind, "novelty causeth admiration, and admiration curiosity, which is a delightful appetite of knowledge."[33] Hobbes's entry into the neoclassical debates thus ironically did more to shift the aesthetic balance away from pedagogy and toward the passions than Sidney's *Defence of Poesy*. Influencing critics from Dennis to Burke, he also contributed to Coleridge's exaltation of the "esemplastic imagination" by way of David Hartley's vibration theory. By then, however, the Romantics tended to regard imagination and reason as opposites, not complements, which gradually moved the balance further from the "prudence" Hobbes regarded as their natural arbiter.[34]

Milton's contribution to the development of neoclassicism is less direct, although he early joined Bacon and his followers on the "Modern" side of the aesthetic controversy between Tasso and Jacopo Mazzoni. Like his ambivalence about rhetoric, Bacon's anxiety about the imagination centered on the danger of fashioning a false copy or model of the natural world that would thwart his program much as it had thwarted the Ancients: "God forbid that we should give out a dream

---

[32]   Ibid., p. 35; on Bacon's metaphorical clarity, see p. 31.

[33]   Thomas Hobbes, *The Whole Art of Rhetoric* (1681), cited in Clarence DeWitt Thorpe, *The Aesthetic Theory of Thomas Hobbes* (New York, 1964), p. 140.

[34]   This paragraph is highly indebted to Olson, *Science Deified*, vol. 2, pp. 293–301, cited pp. 294–95.

of our imagination for a pattern of the world" (*Works* 4:32–33). Ronald Levao shows that, as Christian poets commonly dedicated to probing the divine design in human history, Tasso and Milton shared the same dilemma and advocated many of the same solutions to it. Simultaneously exalting the redeemed or "icastic" imagination and deploring its idolatrous or fallen counterpart, they heeded Bacon's warning (in Tasso's case, proleptically) against impressing "our image on the creatures and works of God, instead of carefully examining and recognising in them the stamp of the Creator himself," lest "our dominion over the creatures is a second time forfeited" (*Works* 5:132). Yet in reconceiving rather than utterly banishing "the world-creating drive of Renaissance poetics," both poets continued to validate a form of human invention that "stakes claim to the world [w]e would call real." As a result, just as Bacon's dream of perfectly matching words to things failed to protect him from the attraction of radical metaphor, fable, and fantasy, Milton's dream of envisioning unrevealed aspects of Genesis in *Paradise Lost* ironically created an epic cosmos of radically questionable reality.[35]

The main point of his major epic—positively proving that God is not the author of sin or error, as its invocation claims—considerably lessens this dilemma by identifying the false world-creating "idol" who seduces the human race as Satan. This tactic allows his fallen motives, rhetoric, religion, and imagination, to be exiled to the netherworld of fallen time, while the presently unapproachable reality of unfallen Eden is filtered through fables that the Ancients had "relate[d], / Erring" (*PL* 1.746–47). Eden's "Hesperian Fables true, / If true, here only" (*PL* 4.250–51) finally vanish with the deluge, so that this perfect place can never be idolized (*PL* 11.829–38). This poetics is fully authorized by Bacon's *Wisdom of the Ancients*, which naturalizes "conceits" left dark by poets like Spenser and Sidney, and also by Tasso's *Jerusalemme Liberata*, which carefully confines its allegory to the naturalistic dimension of faculty psychology.[36] Nevertheless, Milton's final two poems show that he considered his former efforts incomplete, since they offered only negative, not positive, examples of how to confront and overcome the fallen imagination. To complete his legacy, he would need to demonstrate how both a perfect Son of God and a faulty exemplar of humanity such as Samson could triumph over the idols.[37] During the 1650s, both his blindness and his intense preoccupation with countering Salmasius and his anonymous Calvinist ally, Pierre du Moulin, would have prevented him from paying close attention to the new aesthetic solutions to these problems worked out in the exchanges between Davenant and Hobbes. Conceived and partly begun with Bacon and Tasso's far "looser" neoclassicism in mind, *Paradise Lost* was fortunately completed at a

[35]   Ronald Levao, "Francis Bacon and the Mobility of Science," *Representations* 40 (1992) pp. 1–32, referenced p. 8.

[36]   On Tasso, see Kenneth Borris, *Allegory and Epic in English Renaissance Literature: Heroic Form in Sidney, Spenser, and Milton* (Cambridge, 2000), p. 88.

[37]   See also Steven N. Zwicker, "Politics and Literary Practice in the Restoration," in Lewalski (ed.), *Renaissance Genres*, pp. 268–98.

time when the darkened mood of both Milton and his nation suited the grand, tragic style adopted in his epic. Yet, as the compromises of Charles II's later reign replaced the chaos of the late Protectorate and the tragic disappointments of the early Restoration, the dramatic heights and depths of *Paradise Lost* could be dismissed as tokens of the "over-luxuriant poetic imagination" partly responsible for those failures.

Dissatisfactions with the Restoration regime further promoted the tendency to scapegoat republican "extremists" such as Milton, whose critics found his baroque epic and its poetic "voice" faulty in both rhetoric and politics. Neoclassically denouncing his copiousness and orotundity, Milton's post-Restoration enemies traced his lack of "true" forensic linearity and clarity to his heresies "'both in Religion and Manners.'" Roger L'Estrange and Samuel Butler closely linked these faults to his "'windy foppery'" in oratory, since, as von Maltzahn relates, they were convinced that his overuse of Ciceronian periods proved his lack of the "stricter, more specific requirements for knowledge." L'Estrange invidiously compared Milton's "'Pedantique, ...too 'Peremptory, and Magisterial'" manner with the "more supple and spoken style" praised by Butler and Hobbes, while Butler personally challenged Milton to stop dealing "'altogether in universals[,] the Region of deceits and falacie,'" and to "'come so near particulars, as to let us know which among diverse things of the same kind you would be at.'" Magniloquence then seemed an important cause of society's problems, not the solution to the nation's decline. As Butler put it, just as "you politiques reach but the outside and circumstances of things and never touch at realities, so you are very solicitous about weeds as if they were charmes, or had more in them then what they signifie," which is "'mere word[s].'" As "'the cleverest and most penetrating of all the criticism ever leveled at [Milton] by his contemporaries,'" Butler's satires in *The Character of the Rump*, *The Censure of the Rota*, and *Hudibras* (which even Marvell praised) gravely undermined both the old revolutionary's poetic authority and his republican ethos by redescribing "the eloquence that Milton offered as an expression of virtue as merely an expression of fantasy and personal ambition."[38]

It is virtually impossible to imagine the same author who so fulsomely defended himself against Salmasius in the *Defensio Secunda* and the imaginary "Morus" in *Pro Se Defensio*—and even got his nephew John Phillips to defend him against lesser enemies—not wanting to set the record straight by controverting these damning charges, if only in verse. After the Restoration, he would have had ample time to consult Hobbes's famous *Answer to Davenant's Preface to "Gondibert,"* which further tightened the criteria for eliminating the Baconian "idols" of superfluous eloquence, including "Ancient" conventions like the standard Homeric invocation. Complaining that no rational Christian "enabled to speak wisely from

---

[38]   Von Maltzahn, "From Pillar to Post," pp. 265–85; cited pp. 274–76. Von Maltzahn cites *Treason Arraign'd* (London, 1660), p. 1; L'Estrange, *No Blinde Guides* (London, 1660), p. 3; and Samuel Butler, *Censure of the Rota* (London, 1660), pp. 3, 4, 5, 11–14. See also his essay, "Samuel Butler's Milton."

the principles of nature and his own meditation" would presume to "profane the true God or invoke a false one" by pretending "to speak by inspiration, like a bagpipe," Hobbes added enormous fuel to Davenant's anti-baroque fire.[39] So did Cowley's poem, "To Sir William Davenant," which sees *Gondibert* ushering in an entirely new, non-fabulous poetic age:

> Methinks *Heroick Poesie* till now
> Like some fantastick *Fairy Land* did show,
> *Gods*, *Devils*, *Nymphs*, *Witches* and *Gyants race*,
> And all but *Man* in *Mans chief work* had place.
> Thou like some worthy *Knight* with sacred Arms
> Dost drive the *Monsters* thence, and end the *Charms*.
> Instead of those dost *Men* and *Manners* plant,
> The things which that rich *Soil* did chiefly want. (1–8)[40]

Cowley was seconded by his friend Sprat, who, as Robert Hinman observes, praised him for portraying the real nature of "men and manners" with "compression and economy, unity and restraint, harmony and form, a wealth of imaginative effect without forcing or grotesqueness, an abundance of art that conceals art"—in short, "a masculine style with the virtues of strength, not smoothness." Both believed that this style would at last extinguish the "idols" of exaggerated language that made "clear thinking and effective writing difficult, if not impossible."[41] Dealing only in the known conditions of nature (its "rich *Soil*"), culture, and history (real "*Men* and *Manners*"), the new aesthetic would constrict fantastic digressions, allegorical episodes, and unwarranted speculation on "*Faiths Myst'eries*." So far as possible, the "boundless Godhead" should be made comprehensible to its truest image, the "*Reasonable Mind*."[42]

The opening invocation to *Paradise Lost* had already paid tribute to the upright mind and heart (*PL* 1.18), but Milton's epic race of fairies, "Gods, Devils, Nymphs, Witches and Gyants" could still be read as "superstitious" by critics like John Beale.[43] Thus, in addition to completing his epic exploration of both the fallen and the redeemed imagination, Milton deeply needed to demonstrate his "reasonable mind." In this, he was not alone: only four years after the first edition of his aptly

---

[39]   Thomas Hobbes, *Answer to Davenant's Preface to "Gondibert,"* in Adams (ed.), *Critical Theory*, p. 214.

[40]   Cited in Abraham Cowley, *Poems*, ed. Waller, pp. 42–43. On Hobbes's influence on Cowley, see Robert Hinman, *Abraham Cowley's World of Order* (Cambridge, MA, 1960), pp. 116–34.

[41]   Hinman, *Abraham Cowley's World*, p. 5.

[42]   See Cowley, "Reason. The use of it in Divine Matters," ll. 41, 30, in *Poems*, pp. 46–47.

[43]   Beale was repulsed by the "long blasphemies" of Milton's demons, which led him falsely to regard *Paradise Lost* as a Calvinist epic; see von Maltzahn, "Laureate, Republican, Calvinist," pp. 192–93.

named *Vanity of Dogmatizing*, Joseph Glanvill radically revised it to conform to the new plain style.[44] The prose of Milton's *Of True Religion* indicates a similarly rapid shift. Only four years after Sprat's *History of the Royal Society*, Milton's tract speaks extremely clear, strong, and in the current idiom—"manly" English—at a time when militant Puritans like Edmund Ludlow still employed the incantatory, apocalyptic rhetoric that John Toland needed radically to prune, soften, and "politen." In order to make Ludlow's *Memoirs* palatable to contemporary Whigs, he also had to expunge its Puritan character by making its "breathless sentences, ... urgency and stridency, ... [and] cries of anger and bitterness" yield to the "measured reflection" of the new literary era into which Toland's Milton already fit.[45]

As Zwicker suspects, the plain style of *Paradise Regained* also seems to answer many of the concerns explored in Dryden's 1668 *Essay of Dramatic Poesy*, which was published the same year that he became poet laureate. Resuming the aesthetic and political debates of the 1650s, Dryden's *Essay* addresses linguistic and social reforms far more relevant to Milton than the problem of rhyme. If the "decadence" of the recent civil wars was to be reversed and England returned to its golden age, Dryden asks whether contemporary poets should imitate the Ancients, or Moderns like the French poets Corneille and Molière, or attempt some synthesis of the two. This question is obviously rhetorical, since Dryden clearly favors the synthetic approach. While granting the validity of Aristotle's norms and the French skill in strictly obeying them, he finds their unities too dry and "inorganic" to suit English taste. While Milton would certainly have agreed, his own views fail to exactly match any of those presented by the three speakers in Dryden's dialogue. Crites upholds his belief in the "Ancient" freedom from the "bondage" of rhyme, but otherwise Milton's aesthetics are closer to those of Neander, the "new man" who stands for Dryden. Loosely following Hobbes, Neander believes that the heroic poem should not simply illustrate character-in-action, as the Aristotelians maintained, but demonstrate the proper management of the human passions. "Modern" Christian art would thereby surpass the Ancient gold standard held up by Crites, who argues that the Greek love of honor inspired them to unparalleled heights, even though "the Asian kings and Grecian commonwealths scarce afforded" them "a nobler subject than the unmanly luxuries of a debauched court, or giddy intrigues of a factious city."[46]

The scornful rejection of these "unmanly luxuries" by the Son of *Paradise Regained* indicates that he shares Dryden's disapproval of the Greek ability to "soar" in verse without any concrete models of virtue to extol; hence overly rigid devotion to the classics clearly will not do. Milton's final heroic poem provides a less rigid but still neoclassical solution to the problem by obeying the Aristotelian unities of place an time but expanding the latter into a three-day temptation. The

---

[44]   Adolph, *Rise*, pp. 90–91.

[45]   Worden, *Roundhead*, p. 80.

[46]   John Dryden, *An Essay of Dramatic Poesy*, in Adams (ed.), *Critical Theory*, p. 231.

poem also disproves Crites's rule that heroic drama should not attempt to express "epitomes of a man's life," the condensed "work of an age," or "more countries than the map can show us," for it not only epitomizes Christ's life but includes an accurate spatio-temporal map of the ancient world.[47]

Finally, Milton's epic practice disproves the norms defended by the third party in Dryden's debate, Lisideius, who fashionably prefers French symmetry over English verisimilitude. Neander feels this preference sacrifices the realistic "studies of humanity" that English poets had long been perfecting, and proposes that a balance between Aristotelian orthodoxy and the native English imagination will best preserve its talent for depicting character and passion, especially if overly "luxuriant" subplots are pruned out. Unlike Elizabethan and Jacobean drama, the new heroic poetry should also avoid mixing tragedy with comedy, but, as in earlier neoclassicism, continue to utilize "some known history" interwoven with fictive "improvements" supporting the theme of virtue rewarded.[48] Milton's two final poems express his basic agreement: the preface to *Samson Agonistes* condemns the "error of intermixing Comic stuff with Tragic sadness and gravity," and diverges from Dryden only in trading French for Italian precedent, which he finds "of much more authority and fame" (Hughes 550), as Sprat, for one, agreed.[49] Milton's tragedy also strictly obeys the Aristotle unities of time and place, although the longer heroic poem bound with it, *Paradise Regained*, appropriately conforms to Neander's looser unities. Yet, as Zwicker remarks, it does not just "occasionally" display these unities or occasionally fall into dramatic colloquies exhibiting the rewards of virtue; "the poem is designed for their display."[50]

The Religious and Linguistic Neoclassicism of *Paradise Regained*

Without rejecting lyric power altogether, Milton's brief epic rigorously demystifies and limits emotive rhetoric to a few conventional gestures and makes prudence the principal virtue of the Son of God himself. Christ's history is so thoroughly "improved" that Laura Lunger Knoppers refers to it as an entirely new gospel according to John [Milton]—a bold replacement of radical suffering and inspiration with natural religion and ethics.[51] Like the Horatian poem of instruction praised

---

[47]   Ibid., p. 233.

[48]   Ibid., p. 239.

[49]   Sprat, *History*, pp. 40–44. Sprat feels that England is less like her "airy and discoursive" French neighbors (p. 40) and (hopefully) more like Italy in the Augustan age (pp. 43–44).

[50]   Zwicker, "Milton, Dryden," p. 146.

[51]   Laura Lunger Knoppers, "*Paradise Regained* and the Politics of Martyrdom," *MP* 90.2 (1992): pp. 200–19, cited p. 219. Knoppers believes that Milton's continuing desire to demystify the legend of Charles Martyr produces this unorthodoxy, although Socinianism may also be a factor.

in the preface to Dryden's *Religio Laici*, it eschews both mystical experience and Ciceronian magniloquence, extravagances that depend too much upon "the vagaries of individual taste" to be broadly instructive.[52] Milton's style had been moving in this anti-enthusiastic, anti-Ciceronian direction from the time when *Areopagitica* mocked St. Jerome's "Ciceronianisms" (*CPW* 2:510) to the final drafts of his post-Restoration *History of Britain* (1670), which fully abandon the looser, more personal, and emotionally charged style of his early work.[53] *Paradise Regained* (1671) complements this shift in prose style by closely following the neoclassical doctrine of verisimilitude. Tightly focused on carefully plotted debates about aims and motives, Milton's dramatic action is stripped of the fulsome, emotional, and incantatory rhetoric deployed in the previous epic. Even its villain is less charismatic, while his "sin" is simply to be less prudent or self-knowing than the hero. Fabulous scenes are limited to a brief council in hell and a mythic banquet, while allegorical figures such as Sin, Death, Discord, Chaos, and Night disappear altogether.

Milton's final critique of Greek rhetoric and learning in the last two books of *Paradise Regained* is also highly indebted to the rules of neoclassical decorum. Its stern but not sweeping denunciation of Greek philosophy leaves room for the "high" moral example set by ancient tragedy, which explains why *Samson Agonistes* is the closest imitation of the form ever rendered in English. Its companion poem thus fails to mount a wholesale attack on ancient rhetoric or mythology in theory or in practice. *Paradise Regained* in fact includes well-known Homeric similes along with allusions to Greek mythology—Ixion's "empty cloud" (*PR* 4.320–21), the riddle of the Sphinx, and the combat of "Jove's son" Hercules with Antaeus (*PR* 4.563–75). Its hero's attack on Greek philosophy is also more limited than it seems, particularly in comparison with the near-contemporary example of the Calvinist Theophilus Gale.[54] Gale's *The Court of the Gentiles* (1660) agrees with Stillingfleet, Wallis, and Bochart that human language, philosophy, and religion originated with the Jews, yet (as Dewey Wallace notes) he emphasizes this primitive purity only to "'beat down that fond persuasion'" that pagan wisdom was "'the product of Natures Light.'" This view sharply contrasts with Milton's affirmation that a common "light of nature" inspired ancient learning (*PR* 4.351–522), which hardly supports Gale's belief that all learning had "become 'a common Strumpet, for carnal Reason to commit follie'" with ever since Adam fell. Ever afterward, according to Gale, man's totally depraved nature has gone whoring after secular philosophy, a critique aimed at the rational forms of Christianity currently promoted by Grotius,

---

[52]   On neoclassical anti-mysticism, see Kroll, *Material Word*, quoted cited p. 256; on its anti-Ciceronianism (as derived from Bacon), see Adolph, *Rise*, p. 45.

[53]   Thomas Corns documents this shift in *The Development of Milton's Prose Style* (New York, 1982).

[54]   For a very different reading, see Achinstein, *Literature and Dissent*, pp. 184–87.

the Latitudinarians, their allies among the Arminians and Socinians, and Milton, who would soon defend them all in *Of True Religion*.[55]

According to Richard Westfall, a belief in the common light of nature similarly led Wilkins, Boyle, and most Royal Society virtuosi to regard the Bible less as an exclusive "record of God's dispensation than as a further and higher revelation of his Omnipotence," although like the hero of *Paradise Regained*, they acknowledged its revelation of things unknowable by reason alone. Milton calls this the true "Light from above, from the fountain of light" (*PR* 4.289), which cannot be revealed by "mere" natural light. Nevertheless, neither Milton's Son of God nor the virtuosi uphold Tertullian's "Calvinist" dictum, "*credo quia impossibile est*," which all considered absurd. As Westfall explains, the virtuosi felt reason is needed not only to show that there are things above reason, but to guide choice in most matters, including faith; for religion is too important merely to be taken on trust, and God far too reasonable a creator to demand that it should be. In promulgating true religion, Boyle therefore believed that Christ always "'propose[d] those truths, which He in so wonderful and so solemn a manner recommended, with at least so much clearness as that studious and well-disposed readers may certainly understand such as are necessary to believe.'" In teaching ethics, Christ could therefore be favorably compared to "unaffected" Ancients like Socrates or Pythagoras, who simply taught that "'two things must ennoble a man—to know truth and to do good.'" Boyle's opponents—not just Calvinists like Gale but scholastics like Meric Casaubon—instead sided with Tertullian's teaching by arguing that God should be worshiped without studying the natural evidence of His Providence.[56]

Hinman finds Milton countering men of their persuasion by refusing to claim certain revelation and by consistently using the lessons of nature to search for a fuller understanding both of scripture and of God's hidden ways.[57] His hero follows the same principles: actively searching for objective "evidence" of God's will, the Son carefully sifts, redefines, and tests every category and question of knowledge/ power put to him by Satan in terms of natural logic. This method requires a close attention to the resemblances between words and things, which, according to Alastair Fowler, at once anticipates Pope's famous dictum about the ideal synthesis of sound and sense, and points toward the "plain style" of much modernist poetry. Ironically, this technique can make *Paradise Regained* sound unexcitingly familiar, but when it was first published it registered a recognizable advance in

---

[55]   Wallace, *Puritans*, pp. 178–79. Theophilus Gale wrote firmly within the Augustinian tradition that Milton so strenuously amends in *Paradise Lost*; see Chapter 6 above. Gale's *The Court of the Gentiles* (Oxford, 1660) is cited in pt. 1, sig. [*4], pt. 2, sig. a2,; see also pt. 3, sigs. A3–4.

[56]   Westfall, *Science and Religion*, pp. 169, 168 172, 125, 126, citing Robert Boyle, *Works* vol. 4, p. 41, and vol. 2, p. 5.

[57]   Hinman, *Abraham Cowley's World*, p. 143.

neoclassical subtlety.[58] With the same generic principles in mind, Milton carefully limits his invocation to a modest ten-line address that even his worst critics could never claim was sonorously "blown" as if by "a bagpipe." Immediately afterward, his hero shows his adversary that all coherence—all inferences, analogies, and metaphors—is constructed by artificial signs and not imposed by divine or (in this case) malign fiat. Replacing the "scholastic tyranny" Milton had long lamented with the new epistemology, the Son further supports his volitional ethics of choice with the "modern" practices of translation and revision in which Milton himself was so adept. Every time his adversary offers him a foreign or classical example to follow, he smoothly recasts it in terms more relevant to contemporary realities. Kroll shows that neoclassicism featured critical practices of this kind due to its need to make increasingly fine discriminations between particular contemporary circumstances and the larger patterns of events. Since translation involves global and double-edged acts of displacement and recuperation, it at once communicates, certifies, and transforms the rules of reading by providing verifiable standards of cross-referencing. For that reason alone, translation constitutes the very essence of both the neoclassical mode and the new standards of truth in ethics, politics, and the liberal arts.[59]

By applying this new standard, the Son easily demolishes Satan's claim to higher knowledge in any of these arts. With the Hebraic simplicity advocated in Stillingfleet's *Origines Sacrae*, he proclaims:

> Our Hebrew Songs and Harps in *Babylon*,
> That pleas'd so well our Victors' ear, declare
> That rather *Greece* from us these Arts deriv'd;
> Ill-imitated, while they loudest sing
> The vices of their Deities, and thir own
> In Fable, Hymn, or Song, so personating
> Thir Gods ridiculous, and themselves past shame.
> Remove their swelling Epithets thick laid
> As varnish on a Harlot's cheek, the rest,
> Thin sown with aught of profit or delight,
> Will far be found unworthy to compare
> With *Sion's* songs, to all true tastes excelling,
> Where God is prais'd aright, and Godlike men,
> …
> Thir Orators thou then extoll'st, as those
> The top of Eloquence, Statists indeed,
> And lovers of thir Country, as may seem;

---

[58]   Alastair Fowler, "*Paradise Regained:* Some Problems of Style," in Piero Boitani and Anna Torti (eds.), *Medieval and Pseudo-Medieval Literature* (Cambridge, 1984), pp. 181–89.

[59]   On these features of neoclassicism, see Kroll, *Material Word*, pp. 86–89.

But to our Prophets far beneath,
As men divinely taught, and better teaching
The solid rules of Civil Government
In thir majestic unaffected style
Than all the Oratory of *Greece* and *Rome*,
In them is plainest taught, and easiest learnt.

(*PR* 4.336–48, 353–61)

The linguistic chastity and clarity of this speech exactly mirror its lesson: plain truth plainly spoken. The Son perfectly practices what he preaches: wholly avoiding radical metaphor and using only a single, standard neoclassical simile, he concretely compares extraneous "epithets" to paint on a harlot's cheek. Like the "persuasive Rhetoric / That sleek't" Satan's "tongue, and won so much on" the inexperienced Eve (*PR* 4.4–5), these false "colors" allure only the unwise, the unwary, or the immature. Since the Son's "Reasonable Mind" finds such attractions as unsubstantial and unwelcome as the buzzing of "flies in vintage time," he easily brushes aside Satan's twin allures of false rhetoric and false flattery (*PR* 4.15). His "weak arguing and fallacious drift" (*PR* 3.4) become nothing but a "vain batt'ry" ending "in froth or bubbles," like "surging waves against a solid rock" (*PR* 4.20, 18). By long studying "what is of use to know, / What best to say" and do, the Son easily adheres to the original and "true" purpose of language, which is to give "perfect shape" and "utterance due" to all that is "good, wise, just" (*PR* 3.7–8, 10–11).

At this point, Milton famously charges Plato and his heirs with departing from this model in both theory and in practice. Because he failed humbly to collect "gross particulars," Plato condemned learning to impracticality, utopianism, and romanticism. With all their vaunted objectivity, the Stoics failed to correct his habit of "leaping" to universal conclusions, for, as the Son complains, they confused philosophical detachment with foolish insensibility to fate. Sprat and the Royal Society Baconians fully agreed that these and related errors explained the stagnation of Ancient philosophy and science. Sprat contends that rather than seeking real trials, the Ancients were content to "enlarge the fancy, and fill the head with the matter and artifice of discours," which "breaks the force of things … [with] the subtilty of words," "weakens mens arms, and slackens all the sinews of action."[60] Only adopting opposite methods will counteract this "effeminacy"; pragmatic, cooperative methods will "break" the force of elitist rhetoric by teaching that the "*ordinary way*" triumphs over the Ancient conviction "that nothing ought to be done, though never so common, but by some device of *Art*, and trick of unusual *wisdom*." Sprat complains that this "Greek" or dogmatic method condemns the student to "invent" what one knows and "does out of himself" alone, while the true philosopher "gathers it from the footsteps and progress of *Nature*." Milton's Son follows a very similar version of the latter method as he "indevors rather to know, than to admire," to prove everything by experience rather than resting

---

[60]   Sprat, *History*, p. 332.

upon an "empty cloud" of hearsay authority not warranted by any experience or judgment "equal or superior" to his own (*PR* 4.321, 324).[61] Unlike the subtle philosophers admired by Satan, he knows how useless it is to be "deep verst in books" but "shallow in himself," which makes the Greeks appear to him like children "gathering pebbles on the shore" (4.327, 330).

Milton had long been attracted to the anti-authoritarian aspect of Bacon's empirical program, which Sprat also stresses in critiquing the destructive authority of conformity. Conformists hide behind a "solemn appearance of *Wisdom*," perversely "sticking to the same things in *all times*," while real truth-seekers reject their prescriptive approach. [62] The Son sagely applies the same critique to Satan's outdated rules for world conquest, rules that would prevent him from adjusting his perceptions to changing circumstances and unpredictable situations. Rather than dwelling on the heroes or the imagined perfections of the past, he overcomes new obstacles with the simple patience and fortitude that Sprat also attributes to Christ and his apostles, who combined dovelike innocence with the craftiness of serpents. As practical men, they "craftily" earned their living through trades, but even in spiritual matters, they pragmatically focused on charitable works. These, not theological niceties, are the truest and most innocent "fruits" of religion. New philosophers should follow their example by fusing the skills of the abstract or contemplative thinker with those of the prudent or active man. This synthesis will not only promote scientific progress but also end intemperance, idleness, and vanity without the need for "sour" or repressive rules.[63] Milton's hero practices the same ethic by combining "Saintly patience" (*PR* 3.93) with artisan-like prudence, temperance, fortitude, and skill. Although Satan accuses him of "sourly" despising action, his contemplative habits well prepare him for Job-like trials. For as the Son affirms, only those "who best / Can suffer, best can do; best reign, who first / Well hath obey'd ... [under] just trial" (3.194–96). According to both Milton and Sprat, the rewards of this self-discipline far exceed mere release from death. By freeing men from fear—God's principal curse on the wicked—they are released from both the tyranny of the Ancients, and all the furies, ghosts, and chimeras of the nether world (4.422).

Milton summarizes these lessons in his most strikingly non-scriptural episode, the "ghostly storm" laughed off by the Son, which obliquely recalls Sprat's Baconian proverb: in the dark ages of ignorance, men were not more religious, as conventional wisdom has it, but only more superstitious, and therefore *least* religious. Sprat affirms that Genesis, Job, and Psalms all demonstrate this truism, as do Christ's miracles, which equally testify to the ultimate consonance of divine and natural philosophy. Best understood as "*Divine Experiments*" designed to prove his power to the simple but honest tradesmen who followed him, their intent was to liberate them, not to make them superstitious. This effect is proved by the

---

[61]   Ibid., pp. 334, 335. On the connection to "Ancient" dogmatism, see p. 28.
[62]   Ibid., p. 335.
[63]   Ibid., pp. 366–69, 342–44.

apostles' scant attention to the metaphysical or mysterious aspects of Christianity. While necessary, the mysterious aspects of faith are less practical and conducive to charity because they are most open to contention. The hero of *Paradise Regained* essentially agrees when he ridicules Greek metaphysics or "soul teaching" but offers none of his own, hardly a surprising step given the harsh view of metaphysics presented in *De Doctrina Christiana*. *Paradise Regained* conventionally concedes Christ's incarnation, but refuses to address its "mystery" even in metaphorical terms. This decision conforms to the post-Restoration bias against what Sprat calls assuming a "New *Prophetical Spirit*" that usurps the Almighty's prerogative of concealing his secret will.[64] Those who violate this prerogative not only fail to "reverence the *Power* of *God*," but unwittingly promote "the Passions, and interests, and revenges of men."[65] Milton's Son supports this bias, not only by refusing to perform miracles but also by rejecting all the passions and interests Satan seeks to "inspire" in him. He just as easily penetrates Satan's feigned admiration of his own supposedly "smooth," easy approach to the "Hard ... ways of truth," for more than Satan knows, the knowledge of "hard truths" is earned only through the "rough ... walk" of real experience (*PR* 1.478–79).

Malcolm Kelsall's study of *Paradise Regained* further confirms that its scriptural and historical hermeneutics closely conform to the neoclassical values defended by Sprat and analyzed by Kroll. By using historical context as the key to biblical exegesis, Milton carefully limits typology and allegory, and confines even theology to plausible, non-miraculous events and historically situated explanations of human behavior. Colet's famous Oxford lectures had earlier shown that all careful exegesis should employ this method, but Milton's application of it is more neoclassical. His presentation of the circumstances, actions, and characters described in the gospels and other contemporary histories is based on the broader assumption that "just as the historian may correctly infer the contents of secret negotiations from their consequences in public acts, so too the inspired intuition of the poet may be able to deduce from the memorial of Scripture the contextual and general implications of fragmentarily reported but literally credited words and actions." As Kelsall shows, Milton's sources range from the Hebrew prophets to Livy and Thucydides, the latter of whom he closely follows by freely inventing plausible speeches based on surrounding circumstances. These prominently include such details as the oppression and decadence of the contemporary Romans and the

---

[64] Ibid., pp. 350–52, 358. Sprat also warns that fires and plagues are difficult to interpret as signs of wickedness without evidence of who the wicked are. The new natural philosopher accepts commentaries on prophecy, new predictions and analyses of causes, but does not assign God's finger to all extraordinary events, nor does he agree that all raptures and revelations come from God, but assigns these to natural physical causes wherever possible (pp. 360–64).

[65] Sprat, *History*, p. 360.

inherent instability of Tiberius's line of succession.[66] The final two books of the epic are thus grounded in an impressive range of historical and geographical detail, while the first two present a brief, matter-of-fact, classically balanced account of the Son's baptism and journey into the wilderness. These key events are surrounded by non-allegorical councils in heaven and hell that recall Cowley's subdued handling of comparable episodes, while mental flashbacks allow the Son naturalistically to review his previous life and Judea's politico-historical situation.

The True Wit of "Paradise Regained"

The opening scenes of *Paradise Regained* are especially remarkable for their lack of inspired or supernatural emphasis: the Son seems to have no foreknowledge of his future and he receives no signs from above aside from the well-attested declaration at his baptism that he is the Father's "beloved Son." In true rationalist fashion, this event is confirmed by many factual witnesses: Mary and John the Baptist are further supported by the rabbis who formerly examined the young Jesus in the temple. Even after the Spirit leads him into the wilderness, it operates ambiguously, apparently more as a mental impulse than as a divine intervention. Somehow sensing that he should no more "live obscure" and should now begin his public, messianic ministry (*PR* 1.287), the Son begins his journey with no real idea how, when, or where to start. This lack of clear leading also supplies a naturalistic reason for Satan to enter the scene, since moments of uncertainty or doubt are always conducive to leading youth astray. The Son is of course no ordinary youth, yet, aside from his sinless birth, he seems completely human, non-omniscient, and comparatively uninstructed in what "best becomes / The Authority which I deriv'd from heaven." Following "some strong" but undefined "motion," he sets forth on a solitary search for "what concerns my knowledge" (*PR* 1.288–90, 293), but, like most humans, he encounters false knowledge first. His response to this test is completely rational and even empirical: he relies on skeptical questioning, probing, and an "experimental" synthesis of scriptural record, past experience, and natural prudence to overcome his adversary's fictions with plain fact. As commonly noted, this treatment not only turns Satan into a fully human character—a weary and desperate worlding peddling a sad assortment of Ancient errors—but also causes the Son to appear as a completely earthly persona with a divine mission but no divine powers.

These striking departures from the more mysterious style and substance of *Paradise Lost* are signaled from the very beginning. Based on his prior study and a careful "waiting" upon the Law and Prophets (*PR* 1.260–61), the Son is straightforwardly advised by Satan to end his wandering "by Miracle" (*PR* 1.337). Plainly garbling his history (368–96), he tempts him to justify his

---

[66]   Malcolm Kelsall, "The Historicity of *Paradise Regained*," *Milton Studies* 12 (1978): pp. 235–51, cited pp. 237–39, quoted p. 239.

divine "prerogative" by turning a stone into bread. Here Milton takes advantage of a highly canonical moment to present a neoclassical (and not very biblical) repudiation not just of unauthorized miracles but of all "presages and signs, / And answers, oracles, portents and dreams, / Whereby [mankind] … may direct their future life" (*PR* 1.394–96). In other words, Milton does not wait for the Son's death and resurrection to show that "henceforth Oracles are ceast," but long before the temple veil is rent at his crucifixion, he already considers them defunct. All superstitious "Pomp and Sacrifice" thus gives way to the one "living Oracle," the "Spirit of Truth" (*PR* 1.456–57, 460, 462). As usual, the narrator refuses precisely to identify this "Spirit of Truth," which may ambiguously refer either to the "Holy Ghost" of Pentecost or to right reason. Even the Spirit who descends "like a Dove" has no absolute authority until the Son hears the rational "voice" of the Father, "the sum of all" (*PR* 1.282–83). As in *Comus, Of Civil Power*, and *De Doctrina Christiana*, this Spirit is thus clearly a supplement to, not a replacement for, reason: it fortifies "pious Hearts" (*PR* 1.463) assisted but not overwhelmed by its presence, stimulates the mind's natural powers, and supplies signs of divine support—although these functions are far inferior to the internal strength of the Son himself (*CPW* 6:282, 288, 298).

Since no amount of Satan's "pleasing" and "tunable" talk can replace the Son's vigorous fusion of action and contemplation, the poem's second book opens in much the same way as the first: with a concrete survey of the sites explored in the Son's "walk," their relation to his life history, and the thoughts of his family and followers in his absence. This cultural map is further complicated by the multiple perspectives provided by his mother Mary and his humble artisan followers (*PR* 2.27). These historical and personal flashbacks frame Satan's and the Son's very different constructions of the Holy Land and complement the lessons of the first book by further demystifying the "oracles" of classical myth. Milton embodies its "superstitions" in the fallen imagination of Belial, the "spirit of worthlessness" who supposes that "Some beauty rare, *Calisto, Clymene, / Daphne*, or *Semele, Antiopa, / Or Amymone, Syrinx*, many more / Too long" to mention may entrap their common enemy. In confusing the Son with the pagan suitors of these nymphs—Apollo, Neptune, Jupiter, Pan, or one of his satyrs or fauns—Belial fully embodies the "barbarous dissonance" of the Greeks' pseudo-heroic assumptions (*PR* 2.186–91). The poet emphasizes this dissonance with a clashing combination of "c," "s," and "anti"/"amyn" sounds naming Belial's "idols." Satan himself rebukes Belial for fondly believing in something like "magnetic attraction," since if even lesser heroes like Alexander could resist the allure of beauty, the magic charms of the fabulous "Zone of *Venus*" (*PR* 2.214) have obviously ceased for the Son. Seeking "manlier objects" to entrap his foe, Satan hopes to entice him with the "lawful desires of Nature," not the "trivial toy[s]" that ensnared the pseudo-heroes of the past (*PR* 2.225, 230, 223).

The abrupt failure of these enticements foreshadows the Son's fully modern fact/fiction dichotomies, which effortlessly distinguish the "carnal appetite" awakened by the dreaming or unconscious body from the actual needs of his rational, sentient mind and flesh. As Satan had promised Belial, the Son's initial dream of Elijah's or Daniel's physical refreshment is perfectly natural and lawful in itself (*PR* 2.264–65), although projecting those conditions upon the enchanted banquet that Satan offers is not. The Son's anti-idolatrous separation of wish-fulfillment from natural refreshment forms a strong and obvious contrast with Eve's self-abandonment to the pastoral "magic" of the apple. Although "Nature taught Art" how to adorn the grove where the banquet is offered much as it did Eden's garden, its "Wood Gods and Wood Nymphs" are now credited only by "a Superstitious eye" (*PR* 2.295–97). Nevertheless, they have real contents that the Son must carefully decode before proceeding to higher temptations. Ironically overriding his own advice to Belial, Satan now plies him with all the sumptuous delights of the Ancients "disguised" as lawful Hebrew entertainment: food imported from "*Pontus* and *Lucrine* Bay, and *Afric Coast*," "fruit and flowers from *Almathea*'s horn," "stripling youths rich clad, of fairer hue / Than *Ganymede* or *Hylas*," "Nymphs of *Diana*'s train," "Ladies of th' *Hesperides*" attended by bravest knights, and all set off by charmed music and sweetest "*Arabian* odors" (*PR* 2.347, 352, 355–57, 364). Some of these delights are actually forbidden by Hebrew law, but Milton's conviction that this law too has "ceast" means that his Son must reject them not as illegal but as "pompous Delicacies" adored by the fallen imagination, not by plain truth-seekers (*PR* 2.390). In essence, this refusal exposes Satan's false methods, which consist in overvaluing the "device of *Art*, and trick of unusual *wisdom*," when what Sprat calls the "vulgar" way is forty times more nourishing. Daniel's humble "pulse" and Elijah's desert forage (*PR* 2.266–78) at once represent this more nourishing and humble way, and reveal Satan's preference for magically glorified pomp rather than true refreshment. Unlike Eve but like Sprat, the Son knows that toil justifies and heightens appetite, but instant gratification spoils it.[67]

After exposing these temptations as trivial, the second book shows the Son facing the "manliest" allures acknowledged by Milton's age, "Money, … Honor, Friends, Conquest, and Realms" (*PR* 2.422). As Zwicker notes, these temptations naturalistically ascend "from the feast in the wilderness to Demosthenes and Pericles, Socrates and Plato"—that is, from the idols of the flesh, to crude power, to the most refined "rhetorical skill and philosophical authority."[68] Thus only after rejecting the cruder but "manlier" lures of the carnal imagination—wealth and warfare, aristocratic and political prestige—does the Son face the more subtle "charms" of Greek sophistry and philosophy. Skillfully handling this final temptation requires Milton to present two quite different versions of Socrates: one, the hero of patience and right reason, the other, the unwilling forefather of "fanciful" Platonism. Through it all, his careful analysis of the known patterns of human behavior, manners, and culture shows that his enemy is the fallen imagination, but not reason or learning per se. As a result, Aristotle's ethics,

---

[67] Sprat, *History*, pp. 33–34, 67, 111, 393–94.
[68] Zwicker, "Milton, Dryden," p. 149.

poetics, and politics (which unlike his pseudo-science, remained important to Milton and his contemporaries) are excluded from this "fabling" category.

The Son begins his "witty" cross-examination of carnal power by empirically proving that both the future and past situation of Rome doom the Stoic attempt to rectify it. Nevertheless, Kelsall shows that "Christ's dilemma is neo-Stoic" as well as neo-Socratic, for, while neither Milton nor his hero adopt these creeds:

> It was the Stoic opposition to Caesarism that bore at this time the heaviest weight of imperial proscription and persecution. The cause of the republic, of liberty and of virtue, was guttering out, and the young and idealistic of heart (Lucan), or the lofty of spirit (Seneca), "for truth's sake suffered death unjust" in future years. It is not surprising, therefore, when Christ asks himself how he is going to act under Caesar, that *Paradise Regained* becomes redolent with Stoic allusion. That was the currency of the hour. The martyr Socrates, the Herculean hero, the republican types whom Christ "esteems"—Cincinnatus, Curius, Fabricius, Regulus—these are standard figures from the pantheon of Christ's contemporary, Seneca, and are the only classical figures of moral weight in the poem.[69]

This background further explains the otherwise peculiar predominance of the Stoic/Aristotelian virtues of temperance and magnanimity in a poem that officially criticizes these virtues while not-so-subtly recasting them in Christian form. The Son's simultaneous absorption and transvaluation of these values is most apparent as he reviews and rejects the kingdoms of Babylon, Parthia, and Rome, all of which exemplify false glory, the folly of "pure" military pride. True glory is neither authoritarian nor imperial: it asks us to "show forth ... and impart" the "good communicable to every soul / Freely," requiring in return only the mutual "benediction, that is thanks" (*PR* 3.125–27).

False glory is also associated with the Christian imperial ethos promoted in the heroic romances of Roman Christendom, whose chivalric "fablers" (especially Boiardo and Ariosto) were foolishly captivated by classical values (*PR* 3.339–44). As a result, the Son cultivates a strong skepticism not just about the imagined perfections and power of the past but also of the future, where military dreamers will continue to idolize traditional means of conquest. Yet, much as in the banquet scene, these satanic "visions" were never truly glorious. As Annabel Patterson remarks, the Son's "refusal to intervene in the history of either Rome or Jerusalem implies a rebuke to any political interpretation of his messianic role—that is, any idea of a religious or national crusade."[70] Thus, when the Son asks with quasi-Senecan austerity, *Quis enim placere populo potest, cui placet virtus?* ("Who that is pleased by virtue can please the crowd?"), the only possible answer is that no worthy leader will force his life or work into the mold formed by this empty

---

[69]   Kelsall, "Historicity," p. 241.

[70]   Annabel Patterson, "*Paradise Regained*: A Last Chance at True Romance," *Milton Studies* 17 (1983), pp. 187–208, cited p. 202.

cloud or crowd. Hence the Son refuses to tamper with the divine "experiment" by making himself "Plausible to the world," which "to mee [is] worth naught" because it leads only to false "prediction" (*PR* 3.393–94) and pride.

The Son's unflagging hostility to superstitious "signs" at last leads Satan to display his supreme temptations through the lens of the most scientific instruments of Milton's time—the telescope and recently invented microscope (*PR* 4.40–43, 57). These instruments serve Milton's neoclassical turn by eliminating all magical, fantastic, or even biblical machinery from his most supernatural episodes. Their false content mirrors their form as the Son scorns what he clearly sees as "degenerate" and idolatrous empires "by themselves enslav'd" and unworthy of conquest (*PR* 4.144). This tactic forces Satan to withdraw his specious claim that he can teach him how to rule "Empires, and Monarchs, and thir radiant Courts" through the "best school of best experience" (*PR* 3.237–38), or even alternatively, how to wear the unworldly "Crown" of "contemplation and profound dispute" (*PR* 4.213, 214). Although a generation of scholars trained in classical rhetoric and philosophy equated the Son's stance with the wholesale rejection of humanistic learning, any unbiased observer can see that this "temptation" simply places himself among those Moderns seeking to sift the solid wheat from the superficial chaff. As "both Judge and Savior" (*PL* 10.209), he follows Solomon's "Socratic" example by allowing the guilty party to fall ever deeper into his own "fallacious drift," which in this case, means allowing him to expose the worst defects of Hellenistic music, poetry, political science, and religion. Looking forward to the new utility these arts will gain in the reformed Christian era, the Son reminds Satan that he has explored both their pristine, Hebrew sources and their Greek elaborations, never falling "short / Of knowing what I ought" (*PR* 4.287–88).

Additionally, of course, he possesses that "Light from above, from the fountain of light," the essential or "saving" knowledge of salvation (*PR* 4.289) that utterly trumps "exalted" Greek metaphysics. While their philosophers talk "Much of the Soul," except for Socrates, their "fabling ... and smooth conceits" have only obscured its nature (*PR* 4.295). Socrates' greatest disciple, Plato, adopted the near-Eastern "romance" of the transmigration of souls, while his Stoic descendants sought an impossibly godlike perfection that belongs to the Creator alone. Since their failures led them to further wrong God "under usual names, / Fortune and Fate, as one regardless quite / Of mortal things" (*PR* 4.316–18), whoever "seeks in these / True wisdom, finds her not, or by delusion / Far worse, her false resemblance only meets, / An empty cloud" (*PR* 4.318–21). Sprat, the future Anglican bishop, voiced the same Baconian opinion of the ancient philosophical sects in almost the same words. Where Milton's Son accuses them of giving their followers indigestible "pebbles" or "bones" instead of solid food, Sprat observes that "when the minds of men requir'd *bread*, [they] gave them only a *stone*, and for *fish* a *serpent*." Yet this "sharp" but "empty" learning is only what can be expected from valuing "the subtilty of mens wits, [more] than ... their thickness"; for in thought as in weaving, "those threads, which are of too fine spinning, are found to be more useless, than those which are homespun, and gross."[71] In much the same spirit, the Son accuses the Greeks of offering only feeble "toys" for the "crude or intoxicate," pebbles or "trifles" not "worth a sponge" (*PR* 4.328–30). Divorced from both political and historical reality, the Ancients lack "a spirit and judgement" equal to the Son's humble self-knowledge and practical methods, which is why they failed to produce true science, poetry, or history.

Milton's theory of history explains this failure as follows:

> He who would write worthily of worthy deeds ought to write with no less largeness of spirit and experience of the world than he who did them, so that he can comprehend and judge as an equal even the greatest, and, having comprehended, can narrate them gravely and clearly in plain and temperate language. For I do not insist on ornate language; I ask for a historian, not an orator. Nor would I favor injecting frequent maxims or judgments on historical exploits, lest by breaking the chain of events, the historian invade the province of the political writer; if, in explaining plans and narrating deeds, he follows to the best of his ability not his own invention or conjecture but the truth, he truly fulfills his function. (*CPW* 7:501)

Mirroring Milton's earlier, more famous dictum that the true poet must make his real life a "true Poem" (*CPW* 1:890), these Baconian remarks on history explain why the Son rightly considers himself the best and only "historian" of his own time and place. By rejecting "ornate language" and over-frequent "maxims or judgments on historical exploits," he has become a truly modern exemplar of truth. His "secret history" thus appropriately ends with an easy dismissal of the "Infernal Ghosts, and Hellish Furies," "grisly Specters, which the Fiend had rais'd / To tempt the Son of God with terrors dire" (*PR* 4.422, 430–31), and also to avenge his refusal of the false "pinnacle" of ancient learning.

Afterwards, there remains only the final, most easily met temptation of standing on the top of the Hebrew temple rather than testing God's love by hurling himself from it. In the process, the temple's sacred protective power is dismissed along with other "cobwebs" of the past. Like the astrological "Prophecies" that Satan still credulously believes will spell out the Son's future along with the "Real or Allegoric" nature of his kingdom, oracles only prove the futility of trying to unriddle the future kingdom of God into "either/or" dichotomies. The Son drives this point home with true Royal Society wit on the following morning, when the he tells Satan that he is no "worse than wet" from his spells (*PR* 4.381, 390, 486). For while accurately predicting the sorrow, scorn, "and lastly cruel death" he must suffer, the storm contains false "portents" and terrors (*PR* 4.386–88, 491) that pale in comparison with the triumph to follow. Until his Second Coming, Christ's simultaneously allegoric *and* real kingdom will remain a synthesis of real and partial victory—real for those who understand it, partial, ambiguous or "broken"

[71]   Sprat, *History*, pp. 153, 326.

for the rest. Appropriately presented in carefully pruned classical imagery closely linked to Hebrew truth, the epic's brief conclusion shows that, by practicing the temperance of an "Eremite," the patience of Job, and the legitimate skepticism of Socrates, the Christian hero can "reweave" the true magnanimity of Hercules (*PR* 4.565), the epitome of active, public virtue first tested in solitary, "secret" strife. The Son's victory over Satan thus requires no authorial intervention any more than it requires the fabulous "wing / Of *Hippogrif*" to conduct him to his symbolic triumph "through the Air Sublime" (*PR* 4.541–42). Even this relatively elaborate trope is strictly in keeping with the new ethics of the new heroic poetry. Continuing the strenuous rejection of the idols begun by Tasso and refined by Bacon, Davenant, Hobbes, Dryden, and Sprat, Milton shows that the mythic tamers of earthly idols like Antaeus or the Sphinx all follow the simple underlying pattern of prudent constancy set by the Son of God. After his brief, modest elevation to a simple banquet of "Celestial Food," drink, and song (*PR* 4.588–90, 593–94), the Son appropriately returns to the humble "private house" (*PR* 4.639) where he and the Royal Society's founders humbly began—and where, for all of them, all truly "high" Christian endeavors always begin and end.[72]

---

[72] Sprat recalls the founding members of the Royal Society assembled in a private house "to reason freely upon the works of Nature, to pass Conjectures, and propose Problems, on any Mathematical, or Philosophical Matter, which comes their way. And this is an Omen, on which I will build some hope, that ... they will go on farther" than previous generations (*History*, p. 56). Milton is obviously not alluding to Sprat, but to a common Christian symbol of humble but hopeful discipleship.

Chapter 8

The Classical Republican Tragedy of Defeat in *Samson Agonistes*

The character of priest will give place to that of true patriot

—Sir Robert Molesworth, 1694[1]

The current tendency to interpret *Samson Agonistes* as a tribute to the tragic sufferings of post-Restoration Dissenters conflates distinctly different moral, political, and aesthetic notions of "tragedy."[2] Most Dissenters saw their plight not as a historical turning point signaling the providential return of justice to human affairs, but as an "agon" that did not truly test the truth of good versus evil or enact a sudden "conversion" to righteousness. Instead, it merely proved that human sin and suffering would prevail until the Last Day, although even this truth was not universal but "intelligible only to those who tried to see it as a God sees it." As Gerald Cragg adds, their suffering was also a reminder of the fact that "we dare not forget that in God's sight we always deserve persecution. Neither our character nor our achievements entitle us to stand complacently in God's presence and claim his approbation," and violence against us is merely a symptom of the evil common to all, although "wicked men" and the devil increase it. Persecution should be nevertheless welcomed as a testimony of the saint's eternal faith, righteousness, and communal ability to endure, but not, until the final Apocalypse, as a vehicle of temporal change. What sustained him was precisely the knowledge that "'the happiness of his glorified estate' would infinitely outweigh 'the misery of his

---

[1] Sir Robert Molesworth, *An Account of Denmark* (London, 1694), sig. b3r. As Mark Goldie points out, this manifesto was the ultimate outcome of the Reformed belief in the "priesthood of all believers" advocated throughout the Enlightenment by Whigs who had canonized the politics of Milton, Harrington, and Locke. See Goldie, "The Civil Religion of James Harrington," in Anthony Pagden (ed.), *The Languages of Political Theory in Early-Modern Europe* (Cambridge, 1987), pp. 197–222, cited p. 200.

[2] Differing versions of this argument can be found in Hill, *Milton*, and *The Experience of Defeat: Milton and Some Contemporaries* (London, 1984); Loewenstein, *Representing Revolution*, pp. 269–91, 294–95; and Achinstein, *Literature and Dissent*, pp. 48–58, 138–53. Annabel Patterson sharply critiques Hill for not noticing "the contradiction between his own two theories—the argument for Christian [or Quakerish] resignation and that for encoded political defiance." See "The Good Old Cause," in *Reading between the Lines*, p. 249.

present afflictions.'"[3] The "agon" of Milton's Samson instead builds on an utterly different, neo-Roman view of historical transformation through suffering gleaned from Machiavelli, Cicero, and the great Roman historians. Thus, while Samson's victory over his Philistine oppressors is not transcendentally apocalyptic, it is depicted as a particular historical "deliverance" in if not "from" time.

As Barbara Lewalski observes, Milton, both as a poet and commentator on contemporary events, utterly lacked the apocalyptic "temper." He consistently fails to regard

> specific contemporary events—wars, plagues, fires, apostasies, blasphemies— as signs of impending apocalypse, ... [to] make ... mathematical calculations about dates and times ...[, or] ever look to the Book of Revelation for a model of or a sanction for government by the saints now. Arminian that he was, Milton did not suppose that the saints could be identified with any certainty, and in any case, he always supposed that it is for Christ to install their rule, not for them to preempt it. When reformation seemed to be going well, he imagined that the millennium might be close at hand, ... [but] in what is probably a late addition in *De Doctrina*, [he declared] that Christ "will be slow to come" (*CP* VI.618) ... because he [God] is longsuffering, "not willing that any should perish, but that all should come to repentance" (2 Pet. 3:9).[4]

In all these respects he strikingly differed from "Bible republicans" like Edmund Ludlow or his suffering fellow Dissenters. The Puritan Ludlow was overcome by an overwhelming sense of personal and national sin that made him accept God's "just" verdict on his party, although he escaped to Switzerland where he recorded continued "prodigies" and other signs of God's impending wrath on his enemies. Dissenters such as John Owen and George Fox were more peacefully resigned to their fate since they worshiped a Calvinist deity "who is the same yesterday, to-day, and forever," and who ever since Adam has always made "affliction ... part of the provision ... for his children."[5]

Classical republicans also believed in God's constant laws, but they were mainly empirical laws of political behavior that applied differently in changing historical circumstances. Machiavelli had said that in all "'peoples there are the same desires and the same passions as there always were,'" although as both he and Harrington knew, "'ancient prudence'" and the "'eternal principles of reason'" showed that

---

[3]   Gerald R. Cragg, *Puritanism in the Period of the Great Persecution 1660–1688* (Cambridge, 1957), pp. 71, 72, 86. Cragg paraphrases John Bunyan and John Owen, and cites Thomas Manton in these passages.

[4]   Barbara Lewalski, "Milton and the Millennium," in Cummins (ed.), *Milton and the Ends of Time*, p. 15.

[5]   Cragg, *Puritanism*, p. 82, citing John Owen, *The Person of Christ*, vol. 1, p. 116, in *Works*, ed. W.H. Gould (16 vols., Edinburgh, 1850–53), and George Fox, *Journal*, vol. 2, p. 206. Cragg does not indicate which edition of the *Journal* he cites.

they worked to differing effect on different occasions. According to Worden, that meant that the basic principles of good government are constant even though its forms are not.[6] Yet, for the saints, the exact opposite was true: all human "forms" are illusions in the constant battle against Antichrist, the only warfare against evil government that matters. In contrast, by the age of thirty, Milton had already committed himself to isolating the underlying historical patterns behind each nation state's gain or loss of liberty. Seeking the political rules that the "greatest wisdom" of the "ages has taught to be best," as he informs his closest friend, Charles Diodati (*CPW* 1:327), he was early convinced by Aristotle's *Politics* that societies naturally evolve from a "mild Aristocracy of elective Dukes, and heads of Tribes" to a "Senat at home." In the case of the "ancient Republick of the Jews," the pattern was modified by the added authority of a "Roman Senat from without" (*CPW* 1:574–75), but that circumstance only further confirmed that God's will for his chosen people and his natural laws (which were all that the Romans had) were the same. Both favored representative or republican government in either a full or limited sense.

Yet if God universally wills this freer form of government, it does not descend from above, but ascends from a renewed human awareness of his natural laws. By the same token, liberty naturally declines whenever man allows "unworthy Powers" to subjugate "free Reason" (*PL* 12.91), until finally

> God in Judgment just
> Subjects him from without to violent Lords;
> Who oft as undeservedly enthral
> His outward freedom: Tyranny must be,
> Though to the Tyrant thereby no excuse.
> Yet sometimes Nations will decline so low
> From virtue, *which is reason*, that no wrong,
> But Justice, and some fatal curse annext
> Deprives them of their outward liberty,
> Thir inward lost.
>
> (*PL* 12.92–101, emphasis added)

Other classical republicans such as Edward Sexby, who participated in the failed "Overton Plot" against Cromwell, had concluded that England had brought just such a curse upon herself by submitting to Protectorate tyranny. Turning to Samson and other biblical examples, Sexby also cited Cicero as a classical precedent for the lawfulness of violently ending not just outright tyranny but aspiring tyrants. His *Killing Noe Murder* (1656) nevertheless avoids giving the Ciceronian term *"pater patriae"* to tyrant-killers since the term had been recently bestowed on

---

[6]   Worden, "Classical Republicanism," p. 194. Worden cites Machiavelli, *Discourses*, 1, chapter 39, and Harrington, *The Political Works of James Harrington*, ed. G.A. Pocock (Cambridge, 1977), p. 161.

Cromwell; instead, like Milton in *Samson Agonistes*, he considers true heroes not as fathers but as "deliverers" of their country.[7] Milton's decision to use Samson as the subject of his tragedy doubly avoids making him a father of his country, for his biblical hero is not only literally childless but unable fully to "deliver" the nation to which he would give birth. Samson's initially despairing situation thus responds directly to the defeated republicans' concerns, especially since he and his tribe are portrayed as having inflicted a biblical "curse" upon themselves by condoning Philistine tyranny. Yet the Hebrews soon discover that this curse is neither eternal, irreparable, nor exclusively supernatural in origin, although it seems all those things once they have willingly forfeited their outward with their inward liberty.

The Danites' darkened view of themselves has led many recent readers to question whether Samson and his desperate friends are truly heroic, or (in the terms of the standard Puritan reading) "regenerated" saints.[8] Yet this perfectly reasonable perplexity begs the larger question of whether Milton's hero ever represented a suffering saint or Dissenter, and, if he did, why he chose to celebrate his recovery in a form despised by nearly every type of Puritan. Published two years after *Samson Agonistes*, the "liberal" Richard Baxter's *Christian Directory* lists fifteen separate objections to plays of all sorts, including closet dramas. Tragedy is particularly objectionable because it incites sympathy for the sinful, not the instant hatred or disgust we should feel at the first appearance of vice.[9] Due either to his republicanism or to his obvious debts to pagan philosophers and tragedians, Milton never made Baxter's list of acceptable poets, even though Puritans generally accepted Samson as a hero of faith.[10] Milton actually seems to have invited this kind of reaction by writing a tragic preface announcing his ambition to join Dionysius the elder, Seneca, Gregory Nazianzen, and the three Greek "Tragic Poets unequall'd yet by any"—"*Aeschylus, Sophocles,* and *Euripides*" (Hughes 549, 550). Claiming that ancient "tragedy ... hath been ever held the gravest, moralest, and most profitable of all other Poems" (Hughes 549), his defense of the form also builds on his earlier refutation of a favorite Puritan proof text against the classics: St. Jerome's dream that he was punished by an angel for reading pagan literature (*CPW* 2:510).[11] Milton voices objections against the related censures of Cyprian and Lactantius in his *Commonplace Book*, which faults them for promoting a view "absurd beyond measure," the idea that "dramatic art" promotes "moral error"; for "what in all philosophy is more important or more sacred or more exalted than a tragedy rightly

---

[7]   Ng, *Literature and the Politics*, pp. 110–12.

[8]   See Joseph A. Wittreich, *Interpreting "Samson Agonistes"* (Princeton, 1986). Wittreich's publication has incited a firestorm of controversy too extensive to cite here.

[9]   Baxter, *Christian Directory* (1673), pp. 877–78. See also Sasek, *Literary Temper*, pp. 95–98, 101–102.

[10]   Wittreich also shows there were some important exceptions to this rule, and that the Samson story was adapted to vastly different polemical purposes throughout the period; see *Shifting Contexts: Reinterpreting Samson Agonistes* (Pittsburgh, 2002).

[11]   William Prynne approvingly cites Jerome's dream in *Histriomastix*, pp. 925–26.

produced, what more useful for seeing at a single view the events and changes of human life?" (*CPW* 1:490, 491).

The preface to *Samson Agonistes* continues this line of thought by adopting the "non-purgative" view of tragic catharsis favored by Hobbes and Dennis: fear and pity are not cast out, but mixed with positive emotions that overcome our natural response to sudden catastrophe. For Dennis, these feelings bring true emotional release, not just relief *or* guilt at escaping suffering. Reason alone would make "us miserable by setting our impotence or our guilt before us," but passionate identification with the victim's plight empathetically transports us beyond the "ordinary state of men."[12] Milton's view is similar if not identical: catharsis should "temper and reduce" the passions "with a kind of delight, stirr'd up by reading or seeing those passions well imitated," and also by naturally setting "sour against sour, salt to remove salt humors" (Hughes 549). Milton's formal commitment to the tragic mode is equally obvious: *Samson Agonistes* includes six choral odes cast in "*Monostrophic*, or rather *Apolelymenon*" stanzas (Hughes 550). Such "high flourishes" and "affecting strains" were often excised by the godly, even from "sacred dramas" like the Song of Solomon, since "such eloquence but feedeth the outward ear."[13]

Nevertheless, the republican "experience of defeat" cannot be rigidly separated from the Puritan experience of suffering. Samson-like exile, imprisonment, public humiliation, and feelings of divine desertion united a broad spectrum of defeated republicans ranging from Ludlow to Algernon Sidney and Sir Henry Vane, to name but a few. Yet, if their experiences were similar, their responses were often very different. Vane was imprisoned for two years before his execution in 1662 for refusing to submit to the restored king. During his imprisonment, like Ludlow, he waited upon God either to restore the saints to power or to lead them to martyrdom. Both contributed to the great "books of suffering" compiled by Dissenters, and both Milton's tragedy and his *Readie and Easie Way* contain some obvious parallels with those books. The "Jeremiad" at the end of the second edition of *The Readie and Easie Way* foreshadows the anguished protests of Samson's chorus and the hero himself "at the destruction of the cause … 'making vain … the blood of so many thousand valiant Englishmen, who left us in this libertie, bought with their lives.'" As Jonathan Scott observes, for Milton, God's "Israelites" have again proved themselves a "worthless … inconstant, irrational and image-doting rabble" incapable of learning the lesson inscribed in his *History of Britain*: that "*Liberty hath a sharp and double edge*, fit only to be handled by just and virtuous men." Scott similarly finds Sidney Miltonically bewailing his betrayal by a people who "could never be contented 'till we return'd againe into Egypt, the house of our bondage," an exact paraphrase of *The Readie and Easie Way*'s conclusion (*CPW* 7:463). Yet, as he adds, the republicans did not simply blame "the people." Their

---

[12]   John Dennis, *The Usefulness of the Stage*, in Henry Hitch Adams and Baxter Hathaway (eds.), *Dramatic Essays of the Neoclassic Age* (New York, 1947), p. 203.

[13]   T.S., *The Book of the Song of Solomon in Meeter* (1697), fol. A3.

essentially secular view of history dictated that the national tragedy would follow its classic script to the end: *hubris* or overweening ambition must be followed by *nemesis* or retribution before the "fatal curse annext" to the nation could be removed.[14]

Milton's and Sidney's perspective differs from the godly republicans in another especially telling respect: they strenuously avoided the martyr-complex cultivated by Vane, Ludlow, and the majority of the radical Dissenters. Although Sidney finally did suffer a martyr's death, he never sought it but strove to keep republicanism alive by covert means. Worden regards his synthesis of Protestant providentialism and neo-Roman republicanism to be the closest equivalent to Milton's outlook, especially since Sidney actually echoes Milton more than any other republican. He similarly saw "'liberty' as the natural ally of 'discipline,' of 'frugality,' 'industry,' 'temperance,' 'sobriety,' 'honesty [*sic*] poverty,'" and similarly regarded "'tyranny' as the natural ally of 'licence,'... 'luxury' ... [and] 'idolatry.'" Of course, republicans of this type clearly feared that a "'besotted and degenerate baseness of spirit'" would make their countrymen unfit "for that liberty which they cri'd out and bellow'd for'" (*CPW* 3.344, 488, 581; Sidney, "Court Maxims," 13, 178, 180, 198). Yet these concerns were remote from Ludlow's careful recording of "continued prodigies" in order to stave off the Puritan fear that he had secretly or unwittingly committed Achan's "trespass in the accursed thing" (Joshua 7:1, 20).[15]

Secular seventeenth-century republicanism nevertheless remains difficult to define because it was "a language, not a programme," a broadly ethical rather than a narrowly constitutional approach to politics loosely based on Aristotle's and Cicero's views of balanced government. Yet all classical republicans supported a liberal version of social contract theory where "all power derived originally from the people and could be resumed by the people," even though the ethical component in their thought was equally prominent. They were convinced that "popular sovereignty answers to reason," while the hereditary principle answers only to passion and will, but again, largely because they found hereditary privilege morally corrupting. As Worden observes, this creed was in its own way elitist, most obviously in denouncing a "deluded people" for returning to the irrational "idol" of hereditary monarchy. Yet it was also far removed from the pessimistic theology and politics of Calvinists like Ludlow, who considered all government a necessary consequence of the Fall. "True" classical republicans instead tended to

---

[14] Jonathan Scott, "English Republican Imagination," pp. 51, 53, 49. Scott does not discuss *Samson Agonistes*, although his remarks imply the connection.

[15] Blair Worden, "Milton, *Samson Agonistes*, and the Restoration," in Maclean (ed.), *Culture and Society*, pp. 111–36; see pp. 113–14, 125, 117. Worden cites "Court Maxims" from Algernon Sidney's *Discourses concerning Government*, ed. Thomas G. West (Indianapolis, 1990), pp. 164–65, 184, 254, 350, and Edmund Ludlow, *A Voyce from the Watchtower*, in *A Voyce from the Watch Tower, Part 5: 1660–1662*, ed. Blair Worden (London, 1978), p. 294.

be religious rationalists strongly attracted to the free will ethics of Arminianism or Socinianism. "Cheerful anti-clericalists" like Milton and Harrington eagerly embraced the anti-authoritarian implications of this outlook while Puritans like Ludlow were appalled by their rationalist tendency to read "the Bible ... [as] a political manual ... [or] history book," a tendency equally notable in Thomas Chaloner, Henry Marten, and Henry Neville. All were "as far from being a puritan as the east from the west"—as Aubrey remarked of Chaloner—but most remained committed to the Protestant providentialism expressed in *Samson Agonistes* and *The Readie and Easie Way*.[16]

"Elect above the Rest": Saints, Martyrs, and Samson

While there are many reasons to believe that Milton strongly sympathized with his hero, his Arminianism effectively prevented him from identifying himself with God's "Elect," since, as Lewalski remarks above, he "did not suppose the saints could be identified with any certainty." Like Sidney, Milton did not even remotely desire the special "election" of martyrdom, which he skillfully avoided.[17] Wrongly but briefly imprisoned, he lived to enjoy a successful third marriage, enormous literary fame, and an unimpaired international reputation among the lovers of liberty. Aubrey shows that the plight of the "much visited" Milton was so remote from that of the neglected Samson that he actually desired less company than he received (Hughes 1023). Although Samson similarly seeks solitude, he retreats from the visitations of his bad conscience and his despairing allies, not from the admirers who slowed Milton's work. Samson does of course suffer a form of martyrdom, but it comes unsought and unexpected, the conclusion of his long political struggle with the Philistines. Hence the "trial" or "agon" of this public freedom fighter is actually remote from the private struggles of Nonconformists, who "redeemed" their persecution by recording it in vivid autobiographical detail to justify themselves and their brethren.[18] There is even some question as to whether Samson's very different trial makes him a spiritual martyr at all. He is certainly not a false martyr like the misnamed "Charles Martyr" or a distracting "idol" like the post-apostolic martyrs Milton dismisses in *Of Prelatical Episcopacy*, who were ironically "worshipped" in ways not unlike the suffering post-Restoration saints. Milton explains that the faithful liked to dote on each detail of the martyr's life and suffering: "O happy this house that harbour'd him, and that cold stone whereon he rested, this Village wherein he wrought such a miracle, and that pavement

---

[16]   Worden, "Classical Republicanism," p. 195.

[17]   Mary Ann Radzinowicz traces these sympathies in "*Samson Agonistes* and Milton the Politician in Defeat,"*PQ* 44 (1965): 454–71.

[18]   On the "great books of suffering" composed by dissenting men and women, see Elizabeth Sauer, "The Experience of Defeat: Milton and Some Female Contemporaries," in Martin (ed.), *Milton and Gender*, pp. 133–52.

bedew'd with the warme effusion of his last blood, that sprouted up into eternall Roses to crowne his Martyrdome." He feels that "by this meanes" Christians "lost their time, and truanted in the fundamentall grounds of saving knowledge" (*CPW* 1:642). Significantly, the classical monument that Manoa plans for his son Samson will avoid this mindless idolatry by providing a "site" for the dissemination of "saving knowledge" about ecclesiastical, domestic, and civil liberty, the threefold cause for which both Milton and his hero fight (*CPW* 4.1:624).

Milton's *Eikonoklastes* establishes another test of true martyrdom directly relevant to Milton's tragedy: "to die for *the testimony of his own conscience*" is not "anough to make" anyone a martyr, for in that case the most deluded heretics "dying for direct blasphemie" could "boast a Martyrdom." Moreover, since "Law in a Free Nation hath bin ever public reason, ... privat reason ... to us is no Law" to be honored or obeyed (*CPW* 3:576, 360). Neither suffering nor civil disobedience in themselves makes anyone a martyr, as Dissenters believed, for, if it did, we may as well imagine that "*Sampson* had bin mov'd *to the putting out his eyes, that the Philistims* [*sic*] *might abuse him*" as a "testimony" to God's glory (*CPW* 3:461). Later, Milton is even uncertain whether the biblical Samson was spiritually "elected" to his role as deliverer: his *Defence of the People of England* calls Samson a champion of liberty prompted to make "war single-handed on his masters" and "tyrants over his country" *either* "by God or by his own valor ... even though most of her citizens did not balk at slavery" (*CPW* 4.1:402). Milton does, however, believe in special "election," as the God of *Paradise Lost* himself announces: he dispenses sufficient grace to all, but he has chosen some "of peculiar grace / Elect above the rest" to be his champions (*PL* 3.183–84). These lines refer to the heroes of faith described in Hebrews (11:17–32), which explain the persistence of the faithful in even the darkest and most degenerate ages. According to the Anglican Robert Sanderson, to insure that "the whole species of so noble a creature might not perish," God elected "a certain number of particular persons ... passing by the rest."[19] This concept is essentially alien to Calvinism, which instead held that God arbitrarily chose all his Elect from all eternity, who were thus equally enrolled in God's "Book of Life," although some might have special "callings" or destinies marked out for them.[20] Arminians, on the other hand, needed to explain why God's renewal of man's "lapsed powers" after the Fall sometimes fails to "call" more than a bare minority (such as Noah and his family) to the true faith (*PL* 3.175–76, 185–86). For Milton, the answer is of course the "fatal curse annext" to some dark ages, while the solution to the problem is the restorative work of judges like Samson, although again, this work is largely educative, not

---

[19]   Robert Sanderson, *Pax Ecclesiae*, in *The Works of Robert Sanderson*, ed. William Jacobson (6 vols., Oxford, 1854), vol. 5, pp. 267, 268.

[20]   As Lewalski shows, those "Elect above the rest" cannot be identified with "the absolute elect of the orthodox," as Paul Sellin (and more recently Stephen Fallon) erroneously maintain, since orthodox Calvinism denies both universal grace and gradations of grace or election; see "Milton and *De Doctrina*," pp. 220–21.

sacrificially or sacramentally "redemptive" in the sense condemned in *Of Prelatical Episcopacy*. Even this work has a strong voluntary component, since at no point in the drama do we feel that Samson is "predestined" to defeat the Philistines; at each stage of his agon he must consciously *choose* to continue the fight.

Thus, while God's prophets and judges may be specially chosen, their end is not. Completing a liberation project that Milton consistently refuses to separate into secular and spiritual parts demands their full and unselfish cooperation with God's "leadings" and warnings, which are universally given to all sinners (*PL* 3.185–97). As in *Eikonklastes* and Milton's first *Defence*, this guidance is ambiguous since suffering alone cannot confirm divine approval or disapproval. God waits on man's free response to his will, which is itself intended to promote freedom. Heeding apparently obvious signs of abandonment or "election" is thus equally dangerous since it tempts the afflicted with self-pity or lowered self-expectation and the victorious with pride. Milton appropriately reiterates these convictions in his sonnets on his blindness. In Sonnet 19, "Patience" alone prevents the insidious "murmur" (9) that afflictions come from God to punish revealed or unknown sins. By the time he pens Sonnet 22, he is actually able to regard the loss of sight as a positive reminder of the worthy sacrifices to be made in a just cause, an attitude that his Samson must also learn to adopt. In response to Cyriack Skinner's actual or imagined question, "What supports me, dost thou ask," Milton answers that his still "spotless" or unblemished eyes reflect his inner clarity, that is, his conscientious assurance that "heav'n's hand or will" approves his efforts "in liberty's defense, my noble task, / Of which all Europe talks from side to side" (1–2, 7, 9, 11–12). Samson initially takes the despairing view of his blindness that tempts Milton in Sonnet 19 before coming to much the same conclusion arrived at in Sonnet 22: the loss of his eyes is less a sign of divine rejection than a potential source of strength. Hence God's "Promise ... that I / Should *Israel* from *Philistinian* yoke deliver" (*SA* 38–39) has not yet been foreclosed by a fateful deity, because only his "own default," dereliction or doubt prevents its fulfillment (45). Like any other human, he can thus take the promise into his own hands, even if his nation continues loving "Bondage with ease [more] than strenuous liberty" (271). Asking the ultimate classical republican question—"Whom have I to complain of but myself"? (46)—he begins to understand that, like his countrymen, he has "served" the Philistines more than he realized.

Passages like these clearly make Samson a composite example not just of Milton's mistakes and those of his allies but of England's common "default," the characteristic English lapse traced throughout Milton's contemporaneous *History of Britain*. Nor is there much doubt that Milton felt complicit in his country's "curse" of slavishness. He, too, had served many false "masters": first Parliament (*CPW* 5:443, 449), then Cromwell, and finally General Monck who, rather than fulfilling Milton's hopes by serving as an interim king, engineered the Stuart restoration (*CPW* 7:465). Hence, if Milton's theology prevented him from considering himself an "Elect" Nazirite "separate to God" (*SA* 31), his ongoing aspirations for his "elect" nation and his careful preparation for some great role in national affairs or literature would have prompted this final literary attempt to reawaken England to the ongoing hope and uplifting "yoke" of liberty. No angel had presided over his birth, although he had indeed been semi-Nazaritically set apart "by the ceaselesse diligence and care" of his father. Afterwards, "an inward prompting ... grew daily upon" him that he might "by labour and intent study ... joyn'd with the strong propensity of nature," significantly contribute "to Gods glory by the honour and instruction of my country" (*CPW* 1:808, 810). Later, when the nation balked at further reform, he began to realize that, like Samson, the "ignominy" directed against him was really directed against what he earlier called his "Evangelick doctrine." All these circumstances conspired to assign him a partly innate, partly acquired or self-chosen role to play in a nation where, much like his hero, he was not acting privately as "mine own person." Toward the end of his life he apparently still saw himself as he did at first: as someone "incorporate into that truth whereof I was perswaded, and whereof I had declar'd openly to be a partaker. Whereupon I thought it my duty, if not to my selfe, yet to the religious cause I had in hand, not to leave on my garment the least spot, or blemish in good name so long as God should give me to say that which might wipe it off. Lest those disgraces which I ought to suffer, ... *through my default*" reflected badly on his reformist cause (*Apology*, *CPW* 1:871, emphasis added).

A little later in the *Apology* cited above, Milton explains how he derived his "Nazaritic" vow of chastity both from the biblical doctrine "that *the body is for the Lord and the Lord for the body*" (*CPW* 1:892) and from humanistic admonitions against "wantonnesse and loose living." Taught by the "care ... ever had of me, with my earliest capacity not to be negligently train'd in the precepts of Christian Religion" and by the "lofty Fables and Romances" produced by the "Laureat fraternity of Poets" and philosophers (chiefly the "divine volumes of *Plato*, and his equall *Xenophon*"), he had imbibed only from the "charming cup [which] is only vertue" (*CPW* 1:891, 892). Although Samson's own vow concerns abstinence from wine, not women, as often suspected, these details help to make *Samson Agonistes* Milton's most autobiographical poem. Through three fundamental revisions to the biblical story, it especially recalls the poet's threefold dedication to religious, domestic, and political liberty, the triad listed in his *Second Defence*.[21] In order to justify domestic liberty in his drama, he makes Dalila Samson's wife, not his concubine; to justify true religion, he deletes Samson's prayer for personal vengeance; to justify political liberty, he ascribes priestly, military, and civic corruption to Samson's enemies, the "imperial" rulers of Philistia who exhibit late Roman signs of decadence.

---

21   See Northrop Frye, "Agon and Logos: Revolution and Revelation," in Balachandra Rajan (ed.), *The Prison and the Pinnacle* (London, 1973), pp. 135–73, especially p. 154; and my essay on "The Phoenix and the Crocodile: Milton's Natural Law Debate with Hobbes Retried in the Tragic Forum of *Samson Agonistes*," in Claude Summers and Ted Pebworth (eds.), *The English Civil Wars in the Literary Imagination* (Columbia, MO, 1999), pp. 242–70.

Yet Milton's most important political innovation is to divide the Philistines into two distinct groups. He does this by cleverly suggesting that Dagon's temple is a relatively small near-Eastern "theater" supported by two main pillars broad enough to include its elite but not the throngs who sit outside "on banks and scaffolds under Sky" (*SA* 1605–10, 1651–56). This addition also makes the outcome of Samson's "trial" more providentially and naturalistically plausible, since any greatly "roused" giant might summon enough adrenalin to destroy such a temple. Subliminally, this single-handed feat also links Samson's triumph to Milton's poetic power. While he recognized that the poet's "Truth is properly no more then Contemplation; and her utmost efficiency is but teaching," not enacting "Justice," "in her very essence" the rousing motions inspired by his portrayal of truth and especially Justice are "all strength and activity; and hath a Sword put into her hand, to use against all violence and oppression on earth. Shee it is most truely, who accepts no Person, and exempts none from the severity of her stroke. Shee never suffers injury to prevaile, but when falshood first prevailes over Truth; and that also is a kind of Justice don on them who are so deluded" as to justify tyranny (*CPW* 3:584). This passage in *Eikonoklastes* applies especially to *Samson Agonistes* since it clearly links human liberation to the power of vividly *portraying* Justice. By symbolically putting that "sword" in his reader's hands, Milton hopes to inspire their resistance to all the forces that promote servility—idols, priests, and hereditary monarchs—a resistance that Samson can model and teach, but not force on his people. He may wreck Dagon's temple and destroy the Philistine autocracy, yet as most critics now agree, that is all: there is nothing of millennial renewal in Milton's final poem.[22] Despite the apocalyptic overtones of Samson's cataclysmic act, the tragic ending imagines only a potential future for the "Hebrews." In this future "Israel might recognize Samson's act as providing a political *occasione* in Machiavelli's sense," as Lewalksi says, but again it might not—and did not. For either Israel or England, seizing the "sword of Justice" and establishing a truly new order cannot proceed without first acknowledging and correcting the flaws of the people and their misguided or corrupt leaders, who (like Milton) must accept full responsibility.[23] Since Samson's name literally means "here a second time," Milton's review of his people's deeply flawed past ideally models the necessary acknowledgment of failure than may eventually lead this second Israel to seize a new *occasione*.

A synthetic religio-political reading such as the one sketched above has two major advantages: (1) it closes the apparent gulf between Samson's activism and the apparent quietism of the Son of and *Paradise Regained*; and, (2) unlike exclusively religious readings, it does not obscure the vast political differences separating the appearance of these final poems from the first publication of *Paradise Lost*. As Andrew Milner points out, the later poems were issued at time when the "endemic

---

[22]   This reading has become relatively standard in the wake of Mary Ann Radzinowicz's *Toward Samson Agonistes: The Growth of Milton's Mind* (Princeton, 1978).

[23]   Lewalski, "Milton and the Millennium," p. 26.

instability of the restored monarchy became increasingly discernible" and classical republicans increasingly turned from quietism to activism. Their situations thus resembled those encountered by both Milton's Samson and his Son. The latter well understands the lack of opportunity in imperial Rome, and cautiously waits for the right conditions for action to present themselves. Samson represents the more hopeful side of his caution, but the contrast fails to justify identifying the Son with the "tone of patient stoicism which informed the Quaker–quietist response to the Restoration." His rejection of the kingdoms of the world is in fact conditional, not absolute, "a tactic rather than a strategy, an expedient rather than a principle," as it was with the followers of Fox who "abandon[ed] politics altogether." From this perspective, Milton's Son is more concerned with the tactical appropriateness than with the negative spiritual consequences of political action. As a result, he never unilaterally rejects activism any more than he entirely rejects the pursuit of learning. Samson's initial despair of acting is similarly tactical, not spiritual: he simply believes that his blindness precludes him from making any future contribution to defeating the Philistines. For far from believing with Robert Bolton and his disciple Richard Baxter that "Grace once truly rooted in the heart can never be removed" from God's Elect, he initially believes that God has deserted him and his people—at least for the time. Samson's new "acquist / Of true experience" (1755–56) is thus at one with the return of his martial vigor and political faith, which include the threefold force of renewed personal or domestic, spiritual, and civil liberty.[24]

Tragic Retribution, Republican Renewal, and Autobiographical Reflection

Understanding the *hubris/nemesis* complex touched on by Scott above requires close attention to both the classical and Judeo-Christian meaning of retribution and judgeship, for in the seventeenth century these terms possessed far broader and less negative meanings than at present. Seventeenth-century humanists freely synthesized the Greco-Roman and Judeo-Christian senses of "retribution" since they regarded both biblical judges and classical avengers as *deliverers.* The word "*nemesis*" could also refer to a positive "deliverance" from *hubris* or overweening pride, which would otherwise prevent God's agents from fulfilling their proper destiny. Only if they failed to maintain this aspect of their "covenant" did *nemesis* become identical with divine vengeance, yet even then, it was not synonymous with "revenge." Like retribution, it was rather a two-edged sword that at once punished and freed the people from their enemies, which was not an act of vengeance but of justice. Milton's Cambridge manuscript clearly shows that he personally understood "deliverance" as a self-sacrificial "labor" not unlike childbirth, which at once corrects human error or "barrenness" and pays tribute

---

[24]   Andrew Milner, *John Milton and the English Revolution: A Study in the Sociology of Literature* (London, 1981), pp. 182, 174; Bolton, *Some General Directions*, p. 22.

to divine mercies. In the Judeo-Christian tradition, tribute is also rendered to God when man's *hubris* incites the deity to intervene in history, which may require a violent but no less merciful "deliverance." God punishes those he loves, both to purge and to heal their sins. This punishment/liberation is also the root meaning of the retribution rendered by the biblical judges, who at once scourge the faithless and redeem the community from bondage.[25] These combined Judeo-Christian as well as classical assumptions go straight to the heart of the current controversy over *Samson Agonistes*, since most "anti-regenerationists" conceive of judgment as the Hebraic antithesis to Christian charity or love. Yet reading any tragedy—classical or Miltonic—in terms of these simple antitheses inevitably deprives it of the sense of paradox on which the entire conception of justice turns. For instance, Euripides' *Medea* forces its audience to "choose" between a murderous, vindictive mother who is also a deeply wronged wife, and a heartless, womanizing husband who deserves most of the torment he receives. Since neither antithesis is acceptable, the audience must acknowledge the injustices inherent in both "patriarchal" bondage and feminine wrath, which can only end in destructive retribution. Similar paradoxes apply in *Samson Agonistes*, where the injustice inherent in the enslavement of neighbors makes the retribution inflicted on Philistia's rulers a counterpart of Israelite liberation.

Yet, as Milton's consideration of martyrdom shows, neither destruction, "divine" vengeance, nor personal suffering is automatically redeemed in the so-called service of God. Samson must therefore prove that he is not a "private" individual "but a person rais'd / With strength sufficient and command from Heav'n / To free my Country," someone entitled to wage war on behalf of his leaderless nation. This mission is justified even if the "servile minds" of his countrymen reject "Me their Deliverer" (*SA* 1211–14), because, in classical republican thought, slavery is by definition an unnatural and degenerate condition. This line of thought is the opposite of either ancient or contemporary concepts of "just" tribal warfare, where the concept of vengeance is amorphous and unlimited. Ending or at least "judging" degeneracy is by comparison the much more limited and proper function of *nemesis*, which in Greek means a literal "dealing out" of justice to release a naturally free people from bondage both to their enemies and themselves. In Milton's republican tragedy, this bondage is as clearly personal as it is national, which is why Samson can end it only by rejecting his own, his father's, and Dalila's tribal pride. The *hubris* of Manoa and his fellow Danites is clearly shown as they cringe at their hero's fallen state, reify his former glory, and blame all of his crimes on his Philistine wife. Only by inverting this "blame game" and understanding the real sources of his own and his nation's "default" can Samson justly counter Harapha's accusation that he is a mere robber, raider, or self-appointed martyr-avenger of the kind condemned in *Eikonoklastes* (*CPW* 3:574 n. 17). Nevertheless, his creative "deliverance" would remain incomplete without

[25] See Barbara Lewalski, "*Samson Agonistes* and the 'Tragedy' of the Apocalypse," *PMLA* 85 (1970): pp. 1050–62.

the external destruction of Dagon's temple, which represents tribal laws, rites, and "idols," Hebrew as well as Philistine. Only by turning to a higher and more universal understanding of God's natural laws can Samson understand the true nature of his election and the true causes of his failure. His "sudden apprehension" of both reinvigorates his dedication to the historical work needed to redeem the promise that God first entrusted to the Jews but actually gives to all mankind.

Like the republicans of Milton's era, Samson must begin by questioning where he went wrong: in mistaking the divine will, the people's will, his own destiny, or (as he soon discovers) all three. He naturally begins at the most immediate and personal level, asking why he failed even though his breeding was "prescrib'd / As of a person separate to God, / Design'd for great exploits," or "some great act / Or benefit ... to *Abraham's* race?" (*SA* 28–31). This personal self-examination ultimately leads to a far more universal and synthetic sense of historical obligation and election, so that the Jews begin to signify the "divine right" of liberty itself. More immediately, however, it leads to a confession of personal *hubris*. Samson acknowledges that his services to his people made him feel entitled to Dalila's "charming cup," which he at first "demonizes" as contaminating in itself. Despising himself as thus unclean and unfit to "serve / My Nation, and the work from Heav'n impos'd" (564–65), he wonders why he could so easily abstain from wine ("the grape / Whose heads that turbulent liquor fills with fumes"), but not from "another object more enticing," Philistine women (551–52, 559). Ironically, Milton—who was similarly abstemious but shared Samson's weakness for attractive women— might have asked himself the same question. Figuratively speaking, however, both the poet and his hero question why Samson was bound to serve an "effeminate" nation. In the language of classical republicanism, *effeminacy* stands for both masculine immaturity and a nation's susceptibility "to love Bondage ... with ease [more] than strenuous liberty" (270–71).[26] From this perspective, Dalila's charms begin to seem less literally entrapping than the more mysterious failure of will that similarly doomed the "Good Old Cause," the temptation to settle for superficially attractive and easy detours rather than the more permanent solutions urged in Milton's *Readie and Easie Way*. The Danite chorus obliquely gesture toward this temptation when they question which is worse, "Thy Bondage or lost Sight, / Prison within Prison / Inseparably dark," 152–54). Samson's reply firmly links his "effeminate" imprisonment by Dalila to a much broader personal and national blindness, a blindness that is also bondage. As in Sonnet 19 (3–5), the sightless victim at first feels that he has been unjustly left with "that one Talent which is death to hide, / Lodg'd with me useless, though my Soul more bent / To serve therewith my Maker." In much the same terms, Samson asks why his "high gift of strength" was "lodg'd" in a visual source so "easily bereft me" (*SA* 47–48), and so soon gone for good.

---

    26   See Gina Hauskneckt, "The Gender of Civic Virtue," in Martin (ed.), *Milton and Gender*, pp. 19–33; and Skinner, *Liberty before Liberalism*.

Milton addressed sonnets to Cromwell and Vane in the same year that "When I consider how my light is spent" was probably composed (1652), which together reveal the same deep anxieties about the state of national blindness that later erupt in *The Readie and Easie Way* (1660) and again in *Samson Agonistes* (1671). Stressing the need for republican restraint amidst the rising tide of clerical "enthusiasm" for propagating Puritan religion, Milton urges both politicians "to know / Both spiritual power and civil, what each means, / What severs each" (Sonnet 17, 9–11). Only by this means may they keep the reins of government in the "firm hand" he can no longer "see" or actively support. At the same time, an anonymous 1652 inscription in Milton's *Eikonoklastes* reflects the widespread sentiment that God's judgment had come down on the poet who is now blindly "led up and downe," and, according to popular opinion, that "curse" already applied to his cause.[27] Sonnet 22 shows that he believed no such thing, but like Samson he could not ignore the fact that his condition incited the fierce ridicule of "Idolists, and Atheists" (*SA* 453) both at home and abroad: the worshipers of the "icon" of monarchy and the disbelievers in God's providential law of freedom. Their apparent triumph over him no doubt fueled Milton's deep, Samson-like sense of "impotence," both personal and political. No doubt recalling those days, he has his hero reflect on how "Deceivable, in most things as a child / Helpless, ... easily contemn'd, and scorn'd, / And last neglected" he has become (942–44). This is perhaps the drama's most autobiographical passage, since it seems to revisit the real domestic situation Milton suffered when his children conspired against their blind father. These and other commonalities explain the strongly personal sense of humiliation and despair readers have always found in this tragedy, yet, like his protagonist, Milton never ceased to question "To what can I be useful, wherein serve / My Nation, and the work from Heav'n imposed." Their answers were also virtually identical: both refused to "sit idle on the household hearth, / A burdenous drone; to visitants a gaze, / Or pitied object" consigned "To a contemptible old age obscure" (564–68, 572).

As a lesser official in Cromwell's government, Milton was never really very close to the seat of power, and the legends of the Lord Protector visiting him after he lost his sight are late and apocryphal.[28] Nevertheless, the simultaneous onset of his blindness, the loss of his first wife and only son, and the waning of republican hopes all seem reflected in this final work, whose childless national "son's" defeat seems to spell his country's downfall. Milton's exhortation/encomium to Cromwell's restraint in the *Second Defence* and in Sonnet 16 indicates that he used all his persuasive power in attempting to avert this downfall, yet (as Austin Woolrych notes) his attempts "probably did more than anything else to alienate

---

[27]   This anonymous inscription is dated 11 July 1652 according to Gordon Campbell, *Milton Chronology*, p. 139; similar understandings of his "curse" appear soon after (see pp. 144–45) and follow Milton to his grave. They strengthen the traditional date for Sonnet 19 preferred by Hughes (1652), but 1651 and 1655 are also possible.

[28]   See Worden, *Roundhead*, pp. 237–38.

him from the Protectorate." The final drafts of Milton's *History of Britain* project his view of these dark years and the subsequent Restoration on to the early Britons, who were similarly brought down by "false fears and effete traditionalism" combined with "pusillanimity, corruption[,] ... lack of vision," and a consistent failure "to rise to their great opportunity."[29] Yet Milton's tragedy far transcends "mere" autobiography. More importantly, it reminds his political sympathizers of their common plight, in part by making a deep mystery of what the Bible regards as a simple fact. In the Book of Judges, Samson simply loses his miraculous strength by telling Delilah that its source lies in his unshorn hair, but in *Samson Agonistes* his shorn locks become a sign of a deeper inability to retain the mysterious "seal" of his covenant with God. This failure remains connected to Dalila through the effeminacy/slavery complex noted above, which in turn makes her less the siren of popular legend than the hidden voice of Philistine power. Like the apple in *Paradise Lost*, Samson's hair in turn becomes an arbitrary marker of obedience to something much higher than a vow: it seals his pledge of unconditional love, trust, gratitude, and respect for God and his gifts, particularly liberty. When spurned or unheeded, these gifts are not simply destroyed, but turn into a *nemesis* or curse calling for retribution/restoration. Samson's strength then becomes not only his "bane, / ... the source of all my miseries" (*SA* 63–64) but also an emblem of his nation's miserable slavery. Yet, as his hair grows back, the same "*nemesis*" becomes the sign and source of their joint recovery.

The "false fears and effete traditionalism" of the chorus initially prevent them from understanding this complex, so they strictly interpret Samson's violation of his Nazarite vow as the sole cause of his double curse, blindness and captivity. In their view, violating the taboo on his hair has doomed him to the virtual "castration" symbolized by his sightlessness and military impotence. These assumptions reveal their failure to grasp the real nature of his "high office," which they narrowly conceive as a series of martial conquests that God perversely fails to honor after he has "with gifts and graces eminently adorn'd" and "solemnly elected" him like his other judges "To some great work, thy glory, / And people's safety, which in part they effect." Once "thus dignifi'd," his officers all too often find that "amidst thir height of noon" (*SA* 678–83), God

> Changest thy count'nance and thy hand, with no regard
> Of highest favors past
> From thee on them, or them to thee of service.
>   Nor only dost degrade them, or remit
> To life obscur'd, which were a fair dismission,
> But throw'st them lower than thou didst exalt them high,
> Unseemly falls in human eye,
> Too grievous for the trespass or omission,
> Oft leav'st them to the hostile sword

---

[29]   Austin Woolrych, "Date of the Digression," pp. 241, 230.

Of Heathen and profane, thir carcases
To dogs and fowls a prey, or else captiv'd:
Or to the th' unjust tribunals, under change of times,
And condemnation of the in'grateful multitude.
If these they scape, perhaps in poverty
With sickness and disease thou bow'st them down,
Painful diseases and deform'd
In crude old age.

(*SA* 684–700)

This passage has long been the touchstone for nearly all political readings of the drama, since it transparently presents a collective portrait of the unjust retribution God apparently dealt to Milton and his revolutionary allies: Cromwell's body was exhumed, exposed, and decapitated; Vane and Sidney were tried by "unjust tribunals," all suffered some degree of public humiliation; and Milton's personal health was declining with "crude old age." Yet in reprising this classical theme of divine *nemesis*, the drama again reflects a republican rather than saintly answer to the chorus's tragic question. Misunderstanding both his gifts and his curse, Samson and the Danites at first assume that God has cruelly "saved" their hero only to abandon him to poverty, blindness, and physical decay; utterly overlooking his former service, God proves himself either unjust or "Calvinistically" incomprehensible. Yet these assumptions have been corrected in advance by Samson's complex republican response. Recalling the case of other "glorious Champion[s]" (*SA* 705) of liberty who have unwillingly "brought scandal," "diffidence of God, and doubt / In feeble hearts, propense enough before / To waver, or fall off and join with Idols" (453–56*)*, he knows that his "fate" has been suffered by most of the Israelite judges who attempted to free their people. Milton himself has suffered it, since—if not precisely like Samson, Gideon or Jephthah—he too pursued "vanquisht Kings" from the promised land and "by argument, / Not worse than by his shield and spear / Defended *Israel* from the *Ammonite*" (281, 283–85) before falling into national disrepute.

The libertarian aspect of these Israelite judgeships is appropriately embedded in the biblical passages to which Milton alludes (Judges 8:4–9, 11:12–33, 12:5–6), which focus on Israel's repeated refusal to support her political saviors. Israel figuratively tore down her own towers by failing to support Gideon in Penuel (Judges 8:6–8, 17), which caused the nation to be "judged" in a double sense, both by its leaders and by its enemies. These allusions reflect post-Restoration England's "tearing down" of her republic and her harsh judgment by enemies at home and abroad. The French were not so secretly plotting to "enslave" her at home, while abroad she was suffering disastrous defeats in the Anglo-Dutch wars. Unlike his chorus, however, Samson understands that God permits this national "shame" because his judges never were conventional avengers. As he (or Milton) clearly recognizes, they were purgative historical forces teaching God's people that their pusillanimity will only gain them the deeper slavery they experience immediately after Gideon's death (Judges 8:33–35). By unmasking the arrogance and ignorance of kings and their "high places," the judges offered their people a permanent historical alternative—a community united under just, iconoclastic leaders. This eternal alternative remains as potentially real for England as it did for Israel, a point Milton underscores by alluding to Jephthah's running debate with the king of Ammon. By linking Ammon's treachery and tyranny to his forefather, King Sihon, Jephthah demonstrated the continuities between monarchy and mystification, which in the "Philistine" situation is doubly embodied in Dalila and Harapha.

As Samson's wife, Dalila appropriately defines the domestic aspects of tyranny, but not without the civic and spiritual implications also discussed in Milton's divorce tracts. Here he shows that the inability to exercise domestic freedom simultaneously curtails personal and spiritual development, priorities so important that marriage must be understood as a civil ordinance that becomes invalid as soon as it violates the ends for which it was ordained. Since "the great and almost only commandment of the Gospel, is to command nothing against the good of man," no civil command should ever militate against one's civil *or* spiritual good (*CPW* 2:638–39). Milton grounds these principles both in Christian liberty and in God's universal natural law: "no ordinance human or from heav'n can binde against" that good, for to enforce edicts that violate those principles is effectively "to breake them" in God's eyes (*CPW* 2:588). Milton further developed these views in the wake of pamphlet wars with royal apologists who argued that any limitation or resistance to the king's prerogative is both illegal and sinful. Henry Parker led the assault against this argument by maintaining that the great "Charter of nature" made not the king's but the whole people's preservation paramount, which accordingly meant that "there bee ... tacite trusts and reservations in all publike commands, though of the most absolute nature that can be supposed." Milton and other Parliamentarians explicitly compared the natural law of self-preservation to the marriage covenant, which allowed for separation if either party was wronged by adultery or violence.[30] Milton further added loss of emotional peace or contentment to his definition of this "violence" when he argued that:

> He who marries, intends as little to conspire his own ruine, as he that swears Allegiance: and as a whole people is in proportion to an ill Government, so is one man to an ill mariage. If they against any authority, Covnant, or Statute, may by the soveraign edict of charity, save not only their lives, but honest liberties from unworthy bondage, as well may he against any private Covnant, which hee never enter'd to his mischief, redeem himself from unsupportable disturbances to honest peace, and just contentment. (*CPW* 2:229)

---

[30] Henry Parker, *Observations upon Some of His Majesties Late Answers and Expresses* (1642), p. 4. See also Zagorin, *Milton*, pp. 44–46, and on the Parliamentarian pamphlets and Miltonic arguments that advance the analogy of marriage and government, Barker, *Milton*, pp. 108–20, and Sirluck, *CPW* 2:152–53.

Since this claim was still bitterly contested by prominent royalists of the period, Milton has Samson reassert the idea that these universal principles are found both in the primordial law of nature and in "the *secondary law of nature and of nations*" (*CPW* 2:661), which Samson refers to as "the law of nature, law of nations" (*SA* 890). In fact, his consistent recollection of the divorce tracts seems to make the older allegorical reading of Dalila as a royalist roughly based on Mary Powell not quite as meritless as usually supposed. Like Samson's, Milton's marriage caused him (as he told Carlo Dati) "to bewail my lot, to lament that those whom perhaps proximity or some unprofitable tie has bound to me, whether by accident or by law, those, commendable in no other way, daily sit beside me, weary me—even exhaust me, in fact—as often as they please; ... [so] that I am forced to live in almost perpetual solitude" (*CPW* 2:762–63). Dalila also presumes upon Samson's forgiving nature as Mary did: Samson claims that he was always "With goodness principl'd not to reject / The penitent, but ever to forgive" (*SA* 760–61) in ways that reflect Edward Phillips's portrait of his uncle's "generous nature, more inclinable to reconciliation than to perseverance in anger and revenge" toward his wandering wife (Hughes 1032). Yet Milton's hero obviously reverses this capitulation by subjecting forgiveness to the higher demands of justice, which effectively allows him to divorce both Dalila and her people after they repeatedly break "all faith, all vows." Deceiving, betraying, and manipulating her husband, she has too often "reconcilement move[d] with feign'd remorse," pretended to

> Confess, and promise wonders in her change,
> Not truly penitent, but chief to try
> Her husband, how far urg'd his patience bears,
> His virtue or weakness which way to assail:
> Then with more cautious and instructed skill
> Again transgresses, and again submits;
> That wisest and best men full oft beguil'd,
> With goodness principl'd not to reject
> The penitent, but ever to forgive,
> Are drawn to wear out miserable days.

(SA 752–62)

As we have seen, this complex fusion of the personal and ethical with the political is typical of classical republicans, which is why Milton's animus towards "idolatrous" queens like Henrietta Maria and Mary of Scotland, Charles II's grandmother, also resurfaces in Dalila. Reflecting the typical republican association of deceptive, domineering women with imperial corruption, Dalila not only excels in seductive rhetoric but also exhibits the strong "manly" character that Milton's sonnets extol in good women, yet which in "queenly" women contributes to masculine weakness by extorting submission. Dalila clearly exhibits all these traits when she hypocritically claims that domestic "liberty" is dangerous to Samson, since it "Would draw thee forth to perilous enterprises, / While I at home sat full of care and fears." She then "cavalierly" pleads that she merely wished to "enjoy thee day and night" (803–5, 807), although, by her own admission, the "safe custody" she sought (802) is virtually equivalent to house arrest ("Love's prison ...," 808). Depriving her victim of both the proper "ends" of marriage and his political freedom, her logic seems to parody lyrics like Lovelace's "To Lucasta, from Prison" by implicitly asking "How could I keep from making you love's prisoner since you loved your country's honor more?" Yet if love of country characterizes Samson, it does not actually apply to Dalila. She cares nothing for her country's "real" honor but merely for its material gain. Sharing in these profits, she is perfectly content to serve its priests and politicians despite their falsehood and injustice. As Samson points out, her betrayal of her husband to them for political ends violates both the universal and national laws shared by their tribes, which means that the Philistines, not he, have become "private persons" without legitimate authority or legitimate gods. The servants of Dagon are flatly "unable / To acquit themselves and prosecute their foes / But by ungodly deeds, the contradiction / Of their own deity" (896–99).[31] Thus

> if aught against my life
> Thy country sought of thee, it sought unjustly,
> Against the law of nature, law of nations,
> No more thy country, but an impious crew
> Of men conspiring to uphold thir state
> By worse than hostile deeds, violating the ends
> For which our country is a name so dear;
> Not therefore to be obey'd ...
>
> (*SA* 888–95)

As noted above, this objection against Philistine justice clearly reprises Milton's divorce tract citations of Cicero's *De Legibus* (II, 5) and Selden's *De Jure Naturali et Gentium* (cf. *CPW* 2:350 n. 1) to establish a higher "*law of nature and of nations*" (*CPW* 2:661). His dramatic preface to his tragedy places the republican Cicero among the "Philosophers and other gravest Writers" who defend the moral tenor of tragic poetry (Hughes 549), while false heroes like Dalila and Harapha can only appreciate the amoral "sorceries" (*SA* 937) of absolutist ideology. Harapha clearly represents the masculine and military aspect of Dalila's "domestic" tyranny, although he is actually more childish, superstitious, and appropriately "effeminate" than she. Whereas Dalila's "sorceries" have strong emotional and sexual sources, Harapha's are merely imaginary. In replying to his accusations of witchcraft, Samson thus replies that only his enemy believes in the false "magic" of "glorious arms / Which greatest Heroes have in battle worn, / Thir ornament and

---

[31]   Milton's knowledge of John Selden's studies made him well aware that the Jews and Canaanites shared many sacred laws, texts, and customs; see also Frank Cross, *Canaanite Myth and Hebrew Epic* (Cambridge, MA, 1973).

safety." Once the Hebrew champion demystifies these superficial "ornaments," the Philistine giant suddenly feels helpless against a primal power he ineptly compares both to "black enchantments" and "chaft wild Boars, or ruffl'd Porcupines" (1130–33, 1138). In fact, Samson's strength is neither exclusively natural or supernatural, but something of each: it is the gift of a living God who can make use of even the weakest instruments. Suddenly petrified by Samson's recovering strength, his "Giantship" hides behind empty name-calling: this Hebrew is too dirty, blind, slavish, and animalistic for him to touch, especially since the issue of "whose god is God" (1176) has already been "settled" by nationalistic might:

> Is not thy Nation subject to our Lords?
> Thir Magistrates confest it, when they took thee
> As a League-breaker and deliver'd bound
> Into our hands: ...
> ...
> The *Philistines*, when thou hadst broke the league,
> Went up with armed powers thee only seeking,
> To others did no violence nor spoil.
>
> (*SA* 1182–85, 1189–91)

This charge leads to Harapha's closely related claim that Israel's champion is merely "A Murderer, a Revolter, and a Robber" (1180) who proleptically violates the injunction of Romans 13 against disobeying the "higher powers," an anti-republican charge that Milton had earlier rebutted in *The Tenure of Kings and Magistrates*. Again following Parker, his *Tenure* makes civil obedience conditional upon the higher authority's adherence to its covenant both with the people and with God's natural laws. When David refused to rebel against his kingly oppressor, Saul, he did so because "the matter between them was not tyranny, but privat enmity, and *David* as a privat person had bin his own revenger, not so much the peoples" (*CPW* 3:216).[32] Yet once Saul, who in so many ways resembles Harapha, became an actual tyrant, David was justified in fighting to preserve the life and liberty of his people. In fact, even an *apparently* "private person" may resist civil power illegally maintained by "force of Conquest," for, as Samson says, "force with force / Is well ejected when the Conquer'd can." Like David, such a private person is not a "league-breaker" even if the "servile minds" of his countrymen refuse to defend him, for his commitment to liberty belongs neither to himself nor to them, but to God's eternal laws—the "part from Heav'n assign'd" (1206–7, 1209, 1213, 1217)—which overrides all merely local customs and laws. At this point, Milton's hero becomes one with the libertarian Samson first

---

[32]   As Hughes notes, Milton responds to a treatise by a group of Presbyterian divines, *A Serious and Faithfull Representation of the Judgements of Ministers of the Gospel within the Province of London* (January 18, 1649); see *CPW* 3:39–100, cited p. 73.

described in his *Defence of the People of England* (*CPW* 4.1:402): a hero *more* political than religious.

The Tragic Past and the Inevitable Future of Freedom

Even after the failure of his *Readie and Easie Way*, Milton once again addressed the issues of religious, domestic, and civil liberty only a month before the Restoration. His final pamphlet written without fear of censorship, *Brief Notes Upon a Late Sermon, Titl'd "The Fear of God and King,"* replies to Matthew Griffin's vindictive parody of all who had opposed Charles I and governed in his place. Here Milton vehemently denies that a restored king would "like Samson, avenge his father and himself upon Presbyterians, Independents, and sectaries alike" (*CPW* 7:464), a "prophecy" that Griffin felt confident enough to publish in a volume dedicated to General Monck. Griffin was promptly imprisoned, yet Milton nevertheless thought he deserved a reply, which he issued with his unheeded warning to Monck to uphold his reiterated pledges to maintain the Commonwealth. He also wished to assure the nation that even a doctor of divinity like Griffith could be ignorant of the fundamental laws of nature and right reason "commonly call'd *moral law.*" This moral law decrees that the "choice of Government is so essential" to a people's freedom that without it "they are not free," and that the English people's earlier conquest of their king "was also just by the Law of Nations" even if not sanctioned by a full parliament (*CPW* 7:479, 481). These pronouncements became bitterly ironic only a month later, as a newly restored and full parliament conspired with Monck to return Charles Stuart to the throne. However, in subsequent years Milton no doubt began to feel (if he had ever wavered) that his long-term view was correct: "Free Commonwealths have bin ever counted fittest and properest for civil, vertuous and industrious Nations, abounding with prudent men worthie to govern: monarchie fittest to curb [or in the case of Charles II, encourage] degenerate, corrupt, idle, proud, luxurious people" (*CPW* 7:481–82).

To avert the nightmare of falling into this "unworthiness," Milton had been willing to accept the temporary "judgeship" of someone like Monck, although he knew it signaled both despair "of our own vertue, industrie and the number of our able men." It also signaled England's

> sadly ... befitting thralldom: yet chusing out of our own number one who hath best aided the people, and best merited against tyrannie, the space of a raign or two we may chance to live happily anough, or tolerably. But that a victorious people should give up themselves again to the vanquishd, was never yet heard of; seems rather void of all reason and good policie, and will in all probabilitie subject the subduers to the subdu'd, will expose to revenge, to beggarie, to ruin and perpetual bondage the victors under the vanquishd: then which what can be more unworthie? (*CPW* 7:482)

Much later, he used the Philistine government to represent the temporary "thralldom" which republicans continued to hope would last no longer than a "raign or two," which was in fact exactly how long the Stuarts lasted. Israel/England did not, as Milton hoped, find anyone like Monck to prevent the return of monarchy, but it did face a new succession crisis that republicans hoped would open a way for change. Samson's sudden turn toward a non-tribal God "whose ear is ever open; and his eye / Gracious to re-admit the suppliant" (*SA* 1172–73) thus suggests that God's curse upon a once victorious people who had given "themselves again" to be "vanquishd" might at last be lifted. In Miltonic terms, that would mean overturning a hollow idol no more supportable than his "Giantship" himself: the "Dagon" of monarchy. Samson's parting words to Harapha stress this hollowness, for after refusing a fair trial of reason, right, *or* force, this great "bulk without spirit vast" has shown itself as "slight inform'd" of truth as his idolatrous and shallow people. Like Dalila, he illustrates how undisciplined vice masquerading as virtue can be laid low "with one buffet" or dashed "down / To the hazard of thy brains and shatter'd sides," much like their symbolic temple of tyranny (1229, 1238–41).

Hence, as the drama's anti-regenerationists fail to note, Samson's violence is also largely symbolic. Like the "unactive, and livelesse *Colossus*" of Antiquity that Milton figuratively "buffeted" and shattered in his antiprelatical tracts, Dagon and his "Gyant" champion are empty shells. Dagon's "*Pigmee*" supporters may "turne and wind him" to support their feeble cause, but his collapse will inevitably redound on their "owne heads" (*CPW* 1:699–700). This language suggests the necessary and fateful end of false power but not its means, whether comic or tragic. Harapha's slinking back to his authorities to "tell" on Samson (*SA* 1242–43) in fact suggests comic possibilities, although the biblical account demands that, once Samson has performed his part, his God will be tragically vindicated. Nevertheless, since the destruction of the Philistine temple occurs completely off stage, Samson's great feat is not unlike the Son's purely symbolic "destruction" of the Antichrist who simply falls flat after making an idol of himself in *Paradise Regained.* Like Satan/Antaeus, Harapha is no stronger than his fallible "mother Earth," and even weaker once detached from his native soil, so he is easily "throttled" in mid-air (*PR* 4.563–68). The symbolic continuities in these paired conclusions further explain the underlying parallels between Samson's and the Son's victories, which confirm two sometimes contested "facts" about *Samson Agonistes* and *Paradise Regained*: that they were written in close conjunction with one another, and that Milton regarded the Son's bloodless triumph as a true parallel of Samson's more "strenuous" victory.[33] What remains paramount in either case is thus not the "clotted gore" (1728) inherent in the site of destruction, but the liberating "flight" that both heroes "deliver" to their communities:

---

[33]   As Von Maltzahn notes, Milton and his heroes are usually quite consistent: both *Samson Agonistes* and the *History of Britain* show a characteristic pattern of sudden action after "hesitation and delay" give way to renewed vigor; see *Milton's "History,"* p. 23.

Oh how comely it is and how reviving
To the Spirits of just men long opprest!
When God into the hands of thir deliverer
Puts invincible might
To quell the mighty of the Earth, th' oppressor,
The brute and boist'rous force of violent men
Hardy and industrious to support
Tyrannic power, but raging to pursue
The righteous and all such as honor Truth;
Hee all thir Ammunition
And feats of War defeats
With plain Heroic magnitude of mind
And celestial vigor arm'd,
Thir Armories and Magazines contemns,
Renders them useless, while
With winged expedition
Swift as the lightning glance he executes
His errand on the wicked, who surpris'd
Lose thir defense, distracted and amaz'd.

(SA 1268–86)

As in all great tragedy, this final victory is at once historical/particular and historical/universal. It concretely vindicates Israel's champion and his cause, but also projects the retribution that all enslaved peoples will win against their oppressors into the future. The "tyrannic power" of brute force will be overturned, while "the righteous and all such as honor Truth" will be vindicated "with winged expedition." England herself would not long after be "delivered" by the Glorious (and it turned out, bloodless) Revolution increasingly anticipated by classical republicans at the time of Milton's writing.[34] Samson's triumph is of course neither bloodless nor painless, but the moans and groans of the fallen hero and his enemies imaginatively merge with the birth pangs that Manoa and the chorus "hear" as they "see" their nation's phoenix-like resurrection. Milton's yearning for this vindication seems far from selfless, yet it is not entirely selfish either. Proclaiming God's enduring "covenant" of Christian and classical liberty, his tragedy again reasserts his Areopagitican vision of England as a composite Samson, "a noble and puissant Nation rousing herself like a strong man after sleep, and shaking her invincible locks," like an eagle molting and renewing "her mighty youth, and kindling her undazl'd eyes at the full midday beam; purging and unscaling her long abused sight at the fountain it self of heav'nly radiance; while the whole noise of timorous and flocking birds, with those also that love the twilight, flutter about, amaz'd at what she means" (*CPW* 2:558). According to Corns and Campbell, the tragedy also accompanies Milton's final return to

---

[34] See Hill, *Milton*, p. 402.

political activism both in promoting religious toleration and the institution of elective monarchy, a cherished principle among classical republicans who, like him and Chaloner, could find no superiority in the "mere begetting" or physical conception of kings. No doubt stimulated by privileged knowledge gained from Marvell and Arthur Annesley concerning the continuing decline of Charles II's power and prestige, his simultaneously anti-court and anti-clerical tragedy functions both as a form of wish-fulfillment forecasting the Stuart overthrow and as a summation of his own brilliant but flawed career.[35]

Yet Milton's tragicomic vision also possesses a strong trans-historical component. After the "revolution of 1688 and the establishment of press freedom in the eighteenth century," Milton's lifelong opposition to licensing and religious intolerance was largely vindicated. The first English Deist, Charles Blount, issued a continuation of *Areopagitica* in 1679 that helped persuade the nation to let its censorship laws lapse, and its main principles were later enshrined in Sir William Blackstone's famous *Commentaries on The Laws of England* (1765–69). The latter declares free information to be essential to liberty, so that "every freeman had the right to publish what he pleased but must take the consequences if he published dangerous or offensive writings."[36] Milton's proposed separation of religion from state control also gained acceptance slowly but steadily throughout the eighteenth century until it was finally enshrined in the American Bill of Rights. By the early nineteenth century, domestic liberty (in some cases including the right to divorce on grounds other than adultery) was again being actively debated in both England and America.

Finally, whether or not we approve violence in the cause of freedom, Milton undoubtedly did approve it under the legally limited circumstances described in his tragedy. Here "Patience and Heroic Martyrdom" (*PL* 9.32) are both real opposites and real options, but martyrdom is only heroic when combined with a public defense of universal principles. This explains why Milton's Samson is ultimately so different from the Fifth Monarchists, Ranters, or Quakers, who (ironically like Charles I) assumed a Christlike spirituality when, unlike Christ, they did or could not rationally defend their faith against "Pharisees" who questioned their legitimacy. The fact that Milton himself serenely chose patience rather than martyrdom may explain why *Paradise Regained* was his favorite poem, but it hardly suggests that he silently criticizes Samson for acting out a personal revenge fantasy, as some revisionist critics propose. By carefully deleting Samson's biblical plea for vengeance and replacing it with an ambiguous silence—the Messenger cannot tell whether Samson is saying a silent prayer or merely reflecting on his options before he enters the temple—Milton suggests that he died for a far higher cause than the tribal or personal vindication Milton denied even to David. Finally, if he had actually disapproved of Samson's militant defense of liberty, he would hardly

---

[35] Campbell and Corns, *John Milton*, pp. 370, 347–50, 361. They also summarize the important differences between Milton and his hero; see p. 360.

[36] Zagorin, *Milton*, p. 55.

have inscribed "Samson's" poem with so many obvious allusions to his own life, beliefs, and works.

As for Dalila and her people, Milton had long before made her a composite symbol of political and religious oppression. His *Reason of Church Government* imagines someone like her and her priestly "strumpets" putting "out the fair, and farre-sighted eyes of [Samson's] ... natural discerning" in order to make him "grinde ... in the prison house of their sinister ends and practices." The solution to this unjust slavery remains uncannily consistent with the conclusion of *Samson Agonistes*: the very "rasor ... [which] bereft him of his wonted might" must be turned against his oppressors, as the hero showers "thunder with ruin upon the heads of those his evil counsellors, but not without great affliction to himselfe." In *Samson Agonistes*, "the whole roof [falls] ... with burst of thunder / Upon the head of all who sat beneath," including Samson (*SA* 1651–52). Yet, in both cases, all is not lost: in *The Reason of Church Government* "his puissant hair, the golden beames of Law and Right," again flourishes like the phoenix heralded at the end of the tragedy (*CPW* 1:859). In both allegories, "he" ambiguously alludes to Milton's nation, to the universal forces of "Law and Right," and to the reforming principles of the disillusioned divinity student himself. Fortunately, these allusions need not be strictly distinguished: Milton the poet at last acquits himself like Samson—and like Milton, the great eagle/phoenix of English liberty who never ceased to "look ... forward to unborn generations" to renew it.[37]

---

[37] Woolrych, "Date of the Digression," p. 232.

Milton and the Early Development of Toleration in England

The mature Milton's relationship to the cause of religious toleration cannot be properly understood without first defining his position on three closely related issues: ecclesiastical "comprehension," Protestant ecumenicism, and freedom from censorship. Although his strong defense of freedom from censorship is clear, his positions on Dissent, church comprehension, and authority are far less widely understood. In no small part, this is due to the fact that Milton combined the thoroughly modern principles of voluntary association and ecumenicism with the considerably less modern ideal of church comprehension. These distinctions remain important, since while Dissenters shared Milton's commitment to the principle of fully voluntary church government and attendance, many rejected on principle his commitment to ecumenicism, and the radicals rejected church comprehension as well. For conservative Dissenters like the Presbyterians, ecumenicism ignored the key distinction between the Elect and the Reprobate, while for the radicals, inclusion or "comprehension" in the national church ignored their right to form separate congregations "gathered" by lay, and in many cases, non-university-trained or even self-taught ministers. In practice, that meant that, while conservatives favored comprehension, they did not wish to "tolerate" indiscriminately, and radicals did not wish to be tolerated or "validated" by the establishment. Dissent additionally included important and influential moderates like Richard Baxter, who worked toward both comprehension and ecumenicism, yet modern church historians have cast considerable doubt on the older idea promoted by W.K. Jordan, William Haller, and their successor, Christopher Hill, that Dissent was the "mother" of religious toleration. For, while all Dissenters certainly promoted the cause of freedom from state persecution, neither they nor their Puritan predecessors espoused anything like the modern concept of complete freedom of opinion or skeptical inquiry into doctrinal or ceremonial issues. Except for minorities like the Quakers, Ranters, and Seekers, nearly all Puritans still regarded deviation from Calvinist orthodoxy as heretical, and even Quakers and Seekers maintained a rigidly orthodox and inflexible anti-ceremonialism.

Thus, despite the continued expansion of the moderate center, the post-Restoration situation still largely mirrored the internal conflicts that became apparent soon after the outbreak of the civil wars. As Gerald Cragg remarks, Puritans as a whole did not hesitate "to classify as 'godless' those who differed from them, and condemnation by the one side had awakened an answering contempt in the other."

Yet mutual religious hostility and condemnation did not follow a simple pattern of "Anglicans" versus "Puritans." Some who sympathized with the Dissenters' plight opposed their political and religious principles, while many of their worst enemies simply welcomed the chance to repay them for the "irksome restraints" of the Puritan past or to demonstrate their newfound zeal for the monarchy.[1] Church historian W.M. Spellman shows that, in this climate, the Puritan need to harden the understanding of Holy Writ not only splintered the sects but produced a virtually Roman Catholic codification of their positions into clearly articulated confessional dogmas. In these confessions no "quarter was to be given to those who sought to maintain the inaugural goal of the Reformation: individual access to and interpretation of Scripture," a problem Spellman traces to the foundational dispute between Luther and Erasmus. Erasmus attempted but failed to convince Luther that some conflicting interpretations were undecideable and therefore unenforceable: "'I merely want to analyze and not to judge,' Erasmus wrote, 'to inquire and not to dogmatize. I am more ready to learn from anyone who advances something more accurate or reliable.'" Luther's response would prove typical of the Calvinist Dissenters who believed that scriptural teachings on key issues such as predestination and anti-ceremonialism were clear and incontrovertible. "'Not to delight in assertions,'" said Luther, "'is not the mark of a Christian heart. Indeed, one must delight in assertions to be a Christian at all!'" For Spellman and others, the hermeneutic divide between scriptural certitude and open-endedness explains the religious wars of the sixteenth century, which carry over, "with equally tragic consequences, into mid-seventeenth century England." After the Restoration, it predicts that the deepest philosophical divide would emerge between dogmatic Dissenters or radical sectarians and their more skeptical and tolerant counterparts within the church, the Latitudinarians.[2]

Yet, as noted above, this is not to say that there was no middle ground, still less that Dissenters played no role in the gradual shift toward religious toleration. Baxter and Thomas Manton worked in this direction with John Wilkins, credited by most as the founding spirit of Latitudinarianism, and far less cooperative souls promoted the cause of toleration simply by exemplifying the unacceptable consequences of legal intolerance. The spectacle of pious, ultra-conscientious Christians being severely fined and imprisoned simply for refusing to join a national church they found ungodly or otherwise offensive to their "tender consciences" gradually persuaded their countrymen and women of the barbarity—and worse, the unchristianity—of legally enforcing the Church of England's insistence on "moderate" or *via media* ceremonialism. Cragg adds that the Puritan experience in the Great Persecution also sparked national interest in creating an independent judiciary. The infamous Judge Jeffries ironically produced Dissent's finest hour when, as John Tillotson remarked, "Baxter stood at bay, berogued, abused, despised; never more great than then." Equally ironic was the fact that Dissenters were victims of their own anti-

---

[1]   Cragg, *Puritanism in the Period*, p. 33.
[2]   Spellman, *Latitudinarians*, p. 14.

Papism, since many of the laws used against them had been devised to prosecute Catholics, although that circumstance hardly justified their oppressors.[3] Roger Williams's irenic response aptly captures this double irony: is it "not a true mark and character of a false Church to Persecute?" Are not "the States of *Holland* who tollerate ... nearer the *holy Pattern & commad* [sic] of the Lord Jesus?"[4] In the post-Restoration climate, such questions began to unsettle old certitudes about the need for a comprehensive national church.

Yet, until the specter of a reascendant Catholicism began to unify Protestant opposition to James II, the godly might unite against established authority or in gaining the support of their liberal friends, but their sense of innate righteousness could still set them against one another. Without any national church or leader to settle their disputes, Dissenters actually tended to harden in their own beliefs while stereotyping their neighbors' convictions. In contrast, the Latitudinarians' more Erasmian approach to this problem provided far greater flexibility if also less crusading zeal: they simply trusted in their probability or "uncertainty" principle to foster tolerant exchange, although that trust in turn led to confusions about the nature and limits of reason.[5] This aspect of their faith also left them liable to charges of "lukewarmness" or lack of principle by both their High Church and their Puritan opponents, even though the "Latitude-men" essentially agreed that Christianity consists in assertions of faith and not in "mere" morality. Where they did legitimately differ was on core doctrines, since, like both Milton and Locke, they advocated a simplified form of faith which held that the central articles of saving faith were few, clear, and easily apprehended by all. More obscure Christian teachings were not unimportant, but these obscurities could only be clarified through skeptical inquiry, dispassionate interchange of ideas, and a tolerant ecumenicism. Like Wilkins himself, many Latitudinarians were actually drawn in this direction by their Puritan roots, which led them to recognize the limitations of excessive zeal. Seventeenth-century Quakers veered in the opposite direction and soon became notorious for disrupting church meetings and shouting down other believers, which in turn led even religious radicals like Lodowick Muggleton to compare them to the "grosly rude" and bigoted Ranters: "Quakers that were upon the Rant are the best able to maintain the Quakers principle of Christ within them," he wryly remarked, since it convinced them of their own infallibility.[6]

Recent scholars like Ronald Knox have concurred: George Fox and his followers generally did not "*tolerate*, in the sense of allowing other people to go their own way, to follow the light which was in them if it conflicted with the light which was

---

[3]   Cragg, *Puritanism in the Period*, pp. 49–52, cited p. 49. Cragg quotes from John Tillotson's letter to M. Sylvester, Baxter MSS (Letters), vol. 2: ff. 76, a, b–77 b.

[4]   Roger Williams, *Queries of Highest Consideration, Proposed to the five Holland Ministers and the Scotch Commissioners (So Called)* (London, 1644), p. 12.

[5]   See John Spurr, "'Rational Religion' in Restoration England," *JHI* 49.4 (1988): pp. 563–85.

[6]   Lodowick Muggleton, *A Looking-Glass for George Fox* (London, 1668), p. 46.

in him." Knox cites Baxter's supporting complaint that "There is scarce a scold heard among us in seven years' time that useth so many railing words ... as these people will use familiarly in their religious exercises against the faithful servants of Christ.'" Of course, as Knox reminds us, "Quakerism, from the first, had no sympathy with coercion. But it did not tolerate" in the modern sense of admitting uncertainty about one's own or another's convictions, simply because single-minded evangelism and "agitation, of its very nature, is intolerant."[7] Cragg reads the Quakers' courageous Nonconformity more sympathetically but comes to much the same conclusion. When asked whether "loyalty to the truth [was] consistent with any latitude in interpreting its demands," Quakers "inevitably "returned an answer completely consistent with their literal interpretation of the injunctions of the Gospel. People who refused to compromise even with relatively innocuous forms of customary courtesy were not likely to heed prudential arguments" for moderation. Their witness was therefore marked with an absolutism that forbade any concessions for the sake of safety, and while their courage largely redeemed them from the "taint of doctrinaire perversity," it also "exposed them ... to the perils of spiritual pride" and "inflexibility" toward fellow Nonconformists.[8]

Ironically, then, the pacific, non-violent Quaker and "free-thinking" Dissenter of popular memory largely came into existence after the religious rationalists they despised at last succeeded in separating church and state. This separation of faith from legal regulation permitted uncivil zeal but ultimately limited it to the private sphere where each man and woman could freely pursue his or her inner light. Yet Wilkins's personal failure to spread this "gospel" in his own time was inhibited not just by his fellow churchmen and Baptists like Bunyan, who satirized the liberal position in *Pilgrim's Progress*, but by his own inability fully to understand the Dissenters' mutual and deep concern with apparently "minor" matters such as the prayer book and church ceremony. His insensitivity to their concerns betrayed another common failure among Latitudinarians and other moderates, which was to realize that in doubtful matters the church was primarily responsible for yielding its coercive authority, and that Presbyterian or sectarian adherence to principle was a far different thing from simple "obstinacy" or "malign prejudice."[9] Yet the insensitivities cut both ways, since there was much truth to the conformists' claim that the Presbyterian distinction between the godly community and the unregenerate majority seemed "arrogant" and "exclusivist" from a more tolerant perspective. Cragg also shows that, while Dissenters were strengthened and consoled in their sufferings by the belief that great "benefits accrued from the afflictions of the faithful," who could "trace even in their sufferings the hand of God," their belief in divine guidance hardly served to soften their doctrinal convictions.[10]

---

[7]   Knox, *Enthusiasm*, p. 146, citing Baxter, *One Sheet against the Quakers* (London, 1657), p. 4.

[8]   Cragg, *Puritanism in the Period*, p. 67.

[9]   Spellman, *Latitudinarians*, pp. 39, 43.

[10]   Cragg, *Puritanism in the Period*, pp. 73, 75.

Williams is thus generally considered a more ideal example of Nonconformity, since he in fact went far beyond Milton and the Latitudinarians in arguing for the toleration not just for all Christians, including Roman Catholics "upon good assurance given of *civill obedience* to the *civill state*," but also of Turks and Jews.[11] Nor was his position unique; George H. Williams traces the widespread development of "sectarian ecumenicity" among the bearers of the "Radical Reformation," who liberally enhanced "the status of infidels relative to the beneficiaries of cultural Christianity." Yet, as he observes, they generally did so only at the price of "putting unregenerate Protestants and Catholics on the level of adherents of the Old Covenant and of the infidels."[12] Sharply distinguishing between the two covenants on a basis "roughly comparable to the ancient division between Judah and Israel, later between Judea and Samaria," they drew a firm line between "the righteous remnant living by the covenant written on the heart" and all the rest of so-called Christendom. The results were thus mixed: their cancellation of any absolute "law–grace tension" permitted both an "eschatological interpretation of the destiny of the Jews" and a "prophetic interpretation of the Turks," but in the end, they ultimately failed to escape the "acute Judaizing of Christianity" that characterized the magisterial Reformers, Luther and Calvin. For, by identifying themselves with the "suffering righteous remnant," they "escaped the legalism of the Old [covenant] only to become in many cases more tightly bound by a legalism based on the New." With some justice, they were therefore accused by mainline Protestants of losing the benefits of salvation by faith, and also of prolonging medieval Christianity through a "married" form of monasticism.[13] Su Fang Ng's recent study, *Literature and the Politics of Family in Seventeenth-Century England*, confirms that seventeenth-century Quakers were among those who adopted a highly legalistic approach toward marriage.[14] Like other radicals, they also "maintained both their distinctive witness and their aloofness from all other groups," while more mainstream Presbyterians and Independents (by far the largest category of Dissenters) were initially drawn together by their high Calvinism. Yet, as Cragg points out, these old opponents soon returned to the conflicts earlier fought in the Westminster Assembly, so even this experiment in ecumenicism was short-lived.[15]

Later in the period, Presbyterians ironically became "more moderate Calvinists than the Independents," who in the tradition of their leader, John Owen, were horrified that "extravagant" moderation had come under the aegis of what was once the strictest school of Calvinism. In the same spirit, the Independents maintained their aloofness from the temptations of "Antinomianism," although their ongoing

---

[11]   Williams, *Queries*, 2:107.

[12]   George Huntston Williams, *The Radical Reformation* (Philadelphia, 1962), 833. Williams writes as a self-declared descendant of this tradition.

[13]   Ibid., pp. 832, 833, 834.

[14]   Ng, *Literature and the Politics*, pp. 195–221.

[15]   Cragg, *Puritanism in the Period*, pp. 252–53.

fear of anything remotely Arminian inclined them to be more indulgent toward some of the excesses of the more rabid Calvinists. As for the liberal theology of the Latitudinarians, to them it merely appeared a gateway "to the insidious contamination of Socinianism." And, in fact, Socinians and Deists began to crop up in the Latitudinarian ranks, where their views were consulted if not necessarily welcomed. This example nevertheless contrasts with the Nonconformists, whom Cragg finds fighting "singularly sterile controvers[ies]" over narrow distinctions that ultimately sapped the spirit of Puritanism from within. Baxter conventionally blamed the subsequent increase in skepticism and debauchery on "heresy," not dogmatism, but in reality, most scholars have agreed, its root cause lay in the bitter ill will that divided Calvinists and defied all attempts at mediation, which in turn produced a "coolness of faith" and loss of the spiritual vigor needed to confront the demands of a new age.[16]

The case for both ecumenicity and civil toleration or comprehension was therefore left to the Latitudinarians and their friends, the Dutch Arminians, Milton, and Locke. All realized that separatism by definition marked a clear gain for voluntary civil association, but in their view it also marked a loss for open religious dialogue and ecumenical progress. During this period and long afterward, the absence of open dialogue sustained unreasoning and unreflective religious biases among all parties, wrongly associated both Calvinist and Quaker Nonconformity with political sedition, and increased hatred of antitrinitarian, Socinian, and Deist "heretics" on nearly every front. Spellman shows that the Latitudinarian disposition to respect the theological sincerity of both Socinians and moderate Dissenters was thus closest thing to a middle path at a time when most Englishmen continued to despise "'that tender regard to weak brethren, that upon occasion … can see the inside of a conventicle, be of any synagogue but that of Satan and can show more signs of devotion'" in extempore worship than in "'the flat forms of the undignified liturgy.'"[17] So said Henry Sacheverell, who had in mind men like Joseph Glanvill, a Latitudinarian churchman who publicly declared his admiration for Baxter, although his concept of Protestant ecumenicism was hardly identical with fully modern or secular notions of religious toleration. That cause thus became the property of the Latitudinarians' much more secular descendants, the Deists, by far the most widely despised and persecuted minority of the era. Their fully secular view of man as a rational animal governed by universal, natural moral laws, not by revealed faith, remained reprehensible to most contemporary Christians, who particularly deplored their complete rejection of Christian mystery.

Unlike the Deists but like Milton and Locke, the Latitudinarians lessened or rationalized Christian mystery wherever possible, but accepted core Christian beliefs such as original sin (if not "total depravity"), the Incarnation, and the Atonement. The Deist elimination of all these beliefs thus places them closer to modern Unitarians than to seventeenth-century antitrinitarians, although Locke's

---

[16]   Ibid., pp. 254–58.

[17]   Spellman, quoting Henry Sacheverell in *Latitudinarians*, p. 158.

rejection of innate ideas, innate "depravity," and the trinitarian godhead were all fundamental to the Deist case. By rejecting the ancient Platonic and Thomistic view of reason as a mirror of the mind of God, at least in retrospect, Locke's *Essay of Human Understanding* anticipates the modern conception of reason as a far more modest instrument than the divine "vehicle" it had formerly been. Yet even here, there were gains as well as losses: reason eventually acquired renewed respectability as a reliable means of sorting and recording the objective data of experience, while it never really lost its role in confirming matters of faith until the late eighteenth or early nineteenth century. Locke in particular "proved" that revelation and reason were compatible, for, according to his famous *Essay*, "Reason is natural revelation, whereby the eternal Father of Light and Fountain of all knowledge, communicates to mankind that portion of truth which he has laid within the reach of their natural faculties." Reason's "light" thus continues to embrace even extraordinary revelation, which " is natural reason enlarged by a new set of discoveries communicated by God directly, which reason vouches the truth of by the testimony and proofs it gives that they come from God." Only the early Deists questioned Locke's second and "crucial qualification, this Latitudinarian axiom" concerning revelation, for in their view, to admit any doctrines that the "human mind could not fully understand was to open the door to arbitrary authority and interpretive confusion."[18]

Yet, for that very reason, the Deist "disenchantment" of right reason proved a powerful tool for securing fully secular forms of toleration based on a more optimistic assessment of basic human rights and capacities than the mainline Christian tradition permitted. In rejecting the Puritans' gloomier assessment of fallen human reason and "immediate" rather than "mediate" dependence upon God, the Deists liked to cite Milton as an important predecessor. Their most famous and, by the next century, most influential spokesman was John Toland, who supported his agenda by synthesizing Milton's writings on religious toleration with the skeptical empiricism of Locke's *Essay*, unconsciously or perhaps deliberately confusing Locke's epistemology with his anthropology. Spellman shows that the distinction between the two is nevertheless crucial, since Locke's anthropology is much more Christocentric and conventional in accepting original sin, if mainly in Taylor's sense, as a "propensity" toward evil rather than a permanent blot on the mind and soul.[19] Yet not all early Deists misappropriated their "originals," including their founder, Charles Blount, who would prove a more effective voice for toleration than either the Latitudinarians or their "fellow-traveler," Milton, who had politically supported them in *Of True Religion*.

Spellman traces the Latitudinarians' long-term failure to many factors: "disappointments in Parliament, royal prevarication and deceit, High Church

---

[18] Spellman, *Latitudinarians*, p. 152. Spellman cites Locke's *Essay on Human Understanding*, 4.19.4.

[19] Spellman, *Latitudinarians*, pp. 147–53. On Toland's use of Milton, see Darbishire, *Early Lives*, pp. 83–97.

opposition, periodic impatience with and insensitivity towards their dissenting opposites, and, of greatest moment, a desire to restore a Christian ideal of temporal society where the church would speak with a single voice on matters of behavior in this world pursuant to one's fortune in the next." This dream of a reunited Protestant church with room for internal divisions ultimately looked back to the Elizabethan settlement, but the Latitudinarians lived in a new world where, aside from the "commonplace" and ongoing fear of Catholicism, their unifying efforts were thwarted by the complex realities of securing political patronage during successive regimes. After the "non-juror" clergymen refused to join them in supporting the "particular providence" of William of Orange's ascent to the English throne, Archbishop Tillotson had "little room to formulate, much less to implement, a program of renewal for the church which included concessions to the Dissenters."[20] Blount's advantage over both Tillotson and the earlier Latitudinarians was twofold. First and foremost, he stood apart from the widening cultural and theological "dichotomy between 'church' and 'chapel.'" Second, he greatly benefitted from his Deist conviction (gleaned ultimately from Lord Herbert of Cherbury) that "no single set of beliefs could be uniquely salvific."[21]

This conviction was "enlightened" in respect to other believers, although it somewhat complacently overlooked the inadequacy of reason to solve spiritual mysteries that remain insoluble by either religion or science. For Spellman, these include "the relation of soul to body, the origin of evil, the nature of wisdom and goodness," and the means of attaining them. Arguing with many modern thinkers that evil is either illusory or the product of a bad environment or upbringing, and that, without either disadvantage, humans always act in their own best interests, the Deists effectively reduced Christianity to ethics—as the Latitudinarians did not. This placed them at the outmost limits of rational theology, yet (as Spellman concedes) it also allowed them to find "constructive alternatives to the incessant feuding within the family of English Protestants." They achieved this goal through an oddly proto-modern synthesis of skepticism and conviction: all religious doctrines were subject to question, except, of course, the Deists' conviction that all such doctrines could be made compatible with their own idea of reason.[22] Blount's combination of these convictions along with his adept and accurate use of Milton's arguments for the free circulation of ideas allowed him to make the broadest post-Restoration case for fully secular toleration in the public sphere of the time. Yet, unlike Toland, he accomplished this task not by illegitimately extrapolating Milton's many writings on religion, but by effectively reducing his case against censorship to its rationalist core. Moreover, while succinctly paraphrasing *Areopagitica* for the "new communication age," Blount did not erase its ecumenical Christian overtones. Probably more than any other factor, that wise

---

[20]   Spellman, *Latitudinarians*, pp. 157, 140, 143.

[21]   Ibid., pp. 139, 147.

[22]   Ibid., pp. 149, 154.

decision helped to secure the abolition of press censorship and the passage of the Toleration Bill of 1689.

Just fifty-one years after *Areopagitica*'s initial publication to an unreceptive audience, press licensing was finally allowed to lapse in 1695, although this victory was neither dramatic, decisive, nor productive of widespread public debate. George Sensabaugh nevertheless shows that Milton's ideas definitely played an important part in the long campaign begun in May of 1679 with the publication of Blount's *Just Vindication of Learning*. Two years later, William Denton followed with *An Apology for the Liberty of the Press* (1681), which further fueled the national uproar over Milton's tolerationist principles begun by Blount. Although the exact extent to which they "turned public opinion against the renewal of the Press Act and hence the measure of Milton's contribution to this phase of the attempted Whig revolution will perhaps never be known," Blount in particular would have pleased his mentor by publicly demonstrating the "'Ignorant, Imperious and Remiss, or basely Mercenary'" nature of press licensers like Edmund Bohun and Milton's old enemy, Roger L'Estrange.[23] Significantly, Blount's Deist rejection of dogmatic orthodoxy and anti-scientific subjectivism also remained essentially true to Milton's core beliefs. By recognizing that "illuminism quickly descends into illusionism," and that "the personal element in Protestant theology" can actually become anti-individualistic unless subjected to "more critical and pragmatic criteria," Milton can be seen as an authentic pre-Deist defender of autonomous rational judgment.[24] For, while Blount's appropriation of the poet carried the Reformation doctrine of individual interpretation to its logical extreme, it did not effectively overturn that doctrine, as many Dissenters unwittingly did. Even after the passage of the Toleration Bill, this right remained precarious, as shown by the fate of one of Blount's disciples, the young Scottish university student Thomas Aikenhead, who was executed in 1697 for the "blasphemy" of making his beliefs public, not in print, but merely in discussions with fellow students.[25] Toleration for Roman Catholics was even longer delayed, but Blount's *Just Vindication of Learning* at least helped to end press licensing in England before the end of the century.

---

[23] Sensabaugh, *That Grand Whig*, pp. 58–65, 155–60, cited pp. 64, 160.

[24] Views expressed by Roger Haight, *The Experience and the Language of Grace* (New York, 1979), p. 11, and Spellman, *Latitudinarians*, p. 101, although not in regard to Milton.

[25] See Michael Hunter, "'Aikenhead the Atheist,'" in *Science and the Shape of Orthodoxy*, pp. 308–332. As Hunter points out, the case was particularly shocking because the Blasphemy Act passed in 1661 by the first Scottish parliament of Charles II officially released minors like Aikenhead from the death penalty. Macaulay regarded the case as an intolerant "'crime such as has never since polluted the island'" (p. 308), a view shared by most other nineteenth-century commentators (p. 318). One of Aikenhead's "crimes" was citing Blount's 1693 *Oracles of Reason* (p. 323).

Both Blount's subtitle, *An Appeal to Parliament on behalf of the Liberty of the Press*, and his content discredit the specious charges of plagiarism often brought against him: he proudly cites his "original" on nearly every page.[26] In the person of the patriotic Philopatris, Blount even adopts the familiar Miltonic language of Protestant millenarianism in his opening claim that the "Angel of Darkness" and his chief affliction, the "Plurisie of Poperie," will never be banished from England until censorship ceases. As in *Areopagitica*, press licensing is the last scourge of popery, that obvious "evil" still denounced by all Englishmen, whether Tory or Whig, due to the "Inquisition or Embargo" it places "upon science" (*Proem*).[27] Completely inconsistent with ancient liberty and "true" only to Popish precedent, this embargo has impaired Blount's free, virtuous, and wise nation fully as much as the Inquisition has harmed Counter-Reformation Europe. He credits this "discovery" to "Mr. Milton" (*Just Vindication*, p. 3), his inspiration and predecessor, something anyone remotely familiar with *Areopagitica* would already know.

Blount's acknowledged and unacknowledged citations continue throughout all nine heads of his argument, the first of which repeats his (and Milton's) opening point in detail. The wisest "Ancients" not only refused to censor their most ribald satirists but actually approved the "scandalous" plays of Aristophanes, an artistic license never retracted until the Council of Trent began to suppress the Protestant cause. This point leads to his second, equally Miltonic, argument: to censor any "free and knowing spirit" is to subject him to the "Ferula" or rod of a pupil–teacher who knows neither the art, the industry, nor the worth of what he reads (p. 6). Third, this humiliation creates "a great prejudice even to the Book it self" by subjecting it to "the partiality and ignorant approbation of a *Licenser*" or "*Imprimatur.*" These arguments freely employ not just *Areopagitica*'s metaphors and its examples but its citations from Bacon (p. 8), as does Blount's fourth point: censorship underrates and insults the entire nation by setting such "small value" on "Truth and Understanding" that they become wares to be "monopolized and Traded" under a "servitude, like that imposed by the *Philistines*" who barred the Jews from sharpening their own axes (p. 9). Taken verbatim from *Areopagitica*, this remark leads to Blount's fifth objection to censorship: it is no religious duty but rather an insult both to the church and to the clergy, of "whose labors we should hope better" than that "after all this Light of the Gospel, all this continual Preaching, they should be still frequented with such an un-principled, un-edify'd and Laick rabble, as that the Whiff of every new Pamphlet should stagger them out of their Catechism and Christian walking" (p. 10). These obvious Miltonic paraphrases are fortified with his example of how great "*Italian* wits" like Galileo

---

[26]   See J.A. Redwood, "Charles Blount (1654–93), Deism, and English Free Thought," *JHI* 35.3 (1974): pp. 490–98, especially pp. 495–98.

[27]   On the united Tory and Whig front against Catholicism, Collinson, *Birthpangs*, p. 148.

suffered inquisitorial injustices simply for "thinking otherwise in Astronomy, then the *Dominican* and *Franciscan* Licensers thought" (p. 11).

Blount's sixth, seventh, and eighth arguments continue in the same vein: book licensing constitutes a dangerous and oppressive state monopoly directly contrary to a national spirit "ever famous and bold in the Atchievements of Liberty." It oppresses the licensors themselves, but still worse, it "robs us of the great Argument we make use of against the *Mahometans*, and ... Popish Religion" by encouraging "Laicke Ignorance" (p. 13) or implicit faith. This point calls for a judicious display of *Areopagitica*'s famous rhetorical flourish: "Let her [Truth] and Falshood grapple; who ever knew Truth put to the worst in a free and open Encounter?" He then cites Milton's Baconian aphorism, *"The punishing of Wits [only] enhaunces their Authority, and forbidden writing is thought to be a certain spark of Truth that flyes up in the Faces of them who seek to tread it out."* Finally, Blount cites *Areopagitica*'s most famous passage: "When a man hath been working at the hardest Labour in the deep Mines of Knowledge, and hath furnisht himself out in all Equipage, drawn forth his Reasons as it were in Battail-array; scattered and defeated all objections in his way, summons his Adversary into the field, offers him the advantage of Wind and Sun if he pleases ...; for his opponent then to Sculk & lie in Ambuscade, to keep a narrow Bridge of Licensing, where the Challenger should pass; this, though it be courage enough in a Souldier, is but Weakness and Cowardice in the Wars of Truth" (p. 14). Blount thus reveals that he reads his Milton very like Locke and his modern literary critics but very unlike any of his Puritan readers, who, as Haller showed,[28] either never read or never liked what they found in *Areopagitica*.

Blount's ninth and final proof intriguingly reveals just how and why Deists like himself could still regard Milton as the *chief* champion of the embattled cause of toleration and freedom of conscience in 1679. No longer merely collecting *Areopagitica*'s best sallies, this section astutely summaries its underlying argument: "Licensing and Persecution of Conscience are two Sisters that ever go hand in hand together, being both founded upon one and the same Principle" (p. 15) of coercion. Here Blount additionally alludes to the respectable Latitudinarian lineage supporting both him and Milton by citing Taylor's *Liberty of Prophesying*: if *"all men would use* [one] *another so gently and so charitably, ... no violent Compulsion should introduce Hypocrisy, and render Sincerity as well troublesome as unsafe."* As Taylor also proved, not only is it unchristian and uncivil to "hate men because their Understandings have not been brought up like mine, have not the same Masters, have not met with the same Books, nor the same Company," but, as Bacon, Robinson, and Milton earlier taught, it is impractical and ineffectual as well (p. 15). Here Blount appends the Latitudinarian point that, if certitude on every obscure point of dogma were as necessary to salvation as Calvinists believe, the vast majority of men must be damned and God rightly accused of injustice. True, atheists and innovators may thrive under his proposed "latitude," but they

---

[28]   Haller. *Tracts*, Appendix B.

are properly punished or excommunicated by their own churches, not the state. He further justifies this point by bringing in Deist or "natural religionist" examples: even pagans like Tamburlaine the Great realized that greater understanding, civility, and sincerity would flourish wherever diversity of religion is permitted (p. 16). Any additional civil laws against heresy or blasphemy are thus ill-advised, for they would not benefit *either* church or state: just as the church profits from the voluntary association of like-minded believers, so the state and its institutions profit from pluralism, open debate, free exchange, and the advancement of *all kinds* of learning liberated from Bacon's "Idols of the Cave"— personal prejudice and ingrained habit.

Blount's ideas thus anticipate Locke's *Letter Concerning Toleration*, another often ignored aspect of *Areopagitica*'s lineage, although, as John Shawcross points out, Locke's *Letter* "comes straight out of Milton's tracts, especially *Of True Religion, Haeresie, Schism, Toleration*, which is so meaningful for the separation of church and state.'" He further notes that one of Locke's key passages closely parallels the wording of Milton's late tract: "The one only narrow way which leads to heaven is not better known to the magistrate than to private persons, and therefore I cannot safely take him for my guide, who may probably be as ignorant of the way as myself, and who certainly is less concerned for my salvation than I myself am."[29] Ironically, all three men—Locke, Milton, and Blount—were antitrinitarian rationalists who would have been persecuted and penalized under Cromwell's Puritan regime, reviled by most post-Restoration Dissenters, and exempted from the Toleration Bill, which withdrew the penalties of the Clarendon Code only from all trinitarian Protestants. Yet, despite its imperfections and the political infeasibility of achieving a true separation of church and state in the dawning Enlightenment era, the Latitudinarians' charitable attempt to minimalize the conditions for church comprehension had at least been a step in the right direction. Milton clearly recognized this in *Of True Religion*, and when the Toleration Bill was finally passed it essentially sanctioned the Latitudinarian belief that saving faith depends upon the individual's relationship with God, not on rigor of form, ceremony, or doctrine. Yet, at the same time, the failure of their companion Comprehension Bill finally ended their ecumenical hopes. Rather than solving the problem of dissent through liberal theology, the Latitudinarians were thus reluctantly forced to embrace "diversity" through the legalized self-exclusion of Nonconformists.

The Dissenters themselves had by then abandoned the ideal of a mixed Protestant community and retreated into separate church orders, ministries, and academies devoted to preaching and teaching their distinctive denominational doctrines.[30] Many of these institutions would long produce impressive offspring, although (as Hill points out) the "excluded" Nonconformists became "more utilitarian,

---

[29]   John T. Shawcross, *John Milton and Influence: Presence in Literature, History, and Culture* (Pittsburgh, 1991), p. 143.

[30]   Spellman, *Latitudinarians*, p. 138.

more critical, more democratic," yet also more focused on the practical benefits of trade and industry than on the religious zeal of their forefathers.[31] Another unexpected result was that the exclusive and residually combative branches of Protestant faith, Anglicanism and Nonconformity, continued their traditions of mutual suspicion and hostility well into the twentieth century. It is hard to imagine that this anti-ecumenical outcome would have seemed ideal to Milton or that his own disestablishmentarian principles envisioned it. Yet at least in the New World, where many of his principles were first adopted on the broadest scale, he would have been neither surprised nor sorry to discover that they generally fostered the fertile growth of religion and, to a more limited degree, of ecumenicism as well.[32] Although we now recognize toleration to be at odds with any state system of church comprehension, inclusive or not, it remains difficult to condemn Milton's hope of combining these ideals as the first "century of revolution" and the wounds it tore in the "body" of Christendom drew to a close.

---

[31] Christopher Hill, *The Century of Revolution* (New York, 1961), pp. 293–94.

[32] On the development of Milton's ideas in the New World, see my article, "Milton and the Pursuit of Happiness," *UTQ* 77.3 (2008): pp. 876–902.

Bibliography

Primary Sources

Adams, Hazard (ed.), *Critical Theory Since Plato* (San Diego: Harcourt, Brace, Jovanovich, 1971).

Ames, William, *The Marrow of Sacred Divinity* (London, 1642).

Andrewes, Lancelot, *XCVI Sermons* (1629).

Aubrey, John, *Brief Lives*, ed. Oliver Lawson Dick (London: Secker and Warburg, 1960).

Bacon, Francis, *Certaine Considerations Touching the Better Pacification and Edification of the Church of England*, in Charles R. Gillet (ed.), *Catalogue of the McAlpin Collection of British History and Theology* (5 vols., New York: Union Theological Seminary, 1927–30).

———, *The Philosophy of Francis Bacon*, ed. Benjamin Farrington (Liverpool: Liverpool University Press, 1964).

———, *The Works of Francis Bacon*, ed. James Spedding, Robert Ellis, and Douglas Heath (14 vols., London: Longman & Co., 1860).

Bacon, Robert, *Spirit of Prelacie* (London, 1646).

Baillie, Robert, *A Dissvasive from the Errours of the Time* (1645).

Barclay, Robert, *An Apology for the true Christian divinity, as the same is held forth and preached by the people, called in scorn, Quakers* ([Aberdeen?],1678).

Bastwick, John, *The Litany* (1637).

Baxter, Richard, *A Breviate of the Life of Margaret, the daughter of Francis Charlton of Appleby in Shropshire esquire ...* (1681).

———, *Christian Directory* (1673).

———, *One Sheet against the Quakers* (London: Robert White, 1657).

———, *Poetical Fragments* (1781).

———, *The Practical Works of Richard Baxter* (4 vols., 1707).

———, *Reliquiae Baxterianae*, ed. Matthew Sylvester (London, 1696).

———, *The Saints Everlasting Rest* (London, 1650).

Bayly, Lewis, *The Practice of Piety* (1611).

Bernard, Richard, *The Faithful Shepherd* (London, 1621).

Blount, Charles, *Just Vindication of Learning* (1679).

———, *Oracles of Reason* (1693).

Bolton, Robert, *Some General Directions for a Comfortable Walking with God*, 3rd. ed. (1626).

Borel, Pierre, *Discours nouveau prouvant la pluralité des mondes* (Genève, 1657); English edn., *A New Treatise Proving a Multiplicity of Worlds* (London, 1658).

Boyle, Robert, *The Works of the Honourable Robert Boyle*, ed. Thomas Birch (6 vols., London, 1772).

Brinsley, John, *The Third Part of the True Watch* (1622).

Browne, Sir Thomas, *Pseudodoxia Epidemica* (London: TH for Edward Dod, 1646).

Bulkeley, Peter, *Gospel-Covenant* (London, 1651).

Bunyan, John, *Pilgrim's Progress*, ed. Roger Sharrock (London: Edward Arnold, 1966).

———, *The Works of John Bunyan*, ed. George Offor [rpt. 1856] (3 vols., New York: AMS Press, 1973).

Burton, Henry, *For God and King* (London?: F. Kingston, 1636).

Butler, Samuel, *The Censure of the Rota* (London, 1660).

Calvin, John, *A Commentarie upon S. Paules Epistles to the Corinthians*, trans. T. Timme (London, 1577).

———, *Commentaries on the First Book of Moses* (1554).

———, *The Institutes of the Christian Religion*, trans. John Allen (2 vols., Philadelphia: Presbyterian Board of Christian Education, 1936).

Canne, John, *A Second Voyce from the Temple* (London, 1653).

Cary, Mary, *The Little Horns Doom* (1651).

Chillingworth, William, *The Religion of Protestants* (1637).

Clagett, William, *A Discourse Concerning the Operations of the Holy Spirit* (1678).

Clarkson (Claxton), Lawrence, *The Lost Sheep Found* (1660).

Cleaver, Robert, and John Dod, *A Godlye Form of Household Government* (London, 1621, 1st ed. 1614).

Comenius, John Amos, *The Great Didactic*, trans. M.W. Keatinge (London: Adam and Charles Black, 1896).

———, *Naturall philosophie reformed by divine light, or A synopsis of physicks* (1651).

———, *Reformation of Schooles* ..., trans. Samuel Hartlib (London, 1642).

Cowley, Abraham, *Poems*, ed. A.R. Waller (Cambridge: Cambridge University Press, 1905).

———, *A Proposition for the Advancement of the Experimental Philosophy*, in *The Complete Works in Verse and Prose of Abraham Cowley*, ed. Alexander B. Grosart (2 vols., New York: AMS Press, 1967).

Cradock, Walter, *Divine Drops Distilled* (1650).

Cromwell, Oliver, *The Writings and Speeches of Oliver Cromwell*, ed. W.C. Abbott (4 vols., Cambridge, MA: Harvard University Press, 1937–47).

Darbishire, Helen (ed.), *Early Lives of Milton* (New York: Barnes & Noble, 1932).

Dell, William, *Christ's Spirit a Christian's Strength* (London, 1651).

———, *The Way of True Peace and Unity* (1649), in Woodhouse (ed.), *Puritanism and Liberty*.

Dennis, John, *The Usefulness of the Stage*, in Henry Hitch Adams and Baxter Hathaway (eds.), *Dramatic Essays of the Neoclassic Age* (New York: Columbia University Press, 1947).

Denton, William, *An Apology for the Liberty of the Press* (1681).

Dewsbury, William, *A True Prophecy of the Mighty Day of the Lord* (Feb. 6, 1654).

Dryden, John, *Of Dramatic Poesy and Other Critical Essays*, ed. George Watson (2 vols., London: J.M. Dent & Sons, 1962).

———, *The Poetical Works of Dryden*, ed. George R. Noyes (Boston: Houghton Mifflin, 1950).

Du Bartas, Guillaumne de Salluste, *Bartas: His Devine Weekes and Works* (rpt. 1605), trans. Joshua Sylvester, ed. Francis C. Harber (Gainesville, FL: Scholar's Facsimiles and Reprints, 1965).

"E.F.," *The Marrow of Modern Divinity*, ed. C.G. McCrie (Glasgow, 1902).

Evelyn, John, *Diary and Correspondence* (4 vols., London, H. Colburn, 1857).

Fenwick, John, *Zions Joy* (1643).

Fowler, Edward, *The Principles and Practices, of Certain Moderate Divines of the Church of England* (1670).

Franck, Sebastian, *The Forbidden Fruit* (London,1642).

Gale, Theophilus, *The Court of the Gentiles* (Oxford: Henry Hall, 1660).

Gardiner, Samuel R. (ed.), *Constitutional Documents of the Puritan Revolution 1625–1660* [rpt. 1889] (Oxford: Clarendon Press, 1958).

Geddes, William, *The Saints Recreation* (Edinburgh, 1683).

Geree, John, *The Character of an Old English Puritane or Non-Conformist* (1646).

Glanvill, Joseph Glanvill, *Collected Works of Jospeh Glanvill*, ed. Bernhard Fabian (9 vols., Hildesheim: George Olms, 1979).

Goodwin, John, *Right And Might well met* (1649).

Goodwin, Thomas, *The Works of Thomas Goodwin* (12 vols., Edinburgh: Nichols Series of Standard Divines, 1861–65).

Gott, Samuel, *An Essay of the true Happiness of Man* (1650).

Greville, Robert, Lord Brooke, *A Discourse Opening the Nature of ... Episcopacie* (1642), in Haller (ed.), *Tracts on Liberty in the Puritan Revolution, 1638–1647*.

———, *The Nature of Truth* (1640).

Hakewill, George, *An Apologie or Declaration of the Power and Providence of God in the Government of the World* (Oxford: Lichfield and Turner, 1627).

Hales, John, *Golden Remains of the Ever Memorable M. John Hales* (London, 1659).

Hall, John, *The Advancement of Learning* (1649), ed. A.K. Croston (Liverpool: Liverpool University Press, 1953).

———, *Confusion Confounded, ... Wherein Is Considered the Reason of the Resignation of the late Parliament and the Establishment of a Lord Protector* (London, 1654).

Hall, Joseph, *Quo Vadis? A Just Censure of Travell, As It Is Commonly Undertaken by the Gentlemen of Our Nation* (1617).

Hall, Thomas, *Vindiciae Literarum* (London: W.H., 1554).

Haller, William (ed.), *Tracts on Liberty in the Puritan Revolution, 1638–1647* (3 vols., New York: Columbia University Press, 1934).

——, and Godfrey Davies (eds.), *The Leveller Tracts, 1647–1653* (New York: Columbia University Press, 1944).

Hardison, O.B., Jr. (ed.) *English Literary Criticism: The Renaissance* (New York: Appleton-Century-Crofts, 1963).

Harrington, James, *The Political Works of James Harrington*, ed. J.G.A. Pocock (Cambridge: Cambridge University Press, 1977).

Hartlib, Samuel, *A Description of the Famous Kingdome of Macaria; shewing its Excellent Government* (London, 1641).

Heylyn, Peter, *Microcosmus* (Oxford, 1621).

Hildersam, Arthur, *CLII Lectures upon Psalm LI* (London, 1642).

Hobbes, Thomas, *Answer to Davenant's Preface to "Gondibert,"* in Adams (ed.), *Critical Theory since Plato.*

——, *Behemoth, or The Long Parliament*, ed. Ferdinand Tonnies (Chicago: University of Chicago Press, 1990).

——, *Leviathan*, ed. C.B. Macpherson (Harmondsworth: Penguin, 1968).

Hooker, Thomas, "The Danger of Desertion" (1631), in *Thomas Hooker: Writings in England and Holland, 1626–1633*, ed. George H. Williams (Cambridge, MA: Harvard University Press, 1975).

Hutchinson, Lucy, *Memoirs of the Life of Colonel Hutchinson*, ed. Julius Hutchinson and revised C.H. Firth (2 vols., London: Jon C. Nimmo, 1885).

Jackson, Thomas, *Works* (12 vols., Oxford, 1844).

Jane, Joseph, *Eikon Aklastos, The Image Unbroken* (1651).

Johnson, Samuel, *Lives of the English Poets* (2 vols., London: J.M. Dent & Sons, 1925).

Johnson, Samuel, *The Lives of the Most Eminent English Poets: with Critical Observation on Their Works* (4 vols., London: J. Buckland, 1793).

Jonson, Ben, *Pleasure Reconciled to Virtue*, in David Lindley (ed.), *Court Masques: Jacobean and Caroline Entertainments 1605–1640* (New York: Oxford University Press, 1995).

L'Estrange, Roger, *No Blinde Guides* (London, 1660).

Lilburne, John, *An Answer to Nine Arguments* (1645).

——, *Come Out of her my People* (Amsterdam, 1639).

Locke, John, *The Second Treatise of Government and A Letter Concerning Toleration*, ed. J.W. Gough (Oxford: Basil Blackwell, 1946).

Ludlow, Edmund, *A Voyce from the Watchtower*, in *A Voyce from the Watch Tower, Part 5: 1660–1662*, ed. Blair Worden (London: Offices of the Royal Historical Society, 1978).

Marten, Henry, *The Independency of England Endeavoured to be Maintained* (1648).

Marvell, Andrew, *The Poems of Andrew Marvell*, ed. Nigel Smith (London: Pearson Longman, 2003).

Milton, John, *The Complete Prose Works of John Milton*, ed. Don M. Wolfe et al. (8 vols., New Haven: Yale University Press, 1953–82).

———, *John Milton, The Complete Poetry and Major Prose*, ed. Merritt Y. Hughes (New York: Odyssey Press, 1957).

———, *John Milton: Political Writings*, ed. Martin Dzelzainis (Cambridge: Cambridge University Press, 1991).

———, *A Maske: The Earlier Versions*, ed. Samuel E. Sprott (Toronto: University of Toronto Press, 1973)

Molesworth, Sir Robert, *An Account of Denmark* (London, 1694).

More, Henry, *Philosophicall Poems* (Cambridge: R. Daniel, 1647).

Muggleton, Lodowick, *A Looking-Glass for George Fox* (London, 1668).

Neal, Daniel, *History of the Puritans or the Protestant Nonconformists* (London: William Baynes & Son, 1822).

Nuttall, Geoffrey (ed.), *Early Quaker Letters from the Swarthmore mss. to 1660* (London: Friends House Library, 1952).

Owen, John, *Works*, ed. W.H. Gould (16 vols., Edinburgh, 1850–53).

Owen, John, and Philip Nye, *A Declaration of Faith and Order* (rpt. 1688; London: John Field, 1658).

Parker, Henry, *A Discourse Concerning Puritans* (London, 1641).

———, *Jus populi* (London, 1644)

———, *Observations upon some of his majesties late answers and expresses* (London, 1642).

———, *Scotlands holy war* (London, 1651).

Parr, Elnathan, *Grounds of Divinitie* (London, 1651).

Patrick, Simon, *A Brief Account of the New Sect Called Latitude-Men* (London, 1662).

Penington, Isaac, *Divine Essays; or, Considerations about Several Things in Religion* (London: Giles Calvert, 1654).

———, *Light or Darknesse* (London, 1649).

Perkins, William, *Workes of that Famovs and VVorthy minister of Christ ...* (3 vols., Cambridge, 1608, 1609).

———, *The Work of William Perkins*, ed. Ian Breward (Abingdon: Sutton Courtenay, 1970).

Petty, William, *The Petty Papers: Some Unpublished Writings of Sir William Petty*, ed. Marquis of Lansdowne (2 vols., London: Constable, 1927).

Preston, John, *Breast-Plate of Faith and Love*. 3 pts. (London, [2nd ed.]1630).

———, *A Liveles Life: Or, Mans Spirituall death in Sinne*. 2 pts. (London, [3rd ed.] 1635).

Prynne, William, *Histriomastix* (London, 1633).

Robinson, Henry, *An answer to Mr. William Prynn's Twelve Questions concerning Church Government, etc.* (London, 1644).

———, *John the Baptist* (London, 1644).

———, *Liberty of Conscience* (1644) in Haller (ed.), *Tracts on Liberty in the Puritan Revolution, 1638–1647.*

———, *A Short Answer to A.S. alias Adam Stewart's second part of his overgrown Duply* (London, 1645).

———, *Some few considerations* (London, 1646).

Rutherford, Samuel, *Lex, Rex* (1644).

Rudrum, Alan, et al., *The Broadview Anthology of Seventeenth-Century Verse & Prose* (Petersborough, ON: Broadview Press, 2000).

Salkeld, John, *A Treatise of Paradise* (London: E. Griffin, 1617).

Saltmarsh, John, *Sparkles of Glory* (1647).

Sanderson, Robert, *The Works of Robert Sanderson*, ed. William Jacobson (6 vols., Oxford: Oxford University Press, 1854).

Selden, John, *De Jure Naturali et Gentium, juxta Disciplinam Ebraeorum* (1640).

———, *Table Talk* (1689).

A Serious and Faithfull Representation of the Judgements of Ministers of the Gospel within the Province of London (January 18, 1649).

Sidney, Algernon, *Discourses concerning Government*, ed. Thomas G. West (Indianapolis: Liberty Classics, 1990).

Sidney, Sir Philip, *An Apology for Poetry*, in Adams (ed.), *Critical Theory Since Plato.*

Smith, John, *Select Discourses* (1660, 1673).

Spenser, Edmund, *Edmund Spenser, "The Faerie Queene,"* ed. A.C. Hamilton [rev. ed.] (Harlow: Pearson Longman, 2007).

Sprat, Thomas, *History of the Royal Society*, ed. Jackson I. Cope and Harold Whitmore Jones (St. Louis: Washington University Press, 1966).

Stennett, Joseph, *Hymns* (London: J. Darby, 1697).

Sterry, Peter, *The Spirits conviction of Sinne* (London: Matth. Simmons, 1645).

Taylor, Jeremy, *The Whole Works of the Right Rev. Jeremy Taylor*, ed. Reginald Heber (12 vols., London: C. and J. Rivington, 1828),

Taylor, Thomas, *Japhets First Public Perswasion* (Cambridge, 1612).

Trenchard, John and Thomas Gordon, *Cato's Letters*, ed. Ronald Hamowy (2 vols., Liberty Fund, 1995).

T.S., *The Book of the Song of Solomon in Meeter* (1697).

Twisse, William, *A Treatise of Mr. Cottons, Clearing Certaine Doubts Concerning Predestination. Together with an Examination thereof ...* (London, 1646).

Wallis, John, *A Defence of the Royal Society* (London, 1678).

Walwyn, William, *A Compassionate Samaritan* (1644).

———, *The Vanitie of the Present Churches* (1649).

Ward, Seth, *Vindiciae Academiarum* (Oxford, 1654).

Webster, John, *Academiarum Examen* (1654).

Welde, Thomas, *Rise, reign, and ruine* (London, 1644)

Whichcote, Benjamin, *Moral and religious Aphorisms, to which are added Eight Letters ... between Dr. Whichcote ... and Dr. Tuckney*, ed. Samuel Salter (London: J. Payne, 1753).

————, *Select Sermons* (1698).

Wilkins, John, *Discourse Concerning a New Planet* (London: John Maynard, 1640).

————, *A Discovery of a New World in the Moone* (London: Jon Maynard, 1638).

————, *Mathematical Magick: Or, the Wonders That May be performed by Mechanichal [sic] Geometry* [rpt. 1638] (London, 1680).

Williams, Roger, *The Bloody Tenant of Persecution* (1644), in Woodhouse (ed.), *Puritanism and Liberty*.

————, *Queries of Highest Consideration, Proposed to the five Holland Ministers and the Scotch Commissioners (So Called)* (London, 1644).

————, 16 December 1649, *Collections of the Massachusetts History Society* 4th ser., vol. 6 (Boston, 1863).

Wilson, Thomas, *Davids Zeale for Zion* (London, 1641).

Wither, George, *Haleluiah, or, Britans Second Remembrancer* (1641).

Woodhouse, A.S.P. (ed.), *Puitanism and Liberty* (Chicago: University of Chicago Press, 1951).

Secondary Sources

Aarsleff, Hans, *From Locke to Saussure* (Minneapolis: University of Minnesota Press, 1982).

Achinstein, Sharon, *Literature and Dissent in Milton's England* (Cambridge: Cambridge University Press, 2003).

————, "Milton Catches the Conscience of the King: *Eikonoklastes* and the Engagement Controversy," *Milton Studies* 29 (1992): 143–63.

————, *Milton and the Revolutionary Reader* (Princeton: Princeton University Press, 1994).

Adolph, Robert, *The Rise of Modern Prose Style* (Cambridge, MA: MIT Press, 1968).

Appelbaum, Robert, *Literature and Utopian Politics in Seventeenth-Century England* (Cambridge: Cambridge University Press, 2002).

Armitage, David, Armand Himy, and Quentin Skinner, *Milton and Republicanism* (Cambridge: Cambridge University Press, 1995).

Aston, Margaret, "Puritans ard Iconoclasm, 1560–1660," in Durston and Eales (eds.), *The Culture of English Puritanism 1560–1700*, pp. 92–121.

Aylmer, G.E., *The State's Servants* (London: Routledge & Kegan Paul, 1973).

Baker, Herschel, *The Wars of Truth* (Cambridge, MA: Harvard University Press, 1952).

Barker, Arthur E., *Milton and the Puritan Dilemma 1641–1660* (Toronto: University of Toronto Press, 1942).

Barbour, Reid, "Lucy Hutchinson, Atomism and the Atheist Dog," in Lynette Hunter and Sarah Hutton (eds.), *Women, Science and Medicine 1500–1700:*

Mothers and Sisters of the Royal Society (Stroud: Sutton Publications, 1997), pp. 122–37.

Benedict, Philip, *Christ's Churches Purely Reformed: A Social History of Calvinism* (New Haven: Yale University Press, 2002).

Bennett, Joan S., *Reviving Liberty: Radical Christian Humanism in Milton's Great Poems* (Cambridge, MA: Harvard University Press, 1989).

Bethell, S.L., *The Cultural Revolution of the Seventeenth Century* (London: Dennis Dobson, 1951).

Borris, Kenneth, *Allegory and Epic in English Renaissance Literature: Heroic Form in Sidney, Spenser, and Milton* (Cambridge: Cambridge University Press, 2000).

Bozeman, Theodore Dwight, *To Live Ancient Lives: The Primitivist Dimension in Puritanism* (Chapel Hill: University of North Carolina Press, 1988).

Brodwin, Leonora L., "The Dissolution of Satan in *Paradise Lost*," *Milton Studies* 8 (1975): 165–207.

Bremer, Francis J. (ed.), *Puritanism: Transatlantic Perspectives on a Seventeenth-Century Anglo-American Faith* (Boston: Massachusetts Historical Society, 1993).

Breward, Ian, "The Abolition of Puritanism," *Journal of Religious History* 7 (1972): 20–34.

Brown, Cedric C., *Milton's Aristocratic Entertainments* (Cambridge: Cambridge University Press, 1985).

Brydon, Michael, *The Evolving Reputation of Richard Hooker: An Examination of the Responses 1600–1714* (Oxford: Oxford University Press, 2006).

Buhler, Stephen M., "Counterpoint and Controversy: Milton and the Critiques of Polyphonic Music," *Milton Studies* 36 (1998): 18–40.

Burbery, Timothy J., *Milton the Dramatist* (Pittsburgh: Duquesne University Press, 2007).

Burgess, Glenn, *Absolute Monarchy and the Stuart Constitution* (New Haven: Yale University Press, 1996).

———, *The Politics of the Ancient Constitution* (Basingstoke: Macmillan, 1992).

———, "Was the Civil War a War of Religion?," *Huntington Library Quarterly* 2 (1998): 173–201.

Burns, Norman, *Christian Mortalism from Tyndale to Milton* (Cambridge, MA: Harvard University Press 1972).

Bush, Douglas, *English Literature in the Earlier Seventeenth Century* (Oxford: Clarendon Press, 1945).

———, *John Milton: A Sketch of His Life and Writings* (New York: Macmillan, 1964).

Butler, Martin, *Theatre in Crisis 1632–42* (Cambridge: Cambridge University Press, 1984).

Butterfield, Herbert, *The Whig Interpretation of History* (London: G. Bell and Sons, 1931).

Campbell, Gordon, *A Milton Chronology* (Basingstoke: Macmillan, 1997).

————, and Thomas N. Corns, *John Milton: Life, Work, and Thought* (Oxford: Oxford University Press, 2008).

Capkova, Dagmar, "Comenius and his ideals: escape from the labyrinth," in Greengrass et al. (eds.), *Samuel Hartlib and Universal Reformation*, pp. 75–91.

Capp, Bernard, "The Fifth Monarchists and Popular Millenarianism," in McGregor and Reay (eds.), *Radical Religion in the English Revolution*, pp. 165–89.

Chaplin, Gregory, "'One Flesh, One Heart, One Soul': Renaissance Friendship and Miltonic Marriage," *MP* 99.2 (2001): 266–92.

Chaney, Edward, *The Grand Tour and the Great Rebellion: Richard Lassels and the "Voyage of Italy" in the Seventeenth Century* (Geneve: Slatkine, 1985).

Chernaik, Warren, "Christian Liberty in Marvell and Milton," in Richardson and Ridden (eds.), *Freedom and the English Revolution*, pp. 45–71.

Christopher, Georgia, *Milton and the Science of the Saints* (Princeton: Princeton University Press, 1982).

Clark, Donald Lemen, *John Milton at St. Paul's School* (New York: Columbia University Press, 1948).

Clark, J.C.D., *Revolution and Rebellion: State and Society in England in the Seventeenth and Eighteenth Centuries* (Cambridge: Cambridge University Press, 1986).

Clark, Peter, "The Alehouse and the Alternate Society," in Pennington and Thomas (eds.), *Puritans and Revolutionaries*, pp. 42–72.

Coffey, John, *John Goodwin and the Puritan Revolution* (Woodbridge: Boydell, 2006).

————, "Puritanism and Liberty Revisited: The Case for Toleration in the English Revolution," *Historical Journal* 41.4 (1998): 961–85.

Cogswell, Thomas, Richard Cust, and Peter Lake (eds.), *Politics, Religion and Popularity in Early Stuart Britain: Essays in Honour of Conrad Russell* (Cambridge: Cambridge University Press, 2002).

Collinson, Patrick, *The Birthpangs of Protestant England: Religious and Cultural Change in the Sixteenth and Seventeenth Centuries* (New York: St. Martin's Press, 1988).

————, "A Comment: Concerning the Name Puritan," *Journal of Ecclesiastical History* 31 (1980): 483–88.

————, *From Iconoclasm to Iconophobia* (Reading, UK: University of Reading Press, 1986).

————, *Godly People* (London: Hambledon Press, 1983).

————, *The Religion of Protestants* (Oxford: Clarendon Press, 1982).

————, "Sects and the Evolution of Puritanism," in Bremer (ed.), *Puritanism: Transatlantic Perspectives*, pp. 147–66.

Como, David, *Blown by the Spirit: Puritanism and the Emergence of an Antinomian Underground in Pre-Civil-War England* (Stanford: Stanford University Press, 2004).

Coolidge, John S., *The Pauline Renaissance in England: Puritanism and the Bible* (Oxford: Clarendon Press, 1970).

Condren, Conal, *The Language of Politics in Seventeenth-Century England* (New York: St. Martin's Press, 1994).

Cope, Jackson, I., "Seventeenth-Century Quaker Style," *PMLA* 71.4 (1956): 725–54.

Corns, Thomas N., *The Development of Milton's Prose Style* (New York: Oxford University Press, 1982).

———, "Milton before 'Lycidas,'" in Parry and Raymond (eds.), *Milton and the Terms of Liberty*, pp. 23–36.

———, "Milton's Antiprelatical Tracts and the Marginality of Doctrine," in Dobranski and Rumrich (eds.), *Milton and Heresy*, pp. 39–48.

———, "Milton's Quest for Respectability," *Modern Language Review* 77.4 (1982): 769–79.

Coudert, Allison, "Henry More, the Kabbalah, and the Quakers" in Kroll et al. (eds.), *Philosophy, Science, and Religion in England 1640–1700*, pp. 31–67.

Cragg, Gerald R., *Freedom and Authority: A Study of English Thought in the Early Seventeenth Century* (Philadelphia: The Westminster Press, 1975).

———, *From Puritanism to the Age of Reason* (Cambridge: Cambridge University Press, 1950).

———, *Puritanism in the Period of the Great Persecution 1660–1688* (Cambridge: Cambridge University Press, 1957).

Creaser, John, "'The present aid of this occasion': The setting of *Comus*," in David Lindley (ed.), *The Court Masque* (Manchester: Manchester University Press, 1984), pp. 111–34.

Cross, Frank, *Canaanite Myth and Hebrew Epic* (Cambridge, MA: Harvard University Press, 1973).

Cummins, Juliet (ed.), *Milton and the Ends of Time* (Cambridge: Cambridge University Press, 2003).

Danielson, Dennis, *Milton's Good God* (Cambridge: Cambridge University Press,1982).

Davies, Godfrey, *The Restoration of Charles II* (London: Oxford University Press, 1955).

Davies, Horton, *The Worship of the English Puritans* (Glasgow: Robert Maclemore, 1948).

———, *Worship and Theology in England: From Andrewes to Baxter and Fox, 1603–1690* (Princeton: Princeton University Press, 1975).

Davis, J.C., "The Levellers and Christianity," in Manning (ed.), *Politics, Religion, and the English Civil War*, pp. 225–50.

———, "The Millennium as the Anti-Utopia of Seventeenth Century Political Thought," *Anglophonia: French Journal of English Studies* 3 (1998): 57–66.

———, "Religion and the struggle for freedom in the English Revolution," *Historical Journal* 35.3 (1992): 507–30.

———, *Utopia and the Ideal Society: A Study of English Utopian Writing, 1516–1700* (Cambridge: Cambridge University Press, 1981).

Dean, Margaret Justice, "Choosing Death: Adam's Temptation to Martyrdom in *Paradise Lost*," *Milton Studies* 46 (2007): pp. 30–56.

Debus, Allen G., *Science and Education in the Seventeenth Century: The Webster–Ward Debate* (London: Macdonald, 1970).

Dick, Steven J., *Plurality of Worlds: The Origins of the Extraterrestrial Life Debate from Democritus to Kant* (Cambridge: Cambridge University Press, 1982).

Dobranski, Stephen B., and John P. Rumrich (eds.), *Milton and Heresy* (Cambridge: Cambridge University Press, 1998).

Duffy, Eamon, "The Godly and the Multitude in Stuart England," *The Seventeenth Century* 1.1 (1986): 31–55.

Dugas, Don-John, "'Such Heav'n-Taught Numbers should be more than read': *Comus* and Milton's Reputation in Mid-Eighteenth-Century England," *Milton Studies* 34 (1996): 137–57.

Duncan, Joseph E., *Milton's Earthly Paradise: A Historical Study of Eden* (Minneapolis: University of Minnesota Press, 1972).

Durston, Christopher, and Jacqueline Eales (eds.), *The Culture of English Puritanism, 1560–1700* (New York: St. Martin's Press, 1996).

Eccleshall, Robert, "Richard Hooker and the Peculiarities of the English: The Reception of the *Ecclesiastical Polity* in the Seventeenth and Eighteenth Centuries," *History of Political Thought* 2.1 (1981): 63–117.

Edwards, Karen, *Milton and the Natural World* (Cambridge: Cambridge University Press, 2001).

Eire, Carlos M.N., *War against the Idols* (Cambridge: Cambridge University Press, 1986).

Fallon, Stephen M., *Milton's Peculiar Grace: Self-Representation and Authority* (Ithaca, NY: Cornell University Press, 2007).

Farr, David, *Henry Ireton and the English Revolution* (Rochester, NY: Boydell & Brewer, 2006).

Finlayson, Michael G., *Historians, Puritanism, and the English Revolution: the Religious Factor in English Politics before and after the Interregnum* (Toronto: University of Toronto Press, 1983).

Firth, Charles H., *The Last Years of the Protectorate* (2 vols., London: Longmans, Green, and Co., 1909).

Firth, Katharine R., *The Apocalyptic Tradition in Reformation Britain 1530–1645* (New York: Oxford University Press, 1979).

Fisch, Harold, *Jerusalem and Albion* (New York: Schocken Books 1964).

Fish, Stanley E., *Self-Consuming Artifacts: The Experience of Seventeenth-Century Literature* (Berkeley: University of California Press, 1972).

———, *Surprised by Sin: The Reader in "Paradise Lost"* (Berkeley: University of California Press, 1967).

Fixler, Michael, *Milton and the Kingdoms of God* (Evanston: Northeastern University Press, 1964).

Fletcher, Anthony, *The Outbreak of the English Civil War* (London: Edward Arnold, 1981).

———, "The Protestant Idea of Marriage in Early Modern England," in Fletcher and Roberts (eds.), *Religion, Culture, and Society in Early Modern Britain*, pp. 161–81.

———, and Peter Roberts (eds.), *Religion, Culture, and Society in Early Modern Britain: Essays in Honour of Patrick Collinson* (Cambridge: Cambridge University Press, 1994).

Fletcher, Harris Francis, *The Intellectual Development of John Milton* (2 vols., Urbana, IL: University of Illinois Press, 1961).

Foster, Andrew, "The Clerical Estate Revitalised," in Kenneth Fincham (ed.), *The Early Stuart Church, 1603–1642* (Stanford: Stanford University Press, 1993), pp. 139–60.

Fowler, Alastair, "*Paradise Regained:* Some Problems of Style," in Piero Boitani and Anna Torti (eds.), *Medieval and Pseudo-Medieval Literature* (Cambridge: D.S. Brewer, 1984), pp. 181–89.

Fried, Daniel, "Milton and Empiricist Semiotics," *MQ* 37.3 (October 2003): 117–38.

Frye, Northrop, "Agon and Logos: Revolution and Revelation," in Balachandra Rajan (ed.), *The Prison and the Pinnacle* (London: Routledge & Kegan Paul, 1973), pp. 135–73.

Gardiner, Samuel R., *History of the Commonwealth and Protectorate* (4 vols., London, 1903).

———, *History of England from the Accession of James I to the Outbreak of the Civil War, 1603–42* (10 vols., London: Longmans, Green, and Co., 1883–84).

———, *History of the Great Civil War, 1642–1649* (4 vols., London: Longmans, Green, and Co., 1893).

Garnett, Richard, *The Life of Milton* (London: W. Scott, 1890).

Gay, David, "'Rapt Spirits': 2 Corinthians 12.2–5 and the Language of Milton's *Comus*," *MQ* 29.3 (1995): 76–86.

George, Charles H., "Puritanism as History and Historiography," *Past and Present* 41 (1968): 77–104.

———, and Katherine George, *The Protestant Mind of the English Reformation 1570–1640* (Princeton: Princeton University Press, 1961).

Gentles, Ian, John Morrill, and Blair Worden (eds.), *Soldiers, Writers, and Statesmen of the English Revolution* (Cambridge: Cambridge University Press, 1998).

Goldie, Mark, "The Civil Religion of James Harrington," in Anthony Pagden (ed.), *The Languages of Political Theory in Early-Modern Europe* (Cambridge: Cambridge University Press, 1987), pp. 197–222.

Grafton, Anthony, *Defenders of the Text* (Cambridge, MA: Harvard University Press, 1991).

Greaves, Richard L., *The Puritan Revolution and Educational Thought: Background for Reform* (New Brunswick, NJ: Rutgers University Press, 1969).

Greenblatt, Stephen, *Renaissance Self-Fashioning* (Chicago: University of Chicago Press, 1980).

Greengrass, Mark, Michael Leslie, and Timothy Raylor (eds.), *Samuel Hartlib and Universal Reformation* (Cambridge: Cambridge University Press, 1994).

Guibbory, Achsah, *Ceremony and Community from Herbert to Milton: Literature, Religion, and Cultural Change in Seventeenth-Century England* (Cambridge: Cambridge University Press, 1998).

Haight, Roger, *The Experience and the Language of Grace* (New York: Paulist Press, 1979).

Halkett, John, *Milton and the Idea of Matrimony: A Study of the Divorce Tracts and Paradise Lost* (New Haven: Yale University Press, 1970).

Hall, Basil, "Puritanism: the Problem of Definition," in *Studies in Church History* 2 (1965): 283–96.

Haller, William, *The Rise of Puritanism* (1938; rpt. New York: Harper & Row, 1957).

———, and Malleville Haller, "'Hail Wedded Love,'" *ELH* 13 (1946): 79–97.

Hanford, James Holly, "The Chronology of Milton's Private Studies," *PMLA* 36.2 (1921): 251–314.

Hardie, Philip, "The Presence of Lucretius in *Paradise Lost,*" *MQ* 29.1 (1995): 13–24.

Hardin, Richard F., *Civil Idolatry: Desacralizing and Monarchy in Spenser, Shakespeare, and Milton* (Newark, DE: University of Delaware Press, 1992).

Haskin, Dayton, *Milton's Burden of Interpretation* (Philadelphia: University of Pennsylvania Press, 1994).

Hauskneckt, Gina, "The Gender of Civic Virtue," in Martin (ed.), *Milton and Gender*, pp. 19–33.

Hawkes, David, "Milton and Usury," Paper read at the Ninth International Milton Symposium, July 11, 2008.

Heinemann, Margot, *Puritanism and the Theatre: Thomas Middleton and Opposition Drama under the Early Stuarts* (Cambridge: Cambridge University Press, 1986).

Heal, Felicity, "The Idea of Hospitality in Early Modern England," *Past and Present* 102 (1984): 66–93.

Helgerson, Richard, *Self-Crowned Laureates: Spenser, Jonson, Milton and the Literary System* (Berkeley: University of California Press, 1983).

Henry, Nathaniel H., "Who Meant License When They Cried Liberty?" *MLN* 66.8 (1951): 509–13.

Herendeen, Wyman, "Milton and Machiavelli: The Historical Revolution and Protestant Poetics," in Mario di Cesare (ed.), *Milton in Italy* (Binghamton, NY: Medieval and Renaissance Texts and Studies, 1991), pp. 427–44.

Herman, Peter, *Destabilizing Milton: "Paradise Lost" and the Poetics of Incertitude* (New York: Palgrave Macmillan, 2005).

Hexter, J.H., "Storm over the Gentry," in *Reappraisals in History* (Evanston, IL: Northwestern University Press, 1962), 117–62.

Hill, Christopher, *The Century of Revolution* (New York: Norton, 1961).

——, *Change and Continuity in Seventeenth-Century England* (London: Weidenfeld and Nicolson, 1974).

——, *The Experience of Defeat: Milton and Some Contemporaries* (London: Faber & Faber, 1984).

——, "From Lollards to Levellers," in Maurice C. Cornforth (ed.), *Rebels and their Causes* (London: Lawrence and Wishart, 1978), pp. 49–67.

——, *The Intellectual Origins of the English Revolution* (Oxford: Clarendon Press, 1965).

——, *Milton and the English Revolution* (London: Faber & Faber, 1977).

——, *Puritanism and Revolution* (New York: Schocken Books, 1964).

——, *Society and Puritanism in Pre-Revolutionary England* (New York: Schocken Books, 1964).

——, *The World Turned Upside Down* (London: Temple Smith, 1972).

Hill, John Spencer, *John Milton: Poet, Priest and Prophet* (London: Macmillan, 1979).

Hinman, Robert B., *Abraham Cowley's World of Order* (Cambridge, MA: Harvard University Press, 1960).

Hirst, Derek, *Authority and Conflict in England 1603–1658* (London: Edward Arnold, 1986).

——, "The Failure of Godly Rule in the English Republic," *Past and Present* 132 (1991): 33–66.

Hiscock, W.G., *John Evelyn and Mrs. Godolphin* (London: Macmillan, 1951).

Hobby, Elaine, "A woman's best setting-out is silence: The Writings of Hannah Wooley," in Maclean (ed.), *Culture and Society in the Stuart Restoration*, pp. 179–200.

Hollander, John, *The Untuning of the Sky: Ideas of Music in English Poetry 1500–1700* (Princeton: Princeton University Press, 1961).

Holstun, James, *Ehud's Dagger: Class Struggle in the English Revolution* (New York: Verso, 2000).

——, *Towards a Rational Millennium* (New York: Oxford University Press, 1987).

Honeygosky, Stephen R., *Milton's House of God: The Invisible and Visible Church* (Columbia: University of Missouri Press, 1993).

Hoopes, Robert, *Right Reason in the English Renaissance* (Cambridge, MA: Harvard University Press, 1962).

Hoxby, Blair, *Mammon's Music: Literature and Economics in the Age of Milton* (New Haven: Yale University Press, 2002).

Huehns, Gertrude, *Antinomianism in English History, with Special Reference to the Period 1640–1660* (London: Cresset, 1951).

Hughes, Ann, "The Frustrations of the Godly," in Morrill (ed.), *Revolution and Restoration*, pp. 70–90.

——, *"Gangraena" and the Struggle for the English Revolution* (Oxford: Oxford University Press, 2004).

Hume, Robert, "The Aims and Limits of Historical Scholarship," *RES* 53 (August 2002): 399–422.

Hunt, William, *The Puritan Moment* (Cambridge, MA: Harvard University Press, 1983).

Hunter, Michael, *Establishing the New Science: The Experience of the Early Royal Society* (Woodbridge: Boydell Press, 1989).

———, *John Aubrey and the Realm of Learning* (New York: Science History Publications, 1975).

———, *Science and the Shape of Orthodoxy: Intellectual Change in Late Seventeenth-Century Britain* (Woodbridge: Boydell Press, 1995).

———, *Science and Society in Restoration England* (Cambridge: Cambridge University Press, 1981).

Hunter, William B., Jack H. Adamson, and C.A. Patrides, *Bright Essence: Studies in Milton's Theology* (Salt Lake City: University of Utah Press, 1971).

———, *The Descent of Urania: Studies in Milton 1949–1988* (Lewisburg: Bucknell University Press, 1989).

———, *Visitation Unimplor'd: Milton and the Authorship of De Doctrina Christiana* (Pittsburgh: Duquesne University Press, 1998).

Huntley, Frank L., *Jeremy Taylor and the Great Rebellion* (Ann Arbor: University of Michigan Press, 1970).

Hutton, Sarah, "Edward Stillingfleet, Henry More, and the Decline of *Moses Atticus*: A Note on Seventeenth-Century Anglican Apologetics," in Kroll et al. (eds.), *Philosophy, Science, and Religion*, 68–84.

———, "Mede, Milton, and More: Christ's College millenarians," in Cummins (ed.), *Milton and the Ends of Time*, pp. 29–41.

Jacob, Margaret, *The Newtonians and the English Revolution, 1689–1720* (Ithaca: Cornell University Press, 1976).

———, *The Radical Enlightenment: Pantheists, Freemasons, and Republicans* (Boston: Allen & Unwin, 1981).

Johnson, F.R., *Astronomical Thought in Renaissance England* (Baltimore: Johns Hopkins University Press, 1937).

Jones, Hugh Lloyd, Valerie Pearl, and Blair Worden (eds.), *History and Imagination: Essays in Honour of H.R. Trevor-Roper* (London: Duckworth, 1981).

Jones, Richard Foster, *Ancients and Moderns* (St. Louis: Washington University Press, 1936).

———, *The Seventeenth Century* (Palo Alto: Stanford University Press, 1951).

Jordan, W.K., *Men of Substance: A Study of the Thought of Two English Revolutionaries, Henry Parker and Henry Robinson* (Chicago: Chicago University Press, 1942).

Kahn, Victoria, *Machiavellian Rhetoric: From the Counter-Reformation to Milton* (Princeton: Princeton University Press, 1994).

———, *Wayward Contracts: The Crisis of Political Obligation in England 1640–1674* (Princeton: Princeton University Press, 2004).

Kane, Sean, *Spenser's Moral Allegory* (Toronto: University of Toronto Press, 1989).

Katz, David S., "The Language of Adam in Seventeenth-Century England," in Jones et al., *History and Imagination*, pp. 132–45.

Keeble, N.H., "Milton and Puritanism," in Thomas N. Corns (ed.), *A Companion to Milton* (Oxford: Blackwell, 2001), pp. 124–40.

———, *The Literary Culture of Nonconformity* (Athens, GA: University of Georgia Press, 1987).

Kelley, Mark R., Michael Lieb, and John T. Shawcross (eds.), *Milton and the Grounds of Contention* (Pittsburgh: Duquesne University Press, 2003).

Kelsall, Malcolm, "The Historicity of *Paradise Regained*," *Milton Studies* 12 (1978): 235–51.

Kendall, R.T., *Calvin and English Calvinism to 1649* (Oxford: Oxford University Press, 1979).

Kennington, Richard, *On Modern Origins*, ed. Pamela Kraus and Frank Hunt (Lanham, MD: Lexington Books, 2004).

Kenyon, J.P., *The Stuart Constitution, 1603–1688* (Cambridge: Cambridge University Press, 1966).

King, John N., *English Reformation Literature: The Tudor Origins of the Protestant Tradition* (Princeton: Princeton University Press, 1982).

———, *Milton and Religious Controversy: Satire and Polemic in "Paradise Lost"* (Cambridge: Cambridge University Press, 2000).

———, *Spenser's Poetry and the Reformation Tradition* (Princeton: Princeton University Press, 1990).

Kishlansky, Mark, "Ideology and Politics in the Parliamentary Armies, 1645–9," in Morrill (ed.), *Reactions to the English Civil War 1642–1649*, pp. 163–83.

Klein, Joan Larson, "Some Spenserian Influences on Milton's *Comus*," *Annuale mediaevale* 5 (1964): 27–47.

Knight, David, "Science Fiction of the Seventeenth Century," *The Seventeenth Century* 1.1 (1986): 69–79.

Knoppers, Laura Lunger, "*Paradise Regained* and the Politics of Martyrdom," *MP* 90.2 (1992): 200–19.

——— (ed.), *Puritanism and Its Discontents* (Newark: University of Delaware Press, 2002).

Knott, John R., Jr., "'Suffering for Truths sake: Milton and martyrdom," in Loewenski and Turner (eds.), *Politics, Poetics, and Hermeneutics in Milton's Prose*, pp. 153–70.

———, *The Sword of the Spirit* (Chicago: University of Chicago Press, 1980).

Knox, Ronald, *Enthusiasm: A Chapter in the History of Religion* (New York: Oxford University Press, 1950).

Kroll, Richard W.F., *The Material Word: Literate Culture in the Restoration and Early Eighteenth Century* (Baltimore: Johns Hopkins University Press, 1991).

———, Richard Ashcraft, and Perez Zagorin (eds.), *Philosophy, Science, and Religion in England 1640–1700* (Cambridge: Cambridge University Press, 1992).

Lake, Peter, *Anglicans and Puritans? Presbyterians and English Conformist Thought from Whitgift to Hooker* (London: Unwin Hyman, 1988).

———, "Anti-popery: the structure of a prejudice," in Richard Cust and Ann Hughes (eds.), *The English Civil War* (London: Arnold, 1997), pp. 181–210.

———, "Defining Puritanism—again?" in Bremer (ed.), *Puritanism: Transatlantic Perspectives*, pp. 3–29.

———, "'A Charitable Christian Hatred': The Godly and Their Enemies in the 1630s," in Durston and Eales (eds.), *The Culture of English Puritanism, 1560–1700*, pp. 145–83.

———, "Presbyterianism, the National Church and the Argument from Divine Right," in Peter Lake and Maria Dowling (eds.), *Protestantism and the National Church* (London: Croom Helm, 1987), pp. 193–224.

———, and Kevin Sharpe (eds.), *Culture and Politics in Early Stuart England* (Basingstoke: Macmillan, 1997).

Lamont, William, *Godly Rule: Politics and Religion 1603–1660* (New York: St. Martin's Press, 1969).

———, "Pamphleteering, the Protestant consensus and the English Revolution," in Richardson and Ridden (eds.), *Freedom and the English Revolution*, pp. 72–92.

———, *Puritanism and Historical Controversy* (Montreal: McGill-Queens University Press, 1996).

———, *Richard Baxter and the Millennium* (London: Croom Helm, 1979).

———, "The Two 'National Churches' of 1691 and 1829," in Fletcher and Roberts (eds.), *Religion, Culture, and Society in Early Modern Britain*, pp. 335–52.

Lang, Timothy, *The Victorians and the Stuart Heritage: Interpretations of a Discordant Past* (Cambridge: Cambridge University Press, 1995).

Lecler, Joseph, *Toleration and the Reformation* (2 vols., London: Longmans, Green, & Co., 1960).

Lemmi, Charles W., *The Classic Deities in Bacon: A Study in Mythological Symbolism* (Baltimore: Johns Hopkins University Press, 1933).

Levao, Ronald, "Francis Bacon and the Mobility of Science," *Representations* 40 (1992): 1–32.

Leverenz, David, *The Language of Puritan Feeling: An Exploration in Literature, Psychology, and Social History* (New Brunswick, NJ: Rutgers University Press, 1980).

Levine, Joseph, "Latitudinarians, Neoplatonists, and Ancient Wisdom," in Kroll et al. (eds.), *Philosophy, Science, and Religion in England 1640–1700*, pp. 85–108.

Lewalski, Barbara K., *The Life of John Milton* (Malden, MA: Blackwell, 2003).

———, "Milton and *De Doctrina Christiana:* Evidences of Authorship," *Milton Studies* 36 (1998): 203–28.

——, "Milton on Learning and the Learned Ministry Controversy," *HLQ* 24.4 (1961): 267–81.

——, "Milton and the Millennium," in Cummins (ed.), *Milton and the Ends of Time*, pp. 13–28.

——, "Milton's *Comus* and the Politics of Masquing," in David Bevington and Peter Holbrook (eds.), *The Politics of the Stuart Court Masque* (Cambridge: Cambridge University Press, 1998), pp. 296–320.

——, *Protestant Poetics and the Seventeenth-Century Religious Lyric* (Princeton: Princeton University Press, 1979).

—— (ed.), *Renaissance Genres: Essays on Theory, History, and Interpretation* (Cambridge, MA: Harvard University Press, 1986).

——, "*Samson Agonistes* and the 'Tragedy' of the Apocalypse," *PMLA* 85 (1970): 1050–62.

——, "'To try, and teach the erring Soul': Milton's Last Seven Years," in Parry and Raymond (eds.), *Milton and the Terms of Liberty*, pp. 179–90.

Lewis, C.S., *A Preface to "Paradise Lost"* (New York: Oxford University Press, 1961).

Lieb, Michael, "Milton and the Socinian Heresy," in Kelley et al. (eds.), *Milton and the Grounds of Contention*, pp. 234–83 and 318–33.

Little, Patrick (ed.), *The Cromwellian Protectorate* (Rochester, NY: Boydell & Brewer, 2007).

Liu, Tai, *Discord in Zion: The Puritan Divines and the Puritan Revolution 1640–1660* (The Hague: Nijhoff, 1973).

Loewenstein, David, *Representing Revolution in Milton and His Contemporaries: Religion, Politics, and Polemics in Radical Puritanism* (Cambridge: Cambridge University Press, 2001).

——, "Writing and the Persecution of Heretics in Henry VIII's England: The Examination of Anne Askew," in Loewenstein and Marshall (eds.), *Heresy, Literature, and Politics in Early Modern English Culture*, pp. 11–39.

——, and John Marshall (eds.), *Heresy, Literature, and Politics in Early Modern English Culture* (Cambridge: Cambridge University Press, 2006).

——, and James Grantham Turner (eds.), *Politics, Poetics, and Hermeneutics in Milton's Prose* (Cambridge: Cambridge University Press, 1990).

Lynch, William T., *Solomon's Child* (Palo Alto: Stanford University Press, 2001).

Macaulay, Thomas, "Lord Bacon" (July 1837), in *Literary Essays Contributed to the Edinburgh Review* (London: Oxford University Press, 1913), pp. 203–322.

——, "Milton" (August 1825), in *Literary Essays*, pp. 3–51.

Maclean, Gerald (ed.), *Culture and Society in the Stuart Restoration: Literature, Drama, History* (Cambridge: Cambridge University Press, 1995).

Malcolm, Noel, "Hobbes and the Royal Society," in G.A.J. Rogers and Alan Ryan (eds.), *Perspectives on Thomas Hobbes* (Oxford: Clarendon Press, 1988).

Manning, Brian (ed.), *Politics, Religion, and the English Civil War* (London: Edward Arnold, 1973).

————, "Religion and Politics: The Godly People," in Manning (ed.), *Politics, Religion, and the English Civil War*, pp. 83–123.

Marcus, Leah S., *The Politics of Mirth: Jonson, Herrick, Milton, Marvell, and the Defense of Old Holiday Pastime* (Chicago: Chicago University Press, 1986).

Martin, Catherine G., "The Feminine Birth of the Mind: Regendering the Empirical Subject in Bacon and His Followers," in Julie R. Solomon and Catherine G. Martin (eds.), *Francis Bacon and the Refiguring of Early Modern Thought* (Aldershot: Ashgate, 2005), pp. 69–88.

———— (ed.), *Milton and Gender* (Cambridge: Cambridge University Press, 2004).

————, "Milton and the Pursuit of Happiness," *UTQ* 77.3 (2008): 876–902.

————, "The Phoenix and the Crocodile: Milton's Natural Law Debate with Hobbes Retried in the Tragic Forum of *Samson Agonistes*," in Claude Summers and Ted Pebworth (eds.), *The English Civil Wars in the Literary Imagination* (Columbia, MO: University of Missouri Press, 1999), pp. 242–70.

————, *The Ruins of Allegory: "Paradise Lost" and the Metamorphosis of Epic Convention* (Durham: Duke University Press, 1998).

————, "Rewriting Cromwell: Milton, Marvell, and Negative Liberty in the English Revolution," *Clio* 36.3 (2007): 307–32.

————, "Rewriting the Revolution: Milton, Bacon, and the Royal Society Rhetoricians," in Juliet Cummins and David Burchell (eds.), *Science, Literature, and Rhetoric in Early Modern Europe* (Aldershot: Ashgate, 2007), pp. 95–123.

————, "Self-Raised Sinners and the Spirit of Capitalism: *Paradise Lost* and the Critique of Protestant Meliorism," *Milton Studies* 30 (1994): 109–33.

————, "What If the Sun Be Centre to the World?': Milton's Epistemology, Cosmology, and Paradise of Fools Reconsidered" *MP* 99.2 (2001): 231–65.

————, "Unediting Milton: Historical Myth and Editorial Misconstruction in the Yale Prose Edition," in Christophe Tournu (ed.), *Milton, Rights and Liberties* (New York: Peter Lang, 2006), pp. 113–30.

Masson, David, *The Life of John Milton* [rpt. 1874] (6 vols., New York: Peter Smith, 1946).

Maule, Jeremy, "Milton's Hammersmith," Paper read at the Fifteenth British Milton Seminar, Birmingham, March 1997.

McAdoo, H.R., *The Spirit of Anglicanism* (New York: Charles Scribner's Sons, 1965).

————, *The Structure of Caroline Moral Theology* (London: Longmans, Green and Co., 1949).

McDowell, Nicholas, "Family Politics: How John Phillips Read His Uncle's Satirical Sonnets," *Milton Quarterly* 42.1 (March 2008): 1–21.

McGee, J. Sears, *The Godly Man in Stuart England: Anglicans, Puritans, and the Two Tables, 1620–1670* (New Haven: Yale University Press, 1976).

McGregor, J.F., "The Baptists: Fount of all Heresy," in McGregor and Reay (eds.), *Radical Religion in the English Revolution*, pp. 23–64.

————, and B. Reay (eds.), *Radical Religion in the English Revolution* (London: Oxford University Press, 1984).

McGuire, Maryann Cale, *Milton's Puritan Masque* (Athens, GA: University of Georgia Press, 1983).

McKnight, Stephen A., *The Religious Foundations of Francis Bacon's Thought* (Columbia, MO: University of Missouri Press, 2006),

McLachlan, Herbert John, *The Religious Opinions of Milton, Locke and Newton* (Manchester: Manchester University Press, 1941).

————, *Socinianism in Seventeenth-Century England* (London: Oxford University Press, 1951).

Mendle, Michael, *Henry Parker and the English Civil War: The Political Thought of the Public's "Privado"* (Cambridge: Cambridge University Press, 1995).

Miller, Leo, "Milton's Clash with Chappell: A Suggested Reconstruction," *MQ* 14.3 (1980): 77–87.

Miller, Perry, *The New England Mind: The Seventeenth Century* (Cambridge, MA: Harvard University Press, 1956).

Milner, Andrew, *John Milton and the English Revolution: A Study in the Sociology of Literature* (London: Macmillan, 1981).

Milton, Anthony, "Licensing, Censorship, and Religious Orthodoxy in Stuart England," *The Historical Journal* 41.3 (1998): 625–51.

————, "The Unchanged Peacemaker? John Dury and the politics of irenicism in England, 1628–1643," in Greengrass et al. (eds.), *Samuel Hartlib and Universal Reformation*, pp. 95–117.

Miner, Earl, "Dryden's Admired Acquaintance, Mr. Milton," *Milton Studies* 11 (1978): 3–27.

Moore, Susan Harman, "Popery, Purity, and Providence: Deciphering the New England Experiment," in Fletcher and Roberts (eds.), *Religion, Culture, and Society*, pp. 257–89.

More, Ellen, "John Goodwin and the Origin of the New Arminianism," *Journal of British Studies* 21.1 (1982): 50–70.

Morgan, John, *Godly Learning: Puritan Attitudes toward Reason, Learning, and Education, 1560–1640* (Cambridge: Cambridge University Press, 1986).

Morrill, John, "A Liberation Theology?," in Knoppers (ed.), *Puritanism and Its Discontents*, pp. 27–48.

————, "The Making of Oliver Cromwell," in *Oliver Cromwell and the English Revolution*, pp. 19–48.

————, *The Nature of the English Revolution* (London: Longman, 1993).

———— (ed.), *Oliver Cromwell and the English Revolution* (London: Longman, 1990).

———— (ed.), *Reactions to the English Civil War 1642–1649* (New York: St. Martin's Press, 1982).

———— (ed.), *Revolution and Restoration* (London: Collins & Brown, 1992).

Morton, A.L., *The World of the Ranters* (London: Lawrence & Wishart, 1970).

Mueller, Janel, "Embodying Glory: the Apocalyptic Strain in *Of Reformation*," in Loewenstein and Turner (eds.), *Politics, Poetics, and Hermeneutics in Milton's Prose*, pp. 9–40.

———, "Milton on Heresy," in Dobranski and Rumrich (eds.), *Milton and Heresy*, pp. 21–38.

Murray, Iain H., *The Puritan Hope: A Study in Revival and the Interpretation of Prophecy* (London: Banner of Truth Trust, 1971).

Nardo, Anna K., "Academic Interludes in *Paradise Lost*," *Milton Studies* 27 (1991): 209–41.

Netland, John, "Of Philistines and Puritans: Matthew Arnold's Construction of Puritanism," in Knoppers (ed.), *Puritanism and Its Discontents*, pp. 67–82.

Ng, Su Fang, *Literature and the Politics of the Family in Seventeenth-Century England* (Cambridge: Cambridge University Press, 2007).

Nohrnberg, James, "Paradise Regained by One Greater Man: Milton's Wisdom Epic as a Fable of Identity," in Eleanor Cook (ed.), *Centre and Labyrinth: Essays in Honour of Northrop Frye* (Toronto: University of Toronto Press, 1983), pp. 83–114.

Norbrook, David, *Poetry and Politics in the English Renaissance* (London: Routledge & Kegan Paul, 1984).

———, *Writing the English Republic: Poetry, Rhetoric, and Politics 1627–1660* (Cambridge: Cambridge University Press, 1999).

Nuttall, A.D., *Overheard by God* (London: Metheun, 1980).

Nuttall, Geoffrey F., *The Holy Spirit in Puritan Faith and Experience* (Chicago: University of Chicago Press, 1992).

———, *Visible Saints: The Congregational Way 1640–1660* (Oxford: Basil Blackwell, 1957).

Oakley, Francis, *Omnipotence, Covenant, and Order* (Ithaca: Cornell University Press, 1984).

Olson, Richard, *Science Deified and Science Defied: The Historical Significance of Science in Western Culture* (2 vols., Berkeley: University of California Press, 1990).

Ong, Walter, *Interfaces of the Word: Studies in the Evolution of Consciousness and Culture* (Ithaca: Cornell University Press, 1977).

———, *Orality and Literacy* (London: Methuen, 1982).

Pagels, Elaine, *Adam, Eve, and the Serpent* (New York: Random House 1988).

Parker, William R., *Milton: The Life* (Oxford: Clarendon Press, 1968).

———, *Milton's Contemporary Reputation* (Columbus, OH: Ohio State University Press, 1940).

Parry, Graham, *The Seventeenth Century* (London: Longman, 1989).

———, and Joad Raymond (eds.), *Milton and the Terms of Liberty* (New York: D.S. Brewer, 2002).

Patterson, Annabel, "The Civic Hero in Milton's Prose," *Milton Studies* 8 (1975): 71–101

——, *Early Modern Liberalism* (Cambridge: Cambridge University Press, 1997).

——, "'Forc'd Fingers': Milton's Early Poems and Ideological Constraints," in Claude J. Summers and Ted-Larry Pebworth (eds.), *"The Muse's Common-Weale": Poetry and Politics in the Seventeenth Century* (Columbia, MO: University of Missouri Press, 1988), pp. 9–22.

——, "*L'Allegro, Il Penseroso* and *Comus*: The Logic of Recombination," *MQ* 9.3 (1975): 75–79.

——, *Nobody's Perfect: A New Whig Interpretation of History* (New Haven: Yale University Press, 2002).

——, *Paradise Regained:* A Last Chance at True Romance," *Milton Studies* 17 (1983): 187–208.

——, "Pastoral versus Georgic: The Politics of Virgilian Quotation," in Lewalski (ed.), *Renaissance Genres*, pp. 241–67.

——, *Reading between the Lines* (Madison: University of Wisconsin Press, 1993).

Pennington, Donald, and Keith Thomas (eds.), *Puritans and Revolutionaries: Essays in Seventeenth-Century History Presented to Christopher Hill* (Oxford: Clarendon Press, 1978).

Picciotto, Joanna, "Reforming the Garden: The Experimentalist Eden and *Paradise Lost*," *English Literary History* 72 (2005): 23–78.

Pincus, Steven, *Protestantism and Patriotism: Ideologies and the Making of English Foreign Policy, 1650–1668* (Cambridge: Cambridge University Press, 1996).

Pinto, V. De Sola, "Isaac Watts and the Adventurous Muse," *Essays and Studies* 20 (1934): 86–107

Pocock, J.G.A., *The Ancient Constitution and the Feudal Law* (Cambridge: Cambridge University Press, 1957).

Poole, Kristen, *Radical Religion from Shakespeare to Milton* (Cambridge: Cambridge University Press, 2000).

Poole, William, *Milton and the Idea of the Fall* (Cambridge: Cambridge University Press, 2005).

——, "Two Early Readers of Milton: John Beale and Abraham Hill," *MQ* 38.2 (2004): 76–99.

Price, Bronwen (ed.), *Francis Bacon's "New Atlantis": New Interdisciplinary Essays* (Manchester: Manchester University Press, 2002).

Prince, Frank T., *The Italian Element in Milton's Verse* (Oxford: Clarendon Press, 1954).

Quilligan, Maureen, *Milton's Spenser: The Politics of Reading* (Ithaca: Cornell University Press, 1983).

Radzinowicz, Mary Ann, "*Samson Agonistes* and Milton the Politician in Defeat," *PQ* 44 (1965): 454–71.

——, *Toward Samson Agonistes: The Growth of Milton's Mind* (Princeton: Princeton University Press, 1978).

Rajan, Balachandra, and Elizabeth Sauer (eds.), *Milton and the Imperial Vision* (Pittsburgh: Duquesne University Press, 1999).

Raven, Charles E., *Organic Design: A Study of Scientific Thought from Ray to Paley* (London: Oxford University Press, 1954).

———, *Science, Religion, and the Future* (New York: Macmillan, 1943).

Redwood, J.A., "Charles Blount (1654–93), Deism, and English Free Thought," *JHI* 35.3 (1974): 490–98.

Revard, Stella P., *Milton and the Tangles of Naera's Hair* (Columbia, MO: University of Missouri Press, 1997).

Richardson, R.C. and G.M. Ridden (eds.), *Freedom and the English Revolution* (Manchester: Manchester University Press, 1986).

Rivers, Isabel, *Reason, Grace, and Sentiment: A Study of the Language of Religion and Ethics in England, 1660–1780* (2 vols., Cambridge: Cambridge University Press, 1991).

Robbins, Caroline, *The Eighteenth-Century Commonwealthmen* (Cambridge, MA: Harvard University Press, 1961).

Rosenblatt, Jason, *Torah and Law in "Paradise Lost"* (Princeton: Princeton University Press, 1994).

Rumrich, John P., "Mead and Milton," *MQ* 20.4 (1986): 136–41.

———, "Milton's Arianism: Why It Matters," in Dobranski and Rumrich (eds.), *Milton and Heresy*, pp. 75–92.

———, *Milton Unbound: Controversy and Reinterpretation* (Cambridge: Cambridge University Press, 1996).

Russell, Conrad, *The Causes of the English Civil War* (Oxford: Clarendon Press, 1990).

——— (ed.), *The Origins of the English Civil War* (New York: Barnes & Noble, 1973).

Salzman, Paul, "Narrative Contexts for Bacon's *New Atlantis*," in Price (ed.), *Francis Bacon's "New Atlantis*," pp. 28–47.

Samuel, Raphael, "The Discovery of Puritanism, 1820–1914: A Preliminary Sketch," in Alison Light (ed.), *Island Stories: Unravelling Britain* (London: Verso, 1998), pp. 276–322.

Sánchez, Rueben Márquez, Jr., "'The Worst of Superstitions: Milton's *Of True Religion* and the Issue of Religious Tolerance," *Prose Studies* 9.3 (December 1986): 21–38.

Sauer, Elizabeth, "The Experience of Defeat: Milton and Some Female Contemporaries," in Martin (ed.), *Milton and Gender*, pp. 133–52.

Sasek, Lawrence A., *The Literary Temper of the English Puritans* (Baton Rouge: Louisiana State University Press, 1961).

Saurat, Denis, *Milton, Man and Thinker* [rpt. 1925] (London: J.M. Dent & Sons, 1944).

Schoen, Raymond, "Milton and Spenser's Cave of Mammon Episode," *PQ* 54 (1975): 684–89.

Schultz, Howard, *Milton and Forbidden Knowledge* (New York: Modern Language Association, 1955).

Scodel, Joshua, *Excess and the Mean in Early Modern English Literature* (Princeton: Princeton University Press, 2002).

Scott, Jonathan, *England's Troubles: Seventeenth-Century English Political Instability in European Context* (Cambridge: Cambridge University Press, 2000).

——, "The English Republican Imagination," in Morrill (ed.), *Revolution and Restoration*, pp. 35–54.

Sedley, David, *Sublimity and Skepticism in Milton and Montaigne* (Ann Arbor: University of Michigan Press, 2005).

Sensabaugh, George, *That Grand Whig Milton* (Stanford: Stanford University Press, 1952).

Serjeantson, Richard, "Natural Knowledge in the *New Atlantis*," in Price (ed.), *Francis Bacon's "New Atlantis,"* pp. 82–105.

Sewell, Arthur, *A Study in Milton's Christian Doctrine* (New York: Oxford University Press, 1939).

Shapin, Steven, and Simon Schaffer, *Leviathan and the Air Pump: Hobbes, Boyle, and the Experimental Life* (Princeton: Princeton University Press, 1989).

Shapiro, Barbara, "History and Natural History in Sixteenth- and Seventeenth-Century England: An Essay on the Relationship between Humanism and Science," in *English Scientific Virtuosi in the 16th and 17th Centuries* (Los Angeles: William Andrews Clark Memorial Library, 1979).

——, *John Wilkins 1614–1672: An Intellectual Biography* (Berkeley: University of California Press, 1969).

——, *Probability and Certainty in Seventeenth-Century England* (Princeton: Princeton University Press, 1983).

Sharpe, Kevin, *The Personal Rule of Charles I* (New Haven: Yale University Press, 1992).

Shawcross, John T., *The Arms of the Family: The Significance of Milton's Friends and Associates* (Lexington: University of Kentucky Press, 2004).

——, "The Deleterious and the Exalted: Milton's Poetry in the Eighteenth Century," in Kelley et al. (eds.), *Milton and the Grounds of Contention* (Pittsburgh: Duquesne University Press, 2003), pp. 11–36.

——, *John Milton and Influence: Presence in Literature, History, and Culture* (Pittsburgh: Duquesne University Press, 1991).

Sheils, W.J., *Puritans in the Diocese of Peterborough 1558–1610* (Northampton: Northampton Record Society vol. 30, 1979).

Shuger, Debora K., *Sacred Rhetoric: The Christian Grand Style in the English Renaissance* (Princeton: Princeton University Press, 1988).

Shullenberger, William, *Lady in the Labyrinth: Milton's "Comus" as Initiation* (Cranberry, NJ: Farleigh Dickinson University Presses, 2008).

Simpson, Ken, "'That sovran Book': The Discipline of the Word in Milton's Anti-Episcopal Tracts," in P.G. Stanwood (ed.), *Of Poetry and Politics: New Essays on Milton and His World* (Binghamton, NY: Medieval and Renaissance Texts and Studies, 1995), pp. 313–25.

Skinner, Quentin, *Liberty before Liberalism* (Cambridge: Cambridge University Press, 1998).

——, *Visions of Politics* (3 vols., Cambridge: Cambridge University Press, 2002).

Smith, Nigel, "*Areopagitica*, Voicing Contexts 1643–5," in Loewenstein and Turner (eds.), *Politics, Poetics, and Hermeneutics in Milton's Prose*, pp. 103–22.

——, *Perfection Proclaimed: Language and Literature in English Radical Religion 1640–1660* (Oxford: Clarendon Press, 1988).

Sokol, B.J., "'Tilted Lees.' Dragons, *Haemony*, Menarche, Spirit, and Matter in *Comus*, *RES* n.s. 41.163 (1990): 309–24.

Solt, Leo, *Saints in Arms* (Stanford: Stanford University Press, 1959).

Sommerville, C. John, *Popular Religion in Restoration England* (Gainesville: University of Florida Press, 1977).

Sommerville, J.P., *Politics and Ideology in England, 1603–1640* (Harlow: Longman, 1986).

Spellman, W.M., *The Latitudinarians and the Church of England, 1660–1700* (Athens, GA: University of Georgia Press, 1993).

Spurr, John, "'Rational Religion' in Restoration England," *JHI* 49.4 (1988): 563–85.

Stachniewski, John. *The Persecutory Imagination: English Puritanism and the Literature of Religious Despair* (Oxford: Clarendon Press, 1991).

Stavely, Keith F.M., *Puritan Legacies: "Paradise Lost" and the New England Tradition, 1630–1890* (Ithaca: Cornell University Press, 1987).

Steadman, John M., *Moral Fiction in Milton and Spenser* (Columbia, MO: University of Missouri Press, 1995).

Stone, Lawrence, *The Causes of the English Revolution* (New York: Harper & Row, 1972).

——, *The Crisis of the Aristocracy, 1558–1641* (Oxford: Clarendon Press, 1965).

Strier, Richard, "Milton against Humility," in Claire McEachern and Debora Shuger (eds.), *Religion and Culture in Renaissance England* (Cambridge: Cambridge University Press, 1997), pp. 258–86.

Strider, Robert E.L., *Robert Greville, Lord Brooke* (Cambridge, MA: Harvard University Press,1958).

Swaim, Kathleen M., "Myself a True Poem: Early Milton and the (Re)formation of the Subject," *Milton Studies* 38 (2000): 66–95.

Tanner, John S., "'And Every Star Perhaps a World of Destined Habitation': Milton and Moonmen," *Extrapolation* 30.3 (Fall 1989): 267–79.

Tawney, R.H. "Harrington's Interpretation of His Age," *Proceedings of the British Academy* 27 (1941): 199–223.

———, "The Rise of the Gentry: A Postscript," *Economic History Review*, 2nd series 7.1 (1954): 91–97.

Taylor, George Coffin, *Milton's Use of Du Bartas* (Cambridge, MA: Harvard University Press, 1934).

Thomas, Keith, "The Puritans and Adultery: the Act of 1650 Reconsidered," in Pennington and Thomas (eds.), *Puritans and Revolutionaries*, pp. 257–82.

Thorpe, Clarence DeWitt, *The Aesthetic Theory of Thomas Hobbes* (New York: Russell and Russell, 1964).

Todd, Margo, *Christian Humanism and the Puritan Social Order* (Cambridge: Cambridge University Press, 1987).

———, "Puritan Self-Fashioning," in Bremer (ed.), *Puritanism: Transatlantic Perspectives*, pp. 57–87.

Tolmie, Murray, *The Triumph of the Saints The Separate Churches of London, 1616–1649* (Cambridge: Cambridge University Press, 1977).

Toon, Peter, *Puritans and Calvinism* (Swengel, PA: Reiner Publications, 1973).

Treip, Mindele Anne, *Allegorical Poetics and the Epic: The Renaissance Tradition to "Paradise Lost"* (Lexington, KY: University of Kentucky Press, 1994).

Trevelyan, G.M., *Tudors and the Stuart Era* (Garden City, NJ: Doubleday, 1954).

Trevor-Roper, Hugh R., *Catholics, Anglicans and Puritans: Seventeenth Century Essays* (Chicago: University of Chicago Press, 1987).

———, "The Gentry, 1540–1640," *Economic History Review*, Supplement I (1953).

———, *Historical Essays* (London: Macmillan, 1957).

———, *Religion, the Reformation, and Social Change* (London: Macmillan, 1967).

Tuck, Richard, "'The Ancient Law of Freedom': John Selden and the Civil War," in Morrill (ed.), *Reactions to the English Civil War*, pp. 137–61.

———, *Natural Rights Theories: Their Origin and Development* (Cambridge: Cambridge University Press, 1979),

———, *Philosophy and Government 1572–1651* (Cambridge: University Press, 1993).

Turner, James Grantham, *One Flesh: Paradisal Marriage and Sexual Relations in the Age of Milton* (Oxford: Clarendon Press, 1987).

Tuveson, Ernest Lee, *Millennium and Utopia* (New York: Harper & Row, 1964).

Tyacke, Nicholas, *Anti-Calvinists: The Rise of English Arminianism c.1590–1640* (New York: Oxford University Press, 1990).

———, *Aspects of English Protestantism c.1530–1700* (New York: Manchester University Press, 2001).

———, "Science and Religion at Oxford before the Civil War," in Pennington and Thomas (eds.), *Puritans and Revolutionaries*, pp. 73–93.

———, "Puritanism, Arminianism, and Counter-Revolution," in Russell (ed.), *The Origins of the English Civil War*, pp. 119–43.

Van Beek, Marinus, *An Enquiry into Puritan Vocabulary* (Groningen: Wolters-Noordhoff, 1969).

Vicari, Patricia, "The Triumph of Art, the Triumph of Death: Orpheus in Spenser and Milton," in John Warden (ed.), *Orpheus: The Metamorphoses of a Myth* (Toronto: Toronto University Press, 1982), pp. 207–30.

Viswanathan, Guari, "Milton and Education," in Rajan and Sauer (eds.), *Milton and the Imperial Vision*, pp. 271–93.

Von Maltzahn, Nicholas, "Acts of Kind Service: Milton and the Patriot Literature of Empire," in Rajan and Sauer (eds.), *Milton and the Imperial Vision*, pp. 233–54.

———, "The First Reception of *Paradise Lost*," *RES* 47.188 (1996): 479–99.

———, "From Pillar to Post: Milton and the Attack on Republican Humanism at the Restoration," in Ian Gentles et al. (eds.), *Soldiers, Writers, and Statesmen*, pp. 265–85.

———, "Laureate, Republican, Calvinist: An Early Response to Milton and *Paradise Lost* (1667)," *Milton Studies* 29 (1992): 181–98.

———, *Milton's "History of Britain": Republican Historiography in the English Revolution* (Oxford: Clarendon Press, 1991).

———, "Samuel Butler's Milton," *SP* 92 (1995): 482–95.

Von Rohr, John, *The Covenant of Grace in Puritan Thought* (Atlanta, GA: University of Georgia Press, 1986).

Waddington, Raymond B. "Milton Turned Upside Down," *Journal of Modern History* 51 (1979): 108–12.

———, "Murder One: The Death of Abel. Blood, Soil, and Mortalism in *Paradise Lost*," *Milton Studies* 41 (2002): 76–93.

———, "A Musical Source for *L'Allegro?*" *MQ* 27.2 (1993): 72–74.

Walker, William, *"Paradise Lost" and Republican Tradition from Aristotle to Machiavelli* (Turnhout, Belgium: Brepols, 2009).

———, "Reassessing Milton's Republicanism," in Charles W. Durham and Kristin A. Pruitt (eds.), *Uncircumscribed Mind: Reading Milton Deeply* (Selinsgrove: Susquehanna University Press, 2008), pp. 183–205.

Wallace, Dewey M., Jr., *Puritans and Predestination: Grace in English Protestant Theology, 1525–1695* (Chapel Hill: University of North Carolina Press, 1982).

Wallace, John M., "John Dryden's Plays and the Conception of an Heroic Society," in Zagorin (ed.), *Culture and Politics*, pp. 113–34.

Weber, Max, *Economy and Society*, ed. Guenther Roth and Claus Wittich (New York: Bedminster Press, 1978).

Webster, Charles, *The Great Instauration: Science, Medicine and Reform 1626–1660* (New York: Holmes & Meier, 1976).

——— (ed.), *The Intellectual Revolution of the Seventeenth Century* (London: Routledge & Kegan Paul, 1974).

———, "New Light on the Invisible College," *Transactions of the Royal Historical Society*, 5th series, col. 24 (London: Royal Historical Society Transactions, 1974), pp. 19–42.

———, *Samuel Hartlib and the Advancement of Learning* (Cambridge: Cambridge University Press, 1970).

Webster, Tom, *Godly Clergy in Early Stuart England* (Cambridge: Cambridge University Press, 1997).

Westfall, Richard S., "Isaac Newton in Cambridge: The Restoration University and Scientific Creativity," in Zagorin (ed.), *Culture and Politics*, pp. 135–64.

———, *Science and Religion in Seventeenth-Century England* (New Haven: Yale University Press, 1958).

Whitaker, Virgil K., *The Religious Basis of Spenser's Thought* (Palo Alto: Stanford University Press, 1950).

White, R.S., *Natural Law in English Renaissance Literature* (Cambridge: Cambridge University Press, 1996).

Whiting, George W., *Milton's Literary Milieu* (New York, Russell & Russell, 1964).

———, "Milton and Lord Brooke on the Church," *Modern Language Notes* 51 (1936): 161–66.

Whitney, Charles, *Francis Bacon and Modernity* (New Haven: Yale University Press, 1986).

Willey, Basil, *The Seventeenth Century Background*, [rpt. 1934] (New York: Columbia University Press, 1962).

Williams, C.M. "The Anatomy of a Radical Gentleman: Henry Marten," in Pennington and Thomas (eds.), *Puritans and Revolutionaries*, pp. 118–38.

Williams, George Huntston, *The Radical Reformation* (Philadelphia: Westminster Press, 1962).

Williamson, George, "The Restoration Revolt against Enthusiasm," *SP* 30 (1933): 571–603.

Wilson, John F., *Pulpit in Parliament: Puritans in the English Civil Wars 1640–1648* (Princeton: Princeton University Press, 1969).

Wittreich, Joseph A., *Interpreting "Samson Agonistes"* (Princeton: Princeton University Press, 1986).

———, *Shifting Contexts: Reinterpreting Samson Agonistes* (Pittsburgh: Duquesne University Press, 2002).

Wood, Louis Aubrey, *The Form and Origin of Milton's Antitrinitarian Conception* (London, Ont.: Advertiser Press, 1911).

Woodhouse, A.S.P, "The Argument of Milton's *Comus*," *UTQ* 11 (1941): 46–71.

———, "Nature and Grace in 'The Faerie Queene,'" *ELH* 16 (1949): 194–228.

Woods, Susanne, "The Context of Jonson's Formalism," in Claude J. Summers and Ted-Larry Pebworth (eds.), *Classic and Cavalier* (Pittsburgh: Duquesne University Press, 1982), pp. 77–89.

———, "Elective Poetics and Milton's Prose: *A Treatise of Civil Power* and *Considerations Touching the Likeliest Means to Remove Hirelings Out of the Church*," in Loewenstein and Turner (eds.), *Politics, Poetics, and Hermeneutics in Milton's Prose*, pp. 193–211.

Woolrych, Austin, "The Date of the Digression in Milton's *History of Britain*," in Richard Ollard and Pamela Tudor-Craig (eds.), *For Veronica Wedgewood These: Studies in Seventeenth-Century History* (London: Collins, 1986), pp. 217–46.

Worden, Blair, "Classical Republicanism and the English Revolution," in Jones et. al. (eds.), *History and Imagination*, pp. 182–200.

———, "John Milton and Oliver Cromwell," in Gentles et al. (eds.), *Soldiers, Writers, and Statesmen of the English Revolution*, pp. 243–85.

———, "Milton, *Samson Agonistes*, and the Restoration," in Maclean (ed.), *Culture and Society in the Stuart Restoration*, pp. 111–36.

———, "Oliver Cromwell and the Council," in Little (ed.), *The Cromwellian Protectorate*, pp. 82–104.

———, "Providence and Politics in Cromwellian England," *Past and Present* 109 (1985): 55–99.

———, "The Question of Secularization," in Alan Houston and Steve Pincus (eds.), *A Nation Transformed: England after the Restoration* (Cambridge: Cambridge University Press, 2001), pp. 20–40.

———, Review of Paul S. Seaver, *Wallington's World: A Puritan Artisan in Seventeenth- Century London* (1985), *LRB* (23 January–6 February 1986): 16–17.

———, *Roundhead Reputations: The English Civil Wars and the Passions of Posterity* (London: Penguin Press, 2001).

———, "Toleration and the Cromwellian Protectorate," *Studies in Church History* 21 (1984): 199–233.

Zagorin, Perez (ed.), *Culture and Politics: From Puritanism to the Enlightenment* (Berkeley: University of California Press, 1980).

———, *A History of Political Thought in the English Revolution* (London: Routledge & Kegan Paul, 1954).

———, *Milton: Aristocrat and Rebel: The Poet and His Politics* (New York: D.S. Brewer, 1992).

Zakai, Avihu, "Religious Toleration and its Enemies: The Independent Divines and the Issue of Toleration during the English Civil War," *Albion* 21.1 (1989): 1–33.

Zaret, David, *The Heavenly Contract: Ideology and Organization in Pre-Revolutionary Puritanism* (Chicago: University of Chicago Press, 1985).

———, *Origins of Democratic Culture: Printing, Petitions, and the Public Sphere in Early-Modern England* (Princeton: Princeton University Press, 2000).

———, "Religion and the Rise of Liberal-Democratic Ideology," *American Sociological Review* 54.2 (1989): 163–79.

Zwicker, Steven N., "Milton, Dryden, and the Politics of Literary Controversy," in Maclean (ed.), *Culture and Society in the Stuart Restoration*, pp. 137–58.

———, "Politics and Literary Practice in the Restoration," in Lewalski (ed.), *Renaissance Genres*, pp. 268–98.

Index

Abbott, George 108
Achinstein, Sharon 1, 15, 26, 172, 189, 255
Acontius, Jacob 98
Adiaphora 34, 125, 138
Adolph, Robert 248–49
Aeschylus 282
Agrippa, Cornelius 190, 219
Aikenhead, Thomas 313
Alymer, Gerald 22
Ames, William 72, 152
Anabaptists 17, 34, 38–39, 73, 75, 79–80,
    97, 219
Andrewes, Lancelot 68, 76, 100, 102, 153,
    162
Anglicans, Anglicanism 1–2, 9(n.), 12, 16,
    34, 62, 95, 145, 170, 176, 178, 189,
    192, 243, 257, 286
    liberal wing of the church see
    Latitudinarians
Annesley, Arthur 303
Anti-ceremonialism 3, 24, 33, 38, 53, 55,
    61, 77, 115, 305–6
Anti-clericalism 2, 56–57, 61–62, 88, 285
Antinomianism, Antinomians 4–5, 14–16,
    34–35, 38–39, 43, 45–46, 48, 73,
    101, 102(n.), 153, 161, 188, 193–
    95, 231–33, 237, 239, 254, 309
Appelbaum, Robert 235
Aquinas, St. Thomas 102–3, 153, 179–80,
    182
Ariosto, Ludovico 116, 154, 221, 274
Aristophanes 314
Aristotle 60, 80, 118, 129, 151, 181, 188,
    194, 197–99, 207, 217, 235, 246,
    263–64, 273–74, 281, 284
Arminianism, as doctrine 4–5, 7, 22, 40, 43,
    48, 50, 56, 62–63, 67–68, 75, 78,
    84, 96–100, 102, 107, 109–10, 129,
    144, 147–54, 178, 182, 192, 194,
    243, 245, 255, 266, 285–86, 310

Arminians, as a movement in the English
    church 4, 7, 22, 53, 56, 62–63, 67,
    107, 113(n.), 129, 149, 194
Askew, Anne 34
Aston, Margaret 169
Aubrey, John 9, 69, 185, 210, 285
St. Augustine 178, 181, 228, 238–39,
    243–46
Ayers, Robert 89

Bacon, Francis 3, 31, 41, 42, 53, 77–79,
    86, 99, 114, 117–18, 128–40, 175,
    178–80, 182–83, 186–88, 197–201,
    211, 217–18, 223, 228–29, 242,
    254, 258–60, 269, 277, 314–16
    The Advancement of Learning 77, 129,
        132–33, 166, 187, 198, 215, 217,
        224, 229–32, 235, 249, 257
    Advertisement Touching the
        Controversies of the Church of
        England 136–38, 140
    Aphorisms on the Composition of
        Primary History 258
    Certaine Considerations 136(n.), 138
    Descripti Globi Intellectualis 217
    The Great Instauration 53, 131, 260
    Of the Interpretation of Nature 78, 218
    New Atlantis 48, 71, 131, 185, 204,
        208, 229
    Novum Organum 132, 135, 236–37
    Sylva sylvarum 164
    The Wisdom of the Ancients (Sapientia
        Veterum) 142, 145–47, 163–66,
        225, 257, 260
    A Wise and Moderate Discourse; see
        Advertisement above
Baconians, Baconianism 3, 11, 21, 48,
    66, 77–78, 84, 105, 125–40, 175,
    178, 180, 183–88, 190, 192–93,
    196–204, 207–11, 217, 219, 222,

237, 239, 246, 259, 261, 268, 275–76

Bacon, Robert 35
Baillie, Robert 38
Bainbridge, Thomas 128
Baker, Herschel 39, 134
Bale, John 42
Baptists 38, 46, 74, 88, 96
Barbour, Reid 190
Barclay, Robert 74–75
Barebones Parliament; *see* Nominated Parliament
Barker, Arthur 13, 98, 117, 192
Barry, Richard 184
Bastwick, John 40, 42, 62, 108–9
Baxter, Richard 7, 9, 13, 19, 23, 33, 40, 43, 48, 50(n.), 52, 56, 60, 71, 92–94, 96–97, 101, 152, 172, 188–89, 191, 194–95, 205, 282, 290, 305–6, 308, 310
Bayly, Lewis 171
Beale, John 208, 262
Benedict, Philip 17
Bennett, Joan S. 101, 151
Bentley, Richard 196
Bernard, Richard 129
Bethel, S.L. 196
Biddle, John 58, 97
Birch, Thomas 184
Blackstone, Sir William 303
Blake, William 254
Blount, Charles 80, 303, 311–16
Bochart, Samuel 257, 265
Bodley, Sir Thomas 187
Boehme, Jacob 199
Bohun, Edward 313
Bolton, Robert 45, 50, 290
Borel, Pierre 222
Boyle, Robert 21, 48, 75, 178, 181, 184, 186–87, 197, 266
Bozeman, Theodore 47, 105, 222
Brahe, Tycho 198, 219
Brass, Henry de 225
Brightman, Thomas 42
Brinsley, John 17
Brodwin, Leonara L. 97
Brooke, Samuel 100
Browne, Sir Thomas 75, 175, 198

Bruno, Giordano 221
Bucer, Martin 73–74, 98, 210
Buchanan, George 182
Bulkeley, Peter 35
Bunyan, John 11, 71, 96–97, 172–73, 176, 187, 232, 255, 280, 308
    Life and Death of Mr Badman 72–73
    Pilgrim's Progress 153–54, 192(n.), 308
Burbery, Timothy 70, 142(n.)
Burgess, Glenn 54
Burke, Edmund 254, 259
Burns, Norman 14, 24
Burroughs, Jeremiah 79
Burton, Henry 40, 62, 65, 108–9
Burton, Robert 258
Bush, Douglas 6, 8
Butler, Martin 42
Butler, Samuel 20, 94, 261

Calamy, Edward 4
Calvin, John, Calvinism, Calvinists 4–5, 13–14, 17–18, 33–39, 45–46, 50, 58, 98–100, 102–3, 117–18, 151, 153, 163, 169–71, 175–82, 188–89, 192–95, 216, 221, 231, 236, 238, 243, 245, 266, 286, 309, 310, 315
Cambridge Platonists 75, 76(n.), 97, 104, 180, 182, 187, 194–96, 216
Campbell, Gordon, and Thomas Corns 7, 54–55, 66(n.), 67, 73–74, 77(n.), 82, 84(n.), 117, 136(n.), 252(n.), 302–3
Canne, John 81
Capp, Bernard 46–47, 232
Cardan, Jerome 221
Carlyle, Thomas 11–12, 177, 182
Caro, Hannibal 252
Carpenter, Nathaniel 181, 186
Cartwright, Thomas 34–35, 56
Cary, Lucius, Second Viscount (Lord) Falkland 63, 183
Cary, Mary 79, 232
Casaubon, Isaac 198
Casaubon, Meric 196, 266
Cavendish circle 190
Chaloner, Thomas 285, 303
Chaney, Edward 10, 20

Chappell, William 67, 113, 126, 128–30
Charles I 18, 31, 40–42, 48, 52, 54–56, 63,
　　　119, 121–23, 144, 285, 300, 303
Charles II 19, 261, 297, 300, 303
Charlton, Margaret 33
Charron, Pierre 20
Chaucer, Geoffrey 116
Chidley, Katherine 83
Chillingworth, William 191, 192(n.), 194
Chrysostom 243–45
Cicero, Marcus Tullius 60, 80, 182, 280,
　　　281, 284, 298
Clagett, William 195
Clark, Donald C. 24(n.), 68–69
Clarkson, Lawrence 15, 46, 239(n.)
classical republicans, republicanism 2,
　　　9–10, 20–21, 24, 40, 49, 59–60,
　　　75–77, 94, 128–29, 158, 183,
　　　229, 234, 243, 246–47, 261, 274,
　　　280–85, 287, 290–303
Cleaver, Robert 171
Coffey, John 5(n.), 9(n.), 84
Cogswell, Thomas 22–23
Coleridge, Samuel T. 259
Colet, John 270
Collier, Thomas 14, 48
Collinson, Patrick 18–19, 32, 52
Comenius, John Amos 183, 185–88, 190,
　　　196–97, 99, 204, 207, 241
Como, David 14
Comte, Auguste 17
Congregationalists *see* Independents
Coolidge, John S. 34–36, 58
Cope, Jackson 187
Copernicus, Copernican astronomy 188,
　　　197, 201, 216–17, 219, 224
Coppe, Abiezer 48
Corns, Thomas 70, 98, 149
Cotton, John 16
Coudert, Allison 189–90, 193
Cowley, Abraham 80, 92, 110, 185, 210,
　　　226–27, 250, 252, 257–58, 262, 271
Cradock, Walter 193
Cragg, Gerald 47–48, 64, 103, 279–80,
　　　305–6, 308–10
Creaser, John 143, 171
Cromwell, Oliver 11, 16, 19, 21, 33, 44,
　　　45, 48, 50, 55, 58, 60, 79, 84,

86–87, 109, 176–77, 182, 184, 243,
　　　281–82, 287, 293, 295, 316
Culpepper, Sir Cheney 185
Cust, Richard 22–23
St. Cyprian 282

Danielson, Dennis 96
Dante Alighieri 116, 125, 139, 150
Dati, Carlo 297
Davenant, John 38
Davenant, William 260, 277
Davies, Sir John 92
Davies, Horton 33(n.)
Davis, J.C. 44, 79, 89, 115(n.), 235
Dean, Margaret 122
Debus, Allen 197
Dee, John 190
Deists 27, 104, 303, 310–13, 315–16
Dell, William 39, 74–75, 107, 124, 188–89,
　　　199–200, 209
Democritus 190
Demosthenes 273
Denham, John 216
Dennis, John 254, 259, 283
Denton, William 313
Descartes, René 219, 255
De Tocqueville, Alexis 17
Dick, Steven 222–23
Digby, Sir George 63
Diodati, Charles 128–29, 142–43, 281
Dionysus the elder 282
Dissenters 9(n.), 50, 95–96, 103, 189, 195,
　　　209, 216, 253–54, 279–80, 282–86,
　　　305–10, 312–13, 316–17
Dod, John 171, 178
Donne, John 71, 217
Dorislaus, Isaac 68, 128–29
Dryden, John 21, 60, 96, 144, 216, 249–54,
　　　257, 277
　　　Essay of Dramatic Poesy 252, 263–64
　　　Religio Laici 251–52, 265
Du Bartas, Guillaume de Salluste 92, 225,
　　　227–28, 234, 250(n.)
Duffy, Eamon 45
Duncan, Joseph E. 228
Duns Scotus, John 179
Durkheim, Emile 17–18
Dury, John 80, 128, 178, 184–85, 209

Edward VI 108, 122
Edwards, Karen 198
Edwards, Thomas 85
Egerton, Alice 145
Egerton, John, Earl of Bridgewater 143–44
Eire, Carlos 48
Ellwood, Thomas 21, 233, 249, 252, 257
Elton, Geoffrey 32
empiricism, empiricists 178–82, 184–85,
    187, 190, 195–97, 201, 223–24,
    236–37, 255–56, 266–67, 269, 271,
    274, 280, 311; *see also* Baconians
Erasmus, Desiderius 18, 33, 306
Erbery, William 189
Euripides 282, 291
Evelyn, John 19–20, 189, 208
Everard, John 198

Fairfax, Sir Thomas 21
Fallon, Stephen 2–4, 7
Familists, Familism 73
Feake, Christopher 79
Fenwick, John 232
Ficino, Marsilio 198
Field, John 34
Fifth Monarchists, 39, 46, 49, 79, 81, 86,
    303
Filmer, Robert 229
Finlayson, Michael 51
Firmin, Robert 60
Firth, Sir Charles H.11–12, 31, 45
Fish, Stanley E. 6–8, 131
Fixler, Michael 106
Fletcher, Anthony 52, 54
Fludd, Robert 190, 197–201
Foucault, Michel 195–96, 257
Fowler, Alastair 266–67
Fowler, Edward 103
Fox, George 5, 12, 43–44, 192–3, 203,
    280, 290, 307–8
Foxe, John 33, 40, 42, 114, 122–23, 194
Franck, Sebastian 188, 233
Franklin, Edward 136(n.)
Fried, Daniel 181

Gale, Theophilus 265–6
Galileo Galilei 182, 188, 198, 219–21, 224,
    314–15

Gardiner, Samuel 11–12, 16, 31
Gassendi, Pierre 255
Gedes, William 172
Gell, Robert 67
George, C.H. 22, 32
George, Katherine 32
Geree, John 38
Gil, Alexander, the elder 67–68, 99
Gil, Alexander, the younger 67–68, 99,
    126–7
Gilbert, William 188, 221
Glanvill, Joseph 187, 189, 215–16, 263, 310
Goddard, Jonathan 197
Godwin, Frances 221
Goldie, Mark 279(n.)
Goodwin, John 5(n.), 9–10, 20–23, 38, 40,
    50, 84, 88, 92, 94, 98, 103–4, 126,
    133–34
Goodwin, Thomas 43–45, 72, 86–87, 108,
    118, 186
Gott, Samuel 58
Grace, William 102–3
Grafton, Anthony 196
Great Persecution (of Puritan Dissenters)
    19, 283, 285, 306–10
Great Tew circle 95, 180, 182–84, 206
Greaves, Richard L. 189, 191–92, 205
Greenblatt, Stephen 18
Greville, Fulke 92, 128
Greville, Robert, Lord Brooke 55, 62, 109,
    115, 118, 129, 135–36, 138(n.),
    183(n.), 246
    The Nature of Truth 133, 135–36
Griffin, Matthew 300
Grotius, Hugo 20, 78, 98, 182, 228, 255, 265

Habermas, Jürgen 26
Hakewill, George 99–100, 246
Hale, Matthew 59
Hales, John 33, 76, 88, 180–81, 191–92, 194
Halkett, John 239
Hall, Basil 32
Hall, John 21, 79–80, 185, 197, 209–10,
    256–57
Hall, Joseph 76, 78, 90, 98, 107, 112–14,
    116, 121, 127, 136(n.)
    Mundus Alter et Idem 131
Hall, Thomas 186

Haller, William 7, 13, 44, 47, 106–8, 110, 116–18, 140(n.), 170, 305, 315
Halley, Edmond 206
Hanford, James Holly 136(n.)
Harley, Brilliana 169
Harley, Sir Robert 169
Harrington, James 10, 61, 280–81, 285
Hartley, David 259
Hartlib circle 47–48, 57, 88, 95, 118, 120, 125, 134, 182–85, 190, 203–5, 209
Hartlib, Samuel 80, 128, 136(n.), 178, 184–85, 196, 209–10
Haskin, Dayton 107–8
Hatton, Sir Christopher 136(n.)
Haug, Ralph 108, 115
Hawkes, David 67
Helgerson, Richard 116, 143, 226–27
Henrietta-Maria, Queen 56, 145, 297
Henry, Nathaniel 85
Herbert, Edward, Lord Herbert of Cherbury 312
Herbert, George 92, 189
Herendeen, Wyman 78
Hexter, J.H. 23
Heylyn, Peter 106, 131, 194
Hildersam, Arthur 19
Hill, Abraham 216
Hill, Christopher 3–4, 6–8, 10, 13–16, 23, 32, 36, 43, 50–51, 64, 117, 190–92, 211, 279(n.), 305, 316–17
Hinman, Robert 210, 262, 266
Hirst, Derek 189
historical revisionism, revisionists 5, 22–23, 42–64
Hobart, Sir John 216
Hobbes, Thomas 5(n.), 9, 11, 24, 34, 40, 61, 74, 81, 83, 181–2, 193, 199, 209, 246, 257(n.), 259–61, 263, 277, 283
    Answer to Davenant's Preface to "Gondibert" 261–62
    Leviathan 74
Hollander, John 143
Holstun, James 47, 66, 89, 189, 193, 235–36
Homer 154–55, 217, 227, 238–41, 251, 257, 261, 265
Honeygosky, Stephen R. 24–25
Hooke, Robert 48, 187, 208, 256

Hooker, Richard 2, 20, 24, 33, 59, 61, 68, 100, 151, 176, 180, 182, 186, 191, 207
Hooker, Thomas 56, 81
Hoopes, Robert 151, 178–80
Horace 251
How, Samuel 189
Hoxby, Blair 140(n.)
Hughes, Merritt Y. 119, 221, 228, 245
Hume, Robert 253
Hunt, William 80–81
Hunter, Michael 208, 313(n.)
Hunter, William B. 97(n.), 106, 207(n.)
Huntley, Frank 243
Hus, John 33
Hutchinson, Anne 43
Hutchinson, Colonel John 55
Hutchinson, Lucy 190, 225, 253
Hutton, Matthew 114
Hyde, Edward, Earl of Clarendon (Lord Clarendon) 11, 42, 63

iconoclasm 20, 65, 81, 116, 122–23, 169, 197
Independents 17, 212, 40, 46, 56–8, 80–84, 86–87, 90, 300, 309
Invisible College 184
Ireton, Henry 2, 10

Jacob, Margaret 178
James I 54, 56, 138
    Book of Sports 119, 144–45, 156
James II 307
Jane, Joseph 122
St. Jerome 265, 282
Jessey, Henry 79
Johnson, Samuel 2(n.), 12, 225–27, 250(n.)
Jones, Richard, historian 178–79, 195
Jones, Richard, son of Lady Katherine Ranelagh 184
Jonson, Ben 20, 94, 227, 250(n.)
    Pleasure Reconciled to Virtue 162–63
    The Staple of the News 70
Jordan, W.K. 26, 135, 182, 305
Julian of Eclanum 97, 194, 244–45

Kahn, Victoria 116, 125, 237–38
Keeble, N.H. 186(n.), 189, 253

Kelsall, Malcolm 270–71, 274
Kendall, R.T. 36–37
Kepler, Johannes 201, 220
Kiffin, William 189
King, Edward 67–68, 126, 130, 136(n.), 169
King, John N. 151(n.), 240(n.)
Kirk, Rudolf 130
Kishlansky, Mark 52, 55
Klein, Joan Larson 164–65
Knight, David 223–24
Knoppers, Laura Lunger 264
Knott, John R. 116(n.), 123
Knox, Ronald 307–8
Kroll, Richard W.F. 253–54, 256, 267, 270

Lactantius 194, 282
Lake, Peter 22–23, 32–34, 45, 54(n.), 114–15
Lamont, William 17, 22, 40, 42, 58, 109, 116
Latitudinarians, Latitudinarianism 12, 21, 60, 76, 88, 97, 103–4, 178, 184, 187, 191, 206–8, 266, 306–12, 315–16
Laudians, Archbishop William Laud 4, 22, 32, 40–41, 52–55, 62–63, 67–68, 71, 76, 97, 99, 106–10, 114–15, 117, 126, 129, 137, 141–44, 149, 169, 209, 243
Lawes, Henry 70, 117, 122, 144
Le Clerc, Jean 255
Leighton, Alexander 108
Lemmi, Charles 164–65
L'Estrange, Roger 9, 261, 313
Levao, Ronald 260
Levellers 20–21, 24, 40, 44–46, 79, 87–89, 182, 200
Leverenz, David 15, 170–71
Levine, Joseph 113(n.)
Lewalski, Barbara K. 145(n.), 148, 191(n.), 280, 285, 286(n.), 289
    "Milton and *De Doctrina Christiana*" 77, 101–2, 286(n.)
    The Life of John Milton 98–99, 119
Lewis, C.S. 6, 8
Lilburne, John 20, 43–44, 89
Livy 270

Locke, John 9, 34, 76, 81, 97, 134, 196, 206, 259, 307, 310–11, 315–16
Lord Brooke *see* Robert Greville
Lord Clarendon *see* Edward Hyde
Lovelace, Richard 298
Lucretius 190, 225
Ludlow, Edmund 2, 10, 49, 263, 280, 283–85
    A Voyce from the Watchtower 10, 284
Luther, Martin, Lutherans 18, 72, 75, 117, 221, 306, 309
Lydgate, John 250
Lynch, William 210–11

Macaulay, Thomas 8, 12, 66, 95, 313(n.)
Machiavelli, Niccolò 53, 125, 158–59, 280, 289
Maltzahn, Nicholas von 140(n.), 216, 261, 301(n.)
Manning, Brian 55
Manton, Thomas 306
Marcus, Leah 143–45, 156
Marcuse, Herbert 25
Marshall, Stephen 85
Marten, Henry 55–56, 60, 285
Martin, Richard 63
Marvell, Andrew 21, 79–80, 101, 164–65, 249, 253, 261, 303
Marx, Karl; Marxist historiography 11, 17–18, 23, 25, 51, 64
Mary, Queen of Scots 297
Masson, David 3, 7, 8, 11, 89, 95
Mazzoni, Jacopo 259
McAdoo, Henry R. 175, 180–81, 194–95
McDowell, Nicholas 90
McGee, J. Sears 72
McGregor, J. M. 46–47
McLachlan, John Herbert 59, 75
Mede, Joseph 42, 61, 128, 183, 195
Melanchthon, Phillipp 221–22
Mendle, Michael 61–62
Merton, Robert 47
millenarianism 33, 42–43, 46–49, 53, 77–79, 85, 109–10, 140(n.), 183, 190, 193, 280, 289, 314
Miller, Leo 128–29
Miller, Perry 36
Milner, Andrew 289–90

Milton, Anthony, modern religious
    historian 13–14
Milton, Christopher, brother of the poet
    7, 96
Milton, John
    anti-clericalism of 2, 56–57, 71, 86,
        90, 119–20, 127–30, 191, 205–6,
        285, 303
    anti-scholasticism of 118, 126–31, 133,
        179, 185, 191, 202, 204, 209, 267
    astronomical theories of 216–25
    Baconianism of *see* Bacon, Francis
    Cambridge career 67–8, 70, 77,
        99–100, 105–8, 113, 118–19,
        126–30, 216–17
    civic humanism of 39, 60, 71, 78, 89,
        128, 158–59; *see also* classical
        republicanism
    dramatic, stage, and theatrical outlook
        70, 94, 119–21, 141–47, 171, 253,
        282–83, 298
    educational philosophy, outlook 80,
        94, 118, 120, 126–35, 184–86, 188,
        190, 197, 204–5, 207–11, 241; *see
        also* Hartlib Circle
    on learned ministry controversy
        190–92, 202–7
    Spenserianism of 71, 92, 94, 141–44,
        146–48, 150–63, 167–69, 227, 252
    Stoic/Aristotelian ethics of 60, 80,
        150–55, 158–59, 161, 194, 207,
        222, 229, 242, 250, 273–75, 284
    Works
        Poetry
            Ad Patrem 70, 105–6, 110,
                112–13, 129–30
            Comus, or *A Mask Presented at
                Ludlow Castle* 70, 98, 112,
                141–73, 192, 225, 272
            Elegia Prima 70, 129
            *An Epitaph on the Marchioness
                of Winchester* 117
            Il Penseroso 65, 68, 70, 146,
                155–56, 167–68, 252
            L'Allegro 66, 70, 119, 146,
                155–56, 167–68, 252

            Lycidas 68, 86, 108, 126, 128,
                130, 136–40, 142, 163–64,
                168
            Mansus 90–92, 94, 112
            Paradise Lost 2, 3, 5, 25,
                86, 96–97, 101–4, 111,
                121–23, 139, 146(n.), 153,
                164–65, 170, 172, 190,
                194–95, 198, 206, 209,
                215–52, 260–62, 271, 275,
                281, 286–87, 289, 294, 303
            Paradise Regained 104, 123,
                147, 154, 181, 190–91,
                207, 249–77, 289, 301, 303
            Poems of Mr. John Milton
                (1645) 61–62, 66, 116–17,
                121, 143(n.), 170
            Naturam Non Pati Senium 3,
                217, 242
            "On the New Forcers of
                Conscience" 9, 56, 85, 182
            Samson Agonistes 101, 113,
                123, 252, 260, 264–65,
                279–304
            "On Shakespeare" 70
            "At a Solemn Music" 146
            Sonnet 7; 110–12
            Sonnet 9; 75
            Sonnet 11; 85
            Sonnet 12; 85, 121
            Sonnet 16; 17(n.), 84, 86,
                87(n.), 293
            Sonnet 17; 293
            Sonnet 19; 236, 287, 292–93
            Sonnet 22;287, 293
            Sonnet 23; 82
        Prose
            Animadversions 49, 71, 78, 94,
                117, 128, 130, 136, 142,
                168, 301
            An Apology against a Pamphlet
                4, 71, 78, 99, 103, 113, 119,
                127, 128, 136, 149–51,
                208, 276, 288
            Areopagitica 3, 20, 48, 55, 57,
                62, 77–85, 90, 94, 98–99,
                111, 115, 118, 124–25,
                129, 131–37, 140, 143–44,

147–48, 151–53, 161, 181,
    194, 208–9, 217–18, 237,
    265, 302–3, 312–16
*Brief Notes upon a Late
    Sermon* 229, 287, 300
*Character of the Long
    Parliament* [digression
    from *The History of
    Britain*] 44, 90, 287
Of Civil Power 25, 74–77, 87,
    203–8, 272
Commonplace Book 63, 68, 70,
    122, 125, 136, 158, 194,
    282–83
*A Defence of the People of
    England* 77, 102, 186–87,
    300
De Doctrina Christiana
    2–3, 12, 24, 72, 74–75, 88,
    97–103, 117, 123, 150–51,
    153, 202, 205, 226, 236,
    270, 272, 280
*The Doctrine and Discipline
    of Divorce* 57, 73, 78, 99,
    132, 225, 296
Of Education 80, 118, 151,
    175, 184–85, 204–5, 209,
    225
Eikonoklastes 40–41, 54, 119,
    21–24, 129, 243, 284,
    286–87, 289, 291, 293
History of Britain 77, 90, 128,
    208, 225, 254, 265, 283,
    287, 294
Letter to Alexander Gil (1628)
    67, 118, 127
Letter to Carlo Dati 297
Letter to Charles Diodati
    (1637) 128, 141–43, 171,
    281
Letter to a Friend 108, 111–12,
    129
Letter to Henry de Brass 225,
    276
Letter to Thomas Young 67,
    127
*The Likeliest Means to Remove
    Hirelings from the Church*
    57, 74, 77, 80, 82, 191,
    202–5
Of Prelatical Episcopacy 285–86
Prolusions 128–29, 209,
    217–18
Prolusion II 216–17
Prolusion III 129, 179
Prolusion VI 129, 156
Prolusion VII 77–78, 129, 218
Pro Se Defensio 261
The Readie and Easie Way 79–
    80, 86, 89, 94, 204–5, 207,
    209, 283, 285, 292–93, 300
*The Reason of Church
    Government* 39, 61, 91,
    106–12, 114–16, 119–21,
    128, 130, 140, 145, 153,
    172, 216, 288, 304
Of Reformation 62, 74, 76, 86,
    114–17, 119–20, 123, 128,
    131, 146, 281
*A Second Defence of the
    English People* 87, 94, 197,
    228, 261, 286, 288, 293
*The Tenure of Kings and
    Magistrates* 56–57, 77,
    85–86, 98, 245–47, 299
Tetrachordon 20, 85, 98, 256,
    296–98
Of True Religion 74–76, 186,
    191–92, 207, 263, 266,
    311, 316
"At a Vacation Exercise" 40, 119
Milton, John senior, father of the poet 7,
    67–68, 70–71, 98, 105–6, 112–13,
    126, 129–30, 207
Milton, Katherine, wife of the poet *see*
    Katherine Woodcock
Milton, Mary, wife to the poet *see* Mary
    Powell
Milton, Sara, mother of the poet 71
Miner, Earl 251–52(n.)
Molesworth, Sir Robert 279
Monck, General George 287, 300
Montaigne, Michel de 21
More, Henry 33, 88, 194–95, 216, 221,
    234, 257(n.)
More, Thomas 18, 33

Morrill, John 15–16, 50–52, 54, 67
Mosely, Humphrey 117
Moulin, Pierre du 260
Mueller, Janel 123, 127
Muggletonians 39
Muggleton, Lodowicke 40, 307

natural law, natural rights 182, 193, 204,
    223–24, 229
Nayler, James 49, 79
Nazianzen, Gregory 282
Nedham, Marchamont 21, 49
Nelson, Robert 60
Neo-Roman *see* classical republicanism
Neville, Henry 10, 285
New Methodism 101
New Model Army 43, 45, 52, 55, 87(n.)
new philosophy *see* empiricism
Newton, Isaac 97, 201, 223
Ng, Su Fang 309
Nominated Parliament 48–49, 185, 203
Nonconformists, Nonconformity 10–12,
    19, 38, 61, 95–96, 198, 285, 308–
    10, 316–17; *see also* Dissenters
Noy, William 144
Nuttall, A.D. 226
Nuttall, Geoffrey 4, 118, 187(n.)
Nye, Philip 86

Oakley, Francis 179
Oldenburg, Henry 21, 184, 187, 208–10
Overton, Richard 5(n.), 21, 24, 39, 182
Owen, John 58–59, 84, 86–87, 107, 190,
    195, 280, 309

Pagels, Elaine 243–45
Paracelsus 165, 189–90, 197–98
Parker, Henry 57(n.), 60–63, 95, 109, 118,
    124, 132, 246–47, 296, 299
Parker, William Riley 142(n.)
Parr, Elnathan 231
Parry, Graham 143(n.)
Patrick, Simon 103, 206
Patterson, Annabel 60, 71, 146–47, 274,
    279(n.)
Pelagius, Pelagian 99, 194, 243–44
Penington, Isaac 188–89, 219, 233
Penn, William 207

Pericles 273
Perkins, William 16–17, 19, 34–39, 99, 103,
    105(n.), 107, 120, 126, 169–70, 177
Peter, Hugh 79
Petrarch 150
Petty, William 205–6
Phillips, Edward, nephew to Milton. 66,
    72–73, 90, 186, 226(n.), 297
Phillips, John, nephew to Milton, 90, 261
Phillips, Lady Katherine 92
Pindar 110–11
Plato 165, 179–81, 188, 191, 198–99, 217,
    234–35, 238, 246, 256, 268, 273,
    275, 288, 311
Plattes, Gabriel 203–4
Pocock, J.G.A. 22, 54
politiques (secular politicians) 59–60, 94,
    97–98, 133, 261
Poole, William 210, 233
Pope, Alexander 266
postrevisionists *see* historical revisionists,
    revisionism
Powell, Mary 7, 73, 297
Presbyterians 19, 21, 34, 40, 46, 56–58,
    66–67, 70, 77, 82–85, 109, 114,
    117–18, 187, 210, 218, 300, 305,
    308–9
Preston, John 35, 38, 72, 98, 152
Prince, Frank T. 225
Protectorate 21, 50, 53, 59, 62, 87, 97,
    183–84, 261, 281, 293–94
Prynne, William 40, 55–56, 62–63, 82, 85,
    108–9, 141–42, 145, 170–71
Ptolemy, Ptolemaic astronomy 201,
    216–17, 219, 224
Puritan Revolution thesis *see* Whig
    historians, historiography
Puritans, English *see* Puritanism or
    Anabaptists, Antinomians, Baptists,
    Fifth Monarchists, Independents,
    Muggletonians, Presbyterians,
    Quakers, Ranters, and Seekers
Puritanism, English
    anti-theatricalism of 92, 94, 170–73,
        282
    Calvinism of 4–5, 13–14, 18, 33–38,
        45–46, 50, 58, 95–96, 105–6, 134,

151–52, 169–71, 177, 188, 280,
    284, 305, 309–10
  covenant theology of 14, 34–39, 95,
    193, 231, 236, 309
  definition of 13–14, 16–25, 32–39,
    47–49, 60–62, 151–52, 169–70,
    177
  election, predestination in 3, 19, 35–39,
    99–100, 151–52
  martyrs 40–41, 62–63, 68, 85, 108–9,
    306–7
  politics of 1, 40–51, 76–79, 85–89,
    182, 280
  voluntarism of, 36–39, 46, 83, 88, 154,
    176–77, 182
  worship and ecclesiology 33–9, 70–75,
    83–84, 169–70
Puttenham, George 226
Pym, John 42, 55, 63
Pythagoras 216–17, 266

Quakers 4(n.), 12, 17, 19, 24, 38, 46, 48–
    49, 74–76, 79, 154, 178, 186–88,
    190, 192–93, 207, 209, 219, 233,
    290, 303, 305, 307–10
Quarles, Francis 92

Racovian Catechism 87, 97
Ranelagh, Lady Katherine 184
Ranters 39, 46, 48, 79, 209, 303, 305, 307
Raven, Charles E. 195
Richardson, Jonathan 90–92, 96
Rivers, Isabel 103, 254
Roberts, Donald A. 107(n.)
Robinson, John 47, 48
Robinson, Henry 57, 60, 88, 95, 109, 124,
    133–35, 139, 183, 186, 205, 246,
    315
Rohr, John von 35–36
Root and Branch movement 7, 56, 61, 109,
    113, 124, 133, 145, 209
Royal Society 21–22, 130, 178, 183(n.),
    184, 187, 197, 206–11, 218, 254,
    257–58, 266, 268, 276–77
Rudrum, Alan 110
Russell, Conrad 15(n.), 22–23, 52–54, 62,
    66–67
Rust, George 216

Rutherford, Samuel 9, 85, 182, 245

Sacheverell, Henry 310
Sadler, John 184
Salkeld, John 228
Salmasius, Claudius (Claude de Saumaise)
    260–61
Saltmarsh, John 39, 45, 48, 188
Salzman, Paul 131
Samuel, Raphael 10–11
Sanderson, Robert 286
Sandys, George 92
Sarpi, Paolo 33, 61, 101
Sasek, Lawrence 22, 92(n.), 94, 163, 172–73
Saurat, Denis 6–8, 21
Savoy *Declaration of Faith and Order*
    95–97
Schaffer, Simon 218
Schoen, Raymond 148
science, early modern; see empiricism
Scodel, Joshua 149–50, 242
Scott, Jonathan 43–44, 49–50, 64, 67, 247,
    283–84, 290
Scott, Thomas 114
Scrivener, Matthew 103
Sedley, David 2–3, 143
Seekers 38–39, 46, 48, 75, 88, 187,
    189–90, 209, 305
Selden, John 53–57, 60–61, 63, 76, 82, 118,
    129, 133, 135–36, 182–83, 204
    De Jure Naturali et Gentium 133(n.),
      136, 298
    History of Tithes 63
    Table Talk 57
Seneca, Lucius Anneaus 150(n.), 250, 274,
    282
Sensabaugh, George 313
Sewell, Arthur 102
Sexby, Edward 281
Shakespeare, William 70, 92, 94, 162(n.),
    170
    King Henry IV, part 2 126
    Tragedy of King Richard III 121
Shapin, Steven 218
Shapiro, Barbara 177–8, 196
Sharpe, Kevin 54(n.)
Shawcross, John 90, 316
Shuger, Debora 120

Sidney, Algernon 10, 283–5, 295
Sidney, Sir Philip 119–21, 250, 259–60
Simon, Richard 196
Simpson, Ken 70, 109
Simpson, Sidrach 86
Sirluck, Ernest 125, 134, 148(n.)
skepticism 2–3, 11, 109, 123, 125, 134–5,
    178–80, 185–6, 206, 253–6, 274,
    277, 306–7, 310–12
Skinner, Cyriack 287
Skinner, Quentin 9
Smectymnuans 4, 66, 69–70, 109, 117–18,
    126(n.)
Smith, John 242
Smith, Nigel 172–3, 189, 234
Socinians, Socinianism 12, 58–60, 75, 87,
    97–8, 104, 192, 194, 266, 285, 310
Socinus, Faustus 97
Socrates 255, 266, 273–5, 277
Solt, Leo 22, 43–5, 62, 76
Sommerville, J.P. 54
Spellman, W.M. 306, 310–12
Spenser, Edmund 71, 92, 94, 116, 143–4,
    165, 167–9, 227, 250, 252, 260
    Shepheardes Calendar 142, 168, 172
    The Faerie Queene 142–4, 146–8,
    150–64, 167
Sprat, Thomas 21, 181, 184, 186, 208, 211,
    262, 277
    History of the Royal Society 254–5,
    258, 263–4, 268–70, 273, 275–7
Stachniewski, John 15, 176–7, 194(n.), 216
Stavely, Keith 76, 192
Steadman, John M. 227(n.)
Stennett, Joseph 172
Sterry, Peter 79, 118, 120
Stewart, Adam 57(n.), 85
Stillingfleet, Edward 103, 257, 265, 267
Stock, Richard 7, 67
Stone, Lawrence 51, 64
Stubbe, Henry 75, 210
Summers, Joseph 8
Swaim, Kathleen 8
Swift, Jonathan 200
Sylvester, Joshua 92, 234

Tacitus 259
Tanner, John S. 220, 224

Tasso, Torquato 90, 92, 116, 154, 225–6,
    259–60, 277
Taylor, George Coffin 227(n.)
Taylor, Jeremy 1–2, 14, 24, 59, 75–6,
    97, 100, 102, 147–8, 194–5, 207,
    242–6, 311, 315
Taylor, Thomas 17
Tertullian 266
Thomistic theology *see* Aquinas
Thomkins, Thomas 216
Thucydides 270
Thurloe, John 41
Tillotson, John 60, 306, 312
Todd, Margo 80, 189, 192
Toland, John 10, 89–90, 263, 311–12
toleration, religious 3, 12, 16–17, 44–5,
    48, 50, 53, 58–60, 62, 64, 87–8,
    109–10, 117, 135–40, 145, 181,
    194–5, 206–8, 254, 303, 305–17
Tolmie, Murray 22, 84, 87–88
Toon, Peter 16, 95
Trevelyan, G.M. 64
Trevor-Roper, H.R. 10
Tuck, Richard 9, 87(n.), 182
Tuckney, Anthony 60, 194
Turner, James Grantham 239
Twisse, William 151
Tyacke, Nicholas 13, 18, 22, 100, 136(n.)
Tyndale, William 194

Unitarianism 12, 310
Ussher, James 38

Vane, Sir Henry 2, 75, 87, 153, 283–84,
    293, 295
Vicari, Patricia 146, 167
Virgil 138, 227–28, 238, 251
virtuosi *see* empiricists
Vives, Ludovicus 238
Vondel, Joost van den 228

Waddington, Raymond B. 23
Wall, Moses 205
Wallace, Dewey M. Jr. 14, 59(n.), 265
Waller, Edmund 117
Wallis, John 178, 183(n.), 187, 197, 210,
    257, 265

Walwyn, William 5(n.), 20–21, 87–89, 95, 124, 182
Ward, Samuel 192
Ward, Seth 184, 193, 198–203
Ward–Webster debates 193, 196–203
Weber, Max 11, 15(n.), 17–18, 64, 67, 236
Webster, Charles 3, 16, 184–85, 208
Webster, John 39, 193, 198–202, 204, 207, 209
Webster, Tom 24
Wesley, John 22, 207
Westfall, Richard S. 206, 266
Westminster Assembly 56, 123–25, 309
Westminster Directory of Worship 118
Whichcote, Benjamin 186, 194–95
Whig history, historians 5–8, 10–12, 16, 18, 23, 31, 41, 45, 47, 52, 63–65, 254; *see also* Gardiner Samuel; Sir Charles Firth
Whigs (political party of the late seventeenth, eighteenth, and nineteenth centuries) 2, 9–10, 89–90, 94, 177, 254, 263, 313–14
White, R.S. 204
Whitelocke, Bulstrode 41, 56, 60, 63, 70
Whiting, George 10, 136(n.), 227(n.)
Whitney, Charles 139
Wilkins, John 21, 60, 125, 177–9, 181–2, 184, 186, 189, 197, 199–200, 203, 209–11, 221–3, 257, 266, 306–8
William of Ockham 178–80, 186–7, 222

William of Orange, William III of England 312
Williams, George Huntston 309
Williams, Roger 20–21, 124, 307, 309
Willis, Thomas 197
Wilson, Thomas 124
Winstanley, Gerrard 39–40, 43, 46, 235–6
Wither, George 82, 92, 143
Wittreich, Joseph A. 282(n.)
Wolfe, Don M. 7–8, 13, 108–10, 146
Wolsely, Sir Charles 60
Woodcock, Katherine 82
Woodhouse, A.S.P. 7, 43–5, 47, 52
Woods, Susanne 153, 250(n.)
Woolrych, Austin 95, 204, 293–4
Worden, Blair 1(n.), 10–11, 14–15, 25, 31, 58–9, 67, 87, 177, 210, 281, 284–5
Wordsworth, William 165
Worsley, Benjamin 184
Wotton, Sir Henry 76, 117, 144
Wyclif, John 33, 194

Xenophon 150(n.), 288

Yalden, Thomas 1–2, 8, 103
Young, Thomas 7, 67, 69, 127

Zagorin, Perez 7, 13, 77, 87, 116–17, 127
Zaret, David 16–18, 22, 26
Zwicker, Stephen 252–3, 263–4, 273